AIA

Professional 1 Level

PRINCIPLES OF GOVERNANCE & AUDIT

LEARNING & PRACTICE WORKBOOK

In this 2025 edition

- A **user-friendly format** for easy navigation
- **Exam-centred topic coverage**, directly linked to AIA's syllabus
- **Exam focus points** showing you what the examiner will want you to do
- Regular **fast forward** summaries emphasising the key points in each chapter
- **Questions** and **quick quizzes** to test your understanding
- **Practice question bank** containing exam-standard questions with answers
- **Exam question bank**
- 1 Mock exam
- A full index

FOR EXAMS FROM MAY 2025

Second edition October 2024
ISBN 9781 0355 2578 2
eISBN 9781 0355 2606 2

British Library Cataloguing-in-Publication Data
A catalogue record for this book
is available from the British Library

Published by
BPP Learning Media Ltd
BPP House, Aldine Place
142-144 Uxbridge Road
London W12 8AA

learningmedia.bpp.com

Printed in the United Kingdom

All rights reserved. No part of this publication may be reproduced, stored in a retrieval system or transmitted in any form or by any means, electronic, mechanical, photocopying, recording or otherwise, without the prior written permission of BPP Learning Media.

The contents of this book are intended as a guide and not professional advice. Although every effort has been made to ensure that the contents of this book are correct at the time of going to press, BPP Learning Media makes no warranty that the information in this book is accurate or complete and accept no liability for any loss or damage suffered by any person acting or refraining from acting as a result of the material in this book.

We are grateful to the Association of International Accountants for permission to reproduce past examination questions. The suggested solutions in the exam answer bank have been prepared by BPP Learning Media Ltd.

BPP Learning Media is grateful to the IASB for permission to reproduce extracts from IFRS® Accounting Standards, IAS® Standards, SIC and IFRIC. This publication contains copyright © material and trademarks of the IFRS Foundation®. All rights reserved. Used under license from the IFRS Foundation®. Reproduction and use rights are strictly limited. For more information about the IFRS Foundation and rights to use its material please visit www.IFRS.org.

Disclaimer: To the extent permitted by applicable law the Board and the IFRS Foundation expressly disclaims all liability howsoever arising from this publication or any translation thereof whether in contract, tort or otherwise (including, but not limited to, liability for any negligent act or omission) to any person in respect of any claims or losses of any nature including direct, indirect, incidental or consequential loss, punitive damages, penalties or costs.

Information contained in this publication does not constitute advice and should not be substituted for the services of an appropriately qualified professional.

©
BPP Learning Media Ltd
2024

A note about copyright

Dear Customer

What does the little © mean and why does it matter?

Your market-leading BPP books, course materials and e-learning materials do not write and update themselves. People write them on their own behalf or as employees of an organisation that invests in this activity. Copyright law protects their livelihoods. It does so by creating rights over the use of the content.

Breach of copyright is a form of theft – as well as being a criminal offence in some jurisdictions, it is potentially a serious breach of professional ethics.

With current technology, things might seem a bit hazy but, basically, without the express permission of BPP Learning Media:

- Photocopying our materials is a breach of copyright
- Printing our digital materials in order to share them with or forward them to a third party or use them in any way other than in connection with your BPP studies is a breach of copyright

You can, of course, sell your books, in the form in which you have bought them – once you have finished with them. (Is this fair to your fellow students? We update for a reason.) Please note the e-products are sold on a single user licence basis: we do not supply 'unlock' codes to people who have bought them secondhand.

And what about outside the UK? BPP Learning Media strives to make our materials available at prices students can afford by local printing arrangements, pricing policies and partnerships which are clearly listed on our website. A tiny minority ignore this and indulge in criminal activity by illegally photocopying our material or supporting organisations that do. If they act illegally and unethically in one area, can you really trust them?

Copyright © IFRS Foundation

All rights reserved. Reproduction and use rights are strictly limited. No part of this publication may be translated, reprinted or reproduced or utilised in any form either in whole or in part or by any electronic, mechanical or other means, now known or hereafter invented, including photocopying and recording, or in any information storage and retrieval system, without prior permission in writing from the IFRS Foundation. Contact the IFRS Foundation for further details.

The Foundation has trade marks registered around the world (Trade Marks) including 'IAS®', 'IASB®', 'IFRIC®', 'IFRS®', the IFRS® logo, 'IFRS for SMEs®', IFRS for SMEs® logo, the 'Hexagon Device', 'International Financial Reporting Standards®', NIIF® and 'SIC®'.

Further details of the Foundation's Trade Marks are available from the Licensor on request.

Contents

Introduction

The introduction pages contain lots of valuable advice and information. They include tips on studying for and passing the exam, also the content of the syllabus and what has been examined.

How the BPP Learning Media Learning & Practice Workbook can help you pass – Help yourself study for your AIA exams – Syllabus – AIA List of examinable standards – RPQ students UK differences – Command words and learning outcomes – The exam paper – Examinable ISAs

		Page
1	The concept of audit and sustainability	1
2	Regulation of audit	33
3	Corporate governance and internal audit	57
4	Professional ethics	99
5	The audit client	129
6	Internal controls	145
7	Planning and risk	167
8	Audit evidence	207
9	Using the work of others	243
10	Tests of controls: sales, purchases and wages	257
11	Tests of controls: cash, inventory and non-current assets	285
12	Bank and cash	307
13	Non-current assets	321
14	Inventory	337
15	Receivables and revenue	361
16	Liabilities, expenses and capital	383
17	Audit completion and review	413
18	Audit reports	437

Answers to end of chapter questions ... 471
Practice question bank ... 505
Practice answer bank ... 533
Exam question bank ... 577
Mock exam ... 659
Bibliography ... 673
Index ... 677

INTRODUCTION

How the BPP Learning Media Learning & Practice Workbook can help you pass

> It provides you with the knowledge and understanding, skills and application techniques that you need to be successful in your exams

This Learning & Practice Workbook has been targeted at the **Principles of Governance and Audit** syllabus.

- It is **comprehensive**. It covers the syllabus content. No more, no less.
- It is written at the **right level**. Each chapter is written with AIA's syllabus in mind.
- It is aimed at the **exam**. We have taken account of recent exams, guidance the examiner has given and the assessment methodology.

> It allows you to study in the way that best suits your learning style and the time you have available, by following your personal Study Plan (see page vi)

You may be studying at home on your own or you may be attending a course. You may like to read every word, or you may prefer to do a fast read through and learn through doing practice questions the rest of the time. However you study, you will find the BPP Learning Media Learning & Practice Workbook meets your needs in designing and following your personal Study Plan.

INTRODUCTION

Help yourself study for your AIA exams

Exams for professional bodies such as AIA are very different from those you have taken at college or university. You will be under **greater time pressure before** the exam – as you may be combining your study with work. Here are some hints and tips.

The right approach

1 **Develop the right attitude**

Believe in yourself	Yes, there is a lot to learn. But thousands have succeeded before and you can too.
Remember why you're doing it	You are studying for a good reason: to advance your career.

2 **Focus on the exam**

Read through the Syllabus	This tells you what you are expected to know and is supplemented by **Exam focus points** in the text.
Study the Exam paper section	Past papers are likely to be good guides to what you should expect in the exam.

3 **The right method**

See the whole picture	Keeping in mind how all the detail you need to know fits into the whole picture will help you understand it better. • The **Introduction** of each chapter puts the material in context. • The **Syllabus content** and **Exam focus points** show you what you need to **grasp**.
Use your own words	To absorb the information (and to practise your written communication skills), you need to **put it into your own words**. • **Take notes** • Answer the **questions** in each chapter. • Draw **mindmaps**. • Try **'teaching' a subject** to a colleague or friend.
Give yourself cues to jog your memory	The Learning & Practice Workbook uses **bold** to **highlight key points**. • Try **colour coding** with a highlighter pen. • Write **key points** on cards.

4 **The right recap**

Review, review, review	Regularly reviewing a topic in summary form can **fix it in your memory**. The Learning & Practice Workbook helps you review in many ways. • **Chapter roundups** summarise the 'Fast forward' key points in each chapter. Use them to recap each study session. • The **Quick quiz** actively tests your grasp of the essentials. • Go through the **Examples** in each chapter a second or third time.

Developing your personal Study Plan

BPP recommends that you follow a study plan. Planning and sticking to the plan are key elements of learning successfully.

There are five steps you should work through.

Step 1 **How do you learn?**

What types of intelligence do you display when learning? You might be advised to brush up on certain study skills before launching into this Learning & Practice Workbook, but refer to the 'tackling your studies' section below which will help.

Step 2 **What do you prefer to do first?**

If you prefer to get to grips with a theory before seeing how it is applied, we suggest you concentrate first on the explanations we give in each chapter before looking at the examples and case studies. If you prefer to see first how things work in practice, read through the detail in each chapter, and concentrate on the examples and case studies, before supplementing your understanding by reading the detail.

Step 3 **How much time do you have?**

Work out the time you have available per week, given the following.

- The standard you have set yourself
- The other exam(s) you are sitting
- Practical matters such as work, travel, exercise, sleep and social life

Note your time available in box A.   A [____] Hours

Step 4 **Allocate your time**

- Take the time you have available per week for this Learning & Practice Workbook shown in box A, multiply it by the number of weeks available and insert the result in box B.   B [____]
- Divide the figure in box B by the number of chapters in this text and insert the result in box C.   C [____]

Remember that this is only a rough guide. Some of the chapters in this book are longer and more complicated than others, and you will find some subjects easier to understand than others.

Step 5 **Implement**

Set about studying each chapter in the time shown in box C, following the key study steps in the order suggested by your particular learning style.

This is your personal **Study Plan**. You should try to combine it with the study sequence outlined below. You may want to modify the sequence to adapt it to your **personal style**.

Tackling your studies

The best way to approach this Learning & Practice Workbook is to tackle the chapters in order. Taking into account your individual learning style, you could follow this sequence for each chapter.

Key study steps	Activity
Step 1 **Topic list**	This topic list helps you navigate each chapter; each numbered topic is a numbered section in the chapter.
Step 2 **Introduction**	This sets your objectives for study by giving you the big picture in terms of the context of the chapter. The content is referenced to the syllabus, and Exam guidance shows how the topic is likely to be examined. The Introduction tells you **why** the topics covered in the chapter need to be studied.
Step 3 **Fast forward**	Fast forward boxes give you a quick summary of the content of each of the main chapter sections. They are listed together in the roundup at the end of each chapter to help you review each chapter quickly.
Step 4 **Explanations**	Proceed methodically through each chapter, particularly focusing on areas highlighted as significant in the chapter introduction, or areas that are frequently examined.
Step 5 **Key terms and Exam focus points**	• Key terms are definitions of important concepts that you really need to know and understand before the exam. • Exam focus points highlight areas or topics that may be examined.
Step 6 **Note taking**	Take brief notes, if you wish. Don't copy out too much. Remember that being able to record something yourself is a sign of being able to understand it. Your notes can be in whatever format you find most helpful; lists, diagrams, mindmaps.
Step 7 **Examples**	Work through the examples very carefully as they illustrate key knowledge and techniques.
Step 8 **Case studies**	Study each one, and try to add flesh to them from your own experience. They are designed to show how the topics you are studying come alive in the real world.
Step 9 **Questions**	Attempt each one, as they will illustrate how well you have understood what you have read.
Step 10 **Answers**	Check yours against ours, and make sure you understand any discrepancies.
Step 11 **Chapter roundup**	Review it carefully, to make sure you have grasped the significance of all the important points in the chapter.
Step 12 **Quick quiz**	Use the Quick quiz to check how much you have remembered of the topics covered and to practise questions in a variety of formats.
Step 13 **Question practice**	Attempt the quick quiz and end of chapter question suggested at the very end of each chapter. These are designed for you to confirm some of the key concepts set out in each chapter. Some of these questions are designed to cover more than one topic area to develop your ability to apply syllabus learning. You can then attempt the questions related to this chapter, which are contained in the question bank at the end of this Learning & Practice Workbook.

AIA Achieve

AIA provides an interactive course of study AIA Achieve, which offers students the tools, resources and learning environment to study for the exams. The study tools include a course of study e-book, marked practice questions, marked mock exam paper and feedback and technical advice via an e-Tutor. Contact the Study Support team at: Achieve@aiaworldwide.com.

Moving on...

When you are ready to start revising, you should still refer back to this Learning & Practice Workbook.

- As a source of **reference** (you should find the index particularly helpful for this)
- As a way to **review** (the Fast forwards, Exam focus points, Chapter roundups and Quick quizzes help you here)

PQ Qualification Syllabus

The assessment requirements in the AIA exams at the Foundation, Professional 1 and 2 stages reflect a progression of cognitive levels which successful students are expected to demonstrate in satisfying each stage of the qualification. The levels progress from an emphasis on 'knowledge and comprehension' at the Foundation stage, to a predominance of 'application and analysis' at the subsequent Professional 1 and 2 stages and incorporate 'synthesis and evaluation' at the Professional 2 stage.

Indicative weightings for the cognitive levels at each stage of the qualification are defined in the following table.

Stage of qualification	Cognitive levels of learning*			Associated learning outcomes
	Knowledge and comprehension	Application and Analysis	Synthesis and evaluation	
Foundation Level	90%	10%	0%	Outcomes consistent with the International Education Standards Board (IAESB) standards
Professional 1 Level	50%	50%	0%	
Professional 2 Level	10%	70%	20%	

The cognitive levels of learning are associated with the following.

'Knowledge and comprehension' refer to:

The acquisition of concepts, ideas, terms, facts, practices and techniques in accounting and related disciplines, and the understanding of how they relate to the conduct, management, reporting and assessment of the activities of business and other organisations.

'Application and analysis' refer to:

The ability to apply knowledge and comprehension to actual circumstances and situations and to identify constituent components involved (concepts, ideas, terms, facts, practices, and techniques) and the relationship between these elements.

'Synthesis and evaluation' refer to:

The ability to bring together a variety of components in order to form a coherent whole, and to form judgements about the application of, and value of, those components in a particular context or for a particular purpose.

Professional 1 Level Syllabus

Principles of Governance and Audit

It is important for professionally qualified accountants to have awareness of the governance contexts of business. Audit and assurance is a key part of governance and audit is an essential area of professional practice. This paper builds on the Corporate Governance and Audit component included in the Foundation Level and develops the student's detailed knowledge of audit processes, which is imperative to the work of the professional accountant.

The Learning Outcomes are consistent with those of IES 2 Intermediate Standard for Audit and Assurance, and Governance, Risk Management and Internal Control, relevant aspects of IES 4 Professional Values, Ethics and Attitudes, and IES 8 Competence Requirements for Audit professional.

In designing the syllabus and the related examination papers AIA has employed 'intended learning outcomes' as the means to communicate expectations to potential students and stakeholders, and to inform the specification requirements to be tested in the assessment of students.

The use of learning outcomes:

- Is consistent with what is commonly acknowledged as good practice in the higher education sector; and
- Is consistent with the approach embodied in International Accounting Education Standards.

At the Professional 1 Level students are expected to demonstrate that they are able to achieve the following:

Intended Learning Outcomes[1] – Description of expectations	
Professional 1 level	At the Professional 1 level students are expected to demonstrate that they: • Understand basic principles and concepts underpinning accounting and related practices in organisations and can discuss the conceptual rationale that provides the basis for those practices. • Understand the role of accounting and related practices within the financial and governance context of organisations. • Are able to apply relevant regulations and standards in accounting, auditing, law and taxation. • Know and can execute basic recording and measurement techniques relevant to accounting, management and assurance. • Are able to analyse financial information and interpret it for the purpose of supporting decision-making.

---

[1] The description of the levels of proficiency supports the IAESBs use of learning outcomes in its International Education Standards (IESs) 2, 3, and 4.

Relationship to Qualification Structure

Development in Assurance and Accountability — Principles of Governance and Audit — Financial Accounting and Reporting 1

Aims

The aim of this paper is to develop and examine the candidate's:

- Detailed understanding of the components of corporate governance and auditing, including the evaluation of the risk of misstatement in financial statements and evidence procedures used in audit practice.

- Ability to apply this knowledge to practical scenarios and situations.

Principles of Governance and Audit Learning outcomes

In order to successfully complete this paper, candidates will demonstrate that they are able to:

(1) Justify the need for good governance within companies and other organisations and relate that to the assurance provided by the auditor;

(2) Present the components of a modern external audit from acceptance of a new client to drafting the audit opinion;

(3) Determine business risks and audit risks associated with specific audit assignments;

(4) Apply audit principles and theory to develop a detailed audit plan for items within the financial statements; and

(5) Apply audit principles and theory in the preparation of reports to management, shareholders and those charged with governance.

Structure of the Paper

A three hour 15 minute paper (including 15 minutes reading time) consisting of five questions:

Question	Number of marks
Q1: A case scenario question	20
Q2 and Q3: Short form questions worth 30 marks in total	30
Q4 and Q5: Case study/scenario-based questions worth 25 marks each	50
Total	100

All of these questions could assess any of the learning outcomes. The allocation of marks to any parts of a question will be disclosed on the exam paper. Candidates must answer all questions.

Syllabus

1 Background to auditing and independence

Topic Weighting   5%

- The historical development of audit
- Auditing concepts
- The importance of auditor independence
- The importance of corporate governance
- Governance mechanisms, and the relationship with audit independence
- Threats to independence
- Strengthening auditor independence: Ethical and other issues

2 The regulatory background of auditing

Topic Weighting   5%

- The structure and components making up the annual report
- Reporting and auditing requirements
- Auditor regulation. The Companies Act (2006); Accounting standards; Auditing standards; Stock Exchange requirements; The UK Corporate Governance Code; Corporate Governance Code Guidance; Audit Committees and the External Audit: Minimum Standard
- The Integrated Reporting Framework and the Global Reporting Initiative
- IFRS Sustainability Disclosure Standards S1 and S2
- Auditors' duties and rights
- Directors' responsibilities

Note. RPQ (statutory auditor qualification) candidates will be required to answer based on the UK regulatory background, including auditing and accounting standards issued by the FRC.

3 An overview of the audit process

Topic Weighting   15%

- The audit opinion: gathering information to arrive at an opinion
- Types of evidence
- Reviewing systems and internal controls
- Collecting the evidence
- Documentation
- Types of testing
- Audit sampling techniques
- Automated tools and techniques (ATTs) and data analytics

4 The client

Topic Weighting   25%

- Pre-engagement investigation
- Audit engagement letter
- Understanding the client's business and evaluating its controls
- Setting materiality (qualitative and quantitative) and the degree of assurance
- Planning the audit and liaising with the audit committee
- The appropriateness of types of testing
- Designing the audit programme
- Maintaining ethical standards
- Sustainable supply chain

INTRODUCTION

5   Audit approach

Topic Weighting   20%

- Use of assertions
- Business risk and audit risk
- Inherent risk factors and spectrum of risk
- Components of audit risk
- Controlling audit risk
- Tests of controls
- Substantive audit procedures
- Testing different audit areas

6   Audit completion

Topic Weighting   20%

- The form and content of statutory reports
- Responsibilities of auditors
- Auditor requirements to detect and report material misstatements from non-compliance with laws.
- Auditor's responsibilities relating to fraud in an audit of financial statements
- Corporate governance and other reports
- Corporate sustainability disclosure, environmental and social accountability and stewardship
- Written representations
- Subsequent events
- Final analytical procedures
- Final meeting with clients
- Points for future audits
- Quality management
- Revisiting and reviewing other ethical issues

7   Types of audit report

Topic Weighting   10%

- Companies Act 2006
- Types of audit opinion
- Changes in the audit report

Candidates following the Recognised Professional Qualification (RPQ) statutory audit route (Auditor Qualification) will be examined on the relevant UK Financial Reporting Standards (FRS) and ISAs (UK) as well as the Revised Ethical Standard (ES) 2019 for auditors' integrity, objectivity and independence published by the Financial Reporting Council (FRC).

Relationship to Qualification Structure

This paper builds on the Foundation Level Unit component 'Corporate Governance and Audit' and leads to Professional 2 'Developments in Assurance and Accountability'.

Ethics

Candidates are advised that the standards outlined in The Code of Ethics for Professional Accountants issued by the International Ethics Standards Board for Accountants (IESBA Code) are implicit in, and examinable throughout, the AIA syllabus. The Code can be accessed via the AIA website at: www.aiaworldwide.com.

Candidates following the Recognised Professional Qualification (RPQ) statutory audit route (Auditor Qualification) will be expected to refer, where appropriate, to the Revised Ethical Standard (ES) 2019 for auditors' integrity, objectivity and independence published by the Financial Reporting Council (FRC).

Candidates following other routes will not be penalised if they refer to the ES in preference to the IFAC Code of Ethics.

The ES can be accessed via the Financial Reporting Council's website at:
https://www.frc.org.uk/auditors/audit-assurance/standards-and-guidance

Ethical issues are addressed through a review of current professional guidelines and their application in practice. Some questions will have an ethical component built in and the coverage of the paper is consistent with the relevant learning outcomes in IES 4 Professional Values, Ethics and Attitudes.

Recommended Reading

You can purchase any of the books listed quickly and easily on the AIA website through the AIA essential reading list webpage

AIA Magazine – International Accountant
ISSN: 1465-5144

AIA Learning & Practice Workbook
Principles of Governance and Audit
Publisher: BPP Learning Media
ISBN: 9781 0355 2578 2 / eISBN 9781 0355 2606 2

The e-Book is available at: exams@aiaworldwide.com

Contact our publisher BPP for information on purchasing a hard copy of the text book at:
https://www.bpp.com/learning-media-listing/lmlist/6293

You can purchase any of the books listed below quickly and easily through the publisher's website or link stated below.

Auditing (12th Edition UK 2021)
Author: Millichamp, A, and Taylor, J
Publisher: Cengage Learning EMEA
ISBN: 9781 4737 7899 3

Corporate Governance, Principles, Policies and Practices (4th Edition)
Author: Tricker, B
Publisher: Oxford University Press
ISBN: 9780 1988 0986 9

Accounting Standards: Ass assessed in Financial Accounting and Reporting 1 and the Auditing Standards

Principles of External Auditing (4th Edition)
Author: Porter, B, Simon, J, Hatherly, D
Publisher: John Wiley & Sons Ltd
ISBN: 9780 4709 7445 2

The Audit Process - 7th edition, 2019.
Author: Iain Gray, Louise Crawford, Stuart Manson
Publisher: Cengage Learning EMEA
ISBN-10: 1473760186
ISBN-13: 9781 4737 6018 9

AIA List of examinable standards

All extant International Standards on Auditing, International Standards on Quality Management, International Financial Reporting Standards/International Accounting Standards are examinable, subject to the six months rule (refer to New Legislation).

The depth of knowledge of the standards required for the different levels can be defined as:

- **Foundation** – candidates should be aware of the standard and be familiar with the basic concepts involved.
- **Professional 1** – candidates should be aware of all major requirements of the standard and be able to apply it to straight forward situations. Candidates should be able to recognise some of the pitfalls and issues associated with the standard.
- **Professional 2** – candidates must be fully cognisant of the standard and know how to apply it to specialised situations. They must also be fully aware of the important issues, contemporary thinking and criticisms related to the standard.

For RPQ statutory audit route (Auditor Qualification) candidates the relevant UK standards are Financial Reporting Standards (FRS) and the International Standards on Auditing (UK) (ISAs (UK)) and International Standard on Quality Management (UK) (ISQM (UK)), issued by the Financial Reporting Council (FRC).

In respect of auditing, the relevant UK standards are: https://www.frc.org.uk/library/standards-codes-policy/audit-assurance-and-ethics/auditing-standards/

International Accounting Standards (IASs) and International Financial Reporting Standards (IFRS Standards)

In the Financial Accounting component of the Foundation Unit candidates are required to have studied a limited number of IASs and IFRSs, however in Financial Accounting and Reporting 1 (FAR 1) and Financial Accounting and Reporting 2 (FAR 2) the bulk of IASs and IFRSs are examinable. Refer to the syllabi. A list of currently examinable IASs and IFRSs is presented in the table below.

Note. Candidates following the Audit Qualification (AQ) are expected to be aware of the FRC accounting standards. The relevant accounting standards issued by the FRC are Financial Reporting Standards 100 to 105 including FRS 105 The Financial Reporting Standard applicable to The Micro-entities Regime. Accounting standards apply to all companies, and other entities that prepare accounts that are intended to provide a true and fair view. The Foreword to Accounting Standards explains the authority, scope and application of accounting standards. Audit candidates should refer to the FRC website site to view the relevant standards: https://www.frc.org.uk/accountants/accounting-and-reporting-policy/uk-accounting-standards/standards-in-issue

International Accounting Standards (IASs)		Examinable in Paper						
No	Title	FA	MA	CGA	PGA	FAR 1	FAR 2	DAA
1	Presentation of Financial Statements	✓		✓	✓	✓	✓	✓
2	Inventories	✓	✓	✓	✓	✓	✓	✓
7	Statements of Cash Flows	✓		✓	✓	✓	✓	✓
8	Accounting Policies, Changes in Accounting Estimates and Errors					✓	✓	✓
10	Events After the Reporting Period	✓		✓	✓	✓	✓	✓
12	Income Taxes					✓	✓	✓
16	Property, Plant and Equipment	✓		✓	✓	✓	✓	✓
19	Employee Benefits						✓	✓

INTRODUCTION

International Accounting Standards (IASs)		Examinable in Paper						
No	Title	FA	MA	CGA	PGA	FAR 1	FAR 2	DAA
20	Accounting for Governments Grants and Disclosure of Government Assistance					✓	✓	✓
21	The Effects of Changes in Foreign Exchange Rates						✓	✓
23	Borrowing Costs					✓	✓	✓
24	Related Party Disclosures					✓	✓	✓
27	Separate Financial Statements					✓	✓	✓
28	Investments in Associates and Joint Ventures					✓	✓	✓
29	Financial Reporting in Hyperinflationary Economies						✓	✓
32	Financial instruments: Presentation					✓	✓	✓
33	Earnings per Share					✓	✓	✓
34	Interim Financial Reporting					✓	✓	✓
36	Impairment of Assets					✓	✓	✓
37	Provisions, Contingent Liabilities and Contingent Assets	✓		✓	✓	✓	✓	✓
38	Intangible Assets	✓		✓	✓	✓	✓	✓
40	Investment Property					✓	✓	✓

International Financial Reporting Standards (IFRSs)		Examinable in Paper					
No	Title	FA	MA	CGA	PGA	FAR 1	FAR 2
1	First-time Adoption of International Financial Reporting Standards				✓	✓	✓
2	Share-based Payment						✓
3	Business Combinations				✓	✓	✓
5	Non-current Assets Held for Sale and Discontinued Operations				✓	✓	✓
7	Financial Instruments: Disclosures					✓	✓
8	Operating Segments				✓	✓	✓
9	Financial Instruments					✓	✓
10	Consolidated Financial Statements				✓	✓	✓
11	Joint Arrangements					✓	✓
12	Disclosure of Interests in Other Entities				✓		✓
13	Fair Value Measurement						✓
15	Revenue from Contracts with Customers			✓	✓	✓	✓
16	Leases				✓	✓	✓
IFRS for SMEs	IFRS for Small and Medium-sized Entities					✓	✓
S1	General Requirements for Disclosure of Sustainability-related Financial Information					✓	✓
S2	Climate-related Disclosures					✓	✓

For **RPQ statutory audit route (Auditor Qualification)** candidates the relevant UK standards are Financial Reporting Standards (FRS) 1, 3, 5, 10, 12, 15 and 21 issued by the FRC.

Note. Free website providing comprehensive information about IFRS Standards: www.iasplus.com

INTRODUCTION

Other useful reading includes:

IFRS in Your Pocket - latest edition

Website: https://www.iasplus.com/en-gb/tag-types/global/publication-series/ifrs-in-your-pocket

New supporting materials for the IFRS for SMEs Standard available:
https://www.ifrs.org/issued-standards/ifrs-for-smes/
https://www.ifrs.org/supporting-implementation/supporting-materials-for-the-ifrs-for-smes/

Exposure drafts, discussion papers and IFRIC's are not examinable in the Foundation Unit or Financial Accounting and Reporting 1. Those still current (i.e. they have not been superseded by other publications) are examinable in Financial Accounting and Reporting 2 but only an understanding of their basic principles is required.

International Standards on Auditing (ISAs) and International Standards on Quality Management (ISQMs)

A list of currently examinable ISAs and ISQMs is stated in the table.

Candidates can download the Handbook of International Auditing, and Ethics Pronouncements, which is available free of charge as a PDF file from the IFAC website: www.ifac.org, then click on 'standard setting bodies', then IAASB.

Note. Candidates following the Audit route are expected to be aware of the International Standards on Auditing (UK) (ISAs (UK)) and International Standards on Quality Management (ISQM) (UK)) issued by the FRC. In reviewing the standards on the FRC website you should refer to the standards which are of the same title as those listed below: https://www.frc.org.uk/library/standards-codes-policy/audit-assurance-and-ethics/

International Standards on Auditing (ISAs)		Examinable in Paper		
No	Title	CGA	PGA	DAA
AUDITS OF HISTORICAL FINANCIAL INFORMATION				
200–299 GENERAL PRINCIPLES AND RESPONSIBILITIES				
200	Overall Objectives of the Independent Auditor and the Conduct of an Audit in Accordance with International Standards on Auditing	✓	✓	✓
210	Agreeing the Terms of Audit Engagements	✓	✓	✓
220 (Revised)	Quality Management for an Audit of Financial Statements	✓	✓	✓
230	Audit Documentation	✓	✓	✓
240 (Revised)	The Auditor's Responsibilities Relating to Fraud in an Audit of Financial Statements	✓	✓	✓
250 (Revised)	Consideration of Laws and Regulations in an Audit of Financial Statements Candidates following the RPQ route should refer to ISA (UK) 250A	✓	✓	✓
260 (Revised)	Communication with Those Charged with Governance	✓	✓	✓
265	Communicating Deficiencies in Internal Control to Those Charged with Governance and Management	✓	✓	✓
300–499 RISK ASSESSMENT AND RESPONSE TO ASSESSED RISKS				
300	Planning an Audit of Financial Statements	✓	✓	✓
315 (Revised)	Identifying and Assessing the Risks of Material Misstatement	✓	✓	✓
320	Materiality in Planning and Performing an Audit	✓	✓	✓
330	The Auditor's Responses to Assessed Risks	✓	✓	✓
402	Audit Considerations Relating to an Entity Using a Service			✓

INTRODUCTION

International Standards on Auditing (ISAs)		Examinable in Paper		
No	Title	CGA	PGA	DAA
	Organisation			
450	Evaluation of Misstatements Identified during the Audit	✓	✓	✓
500–599 AUDIT EVIDENCE				
500	Audit Evidence	✓	✓	✓
501	Audit Evidence – Specific Considerations for Selected Items	✓	✓	✓
505	External Confirmations	✓	✓	✓
510	Initial Audit Engagements – Opening Balances			✓
520	Analytical Procedures	✓	✓	✓
530	Audit Sampling	✓	✓	✓
540 (Revised)	Auditing Accounting Estimates and Related Disclosures			✓
550	Related Parties			✓
560	Subsequent Events	✓	✓	✓
570 (Revised)	Going Concern	✓	✓	✓
580	Written Representations	✓	✓	✓
600–699 USING WORK OF OTHERS				
600	Special Considerations – Audits of Group Financial Statements (Including the Work of Component Auditors)			✓
610 (Revised)	Using the Work of Internal Auditors	✓	✓	✓
620	Using the Work of an Auditor's Expert	✓	✓	✓
700–799 AUDIT CONCLUSIONS AND REPORTING				
700 (Revised)	Forming an Opinion and Reporting on Financial Statements	✓	✓	✓
701	Communicating Key Audit Matters in the Independent Auditor's Report	✓	✓	✓
705 (Revised)	Modifications to the Opinion in the Independent Auditor's Report	✓	✓	✓
706 (Revised)	Emphasis of Matter Paragraphs and Other Matter Paragraphs in the Independent Auditor's Report	✓	✓	✓
710	Comparative Information – Corresponding Figures and Comparative Financial Statements			✓
720 (Revised)	The Auditor's Responsibilities Relating to Other Information			✓
800–899 SPECIALISED AREAS				
800 (Revised)	Special Considerations – Audits of Financial Statements Prepared in Accordance with Special Purpose Frameworks			✓
805 (Revised)	Special Considerations – Audits of Single Financial Statements and Specific Elements, Accounts or Items of a Financial Statement	✓	✓	✓
810 (Revised)	Engagements to Report on Summary Financial Statements			✓

International Standards on Quality Management (ISQMs)		Examinable in Paper		
No	Title	CGA	PGA	DAA
1	Quality Management for Firms that Perform Audits and Reviews of Financial Statements, and Other Assurance and Related Services Engagements.			✓

INTRODUCTION

Note. For RPQ statutory audit route (Auditor Qualification) candidates the current ISAs (UK) issued by the FRC are examinable except for ISA 402, 510, 540, 550, 600 and 710.

RPQ students – UK differences

Introduction

As has been noted in the syllabus, those candidates taking the RPQ statutory audit route (Audit Qualification) need to be aware of UK auditing standards. The UK has adopted IFAC's International Standards on Auditing, and the requirements in the UK are largely the same as you will read in this book. However, in the UK there are some additional requirements, which you will be responsible for researching. All UK standards can be found on the FRC's website (www.frc.org.uk).

Most important differences in UK standards

Standard
FRC Revised Ethical Standard December 2019. This standard is entirely supplementary to the IESBA Code.
ISA (UK) 250A (Revised November 2019, updated May 2022) *Considerations of Laws and Regulations in an Audit of Financial Statements.* Several paragraphs give supplementary guidance for UK auditors.
ISA (UK) 570 (Revised September 2019, updated May 2022) *Going Concern.* Several paragraphs give supplementary guidance for UK auditors.
ISA (UK) 610 (Revised June 2013, updated May 2022) *Using the Work of Internal Auditors.* The use of internal auditors to provide direct assistance is prohibited in the UK.
ISA (UK) 700 (Revised November 2019, updated May 2022) *Forming an Opinion and Reporting on Financial Statements.* Several paragraphs give supplementary guidance for UK auditors covering areas including, but not limited to, other audit responsibilities, the auditor's signature and the form of opinion.
ISA (UK) 701 (Revised November 2019, updated May 2022) *Communicating Key Audit Matters in the Independent Auditor's Report.* This ISA contains supplementary paragraphs that deal with the responsibility of auditors in the UK to communicate other audit planning and scoping matters in the auditor's report.
ISA (UK) 705 (Revised June 2016) *Modifications to the Opinion in the Independent Auditor's Report.* Paragraphs A26-1 and A27-1 are supplementary guidance for UK auditors. The examples of auditor's reports in the Appendix do not apply to UK auditors.
ISA (UK) 706 (Revised June 2016) *Emphasis of Matter Paragraphs and Other Matter Paragraphs in the Independent Auditor's Report.* Paragraphs A2-1, A5-1, A9-1 and A13-1 are supplementary guidance for UK auditors. The example auditor's reports in the Appendix do not apply to UK auditors.
ISA (UK) 720 (Revised November 2019, updated May 2022) *The Auditor's Responsibilities Relating to Other Information.* This ISA contains additional obligations imposed by law or regulation on auditors in the UK to report on statutory other information.
Example UK auditor's reports can be found in the FRC's August 2021 Bulletin: Illustrative auditor's reports on United Kingdom private sector financial statements for periods commencing on or after 1 February 2020. Any example auditor's report in international ISAs will not conform to UK requirements.
You should be aware in differences in accounting between UK and international standards from your accounting studies.

Command words

The following list contains active command words appropriate for use at the Professional 1 Level of the AIA qualification. Reference to the command words is essential to understanding how the assessment is applied in AIA exams.

Cognitive Levels of Learning	Command Words	Definitions
Professional 1 Application and Analysis 50% Knowledge and Comprehension 50%	Advise	To inform or notify
	Analyse	Examine in detail in order to interpret its meaning or essential features
	Apply	To use information or a technique in a particular situation
	Calculate Compute	Select the appropriate method and techniques and apply your knowledge and understandings to work out and show how figures were arrived at
	Demonstrate	To show or prove by reasoning or evidence
	Determine	Find out or establish
	Perform	Carry out into effect
	Prepare	To make or get ready for use
	Record	Document the information
	Estimate	Make an approximate judgement/calculation
	Journalise	Produce a double entry of events

Please note

1   The word 'calculate' may be used at all levels of the syllabus.

2   The word 'advise' may be used at all levels of the syllabus.

INTRODUCTION

The concept of audit and sustainability

Topic list	Syllabus reference
1 The purpose of auditing	1.2, 2.1
2 The historical development of audit	1.1
3 The objective of an external audit	1.2
4 Responsibilities of directors and auditors	2.5, 6.2
5 The Global Reporting Initiative	2.4
6 IFRS Sustainability Disclosure Standards	2.5

Introduction

In the first section of this chapter we look at the concepts of **agency, accountability and stewardship,** and consider reporting as a means of communication to the different stakeholders who are interested in the financial statements of the company. This section explains why there is a need for assurance in relation to financial and non-financial information. The main reason an assurance service such as an external audit is required is the fact that the ownership and management of a company are not necessarily one and the same.

Second, it is important to understand how the concept of audit has developed over time. The key assurance service which your syllabus concentrates on is the external audit (statutory and non-statutory). Although it is strictly defined, many people do not understand what an external audit is and what it is designed to achieve. This is discussed in Section 3.

In Section 4 we will briefly explain the responsibilities of directors and auditors. This is an area which will be built upon as you progress through your course.

Finally we will consider the increasing desire, on the parts of both companies and stakeholders, for sustainability reporting and disclosures and the need for assurance in relation to this.

1 The purpose of auditing

> **FAST FORWARD**
>
> An audit provides **assurance** (comfort) to the shareholders and other stakeholders of a company on the financial statements because it is **independent and impartial.**

1.1 Accountability and stewardship

The key reason for having an audit or review can be seen by working through the following case study.

Case Study

Laine decides to set up a business selling flowers. She gets up early in the morning, visits the market, and then sets up a stall by the side of the road. For the first year, all goes well. She sells all the flowers she is able to buy and she derives some income from the business.

However, Laine feels that she could sell more flowers if she was able to transport more to the place where she sells them, and also knows that there are several other roads nearby where she could sell flowers, if she could be in two places at once. She could achieve these two things by buying a van, and by employing other people to sell flowers on the other roads.

Laine needs more money to achieve this expansion of her business. She decides to ask her rich friend Glyn to invest in the business.

Glyn can see the potential of Laine's business and wants to invest, but he doesn't want to be involved in the management of the business. He also does not want to have ultimate liability for the debts of the business if the business fails. He therefore suggests that they set up a limited company. He will own the majority of the shares and be entitled to dividends. Laine will be managing director and be paid a salary for her work.

At the end of the first year of trading as a limited company, Glyn receives a copy of the financial statements. Profits are lower than expected, so his dividend will not be as large as he had hoped. He knows that Laine is paid a salary so does not care as much as him that profits are low.

Glyn is concerned by the level of profits and feels that he wants further assurance on the accounts. He doesn't know whether they give a true reflection on the last year's trading, particularly as the profits do not seem as high as those Laine had predicted when he agreed to invest.

The solution is that the **assurance** Glyn is seeking can be given by an independent **audit** of the financial statements. An auditor can provide the two things that Glyn requires:

- A **knowledgeable review** of the company's business and of the accounts
- An **impartial view**, since Laine's view might be biased

Other people will also view the company's accounts with interest, for example:

- Creditors of the company
- Taxation authorities

The various people interested in the accounts of a company are sometimes referred to as **stakeholders**. Although they will all judge the accounts by different criteria, **they will all gain assurance** from learning that the accounts they are reading have been subject to an independent report.

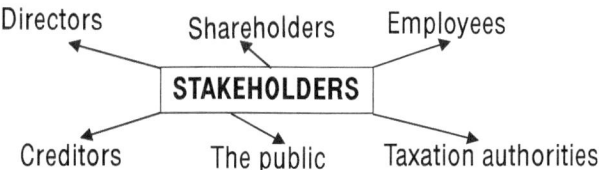

The example of Glyn and Laine is a simple one. In practice companies may have thousands of shareholders and may not know the management personally. It is therefore important that directors are **accountable** to shareholders. Directors act as **stewards** of the shareholders' investments. They are **agents** of the shareholders.

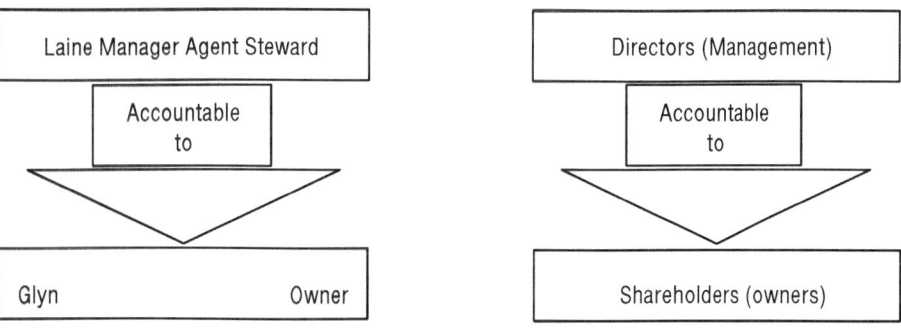

Key terms

Accountability is the quality or state of being accountable, that is, being required or expected to justify actions and decisions. It suggests an obligation or willingness to accept responsibility for one's actions.

Stewardship is the practice of being a steward, that is, someone employed to manage another person's property.

Agents are people employed or used to provide a particular service. In the case of a company, the people being used to provide the service managing the business also have the second role of being people in their own right trying to maximise their personal wealth.

You may ask, 'what are the directors accountable for?'. It is important to understand the answer to this question. The directors are accountable for the **shareholders' investment**. The shareholders have bought shares in that company (they have invested). They **expect a return** from their investment. As the **directors** manage the company, they are **in a position to affect that return.**

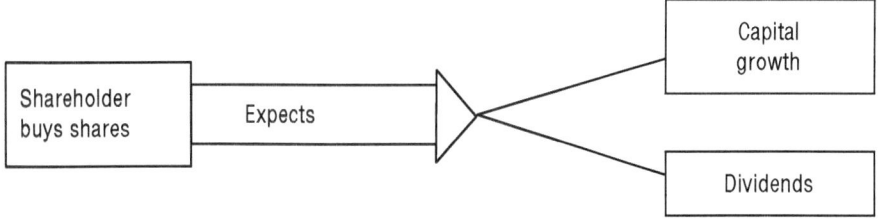

The exact nature of the return expected by the shareholder will depend on the type of company he has chosen to invest in: that is part of his investment risk analysis. Certain issues are true of any such investment, however. For example, if the directors **mismanage** the company, and it goes **bankrupt**, it will neither provide a source of future dividends, nor will it create capital growth in the investment – indeed, the opposite is true, and even the original investment is likely to be lost.

Accountability therefore covers a range of issues:

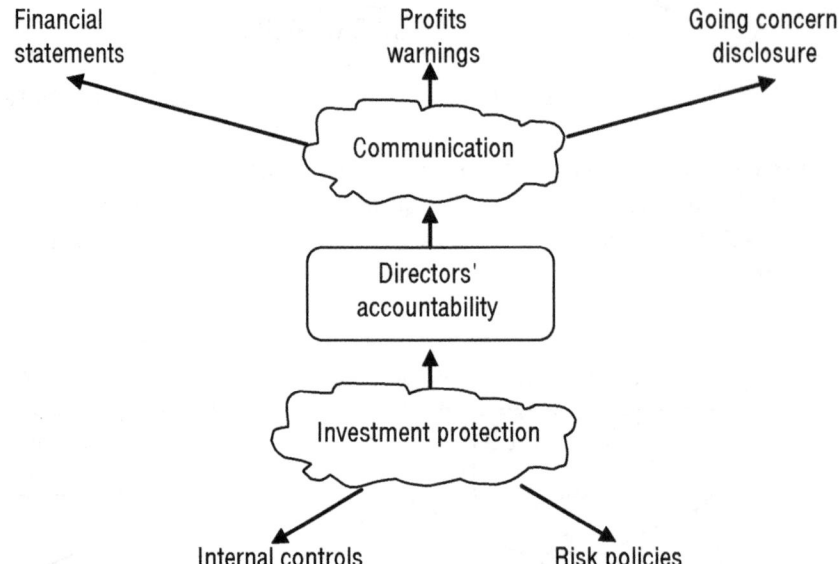

These issues are often discussed under the umbrella title '**corporate governance**', where 'governance' indicates the management (governing) role of the directors, and 'corporate' indicates that the issue relates to companies (bodies corporate). This is illustrated by our scenario, where we saw Laine taking up a corporate governance position in relation to Glyn. We look at corporate governance in more detail in Chapter 3 of this Workbook.

1.2 Assurance engagements

Many of the requirements in relation to corporate governance necessitate **communication** between the directors and the shareholders.

By law, **directors** of all companies are usually **required to produce financial statements** annually which give a **true and fair view** of the affairs of the company and its profit or loss for the period. They are also **encouraged** to **communicate with shareholders** on matters relating to **directors' pay** and benefits (this is required by law in the case of public limited companies), **going concern** and **management of risks**.

But how are the shareholders to know whether the directors' communications are **accurate**, or present a **fair picture?** We are back to the problem that Glyn had in the scenario we presented at the beginning of this section. He knew that Laine's view might be **biased** in a different way to his own, and he sought **assurance** on the information he was presented with. An **assurance engagement** is one where a professional accountant evaluates or measures a subject matter that is the responsibility of another party against suitable criteria, and expresses an opinion which provides the intended user with a level of assurance about that subject matter.

Key term

> An **assurance engagement** is one in which a practitioner aims to obtain sufficient appropriate evidence in order to express a conclusion designed to enhance the degree of confidence of the intended users other than the responsible party about the subject matter information (that is, the outcome of the measurement or evaluation of an underlying subject matter against criteria).

Question — Assurance reports

The concept of assurance is relevant in many aspects of life and is not simply confined to financial reporting.

Consider the following scenarios:

(1) You are currently debating whether or not to buy a house which was built in 1900.

(2) You work for a local council which is just about to issue a $10,000 grant to an organisation which runs sports activity courses for children with special needs.

Required

For each scenario, explain what assurance report you could obtain and who might provide this.

Answer

(1) Here you would want some comfort as to whether or not the house you plan to buy is structurally sound, whether the roof is in a good condition, whether there is any damp and so on. Most house buyers would have a survey carried out by a building surveyor prior to completing a purchase. This survey is carried out by an independent party that is professionally qualified and would give you confidence/comfort that there are no major issues with the property you plan to purchase.

(2) Here the council body will be concerned that the money they have given is used for the designated purpose. They will need assurance that the money has been spent on sports equipment, sports hall premises, staff and so forth rather than on items which are not related to this cause. The council could require the organisation to provide them with a report stating that the money was spent in accordance with the stipulations of the grant. This report would need to be produced by an independent body, perhaps an accountant.

2 The historical development of audit

FAST FORWARD

This syllabus is particularly concerned with the **external audit** (both statutory and non-statutory),

2.1 Statutory and non-statutory audits

Key term

The objective of an **audit** of financial statements is to enable the auditor to express an **opinion** whether the financial statements are prepared, in all material respects, in accordance with an identified financial reporting framework.

The phrases used to express the auditor's opinion are 'give a true and fair view' or 'present fairly, in all material respects', which are equivalent terms. A similar objective applies to the audit of financial or other information prepared in accordance with appropriate criteria.

The purpose of an audit is to enable auditors to **give an opinion** on the financial statements. While an audit might generate by-products such as advice to the directors on how to run the business, the point of an audit is **solely to report to shareholders.**

In most countries, audits are required under **national statute** in the case of a large number of undertakings, including limited liability companies. For example, in the UK the Companies Act 2006 requires companies to have an audit unless they qualify as a small company (this is covered in Chapter 2).

Other organisations and entities requiring a statutory audit may include charities, investment businesses, trade unions and so on.

The statutory audit can bring various advantages to the company and shareholders. The key benefit to shareholders is the impartial view provided by the auditors. However, the company benefits from professional accountants reviewing the accounts and system as part of the audit. Benefits might include recommendations being made in relation to accounting and control systems and the possibility that auditors might detect fraud and error.

Non-statutory audits are performed by independent auditors because the owners, proprietors, members, trustees, professional and governing bodies or other interested parties want them, rather than because the law requires them. In consequence, **auditing may extend** to every type of undertaking which produces accounts, including:

- Clubs
- Charities (some of these will require statutory audits as well)
- Sole traders
- Partnerships

2.1.1 Advantages of the non-statutory audit

In addition to the advantages common to all forms of audit, a non-statutory audit can bring other advantages. For example, the audit of the accounts of a **partnership** may be seen to have the following advantages.

(a) It can provide a means of **settling accounts** between the partners.

(b) Where audited accounts are available this may make the **accounts more acceptable** to the **taxation authorities** when it comes to agreeing an individual partner's liability to tax. The partners may well wish to take advantage of the auditors' services in the additional role of tax advisers.

(c) The **sale** of the business or the **negotiation of loan** or overdraft facilities may be facilitated if the firm is able to produce audited accounts.

(d) An audit on behalf of a **'sleeping partner'** is useful since generally such a person will have little other means of checking the accounts of the business, or confirming the share of profits due to him or her.

Question — Non-statutory audit

Some of the advantages above will also apply in the audit of the accounts of a sole trader, club or charity. Which ones? Can you think of any others?

Answer

The advantages of a non-statutory audit for a partnership may not be relevant to a sole trader, club or charity. However, an audit can be beneficial to these organisations in other ways.

Having an audit can provide credibility with stakeholders and improve relationships with them. It can demonstrate an organisation's commitment to financial transparency. An audit can also identify areas of weakness within an organisation and provide recommendations to improve those weaknesses. This can be particularly advantageous in charities which are unlikely, by their very nature, to operate in the same way as a for profit organisation. Additionally, for charities, an audit may be a prerequisite for eligibility for vital funding.

2.2 History of the audit

There is evidence that auditing procedures existed in the economic activities of many of the earliest civilisations, including those of Rome and ancient Egypt. Sometimes property owners who wanted to verify the activities of their employees undertook the task. In Britain in medieval times independent auditors who were employed by landowners carried out the job. The objective was to verify that the landowners were receiving the correct returns from the tenant farmers who worked on the estates. Early auditing also existed in government, usually related to the collection of taxation revenues.

2.2.1 Evolution of corporate organisations

In the nineteenth century in the UK and its empire, the **evolution of corporate organisations significantly separated ownership from management**, as discussed above. This brought about the need to account to the shareholders of companies by means of published accounts, as well as the corresponding need to verify the quality of the content of the statements.

The Joint Stock Companies Act of 1844 was the first enactment to require all incorporated companies to have their annual financial statements audited. In most cases, the auditor was one of the shareholders, elected by them. The audit report was to state whether the balance sheet (now called the statement of financial position) gave a 'full and fair view' of its state of affairs. In addition there was another major audit objective – to detect fraud and error in the company's accounting records.

The Companies Act 1856 removed the requirement for a statutory audit, but audits continued to be conducted on a voluntary basis. The government also retained the requirement for audit for industries with particularly bad records of dishonest managerial practices, such as the railways and banks.

In 1900 the requirement for an audit was restored for every company. The auditor was still not required to be a professional accountant, although he could not be a director of officer of the company being audited. However, as transactions became more complex, there grew a need for auditors with an accounting expertise sufficient to cope with the increasing complexity of accounting record keeping.

Until the 1920s, **fraud and error detection** continued to be the dominating factor in company audits. Gradually, however, there was a growing awareness of the usefulness of accounting information to investors, and more emphasis than before was placed on the information content of company accounts. The role of the auditor began to be viewed in terms of lending credibility to the financial statements, rather than certifying that they are free from fraud and error.

2.2.2 Accountancy profession develops

Along with this change in audit emphasis came the **emergence of a self-regulated accountancy profession**, whose members were educated and trained sufficiently to take responsibility for the corporate audit. These changes were formally recognised in the Companies Act 1948, which introduced for the first time the requirement that the auditor was to express an opinion as to the truth and fairness of the statement of profit or loss and other comprehensive income (also known as the' income statement' or the 'statement of profit or loss') as well as the statement of financial position. In addition, the auditor was required to possess a recognised professional qualification, and detailed provisions were included regarding their duties, powers and responsibilities. This Act has been amended by subsequent Companies Acts, but its main requirements remain substantially unchanged.

In the late 1940s the first **UK accounting practice guidelines** began to be issued by the Institute of Chartered Accountants of England and Wales. In 1961 the first formal guidance for auditors was issued. For the first time, audit practice was no longer a matter for individual auditors' professional judgement.

In 1980, the main accounting bodies introduced a new series of Auditing Standards and Guidelines intended to set out the basic principles and practices which auditors were expected to follow. We will look more at such regulation of auditing in Chapter 2.

2.2.3 Modern audit

The emphasis of today's company audit has switched from the detailed checking of individual transactions, to an **overall review of the systems** in operation by an **examination of the records and the financial statements**. The detection of fraud is no longer the main objective of the audit, although material discrepancies should be picked up as a result of normal audit procedures.

2.3 Internal audit function

FAST FORWARD

> **Internal auditors** are employed as part of an organisation's system of controls. Their responsibilities are determined by management and may be wide-ranging.

Key term

> The **internal audit function** is a function of an entity that performs assurance and consulting activities designed to evaluate and improve the effectiveness of the entity's governance, risk management and internal control processes (ISA 610 (Revised 2013)).

Up to now in this chapter we have discussed the external audit, where an independent outsider provides an opinion on financial information. However, the syllabus is also concerned with the assurance that can be provided to management by the **internal auditor function**.

As part of their corporate governance duties, listed company directors are required, and all directors are advised, to review the effectiveness of the company's risk management and internal control systems. They should also consider the need for an **internal audit function to help them carry out their duties.** A listed company is one with shares that are listed on a public stock exchange, for example the UK Stock Exchange.

Larger organisations may therefore appoint full-time staff whose **function is to monitor and report on the running of the company's operations**. Internal audit staff members are one type of control. Although some of the work carried out by internal auditors is similar to that performed by external auditors, there are **important distinctions** between the two functions in terms of their responsibilities, scope and relationship with the company. These are discussed further in Chapter 3.

3 The objective of an external audit

FAST FORWARD

> The purpose of an external audit is to enable auditors to **give an independent opinion** on the financial statements.

3.1 Objectives of the auditor

Key term

> In conducting an audit of financial statements, the overall **objectives of the auditor** are:
>
> (a) To obtain reasonable assurance about whether the financial statements as a whole are free from material misstatement due to fraud or error, thereby enabling the auditor to express an opinion on whether the financial statements are prepared, in all material respects, in accordance with an applicable financial reporting framework; and
>
> (b) To report on the financial statements, and communicate as required by the ISAs, in accordance with the auditor's finding.

The purpose of an external audit is to enable auditors to **give an opinion** on the financial statements. While an audit might generate by-products such as recommendations to the directors on improvements to the internal control systems, its objective is **solely to report to the shareholders on the truth and fairness of the financial statements.**

3.2 Truth and fairness

External auditors give an opinion on the **truth and fairness** of financial statements. This is not an opinion of absolute correctness. 'True' and 'fair' are not defined in law or audit guidance, but the following definitions are generally accepted.

Key terms

> **True:** Information is factual and conforms with reality. In addition the information conforms with required standards and law. The financial statements have been correctly extracted from the books and records.
>
> **Fair:** Information is free from discrimination and bias and in compliance with expected standards and rules. The accounts should reflect the commercial substance of the company's underlying transactions.

3.3 Example auditor's report (unmodified)

Below is an example of an auditor's report on an entity's financial statements. This is a report with an **unmodified** opinion (which means the financial statements are true and fair and properly prepared).

INDEPENDENT AUDITOR'S REPORT

To the Shareholders of ABC Company [or other appropriate addressee]

Report on the audit of the financial statements

Opinion

We have audited the financial statements of ABC Company (ABC), which comprise the statement of financial position as at 31 December 20X1, and the statement of comprehensive income, statement of changes in equity and statement of cash flows for the year then ended, and notes to the financial statements, including a summary of significant accounting policies.

In our opinion, the accompanying financial statements present fairly, in all material respects, (or **give a true and fair view of**) the financial position of ABC as at 31 December 20X1, and (of) its financial performance and its cash flows for the year then ended, in accordance with International Financial Reporting Standards (IFRS Accounting Standards).

Basis for opinion

We conducted our audit in accordance with International Standards on Auditing (ISAs). Our responsibilities under those standards are further described in the *Auditor's Responsibilities for the Audit of the Financial Statements* section of our report. We are independent of ABC in accordance with the International Ethics Standards Board for Accountants' *Code of Ethics for Professional Accountants* (IESBA *Code*) together with the ethical requirements that are relevant to our audit of the financial statements in [jurisdiction], and we have fulfilled our other ethical responsibilities in accordance with these requirements and the IESBA *Code*. We believe that the audit evidence we have obtained is sufficient and appropriate to provide a basis for our opinion.

Key audit matters

Key audit matters are those matters that, in our professional judgment, were of most significance in our audit of the financial statements of the current period. These matters were addressed in the context of our audit of the financial statements as a whole and in forming our opinion thereon, and we do not provide a separate opinion on these matters.

[Description of each key audit matter in accordance with ISA 701.]

Other Information

Management is responsible for the other information. The other information comprises the [information included in the X report, but does not include the financial statements and our auditor's report thereon.]

Our opinion on the financial statements does not cover the other information and we do not express any form of assurance conclusion thereon.

In connection with our audit of the financial statements, our responsibility is to read the other information and, in doing so, consider whether the other information is materially inconsistent with the financial statements or our knowledge obtained in the audit, or otherwise appears to be materially misstated. If, based on the work we have performed, we conclude that there is a material misstatement of this other information, we are required to report that fact. We have nothing to report in this regard.

Responsibilities of management and those charged with governance for the financial statements

Management is responsible for the preparation and fair presentation of the financial statements in accordance with IFRS Accounting Standards and for such internal control as management determines is necessary to enable the preparation of financial statements that are free from material misstatement, whether due to fraud or error.

In preparing the financial statements, management is responsible for assessing ABC's ability to continue as a going concern, disclosing, as applicable, matters related to going concern and using the going concern basis of accounting unless management either intends to liquidate the company or to cease operations, or has no realistic alternative but to do so.

Those charged with governance are responsible for overseeing ABC's financial reporting process.

Auditor's responsibilities for the audit of the financial statements

Our objectives are to obtain reasonable assurance about whether the financial statements as a whole are free from material misstatement, whether due to fraud or error, and to issue an auditor's report that includes our opinion. Reasonable assurance is a high level of assurance, but is not a guarantee that an audit conducted in accordance with ISAs will always detect a material misstatement when it exists. Misstatements can arise from fraud or error and are considered material if, individually or in the aggregate, they could reasonably be expected to influence the economic decisions of users taken on the basis of these financial statements.

As part of an audit in accordance with ISAs, we exercise professional judgment and maintain professional scepticism throughout the audit. We also:

- Identify and assess the risks of material misstatement of the financial statements, whether due to fraud or error; design and perform audit procedures responsive to those risks; and obtain audit evidence that is sufficient and appropriate to provide a basis for our opinion. The risk of not detecting a material misstatement resulting from fraud is higher than for one resulting from error, as fraud may involve collusion, forgery, intentional omissions, misrepresentations, or the override of internal control.

- Obtain an understanding of internal control relevant to the audit in order to design audit procedures that are appropriate in the circumstances, but not for the purpose of expressing an opinion on the effectiveness of ABC's internal control.

- Evaluate the appropriateness of accounting policies used and the reasonableness of accounting estimates and related disclosures made by management.

- Conclude on the appropriateness of management's use of the going concern basis of accounting and, based on the audit evidence obtained, whether a material uncertainty exists related to events or conditions that may cast significant doubt on ABC's ability to continue as a going concern. If we conclude that a material uncertainty exists, we are required to draw attention in our auditor's report to the related disclosures in the financial statements or, if such disclosures are inadequate, to modify our opinion. Our conclusions are based on the audit evidence obtained up to the date of our auditor's report. However, future events or conditions may cause ABC to cease to continue as a going concern.

- Evaluate the overall presentation, structure and content of the financial statements, including the disclosures, and whether the financial statements represent the underlying transactions and events in a manner that achieves fair presentation.

We communicate with those charged with governance regarding, among other matters, the planned scope and timing of the audit and significant audit findings, including any significant deficiencies in internal control that we identify during our audit.

We also provide those charged with governance with a statement that we have complied with relevant ethical requirements regarding independence, and to communicate with them all relationships and other matters that may reasonably be thought to bear on our independence, and where applicable, related safeguards.

From the matters communicated with those charged with governance, we determine those matters that were of most significance in the audit of the financial statements of the current period and are therefore the key audit matters. We describe these matters in our auditor's report unless law or regulation precludes public disclosure about the matter or when, in extremely rare circumstances, we determine that a matter should not be communicated in our report because the adverse consequences of doing so would reasonably be expected to outweigh the public interest benefits of such communication.

Report on other legal and regulatory requirements

[The form and content of this section of the auditor's report would vary depending on the nature of the auditor's other reporting responsibilities prescribed by local law, regulation, or national auditing standards. The matters addressed by other law, regulation or national auditing standards (referred to as 'other reporting responsibilities') shall be addressed within this section unless the other reporting responsibilities address the same topics as those presented under the reporting responsibilities required by the ISAs as part of the Report on the Audit of the Financial Statements section. The reporting of other reporting responsibilities that address the same topics as those required by the ISAs may be combined (ie, included in the Report on the Audit of the Financial Statements section under the appropriate subheadings) provided that the wording in the auditor's report clearly differentiates the other reporting responsibilities from the reporting that is required by the ISAs, where such a difference exists.]

The engagement partner on the audit resulting in this independent auditor's report is [name].

[Signature in the name of the audit firm, the personal name of the auditor, or both, as appropriate for the particular jurisdiction.]

[Auditor Address]

[Date]

Exam focus point

You should be able to list the contents of an unmodified audit report. We look at the auditor's report in greater detail in Chapter 18.

RPQ students: In June 2016, the FRC revised ISAs (UK) which are now aligned with the ISAs issued by the IAASB. You can find the revised ISAs (UK) on the FRC's website (www.frc.org.uk) in the standards and guidance section.

Auditor's reports with **modified** opinions may arise because of a number of different reasons and are discussed in Chapter 18.

3.4 Reasonable assurance

The auditor's report refers to the fact that the audit is planned and performed to obtain 'reasonable assurance' whether the financial statements are free from material misstatement.

This is because the auditor cannot check everything and therefore can only provide 'reasonable' not 'absolute' assurance.

Key term

> An auditor's report gives the reader **reasonable assurance** on the truth and fairness of the financial statements, which is a high, but not absolute, level of assurance. The auditor's report does not guarantee that the financial statements are correct, but that they are true and fair within a reasonable margin of error.

One reason an auditor does not give absolute assurance is because of the **inherent limitations** of an audit.

3.5 Limitations of audit

FAST FORWARD

> Audits give **reasonable assurance** that the accounts are free from material misstatement.

The assurance auditors give is governed by the fact that auditors use **judgement** in deciding what audit procedures to use and what conclusions to draw, and also by the limitations of every audit.

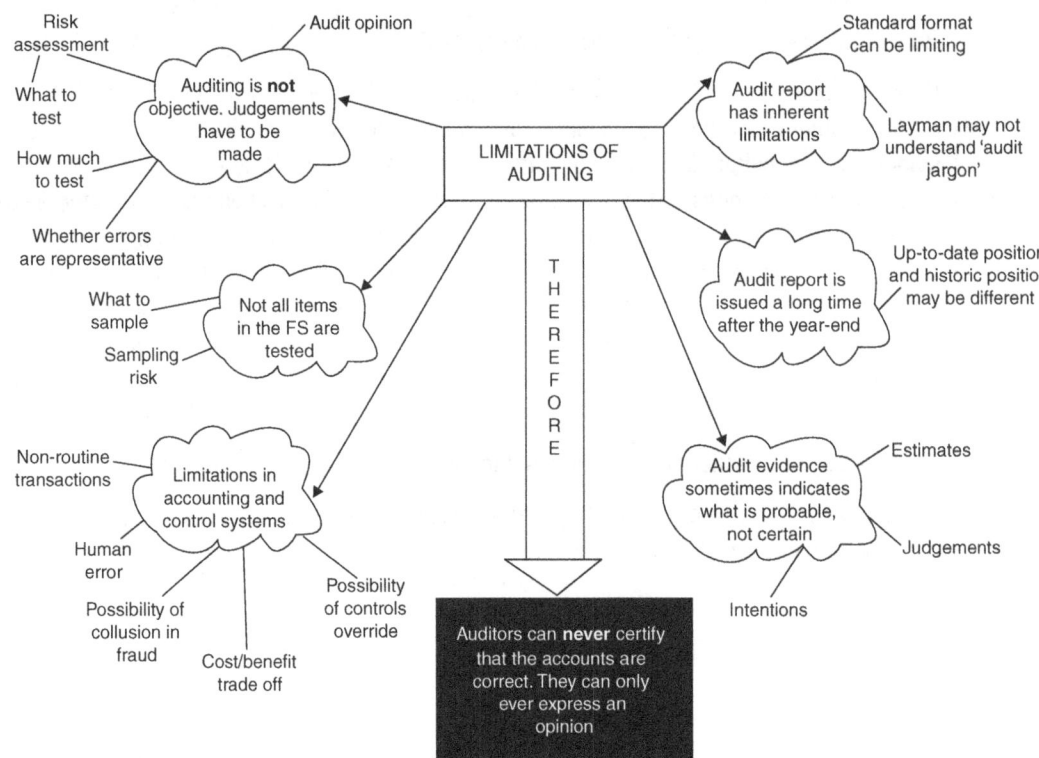

Misstatements which are significant to readers may exist in financial statements and auditors will plan their work on this basis, that is, with **professional scepticism**. The concept of '**significance to readers**' is the concept of materiality.

3.6 Materiality

Misstatements which are significant to readers may exist in financial statements and auditors will plan their work on this basis, that is, with **professional scepticism**. This is the concept of **materiality**.

Key term

> **Materiality** is an expression of the relative significance or importance of a particular matter in the context of financial statements as a whole.
>
> A matter is material if its omission or misstatement would reasonably influence the decisions of an addressee of the auditors' report.
>
> Materiality may also be considered in the context of any individual primary statement within the financial statements or of individual items included in them.
>
> Materiality is not capable of general mathematical definition as it has both qualitative and quantitative aspects.

The auditors' task is to decide whether the financial statements show a **true and fair view**. The auditors are not responsible for establishing whether the financial statements are correct in every particular.

- It can take a great deal of time and trouble to check the accuracy of even a very small transaction and the resulting benefit may not justify the effort.
- Financial accounting inevitably involves a degree of estimation which means that financial statements can never be completely precise.

Although the definition of materiality refers to the decisions of the addressees of the auditor's report (the company's members), materiality levels may well be influenced by other entities that use the financial statements, for example, the bank.

Question — Materiality

Define the term 'not material' and state in which context it might be used.

Answer

Generally speaking, transactions or other events will be seen as material in the context of an entity's financial statements, if their omission or misstatement would reasonably influence the decisions of an addressee of the auditors' report. Therefore, items are judged 'not material' because their omission or misstatement will be judged to not influence the decisions of users. The report lends some credibility to those statements which will have been prepared by the management of the entity.

In order to form an opinion on truth and fairness, the auditors will need to exercise their professional judgement and experience in relation to the question of materiality. It will be important for the auditors to assess materiality not merely in monetary terms but also in the overall context of the company's financial statements, statutory requirements and recognised best accounting and auditing practice.

We will look at materiality in more detail in Chapter 7.

4 Responsibilities of directors and auditors

> **FAST FORWARD**
> The auditors' report clearly describes the respective responsibilities of directors (those charged with governance) and auditors in order to enhance public understanding on the matter.

4.1 Directors' responsibilities

Directors have overall responsibility to run the company in the best interests of the shareholders. These include:

- To prepare and present financial statements which are in accordance with International Financial Reporting Standards (IFRS Accounting Standards) and free from material misstatement, whether due to fraud or error;
- To implement a system of internal controls which is appropriate to manage risk, prevent and detect fraud and prepare financial statements; and
- To make an assessment as to whether the entity can continue as a going concern and make applicable disclosures in the financial statements.

4.2 Auditors' responsibilities

The auditors' responsibilities are really quite simple. They need to obtain an understanding of the client entity so that they can plan and perform their audit to obtain reasonable assurance that the financial statements are free from material misstatement, whether due to fraud or error, and to issue a report that provides that opinion.

The journey that the auditor follows to be in a position to do this will be explained as you work your way through this Workbook.

4.3 Expectations gap

This difference between the actual legal and professional responsibilities of the auditor and the public perception of their responsibilities is part of what is called the '**expectations gap**'.

One response to this was to extend the information provided in the auditor's report concerning the responsibilities of directors and auditors.

Specific misunderstandings are highlighted below.

(a) **Misunderstandings of the nature of audited financial statements**, for example that:

- The statement of financial position provides a fair valuation of the reporting entity.
- The amounts in the financial statements are stated precisely.
- The audited financial statements will guarantee that the entity concerned will continue to exist.

(b) **Misunderstanding as to the type and extent of work undertaken by auditors**

(c) **Misunderstanding about the level of assurance provided by auditors**, for example that:

- An unmodified auditor's opinion means that no frauds have occurred in the period.
- The auditors provide absolute assurance that the figures in the financial statements are correct (ignoring the concept of materiality and the problems of estimation).

Different countries have tackled this problem in different ways. The role of auditors has been included in the debate on corporate governance in many western countries, leading to further rules which are nevertheless voluntary, not mandatory.

5 The Global Reporting Initiative (GRI)

> **FAST FORWARD**
>
> The GRI Standards enable any organisation to understand and report on their impacts on the economy, environment and people in a comparable and credible way.

Earlier in this chapter we explored the concept that the directors of a company have a **stewardship role** and are appointed by the shareholders as **agents** to manage the company in the shareholder's best interests. The directors must produce annual financial statements in order to report the company's financial position and performance to the shareholders who will need **assurance** as to the validity and accuracy of this information. This assurance is provided by the **external auditor** in the form of their auditor's report and so we see that the external auditors also act as **an agent** for the shareholders.

In recent years there has been a shift in focus whereby shareholders and other stakeholders are not solely interested in a company's financial position and performance but also its social and environmental impacts and initiatives. This has prompted companies to include this information in their annual report.

5.1 The history of the Global Reporting Initiative

The Global Reporting Initiative (GRI) was established in 1997 with the objective of creating a **universal standardised framework** for voluntary reporting on the **economic, social, and environmental impacts of corporations** and other entities (White, 1999).

The GRI launched the first global standards for sustainability reporting in October 2016. These Standards empower an organisation to **publicly report its primary impacts** on the economy, environment, and society, including its effects on human rights and its management of these effects. This **fosters transparency** regarding the organisation's impacts and **enhances its accountability**.

The GRI Standards comprise disclosures that enable **consistent and credible reporting** of information about these impacts by organisations. This, in turn, **improves the global comparability and quality** of reported information concerning these impacts, **aiding information users** in making informed evaluations and decisions regarding the organisation's impacts and its contribution to sustainable development (Global Reporting Initiative, 2023).

5.2 The system of GRI Standards

The GRI Standards are structured as a system of interrelated standards that are organised into three series:

- GRI Universal Standards,
- GRI Sector Standards, and
- GRI Topic Standards.

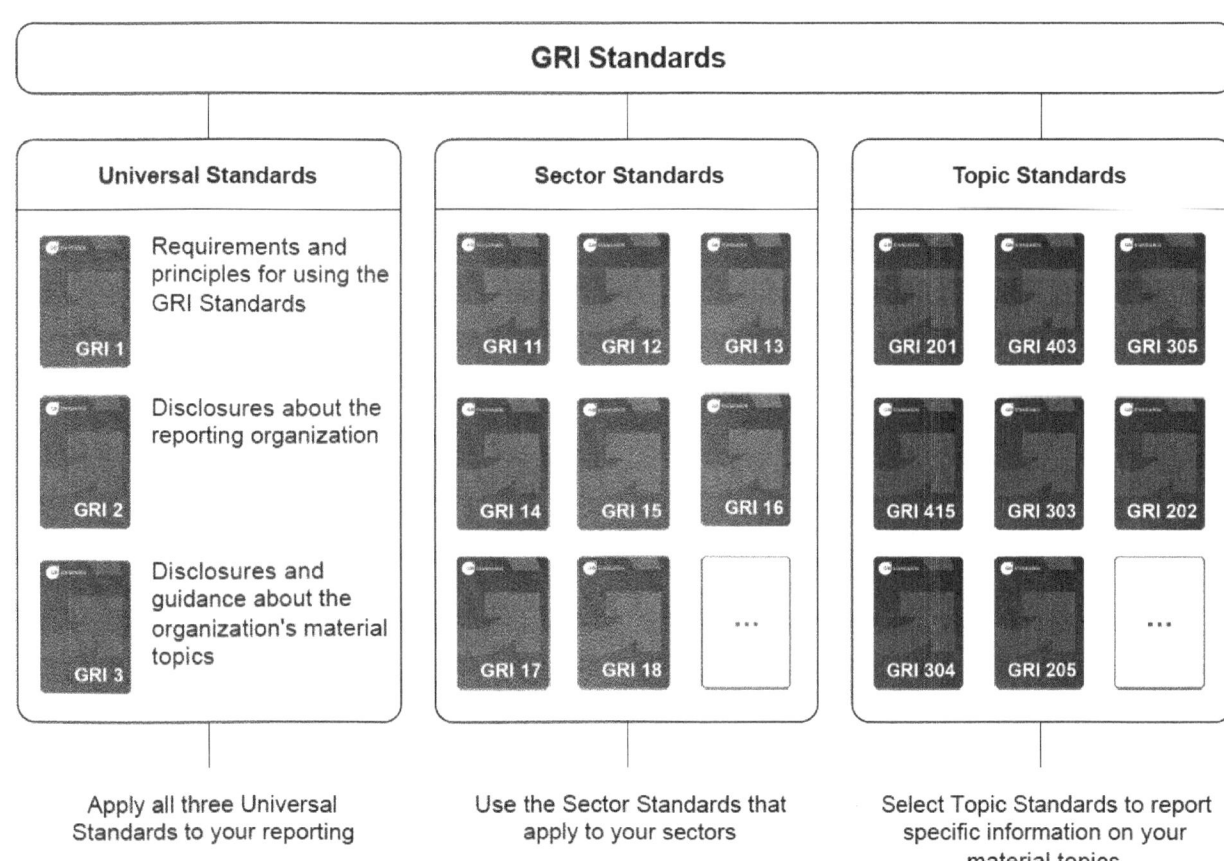

Source: https://www.globalreporting.org/media/s4cp0oth/gri-gristandards-visuals-fig1_family-2021-print-v19-01.png

The *Universal Standards* are used by all organisations when reporting in accordance with the GRI Standards. Organisations use the *Sector Standards* according to the sectors in which they operate, and the *Topic Standards* according to their list of material topics.

5.2.1 Universal Standards

GRI 1 *Foundation 2021* introduces and **outlines the purpose** of the GRI Standards, clarifies critical concepts, and explains how to use the Standards. It lists the requirements that an organisation must comply with to report in accordance with the Standards. It also specifies the principles – such as accuracy, balance, and verifiability – that are fundamental to high-quality reporting.

GRI 2 *General Disclosures 2021* contains **disclosures relating to details about an organisation's structure and reporting practices**; activities and workers; governance; strategy; policies; practices; and stakeholder engagement. These give insight into an organisation's profile and scale and help to provide context for understanding the organisation's impacts.

GRI 3 *Material Topics 2021* provides step-by-step **guidance on how to determine material topics**. GRI 3 explains the steps by which an organisation can determine its material topics and describes how the GRI Sector Standards are used in this process. It also contains disclosures to report the process by which an organisation has determined its material topics; its list of material topics; and how it manages each topic.

5.2.2 Sector Standards

Each Sector Standard lists topics that are likely to be **material** for an organisation in each sector **based on the sector's most significant impacts**. For each likely material topic, the Sector Standards also list disclosures from the GRI Topic Standards for an organisation to report. The Sector Standards are an integral part of reporting using the GRI Standards. Any organisation that wishes to state that its report has been prepared in accordance with the Standards is required to use the applicable Sector Standards, if applicable when determining its material topics.

5.2.3 Topic Standards

Each Topic Standard is **dedicated to a particular topic and contains disclosures relevant to that topic**. Examples include Topic Standards on waste, occupational health and safety, and tax. Each Topic Standard contains an overview of the topic and disclosures for an organisation to report about its impacts concerning the topic, as well as how it manages them. An organisation uses the Topic Standards that correspond to the topics it has determined to be material for reporting.

A list of the available Topic Standards can be found on the GRI website (GRI, 2021). The GRI Universal Standards 2021 have an effective date of 1 January 2023. This means that all information published by an organisation on or after that date must make use of this version of the Universal Standards.

5.3 Reporting in accordance with the GRI Standards

The organisation must **comply with all nine requirements** in this section to report in accordance with the GRI Standards (Global Sustainability Standards Board (GSSB), 2021):

- Requirement 1: Apply the reporting principles.
- Requirement 2: Report the disclosures in GRI 2 *General Disclosures 2021*
- Requirement 3: Determine material topics.
- Requirement 4: Report the disclosures in GRI 3 *Material Topics 2021*
- Requirement 5: Report disclosures from the GRI Topic Standards for each material topic

- Requirement 6: Provide reasons for the omission of disclosures and requirements that the organisation cannot comply with
- Requirement 7: Publish a GRI content index.
- Requirement 8: Provide a statement of use.
- Requirement 9: Notify GRI

If the organisation does not comply with all nine requirements, it cannot claim that it has prepared the reported information in accordance with the GRI Standards.

5.4 GRI Reporting Principles

GRI 1 presents the **reporting principles** that every organisation needs to apply throughout its reporting process to claim that its report has been prepared in accordance with the GRI Standards. The reporting principles are **fundamental to achieving high-quality sustainability reporting** as they guide the organisation in ensuring the quality and proper presentation of the disclosed information. High-quality information allows information users to make informed assessments and decisions about the organisation's impacts and its contribution to sustainable development.

There are eight reporting principles:

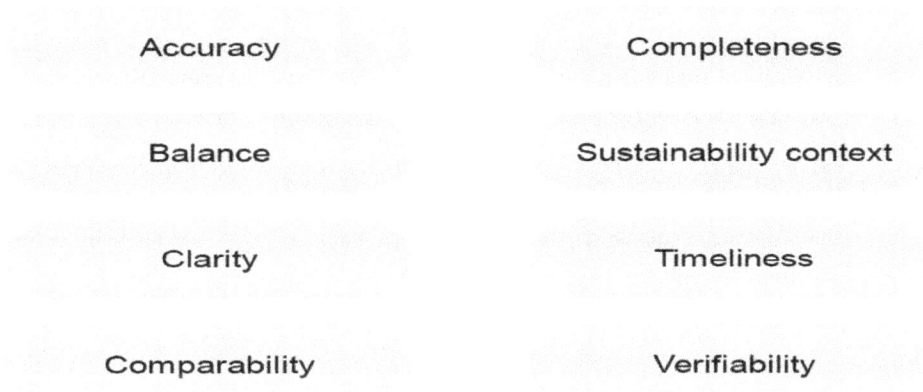

Each reporting principle consists of a requirement and guidance on how to apply it.

Reporting principle	Requirement
Accuracy	The organisation shall report information that is correct and sufficiently detailed to allow an assessment of the organisation's impacts.
Balance	The organisation shall report information in an unbiased way and provide a fair representation of the organisation's negative and positive impacts.
Clarity	The organisation shall present information in a way that is accessible and understandable.
Comparability	The organisation shall select, compile, and report information consistently to enable an analysis of changes in the organisation's impacts over time and an analysis of these impacts relative to those of other organisations.
Completeness	The organisation shall provide sufficient information to enable an assessment of the organisation's impacts during the reporting period.

Reporting principle	Requirement
Sustainability context	The organisation shall report information about its impacts in the wider context of sustainable development.
Timeliness	The organisation shall report information on a regular schedule and make it available in time for information users to make decisions.
Verifiability	The organisation shall gather, record, compile, and analyse information in such a way that the information can be examined to establish its quality.

5.5 Examples of organisations using GRI

The GRI is widely used by organisations worldwide for sustainability reporting. Review the examples of organisations below which are linked to their sustainability reports:

- **Unilever:** Unilever is a multinational consumer goods company. They are known for their commitment to sustainability and have been using GRI guidelines for their reporting. You can find their latest sustainability report on their website: Unilever Sustainability Report

- **Nestlé:** Nestlé is another multinational food and beverage company that utilises GRI guidelines for their sustainability reporting. Their latest sustainability report can be found here: Nestle Sustainability Report

- **Siemens:** Siemens is a global technology company focusing on electrification, automation, and digitalisation. They publish an annual sustainability report following GRI guidelines. You can access their latest sustainability report here: Siemens Sustainability Report

- **IBM:** International Business Machines Corporation is an American multinational technology company headquartered in Armonk, New York and present in over 175 countries. You can access their latest sustainability report here: IBM Sustainability Report and their GRI index can be found here: IBM GRI Index

Below is an example page from IBM's GRI Index, this shows part of their disclosure relating to the topic-specific GRI Standard, GRI 302:

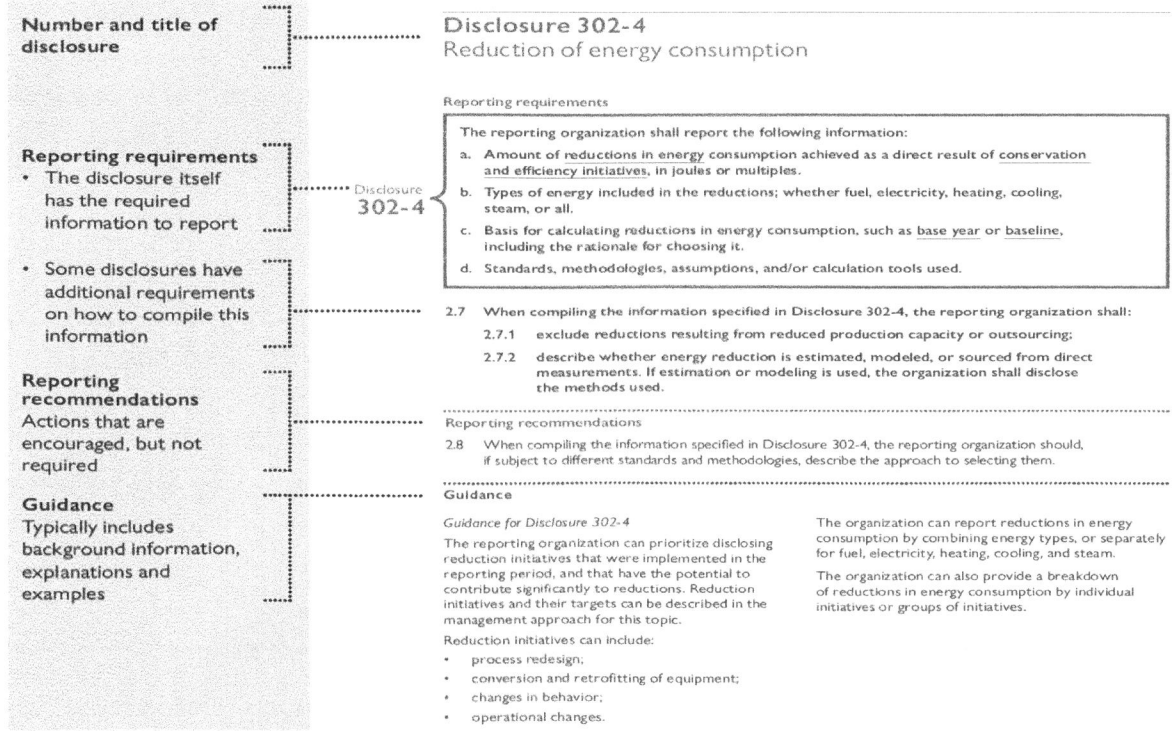

IBM's disclosure of GRI 302-4

These are just a few examples, and many more organisations across various industries use GRI guidelines for their sustainability reporting. You can usually find these reports on the respective company's websites under their sustainability or corporate responsibility sections.

5.6 The Integrated Reporting Framework

An **integrated report** is a concise communication about an organisation's **strategy, governance, performance and prospects**. The report summarises how the organisation **creates value** in the short, medium and long term.

The Integrated Reporting Framework (<IR> Framework) provides a structure that companies can use to explain **how they manage their responses to the external environment** and create value for shareholders. This allows companies to provide information about environmental risks and opportunities and to **connect** this information with information presented in financial statements.

The <IR> Framework was originally published in 2013 by the Value Reporting Foundation (VRF). The VRF merged with the IFRS Foundation in August 2022 and at that time the IFRS Foundation's International Accounting Standards Board (IASB) and International Sustainability Standards Board (ISSB) assumed joint responsibility for the <IR> Framework.

5.6.1 Objective of the <IR> Framework

The <IR> Framework has four objectives:

- The purpose of the Framework is to establish **guiding principles and content elements** that govern the overall content of an integrated report, and to explain the **fundamental concepts** that underpin them.

- The Framework is written primarily in the context of private sector, for-profit companies of any size but it can also be applied, adapted as necessary, by public sector and not-for-profit organisations.
- The Framework identifies information to be included in an integrated report for use in **assessing an organisation's ability to create value**; it does not set benchmarks for such things as the quality of an organisation's strategy or the level of its performance.
- In the Framework, reference to the creation of value includes instances when **value is preserved** and **when it is eroded** and relates to value creation over time.

(<IR> Framework (2013))

5.6.2 Fundamental concepts

There are three fundamental concepts underpinning <IR>:

- Value creation, preservation or erosion for the organisation and for others.
- The **capitals**, which are identified in the Framework as financial, manufactured, intellectual, human, social and relationship, and natural capital.
- Process through which value is created, preserved or eroded.

(<IR> Framework (2013))

5.6.3 Purpose and content of an integrated report

The <IR> Framework sets out the purpose of an integrated report as follows:

> The primary purpose of an integrated report is to explain to providers of financial capital how an organisation creates, preserves or erodes value over time. It therefore contains relevant information, **both financial and other**. An integrated report benefits all stakeholders interested in an organisation's ability to create value over time, including employees, customers, suppliers, business partners, local communities, legislators, regulators and policy-makers.
>
> (<IR> Framework (2013))

An integrated report includes guiding principles and content elements.

Guiding principles underpin the preparation of an integrated report, informing the content of the report and how information is presented. They include:

- Strategic focus and future orientation
- Connectivity of information
- Stakeholder relationships
- Materiality
- Conciseness
- Reliability and completeness
- Consistency and comparability

Content elements describe the key categories of information required to be included in an integrated report under the <IR> Framework. They include:

- Organisational overview and external environment
- Governance
- Business model
- Risks and opportunities
- Strategy and resource allocation
- Performance
- Outlook
- Basis of preparation and presentation

6 IFRS Sustainability Disclosure Standards

FAST FORWARD

Sustainability: "meeting the needs of the present without compromising the ability of future generations to meet their own needs."

The United Nations Brundtland Commission defined 1987

6.1 What is sustainability?

Sustainability is not a new concept. In 1987 the United Nations Brundtland Commission defined sustainability as "meeting the needs of the present without compromising the ability of future generations to meet their own needs."

Sustainability is not just about looking after the natural environment, it includes:

- Environment
- Society
- Economics
- Governance

6.2 The need for sustainability reporting

Investors and other stakeholders are increasingly interested in sustainability including both the **impact an entity has** on the environment and society, as well as understanding **how the entity is dependent** on these factors.

Entities want to ensure that they attract and retain investors, and also appeal to a wide range of stakeholders. They have increasingly been conducting their business in a more sustainable way and providing additional disclosures in the annual report. These disclosures may be within a **strategic report** or a separate **sustainability report** but are **not part of the financial statements** and are **not in the scope of IFRS Accounting Standards**.

6.3 IFRS Sustainability Disclosure Standards

The establishment of The International Sustainability Standards Board (ISSB) was announced during COP26, the United Nations Climate Change Conference. The intention is for **ISSB to deliver a comprehensive global baseline of standards for sustainability-related disclosures**. The standards are to provide investors and other capital market participants with information about the companies' **sustainability-related risks and opportunities**, to help them make informed decisions.

This aims to **improve the reliability and comparability of reporting** by companies on climate and other environmental, social and governance (ESG) matters.

The ISSB issued its first two IFRS Sustainability Disclosure Standards in June 2023, and these address general requirements for the disclosure of sustainability-related information and climate-related disclosures.

- IFRS S1: *General Requirements for Disclosure of Sustainability-related Financial Information*
- IFRS S2: *Climate-related Disclosures*

IFRS S1 sets out the general requirements for disclosing sustainability-related information and refers companies to either other ISSB Standards or other sources for detailed requirements on different topics. For climate-related disclosures, entities should apply IFRS S2. As there are currently no other issued ISSB Standards, an entity should use other sources for guidance on what to disclose on other sustainability-related topics.

The standards are effective for reporting periods beginning from 1 January 2024, though earlier adoption is permitted provided both standards are applied together.

The ISSB Sustainability Standards can be accessed on the IFRS Foundation website here: https://www.ifrs.org/issued-standards/ifrs-sustainability-standards-navigator/

6.4 IFRS S1: *General Requirements for Disclosure of Sustainability-related Financial Information*

6.4.1 Scope and Objective

The objective of IFRS S1 is to require an entity to disclose information about its **sustainability-related risks and opportunities** that is useful to investors when making decisions relating to providing resources to the entity (IFRS S1: para. 1).

IFRS S1 provides a framework for entities to disclose sustainability-related information that is material to their financial performance and prospects. This information can help investors and other stakeholders make informed decisions.

IFRS S1's underlying principle is that an entities' ability to generate cash flows (including raising finance) in the short, medium and long term are inextricably linked to the interactions between the entity and its:

- stakeholders
- society
- the economy
- the natural environment

An entity's business practices can have an **impact** on these, yet at the same time the entity is **dependent** on them. This created both sustainability-related risks and opportunities. (IFRS S1 para. 1–2)

Impacts	'Impacts' refers to **the effect that an entity has** on its stakeholders, society, the economy and the natural environment, through the resources it uses and the relationships it has in its value chain.
	For example:
	- worker rights,
	- human rights,
	- waste,
	- greenhouse gas emissions,
	- water use and use of other natural resources
	Information on impacts is likely to be most useful for **broader stakeholders**, such as governments, consumers, employees and wider society who want to know how the entity's actions and future strategy will **impact both people and planet**.
Dependencies	'Dependencies' refers to **the reliance an entity has on its stakeholders, society, the economy and the natural environment** through the resources it uses and the relationships it has in its value chain.
	For example:
	- worker health,
	- diversity,
	- climate risk,
	- resource availability,
	- consumer expectations,
	- regulatory risk

| | Disclosures on dependencies are likely to be more useful for **investors, lenders and creditors** as **dependencies create risks and opportunities** which can affect the entity's prospects. |

A 'value chain' is defined by the ISSB as 'the full range of interactions, resources and relationships related to a reporting entity's business model and the external environment in which it operates.' (IFRS S1: Appendix A)

Question — Benefits of sustainability reporting

Required

What are some of the potential benefits to investors of entities reporting on sustainability?

Answer

There are many benefits to investors, including:

Assess Future Financial Performance:

An entity's ability to generate cash flows in the short, medium and long term is linked to interactions between the entity and its stakeholders, society, economy and natural environment. By disclosing information about sustainability-related risks and opportunities investors can better understand how the entity is managing these risks and opportunities to affect the entity's prospects.

Investors can assess an entity's ability to adapt to future environmental, social, and technological challenges.

Risk Mitigation:

Sustainability reporting provides investors with insights into a company's exposure to environmental, social, and governance (ESG) risks. By understanding these risks, investors can make informed decisions about their investments and mitigate potential losses. For instance, a company with a poor environmental record may face regulatory fines or reputational damage, which could negatively impact its financial performance, or even lead to going concern issues.

Ethical Investing:

Disclosures enable investors to identify companies that are leading the way in sustainability and make informed decisions about their investment portfolios. By investing in entities that produce sustainability reports, investors can support the broader adoption of sustainable business practices.

6.4.1.1 Core content

IFRS S1 requires a company to disclose how it manages its sustainability-related risks and opportunities under four headings: **governance, strategy, risk management, and metrics and targets** (IFRS S1: paras. 25–53).

Category	Disclosure
Governance	The governance **processes, controls and procedures** the entity uses to **monitor, manage and oversee** sustainability-related risks and opportunities.
	This includes how boards or equivalents and management are **informed, supported and trained** in addressing these risks and opportunities.

Category	Disclosure
Strategy	The approach the entity uses to manage sustainability-related **risks and opportunities** and their **anticipated effects** on the entity's **prospects, business model, value chain, strategy and decision making**. Note that some quantification of these effects is expected alongside these qualitative disclosures.
Risk management	The processes the entity uses to **identify, assess, prioritise and monitor sustainability-related risks and opportunities**. Note that disclosures should consider data sources and how these risks are assessed, including how they should be prioritised relative to other types of risk. Any changes to these processes from previous years should also be reported.
Metrics and targets	The entity's **performance** in relation to sustainability-related risks and opportunities, including **progress towards any targets** the entity has set or is required to meet by law or regulation. Note that metrics can come from a range of sources but should be justified if not ISSB-driven. Details of the metrics used should be provided: for example, whether they are relative or absolute measures, are externally validated and rely on certain assumptions.

6.5 IFRS S2: *Climate-related Disclosures*

6.5.1 Scope and Objective

The objective of IFRS S2 is to require an entity to disclose information about **climate-related risks and opportunities** that are reasonably expected to affect the entity's prospects (IFRS S2: paras. 1–2). Climate-related risks and opportunities arise from an entity's **impacts and dependencies** on people and the environment (IFRS S2: para. BC26):

- **Dependencies**, for example changes in the availability or quality of a resource such as water, **can lead to climate-related risks** for the entity.

- An entity's **impacts can result in climate-related risks and opportunities** if the impact affects the resources or relationships an entity depends on. For example, greenhouse gas emissions (impact) could result in a climate-related risk if there is an expected shift in consumer preference to carbon-neutral alternatives. (IFRS S2: para. BC27–BC28)

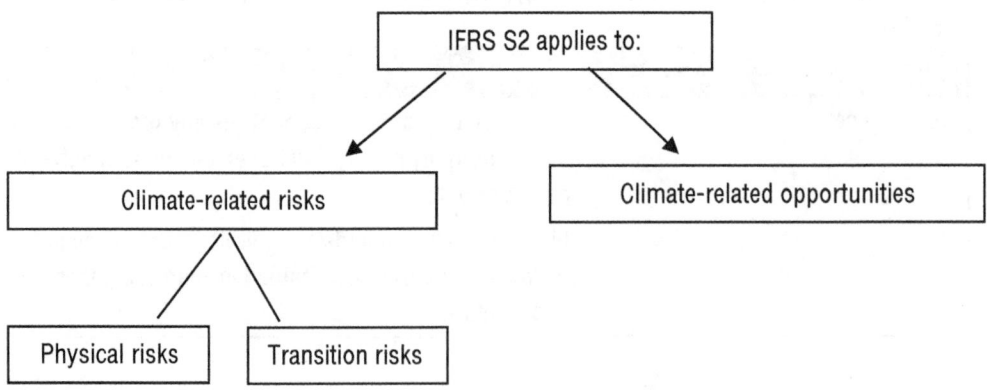

IFRS S2 divides **climate-related risks** into two major categories: **transition risks** and **physical risks** (IFRS S2: paras. 3–4).

Climate-related transition risks:	Risks that arise from efforts to **transition to a lower-carbon economy**. Transition risks include **policy, legal, technological, market and reputational risks**. These risks could carry **financial implications** for an entity, such as increased operating costs or asset impairment due to new or amended climate-related regulations. The entity's **financial performance** could also be affected by shifting consumer demands and the development and deployment of new technology. (IFRS S2: Appendix A)
Climate-related physical risks:	Risks **resulting from climate change** that can be **event-driven** (acute physical risk) or from **longer-term shifts in climatic patterns** (chronic physical risk). Acute physical risks arise from weather-related events such as storms, floods, drought. Chronic physical risks arise from longer-term shifts in climate which could lead to sea level rise, biodiversity loss etc. These risks could carry **financial implications** for an entity, such as costs resulting from direct damage to assets or indirect effects of supply-chain disruption. The entity's **financial performance** could also be affected by changes in water availability, sourcing and quality; and extreme temperature changes affecting the entity's premises, operations, supply chains, transportation needs and employee health and safety (IFRS S2: Appendix A).

IFRS S2 also requires **disclosure of material climate-related opportunities**, as well as risks. Climate related opportunities 'refers to the potential positive effects arising from climate change for an entity. Efforts to mitigate and adapt to climate change can produce climate-related opportunities for an entity' (IFRS S2: Appendix A).

6.5.1.1 Core content

Consistent with IFRS S1, IFRS S2 requires a company to disclose how it manages its climate-related risks and opportunities under four headings: **governance, strategy, risk management, and metrics and targets**.

Category	Disclosure
Governance	The governance **processes, controls and procedures** an entity uses to **monitor, manage and oversee** climate-related risks and opportunities (this includes how boards or equivalents and management are **informed, supported and trained** in addressing these risks and opportunities).
Strategy	To enable users of general-purpose financial reports to understand an entity's strategy for managing climate-related **risks and opportunities**, including those that could affect its **business model, future prospects and overall climate resilience**.
Risk management	An entity's processes to **identify, assess, prioritise and monitor climate-related risks and opportunities**, including whether and

Category	Disclosure
	how those processes are integrated into and inform the entity's overall risk management process. This should include scenario analysis and how an entity might assess the nature, likelihood and magnitude of the effects of those risks.
Metrics and targets	The entity's **performance** in relation to its climate-related risks and opportunities, including progress towards any climate-related **targets** it has set, and any targets it is required to meet by law or regulation. For example, this information could include • Greenhouse Gas (GHG) emissions and the amount and percentage of assets vulnerable to climate-related transition risks and physical risks. • Climate-related opportunities – the amount and percentage of assets or business activities aligned with climate-related opportunities • Capital deployment – the amount of capital expenditure, financing or investment deployed towards climate-related risks and opportunities • Internal carbon prices (a mechanism for an entity to put a value on GHG emissions so they can be considered in decision making) - whether and how internal carbon pricing is used in decision making and the price per tonne of GHG emissions that the entity has used • Remuneration - whether and how climate considerations are factored into remuneration of directors

At this stage, you should be starting to think about how this information relates to assurance providers and what work a professional services firm might need to do if presented with these kinds of disclosures.

6.6 Proposed International Standard on Sustainability Assurance (ISSA) 5000 *General Requirements for Sustainability Assurance Engagements*

6.6.1 Background

In June 2023, the IAASB prepared an exposure draft (ED) of its proposed International Standard on Sustainability Assurance 5000 *General Requirements for Sustainability Assurance Engagements*. Comments on ED-5000 were to be submitted by 1 December 2023 and the final standard is expected to be released in late 2024.

The reason for the proposed ISSA is to address the need for high-quality assurance engagements that enhance the degree of confidence of intended users about sustainability reporting. The documentation published by IAASB refers to the proposed standard as both ED-5000 and ISSA 5000 so you should be aware of both terms.

6.6.1.1 Developing ED-5000

Taking existing best practice from existing ISAs, ISAE 3000, ISAE 3410 and the guidance on Extended External Reporting (EER), ED-5000 will be the primary standard for assurance engagements on

sustainability information, except when a separate conclusion on a greenhouse gas (GHG) statement is required, when ISAE 3410 will continue to be the appropriate standard for such engagements.

ED-5000 will relate to **attestation engagements only**, not direct reporting engagements, meaning that assurance providers will use it to evaluate disclosures that are the responsibility of the reporting entity.

At the time of writing, the IESBA is also considering the **ethics and independence standards** necessary for practitioners conducting sustainability assurance engagements.

The IAASB expects that other ISSAs will be developed over time, and has developed ED-5000 to be **principles-based** to accommodate the following:

- A **broad range of sustainability topics** that could be reported by any organisation in any location
- Variety in **the way such topics are disclosed** (such as integrated reports, part of the annual report, as a stand-alone report)
- The ability to use **different criteria and methodologies** (for example, the GRI, the ISSB standards or even the EU's Corporate Sustainability Reporting Directive (CSRD))
- **Intended users with different requirements** (investors, policy makers and other stakeholders: it is noted that ED-5000 recognises the term 'double materiality' - covered in Chapter 7)
- The availability of **accurate and complete evidence** may vary, meaning that sufficiency and appropriateness of evidence may be subjective
- The ability to issue a conclusion which delivers either **limited assurance or reasonable assurance** to suit the jurisdiction (the IAASB concluded that assurance might also be affected by the extent to which practitioners could obtain an understanding of the reporting entity's **system of internal control**)
- A **range of assurance providers** with different skills and resources (ED-5000 suggests that unlike audits, sustainability engagements could be conducted by **non-accountants**, although the need for relevant **ethical** and **quality standards** would remain)

(IAASB, 2023)

6.6.1.2 Terminology used in ED-5000

To accommodate a range of different assurance providers (some of whom may not be accountants and therefore not familiar with other forms of assurance engagements), ED-5000 has considered some of the terminology it wants to include as follows:

- **Sustainability information** (the equivalent of subject matter information in other assurance standards) is defined as information about sustainability matters
- **Sustainability matters** (the equivalent of underlying subject matter in other assurance standards) includes **environmental, social, economic and cultural matters** (the IAASB have deliberately broadened the definition of sustainability matters beyond environmental, social and governance (ESG) to accommodate the evolving nature of this area)
- The term **engagement leader** will be used instead of engagement partner
- There is a distinction between the criteria used by the assurance provider to measure or evaluate sustainability matters depending on the applicable reporting framework:
    - **Compliance criteria** are used when the framework explicitly requires something to be disclosed
    - **Fair presentation criteria** are used when a departure from the strict requirements of the framework is necessary in order to achieve fair presentation

- **Materiality** needs to be understood if the conclusions reached under ED-5000 are to be meaningful for users of sustainability information, but the variety of topics covered makes materiality levels difficult to set. ED-5000 therefore requires practitioners to do the following:
  - Consider materiality for qualitative disclosures
  - Determine materiality for quantitative disclosures
- Given the underlying subject matter may be complex and technical, and reporting entities may be more geographically spread, the **need for additional expertise** or resource is recognised by ED-5000 and could be one of the following:
  - Practitioner's internal expert (who is a member of the engagement team);
  - Practitioner's external expert (from outside of the firm); or
  - Other Practitioners (including network firms and non-network firms whose work is not subject to directions, supervision and review by the practitioner)

(IAASB, 2023)

6.6.1.3 Other relevant information about ED-5000

The IAASB acknowledges that there is a **risk of fraud** being present in sustainability disclosures and heightened levels of **professional scepticism** should therefore be deployed. The risk of fraud may be higher if the reporting entity has created an expectation that it will be perceived in a certain way, but the underlying facts will not support that perception. Practitioners should be particularly aware of the term 'greenwashing' where sustainability disclosures are made to distract the reader from other unsustainable practices.

In order to align the approach of the practitioner more closely with that of the auditor, the IAASB decided to present the required order of the **assurance report under ED-5000** to mirror the auditor's report as follows:

- Title
- Addressee
- The practitioner's conclusion
- The basis for that conclusion
- Other information
- Responsibilities for the sustainability information
- Inherent limitations in preparing the sustainability information
- Practitioner's responsibilities
- Summary of work completed
- Practitioner's signature, jurisdiction and the date of the report

(IAASB, 2023)

Chapter roundup

- An audit provides **assurance** to the shareholders and other stakeholders of a company on the financial statements because it is **independent and impartial**.
- This syllabus is particularly concerned with the **external audit** (both statutory and non-statutory).
- The purpose of an external audit is to enable auditors to **give an independent opinion** on the financial statements.
- A **statutory external audit** is just **one type of assurance engagement** that is carried out by an auditor to give an independent opinion on a set of financial statements.
- The **degree of assurance** given by the auditor will depend on the nature of the engagement.
- **Internal auditors** are employed as part of an organisation's system of controls. Their responsibilities are determined by management and may be wide-ranging.
- The auditors' report on company accounts is expressed in terms of **truth** and **fairness**. This is generally taken to mean that accounts:
    - Are factual
    - Are free from bias
    - Reflect the commercial substance of the business's transactions
- External audits give **reasonable assurance** that the accounts are free from material misstatement. This assurance can never be **absolute**.
- While having many advantages, the statutory audit also has limitations which may not be understood by users. This leads to what is termed the **expectations gap**.
- There is increased demand from stakeholders for companies to provide information about an organisation's environmental, social, governance and sustainability credentials. However the current limited guidance and regulation in this area could lead to reports being misleading and inconsistent between companies/countries.
- The Global Reporting Initiative (GRI) Standards enable any organisation to understand and report on their impacts on the economy, environment and people in a comparable and credible way.
- The ISSB has issued two IFRS Sustainability Standards (IFRS S1 and IFRS S2) to provide guidance for companies making sustainability-related and climate-related disclosures in their annual reports.
- ED-5000, the proposed International Standard on Sustainability Assurance 5000 aims to provide practitioners with guidance as to how to conduct assurance engagements in the field of sustainability. It is due to be released late 2024

Quick quiz

1. Complete the definition of an audit:

   The objective of an .... of .... is to enable the auditor to .... an .... whether the financial statements are prepared, in all .... respects, in accordance with an identified financial reporting framework. The phrases used to express the auditors' opinion are 'give' a .... and .... view' or '............. .... in all material respects', which are equivalent terms.

2. Link the correct definition to each term.

   (i)   Accountable   (iv) True
   (ii) Steward   (v)   Fair
   (iii) Agent   (vi) Materiality

   (a) An expression of the relative significance or importance of a particular matter in the context of the financial statements as a whole.

   (b) A person employed to provide a particular service.

   (c) Factual and conforming with reality. In conformity with relevant standards and law and correctly extracted from accounting records.

   (d) A person employed to manage other people's property.

   (e) Free from discrimination and bias and in compliance with expected standards and rules. Reflecting the commercial substance of underlying transactions.

   (f) Being required or expected to justify actions and decisions.

3. Give four examples of a non-statutory assurance engagement.

4. A partnership might benefit from having an audit even though it is not required to do so by law. Tick the correct advantages below.

   (a) Means of settling accounts between partners ☐
   (b) Ensures that partners' remuneration will be made public ☐
   (c) May make the accounts more acceptable to tax authorities ☐
   (d) The individual partners will not have to prepare tax returns ☐
   (e) May facilitate the negotiation of a loan ☐
   (f) May benefit a 'sleeping partner' who otherwise has little knowledge of partnership affairs ☐

5. Reasonable assurance is a high, but not absolute, level of assurance.

   True ☐   False ☐

6. What are the benefits of the Global Reporting Initiative Standards?

7. Define sustainability.

Answers to quick quiz

1   Audit, financial statements, express, opinion, material, true, fair, present fairly.

2   (i)   (f)   (iv) (c)
    (ii) (d)   (v)   (e)
    (iii) (b)   (vi) (a)

3   Any from the following:

    - Local authority audit
    - Insurance company audit
    - Bank audits
    - Pension scheme audits
    - Charity audits
    - Solicitors' audits
    - Social auditing
    - Environmental audits
    - Internal audit
    - Value-for-money audit
    - Due diligence
    - Circulation reports (eg for magazines)
    - Web assurance

    Note. This is not an exhaustive listing.

4   (a), (c), (e) and (f). (b) would not necessarily be a result of an audit and would not be an advantage anyway. (d) is simply untrue.

5   True

6   The Global Reporting Initiative Standards assist those reporting information about an entity's impacts on the economy, environment, and society by providing disclosures that enable **consistent and credible reporting** of information about these impacts.

    This **improves the global comparability and quality** of reported information concerning these impacts, which in turn **aids information users** in making informed evaluations and decisions regarding the organisation's impacts and its contribution to sustainable development (Global Reporting Initiative, 2023).

7   Sustainability is defined as "meeting the needs of the present without compromising the ability of future generations to meet their own needs."

End of chapter question

Development (AIA Nov 2004)

Describe the historical development of the external company audit. (15 marks)

Regulation of audit

Topic list	Syllabus reference
1 The statutory audit requirement	2.2
2 Auditor regulation	2.3
3 Auditors' rights and duties	2.4
4 International Standards on Auditing	2.3
5 Auditor liability	2.3

Introduction

This chapter describes the main bodies and the major factors which govern auditing. You should particularly note how the **audit monitoring regime** works and what inspectors are looking for.

The chapter then goes on to discuss the role of the International Federation of Accountants and the scope of the guidance it issues. You should understand the authority of auditing standards. The detailed requirements of the auditing standards you are required to know (most of them) are discussed throughout the rest of this Learning & Practice Workbook.

The regulatory framework for auditors discussed in this chapter and the ethical framework discussed in Chapter 4 are very important. They could be examined together as part of a scenario question on planning or accepting appointment, or in the context of auditors failing to comply with requirements and possible consequences.

1 The statutory audit requirement

Most companies are required to have an audit **by law**, but some small companies are exempt.

1.1 The statutory audit opinion

In Chapter 1 we saw an example of an auditor's report which contained an unmodified opinion.

As discussed, the purpose of a statutory audit is for the auditor to express an opinion on the financial statements, which expresses whether the financial statements give a **true and fair** view, or **present fairly in all material respects**.

The audit opinion may also **imply** certain details are true, because otherwise the audit report would have mentioned them. In the UK, such implications include:

- **Adequate accounting records** have been kept.
- **Proper returns** adequate for the audit have been received from branches not visited.
- The **accounts agree** with the **accounting records** and **returns**.
- **All information and explanations** have been **received** as the auditors think necessary and they have had access at all times to the company's books, accounts and vouchers.
- **Details** of **directors' emoluments** and **other benefits** have been correctly **disclosed** in the financial statements.
- Particulars of **loans** and **other transactions** in favour of **directors** and others have been correctly disclosed in the financial statements.

As noted previously, the majority of companies are required by national law to have an audit. A key exception to this requirement is that given to small companies with many countries having a small company exemption from audit, which is often based on a company's turnover/revenue.

1.2 Small company audit exemption

In most countries, the majority of companies are very small, employing few staff (if any) and are often owner-managed, ie the owner of the company manages the business directly. This is very different from a large business where the owners (the shareholders) devolve the day-to-day running of the business to a group of managers or directors.

Key term

A **small entity** is any enterprise in which:

(a) There is concentration of ownership and management in a small number of individuals (often a single individual); and

(b) One or more of the following are also found:

    (i) Few sources of income and uncomplicated activities

    (ii) Unsophisticated record-keeping

    (iii) Limited internal controls together with potential for management override of internal controls

In the UK all companies who meet **two** of the following criteria **must** have an audit:

- Turnover over £10.2 million
- Total assets over £5.1 million
- Over 50 employees

There has long been a **debate over the benefits of audit to small companies.** As seen above, where small companies are owned by the same people that manage them, there is significantly less value in an independent review of the stewardship of the managers than where management and ownership are divorced. Does the small company audit have value to the users of accounts? From the viewpoint of each type of user, the arguments for and against abolition are as follows.

(a) Shareholders

Against change	Shareholders not involved in management need the reassurance given by audited accounts. Furthermore, the existence of the audit deters the directors from treating the company's assets as their own to the detriment of minority shareholders.
	Audited financial statements are invaluable in arriving at a fair valuation of the shares in an unquoted company either for taxation or other purposes.
For change	Where all the shareholders are also executive directors or closely related to them, the benefit gained from an audit may not be worth its cost.

(b) Banks and other institutional creditors

Against change	Banks rely on accounts for the purposes of making loans and reviewing the value of security.
For change	There is doubt whether banks rely on the audited accounts of companies to a greater extent than those of unincorporated associations of a similar size which have not been audited.
	A review of the way in which the bank accounts of the company have been conducted and of forecasts and management accounts are at least as important to the banks as the appraisal of the audited accounts.
	There is no reason why a bank should not make an audit a precondition of granting a loan.

(c) Trade creditors

Against change	Creditors and potential creditors should have the opportunity to assess the strength of their customers by examining audited financial statements either themselves or through a credit company.
For change	In practice, only limited reliance is placed on the accounts available from the regulatory authority as they are usually filed so late as to be of little significance in granting short-term credit.

(d) Tax authorities

Against change	The authorities rely on accounts for computing corporation tax and checking returns.
For change	There is little evidence to suggest that the tax authorities rely on audited accounts to a significantly greater extent than those, which, whilst being unaudited have been prepared by an independent accountant.

(e) Employees

Against change	Employees are entitled to be able to assess audited accounts when entering wage negotiations and considering the future viability of their employer.
For change	There is little evidence to suggest that, in the case of small companies, such assessments are made.

(f) Management	
Against change	The audit provides management with a useful independent check on the accuracy of the accounting systems and the auditor is frequently able to recommend improvements in those systems.
For change	If the law were changed, the management of a company could, if they so desired, still elect to have an independent audit. It is likely, however, that a systems review accompanied by a management consultancy report would represent a greater benefit for a similar cost.

2 Auditor regulation

FAST FORWARD

Requirements for the **eligibility**, **registration** and **training** of auditors are extremely important as they are designed to maintain standards in the auditing profession.

2.1 National level

The accounting and auditing profession varies in structure from country to country. In some countries accountants and auditors are subject to strict legislative regulation, while in others the profession is allowed to regulate itself. We cannot look at every country, but some examples will show you the divergence of structure and we can make some general points. For the purposes of RPQ route students, we will focus more heavily on regulation in the UK.

2.1.1 United Kingdom

In most countries, company law requires that persons carrying out statutory audits must be approved by the authorities. In the United Kingdom the authority to give this approval is delegated to Recognised Supervisory Bodies (RSBs). An auditor must be a member of an RSB and be eligible under its own rules. In the UK there are a number of different accountancy, or accountancy-related, institutes and associations, such as the Association of International Accountants (AIA) or the Association of Chartered Certified Accountants (ACCA). Some of these are RSBs.

The RSBs are required to have rules to ensure that persons eligible for appointment as a company auditor are either:

- Individuals holding an appropriate qualification; or
- Firms controlled by qualified persons

This section is only relevant for RPQ students.

Persons carrying out audits must have the permission of the relevant authorities. In the UK the relevant authorities are **Recognised Supervisory Bodies** (RSBs), which are defined in the Companies Act 2006.

There are currently five RSBs:

- the Institute of Chartered Accountants in England and Wales (ICAEW),
- the Institute of Chartered Accountants in Ireland (ICAI),
- the Institute of Chartered Accountants of Scotland (ICAS),
- the Association of Authorised Public Accountants (AAPA), and
- the Association of Chartered Certified Accountants (ACCA).

Professional qualifications, which will be prerequisites for membership of an RSB, are offered by **Recognised Qualifying Bodies (RQBs)** approved by the government, of which there are six:

- AIA,
- ICAEW,
- ICAI,
- ICAS,
- ACCA, and
- the Chartered Institute of Public Finance & Accountancy (CIPFA).

Note that **the AIA is an RQB but not an RSB.** Once awarded the Recognised Professional Qualification (RPQ) (Statutory Auditor Qualification), members should seek registration with an RSB who will be responsible for registering and supervising statutory auditors in practice.

The **Financial Reporting Council (FRC)** is the UK's independent regulator for corporate reporting and governance. Its aim is to promote confidence in corporate reporting and governance.

In the area of Codes and Standards the FRC achieves its aims by:

- Setting relevant UK codes and standards and related guidance for governance, accounting, auditing and actuarial work
- Influencing codes and standards at international level
- Researching potential improvements in those areas

In the area of Conduct the FRC achieves its aims by:

- Authorising Recognised Supervisory Bodies (RSBs) and Recognised Qualifying Bodies (RQBs) to approve accountants to carry out audits and to offer a recognised audit qualification respectively, and reviewing the way that the RSBs and RQBs discharge their responsibilities
- Overseeing how the actuarial profession regulates its members
- Inspecting and reporting upon the quality of the work performed by auditors of public interest entities
- Reviewing the reports and accounts of public interest entities to determine compliance with the applicable financial reporting framework
- Investigating possible misconduct by professional accountants and/or actuaries and, where appropriate in the public interest, pursuing disciplinary proceedings
- Part 42 of the Companies Act 2006 sets out the legislative framework for audit regulation. The FRC has published Guidelines on Enforcement Measures against Recognised Supervisory Bodies and Recognised Qualifying Bodies for breach of this part of the Act.

The structure of the FRC is illustrated on the following page.

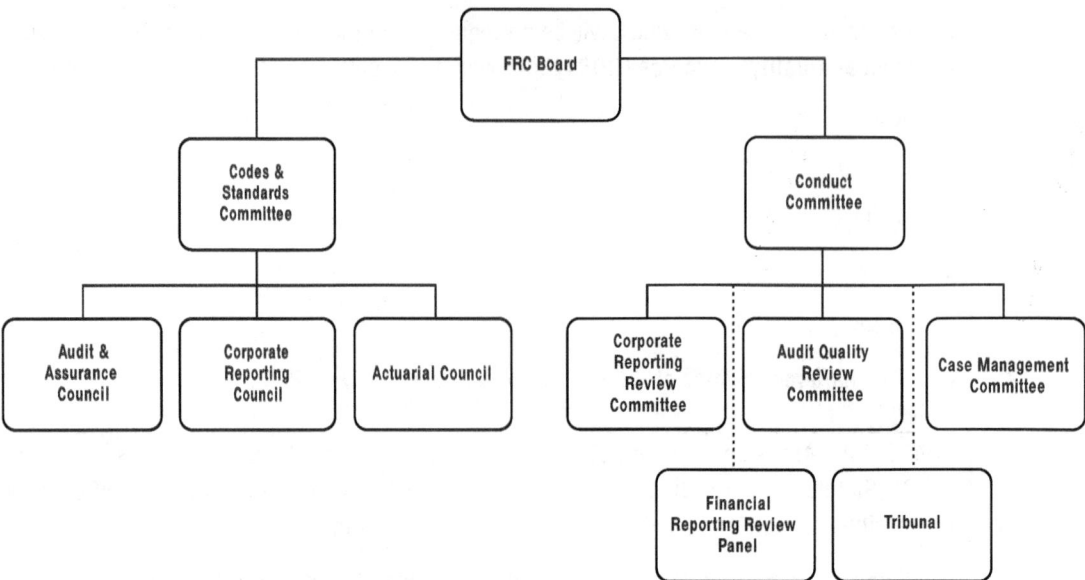

ISAs (UK) are set by the FRC. There are three categories of pronouncement:

- Auditing Standards (quality management, engagement and ethical)
- Practice notes
- Bulletins

The FRC has adopted International Standards on Auditing. The ISAs (UK) were revised in June 2016 and aligned with those issued by the IAASB. Complying with these is a requirement when carrying out statutory audits. RPQ students must familiarise themselves with areas where UK standards have additional requirements from the ISAs that will be outlined in the rest of this text. Where there are significant additional requirements, this will be noted. The FRC's ethical standards are outlined in Chapter 4.

Note that in 2023 there were plans to replace the FRC with a new Audit, Reporting and Governance Authority (ARGA). However at the time of writing this Workbook these plans seemed to have stalled due to a delay in related legislation.

2.1.2 France

In France, the accounting profession is split into three distinct organisations:

- Accountants (Ordre des Experts-Comptables (OEC))
- Auditors (Compagnie Nationale des Commissaires aux Comptes (CNCC))
- Auditors (Haut Conseil du Commissariat aux Comptes (The High Council for Statutory Audits) (H3C))

Most members of the auditors' organisation are also members of the more important accountants' organisation. Examinations, work experience and articles are similar to those of the UK accountancy bodies. The profession's main influence is through the issue of non-mandatory opinions and recommendations of accounting principles relevant to the implementation of the National Plan. The organisations above are members of IFAC (see below).

2.1.3 Germany

The main professional body in Germany is the Institute of Certified Public Accountants (Institut der Wirtschaftsprüfer). Members of this Institute carry out all the statutory audits, and are required to have very high educational and experience qualifications. The Institute issues a form of auditing standard but this is tied very closely to legislation. As well as auditing, members are mainly involved in tax and business management, with no obvious significant role in establishing financial accounting principles and practices. There is no independent accounting standard-setting body. It is a member of IFAC.

The Wirtschaftsprüferkammer (Chamber of Public Accountants (WPK)) is responsible for the following:

- Licensing of auditors (Wirtschaftsprüfer) and audit firms
- Revocation of licenses
- Registration of public accountants and audit firms
- Conducting examinations for auditors
- Setting ethical requirements
- Establishing CPD requirements
- Carrying out quality assurance (QA) reviews
- Carrying out disciplinary procedures for auditors of non-public interest entities (PIEs)

2.1.4 USA

In America, accountants are members of the American Institute of Certified Public Accountants (AICPA), a private sector body. Although the Securities and Exchange Commission (SEC) in the USA can prescribe accounting standards for listed companies, it relies on the Financial Accounting Standards Board (FASB), an independent body, to set such standards. In turn, FASB keeps in close contact with the AICPA, which issues guidance on US standards and which is closely involved in their development.

The audit of public companies in the US is overseen by the Public Company Accounting Oversight Board which is a non-profit corporation created by the Sarbanes-Oxley Act 2002, and is subject to oversight by the SEC.

It can be seen from the above paragraphs that the accounting and auditing profession in most western countries is regulated by legislation to some extent. In the UK and the USA the profession effectively regulates itself, ie regulation is devolved from statute to the private bodies involved in the accountancy profession. In many European countries, statutory control by governments is much more direct.

2.2 EC member states

The EU 8th Directive on company law requires that persons carrying out statutory audits in EC member states must have the permission of the relevant authorities.

The UK is no longer an EU member state and therefore not subject to EU Directives although it may choose to follow these. In the UK the relevant authorities are **Recognised Supervisory Bodies** (RSBs). As well as giving authority, RSBs in the UK supervise and monitor auditors.

In other countries however supervising and monitoring is carried out by a state body or by the national government.

2.3 International level

Regulations governing auditors will, in most countries, be most important at the national level. International regulation, however, can play a major part by:

(a) Setting **minimum standards** and **requirements** for auditors
(b) Providing **guidance** for those countries without a **well-developed national regulatory framework**
(c) Aiding **intra-country recognition** of professional accountancy qualifications

2.4 International Federation of Accountants

The International Federation of Accountants (IFAC) came into being in the 1970s as a result of proposals put forward and eventually approved by the International Congress of Accountants. IFAC's mission is:

> 'The development and enhancement of the profession to enable it to provide services of consistently high quality in the public interest'.

IFAC, based in New York, is a non-profit, non-governmental, non-political international organisation of accountancy bodies.

IFAC co-operates with member bodies, regional organisations of accountancy bodies and other world organisations. Through such co-operation, IFAC initiates, co-ordinates and guides efforts to achieve international technical, ethical and educational pronouncements for the accountancy profession.

Any accountancy body may join IFAC if it is recognised by law or general consensus within its own country as a substantial national organisation of good standing within the accountancy profession. Members of IFAC automatically become members of the International Accounting Standards Committee (IASC).

2.4.1 International Auditing and Assurance Standards Board

The International Auditing and Assurance Standards Board (IAASB) is an independent standard-setting body which is part of IFAC. You will be most concerned with the IAASB because it sets International Standards on Auditing which we will look at in Section 4.

Each country which has a member on the Committee has one vote. The affirmative vote of at least three-quarters of the countries but not less than ten, represented at a meeting, are required to approve a proposed pronouncement for exposure or a definitive pronouncement for issue.

2.5 Regulation, monitoring and supervision

Each country's regulation of external audits will differ. Most regimes do have certain common elements, which we examine in detail below. Briefly these are as follows.

(a) **Education and work experience**: the IFAC has issued guidance on this.

(b) **Eligibility**: there may well be statutory rules determining who can act as auditors. Membership of an appropriate body is likely to be one criteria.

(c) **Supervision and monitoring**: these activities came under particular scrutiny in a number of countries during the 1990s. Questions have been asked about why auditors have failed to identify impending corporate failures, and whether therefore they are being regulated strongly enough. The supervision regime has come under particular scrutiny in countries where regulation and supervision is by the auditors' own professional body (self-regulation). Suggestions have been made in these countries that supervision ought to be by external government agencies.

2.6 Education, examinations and experience

The **International Accounting Education Standards Board (IAESB)** is an independent standard-setting body under the auspices of IFAC which develops guidance to improve the standards of accountancy education around the world. It focuses on two key areas:

- The essential elements of accreditation, which are **education, practical experience and tests of professional competence**

- The nature and extent of **continuing professional education** needed by accountants

The IAESB has produced eight International Education Standards (IESs) and the *Framework for International Education Standards for Professional Accountants and Aspiring Professional Accountants*. The IESs prescribe good practice in learning and development for professional accountants and should be incorporated into the educational requirements of IFAC member bodies. Some of these were revised in 2015.

2.6.1 Education

Initial Professional Development (IPD) may be achieved through a number of pathways, including work experience, study or qualifications.

IFAC member bodies are required to ensure that:

- There are educational entry requirements for professional accounting education programs so that those entering the program are those with a reasonable chance of success
- Education programs achieve learning outcomes in relation to technical competence and professional skills.

2.6.2 Practical experience

IES 5 Initial Professional Development – Practical Experience requires that sufficient practical experience is obtained by the end of IPD. Sufficiency of practical experience is not specifically quantified, however the IES states that 'sufficient practical experience has a blend of depth and breadth, knowledge and application...' The objective is to enable an aspiring professional accountant to demonstrate:

(a) Technical competence
(b) Professional skills
(c) Professional values, ethics and attitudes

Practical experience must be supervised, recorded, reviewed and assessed.

2.6.3 Assessment

IES 6 Initial Professional Development – Assessment of Professional Competence states that:

> 'IFAC member bodies shall formally assess whether aspiring professional accountants have achieved an appropriate level of professional competence by the end of IPD, drawing on the outcomes of a range of assessment activities that are undertaken during IPD'.

This assessment may be undertaken by a range of stakeholders including employers, regulators, licensing bodies, universities, colleges and private education providers.

Assessment activities may include:

(a) A single multi-disciplinary examination conducted at the end of IPD
(b) A series of examinations conducted throughout IPD
(c) A series of examinations and workplace assessments conducted throughout IPD

Specific techniques of assessment could include written examinations, oral examinations, objective testing, workplace assessments and reviews of portfolios of workplace-based evidence.

2.7 Eligibility/ineligibility

Eligibility to act as an auditor is likely to arise from membership of some kind of regulatory body.

Bodies of this type will offer qualifications and set up rules to ensure compliance with any statutory requirements related to auditors. In this way national governments will control who may act as an auditor to limited liability companies, or to any other body requiring a statutory audit.

In some countries, regulation is devolved onto professional accountancy bodies by the statutory authorities. On the other hand, the regulatory body could be a direct extension of national government.

The regulatory body should have rules to ensure that those eligible for appointment as a company auditor are either:

- **Individuals** holding an **appropriate qualification**; or
- **Firms controlled** by **qualified persons**

Regulatory bodies should also have procedures to maintain the competence of members. The regulatory body's rules should:

- Ensure that only **fit and proper** persons are appointed as company auditors
- Ensure that company audit work is conducted **properly** and with **professional integrity**
- Include rules as to the **technical standards** of company audit work (eg following International Standards on Auditing)
- Ensure that **eligible persons** maintain an appropriate level of **competence**
- Ensure that all firms eligible under its rules have arrangements to prevent:
    - Individuals not holding an **appropriate qualification**
    - Persons who are **not members** of the firm from being able to exert influence over an audit which would be likely to affect the independence or integrity of the audit

The regulatory body's rules should provide for adequate monitoring and enforcement of compliance with its rules and should include provisions relating to:

- **Admission** and **expulsion** of members
- **Investigation of complaints** against members
- **Compulsory professional indemnity insurance**

Up-to-date lists of approved auditors and their names and addresses should be maintained by the regulatory body. This register of auditors should be made available to the public.

Membership of a regulatory body is the main prerequisite for eligibility as an auditor. Some countries allow a 'firm' to be appointed as a company auditor. A firm may be either a body corporate (such as a company) or a partnership.

A person should be **ineligible** for appointment as a company auditor if he or she is:

- An **officer or employee** of the company
- A **partner or employee** of such a person
- A **partnership** in which such a person is a partner

There may be further rules about connections between the company or its officers and the auditor, depending on local statutory rules.

Question — Eligibility as auditor

In your country, are the following disqualified from acting as auditor to a company?

(a) A shareholder of the company
(b) A debtor or creditor of the company
(c) A close relative (such as a husband, wife, son or daughter) of an officer or employee of the company

Answer

You may find that the regulations of accountancy bodies such as the AIA applying to their own members are stricter than local statute in this respect.

If during their term of office a company auditor becomes ineligible for appointment to the office, he should vacate office and give notice to the company. If an audit is carried out by an auditor who was ineligible, the authorities may require a second audit, or a review of the first audit, to be conducted by an eligible person. In such a case, the company may be able to recover the costs of complying from the ineligible auditor.

2.8 Supervisory and monitoring roles

Some kind of supervision and monitoring regime should be implemented by the regulatory body. This should inspect auditors on a regular basis.

The frequency of inspection will depend on the number of partners, number of offices and number of listed company audits (these factors may also be reflected in the size of annual registration fees payable by approved audit firms).

The following features should be apparent in each practice visited by the monitoring regulatory body.

(a) A **properly structured audit approach**, suitable for the range of clients served and work undertaken by the practice.

(b) **Carefully instituted quality control procedures**, revised and updated constantly, to which the practice as a whole is committed. This will include:

- Staff recruitment
- Staff training
- Continuing professional development
- Frequent quality reviews

(c) Commitment to **ethical guidelines**, with an emphasis on independence issues

(d) An emphasis on **technical excellence**

(e) Adherence to the **'fit and proper' criteria** by checking personnel records and references

(f) Use of internal and, if necessary, external **peer reviews**, consultations etc

(g) **Appropriate fee** charging per audit assignment

2.9 Auditor appointment (legal requirements)

The auditors should be **appointed by,** and therefore be **answerable** to, the **shareholders**. The table below shows what the position should ideally be, again using the **UK as an example**. The Companies Act 2006 sets out the rules for appointment of auditors. An auditor must be appointed for each financial year unless the directors reasonably resolve otherwise on the grounds that audited financial statements are unlikely to be required. The table summarises who can appoint auditors for UK public companies.

Auditor appointment (UK)	
Directors	Can appoint auditor: (a) Before company's **first period for appointing auditors** (b) Following a period during which the company **did not have an** auditor (as exempt), at any time before the next period for appointing auditors (c) To fill a **casual vacancy**
Members (shareholders)	Can appoint auditor by **ordinary resolution** (>50%): (a) During a **period for appointing auditors** (b) If company **should have** appointed auditor during a period for appointing auditors **but failed to do so** (c) If directors **fail to do so**
Secretary of state	Can appoint auditors if **no auditors** are **appointed** per above

2.9.1 Remuneration

The remuneration of the auditors, which will include any sums paid by the company in respect of the auditors' expenses, will be fixed either by **whoever made** the **appointment** or in **such manner** as the **company in general meeting** may determine.

However, the auditors' remuneration is fixed, in many countries it must be disclosed in the annual accounts of the company.

2.10 Resignation and removal of auditors (legal requirements)

> **FAST FORWARD**
>
> There are various legal and professional requirements concerning the resignation and removal (dismissal) of auditors which must be followed.

The legal requirements for resignation and removal of auditors using the **UK as an example** are discussed below.

It is important that auditors know the procedures because as part of their client acceptance, they have a duty to ensure the old auditors were properly removed from office.

Resignation of auditors (UK)		
1	Resignation procedures	Auditors deposit **written notice** together with **statement of circumstances** relevant to members/creditors.
2	Notice of resignation	Sent by **company** to regulatory authority.
3	Statement of circumstances	Sent by: (a) Auditors to company (b) Company to everyone entitled to receive a copy of accounts
4	Convening of general meeting	**Auditors** can **require directors** to call extraordinary general meeting to discuss circumstances of resignation. Directors must send out notice for meeting within **21 days** of having received requisition by auditors.
5	Statement prior to general meeting	**Auditors** may require company to circulate (different) **statement of circumstances** to everyone entitled to notice of meeting.
6	Other rights of auditors	Can **receive all notices** that relate to: (a) A general meeting at which their term of office would have expired (b) A general meeting where casual vacancy caused by their resignation to be filled Can **speak** at these meetings on **any matter** which **concerns them as auditors**.

Removal of auditors (UK)		
1	Resolution	Auditors may be removed by **ordinary resolution** at a general meeting. **Special notice** (28 days) must be given. Directors must send a copy of the resolution to the auditors immediately on receiving it and convene meeting to take place within reasonable time.
2	Representations	**Auditors** can make **representations** on why they ought to stay in office, and may require company to state in notice representations have been made and send copy to members.
3	If resolution passed	(a) Company must **notify** regulatory authority. (b) Auditors must **deposit statement of circumstances** at company's

		registered office **within 14 days** of ceasing to hold office. Statement must be sent to regulatory authority.
4	Auditor rights	Can **receive notice** of and **speak** at:
		(a) General meeting at which their term of office would have expired
		(b) General meeting where casual vacancy caused by their removal to be filled

The UK's Companies Act 2006 places a requirement on auditors to notify the appropriate audit authority in certain circumstances on leaving office.

Under the UK Companies Act 2006, for a quoted (listed) company an auditor must always submit a **statement of circumstances** surrounding their leaving office, even where there are no matters which the auditor believes should be brought to the attention of members or creditors (Companies Act 2006: s.519).

In the case of a private company (or an unlisted public company), the auditor does not need to submit a statement if they are leaving because their term of office has come to an end. If they are leaving before this, then a statement must be submitted unless the reasons for leaving are 'exempt reasons' (eg the auditor is ceasing to practise as an auditor, or the company is now exempt from audit), and there is nothing that needs to be communicated (*Companies Act 2006*: s. 519(1)–(3)).

The appropriate audit authority in the UK is:

- Secretary of State or delegated body (such as the FRC's Conduct Committee) if a major audit
- Recognised Supervisory Body for other audits

Notice must inform the appropriate audit authority that the auditor has ceased to hold office and be accompanied by a statement of circumstances or no circumstances.

Question — New auditors

You are a partner in Messrs Borg, Connors & Co, Certified Accountants. You are approached by Mr Nastase, the managing director of Navratilova Enterprises Ltd, who asks your firm to become auditors of his company. In return for giving you this appointment Mr Nastase says that he will expect your firm to waive 50% of your normal fee for the first year's audit. The existing auditors, Messrs Wade, Austin & Co, have not resigned but Mr Nastase informs you that they will not be re-appointed in the future.

Required

(a) What action should Messrs Borg, Connors & Co take in response to the request from Mr Nastase to reduce their first year's fee by 50%?

(b) Are Messrs Wade, Austin & Co within their rights in not resigning when they know Mr Nastase wishes to replace them? Give reasons for your answer.

Answer

(a) The request by Mr Nastase that half of the first year's audit fee should be waived is quite improper. If this proposal were to be accepted it could be held that Borg Connors & Co are not charging an audit fee that is sufficient to cover their costs and so may not be able to perform a professional audit in accordance with applicable auditing standards, and that a lower quality audit may be conducted. This would not be acceptable and would contravene the firms' quality review procedures.

Mr Nastase should be informed that the audit fee will be determined by reference to the work involved in completion of a satisfactory audit, taking into account the nature of the audit tasks involved and the resources required to carry out those tasks in an efficient manner. He should also

be told that if he is not prepared to accept an audit fee arrived at in this way and insists on there being a reduction then regrettably the nomination to act as auditor will have to be declined.

(b) Wade, Austin & Co have every right not to resign even though they may be aware that Mr Nastase wishes to replace them. The auditors of a company are appointed by, and report to, the members of a company and the directors are not empowered to remove the auditors. If the reason for the proposed change arises out of a dispute between management and the auditors then the auditors have a right to put forward their views as seen above and to insist that any decision should be made by the members, but only once they have been made aware of all pertinent facts concerning the directors' wishes to have them removed from office.

3 Auditors' rights and duties

FAST FORWARD

> The law gives auditors both rights and duties. This allows auditors to have sufficient **power** to carry out an independent and effective audit.

The audit is primarily a statutory concept, and eligibility to conduct an audit is often set down in statute. Similarly, the rights and duties of auditors can be set down in law, to ensure that the auditors have sufficient power to carry out an effective audit. In this section we look at the rights and duties of auditors in the **UK as an example** (but bear in mind that these may be different in other jurisdictions). The relevant legislation in the UK is the **Companies Act 2006**.

3.1 Duties

The auditors should be required to report on every statement of financial position and statement of profit or loss and other comprehensive income laid before the company in general meeting.

The auditors may also be required to consider the following.

Compliance with legislation	Whether the accounts have been prepared in accordance with the relevant legislation
Truth and fairness of financial statements	Whether the statement of financial position (balance sheet) shows a true and fair view of (presents fairly in all material respects) the company's affairs at the end of the period and the statement of profit or loss and other comprehensive income (and a statement of cash flows) show a true and fair view of the results for the period
Adequate records and returns	Whether adequate accounting records have been kept and proper returns adequate for the audit received from branches not visited by the auditor
Agreement of accounts to records	Whether the accounts are in agreement with the accounting records and returns
Consistency of other information	Whether the other information with the accounts (for example the directors' report) is consistent with the accounts
Directors' benefits	Whether disclosure of directors' benefits has been made in accordance with the Companies Act 2006

3.2 Rights

The auditors must have certain rights to enable them to carry out their duties effectively.

The principal rights auditors should have, excepting those dealing with resignation or removal, are set out in the table below, and the following are notes on more detailed points.

Access to records	A right of access at all times to the books, accounts and vouchers of the company
Information and explanations	A right to require from the company's officers such information and explanations as they think necessary for the performance of their duties as auditors
Attendance at/notices of general meetings	A right to attend any general meetings of the company and to receive all notices of and communications relating to such meetings which any member of the company is entitled to receive
Right to speak at general meetings	A right to be heard at general meetings which they attend on any part of the business that concerns them as auditors
Rights in relation to written resolutions	A right to receive a copy of any written resolution proposed

3.2.1 Rights to information

If auditors have not received all the information and explanations they consider necessary, they should state this fact in their audit report.

The Companies Act 2006 makes it an **offence** for a company's officer to knowingly or recklessly make a statement in any form to an auditor which:

- Conveys or purports to convey any information or explanation required by the auditor; and
- Is misleading, false or deceptive

4 International Standards on Auditing

FAST FORWARD

You must be able to discuss the scope and authority of **International Standards on Auditing (ISAs)**, which are set by the **International Auditing and Assurance Standards Board** (IAASB).

4.1 Rules governing audits

We discussed in Chapter 1 the various stakeholders in a company, and the number of people who might read a company's accounts. Consider also that a number of these readers will not just be reading a single company's accounts, but will also be reading the accounts of a large number of companies, and making comparisons between them.

Readers **want assurance** when making comparisons **that the reliability of the accounts does not vary from company to company**. This assurance will be obtained not just from knowing each set of accounts has been audited, but knowing that each set of accounts has been audited to **common standards**.

Hence there is a need for audits to be **regulated** so that auditors follow the same standards. As we see in this chapter, auditors have to follow rules issued by a variety of bodies. As we saw above, some obligations are imposed by governments in law, or statute. Some obligations are imposed by the professional bodies to which auditors are required to belong (such as the **AIA**).

We have already mentioned that International Standards on Auditing (ISAs) are produced by the International Auditing and Assurance Standard Board (IAASB), a technical standing committee of IFAC.

4.1.1 Working procedures of the IAASB

The working procedure of the IAASB is to select subjects for detailed study by a **sub committee** established for that purpose. The IAASB delegates to the subcommittee the initial responsibility for the preparation and drafting of accounting standards and statements.

As a result of that study, an **exposure draft** is prepared for consideration by the IAASB. If approved, the exposure draft is widely distributed for comment by member bodies of IFAC, and to such international organisations that have an interest in auditing standards as appropriate.

The comments and suggestions received as a result of this exposure are then considered by the IAASB and the exposure draft is **revised** as appropriate. Provided that the revised draft is approved it is issued as a definitive **International Standard on Auditing** and becomes operative.

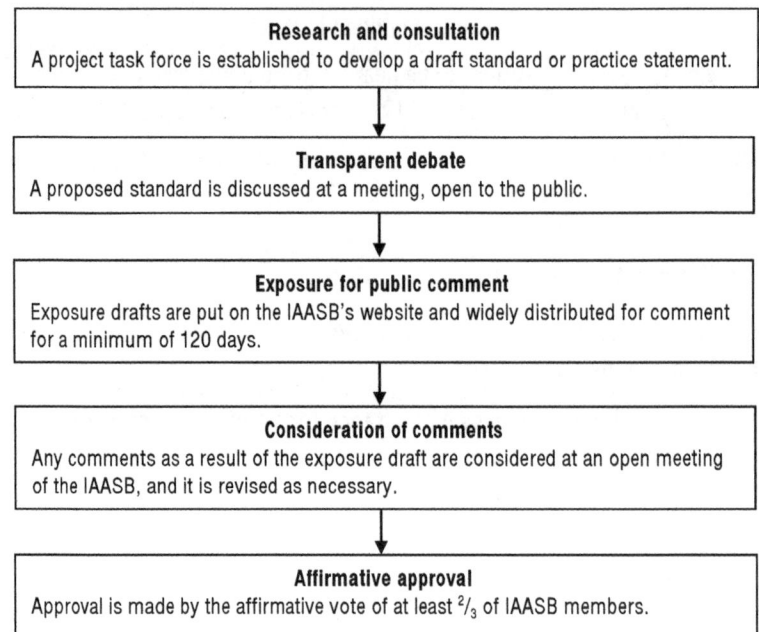

4.2 Current ISAs

International Standards on Auditing	
No	Title
200	Overall Objectives of the Independent Auditor and the Conduct of an Audit in Accordance with International Standards on Auditing
210	Agreeing the Terms of Audit Engagements
220 (Revised)	Quality Management for an Audit of Financial Statements
230	Audit Documentation
240	The Auditor's Responsibilities Relating to Fraud in an Audit of Financial Statements
250 (Revised)	Consideration of Laws and Regulations in an Audit of Financial Statements
260 (Revised)	Communication with Those Charged With Governance
265	Communicating Deficiencies in Internal Control to those Charged with Governance and Management
300	Planning an Audit of Financial Statements
315 (Revised 2019)	Identifying and Assessing the Risks of Material Misstatement
320	Materiality in Planning and Performing an Audit

International Standards on Auditing	
No	**Title**
330	The Auditor's Responses to Assessed Risks
402	Audit Considerations Relating to an Entity Using a Service Organisation
450	Evaluation of Misstatements Identified during the Audit
500	Audit Evidence
501	Audit Evidence – Specific Considerations for Selected Items
505	External Confirmations
510	Initial Audit Engagements – Opening Balances
520	Analytical Procedures
530	Audit Sampling
540 (Revised)	Auditing Accounting Estimates and Related Disclosures
550	Related Parties
560	Subsequent Events
570 (Revised)	Going Concern
580	Written Representations
600	Special Considerations – Audits of Group Financial Statements (Including the Work of Component Auditors)
610 (Revised 2013)	Using the Work of Internal Auditors
620	Using the Work of an Auditor's Expert
700 (Revised)	Forming an Opinion and Reporting on Financial Statements
701	Communicating Key Audit Matters in the Independent Auditor's Report
705 (Revised)	Modifications to the Opinion in the Independent Auditor's Report
706 (Revised)	Emphasis of Matter Paragraphs and Other Matter Paragraphs in the Independent Auditor's Report
710	Comparative Information – Corresponding Figures and Comparative Financial Statements
720 (Revised)	The Auditor's Responsibilities Relating to Other Information
800 (Revised)	Special Considerations – Audits of Financial Statements Prepared in Accordance with Special Purpose Frameworks
805 (Revised)	Special Considerations – Audits of Single Financial Statements and Specific Elements, Accounts or Items of a Financial Statement
810 (Revised)	Engagements to Report on Summary Financial Statements

Note. For RPQ (statutory auditor qualification) candidates the relevant UK standards are all current International Standards on Auditing (ISAs) issued by the Audit and Assurance Council of the Financial Reporting Council (FRC).

Exam focus point

International standards are quoted throughout this text and you must understand how they are applied in practice. Not all the standards listed above are examinable in Principles of Governance and Audit, you should look for the list of examinable documents in the syllabus (reproduced in the front pages of this Workbook). The following are **not examinable**:

ISA 402	Audit Considerations Relating to an Entity Using a Service Organisation
ISA 510	Initial Audit Engagements – Opening Balances
ISA 540 (Revised)	Auditing Accounting Estimates and Related Disclosures
ISA 550	Related Parties
ISA 600	Special Considerations – Audits of Group Financial Statements (Including the Work of Component Auditors)
ISA 710	Comparative Information – Corresponding Figures and Comparative Financial Statements
ISA 720 (Revised)	The Auditor's Responsibilities Relating to Other Information
ISA 800 (Revised)	Special Considerations – Audits of Financial Statements Prepared in Accordance with Special Purpose Frameworks
ISA 810 (Revised)	Engagements to Report on Summary Financial Statements

Examinable documents other than the IAASB pronouncements are:

Other documents
The Code of Ethics for Professional Accountants issued by the International Ethics Standards Board for Accountants (IESBA Code)
International Accounting Standards 1, 2, 7, 10, 16, 37 and 38
International Financial Reporting Standards 1, 3, 5, 8, 10, 12, 15 and 16

The AIA has adopted the *Code of Ethics for Professional Accountants* issued by the International Ethics Standards Board for Accountants (the IESBA *Code*). Ethics will be discussed in Chapter 4 of this Workbook. Note that candidates following the RPQ (statutory auditor qualification) route will be expected to refer, where appropriate, to the *Revised Ethical Standard 2019* (ES) published by the FRC. Candidates following other routes will not be penalised if they refer to the ES in preference to the IESBA *Code*. The ES can be accessed via the Financial Reporting Council's website at https://www.frc.org.uk/library/standards-codes-policy/audit-assurance-and-ethics/ethical-standard-for-auditors/

Candidates should be familiar with International Accounting Standards from their Financial Accounting studies. For RPQ (statutory auditor qualification) candidates the relevant UK standards are Financial Reporting Standards (FRS) issued by the FRC.

5 Auditor liability

If auditors do not follow international standards on auditing they may carry out **negligent** audits.

Negligence is a common law concept. It seeks to provide compensation to a person who has suffered loss due to another person's wrongful neglect. To succeed in an action for negligence, an injured party must prove three things:

(a) A **duty of care** which is enforceable at law existed.

(b) This duty of care was **breached**.

(c) The breach caused the injured party **loss**. In the case of negligence in relation to financial advisers/auditors, this loss must be pecuniary (ie financial) loss.

5.1 Who might bring an action for negligence?

The parties likely to want to bring an action in negligence against the auditors, for example, if they have given the wrong audit opinion through lack of care, include:

- The company
- Shareholders
- The bank
- Other lenders
- Other interested third parties

A key differences between the various potential claimants is the **nature** of the **duty of care** owed to them.

5.2 The audit client

FAST FORWARD

> The auditor owes a duty of care to the audit client automatically under law.

The audit client is the **company**. It is a basic maxim of company law that the company is all the shareholders acting as a body. In other words, the company in this respect, cannot be represented by a single shareholder.

| COMPANY | = | SHAREHOLDERS AS A BODY |

| COMPANY | ≠ | SHAREHOLDER | + | SHAREHOLDER |

The **company** has a **contract** with the audit firm. In the law of many countries, a contract for the supply of a service such as an audit has a duty of reasonable care implied into it by statute.

In other words, whatever the express terms of any written contract between the company and the audit firm, the law always implies a duty of care into it. Therefore, if the company (all the shareholders acting as a body) want to bring a case for negligence, the situation would be as follows.

Client	
Duty of care exists?	AUTOMATIC
Breached?	MUST BE PROVED
Loss arising?	MUST BE PROVED

In order to prove whether a duty of care had been breached, the court has to give further consideration to what the duty of 'reasonable' care means in practice.

5.2.1 The auditors' duty of care

The standard of work of auditors is generally as defined by legislation. A number of judgements made in law cases show how the auditors' duty of care has been gauged at various points in time because legislation often does not state clearly the manner in which the auditors should discharge their duty of care. It is also not likely that this would be clearly spelt out in any contract setting out the terms of an auditors' appointment.

Exam focus point

> An exam question in May 2012 looked at the question of negligence; how a firm could have prevented legal action, to whom they might be held liable and issues relating to protecting auditors from large claims, such as liability capping.

5.3 Recent developments

FAST FORWARD

> As auditor liability is an important practical issue, there are regular developments in this area.

Even with professional indemnity insurance in place and other means of restricting liability there has been great concern throughout the audit profession globally at the remaining risks to firms' survival in the face of claims which might exceed their insurance cover.

The profession has lobbied for further protection in the form of **proportionate liability** or **capping liability**.

Key terms

> **Proportionate liability** would allow claims arising from successful negligence claims to be split between the auditors and the directors of the client company, the split being determined by a judge on the basis of where the fault was seen to lie. This would require the approval of shareholders.
>
> **Capping liability** would set a maximum limit on the amount that the auditor would have to pay out under any claim.

5.3.1 UK Companies Act 2006

The UK Companies Act has a provision for 'liability limitation agreements'. These allow the auditor, with authorisation from the members of the company, to agree a limit to the auditors liability.

The agreement may specify the limit by any mechanism agreed between the auditor and the company. Examples might be:

- A specific sum
- Multiples of the audit fee
- Proportionate liability

A new agreement must be drawn up and authorised for each financial year.

2: REGULATION OF AUDIT

Chapter roundup

- Most companies are required to have an audit by law, but some small companies are exempt.
- Requirements for the **eligibility**, **registration** and **training** of auditors are extremely important as they are designed to maintain standards in the auditing profession.
- Legal requirements govern the appointment, resignation and removal of auditors.
- The law gives auditors both rights and duties. This allows auditors to have sufficient **power** to carry out an independent and effective audit.
- **International Standards on Auditing** are set by the **International Auditing and Assurance Standards Board**. You must be able to discuss the scope and authority of **International Standards on Auditing (ISAs)**.
- The auditor owes a duty of care to the audit client automatically under law.
- As auditor liability is an important practical issue, there are regular developments in this area.

Quick quiz

1. Name four items of information implied by a standard auditor's report.

2. Name three characteristics of accountancy bodies in the UK.

    (1) ……………………………………
    (2) ……………………………………
    (3) ……………………………………

3. List the items that a monitoring regulatory body should find on visiting a firm.

    (1) ……………………………………
    (2) ……………………………………
    (3) ……………………………………
    (4) ……………………………………
    (5) ……………………………………

4. Complete the following diagram showing the stages used by the IAASB to develop ISAs.

    [ ]
     ↓
    [ ]
     ↓
    [ ]
     ↓
    [ ]
     ↓
    [ ]

5. ISAs are to be applied in the audit of financial statements. ISAs are also to be applied, adapted as necessary, to the audit of other information and to related services:

    True ☐
    False ☐

Answers to quick quiz

1. See section 1.1

2. (1) Stringent entrance requirements
   (2) Strict code of ethics
   (3) Technical updating of members

3. (1) Ensure that only **fit and proper** persons are appointed as company auditors
   (2) Ensure that company audit work is conducted **properly** and with **professional integrity**
   (3) Include rules as to the **technical standards** of company audit work (eg following International Standards on Auditing)
   (4) Ensure that **eligible persons** maintain an appropriate level of **competence**
   (5) Ensure that all firms eligible under its rules have arrangements to prevent:
       - Individuals not holding an **appropriate qualification**
       - Persons who are **not members** of the firm from being able to exert influence over an audit which would be likely to affect the independence or integrity of the audit

4.
```
┌─────────────────────────────────────────────────────────────────┐
│                    Research and consultation                     │
│ A project task force is established to develop a draft standard │
│ or practice statement.                                           │
└─────────────────────────────────────────────────────────────────┘
                                ↓
┌─────────────────────────────────────────────────────────────────┐
│                       Transparent debate                         │
│ A proposed standard is discussed at a meeting, open to the public.│
└─────────────────────────────────────────────────────────────────┘
                                ↓
┌─────────────────────────────────────────────────────────────────┐
│                    Exposure for public comment                   │
│ Exposure drafts are put on the IAASB's website and widely        │
│ distributed for comment for a minimum of 120 days.               │
└─────────────────────────────────────────────────────────────────┘
                                ↓
┌─────────────────────────────────────────────────────────────────┐
│                    Consideration of comments                     │
│ Any comments as a result of the exposure draft are considered at │
│ an open meeting of the IAASB, and it is revised as necessary.    │
└─────────────────────────────────────────────────────────────────┘
                                ↓
┌─────────────────────────────────────────────────────────────────┐
│                       Affirmative approval                       │
│ Approval is made by the affirmative vote of at least $2/3$ of    │
│ IAASB members.                                                   │
└─────────────────────────────────────────────────────────────────┘
```

5. True

End of chapter question

Larch Ltd (AIA Nov 2008)

The directors of Larch Ltd are unhappy with the company's current auditor. They have been unable to persuade her to allow them to adopt a particular accounting policy. As a result, they want to replace her with a more compliant auditor.

Required

(a) Explain how statutory legislation should provide safeguards for the auditor against being removed from office. **(12 marks)**

(b) Discuss whether you think that these safeguards will be effective in practice. **(3 marks)**

(Total = 15 marks)

Watkins Ltd (AIA May 2007)

You are the auditor of Watkins Ltd. The company is one of your largest clients, and contributes a substantial amount to your fee income. During the current audit, you have identified certain items in the draft statements where you disagree with the accounting treatment. You have asked the directors to make changes to these figures prior to the publication of the financial statements, but the directors have refused to do so. The directors have also threatened to seek your dismissal at the annual general meeting if you refer to the matter in your report to the shareholders.

Required

Discuss the alternative actions that you could take in this situation. **(15 marks)**

Corporate governance and internal audit

Topic list	Syllabus reference
1 Introduction to corporate governance	2.3
2 The UK Corporate Governance Code	2.3, 6.3
3 Audit committees	2.3
4 Internal control effectiveness	2.3
5 Internal audit	2.3
6 Internal audit assignments	2.3
7 Internal audit reports	6.3
8 Regulation	2.3
9 Outsourcing the internal audit function	2.3

Introduction

In this chapter we will look at the codes of practice that have been put in place to ensure that companies are well managed and controlled. The UK Corporate Governance Code is an internationally recognised code which we will use as an example of a code of best practice. The audit carried out by the external auditors is a very important part of corporate governance, as it is an independent check on what the directors are reporting to the shareholders.

Auditors of all kinds have most contact with the audit committee, a sub-committee of the board of directors. External auditors liaise with the audit committee over the audit, and internal auditors will report their findings about internal control effectiveness to it. We shall look at audit committees in Section 3 and internal control effectiveness in Section 4.

The internal audit function is **established by management** to **assist in corporate governance** by monitoring internal controls and risk management. It can be a department of employees, or, as discussed in Section 9, can be **outsourced** to expert service providers.

The various **assignments** which may be undertaken by internal auditors and their role with regard to **fraud** are outlined in Section 6. While the techniques used may be similar to external auditors, the **focus and reasons** behind the audit may **differ**.

1 Introduction to corporate governance

> **FAST FORWARD**
>
> Good corporate governance is important because the owners of a company and the people who manage the company are not always the same people.
>
> Where this is the case, the owners will need assurance that the company is operated in the owners' best interests, especially where this may conflict with the interests of the managers (board).

1.1 The importance of corporate governance

Key term

> 'Corporate governance is the system by which companies are directed and controlled.'
>
> (Report of the Cadbury Committee (UK))

There are various stakeholders in companies, as we discussed in Chapter 1. The Cadbury Report (a report commissioned by the UK government concerning corporate governance) identified the following:

- **Directors**: responsible for corporate governance
- **Shareholders**: (owners) linked to the directors by the financial statements
- **Other relevant parties**: such as employees, customers and suppliers.

The roles of the parties can be seen in the diagram of two companies shown below.

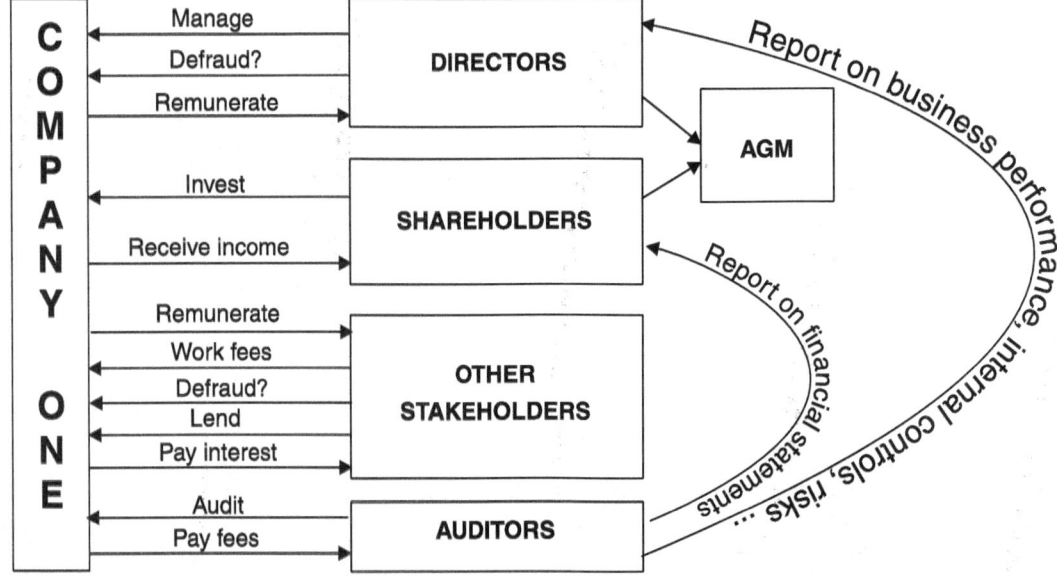

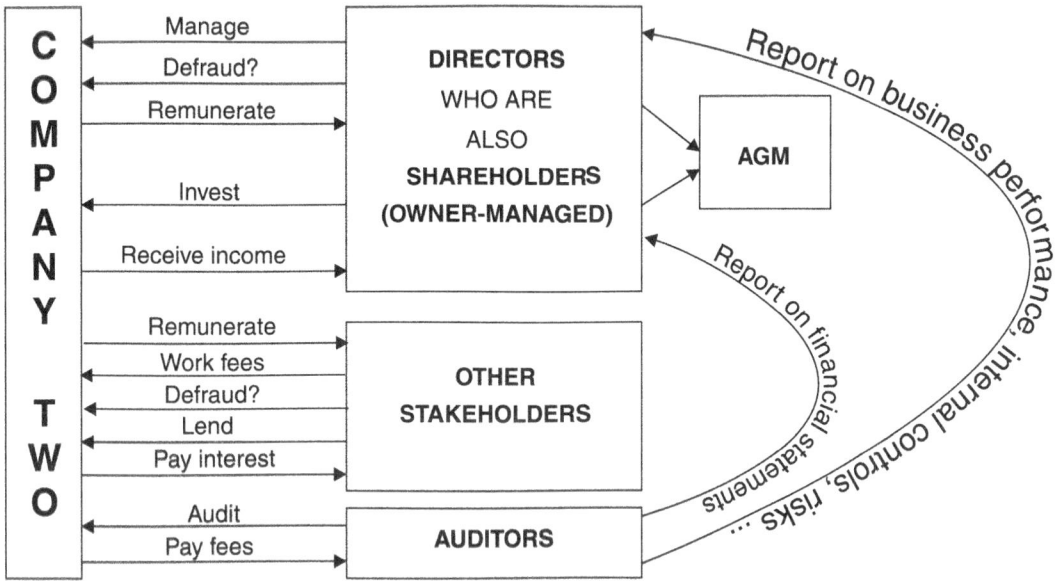

The diagram above shows two companies and their relationships with the key people associated with corporate governance.

The key difference between the companies is that in **company two**, the **shareholders** are **fully informed about** the **management** of the business, being directors themselves, in **company one**, the **shareholders** only have an opportunity to find out about the management of the company at the **Annual General Meeting (AGM)**.

The **day-to-day running of a company is the responsibility of the directors** and other management staff to whom they delegate, and although the company's results are submitted for shareholders' approval at the AGM, there is often apathy and acquiescence in director's recommendations.

AGMs are often very poorly attended. For these reasons, there is the **potential** for **conflicts of interest** between management and shareholders.

The importance of good corporate governance was summed up by another report to the UK government: 'good governance ensures that the constituencies (stakeholders) with a relevant interest in the company's business are fully taken into account' (Hampel Committee Report).

In other words, it is necessary for structures to be in place to ensure that every stakeholder in the company is not disadvantaged. As it is the directors that manage the company, the burden of good corporate governance falls on them. It is important that they manage the company in the best way for the shareholders, employees and other parties.

1.2 G20/OECD Principles of Corporate Governance

FAST FORWARD

The **G20/OECD Principles of Corporate Governance** provide guidance to help policy makers evaluate and improve the **legal, regulatory and institutional framework for corporate governance**, with a view to supporting market confidence and integrity, economic efficiency, sustainable growth and financial stability.

The G20/OECD Principles of Corporate Governance offer guidance on companies' sustainability and resilience, and help companies manage environmental and social risks, with insights on disclosure, the roles and rights of shareholders as well as stakeholders and the responsibilities of company boards

First, they help companies **improve access to finance**, particularly from capital markets. By doing so, they promote investment, innovation, and productivity growth, and foster economic dynamism more broadly.

Second, they **provide a framework to protect investors**, which include households with invested savings. A formal structure of procedures that **promotes the transparency and accountability of board members and executives** to shareholders helps to build trust in markets.

Third, they **support the sustainability and resilience of corporations** which, in turn, contributes to the sustainability and resilience of the broader economy.

An important question to consider is 'Will the same way of managing companies be the best method for all companies?' The answer is likely to be no. Companies are different from each other, and, globally, they operate in different legal systems with different institutions, frameworks and traditions. It would not be possible to construct one single way of operating companies that could be described as good practice for all.

The objectives of the Principles are to help improve companies' access to financial markets in an environment where investor expectations are evolving and to support investor confidence on the basis of more transparent market information and reinforced investor rights.

Shareholders in a company might be a family, they might be the general public or they might be institutional investors representing, in particular, people's future pensions. These shareholders will vary in their degree of interaction with the company and their directors.

The **Principles of Corporate Governance** were issued in 1999 and revised in 2015 and then underwent a **comprehensive review** in 2021-2023 to reflect recent evolutions in corporate governance and capital markets. The revised Principles were adopted by the OECD Council in June 2023 and endorsed by G20 Leaders in September 2023.

The review had **two major objectives**:

- to support national efforts to improve the conditions for companies' access to finance from capital markets, and
- to promote corporate governance policies that support the **sustainability and resilience** of corporations which, in turn, may contribute to the sustainability and resilience of the broader economy.

Accordingly, a major evolution in the Principles is the **new Chapter on "Sustainability and resilience"** which reflects the growing challenges corporations face in managing climate-related and other **sustainability-related risks and opportunities**. This new Chapter also incorporates Chapter IV on "The Role of Stakeholders in Corporate Governance" of the previous version of the Principles.

The Principles aim to provide a robust but flexible reference for policy makers and market participants in each country to **develop their own frameworks for corporate governance**. They are **non-binding** and do not aim to provide detailed prescriptions for national legislation.

The six Principles are as follows:

G20/OECD Principles of Corporate Governance
I **Ensuring the basis for an effective corporate governance framework** The corporate governance framework should promote **transparent and fair markets**, and the **efficient allocation of resources**. It should be consistent with the rule of law and support effective supervision and enforcement.
II **The rights and equitable treatment of shareholders and key ownership functions** The corporate governance framework should **protect and facilitate the exercise of shareholders' rights and ensure the equitable treatment of all shareholders**, including minority and foreign shareholders. All shareholders should have the opportunity to obtain effective redress for violation of their rights at a reasonable cost and without excessive delay.
III **Institutional investors, stock markets, and other intermediaries** The corporate governance framework should provide sound **incentives** throughout the investment chain and provide **for stock markets to function in a way that contributes to good corporate governance**.

IV	**Disclosure and transparency**
	The corporate governance framework should ensure that **timely and accurate disclosure is made on all material matters** regarding the corporation, including the financial situation, performance, ownership, and governance of the company.
V	**The responsibilities of the board**
	The corporate governance framework should ensure the **strategic guidance** of the company, the **effective monitoring** of management by the board, and the board's accountability to the company and the shareholders.
VI	**Sustainability and resilience**
	The corporate governance framework should provide incentives for companies and their investors to **make decisions and manage their risks, in a way that contributes to the sustainability and resilience of the corporation**.

(OECD, 2023)

The G20/OECD Principles can be found on the OECD website at: https://doi.org/10.1787/ed750b30-en

When applying the G20/OECD principles, countries may take a hybrid approach and make some elements of corporate governance mandatory and some voluntary. In addition, national codes also exist. For instance, in the UK, companies are required to comply with **legislation** (such as the Companies Act) and there is also a **voluntary corporate governance code**, the UK Corporate Governance Code, which contains some **mandatory elements** for listed companies. We discuss the provisions of the UK Corporate Governance Code below.

2 The UK Corporate Governance Code

> **FAST FORWARD**
>
> The **UK Corporate Governance Code** contains detailed guidance for UK companies on good corporate governance.

Application

The Code applies to all companies with a **premium listing of equity shares in the UK**, whether incorporated in the UK or elsewhere.

The updated 2024 Code applies to accounting periods beginning on or after 1 January 2025, with the exception of Provision 29. This provision is applicable for accounting periods beginning on or after 1 January 2026.

Reporting

The FCA's Listing Rules require companies to **make a statement of how they have applied** the Principles of the UK Corporate Governance Code in a manner that would **enable shareholders to evaluate how the Principles have been applied**. Reporting should cover the application of the Principles in the context of the particular circumstances of the company, including how the board has set the company's purpose and strategy, met objectives, and achieved outcomes through the decisions it has taken.

The Listing Rules also **require companies to set out their reasons for non-compliance with a Code Provision**. Companies may depart from the Code for a number of reasons, for example the size, complexity, history and ownership structure of a company. Explanations should **set out the background, provide a clear rationale for the action the company is taking and explain the impact that the action has had**. Where a departure from a Provision is intended to be limited in time, the explanation should indicate when the company expects to conform to the Provision.

Corporate governance **reporting should relate to other parts of the annual report** and other complementary information, for example, a sustainability report, so that shareholders can effectively assess the quality of the company's governance arrangements and the board's activities and contributions. (FRC *UK Corporate Governance Code 2024*: pages 4 and 5).

2.1 A history of corporate governance in the UK

Before we discuss the principles of the UK Corporate Governance Code (formerly known as The Combined Code on Corporate Governance) in detail, it is useful to provide a short history of corporate governance in the UK.

As a result of several accounting scandals in the 1980s and 1990s, such as (Mirror Group, BCCI and PollyPeck), the **Cadbury** committee produced a report entitled *Financial Aspects of Corporate Governance*.

The **Cadbury** report provided the following definition of corporate governance:

> *Corporate governance is the system by which companies are directed and controlled.*
>
> (*Cadbury Code: Financial Aspects of Corporate Governance, para. 2.5*).

This means that the Board of Directors has **control** over and is responsible for the manner in which a company is run (governance). The Board should:

- set the company's **strategic aims**;
- provide the **leadership** to put those aims into effect;
- **supervise the management** of the business; and
- **report to shareholders** on their stewardship.

The Board should also set the company's financial policy and oversee its implementation including the use of financial controls which should be embedded within the entity's **system of internal control**.

Throughout, the board's actions are subject to laws, regulations and shareholders in the general meeting.

Where a company is owner-managed and the shareholders (owners) sit on the Board of Directors the individuals making the decisions are the same individuals who are affected by them and so this intuitively encourages good corporate governance as they would only be harming themselves.

However, when **ownership is separated from control** it is imperative that good corporate governance is being exercised and a robust system of internal control exists to identify and manage risk thus protecting the shareholders (owners) from the situation where the members of the Board of Directors might choose to act in their own best interest when this is to the detriment of the owners.

We saw in Chapter 1 that the directors act as **agents** for the shareholders as they are appointed by the shareholders to manage the company's affairs on a day-to-day basis and should do this in the best interests of the shareholders. Most companies are subject to an external audit and so similarly the **external auditor** is also an agent for the shareholders. Their role is to perform an independent audit and to **report to the shareholders** via the auditor's report and give their opinion as to whether the financial statements give a **true and fair view** of (or present fairly) the company's activities during the period. The audit process therefore enhances the need for directors to be **accountable**.

In 1995, the **Greenbury** report added a set of principles on the remuneration of executive directors. The **Hampel** report in 1998 brought the Cadbury and Greenbury reports together to form the first **Combined Code**. In 1999, **Turnbull** produced a report relating to risk management and internal control which ultimately resulted in the Financial Reporting Council (FRC) providing guidance for directors on how to comply with internal control provisions in the Combined Code.

In 2002, the **Higgs report** (*Review of the Role and Effectiveness of Non-executive Directors*) was commissioned to produce a single comprehensive code, which was refined by the FRC to produce the Combined Code. This evolved into the **UK Corporate Governance Code** that is with us today.

Also in 2002, the **Smith report** resulted in recommendations on audit committees. This evolved into the FRC's *Guidance on Audit Committees*, which supplements UK Corporate Governance Code. In May 2023, the FRC issued *Audit Committees and the External Audit: Minimum Standard* which should be read in conjunction with the UK Corporate Governance Code and the FRC *Guidance on Audit Committees*.

Having concluded during its 2009 review that a major reason for corporate governance failings was a lack of interaction between the boards of listed companies and shareholders, the FRC deemed it necessary to also publish a UK **Stewardship Code** in July 2010. This Stewardship Code became the UK Stewardship Code 2020 when it was last updated in October 2019. It provides guidance on good practice for investors and separates out the principles and provisions relevant to institutional shareholders.

In January 2024 the **updated UK Corporate Governance Code** was published, focussing on a limited number of changes to the Code to ensure the right balance is struck between UK competitiveness and positive outcomes for companies, investors and the wider public.

2.2 'Comply or explain'

The UK Corporate Governance Code is structured into a set of **broad principles** and more **specific provisions**, which seek to apply those principles. Companies are only **required to apply the principles** and are **permitted to depart from the specific provisions**. However, if they do depart from the specific provisions then they must explain why they have done this. This is known as the '**comply or explain**' basis, according to which a board must either comply with the specific provisions, or explain why they have not. The board can only choose not to comply with a provision if they believe that doing so would have failed to apply the broad principle, ie if not complying results in a better application of the principle.

The reasons for not complying with a specific provision should be clearly and fully explained to the shareholders. Any explanation must include details of how actual practices are consistent with the overall principle to which a provision related.

2.3 Principles of the UK Corporate Governance Code

The UK Corporate Governance Code, produced by the FRC, sets out standards of good practice that cover a number of different areas: board leadership and company purpose; the division of responsibilities; composition, succession and evaluation; audit, risk and internal control, and; remuneration.

The broad **principles** of the Code are as follows:

Principles of the UK Corporate Governance Code (for listed UK companies)

Board Leadership and Company Purpose

A A successful company is led by an effective and entrepreneurial board, whose role is to promote the long-term sustainable success of the company, generating value for shareholders and contributing to wider society. The board should ensure that the necessary resources, policies and practices are in place for the company to meet its objectives and measure performance against them.

B The board should establish the company's purpose, values and strategy, and satisfy itself that these and its culture are aligned. All directors must act with integrity, lead by example and promote the desired culture.

C Governance reporting should focus on board decisions and their outcomes in the context of the company's strategy and objectives. Where the board reports on departures from the Code's provisions, it should provide a clear explanation.

D In order for the company to meet its responsibilities to shareholders and stakeholders, the board should ensure effective engagement with, and encourage participation from, these parties.

E The board should ensure that workforce policies and practices are consistent with the company's values and support its long-term sustainable success. The workforce should be able to raise any matters of concern.

(FRC *UK Corporate Governance Code 2024*: Section 1)

Division of Responsibilities

F The chair leads the board and is responsible for its overall effectiveness in directing the company. They should demonstrate objective judgement throughout their tenure and promote a culture of openness and debate. In addition, the chair facilitates constructive board relations and the effective contribution of all non-executive directors, and ensures that directors receive accurate, timely and clear information.

G The board should include an appropriate combination of executive and non-executive (and, in particular, independent non-executive) directors, such that no one individual or small group of individuals dominates the board's decision-making. There should be a clear division of responsibilities between the leadership of the board and the executive leadership of the company's business.

H Non-executive directors should have sufficient time to meet their board responsibilities. They should provide constructive challenge, strategic guidance, offer specialist advice and hold management to account.

I The board, supported by the company secretary, should ensure that it has the policies, processes, information, time and resources it needs in order to function effectively and efficiently.

(FRC *UK Corporate Governance Code 2024*: Section 2)

Composition, Succession and Evaluation

J Appointments to the board should be subject to a formal, rigorous and transparent procedure, and an effective succession plan for the board and senior management should be maintained. Both appointments and succession plans should be based on merit and objective criteria. They should promote diversity, inclusion and equal opportunity.

K The board and its committees should have a combination of skills, experience and knowledge. Consideration should be given to the length of service of the board as a whole and membership regularly refreshed.

L Annual evaluation of the board should consider its performance, composition, diversity and how effectively members work together to achieve objectives. Individual evaluation should demonstrate whether each director continues to contribute effectively

(FRC *UK Corporate Governance Code 2024*: Section 3)

3: CORPORATE GOVERNANCE AND INTERNAL AUDIT

> **Principles of the UK Corporate Governance Code (for listed UK companies)**
>
> **Audit, Risk and Internal Control**
>
> M The board should establish formal and transparent policies and procedures to ensure the independence and effectiveness of internal and external audit functions and satisfy itself on the integrity of financial and narrative statements.
>
> N The board should present a fair, balanced and understandable assessment of the company's position and prospects.
>
> O The board should establish and maintain an effective risk management and internal control framework, and determine the nature and extent of the principal risks the company is willing to take in order to achieve its long-term strategic objectives.
>
> (FRC *UK Corporate Governance Code 2024*: Section 4)
>
> **Remuneration**
>
> P Remuneration policies and practices should be designed to support strategy and promote long-term sustainable success. Executive remuneration should be aligned to company purpose and values, and be clearly linked to the successful delivery of the company's long-term strategy.
>
> Q A formal and transparent procedure for developing policy on executive remuneration and determining director and senior management remuneration should be established. No director should be involved in deciding their own remuneration outcome.
>
> R Directors should exercise independent judgement and discretion when authorising remuneration outcomes, taking account of company and individual performance, and wider circumstances.
>
> (FRC *UK Corporate Governance Code 2024*: Section 5)

The UK Corporate Governance Code and a document summarising the 2024 changes to the Code can be found on the FRC website at: https://www.frc.org.uk/library/standards-codes-policy/corporate-governance/uk-corporate-governance-code/#uk-corporate-governance-code-2024-effective-2025-16c7508e

Similarly the FRC website has also provided a Guidance document to help those applying the Code: https://www.frc.org.uk/library/standards-codes-policy/corporate-governance/corporate-governance-code-guidance/

Exam focus point

> Make sure you learn the principles in the table above. You may be presented with a scenario in which you are asked to identify corporate governance deficiencies and make recommendations to improve corporate governance.

2.4 Auditors and the UK Corporate Governance Code

The principles and provisions in the 'Audit, risk and internal control' section of the UK Corporate Governance Code (Section 4) deal with the board's relationship with the auditor.

In the UK, companies affected by the UK Corporate Governance Code will need an annual independent audit of the financial statements. As we have seen, one of the Code's main principles is:

'The board should establish formal and transparent policies and procedures to ensure the independence and effectiveness of internal and external audit functions and satisfy itself on the integrity of financial and narrative statements.'

(FRC *UK Corporate Governance Code 2024*: Section 4 Principle M).

The Code goes on to suggest that in order to maintain an appropriate relationship with the auditor, an audit committee should be set up. We will look at audit committees in detail in the next section.

If information is disclosed and audited according to a high quality, the reliability and comparability of reporting will be increased and investors will be able to make better investment decisions.

2.4.1 Other information

The principles also imply that shareholders will benefit if other information is subject to checks by auditors. This information includes disclosure relating to:

- **Financial and operating results** of the company
- Company objectives
- Major share ownership and voting rights
- **Members of the board and key executives, and their remuneration**
- Material foreseeable **risk factors**
- Material issues regarding employees and other stakeholders
- Governance structures and policies

So for example, auditors could be asked to check whether companies are applying certain aspects of corporate governance codes. What auditors need to check and report on will depend on the laws and regulations applicable in specific countries, however auditors in the UK are required to report on whether listed companies comply with certain aspects of the UK Corporate Governance Code.

2.5 Directors and the UK Corporate Governance Code

> **FAST FORWARD**
>
> Directors should set company policy, including risk policy, and are responsible for the company's systems and controls.

Directors should make sure they set enough time aside, and that they have the necessary experience and skill, to do this effectively.

2.5.1 Policy

Directors are responsible ultimately for managing the company, and this includes setting strategy, budgets, managing the company's people, maintaining company assets, and ensuring corporate governance rules are kept. An important element of setting strategies is determining and managing risks. We shall outline later in this text how internal audit may have a role in this area. The UK Corporate Governance Code requires that there is clear division of responsibility at the head of a company between the chairman and the chief executive (FRC *UK Corporate Governance Code 2024*: Principle G, provision 9). It requires that no one individual has unfettered powers of decision. The chairman also has to meet the same independence criteria as non-executive directors and should not be a former chief executive of the same company except in exceptional circumstances (FRC *UK Corporate Governance Code 2024*: Principle G, provisions 9-10).

The board should be supplied with information in a timely manner to enable it to carry out its duties and should ensure it has the time and resources it needs in order to function effectively and efficiently.

2.5.2 Going concern

The board must state whether it considers it appropriate to adopt the going concern basis of accounting, and should identify any material uncertainties to the company's ability to continue to do so over a period of **at least twelve months** (FRC *UK Corporate Governance Code 2024*: Principle M, provision 30). The board should also explain how it has assessed the prospects of the company, over what period it has done so and why it considers that period to be appropriate (FRC *UK Corporate Governance Code 2024*: Principle N, provision 31).

2.5.3 Systems, controls and monitoring

Directors are responsible for the systems put in place to achieve the company policies and the controls put in place to mitigate risks. These issues will be considered further later in this chapter.

They are also responsible for **monitoring** the effectiveness of systems and controls. **The internal audit function** has an important role in this area, but a key point to remember is that the **directors are responsible** for determining whether to have an internal audit function to assist them in monitoring in the first place.

Under the UK Corporate Governance Code, UK boards (through the audit committee) are required to consider annually whether an internal audit department is required (FRC *UK Corporate Governance Code 2024*: Principle M, provision 25). If there is no internal audit function, the reasons for not having one need to be explained in the annual report (FRC *UK Corporate Governance Code 2024*: Principle M, provision 26).

In the UK, the FRC has published a report called *Guidance on Risk Management and Internal Control and Related Financial and Business Reporting*. This includes the following guidance (paragraph 24):

The board has responsibility for an organisation's overall approach to risk management and internal control. The board's responsibilities are:
Ensuring the design and implementation of appropriate risk management and internal control systems that identify the risks facing the company and enable the board to make a robust assessment of the principal risks.
Determining the nature and extent of the principal risks faced and those risks which the organisation is willing to take in achieving its strategic objectives (determining its risk appetite).
Ensuring that appropriate culture and reward systems have been embedded throughout the organisation.
Agreeing how the principal risks should be managed or mitigated to reduce the likelihood of their incidence or their impact.
Monitoring and reviewing the risk management and internal control systems, and the management's process of monitoring and reviewing, and satisfying itself that they are functioning effectively and that corrective action is being taken where necessary.
Ensuring sound internal and external information and communication processes and taking responsibility for external communication on risk management and internal control.

2.5.4 Non-executive directors

Key term

Non-executive directors are directors who **do not** have day-to-day operational responsibility for the company. They are not employees of the company or affiliated with it in any other way.

An important recommendation of the principles of the UK Corporate Governance Code is that the board contains some non-executive directors to ensure that no one party dominates thinking and causes bias. The UK Corporate Governance Code requires 'an appropriate combination' of executive and non-executive directors on the board and recommends that **at least half the board should comprise independent non-executive directors** (FRC *UK Corporate Governance Code 2024*: Principle G, provision 11).

Such non-executive directors may have a particular role in some sensitive areas such as company reporting, nomination of directors and remuneration of executive directors. It is important, therefore, that they have the appropriate mix of skills, commitment, experience and independence to carry out their roles effectively.

Independence of a non-executive director can be **compromised** by the following:

- **Employment** with the company (or group) in the last **five years**

- **Material business relationships** with the company within the last **three years**
- Remuneration **beyond the basic fees** agreed for the role (this includes share options, bonus schemes and pensions)
- **Close family ties** with any of the company's advisors, directors or senior employees
- Holding **cross-directorships**/having significant links with other directors through involvement in other companies
- Representing a **significant shareholder**
- Serving longer than **nine years** on the board

(FRC *UK Corporate Governance Code 2024*: Principle G, provision 10)

One of the non-executives should be appointed as the **senior independent director** who will be available to shareholders if they have concerns (FRC *UK Corporate Governance Code 2024*: Principle H, provision 12).

All directors should be subject to **annual** re-election (FRC *UK Corporate Governance Code 2024:* Principle K, provision 18).

Because the composition and effectiveness of the board is so important, it is recommended that **board performance reviews** are externally facilitated **at least every three years** for boards of UK FTSE 350 companies (the top 350 listed companies in the UK) (FRC *UK Corporate Governance Code 2024:* Principle L, provision 21).

2.5.5 Nomination committee

The board should establish a **nomination committee**, the **majority of whom should be independent non-executive directors**.

The **purpose** of the nomination committee is to:

- lead the process for appointments to the Board
- ensure plans are in place for orderly succession to both the board and senior management positions; and
- oversee the development of a diverse pipeline for succession

The chair of the board should not chair the nomination committee when it is dealing with the appointment of their successor.

(FRC *UK Corporate Governance Code 2024:* Provision 17)

The nomination committee should evaluate the skills, experience and knowledge on the board, and the future challenges affecting the business, and, in the light of this evaluation, **prepare a description of the role and capabilities required for a particular appointment**. It should then agree the process to be undertaken to identify, sift and interview suitable candidates. It is important to build a proper assessment of values and expected behaviours into the recruitment process.

The nomination committee members along with the chair and company secretary should be responsible for ensuring **all newly appointed directors receive a full, formal and tailored induction** on joining the board.

(FRC *Corporate Governance Code Guidance:* Paras. 104, 107)

2.5.6 Remuneration committee

The board should establish a **remuneration committee of independent non-executive directors**, with a minimum membership of three, or in the case of smaller companies, two. The chair of the board can only be a member if they were independent on appointment and they **cannot chair the committee**. Before

appointment as chair of the remuneration committee, the appointee should have served on a remuneration committee for at least 12 months.

The remuneration committee should have delegated responsibility for **determining the policy for executive director remuneration** and **setting remuneration for the chair, executive directors and senior management**. It should review workforce remuneration and related policies and the alignment of incentives and rewards with culture, taking these into account when setting the policy for executive director remuneration.

The **remuneration of non-executive directors should be determined in accordance with the Articles of Association or, alternatively, by the board**. Levels of remuneration for the chair and all non-executive directors should reflect the time commitment and responsibilities of the role. Remuneration for all non-executive directors **should not include share options or other performance-related elements**.

Remuneration schemes should promote long-term shareholdings by executive directors that support alignment with long-term shareholder interests. Only basic salary should be pensionable.

(FRC *UK Corporate Governance Code 2024:* Provisions 32-34, 36, 39)

Here we have seen that companies will often set up sub-committees of the board, such as the nomination committee and the remuneration committee to deal with specific issues highlighted by the Code. There is one further such sub-committee, the **audit committee**, which we will look at in more detail later in the chapter.

Exam focus point

A question in May 2012 looked closely at the issue of non-executive directors and asked candidates to appraise whether three candidates were appropriate to be non-executive directors of a company. The answer looked closely at issues of independence from executive directors and suitable experience and skills.

Question — Reviewing corporate governance

You are an audit senior and have been asked to review Dress You Like Co's corporate governance report for the year ended 30 September 20X5.

Dress You Like Co
Corporate Governance Report extract for the year ended 30 September 20X5

As a clothing manufacturer, Dress You Like Co operates within a particularly challenging sector. I believe that in order to conquer modern economic challenges, we must continue to act responsibly in all of our business decisions and monitor our performance closely. Strong leadership (governance) and tight control are fundamental to the success of our business.

Board leadership and company purpose

As Chairman of the board of directors, my role is to lead the board and make sure that each of our directors is fulfilling their role effectively. I will ensure that the board is unified, ably supported by our non-executive directors and offers a greater service to the company as a board than its members could individually.

On 1 January 20X5 I appointed Mary Batter to take over from me as Chief Executive Officer. Relinquishing this position has meant that I could concentrate solely on my role as Chairman rather than dividing my time between the two roles.

As Chief Executive Officer, Mary and her team will seek to develop the company's strategy and steer the company through the years ahead.

Composition, succession and evaluation

During the year an independent consultant conducted a board evaluation. This included individual interviews with each director to gather their opinions on issues ranging from how effective the current board is and risk management to how we can better conduct our relationships with shareholders. To be consistent with best practice, this evaluation will now become an annual occurrence.

As mentioned above Mary Batter joined us this year. She was appointed on the recommendation of the Nomination Committee and completed a tailored induction process.

All directors are offered training throughout the year and are subject to annual re-election.

Audit, risk and internal control

The board is responsible for risk management and for maintaining a system of internal controls. The risks affecting the company are widespread; however, key risks are firstly the ability to predict customer demand in terms of tastes and fashions and secondly security of inventory. We have an internal audit department which we outsource to an independent firm.

The audit committee reviews the effectiveness of the board's risk management procedures.

Gary Lewis (Chairman)

Our board	
Gary Lewis (Chairman)	Chairman of Nomination Committee
Mary Batter (CEO)	Member of Nomination Committee
Katie Escombe (Chief Finance Officer)	Executive Director
Bob Part (Non-executive Director)	Chairman of the Audit Committee Member of the Remuneration and Nomination Committees
Adam Knight (Non-executive Director)	Chairman of the Remuneration Committee Member of the Audit and Nomination Committees
Jeremy Flage (Non-executive Director)	Member of the Audit, Remuneration and Nomination Committees

Required

Review the corporate governance report extract below and answer the following questions:

(a) Why should the role of the Chairman and the Chief Executive Officer ideally be carried out by two different people?

(b) How does Dress You Like Co ensure that board members are properly equipped to do their job?

(c) Why do you think the directors are re-elected each year?

(d) How is the responsibility for risk management shared in Dress You Like Co?

(e) Why does the company have both executive and non-executive directors?

(f) Which sub-committees do the non-executive directors form and what are their roles?

3: CORPORATE GOVERNANCE AND INTERNAL AUDIT

Answer

(a) The Chairman's role is to run/direct the board of directors so that its members can undertake their roles effectively. These duties include ensuring that the board is appropriately balanced (in terms of the numbers of executive and non-executive directors) and that each director is aware of their responsibilities and equipped to fulfil them.

The Chief Executive Officer's role is to decide on the company's strategy and put procedures in place to achieve these.

These are very different roles and so should ideally be undertaken by two separate people.

Also separating the roles will not allow one person to have too much power (as in the case of Robert Maxwell from Mirror Group Newspapers).

(b) Dress You Like Co undertakes a board evaluation each year which allows directors to voice their concerns as to how the board is being run.

It also makes training available to its directors and offers a full induction to new directors.

(c) Directors should only remain in position if they are performing in their role. Having the annual re-election of directors allows companies to remove directors who are not performing and also encourages directors to work effectively for the company/shareholders.

(d) Board of directors:

The responsibility for risk management lies with the board of directors. It is the directors' responsibility to assess the risks that the business is exposed to. All businesses are exposed to general risks; however, there are additional, specific risks relevant to each business. Dress You Like Co is a clothing manufacturer and two risks mentioned in the scenario are: changing fashion trends and the security of inventory. These are risks from a number of perspectives. For example, changing fashion trends could lead to obsolete inventory if some lines are unable to be sold due to being out of fashion. This is a business risk as it may lead to loss of money (inventory write off) and profitability for the business. It can also be viewed as a risk to the financial statements in that if the obsolete inventory is not identified, the inventory valuation figure may be overstated on the statement of financial position.

Once the board has identified the key risks to which the business is exposed, it must then implement a system of internal controls (or procedures) to prevent and/or detect these risks occurring.

Internal controls could range from performing continual market research into consumer fashion tastes to installing security cameras in the factory to deter theft of inventory.

The existence of an internal audit function is often cited as a positive form of risk management and internal control.

Audit committee:

As well as giving the board of directors the responsibility for risk management, corporate governance principles require a company to establish an audit committee. This should comprise at least three non-executive directors (two non-executive directors for a small company).

The audit committee has a responsibility to review the company's risk management and internal control systems and should include at least one non-executive director with financial knowledge.

The audit committee must also review the effectiveness of the internal audit department where one exists. If there is no internal audit department, then the audit committee should consider annually whether or not there is a need for one.

(e) Executive directors are responsible for the day to day running of the company and perform operational and strategic business functions such as entering into contracts, safeguarding company assets and managing people.

Non-executive directors are not involved in the day to day running of the business. Instead they should use their experience and expertise to provide independent advice and objectivity to the board as a whole. They also perform a supervisory role and will review and monitor the executive directors to ensure that they are fulfilling their duties and running the company in the best interests of the shareholders.

In order to improve their independence, non-executive directors should not be reliant on the company for their main source of income. They often work part time for the company and can have a specialist role within the organisation.

All directors, executive and non-executive, are required to attend as many board meetings as they reasonably can.

Also there is no legal distinction between executive and non-executive directors – each has the same responsibilities and rights under law.

Dress You Like Co has three executive and three non-executive directors which makes the board very well balanced.

(f) As well as forming part of the board of directors as a whole, the non-executive directors also sit on the audit committee, remuneration committee and nomination committee. These are sub-committees of the board of directors.

The audit committee is responsible, amongst other things, for reviewing the effectiveness of the board's risk management processes.

The remuneration committee is responsible for making sure that the company offers a performance-related remuneration package which is sufficient to attract and retain quality directors (but not excessive).

The nomination committee is responsible for identifying and approving the appointment of new directors to the board, for example Mary Batter, the new Chief Executive Officer.

Non-executive directors have a very important role to play in each of these sub-committees and their independence and objectivity can improve the quality and relevance of the decisions taken.

3 Audit committees

FAST FORWARD

An audit committee can help a company maintain objectivity with regard to financial reporting and the audit of financial statements.

3.1 Role and function of audit committees

Key term

An **audit committee** is a **sub-committee of the board of directors**, usually containing a number of independent non-executive directors.

The role and function of the audit committee is described in the UK Corporate Governance Code:

Extract of UK Corporate Governance Code provisions relating to the audit committee

Provision 24:

'The board should establish an **audit committee of independent non-executive directors**, with a minimum membership of three, or in the case of smaller companies, two.

The chair of the board should **not** be a member.

The board should satisfy itself that **at least one member** has recent and relevant **financial experience**.

The committee as a whole shall have competence relevant to the sector in which the company operates.'

Provision 25:

'The main role and responsibilities should be set out in **written terms of reference** and should include:

- **monitoring the integrity of the financial statements** of the company and any formal announcements relating to the company's financial performance, and reviewing significant financial reporting judgements contained in them
- **providing advice** (where requested by the board) on whether the **annual report and accounts**, taken as a whole, is fair, balanced and understandable, and provides the information necessary for shareholders to assess the company's position and performance, business model and strategy
- following the *Audit Committees and the External Audit: Minimum Standard* (section 3.2)
- **reviewing the company's risk management and internal control framework**, unless expressly addressed by a separate board risk committee composed of independent non-executive directors, or by the board itself
- monitoring and reviewing the **effectiveness** of the company's **internal audit function** or, where there is not one, considering **annually** whether there is a need for one and making a recommendation to the board
- reporting to the board on how it has discharged its responsibilities.'

Provision 26:

'The annual report should describe the work of the audit committee, including:

- the matters set out in the *Audit Committees and the External Audit: Minimum Standard*
- where there is no internal audit function, an explanation for the absence, how internal assurance is achieved, and how this affects the work of external audit.'

3.2 Audit Committees and the External Audit: Minimum Standard

The FRC issued the Standard *Audit Committees and the External Audit: Minimum Standard* in May 2023.

The Standard is **applicable** to Audit Committees of companies with a **Premium Listing on the London Stock Exchange**, and which are included within the **FTSE 350 index**. It should be read in conjunction with the UK Corporate Governance Code and the FRC Guidance on Audit Committees.

3.2.1 Responsibilities

As we have seen Audit Committees are subject to the UK Corporate Governance Code and other guidance, and legislation. This Standard focuses on the following Audit Committee responsibilities:

- Requiring that the company manages its non-audit relationships with audit firms to **ensure that it has a fair choice of suitable external auditors at the next tender** and in light of the need for greater market diversity and any market opening measures which may be introduced.
- **Conducting the tender process and making recommendations** to the board, about the appointment, reappointment and removal of the **external auditor**, and approving the remuneration and terms of engagement of the external auditor.
- Engaging with shareholders on the scope of the external audit, where appropriate.
- Ensuring that the **external auditor has full access to company staff and records**.
- Inviting challenge by the external auditor, **giving due consideration to points raised** and making changes to financial statements in response, where appropriate.
- Reviewing and monitoring the **external auditor's independence and objectivity**.
- Reviewing the **effectiveness of the external audit process**, taking into consideration relevant UK professional and regulatory requirements.
- Developing and implementing policy on the engagement of the external auditor to supply **non-audit services**, ensuring there is prior approval of non-audit services, considering the **impact this may have on independence**, taking into account the relevant regulations and ethical guidance in this regard, and reporting to the Board on any improvement or action required.
- Reporting to the Board and the members of the company on how it has discharged its responsibilities with respect to the external audit.

(Audit Committees and the External Audit: Minimum Standard: para. 4)

3.2.2 Oversight of Auditors and Audit

The Audit Committee is responsible for overseeing and assessing the entity's external audit and its auditors and should create a culture that **encourages challenge** by the auditor. They should also assess the effectiveness of the audit process including an **assessment of external audit quality** in particular, the auditor's skills, character and knowledge, quality control and ability to handle key judgements.

The Audit Committee should also ask the auditor to **explain the risks to audit quality** they have identified and how they have been addressed. They should also review whether the auditor has met the agreed audit plan and **understand the reasons for any changes**, including changes in perceived audit risks.

(Audit Committees and the External Audit: Minimum Standard: paras. 15-17)

3.2.3 Reporting

The annual report should describe the work of the Audit Committee as follows:

- The **significant issues** that the Audit Committee considered relating to the financial statements, and **how these issues were addressed**.
- An explanation of the **application** of the entity's accounting policies.
- Where shareholders have requested that certain matters be covered in an audit and that request has been rejected, an **explanation of the reasons why**.
- An explanation of **how it has assessed the independence and effectiveness** of the external audit process and the **approach taken** to the appointment or reappointment of the external auditor,

information on the length of tenure of the current audit firm, when a tender was last conducted and advance notice of retendering plans.

- Where a regulatory inspection of the quality of the company's audit has taken place, information about the findings of that review, together with any remedial action the auditor is taking in the light of these findings.

- In the case of a board not accepting the Audit Committee's recommendation on the external auditor appointment, reappointment or removal, **a statement from the Audit Committee explaining its recommendation and that of the board**, and the reasons why the Board has taken its different position (this should also be supplied in any papers recommending appointment or reappointment).

- An explanation of **how auditor independence and objectivity are safeguarded**, if the external auditor provides **non-audit services**.

(*Audit Committees and the External Audit: Minimum Standard: para. 24*)

The Standard can be found on the FRC website at:
https://media.frc.org.uk/documents/Audit_Committees_and_the_External_Audit_Minimum_Standard.pdf

3.3 Advantages and disadvantages of audit committees

The key advantage to an auditor of having an audit committee is that a committee of independent non-executive directors provides the auditor with an independent point of reference other than the executive directors of the company, in the event of disagreement arising.

Other **advantages** that are claimed to arise from the existence of an audit committee include:

(a) It will lead to **improved quality** of financial reporting and **increased confidence** in the credibility and objectivity of financial reports. This is because an audit committee should have at least one member with financial expertise and is particularly important for listed companies and companies seeking listing.

(b) By specialising in the problems of financial reporting the internal auditors will be able to assist the directors, allowing the **executive** directors to **devote their attention to management**.

(c) In cases where the interests of the company, the executive directors and the employees conflict, the audit committee might provide an **impartial body** for the auditors to consult. It will also provide a channel for international and external auditors to communicate through.

(d) The internal auditors will be able to report to the audit committee, rather than the main board, **enhancing their independence and objectivity**.

(e) The audit committee can be a **'critical friend'** to the board in ensuring that the company keeps up to date with corporate governance requirements.

Opponents of audit committees argue that:

(a) The executive directors **may not understand** the purpose of an audit committee and may perceive that it detracts from their authority.

(b) There may be **difficulty selecting** sufficient non-executive directors with the necessary competence in auditing matters for the committee to be really effective.

(c) The establishment of such a **formalised reporting procedure** may **dissuade** the **auditors** from raising matters of judgement and limit them to reporting only on matters of fact.

(d) Costs may be increased.

3.4 Voluntary or mandatory?

It should be observed that it can be difficult to find suitably qualified individuals who are prepared to be non-executive directors in companies and serve on audit committees. Allowing such individuals large salaries to recruit them results in a loss of the objectivity they are supposed to bring to the role.

However, this difficulty should not prevent companies from having the correct corporate governance arrangements, and arguably, if audit committees were made mandatory, the corporate culture would have to change, and it might more often become the case that executive directors from the company became non-executives in other companies not in competition with their primary company.

4 Internal control effectiveness

FAST FORWARD — Directors must ensure that a company's system of controls is effective.

4.1 Importance of internal control and risk management

Internal controls are essential to management, as they contribute to

- Safeguarding the company's assets
- Helping to prevent and detect fraud
- Therefore, safeguarding the shareholders' investment

Exam focus point: Good internal control helps the business to run efficiently. A control system reduces identified risks to the business. It also helps to ensure reliability of reporting, and compliance with laws.

4.2 Directors' responsibilities

The **ultimate responsibility** for a company's system of internal controls lies with the board of directors. It should set procedures of internal control and regularly monitor that the system operates as it should.

Part of setting up an internal control system will involve **assessing the risks** facing the business, so that the **system** can be **designed** to ensure those **risks are avoided**.

Internal control systems will always have **inherent limitations**, the most important being that a system of internal control cannot eliminate the possibility of human error, or the chance that staff will collude in fraud.

Once the directors have set up a system of internal control, they are responsible for **reviewing** it regularly, to ensure that it **still meets its objectives**.

The board may decide that in order to carry out their review function properly they have to employ an **internal audit function** to undertake this task. When deciding whether an internal audit function is required, directors will need to consider the extent of systems and controls, and the relative expense of obtaining checks from other parties, such as the external auditors.

If the board does not see the need for an internal audit function, in the UK, the UK Corporate Governance Code requires companies to consider the need for one at least annually, so that the **need for internal audit is regularly reviewed** (FRC *UK Corporate Governance Code 2024*: Principle M, provision 25).

The Code also recommends that the board of directors **reports** on its **review** of the company's **risk management** and **internal controls** systems as part of the annual report.

The board should carry out a robust **assessment of the company's emerging and principal risks** (FRC *UK Corporate Governance Code 2024*: Principle O, provision 28). The board should monitor the company's **risk management and internal control framework** and, at least annually, carry out a review of their

effectiveness and report on that review in the annual report (FRC *UK Corporate Governance Code 2024*: Principle O, provision 29).

The statement should be based on an **annual review of the effectiveness of internal control** which should confirm that the board has considered **all significant aspects** of internal control. In particular the assessment should cover:

- the company's willingness to take on risk (its "**risk appetite**"), the desired culture within the company and whether this culture has been embedded;
- the **operation of the risk management and internal control systems**, covering the design, implementation, monitoring and review and identification of risks and determination of those which are principal to the company;
- the integration of risk management and internal controls with considerations of **strategy and business model**, and with business planning processes;
- the **changes in the nature, likelihood and impact of principal risks**, and the company's ability to respond to changes in its business and the external environment;
- the extent, frequency and quality of the communication of the results of management's monitoring to the board which enables it to build up a cumulative assessment of the state of control in the company and the effectiveness with which risk is being managed or mitigated;
- **issues dealt with in reports** reviewed by the board during the year, in particular the incidence of significant control failings or weaknesses that have been identified at any time during the period and the extent to which they have, or could have, resulted in unforeseen impact; and
- the effectiveness of the company's **public reporting** processes.

(FRC *Guidance on Risk Management, Internal Control and Related Financial and Business Reporting*: para. 43)

4.3 Auditors' responsibilities

Certain jurisdictions may require auditors to review a company's compliance with corporate governance codes as part of their statutory audit. For example, the UK Listing Rules require UK auditors to report on whether listed companies comply with specific provisions within the Code relevant to UK companies. These are:

- Directors' responsibility for preparing the annual report and accounts explained in report
- Effectiveness of the risk management and internal control systems reviewed and reported on
- Audit committee of at least three non-executive directors set up (or at least two non-executive directors for smaller companies)
- Audit committee terms of reference set out in writing
- Audit committee terms of reference available/described in report
- Audit committee arranges methods for staff to report impropriety in financial reporting
- Audit committee monitors and reviews effectiveness of internal audit activities
- Audit committee has primary responsibility for appointment of external auditors
- If external audit provides non-audit services, then the annual report sets out how independence is maintained

If the auditor is required to undertake certain procedures as part of an audit, it is advisable to ensure that both parties understand exactly what the auditor will do (ie by including the nature of the review in the engagement letter and to make sure any reporting is clearly separated from the audit opinion.

Question

There is a growing call internationally for public reporting about the control effectiveness of companies not just from a narrow statutory audit perspective but more from the wider perspective of corporate governance.

Required

(a) Explain the key enquiries that an auditor would make in order to ensure that a company is managing effectively its corporate business risk.

(b) Explain what you understand by the term audit committee.

Answer

(a) **Corporate business risk**

The questions the auditor should ask include:

(i) Does the company address the issues?

The auditors should ensure that the company is aware of the issues raised by internal control guidance for directors and that they have taken steps to follow such guidance. Indicators of such steps might include having one director put in charge of complying with the guidance, and information issued to staff about what this will involve.

(ii) Do the directors identify significant risks?

It is possible that 'risks' are defined narrowly by the directors, in other words that they have tried to set out what issues the company might face, and that other significant risks may slip through the net.

Again, reading the documentation that has been prepared for staff may indicate whether this is the case. It might also emerge in the course of discussions with the director designated to control compliance.

(iii) Does the board evaluate and manage significant risks?

The board must be able to do this stage effectively, or the entire process is pointless. The auditors should assess the director's action plan in the event of significant risks being identified, and perhaps review minutes of past meetings when the directors have had to respond to a risk.

(iv) Does the board consider the probability of the risk arising?

(v) Does the board consider the potential operational and financial impact in the event of the risk arising?

(vi) Has the board implemented controls which would maintain the business risk between certain specified tolerance limits? (Have the directors set specified tolerance limits?)

(vii) Does the board regularly review its processes for identifying and dealing with risks arising?

(viii) Does the board include meaningful reports about the systems to identify and manage risks in the annual report so that shareholders can understand their actions?

(b) An audit committee reviews financial information and liaises between the auditors and the company. It should consist of three (or in the case of smaller companies two) non-executive directors of the company.

5 Internal audit

FAST FORWARD

The internal audit function assists management in achieving corporate objectives, particularly in achieving good corporate governance.

5.1 Definition

Key term

Internal audit function is a function of an entity that performs assurance and consulting activities designed to evaluate and improve the effectiveness of the entity's governance, risk management and internal control processes.

The internal audit function is generally a feature of large companies. It is a function, provided either by employees of the entity or sourced from an external organisation to assist management in **achieving corporate objectives.**

If the internal audit function exists to assist management in achieving corporate objectives, it is important to ask '**what are corporate objectives**?' Obviously, these will vary from company to company, and will be found, for example, in companies' mission statements and strategic plans.

However, other corporate objectives will not vary so much between companies, and are linked to a key corporate issue we have already discussed at length, the issue being **good corporate governance**.

The codes of corporate governance that we have already looked at highlight the need for businesses to maintain **good systems of internal control** to manage the risks the company faces. The **internal audit function** can play a **key role in assessing and monitoring** internal control policies and procedures.

The internal audit function can assist the board in other ways as well:

- By, in effect, acting as auditors for board reports not audited by the external auditors.
- By being the experts in fields such as auditing and accounting standards in the company and assisting in implementation of new standards.
- By liaising with external auditors, particularly where external auditors can use IA work and reduce the time and therefore cost of the external audit. In addition, IA can check that external auditors are reporting back to the board everything they are required to under auditing standards.

The UK Corporate Governance Code highlights the importance of the internal audit function by stipulating that directors of companies that do not have an internal audit department should re-consider the need for one annually.

5.2 Distinction between internal and external audit

FAST FORWARD

Although many of the techniques internal and external auditors use are similar, the basis and reasoning of their work is different.

The best way to see the difference between internal and external audit is to revise a key term.

Key term

An **external audit** is an exercise whose objective is to enable auditors to express an opinion whether the financial statements give a true and fair view (or equivalent) of the entity's affairs at the period end and of its profit and loss for the period then ended and have been properly prepared in accordance with the applicable reporting framework.

Contrast the definition of external audit with the definition of internal audit given at the beginning of this section. The external audit is focused on a very specific item, the financial statements, whereas the internal audit function is focused on the operations of the entire business.

The following table highlights the differences between internal and external audit.

	Internal audit	External audit
Reason	Internal audit is an activity designed to add value and improve an organisation's operations.	External audit is an exercise to enable auditors to express an opinion on the financial statements.
Reporting to	Internal audit reports to the board of directors, or other people charged with governance, such as the audit committee.	The external auditors report to the shareholders, or members, of a company on the truth and fairness of the accounts.
Relating to	Internal audit work relates to the operations of the organisation	External audit work relates solely to the financial statements.
Relationship with the company	Internal auditors are very often employees of the organisation, although sometimes the internal audit function is outsourced.	External auditors are independent of the company and its management. They are appointed by the shareholders.

The table shows that although some of the procedures that the internal audit function undertake are very similar to those undertaken by the external auditors, the **whole basis and reasoning of their work is fundamentally different**.

5.3 Internal audit planning

> **FAST FORWARD**
>
> Internal audit departments need to plan, both at an **annual department level** and at an **individual assignment level**.

Planning internal audit work helps:

- Determine priorities
- Establish the most cost-effective way of doing the work
- Assist in the direction and control of work
- Ensure that attention is devoted to critical aspects of work
- Ensure that work is completed in accordance with pre-determined targets

Key terms

> The **strategic plan** is a long term plan covering a period of between 2 and 5 years. During this time, all major systems should be audited. The plan should set out the audit objectives, areas, types of activity, frequency of audit and resources to be applied.
>
> The **periodic plan** is typically set out for a financial year and it translates the strategic plan for that year into a schedule of assignments to be carried out, allocating staff and resources. It is likely to be approved by management.
>
> **Operational work plans** are those plans produced for each audit assignment. They should cover the objectives and scope of the audit, include time budgets and outline procedures and methods.

All of the types of plan outlined above should be flexible, so that the plans can be adapted to the changing needs of the business.

When the audit plans (above) are formulated, the following stages should be followed:

Stage 1   Identify the objectives of the organisation

Stage 2   Define internal audit objectives

Stage 3   Take account of relevant legal and regulatory changes

Stage 4   Obtain a comprehensive understanding of the systems, structure and operations

Stage 5 Identify, evaluate and rank risks to which the company is exposed

Stage 6 Take account of changes in structure or systems during the period, known strengths and weaknesses in the system, management concerns and expectations

Stage 7 Identify audit areas by service, function and major systems

For example, the team might audit divisions of the business separately, or focus on the Human Resources department, or the sales systems.

Stage 8 Determine the type of audit, for example, systems, verification, value for money.

A systems audit might be conducted on the sales or purchase system, for example. If the internal auditors were investigating a fraud, they might use a verification or substantive approach, trying to substantiate financial results to third party evidence.

Stage 9 Take account of any external audit or review plans

The company will not want internal audit to carry out work that the external audit team plan to carry out as part of their audit as this is not cost-effective. On the other hand, the external audit team might make use of work performed by the internal audit function (see Chapter 8) which might be cheaper for the company.

Stage 10 Assess staff resources and match to requirements.

5.4 Internal audit and risk management

> **FAST FORWARD**
>
> The internal audit function has two key roles to play in relation to organisational risk management:
> - Ensuring the company's risk management system operates effectively
> - Ensuring that strategies implemented in respect of business risks operate effectively

5.4.1 Risk

All companies face risks arising from their activities. This risk is known as business risk.

Key term

> **Business risk** describes risks that may stop the company achieving its financial goals and objectives.

Business risk cannot be eliminated, but it must be **managed** by the company.

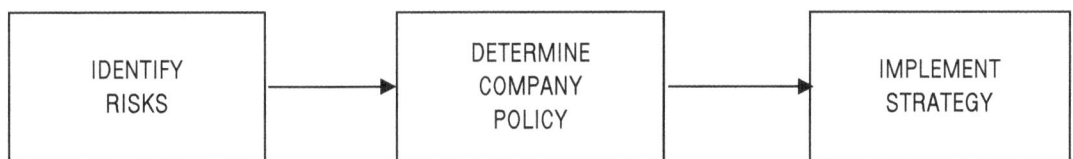

Designing and operating internal control systems is a key part of a company's risk management. This will often be done by employees in their various departments, although sometimes (particularly in the case of specialised computer systems) the company will hire external expertise to design systems.

Exam focus point

> Part of a question in May 2012 focused on business risks and management strategies to address them.

5.4.2 The role of the internal audit function

The internal audit function has a two-fold role in relation to risk management:

- Monitoring the company's overall risk management policy to ensure it operates effectively
- Monitoring the strategies implemented to ensure that they continue to operate effectively

This can be shown as:

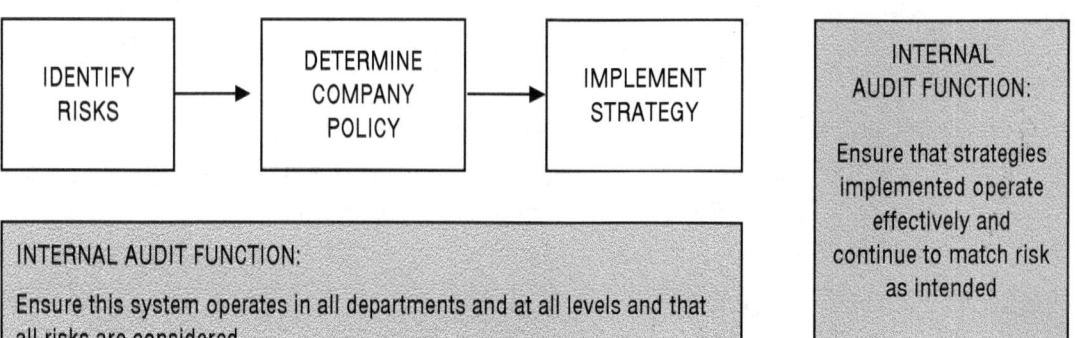

As a significant risk management policy in companies is to implement internal controls to reduce the risks, the internal audit function has a key role in assessing systems and testing controls.

The key role of the internal audit function will be **monitoring the overall process** and in **providing assurance** that the **systems** which the departments have designed **meet objectives** and **operate effectively**.

It is important that the internal auditors retain their **objectivity** towards these aspects of their role so internal auditors will usually not assist in the development of systems as this would detract from their objectivity when monitoring them

6 Internal audit assignments

FAST FORWARD

Internal auditors can be involved in many different assignments as directed by management.

Exam focus point

You should read through the following section to learn **what an internal auditor does** and to **reinforce the difference between the internal audit function and the statutory (external) audit**. However, don't worry too much about the mechanics of **how** they test the following things – you are going to be introduced to the techniques of auditing in the next few parts of the Text.

6.1 Value for money audits

6.1.1 Example

A good example of value for money is a bottle of washing up liquid sold by the leading brand. If we believe the advertising, the leading brand is good 'value for money' (VFM) because it washes half as many plates again as any other washing up liquid. Bottle for bottle it may be more expensive, but plate for plate it is cheaper. Not only this but the leading brand gets plates 'squeaky' clean. To summarise, the leading brand gives us VFM because it exhibits the following characteristics.

- **Economy** (more clean plates per dollar)
- **Efficiency** (fewer squirts required to clean the same number of plates as an alternative product)
- **Effectiveness** (more clean plates per squirt)

These are the three Es of VFM.

6.1.2 The three Es

In 1990 an audit brief by the Consultative Committee of Accountancy Bodies in the UK on VFM audit defined the three Es as follows.

(a) **Economy**: attaining the appropriate quantity and quality of physical, human and financial resources (**inputs**) at lowest cost. An activity would not be economic, if, for example, there was over-staffing or failure to purchase materials of requisite quality at the lowest available price.

(b) **Efficiency**: this is the relationship between goods or services produced (**outputs**) and the resources used to produce them. An efficient operation produces the maximum output for any given set of resource inputs; or it has minimum inputs for any given quantity and quality of product or service provided.

(c) **Effectiveness**: this is concerned with how well an activity is achieving its policy objectives or other intended effects.

The internal auditors will **evaluate these three factors** for any given business system or operation in the company. Value for money can often only be judged by **comparison.** In searching for value for money, present methods of operation and uses of resources must be **compared with alternatives.**

6.1.3 Selecting areas for investigation

Value for money checklists can be used. The following list identifies areas of an organisation, process or activity where there might be scope for significant value for money improvements. Each of these should be reviewed within individual organisations, with a view to assessing its economy, efficiency and effectiveness.

- Service delivery (the actual provision of a public service)
- Management process
- Environment

An alternative approach is to look at areas of spending. A value for money assessment of economy, efficiency, and effectiveness would look at whether:

- Too much money is being spent on certain items or activities, to achieve the targets or objectives of the overall operation.

- Money is being spent to no purpose, because the spending is not helping to achieve objectives.

- Changes could be made to improve performance.

An illustrative list is shown below of the sort of spending areas that might be looked at, and the aspects of spending where value for money might be improved.

- Employee expenses
- Premises expenses
- Suppliers and services
- Establishment expenses
- Capital expenditure

Problems with VFM auditing	
Measuring outputs	For example, the outputs of a fire brigade can be measured by the number of call-outs, but it is not satisfactory to compare a call-out to individuals stuck in a lift with a call-out to a small house fire or a major industrial fire or a road accident etc.
Defining objectives	In not for profit organisations the quality of the service provided will be a significant feature of their service. For example, a local authority has, amongst its various different objectives, the objective of providing a rubbish collection service. The effectiveness of this service can only be judged by establishing what standard or quality of service is required.
Sacrifice of quality	Economy and efficiency can be achieved by sacrificing quality. Neither outputs nor impacts are necessarily measured in terms of quality. For example, the cost of teaching can be reduced by increasing the pupil:teacher ratio in schools, but it is difficult to judge the consequences of such a change on teaching standards and quality.
Measuring effectiveness	For example, the effectiveness of the health service could be said to have improved if hospitals have greater success in treating various illnesses and other conditions, or if the life expectancy of the population has increased, but a consequence of these changes will be overcrowded hospitals and longer medical waiting lists.
Overemphasis in cost control	There can be an **emphasis** with VFM audits on **costs and cost control** rather than on achieving more benefits and value, so that management might be pressurised into 'short term' decisions, such as abandoning capital expenditure plans which would create future benefits in order to keep current spending levels within limits.
Measuring efficiency	In profit-making organisations, the efficiency of the organisation as a whole can be measured in terms of return on capital employed. Individual profit centres or operating units within the organisation can also have efficiency measured by relating the quantity of output produced, which has a **market value** and therefore a quantifiable financial value, to the inputs (and their cost) required to make the output. In NFP organisations, output does not usually have a market value, and it is therefore more difficult to measure efficiency. This difficulty is compounded by the fact that, since NFP organisations often have many different activities or operations, it is difficult to compare the efficiency of one operation with the efficiency of another. For example, with the police force, it might be difficult to compare the efficiency of a serious crimes squad with the efficiency of the traffic police.

6.2 Information technology audits

An information technology audit is a test of control in a specific area of the business, the computer systems. Increasingly in modern business, computers are vital to the functioning of the business, and therefore the controls over them are some of the most important in the business.

It is likely to be necessary to have an IT specialist in the internal audit team to undertake an audit of the controls, as some of them will be programmed into the computer system.

The diagram below shows the various areas of IT in the business which might be subject to a test of controls by the auditors.

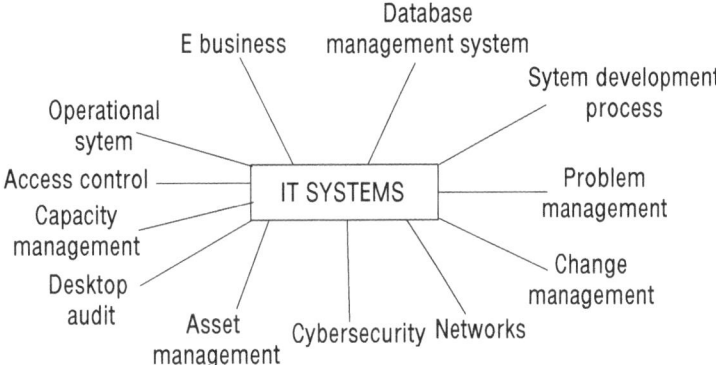

6.3 Financial audits

The financial audit is the internal audit function's traditional role. It involves reviewing all the available evidence (usually the company's records) to substantiate information in management and financial reporting.

This role in many ways echoed the role of the external auditor, and was not a role in which the internal auditors could add any particular value to the business. Increasingly, it is a minor part of the function of the internal audit function.

6.4 Fraud investigations

FAST FORWARD

Internal auditors may have a role in preventing and detecting fraud.

Fraud is a **key business risk**. It is the responsibility of the directors to prevent and detect fraud. As the **internal auditor has a role in risk management** he is involved in the process of managing the risk of fraud.

The internal auditor can help to **prevent** fraud by their work **assessing the adequacy and effectiveness of control systems** and **detect** fraud by **being mindful** when carrying out their work and **reporting any suspicions**.

The very **existence of an internal audit** function may act as a **deterrent** to fraud. The internal auditors might also be called upon to undertake special projects to investigate a suspected fraud.

6.5 Operational audits

FAST FORWARD

Internal auditors traditionally undertake operational audits.

Key term

Operational audits are audits of the operational processes of the organisation. They are also known as management or efficiency audits. Their prime objective is the monitoring of management's performance, ensuring company policy is adhered to.

6.5.1 Approaching operational audits

There are two aspects of an operational audit assignment:

- Ensure policies are **adequate**
- Ensure policies **work effectively**

6.5.2 Adequacy

The internal auditor will have to review the policies of a particular department by:

- Reading them
- Discussion with members of the department

Then the auditor will have to assess whether the policies are adequate, and possibly advise the board of improvement.

6.5.3 Effectiveness

The auditor will then have to examine the effectiveness of the controls by:

- Observing them in operation
- Testing them

This will be done on similar lines to the testing of controls discussed in Section D, even though the controls being tested may differ.

6.6 Procurement audits

Procurement is the process of **purchasing** for the business. A procurement audit will therefore concentrate on the **systems of the purchasing department(s)**.

The internal auditor will be checking that the system achieves key objectives and that it operates according to company guidelines.

Point to note

> The control objectives and systems will be the same as will be discussed when we look at the purchases and expenses system. However, the internal audit function will also be concerned with considerations beyond the scope of the external auditor.

6.7 Marketing

Marketing is the **process of assessing and enhancing demand for the company's products**. Marketing and associated sales are very important for the business, and therefore, the internal auditor but as the **associated systems do not directly impact on the financial statements**, they do not usually concern the external auditor. The external auditor is concerned with systems directly relevant to sales.

It is important for the internal auditor to review the marketing processes to ensure:

- The process is **managed efficiently**
- **Information is freely available** to manager demand
- **Risks** are being **managed** correctly

An audit may be especially critical for a marketing department which may be complex with several different teams, for example:

- Research
- Advertising
- Promotions
- After sales

It is vital to ensure that information is passed on properly within the department, and activities are streamlined.

6.8 Treasury

Treasury is a function within the finance department of a business. It **manages the funds of a business**. It is vital to a business that funds are managed so that cash is available when required.

There are risks associated with treasury, in terms of interest rate risk and foreign currency risk, and the auditor must ensure that the **risk is managed in accordance with company procedures.**

As with marketing audits, it is vital to ensure that **information is available** to the treasury department, so that they can **ensure funds are available when required**.

6.9 Human resources

The human resources department on one hand **procures a human resource** (employee) for the operation of the business and on the other **supports those employees in developing the organisation.**

It is important to ensure that the processes ensure that people are available to work as the business requires them and that the overall development of the business is planned and controlled.

Again, **ensuring company policies are maintained and information is freely available are key factors for internal audit to assess.**

Question — Internal control procedures

The growing recognition by management of the benefits of good internal control, and the complexities of an adequate system of internal control have led to the development of the internal audit function as a form of control over all other internal controls. The emergence of the internal auditors as experts in internal control is the result of an evolutionary process similar in many ways to the evolution of independent auditing.

Required

(a) Explain why the internal and independent auditors' review of internal control procedures differ in purpose.

(b) Explain the reasons why internal auditors should or should not report their findings on internal control to the following selection of company officials:

    (i)   The board of directors
    (ii)   The chief accountant

(c) Explain whether the independent auditors can place any reliance upon the internal auditors' work when the latter's main role is to be of service and assistance to management.

Answer

(a) The internal auditors review and test the system of internal control and report to management in order to improve the information received by managers and to help in their task of running the company. The internal auditors will recommend changes to the system to make sure that the management receives objective information which is efficiently produced. The internal auditors will also have a duty to search for and discover fraud.

The external auditors review the system of internal control in order to determine the extent of the substantive work required on the year end accounts. The external auditors report to the shareholders rather than the managers or directors.

External auditors are required to report on significant deficiencies in internal control and usually issue a letter of weakness to the managers, laying out any areas of weakness and recommendations for improvement in the system of internal control. The external auditors report on the truth and fairness of the financial statements, not directly on the system of internal control. The auditors do not have a specific duty to detect fraud, although they should plan their audit procedures so as to detect any material misstatement in the accounts on which they give an opinion.

(b) (i) **Board of directors**

There may be problems with internal audit reporting to the Board of Directors.

(1) The objectivity of the internal auditors may be reduced if they do not want to appear to criticise their employers, who are responsible for the design and operation of the systems under review.

(2) The members of the Board may not understand all the implications of the internal audit reports when accounting or technical information is required.

(3) The Board may not have enough time to spend considering the reports in sufficient depth. Important recommendations might therefore remain unimplemented.

A way around these problems is to delegate the review of internal audit reports to the audit committee, which is a sub-committee to the main board. The audit committee is made up of non-executive directors who have more time and more independence from the day-to-day running of the company.

(ii) **Chief accountant**

It would be inappropriate for the internal audit function to report to the chief accountant, who is largely in charge of running the system of internal control. It may be feasible for him or her to receive the report as well as the Board. Otherwise, the internal audit function cannot be effectively independent as the chief accountant could suppress unfavourable reports or could just not act on the recommendations of such reports.

(c) The internal audit function is itself part of the system of internal control: it is an internal control over internal controls. As such, the external auditors should be able to test it and, if it is found to be reliable, they can rely on it.

To check the reliability of the work of the internal auditors, I would consider the following matters.

(i) **The degree of independence of the internal auditors**

I would assess the organisational status and reporting responsibilities of the internal auditors and consider any restrictions placed upon them. Although internal auditors are employees of the enterprise and cannot therefore be independent of it, they should be able to plan and carry out their work as they wish and have access to senior management. They should be free of any responsibility which may create a conflict of interest, and of a situation where those staff on whom they are reporting are responsible for their or their staff's appointment, promotion or pay.

(ii) **The scope and objectives of the internal audit function**

I would examine the internal auditors' formal terms of reference and ascertain the scope and objectives of internal audit assignments.

(iii) **Quality of work**

I would consider whether the work of the internal audit function is properly planned, controlled, recorded and reviewed. Examples of good practice include the existence of an adequate audit manual, plans and procedures for supervision of individual assignments, and satisfactory arrangements for ensuring adequate quality control, reporting and follow-up.

(iv) **Technical competence**

Internal audit should be performed by persons having adequate training and competence as auditors. Indications of technical competence may be membership of an appropriate professional body or attendance at regular training courses.

(v) **Reports**

I would consider the quality of reports issued by the internal audit function and find out whether management considers and acts upon such reports.

If I find that the internal auditors' work is reliable, I will be able to place reliance on that work when appropriate. This may mean that I will need to carry out less audit work.

However, it should be emphasised that I cannot rely totally on the internal auditors' work in relation to any particular audit objective. Internal audit work provides only one form of evidence, and the internal auditors are not independent of company management. I may be able to reduce the number of items which I test, but I will not be able to leave a particular type of test (for example, a receivables' confirmation) entirely to the internal audit function. I remain responsible for the opinion which I form on the financial statements.

7 Internal audit reports

FAST FORWARD

The internal auditors' report may take any form as there are no formal reporting requirements for internal review reports.

7.1 Reporting on internal review assignments

Internal auditors prepare reports for directors and management as a result of work they have performed. These reports are internal to the business and are unlikely to be shared with third parties other than the external auditors.

We looked in detail at the types of assignment internal audit will carry out earlier in this chapter. These may be summarised as **'risk-based'**, where the internal auditors consider internal and external risks and discuss company operations and systems in place in respect of them or **'performance enhancement'** where internal audit consider risk and strategy on a higher level.

For the most part, work is likely to be **risk-based**. Regardless of the nature of the assignment, however, all internal audits are likely to result in a formal report.

There are **no formal requirements** for such reports as there are for the statutory audit. As we saw at the start of the chapter, the statutory auditor's report is a highly stylised document whose format is substantially the same for any audit. A report from the internal auditors in relation to an assignment can take essentially any form. However, some points should be borne in mind.

There is a generally accepted format for reports in business, which is laid out below. This format makes reports useful to readers as it highlights the conclusions drawn and gives easy reference to the user.

> **Standard report format**
>
> TERMS OF REFERENCE
> EXECUTIVE SUMMARY – summarising conclusions drawn from assignment
> BODY OF THE REPORT
> APPENDICES FOR ANY ADDITIONAL INFORMATION

The report is likely also to be dated, designated as to whether it is draft or final and have a 'distribution list' of directors and management who should read it attached.

Some internal audit reports will be modified as responses are made to it may various members of staff. If this is the case, the report should clearly state which version it is. The distribution list may also be annotated to show who has commented on the report at any time.

7.2 Contents of the report

The **executive summary** of an internal audit report should give the following information.

- Background to the assignment
- Objectives of the assignment
- Major outcomes of the work
- Key risks identified
- Key action points
- Summary of the work left to do

The **main body** of the report will contain the detail; for example the audit tests carried out and their findings, full lists of action points, including details of who has responsibility for carrying them out, the future time-scale and costs.

8 Regulation

> **FAST FORWARD**
>
> The internal audit function is not regulated in the same way as external audit.

The internal audit function is not regulated in the same ways as statutory auditing. There are **no legal requirements** associated with becoming an internal auditor. The **scope** and **nature** of **internal audit's work** is more likely to be set by **company policy** than by any external guidelines.

The International Auditing and Assurance Standards Board does not issue detailed auditing standards in relation to internal audit work. Where they are **applicable**, the standards set out in International Standards on Auditing are likely to be **good practice**, but they are not prescriptive in the same ways that they are for external auditors.

8.1 Institute of Internal Auditors

> **FAST FORWARD**
>
> Internal auditors may be members of bodies such as AIA or IIA, or both.

In contrast to external auditors, **internal auditors are not required to be members of a professional body** such as AIA. However, this does not mean they cannot be, and many are. There is also a global Institute of Internal Auditors (the IIA) which internal auditors **may** also become members of. Some people are members of both AIA and IIA.

The IIA has over 6,000 members in the UK and Ireland and it is dedicated to representing and promoting the interests of internal auditors.

It issues 'International Standards for the Professional Practice of Internal Auditing'. These are not examinable, so are not detailed in this Learning & Practice Workbook, but you should be aware of the them as being another Code of Good Practice that internal auditors can follow, providing a framework for providing a wide range of internal audit services.

9 Outsourcing the internal audit function

FAST FORWARD

> The internal audit function may consist of employees, or may be sourced from external service providers.

9.1 Sources of internal audit

While, as we have just discussed, the scope of the internal auditor's work is different to that of the external auditor, there are many features that can link them. The key linking factor is that the **techniques** which are used to carry out audits are the same for internal and external auditors.

It can be expensive to maintain an internal audit function consisting of employees. As a result the directors may conclude that the cost is prohibitive.

It is possible that the monitoring and review required by a certain company could be done in a small amount of time and full-time employees cannot be justified.

It is possible that a number of internal audit staff are required, but the cost of recruitment is prohibitive, or the directors are aware that the need for internal audit is only short-term.

In such circumstances, it is possible to **outsource the internal audit function**, that is, purchase the service from outside.

Therefore, many of the **larger accountancy firms offer internal audit services**. It is possible that the same firm might offer one client both internal and external audit services. In such circumstances the firm would have to be aware of the independence issues this would raise for the external audit team.

Exam focus point

> **RPQ candidates** should note that the Financial Reporting Council's *Revised Ethical Standard 2024* (FRC ES) **prohibits** an audit firm from **providing internal audit services** to an entity where it also acts as the entity's external auditor. The FRC ES is covered in Chapter 4.

Question — Independence

The independence issues which would arise through the audit firm offering both internal and external audit services to the same client are referred to above.

(a) What are the independence issues?
(b) Why should the issues affect the external audit team rather than the internal audit team?

Answer

(a) External auditors are employed to give an assurance to the members of a company about the stewardship of the directors and the management of that entity. They are independent verifiers. If the firm provides internal audit services to the entity, two issues arise:

   (i) Internal auditors report to the director so there is a link between the firm and the directors which is a block to independence.

(ii) The firm provides 'other services' to an external audit client, and they must consider whether this affects their objectivity in relation to the audit and renders them no longer impartial.

The specific guidance on auditors' independence will be considered in more detail in Chapter 4.

(b) The issues arise for the external audit team as independence is a key ethical issue for external auditors. As internal auditors provide a service to the directors, by whom they are employed, the issue of independence is a more tricky issue! It relates more to 'independence of mind'. Internal auditors are not required to be 'seen to been independent' in the same way that external auditors are. Ethical issues for internal audit are also discussed in Chapter 4.

9.2 Advantages of outsourcing

FAST FORWARD

Advantages of outsourcing the internal audit function include speed, cost, and a tailored answer to internal audit requirements.

The advantage of outsourcing internal audits is that outsourcing can overcome all the problems mentioned above.

- Staff do not need to be recruited, as the **service provider has good quality staff.**
- The service provider has different specialist skills and can assess what management require them to do. As they are external to the operation, this will not cause operational problems. The company will have access to a broad range of skills.
- Outsourcing can provide an **immediate** internal audit function.
- Associated costs, such as staff training, are eliminated.
- The service contract can be for the **appropriate time scale** (a two week project, a month, etc)
- Because the **time scale is flexible**, a **team of staff** can be provided if required.
- The service provider could also provide less than a team, but, for example, could provide one member of staff on a full-time basis for a short period, as a **secondment.**

Outsourced internal audit services are provided by many audit firms, particularly the large firms. This can range from a team of staff for a short term project, or a single staff member on a long term project. However, problems with such provision may include a high turnover in the staff used to provide IA services.

The fact that internal audit services are typically provided by **external auditors** can raise problems as well:

- The company might wish to **use the same firm** for internal and external audit services, but this may lead to **complications for the external auditors**, particularly in terms of independence.
- The **cost** of sourcing the internal audit function might be high enough to make the directors choose not to have an internal audit function at all.

A key advantage of outsourcing internal audit is that **outsourcing can be used on a short term basis**, to:

- Provide immediate services
- Lay the basis of a permanent function, by setting policies and functions
- Prepare the directors for the implications of having an internal audit function
- Assist the directors in recruiting the permanent function.

9.3 Managing an outsourced department

A company will need to establish controls over the outsourced internal audit function. Controls would include:

- Setting performance measures in terms of cost and areas of the business reviewed and obtaining explanations for variances.
- Ensuring appropriate audit methodology (working papers/reviews) is maintained.
- Reviewing working papers on a sample basis to ensure they meet internal standards/guidelines.
- Agreeing internal audit work plans in advance of work being performed.
- If external auditor is used, ensuring the firm has suitable controls to keep the two functions separate.

Chapter roundup

- Good corporate governance is important because the owners of a company and the people who manage the company are not always the same people.
- The G20/OECD Principles of Corporate Governance provide guidance to help policy makers evaluate and improve the legal, regulatory and institutional framework for corporate governance, with a view to supporting market confidence and integrity, economic efficiency, sustainable growth and financial stability.
- The **UK Corporate Governance Code** contains detailed guidance for UK companies on good corporate governance. Companies must **comply** with the principles of the Code or **explain** their non-compliance in their corporate governance report.
- Directors should set company policy, including risk policy, and are responsible for the company's systems and controls.
- An **audit committee** can help a company maintain objectivity with regard to financial reporting and the audit of financial statements.
- The internal audit function assists management in achieving corporate objectives, particularly, in achieving good corporate governance.
- Internal audit departments need to plan, both at an **annual department level** and at an **individual assignment level**.
- The internal audit function has **two key roles** to play in relation to organisational risk management:
    - Ensuring the company's risk management system operates effectively
    - Ensuring that strategies implemented in respect of business risks operate effectively
- Internal auditors can be involved in many **different assignments as directed by management** including preventing and detecting fraud and undertaking operational audits.
- The internal auditors' report may take any form as there are **no formal reporting requirements** for internal review reports.
- The internal audit function is **not regulated** in the same way as external audit.
- Internal auditors **may be members of bodies such as AIA** or IIA, or both.
- The internal audit function may consist of **employees**, or may be **sourced from external service providers**.
- **Advantages of outsourcing** the internal audit function include **speed, cost**, and **a tailored answer to internal audit requirements**.

Quick quiz

1. An advantage of voluntary codes of corporate governance is that they are flexible and therefore suit different kinds of companies in different situations.

   True ☐

   False ☐

2. The G20/OECD Principles of Corporate Governance strongly recommend:

   A   An annual audit
   B   Internal audit
   C   Directors should not receive pay
   D   Directors should be non-executive

3. Complete the blanks.

   An audit.............is a sub-committee of the.............. ...., usually containing a number of....................... ....directors.

4. When a company cannot easily find non-executive directors it should not have an audit committee.

   True ☐

   False ☐

5. Why are internal controls important in a company?

6. What is the internal audit function?

7. Name three key differences between internal and external audit.

   (1) ....
   (2) ....
   (3) ....

8. It is possible to buy in an internal audit service from an external organisation.

   True ☐

   False ☐

9. Link the value for money 'E' with its definition.

   (a) Economy
   (b) Efficiency
   (c) Effectiveness

   (i)   The relationships between the goods and services produced (outputs) and the resources used to produce them
   (ii) The concern with how well an activity is achieving its policy objectives or other intended effects
   (iii) Attaining the appropriate quantity and quality of physical, human and financial resources (inputs) at lowest cost

10. Name five areas of the computer system which might benefit from an IT audit.

    (1) ....
    (2) ....
    (3) ....
    (4) ....
    (5) ....

11 Define the following areas of a business, which an internal auditor might review:

(a) Procurement
(b) Marketing
(c) Treasury
(d) Human resources

12 There are formal statutory rules governing the format of internal audit reports.

True ☐

False ☐

Answers to quick quiz

1 True

2 A

3 An audit **committee** is a sub-committee of the **board of directors**, usually containing a number of **independent non-executive** directors.

4 False. It should have an audit committee if required, or if the directors feel it is in the best interests of the shareholders, even if it is difficult to find non-executive directors.

5 Internal controls contribute to:

- Safeguarding company assets
- Preventing and detecting fraud
- As a result, safeguarding the shareholder's investment

6 The **internal audit function** is an appraisal activity established by the entity as a service to the entity.

7 (1) External auditors report to members, internal auditors report to directors.

   (2) External auditors report on whether the financial statements are true and fair, internal auditors report on systems, controls and risks.

   (3) External auditors are independent of the company, internal auditors are often employed by it.

8 True, the internal audit function may be outsourced.

9 (a) (iii), (b) (i), (c) (ii)

10 Look back to the diagram in paragraph 6.2.

11 (a) The purchasing department
   (b) The process which assesses and enhances demand for a product.
   (c) Function (often within finance department) which manages funds.
   (d) Department which procures staff and manages development of the organisation.

12 False

End of chapter question

Sparky (AIA May 2005) (amended)

You are the auditor of Sparky Ltd. The board of directors comprises three executive and four non-executive directors. The company is not listed, and so is not required to comply with the UK Corporate Governance Code. The directors are, however, considering setting up an audit committee. They have approached you for advice.

Required

Write a memorandum to the directors of Sparky Ltd explaining:

(a)	The role and responsibilities of an audit committee;	**(7 marks)**
(b)	The possible advantages and disadvantages for Sparky of having an audit committee; and	**(6 marks)**
(c)	Who should be appointed to sit on the committee.	**(2 marks)**

(Total = 15 marks)

Mendelson Ltd (AIA May 2005)

Mendelson Ltd has been in business for several years. Although it operated as a small company initially, over the years it has grown in both size and complexity. At a recent board meeting, the directors expressed concerns that as the company grew, they were finding it increasingly difficult to monitor everyday operations. In particular, they were worried that they might be failing in their responsibilities to safeguard the company's assets and ensure that adequate accounting records are being maintained.

Required

Explain how the internal audit function can assist management to fulfil their responsibilities. **(10 marks)**

Professional ethics

Topic list	Syllabus reference
1 The need for an ethical code	1.3
2 Ethical guidance	1.3
3 IESBA *Code of Ethics for Professional Accountants*	1.5, 1.6, 1.7
4 The FRC's *Ethical Standard*	1.5, 1.6, 1.7

Introduction

The ethical matters covered in this chapter are very important. You must be able to apply the guidance on ethical matters to any given situation, but remember that common sense is usually a good guide.

First we look at the reasons why an ethical code is required and examine the five fundamental principles of professional ethics as defined by IESBA's *Code of Ethics for Professional Accountants*. We then look at the five main threats to compliance with these principles and the sorts of safeguards that can be put in place to mitigate these threats.

The section on the FRC's *Ethical Standard* is **only relevant** to RPQ students.

1 The need for an ethical code

> **FAST FORWARD**
> Professional accountants need an ethical code because they are **relied upon** for their expertise.

Ethics can be defined as a set of principles of right conduct or a system of moral values. In its most basic form, it means knowing the difference between right and wrong and choosing to do what is right. Ethical dilemmas will naturally arise in the workplace and an ethical code provides **guidance** on the best course of action.

Members of all professions, including doctors, lawyers and accountants are **relied upon** for their expertise. Accountants are relied upon by their clients and other stakeholders such as employees, lenders and taxation authorities. Accountants must act, and be seen to act, in the **public interest** rather than in their own interest. By adhering to an ethical code, accountants help to maintain the **integrity** of their profession providing reassurance to both individual stakeholders and the wider community.

An ethical code also provides some **protection** for accountants if they have been accused of acting unethically. An accountant cannot be accused of acting differently from other accountants if they all follow the same ethical code.

2 Ethical guidance

> **FAST FORWARD**
> Sources of ethical guidance include the *Code of Ethics for Professional Accountants* issued by the International Ethics Standards Board for Accountants (the IESBA *Code*) and the FRC's *Ethical Standard*.

The AIA has adopted the **Code of Ethics for Professional Accountants issued by the International Ethics Standards Board for Accountants** (the **IESBA Code**). All AIA members and candidates are expected to follow this guidance. The International Ethics Standards Board for Accountants (IESBA) is an independent standard-setting board of IFAC which is responsible for developing and issuing high quality global ethical standards and other pronouncements. IFAC is the global organisation for the accountancy profession based in New York City. IFAC was founded in 1977 and one of its aims is to establish and promote adherence to high quality international standards. AIA's *Code of Ethics* fully complies with the IESBA *Code* and all members and candidates are expected to comply with it.

Some countries may have their own ethical guidance in additional to the IESBA *Code*. For example, in the UK, the Financial Reporting Council has issued its own **Ethical Standard** (FRC ES) – the 'Revised Ethical Standard 2024' – which provides an additional source of guidance.

> **Exam focus point**
> **RPQ candidates** will be expected to refer as appropriate to this FRC ES. Candidates following other routes will not be penalised if they refer to the FRC ES in preference to the IESBA *Code*. The FRC ES can be accessed via the Financial Reporting Council's website at www.frc.org.uk.

This Learning & Practice Workbook will first cover the IESBA *Code* before looking at the FRC ES. Since the FRC ES is an additional source of country-specific guidance and all AIA candidates must follow the IESBA *Code*, **RPQ candidates must study both sections.** All other candidates can miss out the section on the FRC ES.

3 IESBA *Code of Ethics for Professional Accountants*

3.1 The fundamental principles

> **FAST FORWARD**
> The five **fundamental principles** of professional ethics are integrity, objectivity, professional competence and due care, confidentiality and professional behaviour.

4: PROFESSIONAL ETHICS

The IESBA *Code of Ethics for Professional Accountants* (the *Code*) sets out **five fundamental principles of professional ethics** and provides a conceptual framework for applying those principles. Members must apply this conceptual framework to **identify threats** to compliance with the fundamental principles, **evaluate the significance of the threats** identified and **apply safeguards**, when necessary, to eliminate the threats or reduce them to an acceptable level.

The five fundamental principles are summarised in the table below.

IESBA *Code's* fundamental principles (IESBA *Code* para. 110.1 A1)	
Integrity	To be straightforward and honest in all professional and business relationships.
Objectivity	To exercise professional or business judgment without being compromised by: • Bias; • Conflict of interest; or • Undue influence of, or undue reliance on individuals, organisations, technology or other factors.
Professional competence and due care	To: • Attain and maintain professional knowledge and skill at the level required to ensure that a client or employer receives competent professional service, based on current technical and professional standards and relevant legislation; and • Act diligently and in accordance with applicable technical and professional standards.
Confidentiality	To respect the confidentiality of information acquired as a result of professional and business relationships.
Professional behaviour	To: • Comply with relevant laws and regulations; • Behave in a manner consistent with the profession's responsibility to act in the public interest in all professional activities and business relationships; and • Avoid any conduct that the professional accountant knows, or should know, might discredit the profession.

3.2 Threats and safeguards

FAST FORWARD

The professional accountant must **identify, evaluate and address** threats to compliance with the fundamental principles. Threats may arise in the form of **self-interest, self-review, advocacy, familiarity and intimidation threats**.
Appropriate **safeguards** must be put in place to eliminate or reduce such threats to acceptable levels.

It would be impossible for the IESBA *Code* to define every situation that creates threats to the fundamental principles and specify the appropriate action. Instead, it provides a **conceptual framework** that requires the professional accountant to **identify, evaluate and address** threats to compliance with the fundamental principles.

Threats to the fundamental principles can fall into one or more of the following categories.

(a) A **self-interest threat** is the threat that **a financial or other interest** will inappropriately influence a professional accountant's **judgment or behaviour**.

(b) A **self-review threat** is the threat that a professional accountant **will not appropriately evaluate** the results of a previous judgement made; or an activity **performed by the accountant, or by**

another individual within the accountant's firm or employing organisation, on which the accountant will rely when forming a judgment as part of performing a current activity.

(c) An **advocacy threat** is the threat that a professional accountant will promote a client's or employing organisation's position to the point that the **accountant's objectivity is compromised**.

(d) A **familiarity threat** is the threat that due to a **long or close relationship** with a client, or employing organisation, a professional accountant will be **too sympathetic to their interests** or **too accepting of their work**.

(e) An **intimidation threat** is the threat that a professional accountant will be **deterred from acting objectively** because of actual or perceived pressures, including attempts to exercise undue influence over the accountant.

(IESBA *Code* para. 120.6 A3)

Safeguards are actions or other measures that may **eliminate threats** or **reduce them to an acceptable level**. They fall into two broad categories.

(a) Safeguards created by the **profession, legislation or regulation**
(b) Safeguards in the **work environment**

Safeguards created by the profession, legislation or regulation include the following.

- Educational, training and experience requirements for entry into the profession
- Continuing professional development requirements
- Corporate governance regulations
- Professional standards
- Professional or regulatory monitoring and disciplinary procedures
- External review

Safeguards in the work environment can be **firm-wide or engagement-specific**. Firm-wide safeguards include the following.

- Leadership of the firm that stresses the importance of compliance with the fundamental principles
- Policies and procedures that will enable the identification of interests or relationships between the firm or members of engagement teams and clients
- Policies and procedures to monitor and, if necessary, manage the reliance on revenue received from a single client
- Using different partners and engagement teams with separate reporting lines for the provision of non-assurance services to an assurance client

Examples of engagement-specific safeguards in the work environment include the following.

- Having a professional accountant who was not a member of the assurance team review the assurance work performed or otherwise advise as necessary
- Consulting an independent third party, such as a committee of independent directors, a professional regulatory body or another professional accountant
- Rotating senior assurance team personnel

> **Exam focus point**
>
> Exam questions may present an ethical scenario and ask what to do. Answers should identify threats to the fundamental principles and propose safeguards, where appropriate. Candidates may want to present threats and safeguards in a table to make the answer easier for the examiner to read. Remember that withdrawing from the engagement is always a last resort.

3.3 Integrity, objectivity and independence

The principle of integrity imposes an obligation on all professional accountants to be **straightforward and honest** in all professional and business relationships. Integrity also implies fair dealing and truthfulness.

Objectivity is a state of mind but in certain roles the preservation of objectivity has to be shown by the maintenance of **independence** from those influences which could impair objectivity.

It is very important that the auditor is **impartial** and **independent** of management, so an **objective** view on the financial statements of an entity can be given. The onus is always on the auditor not only to be independent but also to be **seen** to be independent.

Key terms

> **Independence of mind** is the state of mind that permits the expression of a conclusion without being affected by influences that compromise professional judgment, thereby allowing an individual to act with integrity, and exercise objectivity and professional scepticism.
>
> **Independence in appearance** is the avoidance of facts and circumstances that are so significant that a reasonable and informed third party would be likely to conclude that a firm's or an audit or assurance team member's integrity, objectivity or professional scepticism has been compromised.
>
> (IESBA *Code*: para. 120.15 A1)

Independence and objectivity matter because of:

(a) The **expectations** of those directly affected, particularly the members of the company. The audit should be able to provide **objective** assurance on the truth and fairness of the financial statements that the directors can never provide.

(b) The **public interest**. Companies are public entities, governed by rules requiring the disclosure of information.

What can the auditor do to preserve objectivity? The simple answer is to **withdraw from any engagement** where there is the **slightest threat** to objectivity. However there are disadvantages in this strict approach.

- Clients may lose an auditor who knows their business.
- It denies clients the freedom to be advised by the accountant of their choice.

The conceptual framework approach allows the professional accountant to identify the threat to independence and objectivity, evaluate its significance and apply safeguards where necessary to eliminate the threats or reduce them to an acceptable level. If the threats cannot be eliminated or reduced to an acceptable level the accountant shall **withdraw from the engagement or refuse to act**.

3.4 Threats to independence and objectivity

3.4.1 Self-interest

The IESBA *Code* highlights a number of areas in which a self-interest threat might arise. These may arise as a result of the financial or other interests of members or of immediate or close family and are summarised in the diagram below.

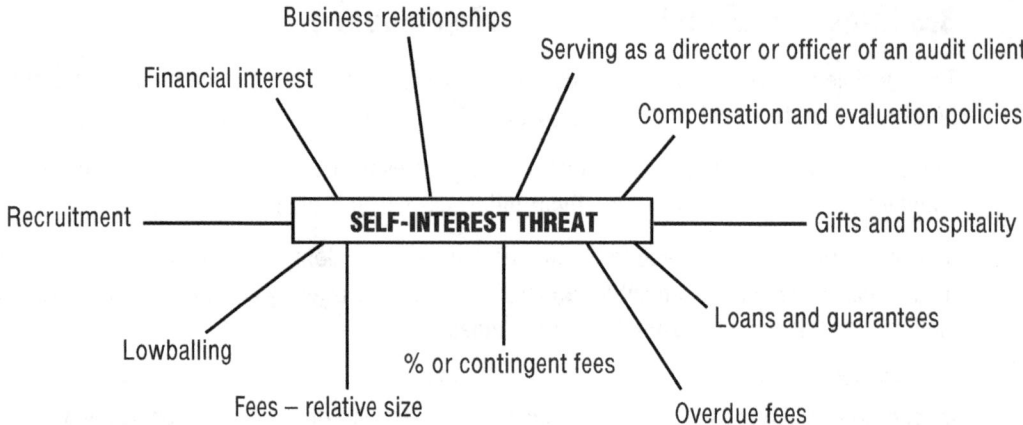

We will look at each of these areas in turn.

(i) **Financial interests**

A financial interest exists where an audit firm has a financial interest in a client's affairs, for example, the audit firm owns shares in the client, or is a trustee of a trust that holds shares in the client. The IESBA *Code* **does not allow** the following to own a direct financial interest or a material indirect financial interest in a client:

- The assurance firm or a network firm
- A member of the assurance team or any member of that individual's immediate family
- Any other partner in the same office (or their immediate family)
- Other partners/managers who provide non-audit services to the audit client

(IESBA *Code*: para. R510.4)

If any of these hold a **direct** financial interest, then **no safeguards would be sufficient** to mitigate the risk created.

For members of the audit team, if the interest is not direct (eg is held by an employee's pension scheme) or is **not material** (so the client cannot exercise significant influence over the auditor), then the following **safeguards** may be relevant:

- Disposing of the interest
- Removing the individual from the audit team
- Having a professional accountant review the work of the member of the audit team
- Exclude the individual from any significant decision-making concerning the audit engagement

(ii) **Loans and guarantees**

The advice on loans and guarantees falls into two categories:

- The client is a bank or other similar institution
- Other situations

If a client is a lending institution which lends an **immaterial amount** to an audit firm or member of the audit team on **normal commercial terms**, there is **no threat** to independence. If the loan were material, it would be necessary to apply safeguards to bring the self-interest threat down to an acceptable level. A suitable safeguard is likely to be an **independent review** (by a partner from another office in the firm) (IESBA *Code*: para 511.5 A3).

Loans to members of the audit team from a bank or other lending institution client are likely to be material to the individual but, provided that they are on normal commercial terms, these do not constitute a threat to independence.

An audit firm or individual on the audit team **should not** enter into any loan or guarantee arrangement with a client **that is not a bank or similar institution** (IESBA *Code*: para. R511.7).

The firm or audit team member **must not make a material loan to a client** (IESBA *Code*: para. R511.4). This rule is important because **overdue fees** from a previous audit could be construed to be a loan, and must therefore be settled before an audit begins.

(iii) **Business relationships**

Examples of when an audit firm and an audit client have an **inappropriately close business relationship** include:

- Having a financial interest in a joint venture with the client
- Arrangements to combine one or more services or products of the firm with one or more services or products of the client and to market the package with reference to both parties
- Distribution or marketing arrangements under which the firm distributes or markets the client's products or services or *vice versa*

(IESBA *Code*: para. 520.3 A2)

Again, it will be necessary for the partners to judge the materiality of the interest and therefore its significance. However, **unless the interest is clearly insignificant, an assurance provider should not participate in such a venture with an assurance client**. Appropriate safeguards are therefore to end the assurance provision or to terminate the (other) business relationship.

If an individual member of an audit team had such an interest, they should be removed from the audit team. However, if the firm or a member (and immediate family of the member) of the audit team has an interest in an entity when the client or its officers also has an interest in that entity, the threat might not be so great (IESBA *Code*: para. R520.5).

Generally speaking, **purchasing goods and services from an assurance client on an arm's length basis does not constitute a threat to independence**. If there are a substantial number of such transactions, there may be a threat to independence and safeguards may be necessary (IESBA *Code*: para. 520.6 A1).

(iv) **Serving as a director of officer of an audit client**

A partner or employee of an assurance firm or network firm should not serve as a director or officer of an assurance client (IESBA *Code*: para. R523.3).

It may be acceptable for a partner or an employee of an assurance firm to perform the role of **company secretary** for an assurance client, if:

- the role is essentially administrative, with no managerial decision-making; and
- if this practice is specifically permitted under local law and professional rules

(IESBA *Code*: paras. R523.4).

Although a partner or employee cannot serve on a client's board, it is possible for them to attend board meetings. This is common practice, and moreover may be necessary if there are issues that need to be raised with management.

(v) **Compensation and evaluation policies**

There is a **self-interest threat** when a member of the audit team is evaluated on **selling non-assurance services** to the client. The significance of the threat depends on:

- The proportion of the individual's compensation or performance evaluation that is based on the sale of such services
- The role of the individual on the audit team
- Whether promotion decisions are influenced by the sale of such services

(IESBA *Code*: para. 411.3 A1)

The firm should either revise the compensation plan or evaluation process, or put in place appropriate safeguards. **Safeguards** include:

- Revising the compensation plan or evaluation process for that individual;
- Reviewing their work; or
- Removing the member from the audit team.

(IESBA *Code*: para. 411.3 A2-3)

(vi) **Gifts and hospitality**

Unless the value of the gift/hospitality is **trivial and inconsequential**, a firm, network firm or a member of an assurance team should not accept it (IESBA *Code*: para. R420.3).

(vii) **Relative size of fees**

When a firm receives a high proportion of its fee income from just one audit client, there is **a self-interest or intimidation threat**, as the firm will be concerned about losing the client. A high percentage fee income does not by itself create an insurmountable threat. This depends on the following.

- The **operating structure** of the **firm**
- Whether the **firm** is well-established or **new**
- The **significance of the client** to the firm

Possible safeguards include **reducing** the **dependence** on the client (eg by increasing the client base) (IESBA *Code*: para. 410.14 A4).

It is not just a matter of the audit firm actually **being** independent in terms of fees, but also of it being **seen to be independent by the public**. It is as much about public perception as reality.

The *Code* also states that a threat may be created where an individual partner or office's percentage fees from one client is high. The safeguards include reducing dependence on the client and, in addition, having an internal quality review performed by an appropriate reviewer who was not involved in the audit engagement (IESBA *Code*: para. 410.14 A7).

For audit clients that are **public interest entities**, the Code states that where **total fees** from the client (for the audit and any non-audit services) represent **more than 15% of the firm's total fees for two consecutive years**, the firm shall:

- **Disclose** this to **those charged with governance** of the audit client

- **Conduct a review**, either by an external professional accountant or by a regulatory body. This review can be either before the audit opinion on the second year's financial statements is issued (a '**pre-issuance review**'), or after it is issued (a '**post-issuance review**').

If total fees **significantly exceed 15%,** then a post-issuance review may not be sufficient, and a **pre-issuance review** will be required (IESBA *Code*: para. R410.18-21).

(viii) **Overdue fees**

In a situation where there are overdue fees, the auditor runs the risk of, in effect, **making a loan to a client**, whereupon the guidance above becomes relevant. If the previous year's fees remain unpaid when the current year's auditor's report is to be signed, then safeguards should be applied such as a pre-issuance review of the audit or obtaining partial payment of overdue fees (IESBA *Code*: para. 410.12 A4).

Audit firms should guard against fees building up and being significant by discussing the issues with those charged with governance, and, if necessary, the possibility of resigning if overdue fees are not paid.

(ix) **Contingent fees**

Key term

> **Contingent fee.** A fee calculated on a predetermined basis relating to the outcome of a transaction or the result of the services performed. A fee that is established by a court or other public authority is not a contingent fee. (IESBA *Code*: para. 410.8 A1).

A firm shall **not enter into a contingent fee arrangement** in respect of an audit. For any assurance engagements provided to audit clients, unless immaterial or unconnected to the audit, a contingent fee would still carry a threat so great that no safeguards could reduce it to an acceptable level (IESBA *Code*: para. R410.9-10).

(x) **Lowballing**

When a firm quotes a **significantly lower fee level** for an assurance service than would have been charged by the predecessor firm, there is a significant self-interest threat. If the firm's tender is successful, the firm must apply safeguards such as:

- Maintaining records such that the firm is able to demonstrate that appropriate staff and time are spent on the engagement
- Complying with all applicable assurance standards, guidelines and quality review procedures

(xi) **Recruitment services**

Providing recruitment services in relation to the senior management of an audit client, particularly those able to affect the financial statements, might create a self-interest, familiarity or intimidation threat (IESBA *Code*: para. 609.4 A1).

Assurance providers must not make management decisions for the client. Their involvement could be limited to:

- Professional qualifications of a number of applicants and providing advice on their suitability for the position
- Interviewing candidates and advising on a candidate's competence for financial accounting, administrative or control positions (IESBA *Code*: para. 609.4 A2)

The client must make all management decisions with respect to hiring, selecting candidates and determining employment terms (such as salary) (IESBA *Code*: para. R609.6).

Prohibited recruitment services include:

- Searching for or seeking out candidates; or
- Checking references for prospective directors or senior management (whose role relates to the financial statements) (IESBA *Code*: para. R609.6)

Question — Threats and safeguards I

You are a manager in the audit firm Check and Co which has annual revenue in the region of $2,400,000. The following situations have arisen with different audit clients of your firm.

(1) In an initial meeting with the finance director of Weadon Co, an audit client, you learn that the entire audit team will be invited to the company's annual summer social event, a weekend at an exclusive spa hotel.

(2) Overdue fees from Evergreen Co have built up to include all invoices submitted by your firm in the last twelve months.

(3) For the last few years your firm's most important client, Emerald Co, has generated a high level of fee income to Check and Co. This year the client has also requested that you perform a detailed review of the company's internal control systems. The fee for this work would be $150,000 and this would take the total revenue earned during the year from Emerald Co to $480,000.

Required

Explain the ethical threats which may affect the independence of Check and Co in respect of each of the client audits, and for each threat explain how it may be reduced.

Answer

Threat	Safeguards
Weadon Co This involves a **self-interest threat** because the auditors may wish to continue enjoying lavish hospitality so may be reluctant to raise any problems in their auditor's report. There is also a **familiarity threat** because involvement in social events with the client is likely to increase the audit staff's familiarity with the client staff and make them more likely to accept explanations without adequate questioning.	Gifts and hospitality should not be accepted unless the value is **trivial** and **inconsequential**. In this case it would be appropriate to decline the weekend away so as not to impair the firm's independence.
Evergreen Co This could be viewed as a combination of a **self-interest threat** and an **intimidation threat**. The auditors' self-interest could lead them to issue a favourable opinion rather than risk losing the amounts owed to them. The directors could use the outstanding fees as a means of pressuring the audit firm into giving a favourable audit opinion.	The firm should: • Use normal credit control procedures to chase payment of all overdue balances. • Have a policy of refusing to start any new work for a client until overdue bills have been paid. • Discuss the outstanding debt with the Audit Committee if one exists • Consider resignation if the overdue fees are not paid
Emerald Co This scenario represents a **self-interest threat** because the firm may issue a favourable opinion rather than risk losing such a significant income stream. If the additional work is undertaken then 20% ($480,000 / $2,400,000) of the firm's income will come from Emerald Co. If the work is not undertaken the percentage will fall to 13¾% ($330,000 / $2,400,000). Completing the additional work may also constitute a **self-review threat** as the auditor may rely on tests of controls as part of their audit and will not want to report any deficiencies noted.	There is no evidence that Emerald Co is a public interest entity, if it were then the additional work should not be undertaken as the firm would generate more than 15% of its total income from one client for two consecutive years. This is a threat to independence. However, even if the client is not a public interest client then the firm must consider how generating such a large proportion of income from one client would be perceived by third parties. The firm should consider not accepting/ resigning from some services. It may also require an external quality review.

3.4.2 Self-review threat

Self-review threats may occur when a previous judgement needs to be re-evaluated by members responsible for that judgement. Circumstances that may give rise to such threats include the following.

The key area in which there is likely to be a self-review threat is where an audit firm provides non-assurance services to an audit client (providing multiple services). There is a great deal of guidance in the AIA and IESBA *Codes* about the various other services that accountancy firms might provide to their clients, and these are dealt with below.

(i) **Preparing accounting records and financial statements**

There is clearly a significant risk of a **self-review threat** if a firm prepares accounting records and financial statements and then audits them.

On the other hand, auditors routinely assist management with the preparation of financial statements and give advice about accounting treatments and journal entries.

Therefore, assurance firms must analyse the risks arising and put safeguards in place to ensure that the risk is at an acceptable level. If this can be done, then **these services may be provided**.

Examples of the kinds of 'routine or mechanical' services **which may be provided** include:

- Preparing payroll calculations or reports for approval and payment by the client
- Calculating depreciation on fixed assets (property, plant and equipment) when the client determines the accounting policy and estimates of useful life and residual values
- Preparing the financial statements based on information in the client-approved trial balance and preparing the related notes based on client-approved records

(IESBA *Code*: para. 601.5 A2)

For audit clients that are **not public interest entities** (ie not listed), assurance firms are only **allowed** to provide services of a routine or mechanical nature, and must consider any threats arising from these services, applying **safeguards** such as using staff members other than audit team members to carry out the work and an independent review.

(IESBA *Code*: para. R601.5, 601.5 A1)

The rules are more stringent when the client is **a public interest entity**. **Firms shall not provide accounting and bookkeeping services for public interest clients**.

(IESBA *Code*: para. R601.6)

Question — Threats and safeguards II

You are a manager in the audit firm Check and Co which has annual revenue in the region of $2,400,000. The following situation has arisen with an audit client, Green Co. Due to time pressure and staff shortages in the accounts department, the finance director of Green Co has sought assistance from your firm with year end procedures including the preparation of the annual financial statements for the company. Green Co is not considered to be a public interest entity.

Required

Explain the ethical threats which may affect the independence of Check and Co in respect of the audit of Green Co and explain the threat may be reduced.

Answer

Threat	Safeguards
Green Co This scenario poses a **self-review threat** as the audit team are unlikely to criticise the financial statements which have been prepared by the firm.	The client is not a public interest entity and so the provision of accountancy services is permitted. However: • The accounting services should not be provided by a member of the audit team. • The client must provide all source data and make decisions on judgemental figures e.g. allowances for receivables. • A review by an independent partner should be undertaken to ensure that the financial statements were thoroughly audited.

(ii) **Valuation services**

If an audit firm performs a valuation which will be included in financial statements audited by the firm, a self-review threat arises.

Audit firms should not carry out valuations for public interest entities on matters which will be material to the financial statements (IESBA *Code*: para. R603.5).

If the client is **not** a public interest entity, then the firm cannot provide a valuation service if the valuation would have a **material** effect on the financial statements **and** it involves a **significant** degree of **subjectivity** (IESBA *Code*: para. R603.4).

If the valuation is for an immaterial matter which is not subjective in nature, the audit firm should apply safeguards to ensure that the risk is reduced to an acceptable level. **Safeguards** include:

• Second partner review
• Using separate personnel for the valuation and the audit   (IESBA *Code*: para. 603.3 A4)

4: PROFESSIONAL ETHICS

(iii) **Taxation services**

The *Code* divides taxation services into five categories.

(a) Tax return preparation
(b) Tax calculations for the purpose of preparing the accounting entries
(c) Tax advisory services
(d) Tax planning services
(e) Tax services involved in valuations
(f) Assistance in the resolution of tax disputes   (IESBA *Code*: para. 604.2 A1)

Guidance in respect of each of these categories is:

(a) **Tax return preparation does not generally threaten independence**, as long as management takes responsibility for the returns.   (IESBA *Code*: para. 604.6 A1)

(b) **Tax calculations for the purpose of preparing material accounting entries may not prepared for public interest entities**. For non-public interest entities, it is acceptable to do so provided that safeguards such as independent reviews and the use of separate teams are applied.   (IESBA *Code*: paras. 604.9 A1-A2, R604.10)

(c) **Tax planning may be acceptable in certain circumstances**, eg where the advice is clearly supported by tax authority or other precedent. However, if the effectiveness of the tax advice depends on a particular accounting treatment or presentation in the financial statements, the audit team has reasonable doubt about the accounting treatment, and the consequences of the tax advice would be material, then the service should not be provided.
(IESBA *Code*: paras. 604.12 A1-A3; R604.13)

(d) **Tax services involving valuations** may be acceptable if the effect on the financial statements is neither direct nor material, but can still provide self-review threats that might not be managed by safeguards. Where appropriate, such engagements can be carried out for all clients with safeguards such as independent review, separate teams and obtaining pre-clearance from the local tax authority.   (IESBA *Code*: paras. 604.17 A1-3)

(e) **Assistance in the resolution of tax disputes may be provided**, depending on whether the firm itself provided the service which is the subject of the dispute, and whether the effect is material to the financial statements.

Safeguards include using professionals who are not members of the audit team to perform the service, and obtaining advice on the service from an external tax professional.   (IESBA *Code*: paras. 604.22 A13, 604.23 A1, 604.24 A1)

(iv) **Internal audit services**

A firm may provide internal audit services to an audit client. However, it should ensure that the client acknowledges its responsibility for establishing, maintaining and monitoring the system of internal controls. The key risk is of **assuming a management responsibility**. The following services would involve assuming a management responsibility, and must **not** be provided:

- Setting strategic policies for the internal audit function
- Performing internal control procedures
- Taking responsibility for designing/maintaining internal controls
- Performing outsourced internal audit with some management responsibility

(IESBA *Code*: para. 605.3 A2)

It may be appropriate to use safeguards, such as ensuring that an employee of the client is designated as responsible for internal audit activities and that the client approves all the work that internal audit does.

If the client is a **public interest entity**, then internal audit services **must not** be provided if they **might create a self-review threat**. Examples of prohibited services include internal audit services that relate to:

- The internal controls over financial reporting;
- Financial accounting systems that generate information for the client's accounting records or financial statements on which the firm will express an opinion; or
- Amounts of disclosures that relate to the financial statements on which the firm will express an opinion (IESBA *Code*: paras. R605.6, R605.6 A1).

(v) **Corporate finance services**

Certain aspects of corporate finance will create self-review threats that cannot be reduced to an acceptable level by safeguards. Therefore, **assurance firms are not allowed to promote, deal in or underwrite an assurance client's shares** (IESBA *Code*: para. R610.5).

Firms must also refrain from providing **advice that interacts with the financial statements** – both when the advice depends on an accounting treatment, and when the advice may have a material effect on the financial statements (IESBA *Code*: para. R610.6).

Other corporate finance services, such as assisting a client in defining corporate strategies, assisting in identifying possible sources of capital and providing structuring advice, may be acceptable, providing that **safeguards** are put in place, such as using different teams of staff and reviewing the work undertaken to ensure no management decisions are taken on behalf of the client (IESBA *Code*: paras. R610.7 A1).

(vi) **Temporary personnel assignments**

Personnel may be loaned to an audit client, but only **for a short period of time. Personnel must not assume management responsibilities**, or undertake any non-assurance work that is prohibited elsewhere in the Code (IESBA *Code*: para. R525.4).

The audit client must be responsible for directing and supervising the activities of the loaned personnel.

Possible safeguards include:

- Conducting an additional review of the work performed by the loaned personnel;
- Not giving the loaned personnel audit responsibility for any function or activity on the audit, that they performed during the temporary staff assignment; or
- Not including the loaned personnel in the audit team.   (IESBA *Code*: para. 525.3 A1)

(vii) **Other services**

The audit firm might sell a variety of other services to audit clients, such as:

- IT services
- Litigation support
- Legal services

The assurance firm should consider whether there are any threats to independence, such as if the firm were asked to design internal control IT systems, which it would then review as part of its audit. The firm should consider whether the threat to independence could be reduced by appropriate safeguards.

In general, firms cannot accept any management responsibilities for an audit client (IESBA Code: para. 600.7 A1) and must always actively consider risk factors such as the nature of the engagement, the nature of the client and the perception of a reasonable and informed third party in determining the extent of any ethical threats.

Question — Other services I

Southern Engineering has undergone a period of substantial growth following its establishment five years ago by two engineers. Because of a lack of accounting expertise within the company it has traditionally looked to its auditors, Smith and Jones, for accounting services in the preparation of annual financial statements as well as for the statutory audit function. Smith and Jones have also provided advice in connection with the company's accounting and internal control systems.

Smith and Jones is a two partner firm of accountants whose clients are mainly sole traders, partnerships and small limited companies. Although Southern Engineering was originally a typical small company client, its growth over the last five years has meant that it now accounts for approximately 20% of Smith and Jones' gross fee income and the company has indicated that it may wish to issue shares on the public exchange in the near future.

Required

(a) Discuss the extent to which it is acceptable and desirable that Smith and Jones have in the past provided the three services of statutory audit, advice in connection with systems, and accountancy services in the preparation of annual financial statements to Southern Engineering.

(b) Discuss the acceptability and desirability of Smith and Jones continuing to act in the future as auditors to Southern Engineering while continuing to provide the other services.

Answer

(a) Auditors, especially of small companies, often provide other, non-audit services. The risk arises that, in such cases, the auditor's objectivity may be impaired. This is particularly possible where the auditor is involved in advising the client on systems, as it becomes difficult for the auditor to remain sufficiently detached to comment critically on any weaknesses or shortcomings which appear when systems are implemented. A clear distinction must be drawn between the auditor's advisory capacity – in systems or accountancy work – and the executive responsibility, which is still that of the company's management. Undue involvement with non-audit services must be avoided, lest it detracts from the auditor's essential independence and objectivity.

(b) The ethical guidance of IESBA recommends that fee income from a public interest client shall not exceed 15% of a practice's total gross fees. As Southern Engineering's fees now represent 20% of fee income and would, presumably, increase when the company makes a public issue (when they would become a public interest entity) it seems Smith and Jones have to consider ways of reducing their dependence on this one client. This might well be done by continuing as auditors but ceasing to provide accounting services and systems advice. Note that the ethical guidelines prohibit the provision of accounting or bookkeeping services to a client that is a public interest entity.

Smith and Jones shall keep the situation under review, even after they have moved to a pure audit role, to ensure that they are not again becoming unduly dependent on Southern Engineering as it expands. They shall keep in communication with those charged with governance, and bear in mind that two years after the flotation, they may need to conduct pre- or –post-issuance reviews.

Question — Other services II

An auditor must ensure that his independence is not being compromised by providing other services to audit clients, and by other actions.

The additional services an auditor may provide include:

(a) Taxation, preparing the company's corporation tax computation and negotiating with the tax authorities; dealing with the tax affairs of the company's directors

(b) Preparing periodic management accounts of the company, quarterly and annual accounts

(c) Advising the directors on legal and accounting matters in relation to the company, for example, preparing submissions to the bank to obtain additional finance, advising on changes in share ownership and capital structure of the company and valuation of the company's shares

(d) Attending meetings of the board of directors

Required

In relation to a private company, of which you are auditor, consider:

(i) The benefits which may arise to the auditor and client in providing each of the above services

(ii) The extent to which providing each of these services may compromise your independence, and the action you would take to minimise the risk to your independence of providing these services

Answer

In all cases, the auditor will of course enjoy income additional to the audit fee. The client will probably benefit from a saving in using the same professional for all these types of work, because information gained on one assignment can be used on others, and the client will not be paying for the learning time of a new advisor. The client's staff and management shall also save time, as they shall not need to explain the business repeatedly to different people. (It has to be admitted, however, that changes in audit and other staff do often result in the client's needing to explain the same point in successive years.) The following individual comments may be made.

(a) **Taxation**. It is customary for the company's taxation liability to be at least checked, and often computed, as part of routine audit work. It is unlikely that independence would be impaired by this, or by routine correspondence with the tax authorities. Similarly, it is normal for an auditor to deal with directors' tax affairs. A problem would, however, arise here if there were any dispute between the company and its directors, as the auditor would suffer a conflict of interests and would probably be best advised to relinquish either the audit or the tax advisory role.

(b) **Accounts preparation**. This clearly gives the auditor a very good opportunity to keep in touch with the company's performance during the year and to take note of any possible audit problems as soon as they arise. There is, however, a risk that the auditor will not be as detached in carrying out the audit of accounts he or she has prepared as would be the case if the client had produced the accounts. Using separate teams of staff for accounts preparation and audit will help.

(c) **Advice to directors**. Clearly, the auditor will be able to draw on knowledge of the company in giving advice. There is a significant risk, however, that independence will be compromised, particularly if the advice turns out to have been mistaken. If the auditor has prepared a profit forecast for submission to the bank which subsequently proves over-optimistic, he or she may find it difficult to require the client to reflect the actual result in the year end accounts. The audit firm must ensure it does not take a management role.

(d) **Board meetings**. There is a risk here that the auditor may completely forfeit independence by becoming too closely involved in the running of the company. Generally, a director is considered by law to be anyone who carries out the functions of a director, and an auditor would be exposed to this presumption if he or she attended meetings regularly. It would therefore be advisable for the auditor to attend only the board meetings at which the annual accounts are approved by the board.

3.4.3 Advocacy threat

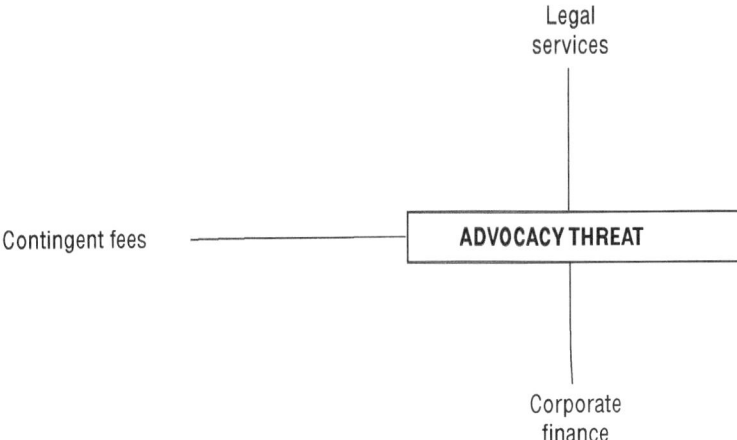

An advocacy threat arises in certain situations where the assurance firm is in a position of taking the client's part in a dispute or somehow acting as their advocate. The most obvious instances of this would be when a firm offered legal services to a client and, say, defended them in a legal case or provided evidence on their behalf as an expert witness. An advocacy threat might also arise if the firm carried out corporate finance work for the client, for example, if the audit firm was involved in advice on debt reconstruction and negotiated with the bank on the client's behalf.

As with the other threats above, the firm has to appraise the risk and apply safeguards as necessary. Relevant safeguards might be using different departments in the firm to carry out the work and making disclosures to the audit committee. Remember, the ultimate option is always to withdraw from an engagement if the risk to independence is too high.

3.4.4 Familiarity threat

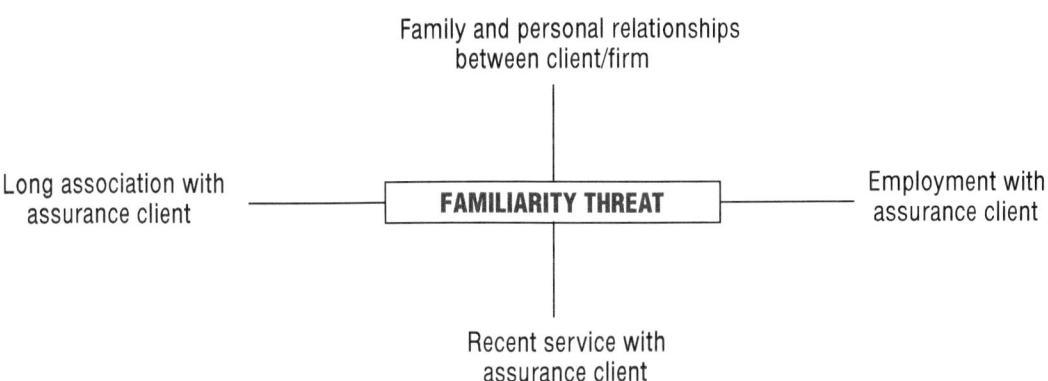

A familiarity threat is the threat that due to a long or close relationship with a client or employer, a professional accountant will be too sympathetic to their interests or too accepting of their work. There is a substantial risk of loss of professional scepticism in such circumstances.

(i) **Long association of senior personnel with audit clients**

Having an audit client for a **long period of time may create a familiarity threat** to independence. The severity of the threat depends on such factors as:

- The length of the relationship between the individual and the client (especially if this extends over employment at more than one firm);
- How long the individual has been on the audit team and the nature of the roles performed;
- The extent of any supervision and review of the individual by senior personnel;

- The extent of the individual's influence over the outcome of the audit;
- The closeness of any personal relationship between the individual and anyone in a responsible position at the client; and
- The nature, frequency and extent of interaction between the individual and anyone in a responsible position at the client.

Other factors can be relevant here, such as the client's accounting and reporting framework or its senior management personnel, including any recent changes. (IESBA *Code*: para. 540.3 A3)

Possible **safeguards** include:

- **Rotating** the **individual** off the **audit team** or **changing** the nature of their **role** or **tasks**;
- Having an **appropriate reviewer** who was not an audit team member review the work of the individual; or
- **Regular** independent **internal or external quality reviews** of the engagement.

(IESBA *Code*: para. 540.3 A6)

The rules for **public interest entities** are stricter. If an individual is a **key audit partner** for **seven years**, they must be rotated off the audit and serve a 'cooling off' period dependent on the roles vacated: for **engagement partners**, this is **five consecutive years**; for **engagement quality reviewers**, **three** years and for **other key audit partners** this is **two years** (IESBA *Code*: para. R540.11-13). During this time they cannot be on the audit team, and cannot consult with the audit team or the client on any issues that may affect the engagement (including giving just general industry advice) (IESBA *Code*: para. R540.21).

The *Codes* do allow some flexibility here: **if** key partner **continuity** is particularly beneficial to **audit quality**, and there is some **unforeseen circumstance** (such as the intended engagement partner becoming seriously ill), then the key audit partner **can remain on the audit for an additional year**, making eight years in total (IESBA *Code*: para. R540.7).

If a client that was not a public interest entity becomes one, then the seven year limit still applies, starting from the date when the key audit partner originally became the key partner for that audit client (IESBA *Code*: para. R540.8).

Finally, it is possible for an independent regulator to give permission for an audit partner to remain a key audit partner indefinitely, provided alternative safeguards are applied (eg external review) (IESBA *Code*: para. R540.9).

(ii) **Recent service with an audit client**

An individual may have recently worked for an audit client. This may give rise to self-interest and self-review threats. If they worked for the client **during the period audited**, then they **cannot be on the audit team** if they:

- Had served as a **director** or officer of the audit client; or
- Were an employee in a position to exert **significant influence** over the accounting records (or financial statements). (IESBA *Code*: para. R522.3).

If the individual had been in one of the above roles in the period prior to the period being audited a threat would still be created. The firm should consider the threat and apply appropriate safeguards, eg obtaining a quality review of the individual's work on the audit (IESBA *Code*: paras. 522.4 A1-3).

(iii) **Employment with an audit client**

It is possible that staff might transfer between an assurance firm and a client, or that negotiations or interviews to facilitate such movement might take place. Both situations are a threat to independence:

- An audit staff member might be motivated by a desire to impress a future possible employer
- A former partner turned finance director has too much knowledge of the audit firm's systems and procedures

In general there may be **self-interest**, **familiarity** and **intimidation threats** when a member of the audit team joins an audit client.

A **'significant connection'** still **remains** between the audit firm and the former employee/partner where:

- The individual is entitled to benefits from the audit firm
- Any amount owed to the individual is material to the firm
- The individual continues to participate in the audit firm's business or professional activities

(IESBA *Code*: para. R524.4)

Any familiarity or intimidation threat depends on the following:

- The **position** the individual has taken at the client
- Any **involvement** the individual will have **with the audit team**
- The **length of time** since the individual was a member of the audit team or partner of the firm
- The **former position** of the individual **within the audit team or firm**; for example, whether the individual was responsible for maintaining regular contact with the client's management or those charged with governance (IESBA *Code*: para. 524.4 A3)

Safeguards could include:

- **Modifying** the **audit plan**;
- **Assigning individuals** to the audit team **who have sufficient experience** in relation to the individual who has joined the client; or
- Having an independent professional accountant **review** the work of the former member of the audit team. (IESBA *Code*: para. 524.4 A4)

Should an audit team member be pursuing employment with an audit client, they should inform the firm of this as soon as possible. Safeguards to address the self-interest threat presented here are to remove the individual from the audit team, and to review their work for any indication of bias (IESBA *Code*: para. 524.5 A2-A3).

If the **audit client** is a **public interest entity**, then 'cooling off' periods are required. Both the AIA and IESBA *Codes* state that **when a key audit partner joins such a client**, either as a director or as an employee with significant influence on the financial statements, the client must have issued audited financial statements covering at least **12 months** before the employment can begin. The partner in question must also not have been a member of the audit team in relation to those audited financial statements (IESBA *Code*: para. R524.6).

In the case of a **senior or managing partner joining an audit client**, **12 months** must have passed (ie there is no requirement for audited financial statements to have been issued) (IESBA *Code*: para. R524.7).

(iv) **Family and personal relationships**

Key term

> **Immediate family:** A spouse (or equivalent) or dependent.
>
> **Close family:** A parent, child or sibling who is not an immediate family member.
>
> (IESBA *Code*: Glossary)

Family or close personal relationships between assurance firm staff and client staff could seriously threaten independence. Each situation has to be evaluated individually.

When an **immediate family member** of someone on the audit team is a director, an officer, or an employee who is in a position to exert direct and significant influence over the financial statements, then the individual should be **removed from the audit team** (IESBA *Code*: para. R521.5). Otherwise, safeguards should be applied, such as such as either removal from the audit team or restructuring someone's role in the firm so they are not dealing with matters under the family member's responsibility (IESBA *Code*: para. 521.4 A3-4)

If the person is only a **'close' family member** (but not an 'immediate' family member), then the threat is evaluated and the same safeguards can be applied (IESBA *Code*: paras. 521.6 A3-4).

If the relationship is not a family relationship but is still close (eg friendship), then the threat is evaluated and safeguards applied (IESBA *Code*: para. R521.7).

A firm should have quality management policies and procedures under which staff should disclose whether a close family member employed by the client is promoted within the client. If a firm inadvertently violates the rules concerning family and personal relationships then they should apply additional safeguards, such as: undertaking a quality review of the audit, or discussing the matter with the audit committee of the client, if there is one.

Question — Threats and safeguards III

You are a manager in the audit firm Check and Co which has annual revenue in the region of $2,400,000. The following situations have arisen with different audit clients of your firm.

(1) Mr Walker has been the engagement partner for a client, Stewards Co, for nine years. He has excellent knowledge of the client and knows all of the directors of Stewards Co very well. Stewards Co is considered to be a public interest entity.

(2) Mrs Sayer is the engagement partner for a client, Aspen Co. Her daughter Holly joined Aspen Co 6 months ago and is working as an assistant to the receivables ledger clerk whilst she studies for her first set of accountancy exams.

Required

Explain the ethical threats which may affect the independence of Check and Co in respect of each of the client audits, and for each threat explain how it may be reduced.

Answer

Threat	Safeguards
Stewards Co This involves a **familiarity threat** because Mr Walker has been the engagement partner for nine years and his long association with the client could mean that he does not question judgements made by the client and does not exercise sufficient professional scepticism.	Mr Walker should be rotated off the audit and another partner assigned to the client. Given that Stewards Co is a public interest entity, key audit partners (such as the engagement partner) should serve for no more than seven years before being rotated off. They should not return to having involvement in the client for a period of five years.
Aspen Co Given that the partner's daughter works for the audit client a **self-interest threat** could arise if the partner did not want to disadvantage her daughter financially from any pay rise/ bonus by identifying errors in her work. An **intimidation threat** could also exist if the daughter tries to pressure her mother into making inappropriate decisions in relation to audit judgements.	Mrs Sayer should be removed from the audit team and replaced by an independent partner. If it is felt that Holly does not have any influence over the audit process and therefore that Mrs Sayer can remain as partner then the Board/ Audit Committee of Aspen Co should be informed. An independent partner review should also be conducted on the audit.

3.4.5 Intimidation threat

An intimidation threat arises when members of the assurance team have reason to be intimidated by client staff.

These are also examples of self-interest threats, largely because intimidation may only arise significantly when the assurance firm has something to lose.

(i) **Actual and threatened litigation**

There may be an intimidation threat when the client threatens to sue, or indeed sues, the audit firm for work that has been done previously. The firm is then faced with the risk of losing the client, bad publicity and the possibility that they will be found to have been negligent, which will lead to further problems. This could lead to the firm being under pressure to produce an unmodified auditor's report when they have been modified in the past, for example.

Generally, audit firms should seek to avoid such situations arising. If they do arise, factors to consider are:

- The materiality of the litigation
- Whether the litigation relates to a prior audit engagement (IESBA *Code*: para. 430.3 A2)

The following safeguards could be considered.

- Removing the individual from the audit team
- Having a professional review the work performed (IESBA *Code*: paras. 430.3 A3-4)

3.5 Conflicts of interest

There are two kinds of conflict of interest:

- Conflicts between the interests of different clients
- Conflicts between members' and clients' interests (IESBA *Code*: para. 310.2)

Audit firms should take reasonable steps to identify circumstances that could pose a conflict of interest.

Examples of conflicts of interest (IESBA *Code*: para. 310.4 A1)
Using **confidential information** obtained during an audit to help another client to acquire the audit client
Advising **two clients at the same time** who are competing to acquire the same company
Providing **services to both a vendor and a purchaser** in relation to the same transaction
Representing **two clients who are in a legal dispute** with each other (eg during divorce proceedings)

The *Code* emphasises the importance of considering potential conflicts of interest **before accepting a new client** (IESBA *Code*: para. R310.5). An issue here is first **identifying that there is a conflict** – it may be that, for example, the engagement partner for a new client is not aware that there is a conflict because they do not know all of the firm's other clients. It is therefore necessary to have an **effective conflict identification process** (IESBA *Code*: para. 310.5 A1-2).

As with all threats, **safeguards** should be applied if necessary. If safeguards would not be enough, then the engagement should be declined or discontinued.

Examples of safeguards (IESBA *Code*: para. 310.9-13)
Disclosure of the nature of the conflict of interest (and related safeguards) to clients affected, to **obtain their consent** to the professional accountant performing the services
Mechanisms to **prevent unauthorised disclosure of confidential information**, such as: • Separate engagement teams • Creating separate areas of practice for specialty functions within the firm • Establishing policies and procedures to limit access to client files
Review of safeguards by a senior individual not involved with the engagement(s)
External **review** by a professional accountant
Consulting with third parties, such as a professional body, legal counsel or another professional accountant

Disclosure is the key safeguard here. If the **client refuses** to give consent, then the engagement giving rise to the conflict should be discontinued.

3.6 Confidentiality

Accountants can only disclose confidential information if authorised by the client, required by law or if there is a public duty or right to disclose and this is permitted by law.

The following are points relate to confidentiality in general.

- Do not disclose information acquired, ie respect the principle of confidentiality (IESBA *Code*: para. R114.1)
- Information **may be disclosed** in certain circumstances, eg where it is required by law (see below) (IESBA *Code*: para. 114.1 A1).

In exchange for this duty of confidence owed by the auditor to the client, the client must agree to disclose in full all information relevant to the engagement. The professional accountant must make the client aware of the duty of confidentiality, and of the fact that it can be overridden where there is a right or duty to disclose.

Maintaining confidentiality means avoiding inadvertent disclosure as much as intentional disclosure (IESBA *Code*: para. R114.1). For instance, information must not be disclosed unintentionally when socialising. The *Code* also notes that the duty of **confidentiality continues even after the end of the relationship with the client** (IESBA *Code*: para. R114.2).

Binding though the duty of confidence is, there are nevertheless exceptions to it. The *Code* identifies three general circumstances where **disclosure may be appropriate**.

- Disclosure is **permitted by law and is authorised** by the client.
- Disclosure is **required by law** (eg for legal proceedings).
- There is a **professional duty or right to disclose** (eg to comply with a quality review by a professional body such as ACCA; to respond to an investigation by a regulatory body; to protect the professional accountant's interests in legal proceedings; to comply with technical and professional standards, including ethics requirements).

(IESBA *Code*: para. 114.1 A1)

3.6.1 Non-compliance with laws and regulations

ISA 250 *Consideration of Laws and Regulations in an Audit of Financial Statements* requires auditors to respond appropriately to non-compliance or suspected Non-Compliance with Laws and Regulations (NOCLAR) identified during the audit. Management, not the auditor, is responsible for preventing NOCLAR.

If the auditor discovers NOCLAR, then they have a professional duty to maintain the confidentiality of client information. This may preclude reporting identified or suspected non-compliance with laws and regulations to a party outside the entity. However, the auditor may take further action in the public interest. This essentially depends on the urgency and seriousness of the matter, and how likely it is to re-occur.

The auditor's legal responsibilities to report NOCLAR vary by jurisdiction and, in certain circumstances the duty of confidentiality may be overridden by statute, the law or courts of law. The auditor may consider it appropriate to **obtain legal advice** to determine the appropriate course of action.

4 The FRC's *Ethical Standard*

> **FAST FORWARD**
>
> The FRC in the UK has released its *Revised Ethical Standard 2024*, which is based on the IESBA *Code*. This is **only examinable for RPQ candidates**.

This section needs to be covered by RPQ candidates only.

The Financial Reporting Council (FRC) in the UK has released its *Ethical Standard* (FRC ES). The ES was developed with IESBA's *Code* in mind, so it is acceptable to apply either piece of guidance to an ethical situation in this exam. Make sure that you refer to the FRC ES rather than the IESBA's *Code* if you are an RPQ candidate.

The key thing to note about the FRC ES is that in some instances it is more stringent than the IESBA *Code*, recommending specific safeguards that are not recommended by the IESBA.

4.1 FRC ES Part B1 *General requirements and guidance*

Part B1 is an example of where the standard makes required practice of the safeguards that the IESBA *Code* recommends. Under the FRC ES, audit firms in the UK are required to:

- Establish policies and procedures to ensure that people connected with the audit are independent of the audit client
- Create a control environment which promotes adherence to ethical procedures above commercial considerations
- Establish policies and procedures to ensure that partners and employees of the firm do not take decisions for the audited entity that are the responsibility of management
- Appoint an Ethics Partner who monitors the firm's policies and procedures, and adherence to them
- Review whether the firm is independent at all stages of an audit (acceptance, planning, forming an opinion, retaining the audit, dealing with ethical issues arising) (this will be done by the audit engagement partner)
- Communicate with those charged with governance (the audit committee) all matters which bear upon the firm's independence

These are all things that are suggested as good practice in the IESBA *Code*.

4.2 FRC ES Part B2 *Financial, business, employment and personal relationships*

The rules concerning staff joining an audit client are more stringent in the FRC ES than in the IESBA Code. Partners, senior members of the engagement team and other members of the engagement team **should notify the firm of any situation involving their potential employment with an audited entity** (FRC ES: para. 2.39). The individual shall be **removed from the team** and any **work performed** by them on the most recent audit shall be **reviewed**.

> **FRC *ES*: para. 2.43**
>
> As required by legislation, a natural person appointed as a statutory auditor or key audit partner for an entity subject to a statutory audit shall not take up:
>
> (a) Any key management position;
>
> (b) Membership of the entity's audit committee; or of any body performing equivalent functions to an audit committee in relation to the entity;
>
> (c) Any other position as director of the entity or, where the entity's affairs are managed by a management body or other committee, membership of that management body or committee;
>
> before the end of:
>
> (a) In the case of a **public interest entity, two years**; and
> (b) In any other case, **one year**.
>
> beginning with the day on which the person ceased to be the entity's statutory auditor or key audit partner in connection with the statutory audit of the entity.

Where the above situation applies to a member of the engagement team the audit firm shall consider whether the composition of the engagement team is appropriate.

If a partner (who is approved as a 'statutory auditor') joins the entity as a director/member of the audit committee/in a key management position within **two years** of having been a covered person, then the firm must **resign from the engagement** (FRC ES: para. 2.45). If the person who joins the entity was not a partner then the firm only need wait for one year.

4.3 FRC ES Part B3 *Long association with engagements and with entities relevant to engagements*

Where audit engagement partners, key audit partners and staff in senior positions have a long association with the audit, safeguards should be applied. **Where they cannot be applied, the audit firm should either resign or not stand for reappointment** (FRC ES: para. 3.1).

Key Audit Partners and Engagement Partners

The firm must establish policies to ensure that:

(a) No one shall act as **audit engagement partner** for more than **five years**

(b) Anyone who has acted as the audit engagement partner for a period of five years shall **not** subsequently **participate in the audit** engagement until a **further period of five years** has elapsed

(c) On completing their rotation, the engagement partner, shall not continue to have significant or frequent interaction with senior management or with those charged with governance of the entity they have previously audited until the cooling off period has elapsed.

(FRC ES: para. 3.10)

The FRC ES specifies the following rules for **engagement quality reviewers**:

(a) No one should act as the engagement quality reviewer for a continuous period of longer than **seven years**.

(b) Where the engagement quality reviewer or a key partner involved in the engagement becomes the audit engagement partner, the combined service in these two positions should not exceed seven years.

(c) People who have held these positions for seven years (continuously or in aggregate) should not return to them for at least five years. (FRC ES: para. 3.19)

4.4 FRC ES Part B4 *Fees, remuneration and evaluation policies, gifts and hospitality, litigation*

The FRC ES looks at the spirit of setting fees for audit work, and states that the audit fee shall reflect the **time spent** and the **skills and experience** of the personnel performing the audit and that they should not be influenced by the possibility of providing non-audit work.

The FRC ES gives clearer guidance than the IESBA *Code* about what constitutes dependence on fees. Where it is expected that the fees for both audit and non-audit services receivable from the audit of a public interest or listed entity and its subsidiaries will regularly exceed **10% of the annual fee income of the audit firm** (15% for non-listed entities that are not public interest entities), the firm shall **not act as the auditors** and shall either resign or not stand for reappointment (FRC ES: para 4.23, 4.24).

Where the above fees from a listed or public interest audited entity and its subsidiaries will regularly exceed **5% of the annual fee income (10% for non-listed entities)** the audit engagement partner shall **disclose** this to the ethics partner and those charged with governance and consider whether safeguards shall be applied.

New firms shall not undertake any audits of listed or public interest companies, where fees would represent 10% or more of the annual fee income of the firm. In addition, for a period not exceeding two years, independent reviews shall be performed on those audits of unlisted entities that represent more than 15% of the annual fee income.

The **total fee income** received from non-audit services from any one client can be **no more than 70% of total fees** – or more precisely, 70% of the average of the fees paid in the last three consecutive financial years (FRC ES: para 4.13). This requirement results from the EU Audit Regulation.

Further, the total fees received by the whole audit firm from non-audit services must not exceed 70% of the firm's total fees.

4.5 FRC ES Part B5 *Non-audit/additional services*

The provisions of Part B5 are broadly the same as the IESBA *Code*.

> **FAST FORWARD** The FRC ES does **not allow** the audit firm to provide **internal audit services, loan staff assignments** (secondments) or to charge any **contingent fees**.

The following services are **prohibited** (FRC ES: Appendix B) for **audits of public interest entities**. The prohibition applies to both the reporting period being audited and the financial year before that.

(a) Tax services relating to:

    (i) Preparation of tax forms;

    (ii) Payroll tax;

    (iii) Customs duties

    (iv) Identification of public subsidies and tax incentives unless support from the statutory auditor or the audit firm in respect of such services is required by law;

    (v) Support regarding tax inspections by tax authorities unless support from the statutory auditor or the audit firm in respect of such inspections is required by law;

    (vi) Calculation of direct and indirect tax and deferred tax; and

    (vii) Provision of tax advice;

(b) Services that involve playing any part in the management or decision-making of the audited entity;

(c) Bookkeeping and preparing accounting records and financial statements;

(d) Payroll services;

(e) Designing and implementing internal control or risk management procedures related to the preparation and/or control of financial information or designing and implementing financial information technology systems;

(f) Valuation services, including valuations performed in connection with actuarial services or litigation support services;

(g) Legal services, with respect to:

    (i) The provision of general counsel;
    (ii) Negotiating on behalf of the audited entity; and
    (iii) Acting in an advocacy role in the resolution of litigation;

(h) Services related to the audited entity's internal audit function;

(i) Services linked to the financing, capital structure and allocation, and investment strategy of the audited entity, except providing assurance services in relation to the financial statements, such as the issuing of comfort letters in connection with prospectuses issued by the audited entity;

(j) Promoting, dealing in, or underwriting shares in the audited entity;

(k) Human resources services, with respect to:

    (i) Management in a position to exert significant influence over the preparation of the accounting records or financial statements which are the subject of the statutory audit, where such services involve:

        (1) Searching for or seeking out candidates for such position; or

        (2) Undertaking reference checks of candidates for such positions;

    (ii) Structuring the organisation design; and

    (iii) Cost control

Chapter Roundup

- Professional accountants need an ethical code because they are **relied upon** for their expertise.
- Sources of ethical guidance include the *Code of Ethics for Professional Accountants* issued by the International Ethics Standards Board for Accountants (the IESBA *Code*) and the FRC's *Ethical Standard*.
- The five **fundamental principles** of professional ethics are integrity, objectivity, professional competence and due care, confidentiality and professional behaviour.
- The professional accountant must **identify, evaluate and address** threats to compliance with the fundamental principles. Threats may arise in the form of **self-interest, self-review, advocacy, familiarity and intimidation threats**. Appropriate **safeguards** must be put in place to eliminate or reduce such threats to acceptable levels.
- Accountants can only disclose confidential information if authorised by the client, required by law or if there is a public duty or right to disclose and this is permitted by law.
- The FRC in the UK has released its **Revised Ethical Standard 2024**, which is based on the IESBA *Code*. This is only examinable for RPQ candidates.

Quick Quiz

1   Complete the table with the definitions of the fundamental principles of professional ethics.

IESBA's fundamental principles of professional ethics	
Integrity	
Objectivity	
Professional competence and due care	
Confidentiality	
Professional behaviour	

2   IESBA's Code of Ethics applies only to statutory audits.

   True ☐
   False ☐

3   A partner may act as audit engagement partner for a listed client for up to seven years, after which they must be rotated off of the audit.

   True ☐   False ☐

4   Give one example of an engagement-specific safeguard in the work environment.

5   Fill in the gaps.

   A **self-interest threat** is the threat that a financial or other interest will …………….. …………….. the professional accountant's …………… or behaviour.

6   Name three situations where accountants can disclose confidential information.

Answers to Quick Quiz

1.

IESBA's fundamental principles of professional ethics	
Integrity	To be straightforward and honest in all professional and business relationships.
Objectivity	Not to compromise professional or business judgments because of bias, conflict of interest or undue influence of others.
Professional competence and due care	To: <ul><li>Attain and maintain professional knowledge and skill at the level required to ensure that a client or employer receives competent professional service, based on current technical and professional standards and relevant legislation; and</li><li>Act diligently and in accordance with applicable technical and professional standards.</li></ul>
Confidentiality	To respect the confidentiality of information acquired as a result of professional and business relationships.
Professional behaviour	To comply with relevant laws and regulations and avoid any action that the professional accountant knows or should know might discredit the profession.

2. False. 'The spirit of the guidance applies equally to other audit situations.'

3. False – there is a limit of five years, not seven.

4. Any from:
   - Having a professional accountant who was not a member of the assurance team review the assurance work performed or otherwise advise as necessary
   - Consulting an independent third party, such as a committee of independent directors, a professional regulatory body or another professional accountant
   - Rotating senior assurance team personnel

5. Inappropriately influence, judgement

6.
   - Disclosure is permitted by law and is **authorised by the client or employer**.
   - There is a **public duty** or right to disclose, when not prohibited by law.
   - Disclosure is **required by law**.

End of chapter question

Independence

It has been suggested that the most important matter affecting the credibility of the auditor is that of 'independence'.

Required

(a) Discuss, giving examples, matters other than independence, which might be relevant in relation to the credibility of the auditor and steps that the accounting profession has taken or might take in relation to them.

(b) Discuss the following situations in the context of the independence of the auditor, showing clearly the principles involved:

(i) The audit manager in charge of the audit assignment of Andrew holds 1,000 $1 ordinary shares in the company (total shares in issue – 100,000). The audit partner holds no shares.

(ii) The audit fee receivable from Janet, a private company is $100,000. The total fee income of the audit firm is $700,000.

(iii) The audit senior in charge of the audit of Margot Bank has a personal loan from the bank of $2,000 on which she is currently paying 6% interest.

(iv) The audit partner is responsible for two audit assignments, Harry and Jean. Harry has recently tendered for a contract with Jean for the supply of material quantities of goods over a number of years. Jean has asked the audit partner to advise on the matter.

The audit client

Topic list	Syllabus reference
1 Accepting appointment	4.1
2 Audit engagement letter	4.2

Introduction

In this chapter we discuss the ethical and competence considerations an auditor should undertake before accepting appointment as auditor and also the process involved in agreeing the audit engagement letter and its contents.

1 Accepting appointment

> **FAST FORWARD**
> Auditors have guidance from AIA on advertising and obtaining professional work.

1.1 Tendering and obtaining work

Members are entitled to advertise their services and products. The advertising medium shall not reflect adversely on the member, AIA or the accountancy profession. Adverts shall not:

- Bring AIA into disrepute or bring discredit to the member, firm or accountancy profession
- Discredit the services of others
- Be misleading
- Fall short of local regulatory or legislative requirements

1.1.1 Fee negotiation and lowballing

The audit fee is a sensitive subject for most companies. It represents a cost for something the company often does not really want and the fees may be perceived as too high just for this reason. The auditors must ensure that they can provide a quality audit for the price.

Many large companies invite **tenders** for their audit work. The directors then have the opportunity to compare directly a range of offers.

Generally, a tender will take the form of detailed written proposals and a presentation. Factors include:

- The **level** of **expertise** each firm has in the industry
- **Similar companies** audited by each firm (good for expertise, bad for confidentiality?)
- **National** and **international presence**
- The proposed fee

Audit firms which tender for such audits will usually give at least an indication of the level of fees in the next few years, including likely overall rate rises. Fee levels are very important to most companies, and are often the determining factor.

In all situations, the auditors shall quote a fee based on the estimated hours worked by each member of staff required on the audit, multiplied by the hourly rate plus any travel as other expenses to be incurred during the audit. They may also charge a premium for more complex audits.

Sometimes it appears that firms are charging less than 'market rate' for an audit, especially when tendering for new clients. This practice is known as **lowballing**.

It is not considered ethically wrong to charge a low price for an audit in itself. However, the auditors must ensure that they carry out an audit of the quality demanded by auditing standards and must ensure that the 'cut-price' audit fee does not call their independence into question.

This is always going to be a topical debate, but in terms of negotiating the audit fee the following factors need to be taken into account.

(a) The audit is perceived to have a **fluctuating 'market price'** as any other commodity or service.

(b) Companies can reduce external audit costs through various **legitimate measures:**
- Extending the size and function of internal audit
- Reducing the number of different audit firms used world-wide
- Selling off subsidiary companies leaving a simplified group structure to audit
- The tender process itself simply makes auditors more competitive
- Exchange rate fluctuations in audit fees

(c) Auditing firms have **increased productivity**, partly through the use of more sophisticated information technology techniques in auditing.

5: THE AUDIT CLIENT

In any case, an auditing firm lays itself open to accusations of loss of independence if it reduces its fees to below a certain level, particularly if it is difficult to see how such fees will cover direct labour costs. This is also true of firms which use the audit as a 'loss leader' to obtain profitable consultancy work from audit clients.

When such non-audit services are offered to a client by the auditors, there can, of course, be an apparent loss of independence. The allegation may arise that the price of an 'acceptable' audit opinion is lucrative taxation or consulting work.

1.2 Appointment ethics

FAST FORWARD

The **present** and **proposed auditors** must **communicate** about the client prior to the audit being accepted.

This section covers the procedures that the **auditors must** undertake to **ensure that their appointment is valid** and that they are clear to act.

1.2.1 Before accepting nomination

FAST FORWARD

The client must be asked to give permission for communication to occur. If the client **refuses** to give **permission,** the proposed auditors must **decline nomination.**

Before a new audit client is accepted, the auditors must ensure that there are no **independence** or **other ethical problems** likely to cause conflict with the ethical code. Furthermore, new auditors shall ensure that they have been appointed in a proper and legal manner.

The nominee auditors must carry out the following procedures:

Acceptance procedures	
Ensure **professionally qualified** to act.	Consider whether disqualified on legal or ethical grounds.
Ensure **existing resources adequate.**	Consider available time, staff and technical expertise.
Obtain references.	Make independent enquiries if directors not personally known.
Communicate with present auditors.	Enquire whether there are reasons/circumstances behind the change which the new auditors ought to know, also courtesy. See flowchart under section 5.2.4 for process

1.2.2 Example letters

This is an example of an initial communication.

To: Retiring & Co
Association of Accountants

Dear Sirs

Re: New Client Co

We have been asked to allow our name to go forward for nomination as auditors of the above company, and we shall therefore be grateful if you would please let us know whether there are any professional reasons why we shall not accept nomination ....

Acquiring & Co

Association of Accountants

Having negotiated these steps the auditors will be in a position to accept the nomination, or not, as the case may be. These procedures can be demonstrated most easily in a decision chart, as shown on the next page.

1.2.3 Procedures after accepting nomination

The following procedures shall be carried out after accepting nomination.

(a) **Ensure** that the **outgoing auditors' removal** or **resignation** has been **properly conducted** in accordance with national legislation.

The new auditors shall see a valid notice of the outgoing auditors' resignation, or confirm that the outgoing auditors were properly removed.

(b) **Ensure** that the **new auditors' appointment is valid**. The new auditors shall obtain a copy of the resolution passed at the general meeting appointing them as the company's auditors.

(c) Set up and **submit a letter of engagement** to the directors of the company.

> **Point to note:** Audit engagement letters are discussed in Section 2 of this chapter.

1.2.4 Other matters

Where the previous auditors have fees still owing by the client, the new auditors need not decline appointment solely for this reason. They shall decide how far they may go in aiding the former auditors to obtain their fees, as well as whether they shall accept the appointment.

Once a new appointment has taken place, the **new auditors shall obtain all books and papers which belong to the client from the old auditors**. The former accountants shall ensure that all such documents are transferred, **unless** they have a lien (a legal right to hold on to them) over the books because of unpaid fees. The old auditors shall also pass any useful information to the new auditors if it will be of help, without charge, unless a lot of work is involved.

5: THE AUDIT CLIENT

Appointment decision chart

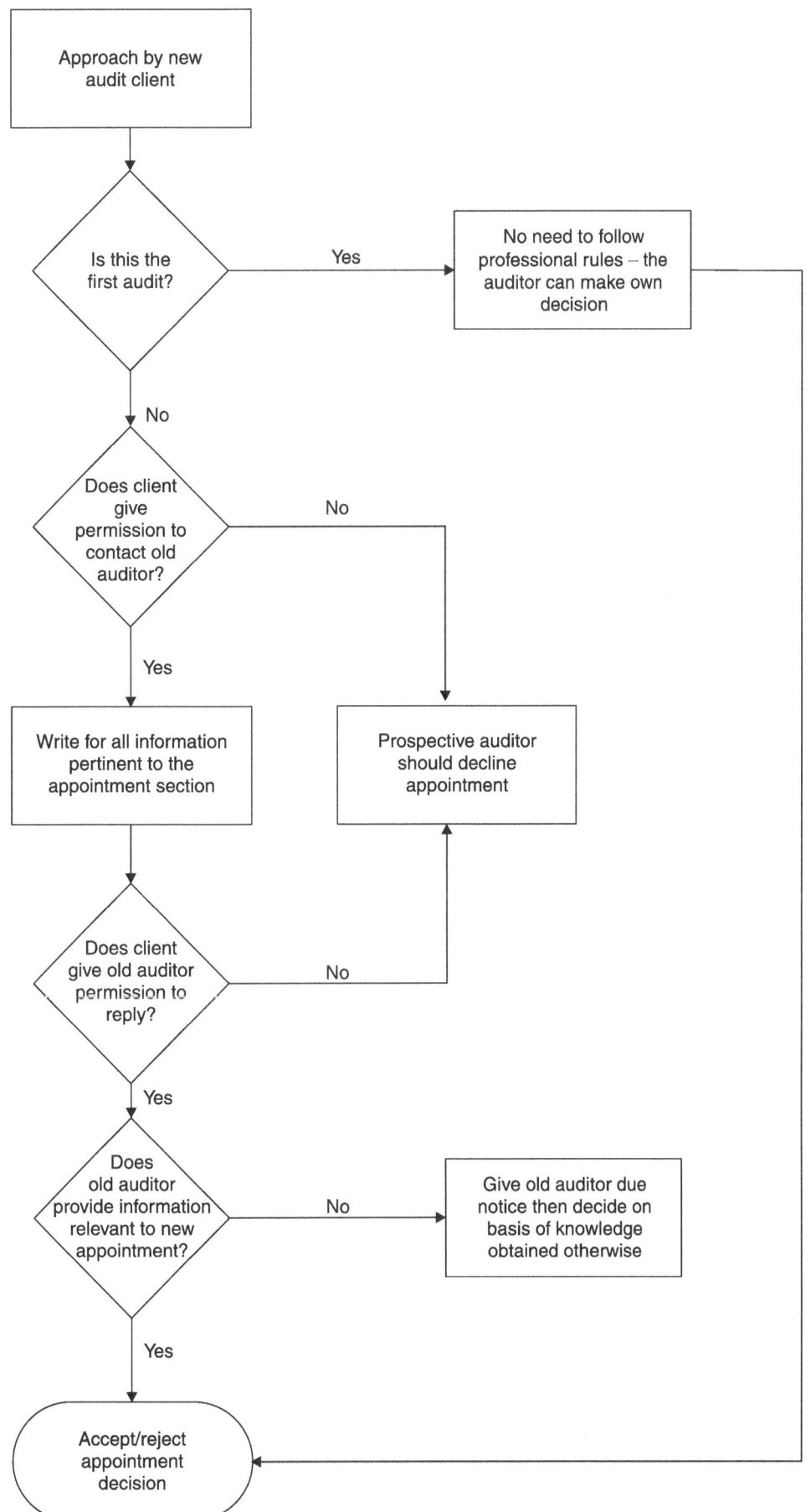

1.3 Client screening

As well as contacting previous auditors many firms, particularly larger firms, carry out **stringent checks** on potential client companies and their management. Some of the basic factors for consideration are given below.

1.3.1 Management integrity

The integrity of those managing a company will be of great importance, particularly if the company is controlled by one or a few dominant personalities.

1.3.2 Risk

The following table contrasts low and high risk clients.

Low risk	High risk
Good long-term prospects	Poor recent or forecast performance
Well-financed	Likely lack of finance
Strong internal controls	Significant control weaknesses
Conservative, prudent accounting policies	Evidence of questionable integrity, doubtful accounting policies
Competent, honest management	Lack of finance director
Few unusual transactions	Significant related party or unexplained transactions

Where the risk level of a company's audit is determined as anything other than low, then the specific risks shall be identified and documented. It might be necessary to assign specialists in response to these risks, particularly industry specialists, as independent reviewers. Some audit firms have procedures for closely monitoring audits which have been accepted, but which are considered high risk.

1.3.3 Engagement economics

Generally, the expected fees from a new client shall reflect the **level of risk** expected. They shall also offer the same sort of return expected of clients of this nature and reflect the overall financial strategy of the audit firm. Occasionally, the audit firm will want the work to gain entry into the client's particular industry, or to establish better contacts within that industry. These factors will all contribute to a total expected economic return.

1.3.4 Relationship

The audit firm will generally want the relationship with a client to be **long-term**. This is not only to enjoy receiving fees year after year; it is also to allow the audit work to be enhanced by better knowledge of the client and thereby offer a better service.

Conflict of interest problems are significant here; the firm shall establish that no existing clients will cause difficulties as competitors of the new client. Other services to other clients may have an impact here, not just audit.

1.3.5 Ability to perform the work

The audit firm must have the **resources** to perform the work properly, as well as any **specialist knowledge or skills**. The impact on existing engagements must be estimated, in terms of staff time and the timing of the audit.

5: THE AUDIT CLIENT

Sources of information about new clients	
Enquiries of other sources	Bankers, solicitors
Review of **documents**	Most recent annual accounts, listing particulars, credit rating
Previous accountants/auditors	Previous auditors shall disclose fully all relevant information.
Review of **rules and standards**	Consider specific laws/standards that relate to industry.

1.4 Approval

Once all the relevant procedures and information gathering has taken place, the company can be put forward for approval. The engagement partner will have completed a client acceptance form and this, along with any other relevant documentation, will be submitted to the managing partner, or whichever partner is in overall charge of accepting clients.

Exam focus point

In the exam you may be given a 'real-life' client situation and asked what factors you would consider in deciding whether to accept appointment.

2 Audit engagement letters

FAST FORWARD

An audit engagement letter shall be sent to all clients.

If an audit engagement letter is not sent to clients, both new and existing, there is scope for argument about the precise extent of the respective obligations of the client and its directors and the auditors. ISA 210 *Agreeing the Terms of Audit Engagements* provides guidance to auditors on this area.

The contents of an audit engagement letter shall be discussed and agreed with management before it is sent.

An engagement letter shall:

- Confirm that the preconditions for an audit exist
- Provide **written confirmation** of the **auditors' acceptance** of the appointment, the scope of the audit and the auditors' responsibilities, the form of their report and the scope of any non-audit services

2.1 Preconditions for an audit

Key term

The **preconditions for an audit** are the use by management of an acceptable financial reporting framework in preparation of the financial statements and the agreement of management and, where appropriate, those charged with governance to the premise on which an audit is conducted.

It is vital that the client understands the nature of an audit and the responsibilities of those charged with governance and the engagement letter is used as a tool to set those out. The auditor is required to:

- Determine that financial statements will be prepared according to an appropriate financial reporting framework
- Obtain management's confirmation that they understand their own responsibilities

Management's responsibilities include:

- Preparing financial statements
- Instituting and maintaining a system of internal control
- Providing the auditors with information and access

ISA 210 states that the auditors shall not accept an audit unless management has confirmed the above matters unless they are legally obliged to do so. They shall also not accept any limitations on the scope of their audit.

2.2 Agreement of terms

The form and content of audit engagement letters may vary for each client, but they must be in writing and include reference to the following.

- The **objective and scope** of the **audit** of financial statements
- **Auditors' responsibilities**
- **Management's responsibilities**
- The **applicable reporting framework**
- Reference to the expected **form and content of any reports** to be issued by the auditor and a statement that there may be circumstances in which a report may differ from its expected form and content

The auditor may wish to include in the letter the following items.

- **Elaboration of scope** of audit, including reference to legislation, regulations, ISAs, ethical and other pronouncements
- Form of **any other communication** of results of the engagement
- The fact that due to the **inherent limitations of an audit** and those of internal control, there is an unavoidable risk that some material misstatements may not be detected, even though the audit is properly planned and performed in accordance with ISAs
- Arrangements regarding **planning and performance**, including audit team composition
- Expectation that management will provide **written representations**
- **Agreement** of management to provide **draft financial statements** and other information in time to allow auditor to complete audit in accordance with proposed timetable
- **Agreement** of management to inform auditor of **facts** that may affect financial statements, of which management may become aware from date of auditor's report to date of issue of financial statements
- Involvement of **other auditors** and **experts**
- Involvement of **internal auditors** and other staff
- Arrangements to be made with the **predecessor auditor**
- Any **restriction of the auditor's liability**
- A reference to any **further agreements** between the auditor and the client
- Any **obligations to provide audit working papers** to other parties

Appendix 1 of ISA 210 includes an example of an audit engagement letter.

2.3 Recurring audits

Once it has been agreed by the client, an engagement letter will, if it so provides, remain effective from one audit appointment to another until it is replaced. However, the engagement letter shall be **reviewed annually** to ensure that it continues to reflect the client's circumstances.

The ISA suggests that the following factors may make the agreement of a new letter appropriate.

- Any indication that the client **misunderstands** the objective and scope of the audit
- Any **revised** or **special terms** of the engagement
- A recent **change of senior management**, board of directors or ownership committee
- A **significant change** in the **nature or size** of the client's business
- **Legal requirements**

2.4 Acceptance of a change in engagement

In the case of a change in the terms of engagement prior to completion, this may result from:

(a) A **change in circumstances** affecting the need for the service

(b) A **misunderstanding** as to the nature of an audit or of the related service originally requested

(c) A **restriction on the scope** of the engagement, whether imposed by management or caused by circumstances

The auditors shall consider such a request for change, and the reason for it, very seriously, particularly in terms of any restriction in the scope of the engagement.

In the case of (a) and (b) above, these would normally be acceptable reasons for requesting a change in the engagement. A change would not be considered reasonable, however, if it seemed to relate to information that is incorrect, incomplete or otherwise unsatisfactory. Any changes in the terms of the agreement must be documented and a new letter of engagement issued.

In addition to the above, an auditor engaged to perform an audit in accordance with ISAs must consider **any legal** or **contractual implications** of **the change**.

The audit report issued after such a change has been agreed (and the relevant audit work carried out) shall be appropriate to the revised terms of engagement. Such an audit report shall **not** include reference to:

- The original engagement
- Any procedures performed under the original engagement

Question — New auditors

You are an audit partner in an accountancy firm. You have recently been approached by the board of Stayman plc, a listed company, with a view to your firm taking over as the company's auditors.

Stayman is an internet gambling company, which has recently been featured prominently in the financial press. Several similar companies, which offer online casino facilities, have unexpectedly been closed down by the US government on the grounds that such trading is both immoral and illegal. Stayman only operates in Europe, and the directors are confident that European law will continue to allow them to operate. Despite this, public confidence in the company has fallen, resulting in the company's share price falling sharply.

The company has announced that it expects to make substantial losses in the coming financial year. This follows the decision to write-off the costs of developing new gambling software, which was found to be unsuitable for the European market. In addition, trading has been lower than anticipated, with the long, hot summer in Europe encouraging many would-be gamblers to remain outside enjoying the sunshine.

The directors have also asked your firm to carry out an independent review of the company's accounting policies for revenue recognition and development costs. The directors have indicated that following this review, your firm will be proposed to be appointed as auditors.

This proposed appointment was discussed at a recent meeting of the partners of your firm.

Your senior partner has expressed concern that your firm knows relatively little about Stayman.

If taken on Stayman could become one of the firm's largest clients. It was agreed that rigorous client acceptance procedures shall be carried out in order for the partners to consider whether or not to agree to accept appointment as auditor.

Required

(a) Explain what is meant by the term 'client acceptance procedures'.

(b) Identify the factors that an audit firm shall evaluate and consider as part of the acceptance procedures.

(c) Set out the client acceptance issues which shall be considered in relation to the invitation to act for Stayman.

Answer

This question assesses students' knowledge of the importance of client acceptance procedures, particularly the identification of high risk potential clients (syllabus reference 4.1 and 4.2).

(a) The term 'client acceptance procedures' is used to describe the procedures that shall be undertaken by auditors in deciding whether or not to accept or reject an engagement. Such procedures shall be used whether the engagement is of a recurring nature, or whether it is a new client.

While it may seem common sense to accept all audit engagements, so that the firm can increase profitability and expand its client base, all engagements expose the firm to a degree of risk.

In order to decide whether to take on a new audit engagement or to continue with an existing one, audit firms need to have an understanding of the risk profile of their clients, and the potential impact on the audit firm. Client acceptance procedures form an integral part of an audit firm's risk management system.

(b) Factors that shall be evaluated and considered as part of the acceptance procedures would include:

- Damage to the reputation of the audit firm; for example, if the client has unscrupulous directors there is a risk of the audit firm being associated with any inappropriate practices.
- Financial loss to the audit firm; for example if the client is unable to pay fees.
- Lack of independence or conflict of interest; for example provision of non-audit work could impact on the objectivity of the audit firm.
- The client's business environment and financial position; for example, a highly geared company may have a greater incentive to manipulate the accounts.
- The complexity and size of client; for example, the audit firm may not have the technical resources to adequately carry out the audit.
- Public profile of the client; for example, problems or issues with high profile audit clients are likely to receive high press attention.

(c) Issues to consider prior to acceptance of Stayman plc:

Previous auditors ceasing to hold office

The audit firm shall obtain the Statement of Circumstances filed by the previous auditors.

It shall also ask permission to contact the previous auditors, and discuss reasons for their resignation/removal with the directors of Stayman. The audit firm will need to establish if there are any reasons why it shall not accept the appointment.

Internet gambling industry

Stayman is a high profile, listed company that has recently featured prominently in the financial press. As Stayman is involved in activities that some people (and some governments) consider to be ethically questionable, any adverse public reaction to its activities could have an adverse effect on the auditors.

Competence/knowledge of the business

Prior to accepting Stayman, the audit firm shall review whether or not it has the technical competence and understanding of this high technology industry. If, as is likely, the firm does not understand the internet gambling industry, it shall ensure that it has the resources and ability to achieve such an understanding prior to commencing the audit.

Losses

Stayman is expecting to make 'substantial losses' in the coming year, with revenue lower than anticipated, and new software is being written off as unsuitable. This places concern over whether or not Stayman will be able to continue as a going concern. The collapse of such a high profile company could affect the audit firm's reputation, and there would also be the risk that audit fees would not be paid.

Closure of other companies

Several other similar companies have 'unexpectedly' been closed down in the US. Although the directors are confident this will not happen in Europe, there is a potential for the law to be changed, resulting in the forced closure of Stayman. This also raises going concern issues and adverse publicity issues for the audit firm.

Falling share price

In addition to the anticipated losses, Stayman's share price has recently fallen sharply. This could result in the risk that the client may be encouraged to use creative accounting techniques, or otherwise try to manipulate the accounts. The audit firm must be alert to this risk if it agrees to act.

Potential 'opinion shopping'

The audit firm has been asked to undertake an independent review of Stayman's accounting policies for revenue recognition and development costs, prior to appointment as auditor. There is a danger that Stayman is attempting to establish which audit firm will agree with potentially inappropriate accounting policies, prior to acting as auditor.

Size of Stayman

If accepted as an audit client, Stayman would become one of the audit firm's largest clients. The firm must ensure that it has adequate resources to staff the assignment.

Level of fee income

Given that Stayman will be one of the firm's largest clients, the firm must ensure that it is not, and is not seen to be, financially dependent on the client. It shall review the likely recurring fee income that will be gained from Stayman, and ensure that it does not question its independence and objectivity.

Independence issues

As with all audit engagements, the firm will need to undertake normal acceptance procedures in respect of independence. Areas that will need to be considered include family and business connections, beneficial interests, and conflict of interest.

Chapter roundup

- Auditors have guidance from AIA on advertising and obtaining professional work.
- The **present** and **proposed auditors** must **communicate** about the client prior to the audit being accepted.
- The client must be asked to give permission for communication to occur. If the client **refuses** to give **permission,** the proposed auditors must **decline nomination.**
- An audit engagement letter shall be sent to all clients.

Quick quiz

1 Complete the questions that shall be in the following diagram.

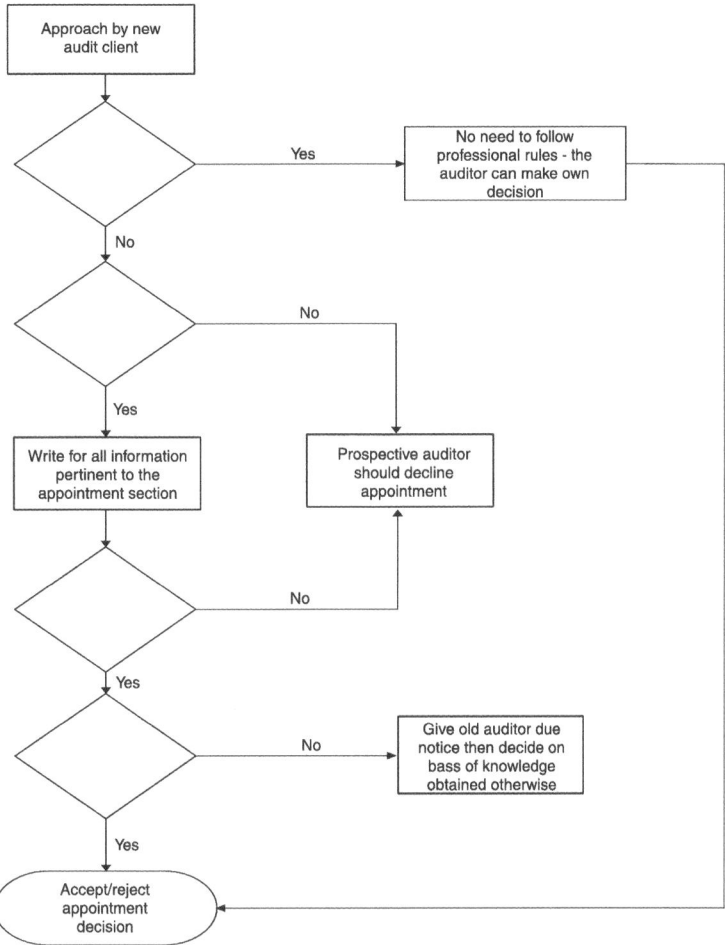

2 An audit engagement letter is only ever sent to a client before the first audit.

True ☐
False ☐

Answers to quick quiz

1
- Is this the first audit?
- Does the client give permission to contact the old auditor?
- Does client give old auditor permission to reply?
- Does old auditor provide information relevant to new appointment?

2   False. It shall be re-issued if there is a change in circumstances.

End of chapter question

PLD Associates

PLD Associates Co, a large quoted company, was founded and controlled by Mr J Scott. The principal business of the company was to develop derelict land in city centres into office accommodation. In 20X3, the taxation authorities became suspicious of the nature of the operations being carried out by the company and an investigation into its affairs commenced.

The resultant report stated that the organisation's internal controls had deficiencies and were non-existent in many cases. The investigators found payments to unknown persons, and fictitious consultancy firms. The auditors were heavily criticised in the report of the investigators.

The firm of auditors, Allcost & Co, had an aggressive marketing strategy and had increased its audit fees by 100% in two years. The audit firm had accepted the appointment in 20X1 after the previous auditors had been dismissed. The auditor's report for the year ended 20X0 had been qualified by the previous auditors on the grounds of poor internal control and lack of audit evidence. J Scott had approached several firms of auditors in order to ascertain whether they would qualify the auditor's report given the present systems of control in PLD Associates Co. Allcost & Co had stated that it was unlikely that they would qualify their report. They realised that J Scott was 'opinion shopping' but were prepared to give an opinion in order to attract the client to their firm.

PLD Associates Co subsequently filed for insolvency and Allcost & Co were sued for negligence by the company's largest loan creditor, its bankers.

Required

(a) Describe the procedures which an audit firm should carry out before accepting a client with potentially high audit risk such as PLD Associates Co. **(5 marks)**

(b) Suggest measures that audit firms might introduce to try to minimise the practice of 'opinion shopping' by prospective audit clients. **(5 marks)**

(Total = 10 marks)

Internal controls

Topic list	Syllabus reference
1 Internal control systems	3.3
2 Limitations of internal control systems	3.3
3 Internal controls in a computerised environment	3.3
4 Documenting systems	3.3

Introduction

In a modern audit the auditor seeks to rely on internal controls and is therefore able to reduce the amount of testing of final balances.

The evaluation of a client's system is essential as the auditor gains an understanding of the entity. In this chapter, we shall look at some of the detailed requirements of ISA 315 (Revised 2019) with regard to internal controls, and shall also set out control issues the auditor may come across.

We shall examine the detailed controls that businesses operate in later chapters, and the tests that the auditors may carry out. You should bear in mind the principles discussed in this chapter when considering the controls needed over specific accounting areas.

1 Internal control systems

FAST FORWARD The external auditors must **understand** the **accounting system** and **control environment** in order to determine the audit approach.

Key term

The **system of internal control** is the system designed, implemented and maintained by those charged with governance, management, and other personnel to provide reasonable assurance about the achievement of an entity's objectives with regard to reliability of financial reporting, effectiveness and efficiency of operations and compliance with applicable laws and regulations.

(ISA 315 (Revised), para. 12(m))

In other words, a system of internal control helps management

- Report reliably
- Operate efficiently
- Comply with legal requirements
- Keep its assets secure from theft or damage

As discussed in the previous chapter, the internal auditors may be required to test controls to ensure that they achieve these objectives. External auditors are required to consider internal controls too, as part of identifying and assessing risks that the financial statements will be misstated. They are required to by ISA 315 (Revised), which we will look at in this chapter. These requirements only apply to external auditors, although internal auditors may carry out the same or similar tests.

ISA 315 (Revised) *Identifying and Assessing the Risks of Material Misstatement* deals with the whole area of controls.

A system of internal control has **five** components:

- The control environment
- The entity's risk assessment process
- The entity's process to monitor the system of internal control
- The information system and communication
- Control activities

In obtaining an understanding of internal control, the auditor must understand the **design** of the internal control and the **implementation** of that control. In the following sub-sections, we look at each of the elements of internal control in turn.

1.1 Control environment

The control environment is the framework within which controls operate. The control environment is very much determined by the management of a business.

Key term

Control environment includes the governance and management functions and the attitudes, awareness and actions of those charged with governance and management concerning the entity's internal control and its importance in the entity.

A strong control environment does not, by itself, ensure the effectiveness of the overall internal control system, but can be a positive factor when assessing the risks of material misstatement. A weak control environment can undermine the effectiveness of controls.

Aspects of the control environment (such as management attitudes towards control) will nevertheless be a significant factor in determining how controls operate. Controls are more likely to operate well in an environment where they are treated as being important. In addition consideration of the control environment will mean determining whether certain controls (internal auditors, budgets) actually exist.

ISA 315 (Revised) states that auditors shall obtain an understanding of the control environment relevant to the preparation of the financial statements. As part of this understanding, the auditor shall evaluate whether:

- Management has created and maintained a culture of honesty and ethical behaviour.
- The strengths in the control environment provide an appropriate foundation for the other components of internal control and whether those components are not undermined by deficiencies in the control environment.

The following table illustrates the elements of the control environment that may be relevant when obtaining an understanding of the control environment.

CONTROL ENVIRONMENT	
Communication and enforcement of integrity and ethical values	Essential elements which influence the effectiveness of the design, administration and monitoring of controls
Commitment to competence	Management's consideration of the competence levels for particular jobs and how those levels translate into requisite skills and knowledge
Participation by those charged with governance	• Independence from management • Experience and stature • Extent of involvement and scrutiny of activities • Appropriateness of actions and interaction with internal and external auditors
Management's philosophy and operating style	• Approach to taking and managing business risks • Attitudes and actions towards financial reporting • Attitudes towards information processing and accounting functions and personnel
Organisational structure	The framework within which an entity's activities for achieving its objectives are planned, executed, controlled and reviewed
Assignment of authority and responsibility	How authority and responsibility for operating activities are assigned and how reporting relationships and authorisation hierarchies are established
Human resource policies and practices	Recruitment, orientation, training, evaluating, counselling, promoting, compensation and remedial actions

The auditor shall assess whether these elements of the control environment have been implemented using a combination of **inquiries of management**, **observation** and **inspection**.

1.2 Entity's risk assessment process

ISA 315 (Revised) says the auditor shall obtain an understanding of whether the entity has a process for:

- Identifying business risks relevant to financial reporting objectives
- Estimating the significance of the risks
- Assessing the likelihood of their occurrence
- Deciding upon actions to address those risks

If the entity has established such a process, the auditor shall obtain an understanding of it. If there is not a process, the auditor shall discuss with management whether relevant business risks have been identified and how they have been addressed.

1.3 The entity's process to monitor the system of internal control

Key term

> **Monitoring of controls** is a process to assess the effectiveness of the performance of the system of internal control over time. It includes assessing the design and operation of controls on a timely basis and taking necessary corrective actions modified for changes in conditions.

The auditor shall obtain an understanding of the entity's process for monitoring the system of internal control relevant to the preparation of the financial statements. This includes ongoing and separate evaluations for monitoring the effectiveness of controls, and the identification and remediation of control deficiencies identified (this may well be carried out by an internal audit function).

If the entity has an **internal audit function**, the external auditors shall obtain an understanding of its **nature and responsibilities**, how it **fits** in the organisational structure, and the **activities** performed/to be performed.

The auditor shall also obtain an understanding of the **sources of the information** used in the monitoring activities and the **basis** on which management considers it reliable.

1.4 The information system and communication

Key term

> The **information system** is a component of internal control that includes the financial reporting system, and consists of the procedures and records established to initiate, record, process and report entity transactions and to maintain accountability for the related assets, liabilities and equity.

The auditor shall obtain an understanding of the entity's information system and communication relevant to the preparation of financial statements.

The auditor shall obtain an understanding of the entity's information processing activities, including its data and information, the resources to be used in such activities and the policies that define: Significant classes of transactions, account balances and disclosures:

- How information flows through the entity's information system.

    This includes how transactions are initiated, recorded, processed, corrected, incorporated in general ledger and reported in the financial statements and how information about events and conditions, other than transactions, is captured, processed and disclosed in the financial statements.

- The accounting records, specific accounts in the financial statements and other supporting records relating to the flows of information in the information system.

- The financial reporting process used to prepare the entity's financial statements, including significant accounting estimates and disclosures.

- The entity's resources, including the IT environment relevant to the points above.

The auditor shall obtain an understanding of how the entity **communicates** significant matters that support the preparation of the financial statements and related reporting responsibilities in the information system and other components of the system of internal control.

1.5 Control activities

Key term

> **Control activities** are those policies and procedures that help ensure that management directives are carried out.

ISA 315 (Revised) states that the auditor shall obtain an understanding of control activities relevant to the audit and how the entity has responded to risks arising from IT.

Control activities include those activities designed to **prevent** or to **detect** and **correct errors**. Examples include activities relating to **authorisation, performance reviews, information processing, physical controls and segregation of duties**.

Examples of control activities	
Approval and control of documents	Transactions should be approved (signature or online/electronic approval) by an appropriate person. For example, overtime should be approved by departmental managers.
Controls over computerised applications	We shall look at computer controls later in this chapter.
Checking the arithmetical accuracy of records	For example, checking to see if individual invoices have been added up correctly.
Maintaining and reviewing control accounts and trial balances	Control accounts bring together transactions in individual ledgers. Trial balances bring together unusual transactions for the organisation as a whole. Preparing these can highlight unusual transactions or accounts. Note that where an entity has a fully integrated accounting system the recording of sales and purchase invoices will automatically update the individual customer and supplier accounts and so control accounts will reconcile with these balances.
Reconciliations	Reconciliations involve comparison of a specific balance in the accounting records with what another source says the balance should be, for example, a bank reconciliation. Differences between the two figures should only be reconciling items.
Comparing the results of cash, security and inventory counts with accounting records	For example, in a physical count of petty cash, the balance shown in the petty cash book or petty cash ledger account should be the same as the amount held.
Comparing internal data with external sources of information	For example, comparing records of goods despatched to customers with customers' acknowledgement of goods that have been received.
Limiting physical access to assets and records	Only authorised personnel should have access to certain assets (particularly valuable or portable ones). For example, ensuring that the inventory store is only open when store personnel are there and is otherwise locked.

1.5.1 Segregation of duties

Segregation implies a **number of people** being involved in the accounting process. This makes it more difficult for fraudulent transactions to be processed (since a number of people would have to collude in the fraud), and it is also more difficult for accidental errors to be processed (since the more people are involved, the more checking there can be). Segregation should take place in various ways:

(a) **Segregation of function.** The key functions that should be segregated are the **carrying out** of a transaction, **recording** that transaction in the accounting records and **maintaining custody** of assets that arise from the transaction.

(b) The various **steps** in carrying out the transaction should also be segregated. We shall see how this works in practice when we look at the major transaction cycles in Chapters 10 and 11.

(c) The **carrying out** of various **accounting operations** should be segregated. For example the same staff should not record transactions and carry out the reconciliations at the period-end.

Question — Control activities

Listed below are several everyday situations:

(1) The postman knocks at your front door and hands you a letter which has been sent by recorded delivery.

(2) You submit a claim for expenses to your line manager.

(3) You need to work an extra day over and above your normal hours to clear a backlog of work and will expect to be paid overtime for this.

(4) You are responsible for maintaining the cash book and have just been passed the latest bank statement.

(5) You have just received a monthly statement from your main supplier.

(6) You are responsible for payroll processing and you have just received notification from human resources that an employee wants to take advantage of a season ticket loan offered by your company. Your password does not give you permission to amend employee deductions.

(7) You have just returned from a three-month holiday and are trying to log on to your computer.

(8) You are preparing to pay an invoice received from a supplier.

(9) You have prepared a bank reconciliation for your supervisor.

(10) You are entering 75 sales invoices into the accounting records and want to check the accuracy of your posting.

(11) You have been working on the computer but have now gone away to make a cup of tea, leaving the computer inactive for a period of time.

(12) You have a Saturday job operating the till in a small corner shop which is closing for the night.

(13) You work in a shop that sells diamond jewellery; the jeweller is very keen to keep their inventory secure.

Required

What checks/internal controls would you expect to be carried out in each of the situations above?

Answer

1 You should be required to sign for the letter on the postman's handset.

2 You should need to evidence the claim by presenting the receipt; the line manager should sign the claim form to authorise payment.

3 You should submit a request that the overtime be authorised prior to it being completed and this authorisation request should be signed by your line manager.

4 You should perform a bank reconciliation to verify the completeness and accuracy of the cash book.

5 You should reconcile the balance per the supplier statement to the purchase ledger balance.

6   You should be provided with a copy of the letter signed by the employee which authorises the deductions and a hierarchical password should be required to amend the standing data.

7   Your password should have expired and the computer should automatically require you to change your password.

8   You should verify that the goods have been received by checking to a goods received note, vouch the prices to the supplier's price list and recalculate the sales tax and addition of the invoice. The invoice should then be authorised for payment and this evidenced by a signature.

9   Your supervisor should review the bank reconciliation to verify it has been done properly and sign to evidence that the review has taken place.

10 You should perform a batch reconciliation whereby you manually count the number of invoices posted and verify to the system or manually total the value of the invoices and verify that the revenue, sales tax and receivables accounts have increased by the corresponding amounts.

    Provided that the invoices are sequentially numbered, you should also perform a sequence check to determine whether any invoice numbers have been omitted.

11 You should log out/lock your computer prior to leaving your work station.

    If you do not lock your computer then the computer should 'time out' after a certain period of time and require you to re-enter your log on/ password details before you can resume work.

12 The cash in the till should be counted at the end of the day and reconciled to the till receipt. Money should be kept in a safe overnight.

13 The shop should have CCTV in operation, the front door should be locked with a door bell which must be rung to gain entry, jewellery should be kept in locked cabinets and stored overnight in a safe/secure vault and grilles pulled down over the shop windows.

1.6 Confirming understanding

In order to confirm their understanding of the control systems, auditors will often carry out 'walk-through tests'. This is where they pick up a transaction and follow it through the system to see whether all the controls they anticipate should be in existence were in operation with regard to that transaction.

1.7 Small companies – the problem of control

Many of the controls which would be relevant to a large enterprise are neither practical nor appropriate for the small enterprise. For these the most important form of internal control is generally the **close involvement** of the **directors or proprietors**. However, that very involvement will enable them to **override controls** and, if they wish, to **exclude transactions** from the records.

Auditors can have difficulties not because there is a general lack of controls but because the evidence available as to their operation and the completeness of the records is insufficient.

Segregation of duties will often appear inadequate in enterprises having a small number of staff. Similarly, because of the scale of the operation, organisation and management controls are likely to be rudimentary at best.

The onus is on the proprietor, by virtue of their day-to-day involvement, to compensate for this lack of controls. This involvement should encompass physical, authorisation, arithmetical and accounting checks as well as supervision.

However it is important to stress that in a well-run small company there will be a system of internal control. In any case, all companies must comply with the provisions of the Companies Act 2006 concerning the maintenance of an adequate accounting system. Under the Small Business, Enterprise and

Employment Act 2015, UK companies must also keep a register of people with significant control over the company. A person with significant control is an individual who owns more than 25% of a company's shares or voting rights.

Where the manager of a small business is not themself the owner, they may not possess the same degree of commitment to the running of it as an owner-manager would. In such cases, the auditors will have to consider the adequacy of controls exercised by the shareholders over the manager in assessing internal control.

Question — Internal control systems

An internal control system has been described as comprising 'the control environment and control activities. It includes all the policies and procedures (internal controls) adopted by the directors and management of an entity to assist in achieving their objective of ensuring, as far as practicable, the orderly and efficient conduct of its business, including adherence to internal policies, the safeguarding of assets, the prevention and detection of fraud and misstatement, the accuracy and completeness of the accounting records, and the timely preparation of reliable financial information'.

Explain the meaning and relevance to the auditors giving an opinion on the financial statements of each of the management objectives above.

Answer

The auditors' objective in evaluating and testing internal controls is to determine the degree of reliance which they may place on the information contained in the accounting records. If they obtain reasonable assurance by means of tests of controls that the internal control system is effective in ensuring the completeness and accuracy of the accounting records and the validity of the entries therein, they may limit the extent of their substantive procedures.

(a) **'The orderly and efficient conduct of its business'**

An organisation which is efficient and conducts its affairs in an orderly manner is much more likely to be able to supply the auditors with sufficient appropriate audit evidence on which to base their audit opinion. More importantly, the level of inherent and control risk will be lower, giving extra assurance that the financial statements do not contain material misstatements.

(b) **'Adherence to internal policies'**

Management is responsible for setting up an effective system of internal control and management policy provides the broad framework within which internal controls have to operate. Unless management does have a pre-determined set of policies, then it is very difficult to imagine how the company could be expected to operate efficiently. Management policy will cover all aspects of the company's activities and will range from broad corporate objectives to specific areas such as determining selling prices and wage rates.

Given that the auditors must have a sound understanding of the company's affairs generally, and of specific areas of control in particular, then the fact that management policies are followed will make the task of the auditors easier in that they will be able to rely more readily on the information produced by the systems established by management.

(c) **'Safeguarding of assets'**

This objective may relate to the physical protection of assets (eg locking monies in a safe at night) or to less direct safeguarding (eg ensuring that there is adequate insurance cover for all assets). It can also be seen as relating to the maintenance of adequate records in respect of all assets.

The auditors will be concerned to ensure that the company has properly safeguarded its assets so that they can form an opinion on the existence of specific assets and, more generally, on whether the company's records can be taken as a reliable basis for the preparation of financial statements. Reliance on the underlying records will be particularly significant where the figures in the financial statements are derived from such records rather than as the result of physical inspection.

(d) **'Prevention and detection of fraud and misstatement'**

The directors are responsible for taking reasonable steps to prevent and detect fraud. They are also responsible for preparing financial statements which give a true and fair view of the entity's affairs. However, the auditors must plan and perform their audit procedures and evaluate and report the results thereof, recognising that fraud or misstatement may materially affect the financial statements. A strong system of internal control will give the auditors some assurance that frauds and misstatements are not occurring, unless management are colluding to overcome that system.

(e) **'Accuracy and completeness of the accounting records'/'timely preparation of reliable financial information'**

This objective is most clearly related to statutory requirements relating to both management and auditors. A company generally has legal obligations to maintain adequate accounting records. The auditors must form an opinion on whether the company has fulfilled these obligations and also conclude whether the financial statements are in agreement with the underlying records.

2 Limitations of internal control systems

FAST FORWARD   There are always inherent limitations to internal controls and therefore internal control systems.

Any internal control system can only provide the directors with **reasonable assurance** that their objectives are reached, because of **inherent limitations**. These include:

- The **costs** of control **not outweighing** their **benefits**
- The **potential** for **human error**
- **Collusion** between employees
- The possibility of **controls** being **by-passed** or **overridden** by management
- Controls being **designed to cope** with **routine** and **not non-routine transactions**

These factors show why auditors cannot obtain all their evidence from tests of the systems of internal control. The key factors in the limitations of controls system are **human error** and **potential for fraud**.

The safeguard of segregation of duties can help deter fraud. However, if employees decide to perpetrate frauds in harness, or management commit fraud by overriding systems, the accounting system will not be able to prevent such frauds.

This is one of the reasons that auditors need to be alert to the possibility of fraud, the subject of ISA 240 *The Auditor's Responsibilities Relating to Fraud in an Audit of Financial Statements*.

3 Internal controls in a computerised environment

FAST FORWARD   There are special considerations for auditors when a system is computerised.

Exam focus point   The examiner expects you to be comfortable with computerised environments.

The internal controls in a computerised environment includes both manual procedures and procedures designed into computer programs. Such manual and computer control procedures comprise two types of control.

Key terms

> **General IT controls** are controls over the entity's IT processes that support the continued proper operation of the IT environment, including the continued effective functioning of information processing controls and the integrity of information (ie, the completeness, accuracy and validity of information) in the entity's information system.
>
> (ISA 315 (Revised): para. 12(d))
>
> **Information processing controls** are controls relating to the processing of information in IT applications or manual information processes in the entity's information system that directly address risks to the integrity of information (ie the completeness, accuracy and validity of transactions and other information).
>
> (ISA 315 (Revised): para. 12(e))

3.1 General controls

GENERAL CONTROLS	
Development of computer applications	Standards over **systems design, programming and documentation**
	Full **testing procedures** using test data
	Approval by **computer users** and **management**
	Segregation of duties so that those responsible for design are not responsible for testing
	Installation procedures so that data is not corrupted in transition
	Training of staff in new procedures and availability of adequate documentation
Prevention or detection of unauthorised changes to programs	**Segregation of duties**
	Full records of program **changes**
	Password protection of programs so that access is limited to computer operations staff.
	Restricted access to **central computer** by locked doors, keypads
	Maintenance of programs logs
	Virus checks on software: use of anti-virus software and policy prohibiting use of non-authorised programs or files
	Back-up copies of programs being taken and stored in other locations
	Control copies of programs being preserved and regularly **compared** with **actual programs**
	Stricter controls over certain programs (utility programs) by use of **read only memory**
Testing and documentation of program changes	Complete **testing procedures**
	Documentation standards
	Approval of changes by computer users and management
	Training of staff using programs
Controls to prevent wrong programs or files being used	**Operation controls** over programs
	Libraries of programs
	Proper job scheduling

GENERAL CONTROLS	
Controls to prevent unauthorised amendments to data files	**Password protection** **Restricted** access to authorised users only
Controls to ensure continuity of operation	**Storing extra copies** of programs and data files off site **Protection of equipment** against fire and other hazards **Back-up power sources** **Emergency procedures** **Disaster recovery procedures** eg availability of back-up computer facilities. **Maintenance agreements** and **insurance**

The auditors will wish to test some or all of the above general IT controls, having considered how they affect the computer applications significant to the audit.

General IT controls that relate to some or all applications are usually interdependent controls, ie their operation is often essential to the effectiveness of information processing controls. As information processing controls may be useless when general IT controls are ineffective, it will be more efficient to review the design of **general IT controls first,** before reviewing the information processing controls.

The purpose of information processing controls is to establish **specific control procedures** over the accounting applications in order to provide reasonable assurance that all transactions are authorised and recorded, and are processed completely, accurately and on a timely basis. Information processing controls include the following.

3.2 Information processing controls

INFORMATION PROCESSING CONTROLS	
Controls over **input: completeness**	Manual or programmed agreement of **control totals** **Document counts** **One for one checking** of processed output to source documents **Programmed matching** of input to an expected input control file Procedures over resubmission of rejected controls
Controls over **input: accuracy**	Programmes to **check data** fields (for example value, reference number, date) on input transactions for plausibility: • Digit verification (eg reference numbers are as expected) • Reasonableness test (eg sales tax to total value) • Existence checks (eg customer name) • Character checks (no unexpected characters used in reference) • Necessary information (no transaction passed with gaps) • Permitted range (no transaction processed over a certain value) • Manual scrutiny of output and reconciliation to source • Agreement of control totals (manual/programmed)
Controls over **input: authorisation**	Manual checks to ensure information input was • Authorised • Input by authorised personnel
Controls over **processing**	Similar controls to input must be completed when input is completed, for example, **batch reconciliations**. **Screen warnings** can prevent people logging out before processing is

INFORMATION PROCESSING CONTROLS	
	complete
Controls over **master files and standing data**	**One for one checking** **Cyclical reviews** of all master files and standing data **Record counts** (number of documents processed) and hash totals (for example, the total of all the payroll numbers) used when master files are used to ensure no deletions **Controls** over the deletion of accounts that have no current balance

Controls over input, processing, data files and output may be carried out by IT personnel, users of the system, or a separate control group, and may be programmed into application software. The auditors may wish to test the following information processing controls.

TESTING OF INFORMATION PROCESSING CONTROLS	
Manual controls exercised by the user	If manual controls exercised by the user of the application system are capable of providing reasonable assurance that the system's output is complete, accurate and authorised, the auditors may decide to limit tests of control to these manual controls.
Controls over system output	If, in addition to manual controls exercised by the user, the controls to be tested use information produced by the computer or are contained within computer programs, such controls may be tested by examining the system's output using either manual procedures or **automated tools and techniques** (ATTs). Such output may be in the form of electronic files or printouts. Alternatively, the auditor may test the control by performing it with the use of ATTs.
Programmed control procedures	In the case of certain computer systems, the auditor may find that it is not possible or, in some cases, not practical to test controls by examining only user controls or the system's output. The auditor may consider **performing tests of controls** by using ATTs, such as test data, reprocessing transaction data or, in unusual situations, examining the coding of the application program.

As we have already noted, general IT controls may have a pervasive effect on the processing of transactions in application systems. If these general controls are not effective, there may be a risk that misstatements occur and go undetected in the application systems. Although deficiencies in general IT controls may preclude testing certain information processing controls, it is possible that manual procedures exercised by users may provide effective control at the **application level**.

4 Documenting systems

FAST FORWARD

The auditors must keep a record of the client's systems which must be updated each year.

There are several techniques for recording the assessment of control risk, that is, the system. One or more may be used depending on the complexity of the system.

- Narrative notes (a long-hand description of the system)
- Flowcharts (a pictorial representation of the system)
- Questionnaires (a list of questions about the system – see below)
- Checklists (a list of expectations about the system and whether they are met)

Whatever method of recording the system is used, the record will usually be retained on the permanent file and updated each year.

4.1 Internal Control Questionnaires (ICQs)

The major question which internal control questionnaires are designed to answer is 'How good is the system of controls?'

Where strengths are identified, the auditors will perform work in the relevant areas. If, however, deficiencies are discovered they should then ask:

- What misstatements or irregularities could be made possible by these deficiencies?
- Could such misstatements or irregularities be material to the accounts?
- What substantive procedures will enable such misstatements or irregularities to be discovered and quantified?

Although there are many different forms of ICQ in practice, they all conform to the following basic principles:

- They comprise a list of questions designed to determine whether desirable controls are present.
- They are formulated so that there is one to cover each of the major transaction cycles.

Since it is the primary purpose of an ICQ to evaluate the system rather than describe it, one of the most effective ways of designing the questionnaire is to phrase the questions so that all the answers can be given as 'yes' or 'no' and a 'no' answer indicates a deficiency in the system. An example would be:

> Are purchase invoices checked to goods received notes before being passed for payment?
> Yes/No/Comments

A 'NO' answer to that question clearly indicates a deficiency in the company's payment procedures.

The ICQ questions below dealing with goods inward provide additional illustrations of the ICQ approach.

> **Goods inward**
>
> (a) Are supplies examined on arrival as to quantity and quality?
>
> (b) Is such an examination evidenced in some way?
>
> (c) Is the receipt of supplies recorded, perhaps by means of goods inwards notes?
>
> (d) Are receipt records prepared by a person independent of those responsible for:
>
>   (i) Ordering functions
>
>   (ii) The processing and recording of invoices
>
> (e) Are goods inwards records controlled to ensure that invoices are obtained for all goods received and to enable the liability for unbilled goods to be determined (by pre-numbering the records and accounting for all serial numbers)?
>
> (f) (i) Are goods inward records regularly reviewed for items for which no invoices have been received?
>
>   (ii) Are any such items investigated?
>
> (g) Are these records reviewed by a person independent of those responsible for the receipt and control of goods?

4.2 Internal Control Evaluation Questionnaires (ICEQs)

In recent years many auditing firms have developed and implemented an evaluation technique more concerned with assessing whether specific errors (or frauds) are possible rather than establishing whether certain desirable controls are present.

This is achieved by reducing the control criteria for each transaction stream down to a handful of key questions (or control questions). The characteristic of these questions is that they concentrate on the significant misstatements or omissions that could occur at each phase of the appropriate cycle if controls are weak. The nature of the key questions may best be understood by reference to the examples on the following pages.

Internal control evaluation questionnaire: control questions

The sales (revenue) cycle

Is there reasonable assurance that:

(a) Sales are properly authorised?
(b) Sales are made to reliable payers?
(c) All goods despatched are invoiced?
(d) All invoices are properly prepared?
(e) All invoices are recorded?
(f) Invoices are properly supported?
(g) All credits to customers' accounts are valid?
(h) Cash and cheques received are properly recorded and deposited?
(i) Slow payers will be chased and that bad and doubtful debts will be provided against?
(j) All transactions are properly accounted for?
(k) Cash sales are properly dealt with?
(l) Sundry sales are controlled?
(m) At the period end the system will neither overstate nor understate trade accounts receivable?

The purchases (expenditure) cycle

Is there reasonable assurance that:

(a) Goods or services could not be received without a liability being recorded?
(b) Receipt of goods or services is required in order to establish a liability?
(c) A liability will be recorded:
 (i) Only for authorised items
 (ii) At the proper amount?
(d) All payments are properly authorised?
(e) All credits due from suppliers are received?
(f) All transactions are properly accounted for?
(g) At the period end liabilities are neither overstated nor understated by the system?
(h) The balance at the bank is properly recorded at all times?
(i) Unauthorised cash payments could not be made and that the balance of petty cash is correctly stated at all times?

Wages and salaries

Is there reasonable assurance that:

(a) Employees are only paid for work done?
(b) Employees are paid the correct amount (gross and net)?
(c) The right employees actually receive the right amount?
(d) Accounting for payroll costs and deductions is accurate?

Internal control evaluation questionnaire: control questions

Inventory

Is there reasonable assurance that:

(a) Inventory is safeguarded from physical loss (eg fire, theft, deterioration)?
(b) Inventory records are accurate and up to date?
(c) The recorded inventory exists?
(d) The recorded inventory is owned by the company?
(e) The cut-off is reliable?
(f) The costing system is reliable?
(g) The inventory sheets are accurately compiled?
(h) The inventory valuation is fair?

Non-current tangible assets

Is there reasonable assurance that:

(a) Recorded assets actually exist and belong to the company?
(b) Capital expenditure is authorised and reported?
(c) Disposals of non-current assets are authorised and reported?
(d) Depreciation is realistic?
(e) Non-current assets are correctly accounted for?
(f) Income derived from non-current assets is accounted for?

Investments

Is there reasonable assurance that:

(a) Recorded investments belong to the company and are safeguarded from loss?
(b) All income, rights or bonus issues are properly received and accounted for?
(c) Investment transactions are made only in accordance with company policy and are appropriately authorised and documented?
(d) The carrying values of investments are reasonably stated?

Management information and general controls

Is the nominal ledger satisfactorily controlled?

(a) Are journal entries adequately controlled?
(b) Does the organisation structure provide a clear definition of the extent and limitation of authority?
(c) Are the systems operated by competent employees, who are adequately supported?
(d) If there is an internal audit function, is it adequate?
(e) Are financial planning procedures adequate?
(f) Are periodic internal reporting procedures adequate?

Each key control question is supported by detailed control points to be considered. For example, the detailed control points to be considered in relation to key control question (b) for the expenditure cycle (Is there reasonable assurance that receipt of goods or services is required to establish a liability?) are as follows.

(1)	Is segregation of duties satisfactory?
(2)	Are controls over relevant master files satisfactory?
(3)	Is there a record that all goods received have been checked for: • Weight or number? • Quality and damage?

(4)	Are all goods received taken on charge in the detailed inventory ledgers: • By means of the goods received note? • Or by means of purchase invoices? • Are there, in a computerised system, sensible control totals (hash totals, money values and so on) to reconcile the inventory system input with the payables system?
(5)	Are all invoices initialled to show that: • Receipt of goods has been checked against the goods received records? • Receipt of services has been verified by the person using it? • Quality of goods has been checked against the inspection?
(6)	In a computerised invoice approval system are there print-outs (examined by a responsible person) of: • Cases where order, GRN and invoice are present but they are not equal ('equal' within predetermined tolerances of minor discrepancies)? • Cases where invoices have been input but there is no corresponding GRN?
(7)	Is there adequate control over direct purchases?
(8)	Are receiving documents effectively cancelled (for example cross-referenced) to prevent their supporting two invoices?

Alternatively, ICEQ questions can be phrased so that the weakness which should be prevented by a key control is highlighted, such as the following.

Question	Answer	Comments or explanation of 'yes' answer
Can goods be sent to unauthorised suppliers?		

In these cases a 'yes' answer would require an explanation, rather than a 'no' answer.

4.3 Advantages and disadvantages of questionnaires

ICQs: advantages

(a) If drafted thoroughly, they can ensure **all controls** are **considered**.
(b) They are **quick** to **prepare**.
(c) They are **easy** to **use** and **control**.

ICQs: disadvantages

(a) The client may be able to **overstate controls.**
(b) They may contain a large number of **irrelevant controls.**
(c) They may not include **unusual controls**, which are nevertheless effective in particular circumstances.
(d) They can give the impression that all controls are of **equal** weight. In many systems one no answer (for example lack of segregation of duties) will cancel out a string of yes answers.

ICEQs: advantages

(a) Because they are drafted in terms of **objectives** rather than specific controls, they are easier to apply to a variety of systems than **ICQs**.

(b) Answering ICEQs should enable auditors to **identify the key controls** which they are most likely to test during control testing.

(c) ICEQs can **highlight areas of weakness** where extensive substantive testing will be required.

ICEQs: disadvantage

They can be **drafted vaguely**, hence **misunderstood** and important controls not identified.

Question — Segregation of duties

Explain the importance of segregation of duties.

Answer

Segregation of duties is important because the more people that are involved in all the stages of processing a transaction, the more likely it is that fraud or error by a single person will be identified. In addition the more people that are involved, the less the chances of fraudulent collusion between them.

Chapter roundup

- The external auditors must **understand** the **accounting system** and **control environment** in order to understand the entity and determine the audit approach.
- There are always inherent limitations to internal controls.
- There are special considerations for auditors when a system is computerised.
- The auditors must keep a record of the client's systems which must be updated each year.

Quick quiz

1. Complete the definition taking the words given below.

   ………………………… includes the governance and management functions and the……………, ………………… and ………… of those charged with …………… and management concerning the entity's internal ……… and its ……………… in the entity.

   > attitudes importance control environment awareness governance actions control

2. Name two **key** inherent limitations of an internal control system.

   (1) ……………………………………………

   (2) ……………………………………………

3. Put the controls below in the correct category.

Information processing controls	General controls

One for one checking	Virus checks	Hash totals
Segregation of duties	Passwords	Program libraries
Review of master files	Training	Controls over account deletions
Back-up copies	Record counts	Back-up power source

4. Explain one advantage and one disadvantage of using narrative notes to document internal control systems.

5. Explain one advantage and one disadvantage of using flowcharts to document internal control systems.

6. Describe the main purpose of an internal control questionnaire.

Answers to quick quiz

1 Control environment, attitude, awareness, action, governance, control, importance

2 Human error

   Possibility of staff colluding in fraud

3

Information processing controls	General controls
One for one checking	Virus checks
Hash totals	Program libraries
Review of master files	Segregation of duties
Record counts	Passwords
	Controls over account deletion
	Training
	Back-up power source
	Back-up copies

4 Advantages, any one from:

- Simple to record and can facilitate understanding by all audit team members
- Flexible and so can be used for any system
- Editing is easier if notes are computerised

Disadvantages, any one from:

- Time consuming to prepare, especially for a detailed system
- Missing internal controls may not be easily identified
- Difficult to update if written manually

5 Advantages, any one from:

- Quick for an experienced user to prepare
- Easy to follow and review
- Highlights salient processes and missing controls

Disadvantages, any one from:

- May not be suitable for non-standard systems
- Difficult to update unless redrawn

6 Internal control questionnaires comprise a list of questions which are designed to determine whether appropriate controls are present in an entity for each major transaction cycle (for example, sales, purchases).

End of chapter question

Internal control

(a) State the objective of a system of internal control. **(3 marks)**

(b) Internal and external auditors may review a system of internal control. Explain the reason for their reviews, distinguishing between them. **(7 marks)**

(Total = 10 marks)

Planning and risk

Topic list	Syllabus reference
1 Audit planning	4.5
2 Understanding the entity and its environment	4.3
3 Risk	5.2, 5.3, 5.4, 5.5
4 Assessing the risk of material misstatement	5.2, 5.3, 5.4, 5.5
5 Responding to the risks of material misstatement	5.2, 5.3, 5.4, 5.5
6 Materiality	4.4
7 Fraud, laws and regulations	5.2, 5.3, 5.4, 5.5
8 Quality management	4.8, 6.9

Introduction

This chapter covers the aspects of the audit which will be considered at the earliest stages, during planning. It is unlikely that you will have direct experience of planning an audit, but you should acquaint yourself with all the planning documentation on any audit you attend.

Key points this chapter covers which you must understand are:

- The **purposes of planning**
- The importance of **understanding the entity and its environment**
- Using that understanding to **assess the risks** of material misstatement and **plan further procedures**

The auditor also needs to consider the risks of fraud and non-compliance with law and regulations in the audit.

1 Audit planning

FAST FORWARD

The auditors formulate an **overall audit strategy** which is translated into a **detailed audit plan** for audit staff to follow.

1.1 The importance of planning

An effective and efficient audit relies on proper planning procedures. The planning process is covered in general terms by ISA 300 *Planning an Audit of Financial Statements* which states that the auditor shall plan the audit so that the engagement is performed in an **effective manner**.

Audits are planned to:

- Help the auditor **devote appropriate attention to important areas** of the audit.
- Help the auditor **identify and resolve potential problems on a timely basis**.
- Help the auditor properly organise and manage the audit so it is performed in an **effective manner**.
- Assist in the **selection of appropriate team members and assignment of work** to them.
- Facilitate the **direction, supervision and review** of work.
- Assist in **coordination of work** done by auditors of components and experts.

Audit procedures should be discussed with the client's management, staff and/or audit committee in order to co-ordinate audit work, including that of internal audit. However, all audit procedures remain the responsibility of the external auditors.

A structured approach to planning will include:

Step 1 Ensuring that ethical requirements are met, including independence

Step 2 Ensuring the terms of the engagement are understood

Step 3 Establishing the overall audit strategy that sets the scope, timing and direction of the audit and guides the development of the audit plan.

- Identify the characteristics of the engagement that define its scope.
- Ascertain the reporting objectives to plan the timing of the audit and nature of communications required.
- Consider significant factors in directing the team's efforts.
- Consider results of preliminary engagement activities.
- Ascertain nature, timing and extent of resources necessary to perform the engagement.

Step 4 Developing an audit plan that includes the nature, timing and extent of planned risk assessment procedures and further audit procedures

1.2 The audit strategy and the audit plan

FAST FORWARD

The audit strategy and audit plan shall be updated and changed as necessary during the course of the audit.

1.2.1 The audit strategy

Key term

The **audit strategy** sets the scope, timing and direction of the audit, and guides the development of the more detailed audit plan.

7: PLANNING AND RISK

The matters the auditor may consider in establishing an overall **audit strategy** are set out in the table below.

The audit strategy: matters to consider	
Characteristics of the engagement	• Financial reporting framework • Industry-specific reporting requirements • Expected audit coverage • Nature of business segments • Availability of internal audit work • Use of service organisations • Effect of information technology on audit procedures • Availability of client personnel and data
Reporting objectives, timing of the audit and nature of communications	• Entity's timetable for reporting • Organisation of meetings with management and those charged with governance • Discussions with management and those charged with governance • Expected communications with third parties
Significant factors, preliminary engagement activities, and knowledge gained on other engagements	• Determination of materiality • Areas identified with higher risk of material misstatement • Results of previous audits • Need to maintain professional scepticism • Evidence of management's commitment to design, implementation and maintenance of sound internal control • Volume of transactions • Significant business developments • Significant industry developments • Significant changes in financial reporting framework • Other significant recent developments
Nature, timing and extent of resources	• Selection of engagement team • Assignment of work to team members • Engagement budgeting

1.2.2 The audit plan

Key term

The **audit plan** converts the audit strategy into a more detailed plan and includes the nature, timing and extent of audit procedures to be performed by engagement team members in order to obtain sufficient appropriate audit evidence to reduce audit risk to an acceptably low level.

The audit plan shall include the following:

- A description of the nature, timing and extent of planned risk assessment procedures
- A description of the nature, timing and extent of planned further audit procedures at the assertion level
- Other planned audit procedures required to be carried out for the engagement to comply with ISAs

The planning for these procedures occurs over the course of the audit as the audit plan develops.

Any changes made during the audit engagement to the overall audit strategy or audit plan, and the reasons for such changes, shall be included in the audit documentation.

2 Understanding the entity and its environment

FAST FORWARD The auditor is required to **obtain an understanding of the entity and its environment** in order to be able to assess the risks of material misstatements.

2.1 Obtaining an understanding

ISA 315 (Revised) *Identifying and Assessing the Risks of Material Misstatement* states that:

> 'The objective of the auditor is to identify and assess the risks of material misstatement, whether due to fraud or error, at the financial statement and assertion levels thereby providing a basis for designing and implementing responses to the assessed risks of material misstatement.'

(ISA 315 (Revised), para. 11)

In order to be able to do this, the auditor needs to have a clear understanding of the entity they will audit.

Summary: Obtaining an understanding of the entity and its environment	
Why?	<ul><li>To identify and assess the risks of material misstatement in the financial statements through performing risk assessment procedures</li><li>To enable the auditor to design and perform further audit procedures</li><li>To provide a frame of reference for exercising audit judgement, for example, when setting audit materiality</li></ul>
What?	<ul><li>Industry, regulatory and other external factors, including the reporting framework</li><li>Nature of the entity, including operation, ownership, investments, finance</li><li>Selection and application of accounting policies</li><li>Objectives and strategies and relating business risks that might cause material misstatement in the financial statements</li><li>Measurement and review of the entity's financial performance</li><li>Internal control relevant to audit</li></ul>
How?	<ul><li>Inquiries of management and others within the entity</li><li>Analytical procedures</li><li>Observation and inspection</li><li>Prior period knowledge</li><li>Discussion of the susceptibility of the financial statements to material misstatement among the engagement team</li></ul>

As can be seen in the table above, the reasons the auditor is to obtain the understanding of the entity and its environment are very much bound up with assessing risks and exercising audit judgement. We shall look at these aspects more in the next two sections of this chapter.

2.2 What?

The ISA sets out a number of requirements about what the auditors must consider in relation to obtaining an understanding of the business. The general areas are shown in the following diagram.

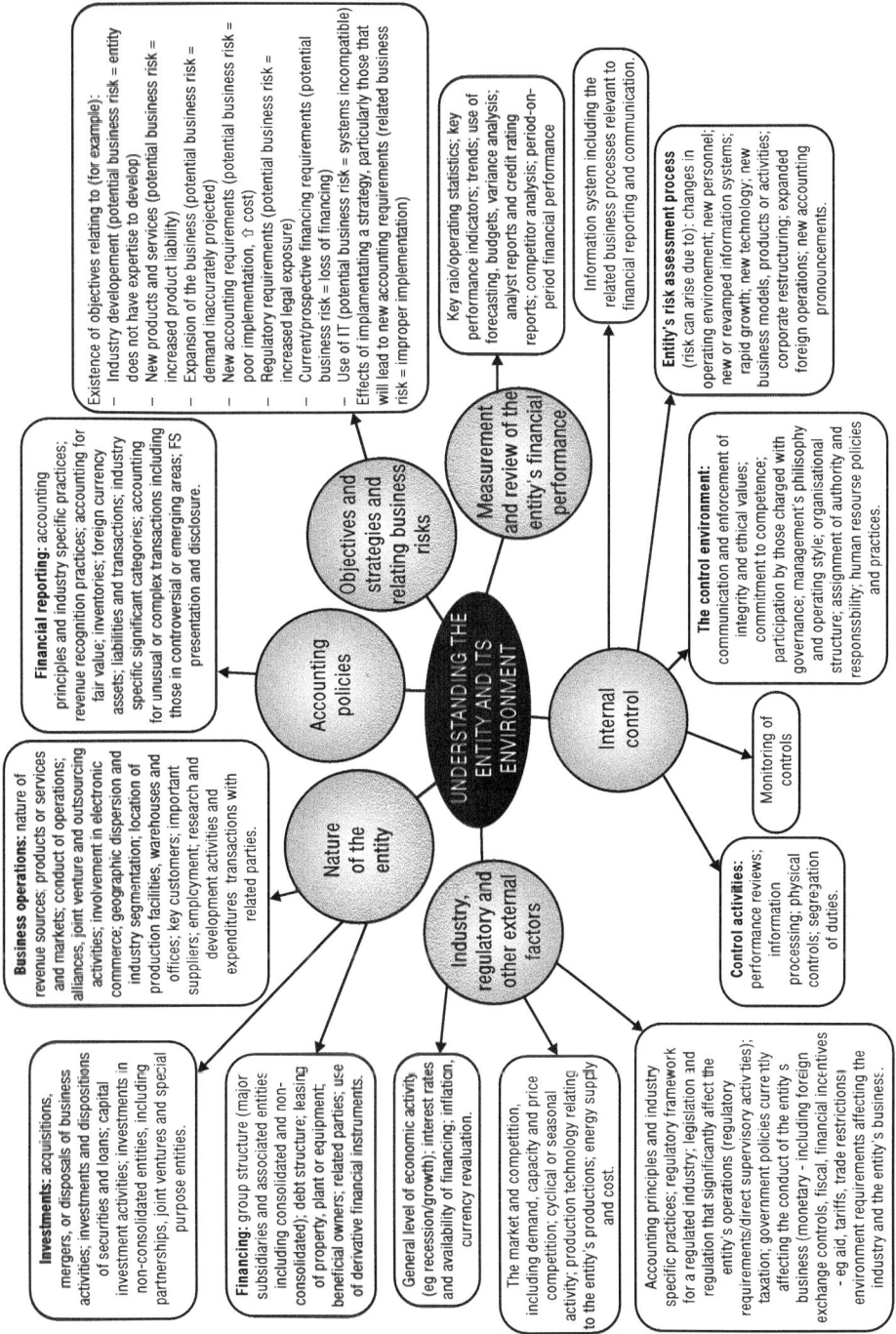

2.3 How?

ISA 315 (Revised) sets out the methods that the auditor **must** use when obtaining the understanding. The auditor does not have to use all of these for each area, but a combination of these procedures should be used. These are:

- **Inquiries** of management and others within the entity, including the **internal audit function**
- **Analytical procedures**
- **Observation and inspection**

(ISA 315 (Revised), para. 14)

The **audit team** is also required by ISA 315 (Revised) to **discuss the susceptibility of the financial statements to material misstatement**. Judgement must be exercised in determining which members of the team should be involved in which parts of the discussion, but all team members should be involved in the discussion relevant to the parts of the audit they will be involved in.

Lastly, if it is a recurring audit, the auditors may have obtained a great deal of knowledge about the entity and the environment in the course of prior year audits. The auditor is entitled to use this information in the current year audit, but he must make sure that he has determined whether any **changes** in the year have affected the relevance of information obtained in previous years.

2.3.1 Inquiries of management and others within the entity

The auditors will usually obtain most of the information they require from staff responsible for financial reporting, but may also need to make enquiries of other personnel, for example, internal audit, production staff or those charged with governance.

2.3.2 Examples

- Those charged with governance may give insight into the environment in which the financial statements are prepared.
- In-house legal counsel may help with understanding matters such as outstanding litigation, or compliance with laws and regulations.
- Sales and marketing personnel may give information about marketing strategies and sales trends.

2.3.3 Analytical procedures

Analytical procedures are a useful tool in risk assessment. They can also be used at other stages of the audit, and we discuss their other uses elsewhere in this Learning & Practice Workbook.

Key term

> **Analytical procedures** consist of the analysis of significant ratios and trends including the resulting investigations of fluctuations and relationships that are inconsistent with other relevant information or which deviate from predictable amounts.

Case Study

The following draft figures have been obtained by the auditors of Grey Co:

EXTRACT DRAFT FIGURES FOR YEAR ENDED 30 SEPTEMBER

	20X1 $	20X0 $
Revenue	6,408,279	7,794,301
Gross profit	2,412,797	2,897,686
Profit before interest and tax	527,112	501,556
Property, plant and equipment	308,947	352,001
Inventories	1,247,487	1,199,384
Receivables	1,491,498	1,792,635
Trade payables	998,123	1,050,754
Other current liabilities (incl. bank)	107,501	81,634

The auditors have calculated the following ratios as part of the planning process:

20X1

Gross profit margin $\quad \dfrac{2,412,797}{6,408,279} \times 100 \quad = 37.65\%$

Receivables collection period $\quad \dfrac{1,491,498}{6,408,279} \times 365 \quad = 85 \text{ days}$

Inventory holding period $\quad \dfrac{1,247,487}{(6,408,279 - 2,412,797)} \times 365 = 114 \text{ days}$

Current ratio $\quad \dfrac{1,247,487 + 1,491,498}{998,123 + 107,501} = 2.47$

Acid test ratio $\quad \dfrac{1,491,498}{998,123 + 107,501} = 1.35$

Return on capital employed $\quad \dfrac{527,112}{(308,947 + 1,247,487 + 1,491,498) - (998,123 + 107,501)} \times 100 = 27.1\%$

20X0

Gross profit margin $\quad \dfrac{2,897,686}{7,794,301} \times 100 \quad = 37.1\%$

Receivables collection period $\quad \dfrac{1,792,635}{7,794,301} \times 365 \quad = 84 \text{ days}$

Inventory holding period $\quad \dfrac{1,199,384}{(7,794,301 - 2,897,686)} \times 365 = 89 \text{ days}$

Current ratio $\quad \dfrac{1,199,384 + 1,792,635}{1,050,754 + 81,634} = 2.64$

Acid test ratio $\quad \dfrac{1,792,635}{1,050,754 + 81,634} = 1.58$

Return on capital employed $\quad \dfrac{501,556}{(352,001 + 1,199,384 + 1,792,635) - (1,050,754 + 81,634)} \times 100 = 22.7\%$

A comparison of the 20X1 and 20X0 figures shows the following areas which may need further investigation together with the additional work which would be included in the audit plan to address the issues identified.

Revenue

The figures show that there has been a drop in revenue of $1,386,022. The auditors would discuss this with the client. It could indicate several things:

- That the company has had a bad year in 20X1, with potential impact on the assessment of going concern
- That the company had a particularly good year in 20X0, and 20X1 is more representative of what the company expected
- A major customer has been lost
- There have been errors in recording sales
- Lack of completeness in the recording of sales
- Misclassification of sales

- Incorrect application of cut-off
- Inaccuracies (eg arithmetical) in the accounting records
- Possible fraud

The auditors should carry out further analysis to assess any explanations given to them by the client. For example, because the gross profit percentage and receivables collection period are similar to last year, that might indicate that there was not an error in sales recording.

Further work would be planned to include a more detailed substantive analytical review on the sales figure, by obtaining detailed analysis of sales by month and by product to see if this reveals any more answers about why the sales figure has dropped in 20X1.

Profit before interest and tax

The auditors might expect the profit before interest and tax figure to drop because the revenue figure has dropped by a significant amount compared to last year. However, the profit before interest and tax figure being approximately the same as it was in 20X0 could indicate several things:

- That the company has implemented cost saving measures and has made substantial savings in administrative expenses
- That there have been errors in recording expenses
- That the amount of interest payable by the company has reduced
- That management has tried to improve profit figures by not recording all relevant expenses for the year

The auditors should discuss this with the client to find out if any cost saving measures have been implemented or if there any other factors which could have resulted in a reduction in expenses. The auditors may also plan to perform detailed testing of expenses at the year end in order to make sure they have been captured in the correct period and not incorrectly recorded in the following year.

Receivables

The receivables collection period is consistent between 20X0 and 20X1 however the actual receivables figure has reduced by $301,137 compared to 20X0. This could indicate several things:

- There were fewer sales in the last few months of this year compared to last year, so there are fewer outstanding receivables at the year end.
- Customers are paying more quickly than they did in the previous year, so there are fewer outstanding receivables at the year end.
- There have been errors in recording sales and receivables.

The auditors should discuss this with the client and plan to perform further analysis based on the results of the detailed month by month revenue testing. The auditors would also plan to perform a more detailed analysis on the age of outstanding receivables compared to last year in order to see if this reveals any more information about why receivables have fallen.

Inventories

The inventories figure has increased slightly compared with 20X0, however the inventory holding period has increased from 89 days to 114 days. The rise in inventory holding period could be due to:

- A reduction in the total number of products sold
- Incorrect valuation of inventories at the year end
- An error in the cost of sales or inventories figures

The auditors should discuss this with the client and could perform further analysis based on the results of the detailed revenue testing. The auditors would also plan to perform additional procedures around the valuation of inventories, as well as carefully reviewing the results of the inventory count testing performed at the year end to check that inventory was counted accurately.

2.3.4 Observation and inspection

These techniques are likely to confirm the answers made to inquiries made of management. They will include observing the normal operations of a company, reading documents or manuals relating to the client's operations or visiting premises and meeting staff.

3 Risk

3.1 Professional scepticism

FAST FORWARD

Auditors are required to carry out the audit with **professional scepticism**.

Key term

Professional scepticism is an attitude that includes a questioning mind, being alert to conditions which might indicate a possible misstatement due to fraud or error, and a critical assessment of evidence.

ISA 200 *Overall Objectives of the Independent Auditor and the Conduct of an Audit in Accordance with International Standards on Auditing* states that auditors shall plan and perform an audit with an attitude of **professional scepticism** recognising that circumstances may exist that cause the financial statements to be materially misstated.

This requires the auditor to:

- Make a critical assessment, with an inquiring mind, of the validity of audit evidence obtained.
- Be alert to audit evidence that contradicts or brings into question the reliability of documents or representations from management.
- Neither assume that management is dishonest or assume unquestioned honesty.

3.2 Overall audit risk

Auditors usually follow a **risk-based approach** to auditing as required by ISAs. In this approach, auditors analyse the risks associated with the client's business, transactions and systems which could lead to misstatements in the financial statements, and direct their testing to risky areas. This is in contrast to a procedural approach which is not in accordance with ISAs.

3.3 Audit risk

FAST FORWARD

Audit risk is the risk that the auditor expresses **an inappropriate audit opinion** when the financial statements are materially misstated. It is a function of the risk of material misstatement (**inherent risk** and **control risk**) and the risk that the auditor will not detect such misstatement (**detection risk**).

Key term

Audit risk is the risk that the auditor expresses an inappropriate audit opinion when the financial statements are materially misstated.

Audit risk has two elements, the risk that the **financial statements contain a material misstatement** and the risk that the **auditors will fail to detect** any material misstatements.

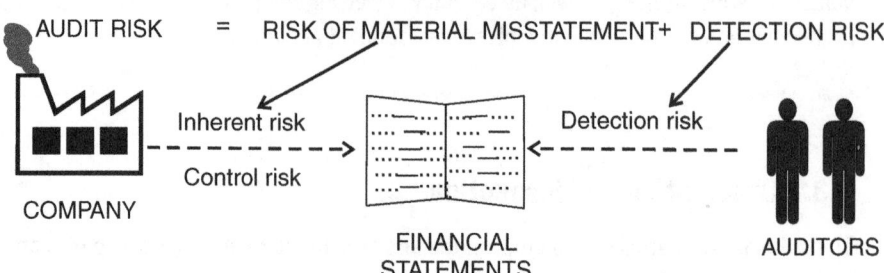

Audit risk has two major components. One is dependent on the entity, and is the risk of material misstatement arising in the financial statements (**inherent risk** and **control risk**). The other is dependent on the auditor, and is the risk that the auditor will not detect material misstatements in the financial statements (**detection risk**). We shall look in detail at the concept of materiality in the next section of this chapter. Audit risk can be represented by the **audit risk model**:

Formula to learn

> Audit risk = inherent risk × control risk × detection risk

3.3.1 Inherent risk

Key term

> **Inherent risk** is the **susceptibility** of an assertion about a class of transaction, account balance or disclosure to a **misstatement** that could be material either individually or when aggregated with other misstatements, **before consideration of any related internal controls**.
>
> (ISA 200: para. 13(ni))

Inherent risk is the risk that items will be misstated due to the characteristics of those items, such as the fact they are estimates or that they are important items in the accounts. The auditors must use their professional judgement and all available knowledge to assess inherent risk. If no such information or knowledge is available then the inherent risk is **high**.

Inherent risk is affected by the **nature of the entity**; for example, the industry it is in and the regulations it falls under, and also the nature of the strategies it adopts. We shall look at more examples of inherent risks later in this chapter.

3.3.2 Control risk

The other element of the risk of material misstatements in the financial statements is control risk.

Key term

> **Control risk** is the **risk that a material misstatement** that could occur in an assertion about a class of transaction, account balance or disclosure and that could be material, either individually or when aggregated with other misstatements, **will not be prevented, or detected and corrected**, on a timely basis by the entity's **internal control**.
>
> (ISA 200: para. 13(nii))

We looked at control risk in detail in Chapter 6 when we discussed internal controls.

3.3.3 Detection risk

Key term

> **Detection risk** is the risk that the **procedures performed by the auditor** to reduce audit risk to an acceptable level **will not detect a misstatement** that exists and that could be material, either individually or when aggregated with other misstatements.
>
> (ISA 200: para. 13e)

The third element of audit risk is detection risk. This is the component of audit risk that the auditors have a degree of control over, because, if risk is too high to be tolerated, the auditors can carry out more work to reduce this aspect of audit risk, and therefore audit risk as a whole.

Detection risk has two components: **sampling risk** and **non-sampling risk**. We look at these in Chapter 8 in the context of sampling.

3.4 Management of audit risk

ISA 200 makes the point that in order to obtain reasonable assurance on the financial statements, 'the auditor must plan and perform the audit to reduce audit risk to an acceptably low level'.

Auditors will want their overall audit risk to be at an acceptable level, or it will not be worth them carrying out the audit. In other words, if the chance of them giving an inappropriate opinion and being sued is high, it might be better not to do the audit at all.

The auditors will obviously consider how risky a new audit client is during the acceptance process, and may decide not to go ahead with the relationship. However, they will also consider audit risk for each individual audit, and will seek to manage the risk.

As we have seen above, it is not in the auditors' power to affect inherent or control risk. These are risks integral to the client, and the auditor cannot change the level of these risks.

The auditors therefore manage overall audit risk by manipulating detection risk, the only element of audit risk over which they have control. This is because the more audit work the auditors carry out, the lower detection risk becomes, although it can never be entirely eliminated due to the inherent limitations of audit.

The auditors will decide what level of overall risk is acceptable, and then determine a level of audit work so that detection risk is as low as possible.

It is important to understand that there is not a standard level of audit risk which is generally considered by auditors to be acceptable. This is a matter of **audit judgement**, and so will vary from firm to firm and audit to audit. Audit firms are likely to charge higher fees for higher risk clients. Regardless of the risk level of the audit, however, it is vital that audit firms always carry out an audit of **sufficient quality**.

Question — Audit risk

Hippo Co is a long established client of your firm. It manufactures bathroom fittings and fixtures, which it sells to a range of wholesalers, on credit.

You are the audit senior and have recently been sent the following extract from the draft statement of financial position by the finance director.

	Budget		Actual	
	$'000s	$'000s	$'000s	$'000s
Non-current assets		453		367
Current assets				
Trade receivables	1,134		976	
Bank	–		54	
Current liabilities				
Trade payables	967		944	
Bank overdraft	9		–	

During the course of your conversation with the finance director, you establish that a major new customer the company had included in its budget went bankrupt during the year.

Required

Identify any potential risks for the audit of Hippo and explain why you believe they are risks.

Answer

Potential risks relevant to the audit of Hippo

(1) **Credit sales**. Hippo makes sales on credit. This increases the risk that Hippo's sales will not be converted into cash. Trade receivables is likely to be a risky area and the auditors will have to consider what the best evidence that customers are going to pay is likely to be. This is further evidenced by the fact that one customer has gone bankrupt during the year.

(2) **Related industry**. Hippo manufactures bathroom fixtures and fittings. These are sold to wholesalers, but it is possible that Hippo's ultimate market is the building industry. This can be a volatile industry, and Hippo may find that their results fluctuate too, as demand rises and falls. This suspicion is added to by the bankruptcy of the wholesaler in the year. The auditors must be sure that accounts which present Hippo as a viable company are in fact correct.

(3) **Controls**. The fact that a major new customer went bankrupt suggests that Hippo did not undertake a very thorough credit check on that customer before agreeing to supply them. This implies that the controls at Hippo may not be very strong.

(4) **Variance**. The actual results are different from budget. This may be explained by the fact that the major customer went bankrupt, or it may reveal that there are other errors and problems in the reported results, or in the original budget.

(5) **Bankrupt wholesaler**. There is a risk that the result reported contains balances due from the bankrupt wholesaler, which are likely to be irrecoverable.

3.5 Business risk

The other major category of risk which the auditor must be aware of is **business risk**. As you saw in Chapter 6 when we looked at internal controls, the auditor is required to consider the company's process of business risk management.

We briefly introduced the concept of business risk in Chapter 6. Remember business risks are risks that may stop the company achieving its financial goals and objectives.

Exam focus point

> It is important that you do not confuse the concepts of audit and business risks. Remember – audit risk is focused on the **financial statements** of a company, whereas business risk is related to the company as a whole. If an exam question asks you to identify audit risks, make sure you explain them in relation to the financial statements. Conversely, if a question focuses on business risks, you must answer in the context of business risks and the impact on the company and its operations, and not focus on the financial statements.

4 Assessing the risks of material misstatement

FAST FORWARD

> When the auditor has obtained an understanding of the entity, he must assess the risks of material misstatement in the financial statements, also identifying significant risks.

4.1 Identifying and assessing the risks

ISA 315 (Revised) says that 'the auditor shall design and perform risk assessment procedures to obtain audit evidence that provides an appropriate basis for the identification and assessment of **risks of material misstatement**, whether due to fraud or error, at the **financial statement** and **assertion levels**'. These risk assessment procedures are the procedures we have just outlined in obtaining an understanding of the entity.

ISA 315 (Revised) requires the auditor to take the following steps:

Step 1   Identify risks throughout the process of obtaining an understanding of the entity (as already set out).

Step 2   Assess the identified risks and whether they are pervasive to the financial statements.

Step 3   Relate the risks to what can go wrong at the assertion level taking account of the controls that the auditor intends to test.

Step 4   Consider the likelihood of the risks causing a misstatement and whether the risks are of a magnitude that could result in a material misstatement.

4.2 Example

The audit team at Ockey Co has been carrying out procedures to obtain an understanding of the entity. In the course of making inquiries about the inventories system, they have discovered that Ockey Co designs and produces tableware to order for a number of high street stores. It also makes a number of standard lines of tableware, which it sells to a number of wholesalers. By the terms of its contracts with the high street stores, it is not entitled to sell uncalled inventories designed for them to wholesalers. Ockey Co regularly produces 10% more than the high street stores have ordered, in order to ensure that they meet requirements when the stores do their quality control check. Certain stores have more stringent control requirements than others and regularly reject some of the inventories.

The knowledge above suggests two risks, one that the company may have obsolescent inventories, and the other that if their production quality standards are insufficiently high, they could run the risk of losing custom.

We shall look at each of these risks in turn and relate them to the assertion level.

Inventories

If certain of the inventories are obsolescent due to the fact that it has been produced in excess of the customer's requirement and there is no other available market for the inventory, then there is a risk that inventory as a whole in the financial statements will not be carried at the **appropriate value**. Given that inventory is likely to be a material balance in the statement of financial position of a manufacturing company, and the misstatement could be up to 10% of the total value, this has the capacity to be a material misstatement.

The factors that will contribute to the likelihood of these risks causing a misstatement are matters such as:

- Whether management regularly review inventory levels and scrap items that are obsolescent
- Whether such items are identified and scrapped at the inventory count
- Whether such items can be put back into production and changed so that they are saleable

Losing custom

The long-term risk of losing custom is a risk that in the future the company will not be able to operate (this is a going concern risk, which we shall look at in more detail in Chapter 17). It could have an impact on the financial statements, if disputed sales were attributed to customers, sales and trade receivables could be overstated, that is, not carried at the correct **value**. However, it appears less likely that this would be a material problem in either area, as the problem is likely to be restricted to a few number of customers, and only a few number of sales to those customers.

Again, review of the company's controls over the recording of sales and the debt collection procedures of the company would indicate how likely these risks to the financial statements are to materialise.

Question — Assessing the risks of material misstatement

You are involved with the audit of Tantpro Co, a small company. You have been carrying out procedures to gain an understanding of the entity. The following matters have come to your attention:

The company offers standard credit terms to its customers of 60 days from the date of invoice. Statements are sent to customers on a monthly basis. However, Tantpro Co does not employ a credit controller, and other than sending the statements on a monthly basis, it does not otherwise communicate with its customers on a systematic basis. On occasion, the receivables ledger clerk may telephone a customer if the company has not received a payment for some time. Some customers pay regularly according to the credit terms offered to them, but others pay on a very haphazard basis and do not provide a remittance advice. Receivables ledger receipts are entered onto the receivables ledger but not matched to invoices remitted. The company does not produce an aged list of balances.

Required

From the above information, assess the risks of material misstatement arising at in the financial statements and discuss factors in the likelihood of the risks arising.

Answer

The key risk arising from the above information is that trade receivables will not be carried at the appropriate **value** in the financial statements, as some may be irrecoverable but may not have been written off. Where receipts are not matched against invoices in the ledger, the balance on the ledger may include old invoices that the customer has no intention of paying.

A key factor that affects the likelihood of the material misstatement arising is the poor controls over the receivables ledger. The fact that invoices are not matched against receipts increases the chance of old invoices not having been paid and not noticed by Tantpro Co. It appears reasonably likely that the trade receivables balance is overstated in this instance.

4.3 Significant risks

FAST FORWARD

Significant risks are complex or unusual transactions, those that may indicate fraud or other special risks.

Once the auditor has obtained an understanding of the entity and its environment, they shall assess the risks of material misstatement in the financial statements and identify significant risks. Where a risk is identified as **significant**, it presents **special audit considerations** for the auditors.

Key term

A **significant risk** is an identified risk of material misstatement
- For which the **assessment of inherent risk** is close to the **upper end** of the **spectrum of inherent risk** due to the degree to which inherent risk factors affect the combination of the likelihood of a misstatement occurring and the magnitude of the potential misstatement should that misstatement occur; or
- That is to be treated as a significant risk in accordance with the requirements of other ISAs.

(ISA 315 (Revised): para. 12l)

The auditor will begin simply by identifying risks, but **will then need to consider how severe each risk is** in terms of the 'spectrum of inherent risk'. Significant risks are essentially the most severe risks.

7: PLANNING AND RISK

Routine, non-complex transactions are **less likely** to give rise to significant risks as client staff are likely to be more used to processing these transactions and such transactions are likely to be **subject to robust internal controls**.

Unusual and complex transactions and matters where **judgement** is required are **more likely** therefore **to pose significant risk**.

The ISA gives the following examples of the inherent risk factors (which we gave above, in the section 'Understanding the entity's system of internal control'). These are the kinds of things that could feature in an exam question and which you therefore need to be able to recognise as risks.

(ISA 315 (Revised): Appendix 2)

Risk factor	
Complexity	Regulatory – lots of **complex regulation**
	Business model – **complex alliances** and joint ventures
	Financial reporting framework – complex accounting measurements
	Transactions – complex arrangements (eg off-balance sheet finance)
Subjectivity	Financial reporting framework:
	• Wide range of possible accounting estimates (eg depreciation)
	• **Management choice** of valuation technique
Change	Changes in:
	Economic conditions – instability (eg current devaluation)
	Markets – exposure to volatility (eg futures trading)
	Customer loss – going concern/liquidity risk
	Industry model – changes in the industry in which the entity operates
	Business model – change in supply chain, new lines of business
	Geography – expanding into new locations
	Entity structure – for example reorganisations, subsidiaries sold
	IT – IT environment change/new IT systems relevant to FR
Uncertainty	Financial reporting – estimation uncertainty
	Pending litigation and contingent liabilities
Susceptibility to misstatement due to management bias or other fraud risk	**Opportunities** for fraudulent financial reporting
	Transactions with **related parties**
	Non-routine or non-systemic transactions
	Transactions recorded based on **management intentions**

Note that ISA 315 (Revised) requires the auditor to consider the risks of material misstatement relating to **both** those due to **error** and those due to **fraud**.

The risk relating to fraud can be significant and this is discussed later in this chapter in the section relating to ISA 240 *The Auditor's Responsibilities Relating to Fraud in an Audit of Financial Statements*. Similarly risks of material misstatement can occur due to an entity's non-compliance with laws and regulations, ISA 250 (Revised) *Consideration of Laws and Regulations in an Audit of Financial Statements* is also covered later in this chapter.

Exam focus point

RPQ students will need to be familiar with ISA (UK) 250A (Revised) *Consideration of Laws and Regulations in an Audit of Financial Statements*.

5 Responding to the risks of material misstatement

> **FAST FORWARD**
>
> The auditor must **formulate an approach** to assessed risks of material misstatement.

The main requirements of ISA 330 *The Auditor's Responses to Assessed Risks* are that 'the auditor shall design and implement overall responses to assessed risks of material misstatement at the financial statement level', and 'the auditor shall design and perform further audit procedures whose nature, timing and extent are based on and are responsive to assessed risks of material misstatement at the assertion level'.

In other words, having assessed the risks of material misstatements in the financial statements, the auditor has to **plan the work** that will be carried out **to ensure** that **they can give an opinion** that the financial statements give a true and fair view, that is, that any material misstatements have been identified and amended if necessary.

5.1 Overall responses

> **FAST FORWARD**
>
> **Overall responses** include issues such as emphasising to the team the importance of professional scepticism, allocating more staff, using experts or providing more supervision.

Overall responses to risks of material misstatement will be changes to the general audit strategy or re-affirmations to staff of the general audit strategy. For example:

- Emphasising to audit staff the need to maintain professional scepticism
- Assigning **additional or more experienced staff** to the audit team
- Providing **more supervision** on the audit
- Incorporating more unpredictability into the audit procedures
- Making general changes to the nature, timing or extent of audit procedures

The evaluation of the control environment that will have taken place as part of the assessment of the client's internal control systems will help the auditor determine whether they are going to take a substantive approach (focusing mainly on substantive procedures) or a combined approach (tests of controls and substantive procedures).

5.2 Responses to the risks of material misstatement at the assertion level

> **FAST FORWARD**
>
> The auditor must also determine **further audit procedures** to address the risks of material misstatement.

As noted above, the ISA says that the auditor should design and perform further audit procedures whose **nature, timing** and **extent** are responsive to the assessed risks of material misstatement at the assertion level. We will consider the extent of audit tests in Chapter 8 when we look at sampling. We shall discuss timing below. Nature refers to the purpose and the type of test that is carried out which we shall consider now.

5.2.1 Tests of controls

Tests of controls are carried out when:

- Auditors expect controls to operate effectively and intend to rely on them for the purposes of reducing substantive testing. (So, for example, if controls over sales and receivables were expected to operate effectively and auditors planned to test these classes of transaction by analytical procedures, auditors should test controls in that area.)

- Substantive procedures alone do not provide sufficient appropriate audit evidence (for example, if the entity conducts its business using IT systems which do not produce documentation of transactions).

In carrying out tests of controls, auditors must use **inquiry**, but must not only use inquiry. Other procedures must also be used. In testing controls, **reperformance** by the auditor will often be a helpful procedure, as will **inspection**.

When considering timing in relation to tests of controls, the purpose of the test will be important. For example, if the company carries out a year-end inventory count, controls over the inventory count can only be tested at the year-end. Other controls will operate all year, and the auditor may need to test that controls have been effective all year.

Some controls may have been tested in prior audits and the auditor may choose to rely on that evidence of their effectiveness. If this is the case, the auditor must obtain evidence about any changes since the controls were last tested and must test the controls if they have changed. In any case, controls should be tested for effectiveness at least once in every three audits.

If the related risk has been designated a significant risk, the auditor should not rely on testing carried out in prior years, but should carry out testing in the current year.

5.2.2 Substantive procedures

> **FAST FORWARD**
>
> Substantive procedures must be carried out on **material** items. There are also a number of substantive procedures that must be carried out on the preparation of the financial statements.

The auditor must always carry out substantive procedures on material items. The ISA says 'irrespective of the assessed risk of material misstatement, the auditor shall design and perform substantive procedures for each material class of transactions, account balance and disclosure'.

In addition, the auditor **must** carry out the following substantive procedures:

- Agreeing the financial statements to the underlying accounting records
- Examining material journal entries
- Examining other adjustments made in preparing the financial statements

As you know, substantive procedures fall into two categories: analytical procedures and other procedures (tests of detail). The auditor must determine when it is appropriate to use which type of substantive procedure.

Analytical procedures tend to be appropriate for large volumes of predictable transactions (for example, wages and salaries). **Other procedures (tests of detail)** may be appropriate to gain information about account balances (for example, inventory or trade receivables), particularly verifying the assertions of existence and valuation.

Tests of detail rather than analytical procedures are likely to be more appropriate with regard to matters which have been identified as **significant risks**, but the auditor must determine procedures that are specifically responsive to that risk, which may include analytical procedures. Significant risks are likely to be the most difficult to obtain sufficient appropriate evidence about.

5.2.3 Timing of substantive procedures and tests of controls

Auditors may carry out their audit work for one year in two or more sittings. When they do so, they call these sittings the **interim audit**(s) and the **final audit**.

Key terms

> The **final audit** is the main period of audit testing, when work is focused on the final financial statements.
>
> **Interim audits** are audits undertaken prior to the final audit, often during the period under review. The auditor is likely to carry out tests of controls at interim audits.

We have already highlighted the need for the auditors to obtain evidence that controls have operated effectively throughout the period. When the auditor obtains evidence about the operating effectiveness of controls during an interim period, the auditor must determine what additional audit evidence should be obtained for the remaining period.

The ISA makes a similar observation with regard to substantive procedures. When substantive procedures are performed at an interim date, the auditor should perform further substantive procedures or substantive procedures combined with tests of controls to cover the remaining period that provide a reasonable basis for extending the audit conclusions from the interim date to the period end.

5.3 Documentation

The need for auditors to document their audit work was discussed in the previous chapter, when we looked at ISA 230 *Audit Documentation*. In this chapter we have referred to two key audit documents: the audit strategy and the audit plan. ISAs 315 (Revised) and 330 contain a number of specific requirements about documentation, and we shall briefly run through those here.

The following matters should be documented:

- The discussion among the audit team concerning the susceptibility of the financial statements to material misstatements, including any significant decisions reached
- Key elements of the understanding gained of the entity including the elements of the entity and its control specified in the ISA as mandatory, the sources of the information gained and the risk assessment procedures carried out
- The identified and assessed risks of material misstatement
- Significant risks identified and related controls evaluated
- The overall responses to address the risks of material misstatement
- Nature, extent and timing of further audit procedures linked to the assessed risks at the assertion level
- If the auditors have relied on evidence about the effectiveness of controls from previous audits, conclusions about how this is appropriate

6 Materiality

FAST FORWARD

> **Materiality** should be calculated at the planning stages of all audits. The calculation or estimation of materiality should be based on experience and **judgement**.

We discussed materiality briefly in Chapter 1. Remember it relates to the level of misstatement that affects the decisions of users of the accounts.

Key term

> **Material:** Information is **material** if its omission or misstatement could reasonably be expected to influence the economic decisions of users taken on the basis of the financial statements.

ISA 320 *Materiality in Planning and Performing an Audit,* requires auditors to set materiality when establishing the strategy for the audit. The assessment of materiality at this stage should be based on the most recent and reliable financial information and will help to determine an effective and efficient audit approach.

The materiality assessment will help the auditors to decide:

- **How many** and **what items** to examine
- Whether to use **sampling techniques**
- What **level of misstatement** is likely to lead to a modified audit opinion

When putting together the audit plan, the auditors should set performance materiality.

Key term

> **Performance materiality** is the amount or amounts set by the auditor at less than materiality for the financial statements as a whole (or individual balances if materiality has been set differently for them) to reduce to an appropriately low level the probability that the aggregate of uncorrected and undetected misstatements exceeds materiality for the financial statements as a whole.

As auditors are testing a sample of items, there is obviously a risk that misstatements will be undetected by them. Auditors set performance materiality to ensure that undetected misstatements cannot be material to the financial statements.

The resulting combination of audit procedures should help to reduce audit risk to an appropriately low level. This is how risk and materiality are closely connected. The value of discovered misstatements should be aggregated at the end of the audit to ensure the total is still below tolerable misstatement (as defined when we look at sampling). **Performance materiality** may be set at planning materiality, but it is usually reduced to, say 75% or even 50% of planning materiality so as to take account of sampling risk.

6.1 Audit judgement in setting materiality

To set the materiality level the auditors need to decide the level of misstatement which would distort the view given by the accounts. This is a matter of audit **judgement**. There are several factors auditors will consider when setting benchmarks:

- Elements of the financial statements (profit, assets, revenue etc)
- Whether there are key elements in the financial statements for users (for example, profit)
- The nature of the entity
- The ownership structure and finance
- The relative volatility of the benchmark chosen

The auditors may then set a percentage of the benchmark – for example 5% of profit.

Note that the auditors will often calculate a range of values, such as those shown below, and then take an average or weighted average of all the figures produced as the materiality level.

Value	%
Profit before tax	5
Gross profit	½–1
Revenue	½–1
Total assets	1–2
Net assets	2–5
Profit after tax	5–10

Materiality can be thought of in terms of the size of the business. Hence, if the company remains a fairly constant size, the materiality level should not change; similarly if the business is growing, the level of materiality will increase from year to year.

The size of a company can be measured in terms of turnover and total assets before deducting any liabilities both of which tend not to be subject to the fluctuations which may affect profit.

However, bear in mind that **materiality has qualitative, as well as quantitative**, aspects. You must not simply think of materiality as being a percentage of items in the financial statements.

This is why planning and performance materiality may be set differently for different balances and classes of transactions in the financial statements, depending on factors such as:

- Legal or reporting framework requirements relating to that matter
- Key disclosures in the industry
- Unusual matters in the financial statements (such as an acquisition)

For example, in the UK, matters relating to directors in financial statements are usually considered material due to the legal disclosures relating to directors' remuneration.

Audit materiality and performance materiality should be documented in the audit strategy.

6.2 Review of materiality

FAST FORWARD

Materiality should be reviewed during the audit.

The level of materiality must be reviewed constantly as the audit progresses and **changes** may be required because:

- **Draft accounts** are **altered** (due to material misstatement and so on) and therefore overall materiality changes.
- **External factors cause changes** in the control or inherent risk estimates.
- Such changes are caused by **misstatements** found during testing.

If these changes require a change in performance materiality, the auditor should adjust performance materiality and extend audit testing as required by that. Changes to audit materiality and performance materiality should be documented.

6.3 Sustainability - materiality considerations

We saw in chapter 1 that many entities now include sustainability and climate-related disclosures in their annual report in response to the demand for such information from investors and other users of financial information.

All entities are **exposed to climate-related risks** as they may affect the supply and demand for their goods and services and therefore inventory valuation; expose an entity to fines or penalties from regulatory breaches; and even impact an entity's going concern. As such the auditor should consider climate-related risks when determining materiality and performance materiality, in terms of both **quantitative and qualitative materiality**.

In their IFRS Sustainability Disclosure Standards, the International Sustainability Standards Boards (ISSB) has stated:

Key term

> An entity shall **disclose material information** about the **sustainability-related risks and opportunities** that could reasonably be expected to affect the entity's prospects.
>
> In the context of sustainability-related financial disclosures, **information is material** if omitting, misstating or obscuring that information **could reasonably be expected to influence decisions** that primary users of general purpose financial reports make on the basis of those reports, which include financial statements and sustainability-related financial disclosures and which provide information about a specific reporting entity.
>
> (IFRS S1: paras. 17-18)

This definition is broadly in line with the financial view of materiality in ISA 320 and is also helpful to auditors and assurance providers as the popularity of sustainability-related assurance increases.

6.3.1 Double materiality

When reporting on sustainability an entity should consider two perspectives: the sustainability risks and opportunities that might impact the entity but also the impact the entity may have on the environment within which it operates.

The European Union's Corporate Sustainability Reporting Directive (CSRD) is a highly impactful regulation that requires entities to identify its **material sustainability impacts, risks and opportunities**. This approach is known as a **double materiality** assessment which broadens the concept of materiality beyond traditional **financial materiality** and considers the entity's impact on stakeholders and society (**impact materiality**).

> **Key term**
>
> **Double materiality** means considering not only the sustainability issues that might create financial risks for the company (financial materiality), but also those sustainability issues where a company's activities materially impact on people and the environment (impact materiality).
>
> **Financial materiality:** This view focuses on how sustainability matters may pose either a prospective material risk or opportunity that could affect a company's financial performance and position over the short, medium and long term. Sustainability matters are considered material for primary users of a company's financial reports if omitting or misstating the information **could influence the users' decisions**.
>
> **Impact materiality:** This view focuses on the actual or potential short, medium and long-term **impacts** on people or the environment that are directly linked to a company's operations and its value chain. These impacts can be **both positive and negative**.

This is illustrated in the diagram below:

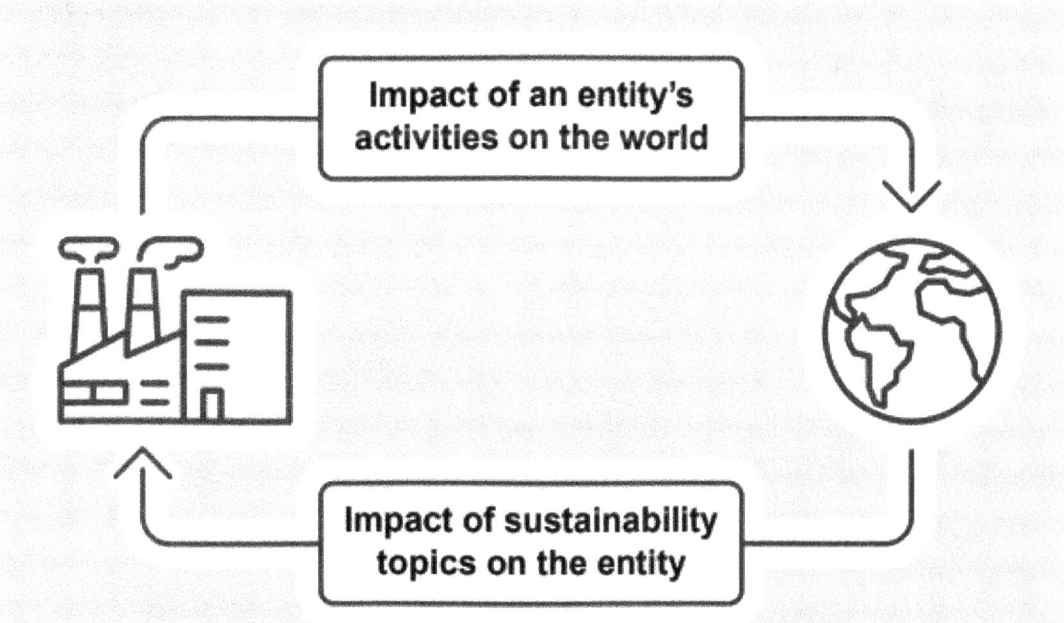

Source: https://www.globalreporting.org/media/rz1jf4bz/gri-double-materiality-final.pdf

7 Fraud, laws and regulations

FAST FORWARD

When carrying out risk assessment procedures, the auditors should also consider the risk of **fraud** and **non-compliance with law and regulations** causing a misstatement in financial statements.

7.1 What is fraud?

Key term

Fraud is an **intentional act** by one or more individuals among management, those charged with governance (management fraud), employees (employee fraud) or third parties involving the use of deception to obtain an unjust or illegal advantage (ISA 240: para. 11(a)).

Fraud may be perpetrated by an individual, or **colluded** in, with people internal or external to the business.

Fraud **risk factors** are events or conditions that indicate an incentive or pressure to commit fraud or provide an opportunity to commit fraud (ISA 240: para. 11(b)).

As we discussed earlier, it is **primarily** the **responsibility of those charged with governance of the entity and management** to **prevent and detect fraud**. This responsibility is discharged **through the use of internal controls**, such as segregation of duties, and having **an internal audit function.**

ISA 240 *The Auditor's Responsibilities Relating to Fraud in an Audit of Financial Statements* states that the **auditor** is responsible for **obtaining reasonable assurance that the financial statements are free from material misstatement, whether caused by fraud or error** (ISA 240: para. 5).

Therefore the **auditor's main concern** is with **fraud** that **causes a material misstatement** in the financial statements. Fraud is distinguished from error, which is when a material misstatement is caused by mistake, for example, in the misapplication of an accounting policy.

It is **not** the **auditors' responsibility to prevent and detect fraud** per se. However ISA 240 clearly places a responsibility on auditors to detect fraud which would have a **material** impact on the financial statements of an entity.

It should be noted that there is a common misconception held by the public in relation to the responsibilities of the auditor in relation to the prevention and detection of fraud. Many members of the public assume this role falls to the auditor, whereas we have seen that the primary responsibility rests with those charged with governance, and that the auditors are responsible for obtaining reasonable assurance that the financial statements are free from material misstatement whether caused by fraud or error. This misconception is called the '**expectations gap**'.

There are two types of fraud causing material misstatement in financial statements:

- **Fraudulent financial reporting**
- **Misappropriation of assets**

7.1.1 Fraudulent financial reporting

This may include:

- Manipulation, falsification or alteration of accounting records/supporting documents
- Misrepresentation (or omission) of events or transactions in the financial statements
- Intentional misapplication of accounting principles

Such fraud may be carried out by overriding controls that would otherwise appear to be operating effectively, for example, by recording fictitious journal entries or improperly adjusting assumptions or estimates used in financial reporting.

7.1.2 Misappropriation of assets

This is the **theft of the entity's assets** (for example, cash, inventory). Employees may be involved in such fraud in small and immaterial amounts, however, it can also be carried out by management for larger items who may then conceal the misappropriation, for example by:

- Embezzling receipts (for example, diverting them to private bank accounts)
- Stealing physical assets or intellectual property (inventory, selling data)
- Causing an entity to pay for goods not received (payments to fictitious vendors)
- Using assets for personal use

7.2 Responsibilities with regard to fraud

7.2.1 Responsibilities of those charged with governance

Those charged with governance of the entity and management are **primarily** responsible for **preventing and detecting fraud**. It is up to them to put a strong emphasis within the company on fraud prevention.

They should take reasonable steps to prevent and detect fraud. This includes:

- Ensuring that the activities of the company are conducted honestly and that its **assets are safeguarded**.
- Implementing **procedures designed to deter fraudulent or other dishonest conduct** and to detect any that occurs.
- Ensuring that, to the best of their knowledge and belief, financial information is reliable.

To prevent and detect fraud, those charged with governance and management should:

- Develop an appropriate **control environment** within the company;
- Implement a Code of Conduct which is clearly communicated to employees, monitor compliance and take appropriate disciplinary action in cases of non-compliance; and
- Implement **systems of internal control**, regularly monitoring their effectiveness and taking corrective action where necessary.

As discussed in Chapter 3, an **internal audit function** and an **audit committee** will help those charged with governance and management to meet their responsibilities with regards to detecting and preventing fraud.

Since it is the responsibility of those charged with governance of the entity and management to prepare financial statements that give a true and fair view of the state of affairs of the company, where material error or fraud has occurred, they must correct the accounting records and ensure that the matter is appropriately reflected and/or disclosed in the financial statements.

7.2.2 Auditor's responsibilities

Auditors are responsible for carrying out an audit in accordance with international auditing standards, one of which is ISA 240 *The Auditor's Responsibilities Relating to Fraud in an Audit of Financial Statements*, the details of which we shall look at now.

The auditors' approach to the possibility of fraud is similar to the approach to the possibility of misstatement, which we have already considered at length in this chapter. The objectives of ISA 240 are as follows:

(a) To **identify and assess the risks of material misstatement** of the financial statements **due to fraud**

(b) To **obtain sufficient appropriate audit evidence** regarding the assessed risks of material misstatement due to fraud

(c) To **respond appropriately** to fraud or suspected fraud identified during the audit

An overriding requirement of the ISA is that auditors are aware of the possibility of there being misstatements due to fraud. The team must have **professional scepticism** and must discuss the possibility of material misstatements due to fraud (how fraud could be perpetrated and by whom, how unpredictability could be added into the audit).

7.2.3 Risk assessment procedures

The **auditor would undertake risk assessment procedures** as set out in ISA 315 (Revised) (discussed in section 4) which would include assessing the risk of fraud. These procedures will include:

- Inquiries of management, those charged with governance and internal auditors (where present)
- Evaluation of fraud risk factors present
- Consideration of unusual or unexpected results of analytical procedures
- Consideration of any other relevant information that indicates risk of material misstatement due to fraud

In identifying the risks of fraud, the auditor is required by the ISA to make specific enquiries of management regarding fraud (for example, what they think the risk is, what their process for identifying and responding to fraud is, management communications on the topic).

Auditors are also required to enquire of management, internal audit or others whether any alleged, actual or suspected fraud has taken place.

Lastly, while obtaining their understanding of the entity, they should consider whether any fraud risk factors are present.

For example, management may have an incentive to report fraudulently if profitability is threatened by market conditions or as a result of new accounting standards, alternatively there may be pressure to meet certain targets to impress shareholders or keep funding.

Alternatively, fraudulent financial reporting could take place because the nature of the entity makes fraud more straightforward for example, if there are significant related parties or the entity is badly managed and there are few controls.

Fraud by misappropriation might be caused by unhappy employees, or opportunities arising out of poor internal controls or because the culture of the organisation is wrong and 'everybody does it'.

The auditors should be alert for evidence of incentives or opportunities for management or employees to carry out frauds.

The process is similar to that set out in ISA 315 (Revised). The auditor:

- Identifies fraud risks
- Relates this to what could go wrong at a financial statement level
- Considers the likely magnitude of potential misstatement
- Comes up with responses to the assessed risks.

The auditor must come up with overall responses and specific procedures to answer the risks of fraud in the audit.

7.3 Reporting

The ISA states:

> 'If the auditor has identified a fraud or has obtained information that indicates that a fraud may exist, the auditor shall communicate these matters on a timely basis to the appropriate level of management in order to inform those with primary responsibility for the prevention and detection of fraud of matters relevant to their responsibilities'.

In addition, 'if the auditor has identified or suspects fraud involving:

- Management
- Employees who have significant roles in internal control, or
- Others, where the fraud results in a material misstatement in the financial statements

the auditor shall communicate these matters to **those charged with governance** on a timely basis.'

The auditor should also make relevant parties within the entity aware of material weaknesses in the design or implementation of controls to prevent and detect fraud which have come to the auditor's attention, and consider whether there are any other relevant matters to bring to the attention of those charged with governance with regard to fraud.

The auditor may have a **statutory duty** to report fraudulent behaviour to **regulators** outside the entity. For example, in the UK, money laundering is covered by the Money Laundering Regulations 2017 (amended 2022). If no such legal duty arises, the auditor must consider whether to do so would breach his **professional duty of confidence**. In either event, the auditor should take **legal advice**.

7.4 Laws and regulations

The auditor is also required to consider the issue of laws and regulations in the audit. Auditors are given guidance in ISA 250 (Revised) *Consideration of Laws and Regulations in an Audit of Financial Statements*.

The **objectives** of the auditor are:

(a) To obtain sufficient appropriate audit evidence regarding compliance with the provisions of those laws and regulations that have a **direct effect** on the determination of material amounts and disclosures in the financial statements

(b) To perform specified audit procedures to help identify non-compliance with other laws and regulations that may have a **material effect** on the financial statements

(c) To respond appropriately to **identified or suspected non-compliance** with laws and regulations identified during the audit (ISA 250: para. 11)

7.4.1 Responsibilities of management and the auditor

It is **management's responsibility** to ensure that the entity **complies with the relevant laws and regulations** (ISA 250: para. 3).

The auditor's responsibility is to obtain reasonable assurance that the financial statements are free from material misstatement whether **due to fraud or error** and, in this respect, the auditor must take into account the legal and regulatory framework within which the entity operates (ISA 250: para. 5).

ISA 250 (para. 6) distinguishes the auditor's responsibilities in relation to compliance with two different categories of laws and regulations and paragraphs 14 and 15 set out the auditor's responsibilities as follows:

Category of laws and regulations	Auditor's responsibilities
The provisions of those laws and regulations that have a **direct effect** on the determination of **material amounts** and disclosures in the financial statements. For example: tax or pension laws and regulations (ISA 250: para. 6a)	The **auditor's responsibility** is to obtain **sufficient appropriate** audit evidence regarding **compliance** with the provisions of laws and regulations that have a **direct effect on the determination of material amounts and disclosures** those laws and regulations (ISA 250: para. 14).

Category of laws and regulations	Auditor's responsibilities
Other laws and regulations that **do not have a direct effect** on the determination of material amounts and disclosures in the financial statements but where compliance may be fundamental to the **operating aspects**, ability to **continue in business**, or to avoid **material penalties** For example: regulatory compliance or compliance with the terms of an operating licence (ISA 250: para. 6b)	The auditor's responsibility is to undertake specified audit procedures to help **identify non-compliance** with laws and regulations that may have a **material effect** on the financial statements. These include enquiries of management; and inspecting correspondence with the relevant licensing or regulatory authorities (ISA 240: para. 15).

7.4.2 Audit procedures

In accordance with ISA 315 (Revised), the auditor shall obtain a general understanding of:

- The applicable legal and regulatory framework
- How the entity complies with that framework

(ISA 250: para. 13)

The auditor can achieve this understanding by using their **existing understanding** and updating it, and making **enquiries of management** about other laws and regulations that may affect the entity, and about its policies and procedures for ensuring compliance and about its policies and procedures for identifying, evaluating and accounting for litigation claims.

The auditor shall remain alert throughout the audit to the possibility that **other audit procedures** may bring instances of non-compliance or suspected non-compliance to the auditor's attention. These audit procedures could include:

- Reading minutes
- Making enquiries of management and in-house/external legal advisers regarding litigation, claims and assessments
- Performing substantive tests of details of classes of transactions, account balances or disclosures

(ISA 250: para. A15)

The auditor shall request **written representations** from management that all known instances of non-compliance or suspected non-compliance with laws and regulations whose effects should be considered when preparing the financial statements have been disclosed to the auditor (ISA 250: para. 16).

7.4.3 Audit procedures when non-compliance is identified or suspected

The following factors may indicate non-compliance with laws and regulations:

- Investigations by regulatory authorities and government departments
- Payment of fines or penalties
- Payments for unspecified services or loans to consultants, related parties, employees or government employees
- Sales commissions or agents' fees that appear excessive
- Purchasing at prices significantly above/below market price
- Unusual payments in cash
- Unusual transactions with companies registered in tax havens

- Payment for goods and services made to a country different to the one in which the goods and services originated
- Payments without proper exchange control documentation
- Existence of an information system that fails to provide an adequate audit trail or sufficient evidence
- Unauthorised transactions or improperly recorded transactions
- Adverse media comment
- Matters raised by 'whistle-blowers'

(ISA 250: para. A17–18)

The following table summarises audit procedures to be performed when non-compliance is identified or suspected (ISA 250: para A20–25).

Non-compliance: audit procedures
Obtain an understanding of the nature of any acts and circumstances
Obtain further information to evaluate the possible effect on the financial statements
Discuss with management and those charged with governance unless laws and regulations in the jurisdiction concerned prohibit such communication (for example, avoiding tipping off in cases of suspected money laundering) meaning legal advice may need to be sought by the auditor before proceeding with such enquiries
Consider the need to obtain legal advice (or consult with others inside or connected to the firm) anyway if sufficient information is not provided and the matter is material
Evaluate the effect on the auditor's opinion if sufficient information is not obtained
Evaluate the implications of any identified or suspected non-compliance on risk assessment and the reliability of any written representations (especially if the auditor possesses evidence of either management or those charged with governance being involved in this non-compliance in some way)

7.4.4 Reporting identified or suspected non-compliance

The auditor shall communicate with **those charged with governance**, but, if the auditor suspects that those charged with governance are involved, the auditor shall communicate with the next highest level of authority, such as the **audit committee or supervisory board**. If this does not exist, the auditor shall consider the need to obtain **legal advice** (ISA 250: paras. 23–25). The auditor shall consider the impact of any identified or suspected non-compliance (including those related to other reporting responsibilities beyond ISAs and any associated with key audit matters) on the **auditor's report** if they conclude that the non-compliance has a material effect on the financial statements and has not been adequately reflected or is prevented by management and those charged with governance from obtaining sufficient appropriate audit evidence to evaluate whether non-compliance is material to the financial statements (ISA 250: paras. 26–28).

The auditor shall determine whether identified or suspected non-compliance has to be reported to **an appropriate authority outside the entity** in line with law, regulation or relevant ethical requirements. This responsibility requires the auditor to make an assessment of when it may be appropriate to report to such an authority (ISA 250: para. 29).

However, in some jurisdictions, reporting or communicating any identified or suspected non-compliance may be prohibited (for example, investigations into an entity by a regulatory authority which may be prejudiced by such disclosure). In any event, legal advice should be sought by the auditor when deciding on how best to discharge reporting and disclosure responsibilities (ISA 250: paras. A26–33).

If legally permitted, **withdrawal** from an audit engagement may be an option for an auditor who believes that any identified or suspected non-compliance is sufficient to raise questions about the client's **integrity**. However, this should only be undertaken after obtaining legal advice and **should not be seen as a way of avoiding other requirements** (such as informing an appropriate authority or even an incoming auditor) (ISA 250: para A25).

> **Exam focus point**
>
> RPQ students should be aware that ISA (UK) 250A (Revised) *Consideration of Laws and Regulations in an Audit of Financial Statements* highlights the link between itself and ISA 315 (Revised) when it emphasises that '**when performing risk assessment procedures and related activities** required by ISA (UK) 315 (Revised July 2020), to obtain an understanding of the entity and its environment, the applicable financial reporting framework and the entity's system of internal control, **the auditor shall consider whether there are any indications of non-compliance with laws and regulations**'.

8 Quality management

> **FAST FORWARD**
>
> ISA 220 (Revised) requires firms to implement quality management procedures over individual audit engagements.

The quality management of individual audits is governed by ISA 220 (Revised) *Quality Management for an Audit of Financial Statements*.

Auditors must implement quality management procedures for each individual audit engagement so that they have reasonable assurance that:

(a) The auditor has fulfilled the auditor's responsibilities, and has conducted the audit, in accordance with professional standards and applicable legal and regulatory requirements; and

(b) The auditor's report issued is appropriate in the circumstances.

(ISA 220 (Revised): para. 11)

8.1 Leadership responsibilities

The **engagement partner** has overall responsibility for managing and achieving quality within an audit engagement including taking responsibility for **creating an environment** for the engagement that emphasises the **firm's culture** and **expected behaviour of engagement team members**. In doing so, the engagement partner shall be sufficiently and appropriately involved throughout the audit engagement such that the engagement partner has the basis for **determining whether the significant judgements made, and the conclusions reached, are appropriate** given the nature and circumstances of the engagement (ISA 220 (Revised): para. 13).

Amongst other things the engagement partner shall ensure that all engagement team members understand that they are responsible for contributing to the management and achievement of quality at the engagement level and for **exercising professional scepticism** throughout the audit engagement.

8.2 Relevant ethical requirements

The engagement partner is responsible for ensuring ethical compliance. This includes identifying and addressing threats, evaluating any breaches and ensuring that engagement personnel take appropriate action (ISA 220 (Revised); paras. 17-21).

Note that ethical compliance includes compliance with the IESBA *Code*, its fundamental principles and all the other detailed requirements we saw in Chapter 4. ISA 220 (Revised) also emphasises the need for independence.

8.3 Acceptance and continuance of client relationships and audit engagements

The engagement partner is required to ensure that the requirements of International Standard on Quality Management 1 *Quality Management for Firms that Perform Audits or Reviews of Financial Statements, or Other Assurance or Related Services Engagements* (ISQM 1) in respect of accepting and continuing with the audit are followed. If the engagement is ethically unacceptable then it is the **partner's responsibility to decline it**.

Note that ISQM 1 itself is not examinable.

8.4 Engagement resources

The engagement partner must ensure that sufficient and appropriate resources are made available to the engagement team including human, technological and intellectual resources.

8.5 Engagement performance

The engagement partner is responsible for the **direction** and **supervision** of the members of the engagement team and the **review** of their work (ISA 220 (Revised): para. 29). Direction, supervision and review is **shared** across members of the engagement team depending on the skills and experience required for each engagement.

8.5.1 Direction

The engagement partner directs the audit and they are required to hold a meeting with the audit team to discuss the audit, in particular the **risks** associated with the audit. Direction of the engagement team includes informing members of the engagement team of their responsibilities such as:

(a) Contributing to the management and achievement of quality at the engagement level through their personal conduct, communication and actions.

(b) Maintaining a questioning mind and being aware of unconscious or conscious auditor biases in exercising **professional scepticism** when gathering and evaluating audit evidence.

(c) Fulfilling relevant ethical requirements.

(d) The responsibilities of respective partners when more than one partner is involved in the conduct of an audit engagement.

(e) The responsibilities of respective engagement team members to perform audit procedures and of more experienced engagement team members to direct, supervise and review the work of less experienced engagement team members.

(f) Understanding the **objectives of the work to be performed** and the detailed instructions regarding the nature, timing and extent of planned audit procedures as set forth in the overall audit strategy and audit plan.

(g) Addressing **threats to the achievement of quality**, and the engagement team's expected response. For example, budget constraints or resource constraints should not result in the engagement team members modifying planned audit procedures or failing to perform planned audit procedures.

(ISA 220 (Revised): para. A85)

8.5.2 Supervision

The audit is supervised overall by the engagement partner, but more practical supervision is given within the audit team by senior staff to more junior staff, as is also the case with review (see below). It includes:

(a) Tracking the progress of the audit engagement

(b) Taking appropriate action to **address issues arising during the engagement**, including for example, reassigning planned audit procedures to more experienced engagement team members when issues are more complex than initially anticipated.

(c) Identifying matters for consultation or consideration by more experienced engagement team members during the audit engagement.

(d) Providing **coaching and on-the-job training** to help engagement team members **develop skills or competencies**.

(e) Creating an environment where engagement team members raise concerns **without fear of reprisals**.

(ISA 220 (Revised): para. A86)

8.5.3 Review

Review of the engagement team's work provides support for the conclusion that the requirements of ISA 220 (Revised) in relation to quality management have been addressed. Review includes consideration of whether:

(a) The work has been performed in accordance with the **firm's policies or procedures, professional standards and applicable legal and regulatory requirements**

(b) **Significant matters** have been **raised for further consideration**

(c) Appropriate **consultations** have taken place and the resulting **conclusions** have been **documented** and implemented

(d) There is a need to **revise** the **nature, timing and extent** of work performed

(e) The work performed **supports the conclusions** reached and is appropriately documented

(f) The evidence obtained is sufficient and appropriate to provide a **basis for the auditor's opinion**

(g) The objectives of the audit procedures have been achieved

(ISA 220 (Revised): para. A88)

Before the audit report is issued, the engagement partner must be sure that sufficient and appropriate audit evidence has been obtained to support the audit opinion.

8.5.4 Consultation

The partner is also responsible for ensuring that if difficult or contentious matters arise the team takes appropriate consultation on the matter and that such matters and conclusions are properly recorded.

If differences of opinion arise between the engagement partner and the team, or between the engagement partner and the engagement quality reviewer, these differences should be resolved according to the firm's policy for such differences of opinion.

All listed entity audits require an engagement quality review to be undertaken before the auditor's report can be signed.

8.5.5 Engagement quality review

The engagement partner is responsible for **appointing** a quality reviewer, if one is required. Engagement quality reviews are **required for audits of listed entities** and any other engagements where the audit firm has determined a quality review is required.

Having appointed a quality reviewer, the engagement partner should:

- **Cooperate** with the quality reviewer, and inform the team that they should cooperate with them too
- Discuss **significant matters and judgements** with the reviewer
- Only date the auditor's report **after** the review

(ISA 220 (Revised): para. 36)

The engagement partner is then responsible for discussing significant matters arising from the review and for not issuing the audit report until the quality review has been completed.

A quality review should include:

- An evaluation of the significant judgements made by the engagement team
- An evaluation of the conclusions reached in formulating the auditor's report

A quality review for a **listed entity** will include a review of:

- The engagement team's evaluation of the **firm's independence** towards the audit
- The **significant risks** identified during the engagement and the responses to those risks (including assessment and response to **fraud**)
- **Judgements** made, particularly with respect to materiality and significant risks
- Whether appropriate consultations have taken place on differences of opinion/contentious matters and the conclusions drawn
- Significance and disposition of corrected and uncorrected misstatements identified during the audit
- Matters to be communicated with management/those charged with governance
- Whether the audit documentation selected for review reflects the work performed in relation to significant judgements/supports the conclusions reached
- The **appropriateness of the proposed audit report**

8.6 Monitoring and remediation

The audit engagement partner is required to consider the results of monitoring of the firm's quality management systems and consider whether they have any impact on the specific audit they are conducting.

Question — Quality management issues

You are an audit senior working for the firm Addystone Fish. You are currently carrying out the audit of Wicker Co, a manufacturer of waste paper bins. You are unhappy with Wicker's inventory valuation policy and have raised the issue several times with the audit manager. The audit manager has dealt with the client for a number of years and does not see what you are making a fuss about. They have refused to meet you on site to discuss these issues.

The former engagement partner to Wicker retired two months ago. As the audit manager had dealt with Wicker for so many years, the other partners have decided to leave the audit of Wicker in their capable hands.

Required

Comment on the situation outlined above.

Answer

Several quality management issues are raised in the above scenario:

Engagement partner

An **engagement partner** is usually appointed to each audit engagement undertaken by the firm, to take responsibility for the engagement on behalf of the firm. Assigning the audit to the experienced audit manager is not sufficient.

The lack of an audit engagement partner also means that several of the requirements of ISA 220 (Revised) about ensuring that arrangements in relation to independence and directing, supervising and reviewing the audit are not in place.

Conflicting views

In this scenario the audit manager and senior have conflicting views about the valuation of inventory. This does not appear to have been handled well, with the manager refusing to discuss the issue with the senior.

The audit engagement partner must take responsibility for settling disputes in accordance with the firm's policy in respect of resolution of disputes as required by ISQM 1. In this case, the lack of engagement partner may have contributed to this failure to resolve the disputes. In any event, at best, the failure to resolve the dispute is a breach of the firm's policy under ISQM 1. At worst, it indicates that the firm does not have a suitable policy concerning such disputes as required by ISQM 1.

Question — Quality management deficiencies

Your firm, PQ & Co is the auditor of Limitless Co, a listed UK company. You are not involved in the audit, but you have been assigned as a mentor for an audit trainee who recently started at the firm and has been working on the audit of Limitless Co. The trainee has sent you the following email:

From: A Trainee

To: A Manager

Subject: Limitless Co – issues

Good morning

I recently returned from my visit to the Limitless Head office where I have been working on the current year audit. I was watching an online tutorial as part of my studies about quality management a few weeks ago and after working on the Limitless audit I am not sure if our firm is reaching the quality management standards expected of a firm like ours.

The team of five trainees was meant to be under the supervision of a senior. However, that senior had been granted leave by the audit manager for the first week. The audit manager sent us an email saying we should follow last year's file until the senior returns.

When the senior returned, I asked if we would be given some background about Limitless because we didn't have a planning meeting. Unfortunately, I was told that this was not needed because it was virtually the same as the last client we worked on together.

Each trainee was given parts of the electronic audit file to complete. The company is struggling with cash flow and I was asked to review forecasts and conclude on the going concern status. I did my best but there were so many variables I just decided to go with the finance director's assumptions in the end. I was hoping the engagement partner would review my working paper on this, but it looks like nobody has reviewed it.

I was thinking about raising some of these points with the audit partner who has been working on the job the last couple of years, but I haven't had a chance yet. Apparently, no other partners have been involved or had anything to do with the client or the audit files.

I am also a bit worried because the partner questioned the amount of time I am taking on some of the work in an email after reviewing my timesheets. The email said the budget is very tight and we need to keep to it as a priority, but I don't think I can work any more quickly than I am and still get enough evidence to conclude on the work.

Maybe we can have a meeting about all this when we are both available?

Required

Describe THREE quality management deficiencies at PQ & Co based on the scenario and provide THREE recommendations to address those deficiencies.

Answer

Quality management deficiency	Recommendation
There is a **lack of supervision** at audits due to it being possible to grant an audit senior annual leave without assigning a replacement. The engagement partner must ensure that **sufficient and appropriate resources** are made available to the engagement team including human resources.	Annual leave policy should take account of the fact the firm needs to ensure **adequate supervision** is given within the audit team by senior staff to more junior staff. Annual leave policy should be such that it cannot be granted during an audit without assigning the responsibility of supervision to another senior unless the manager/partner are on site in their absence.
There was **no planning meeting**. The partner is required by auditing standards to hold a meeting with the audit team to discuss the audit. There has been no opportunity to inform members of the engagement team of their responsibilities, including contributing to engagement quality via their conduct and applying professional scepticism.	Planning meetings should be **compulsory** under the firm's quality management procedures and members of the engagement team should be made aware of their responsibilities for audit quality at that meeting.
The allocation of roles on the audit has been poor with a complex going concern review given to a trainee. Furthermore, there has been **no review** of the work in this area. Under ISA 220 (Revised) the audit partner should review documentation relating to significant matters and judgements. Clearly a going concern review where there is potentially a doubt over the going concern status is one of those matters.	Quality management procedures should make it clear the engagement partner must take responsibility for the direction and supervision of the members of the engagement team and the review of their work. The firm should carry out **periodic reviews of completed files** to detect any issues in this area and action should be taken to ensure these issues do not re-occur following the review. At the planning stage, work should be assigned to audit team members such that the audit engagement partner has sufficient confidence each team member is **experienced enough** to undertake the roles allocated to them.
No other partners have been involved but Limitless Co is a listed client. An engagement quality review is **required for audits of listed clients**.	An **engagement quality reviewer** should be **assigned** for the current and future audits of Limitless. This could be another partner in the firm, or an external reviewer appointed by the firm.

Quality management deficiency	Recommendation
Instead of addressing the threat to quality of a **budget constraint**, the partner has increased the threat by stressing the need to keep within budget. This may lead to work being carried out more quickly and being incomplete, and ultimately there is a risk there will not be sufficient and appropriate evidence to support the audit opinion.	The firm's quality manual should set out that **audit quality should not be compromised** by budgetary constraints and that the engagement partner is responsible for ensuring this. Where engagement partners do not comply, remedial action should be taken.

Note that only three deficiencies were required.

8.7 Taking overall responsibility for managing and achieving audit quality

Before **dating the auditor's report**, the engagement partner shall determine that the engagement partner has taken overall responsibility for **managing and achieving quality** on the audit engagement.

The engagement partner's involvement should have been **sufficient and appropriate throughout the audit** so that they have the basis for determining that the significant judgements made and the conclusions reached are appropriate given the nature and circumstances of the engagement.

8.8 Documentation

The engagement partner should ensure that the requirements of ISA 230 *Audit Documentation* have been satisfied.

Chapter roundup

- The auditors formulate an **overall audit strategy** which is translated into a **detailed audit plan** for audit staff to follow.
- The audit strategy and audit plan shall be updated and changed as necessary during the course of the audit.
- The auditor is required to **obtain an understanding of the entity and its environment** in order to be able to assess the risks of material misstatements.
- Auditors are required to carry out the audit with **professional scepticism**.
- **Audit risk** is the risk that the auditor expresses **an inappropriate audit opinion** when the financial statements are materially misstated. It is a function of the risk of material misstatement (**inherent risk** and **control risk**) and the risk that the auditor will not detect such misstatement (**detection risk**).
- When the auditor has obtained an understanding of the entity, he must assess the risks of material misstatement in the financial statements, also identifying significant risks.
- **Significant risks** are complex or unusual transactions, those that may indicate fraud or other special risks.
- The auditor must **formulate an approach** to assessed risks of material misstatement.
- **Overall responses** include issues such as emphasising to the team the importance of professional scepticism, allocating more staff, using experts or providing more supervision.
- The auditor must also determine **further audit procedures** to address the risks of material misstatement.
- **Materiality** should be calculated at the planning stages of all audits. The calculation or estimation of materiality should be based on experience and judgement.
- Materiality should be reviewed during the audit.
- Substantive procedures must be carried out on **material** items. There are also a number of substantive procedures that must be carried out on the preparation of the financial statements.
- **Double materiality** means considering not only the sustainability issues that might create financial risks for the company (**financial materiality**), but also those sustainability issues where a company's activities materially impact on people and the environment (**impact materiality**).
- When carrying out risk assessment procedures, the auditors should also consider the risk of fraud or non-compliance with law and regulations causing a misstatement in financial statements.
- ISA 220 (Revised) requires firms to implement quality review procedures over individual audit engagements.
- All listed entity audits require an engagement quality review to be undertaken before the auditor's report can be signed.

Quick quiz

1. Complete the definitions:

   An .... is the formulation of a general strategy for the audit.

   An .... is a set of instructions to the audit team that sets out the further audit procedures to be carried out.

2. Complete the definitions.

   .... risk is the risk that .... give an .... opinion when the financial statements are .... misstated.

   .... risk is the .... of an assertion about a ...., account balance or disclosure to ....

3. If control and inherent risk are assessed as sufficiently low, substantive procedures can be abandoned completely.

   True ☐
   False ☐

4. Which of the following procedures might an auditor use in gaining an understanding of the entity?

   (a) Inquiry
   (b) Recalculation
   (c) Analytical procedures
   (d) ATTs
   (e) Observation and inspection

5. The audit team is required to discuss the susceptibility of the financial statements to material misstatements.

   True ☐
   False ☐

6. Name four factors which might indicate a significant risk.

   (1) ....
   (2) ....
   (3) ....
   (4) ....

7. Name any three potential overall responses to assessed risks.

   (1) ....
   (2) ....
   (3) ....

8. Match the percentages to the values for an appropriate calculation of materiality

	%
Profit before tax	5
Gross profit	5–10
Revenue	1–2
Total assets	½–1
Net assets	2–5
Profit after tax	½–1

9   Auditors have a duty to detect fraud.

    True ☐
    False ☐

10 Auditors should always report non-compliance with laws and regulations to the statutory authority.

    True ☐
    False ☐

11 Who carries out the review of audit documentation prepared during an audit of financial statements?

Answers to quick quiz

1 Overall audit strategy, audit plan

2 Audit, auditors, inappropriate, materially

   Inherent, susceptibility, class of transactions, misstatement

3 False

4 (a), (c), (e)

5 True

6 Any of:
   - Risk of fraud
   - Relationship with recent developments
   - Degree of subjectivity in the financial information
   - The fact that it is an unusual transaction
   - Transaction with a related party
   - Complexity of the transaction

7 Any of:
   - Emphasising the need for professional scepticism
   - Assigning additional/more experienced staff
   - Using experts
   - Providing more supervision
   - Incorporating more unpredictability

8

	%
Profit before tax	5
Gross profit	½–1
Revenue	½–1
Total assets	1–2
Net assets	2–5
Profit after tax	5–10

9 False, the external auditor has a duty to plan and perform their audit so that they have a reasonable assurance that they will detect **material** fraud (and error).

10 False, any disclosure of non-compliance with laws and regulations should consider the risks associated with reporting to a third party and in the case of suspected fraud, the auditor should not take action outside the company until they are certain. In each case, the auditor should seek legal advice before proceeding.

11 Audit work is generally reviewed by the staff member who is more senior on the team than the person who did the work. The engagement partner must carry out a review to ensure there is sufficient and appropriate evidence to support the audit opinion. It might also be necessary under the firm's quality management policies to obtain a quality review by a suitable person outside the audit team (the engagement quality reviewer). This will be necessary if the audit is of a listed entity.

End of chapter question

Kudos Ltd (AIA Nov 2006) (amended)

Kudos Ltd is a manufacturer of components for cars and other motor vehicles. It has its manufacturing base in the UK, and has sales offices in several other countries.

You are the audit senior on the audit of Kudos for the year to 30 September 20X6. You are currently at the planning stage of the audit, and are completing the relevant working papers.

You have completed a 'client risk evaluation questionnaire', and have identified certain areas of the company's business as being high risk. Your firm has a policy of working with an overall acceptable audit risk of 5%.

You have obtained the company's management accounts for the eight months to May 20X6, extracts of which are given below.

You have obtained the following additional information:

(i) The company has recently taken on additional long-term loans. As a condition of borrowing, the bank has imposed certain profit targets on the company for the duration of the loans. Failure to meet these will result in the bank reconsidering the terms of the loans. The target for profit before tax for the year to 30 September 20X6 is $800,000.

(ii) For the first time the company has incurred significant development expenditure on a new product that the company plans to launch in early 20X7. Expenditure of $950,000 has been capitalised so far. The original budgeted expenditure for the development of this product was $750,000.

(iii) There have been major additions to tangible non-current assets during the period. These include the cost of $1.5 million for a new factory, built by Kudos' own staff, along with plant and equipment to equip this new facility.

(iv) During the year the company disposed of a piece of machinery which was obsolete. It had cost $500,000, and had been depreciated to $300,000. It was sold for $8,000 as scrap. The disposal of several commercial vehicles resulted in a loss of $$150,000. All other assets realised approximately their book values.

(v) During the year the company started a full physical check of manufacturing plant and machinery, which is now half-complete. The check so far has shown up assets with a net book value of $55,000 which could not be located. The original cost of these items was $375,000.

(vi) During the year the company acquired the entire share capital of Ace Ltd, paying $2.46m for net assets valued at just over $2 million. Ace Ltd produces only one specialised and patented product. Since the acquisition, a competitor has produced a similar product at a cheaper price, resulting in a drop of 70% of Ace Ltd's revenue. Ace Ltd has commenced legal proceedings against the competitor on the ground of patent infringement, but the case is not due to be heard in court until mid-20X7.

KUDOS LTD
EXTRACT FROM MANAGEMENT ACCOUNTS FOR EIGHT MONTHS TO 31 MAY 20X6

STATEMENTS OF PROFIT OR LOSS AND OTHER COMPREHENSIVE INCOME

	Actual 8 months to 31 May X6 $'000	Budget year to 30 Sept X6 $'000	Actual year to 30 Sept X5 $'000
Revenue	49,000	90,000	82,000
Cost of sales	(40,300)	(76,000)	(70,000)
Gross profit	8,700	14,000	12,000
Distribution costs	(3,260)	(5,750)	(5,600)
Administrative expenses	(4,750)	(5,350)	(5,250)
Operating profit	690	2,900	1,150
Financial income	40	150	-
Financial expense	(182)	(275)	(75)
Profit before tax	548	2,775	1,075

STATEMENTS OF FINANCIAL POSITION

	31 May X6 $'000	30 Sept X5 $'000
Assets		
Non-current assets		
Intangible assets	950	-
Property, plant and equipment	8,704	5,846
Investments	2,460	-
	12,114	5,846
Current assets	1,489	4,984
Total assets	13,603	10,830
Equity and liabilities		
Ordinary share capital	5,000	5,000
Retained earnings	3,398	2,850
	8,398	7,850
Non-current liabilities		
Long-term loans	4,880	2,430
Current liabilities	325	550
Total equity and liabilities	13,603	10,830

Required

(a) Explain why the audit firm thinks it is reasonable to accept a 5% risk that a material item will be missed, and as a consequence a wrong audit opinion will be given. **(5 marks)**

(b) Identify the key risk areas that should be addressed during the audit of Kudos Ltd, giving reasons. **(15 marks)**

(Total = 20 marks)

Audit evidence

Topic list	Syllabus reference
1 Audit evidence	3.1
2 Financial statement assertions	5.1
3 Audit procedures	3.2, 3.4, 3.6, 4.6, 4.7, 5.5, 5.6
4 Tests of controls	3.2, 3.4, 3.6, 4.6, 5.5, 5.6
5 Substantive procedures	3.2, 3.4, 3.6, 4.6, 5.5, 5.6
6 Automated tools and techniques (ATTs)	3.8
7 Audit sampling	3.7
8 Documenting audit evidence	3.5

Introduction

Before an auditor can even start putting together a strategy for the audit, they must be aware what kind of **evidence** they will be looking for. In this chapter, we introduce some fundamental auditing concepts of audit evidence, audit sampling and audit documentation.

We also introduce the **financial statement assertions**. These will be particularly important when we consider detailed testing, since audit procedures are designed to obtain **sufficient, appropriate evidence** about the assertions for each balance or transaction in financial statements. Testing may involve **tests of controls** and/or **substantive procedures** and these may be carried out using manual procedures or using automated tools and techniques (ATTs). Whatever type of test is chosen, the auditors need to decide **how they will select the items to be tested** from the whole population. The auditors will want to **select a sample** which reflects, as closely as possible, the characteristics of the population from which the sample has been selected. We will explain **practical aspects of sampling.** Sampling theory is closely associated with the definition of **audit risk** which we look at in detail in the previous chapter.

Lastly, in this chapter we shall look at **how** auditors **document** their work to maintain a written record of work performed on the audit.

1 Audit evidence

FAST FORWARD

Auditors must obtain **sufficient, appropriate** audit evidence. Evidence can be in the form of **tests of controls** or **substantive procedures**.

1.1 The need for audit evidence

The objective of an audit of financial statements is to enable the auditor to express an opinion on whether the financial statements are prepared, in all material respects, in accordance with an identified financial reporting framework (ISA 200: para. 3).

Key term

Audit evidence is all the information used by the auditor in arriving at the conclusions on which the auditor's opinion is based (ISA 500: para. 5(c)).

Audit evidence includes the information contained in the accounting records underlying the financial statements and other information gathered by the auditors, such as confirmations from third parties (ISA 500: para. 5(c)). Auditors are **not expected to look at all the information** that might exist. They will often select **samples** to test, as we shall see in Section 7.

1.2 Sufficient appropriate audit evidence

ISA 500 *Audit Evidence* requires auditors to design audit procedures to obtain **sufficient appropriate** audit evidence. 'Sufficiency' and 'appropriateness' are interrelated and apply to both tests of controls and substantive procedures.

- **Sufficiency** is the measure of the **quantity** of audit evidence.
- **Appropriateness** is the measure of the **quality** of the audit evidence that is, its **relevance** and its **reliability**.

1.2.1 Sufficient

Sufficiency relates to the amount of evidence the auditor should collect. The **quantity** of audit evidence required is affected by the **level of risk** in the area being audited which we looked at in the last chapter.

1.2.2 Appropriateness

Appropriateness is affected by the **quality** of evidence obtained. If the evidence is high quality, the auditor may need less than if it were poor quality. However, obtaining a high quantity of poor quality evidence will not cancel out its poor quality.

The ISA also requires auditors to consider the **relevance and reliability** of the information to be used as audit evidence when designing and performing audit procedures (ISA 500: para. 7).

Relevance deals with the logical connection with the purpose of the audit procedure and the assertion under consideration (we look at assertions in the next section). The relevance of information may be affected by the direction of testing (ISA 500: paras. A27–A28).

Reliability is influenced by the source and nature of the information, including the controls over its preparation and maintenance. The following generalisations may help in assessing the **reliability** of audit evidence (ISA 500: para. A31).

8: AUDIT EVIDENCE

Quality of evidence	
External	Audit evidence from **external sources** is more reliable than that obtained from the entity's records.
Auditor	Evidence obtained **directly by auditors** is more reliable than that obtained indirectly or by inference.
Entity	Evidence obtained from the entity's records is more reliable when related **control system operates effectively**.
Written	Evidence in the form of **documents (paper or electronic)** or **written representations** are more reliable than oral representations.
Originals	Original documents are more realistic than photocopies, or facsimiles.

Auditors will often use information produced by the entity when obtaining audit evidence, although this will not always be a strong form of audit evidence. When doing so, ISA 500 requires the auditor to obtain audit evidence about the **accuracy and completeness** of the information. This may be achieved by testing controls in the related area, or by other methods, for example, computer assisted audit techniques (see Section 6).

Exam focus point

You may be asked to consider how strong certain evidence is from the auditor's viewpoint, for example a confirmation of trade receivables or third party valuation of assets.

2 Financial statement assertions

FAST FORWARD

Audit procedures are designed to obtain evidence about the financial statement assertions.

Key term

Financial statement assertions are the representations of the directors that are embodied in the financial statements. By approving the financial statements, the directors are making representations about the information therein. These representations or assertions may be described in general terms in a number of ways.

ISA 315 (Revised) states that the auditor must consider the assertions for **classes of transactions and related disclosures** (ie statement of profit or loss) and **account balances and related disclosures** (ie statement of financial position) in sufficient detail to form the basis for the assessment of risks of material misstatement and the design and performance of further audit procedures. It gives examples of assertions in these areas.

| Assertions about **classes of transactions and events and related disclosures** for the period under audit | **Occurrence**: Transactions and events that have been recorded or disclosed have occurred, and such transactions and events pertain to the entity.
Completeness: All transactions and events that should have been recorded have been recorded, and all related disclosures that should have been included in the financial statements have been included.
Accuracy: Amounts and other data relating to recorded transactions and events have been recorded appropriately, and related disclosures have been appropriately measured and described.
Cut-off: Transactions and events have been recorded in the correct reporting period.
Classification: Transactions and events have been recorded in the proper accounts.
Presentation: Transactions and events are appropriately aggregated or disaggregated and are clearly described, and related disclosures are relevant and understandable in the context of the requirements of the applicable financial reporting framework. |

Assertions about **account balances and related disclosures** at the period end	**Existence**: Assets, liabilities and equity interests exist.
	Rights and obligations: The entity holds or controls the rights to assets, and liabilities are the obligations of the entity.
	Completeness: All assets, liabilities and equity interests that should have been recorded have been recorded, and all related disclosures that should have been included in the financial statements have been included.
	Accuracy, valuation and allocation: Assets, liabilities and equity interests have been included in the financial statements at appropriate amounts and any resulting valuation or allocation adjustments have been appropriately recorded, and related disclosures have been appropriately measured and described.
	Classification: Assets, liabilities and equity interests have been recorded in the proper accounts.
	Presentation: Assets, liabilities and equity interests are appropriately aggregated or disaggregated and clearly described, and related disclosures are relevant and understandable in the context of the requirements of the applicable financial reporting framework.

This is a key syllabus area and you **must** be very comfortable with the assertions that relate to each area, as the same assertions do not always apply to each area. Exam questions are very likely to test this area in the context of audit procedures to test particular assertions so it's vital that you take the time to learn, understand and test your knowledge.

Exam focus point

When designing audit procedures for specific areas of the financial statements, you should focus on the financial statement assertions.

3 Audit procedures

FAST FORWARD

Audit evidence can be obtained by inspection, observation, inquiry and confirmation, recalculation, reperformance and analytical procedures.

The auditor obtains audit evidence by undertaking audit procedures to do the following:

(a) Obtain an understanding of the entity and its environment to assess the risks of material misstatement at the financial statement and assertion levels (**risk assessment procedures**)

(b) Test the operating effectiveness of controls in preventing, or detecting and correcting, material misstatements at the assertion level (**tests of controls**)

(c) Detect material misstatements at the assertion level (**substantive procedures**)

The auditor must **always** perform **risk assessment procedures** to provide a satisfactory assessment of risks.

Tests of controls are necessary to test the controls to support the risk assessment, and also when substantive procedures alone do not provide sufficient appropriate audit evidence.

Substantive procedures must **always** be carried out for **material** classes of transactions, account balances and related disclosures.

Key terms

Tests of controls are performed to obtain audit evidence about the effectiveness of the:

- Design of the accounting and internal control systems, ie whether they are suitably designed to prevent or detect and correct material misstatements; and
- Operation of the internal controls throughout the period.

Substantive procedures are tests to obtain audit evidence to detect material misstatements in the financial statements. They are generally of two types:

- Analytical procedures
- Other substantive procedures such as tests of detail of transactions and balances, review of minutes of directors' meetings and enquiry.

The audit procedures described in the table below can be used as risk assessment procedures, tests of controls and substantive procedures.

Procedures	
Inspection of tangible assets	Inspection of assets that are recorded in the accounting records confirms existence, gives evidence of accuracy, valuation and allocation, but does not confirm rights and obligations. Confirmation that assets seen are recorded in accounting records gives evidence of completeness.
Inspection of records or documents	Confirmation to documentation of items recorded in accounting records confirms that an asset exists or a transaction occurred. Confirmation that items recorded in supporting documentation are recorded in accounting records tests completeness. Cut-off can be verified by inspecting reverse population ie checking transactions recorded after the reporting date to supporting documentation to confirm that they occurred after the reporting date. Inspection also provides evidence of accuracy, valuation and allocation, rights and obligations and the nature of items (presentation and disclosure). It can also be used to compare documents (and hence test consistency of audit evidence) and confirm authorisation.
Observation	This involves watching a procedure being performed (for example, post opening). It is of limited use, as it only confirms the procedure took place when the auditor was watching.
Inquiry	This involves seeking information from client staff or external sources. Strength of evidence depends on the knowledge and integrity of source of information.
Confirmation	This involves seeking confirmation from another source of details in client's accounting records eg confirmation from bank of bank balances.
Recalculation	Checking arithmetic of client's records for example, adding up ledger account.
Reperformance	Independently executing procedures or controls, either manually or through the use of ATTs (see below).
Analytical procedures	Evaluating and comparing financial and/or non-financial data for plausible relationships.

Question — Audit evidence

(a) Discuss the quality of the following types of audit evidence, giving two examples of each form of evidence.

    (i) Evidence originated by the auditors
    (ii) Evidence created by third parties
    (iii) Evidence created by the management of the client

(b) Describe the general considerations which the auditors must bear in mind when evaluating audit evidence.

Answer

(a) **Quality of audit evidence**

(i) **Evidence originated by the auditors**

Evidence originated by the auditors is in general the most reliable type of audit evidence because there is little risk that it can be manipulated by management.

Examples

(1) Analytical procedures, such as the calculation of ratios and trends in order to examine unusual variations

(2) Physical inspection or observation, such as attendance at physical inventory counts or inspection of a non-current asset

(3) Re-performance of calculations making up figures in the accounts, such as the computation of total inventory values

(ii) **Evidence created by third parties**

Third party evidence is more reliable than client-produced evidence to the extent that it is obtained from sources independent of the client. Its reliability will be reduced if it is obtained from sources which are not independent, or if there is a risk that client personnel may be able to and have reason to suppress or manipulate it. This, for instance, is an argument against having replies to external confirmations sent to the client instead of the auditors.

Examples

(1) External confirmation of trade accounts receivable or payables and other requests from the auditors for confirming evidence, such as requests for confirmation of bank balances.

(2) Reports produced by experts, such as property valuations, actuarial valuations, legal opinions. In evaluating such evidence, the auditors need to take into account the qualifications of the expert, his or her independence of the client and the terms of reference under which the work was carried out.

(3) Documents held by the client which were issued by third parties, such as invoices, price lists and statements. These may sometimes be manipulated by the client, to the extent that items may be suppressed or altered, and to this extent they are less reliable than confirmations received direct.

(iii) **Evidence created by management**

The auditors cannot place the same degree of reliance on evidence produced by client management as on that produced outside the client organisation. However, it will often be necessary to place some reliance on the client's evidence. The auditors will need to obtain audit evidence that the information supplied is complete and accurate, and apply judgement in doing so, taking into account previous experience of the client's reliability and the extent to which the client's representations appear compatible with other audit findings, as well as the materiality of the item under discussion.

Examples

(1) The company's accounting records and supporting schedules. Although these are prepared by management, the auditors have a statutory right to examine such records in full: this right enhances the quality of this information.

(2) The client's explanations of, for instance, apparently unusual fluctuations in results. Such evidence requires interpretation by the auditors and, being oral evidence, only limited reliance can be placed upon it.

(3) Information provided to the auditors about the internal control system. The auditors need to check that this information is accurate and up-to-date, and that it does not simply describe an idealised system which is not adhered to in practice.

(b) **General considerations in evaluating audit evidence**

Audit evidence will often not be wholly conclusive. The auditors must obtain evidence which is **sufficient and appropriate** to form the basis for their audit conclusions. The evidence gathered should also be **relevant** to those conclusions, and sufficiently **reliable** ultimately to form the basis for the audit opinion. The auditors must exercise skill and judgement to ensure that evidence is correctly interpreted and that only valid inferences are drawn from it.

Certain general principles can be stated. **Written evidence** is preferable to oral evidence; **independent evidence** obtained from outside the organisation is more reliable than that obtained internally; and that **evidence generated by the auditors** is more reliable than that obtained from others.

3.1 Designing the audit programme

Once the auditor has determined the audit procedures they need to carry out in order gather sufficient appropriate audit evidence to support the relevant financial statement assertions, they will formalise this in the form of an audit programme.

The audit programme is a **detailed** plan of the audit procedures that will be carried out on each area of the financial statements, for example it will list out all of the procedures that the audit team will conduct in relation to receivables.

These audit procedures may well include a combination of tests of controls and substantive procedures.

4 Tests of controls

Key term

Tests of controls are performed to obtain audit evidence about the effectiveness of the:

- Design of the accounting and internal control systems, ie whether they are suitably designed to prevent or detect and correct material misstatements; and
- Operation of the internal controls throughout the period.

Tests of controls are distinguished from substantive tests which are designed to detect material misstatements in the financial statements.

4.1 Examples

Tests of controls may include the following.

(a) **Inspection of documents** supporting controls or events to gain audit evidence that internal controls have operated properly, eg verifying that a transaction has been **authorised** (signature or online/electronic approval)

(b) **Inquiries about internal controls** which leave no audit trail, eg determining who actually performs each function not merely who is supposed to perform it

(c) **Reperformance of control procedures**, eg **reconciliation** of bank accounts, to ensure they were correctly performed by the entity

(d) **Examination of evidence of management views**, eg minutes of management meetings

(e) Testing of internal controls operating on **computerised systems** or over the overall information technology function, eg access controls

(f) **Observation of controls.** Auditors will consider the manner in which the control is being operated

Auditors should consider:

- **How** controls were applied
- The **consistency** with which they were applied during the period
- **By whom** they were applied

Deviations in the operation of controls (caused by change of staff etc) may increase control risk and tests of controls may need to be modified to confirm effective operation during and after any change.

The use of automated tools and techniques (ATTs) may be appropriate to conduct tests of controls, these are discussed in Section 6.

5 Substantive procedures

Key term

> **Substantive procedures** are tests to obtain audit evidence to **detect material misstatements** in the financial statements. They are generally of two types:
>
> - Analytical procedures
> - Other substantive procedures such as tests of detail of transactions and balances, review of minutes of directors' meetings and enquiry

The types of substantive procedures carried out to obtain evidence about various financial statement assertions are outlined in the table below.

Audit objective	Typical audit tests
Completeness	(a) Review of items from after the date of the financial statements (b) Cut-off testing (c) Analytical procedures (d) External confirmations (e) Reconciliations to control account (f) Sequence checks (g) Review of reciprocal populations
Rights and obligations	(a) Checking invoices for proof that item belongs to the company (b) External confirmations
Accuracy, valuation and allocation	(a) Checking to invoices (b) Recalculation (c) Confirming accounting policy consistent and reasonable (d) Review of payments and invoices after the date of the financial statements (e) Expert valuation

Audit objective	Typical audit tests
Existence	(a) Physical verification (b) External confirmations (c) Cut-off testing
Occurrence	(a) Inspection of supporting documentation (b) Confirmation from directors that transactions relate to business (c) Inspection of items purchased
Accuracy	(a) Recalculation of correct amounts (b) External confirmations (c) Analytical procedures
Classification	(a) Check compliance with law and accounting standards (b) Review of whether true and fair override invoked
Cut-off	(a) Review of transactions either side of the year end (b) Analytical procedures comparing amounts to the previous year
Presentation	(a) Review of financial statement disclosures to ensure compliance with law and IFRS Accounting Standards

Exam focus point

The exam requires a good knowledge of how the **financial statement assertions** determine audit objectives, and the procedures for obtaining audit evidence. Students should be aiming to produce a description of procedures that could be followed by an inexperienced staff member.

5.1 Directional testing

Broadly speaking, substantive procedures can be said to fall into two categories:

- Tests to discover **misstatements** (resulting in overstatement or understatement)
- Tests to discover **omissions** (resulting in understatement)

5.1.1 Tests designed to discover misstatements

These tests will start with the **accounting records** in which the transactions are recorded and **check from the entries to supporting documents or other evidence**. Such tests should detect any overstatement and also any understatement through causes other than omission.

Case Study

Test for misstatements

If the test is designed to ensure that sales are priced correctly, the test would begin with a sales invoice selected from the sales ledger. Prices would then be checked to the official price list.

5.1.2 Tests designed to discover omissions

These tests must start from **outside the accounting records** and then **check back to the accounting records**. Understatements through omission will never be revealed by starting with the account itself as there is clearly no chance of selecting items that have been omitted from the account.

Case Study

Tests for omission

If the test is designed to discover whether all raw material purchases have been properly processed, the test would start, say, with goods received notes, to be checked to the inventory records or purchase ledger.

5.1.3 Directional testing and debits and credits

For most systems auditors would include tests designed to discover misstatements. The type of test, and direction of the test, should be recognised before selecting the test sample. If the sample which tested the accuracy and validity of the sales ledger were chosen from a file of sales invoices then it would not substantiate the fact that there were no misstatements in the sales ledger.

Directional testing is particularly appropriate when testing the **financial statement assertions** of existence, completeness, rights and obligations, and accuracy, valuation and allocation.

The concept of directional testing derives from the principle of double-entry bookkeeping, in that for every **debit** there is a **corresponding credit**, (assuming that the double entry is complete and that the accounting records balance). Therefore, any **misstatement** of a **debit entry** will result in either a corresponding **misstatement** of a **credit entry** or a **misstatement** in the opposite direction, of **another debit entry**.

By designing audit procedures carefully the auditors are able to use this principle in drawing audit conclusions, not only about the debit or credit entries that they have directly tested, but also about the corresponding credit or debit entries that are necessary to balance the books.

Tests are therefore designed in the following way.

Test item	Example
Test debit items (expenditure or assets) for overstatement by selecting debit entries recorded in the nominal ledger and checking value, existence and ownership	If a non-current asset entry in the nominal ledger of $1,000 is selected, it would be overstated if it should have been recorded at anything less than $1,000 or if the company did not own it, or indeed if it did not exist (eg it had been sold or the amount of $1,000 in fact represented a revenue expense).
Test credit items (income or liabilities) for understatement by selecting items from appropriate sources independent of the nominal ledger and ensuring that they result in the correct nominal ledger entry	Select a goods dispatched note and check that the resultant sale has been recorded in the nominal ledger sales account. Sales would be understated if the nominal ledger did not reflect the transaction at all (completeness) or reflected it at less than full value (say if goods valued at $1,000 were recorded in the sales account at $900, there would be an understatement of $100).

A test for the overstatement of an asset simultaneously gives comfort on understatement of other assets, overstatement of liabilities, overstatement of income and understatement of expenses.

Question — Directional testing

Fill in the blank spaces.

(a) Based on double-entry bookkeeping, it can be seen from the matrix that assets can only be **understated** by virtue of:

  (i) Other assets being _____; or
  (ii) Liabilities being _____; or
  (iii) Income being _____; or
  (iv) Expenses being _____.

(b) Similarly, liabilities can only be **overstated** by virtue of:

  (i) Assets being _____; or
  (ii) Other liabilities being _____; or
  (iii) Income being _____; or
  (iv) Expenses being _____.

Answer

(a) (i) Overstated   (b) (i) Overstated
    (ii) Understated   (ii) Understated
    (iii) Understated   (iii) Understated
    (iv) Overstated   (iv) Overstated

So, by performing the primary tests, the auditors obtain audit assurance in other audit areas. Successful completion of the primary tests will therefore result in them having tested all account areas both for overstatement and understatement.

The **major advantage** of the directional audit approach is its **cost-effectiveness.**

(a) Assets and expenses are tested for overstatement only, and liabilities and income for understatement only, that is, items are not tested for both overstatement and understatement.

(b) It audits directly the more likely types of transactional misstatement, that is, unrecorded income and improper expense (arising intentionally or unintentionally).

5.2 Analytical procedures

Analytical procedures are used at all stages of the audit.

5.2.1 Nature and purpose of analytical procedures

Point to note

Analytical procedures consist of evaluation of financial information through the analysis of plausible relationships among both financial and non-financial data.

Analytical procedures also encompass such investigation as is necessary of identified fluctuations or relationships that are inconsistent with other relevant information or that differ from expected values by a significant amount.

ISA 520 *Analytical Procedures* deals with the auditor's use of analytical procedures as substantive procedures. It also deals with the auditor's responsibility to perform analytical procedures near the end of the audit that assist the auditor when forming an overall conclusion on the financial statements (we cover this in Chapter 17). In addition, auditors must use analytical procedures during the planning and risk assessment process.

The ISA states that analytical procedures include:

(a) The consideration of comparisons with:

- **Comparable information** for prior periods
- **Anticipated results** of the entity, from budgets or forecasts
- Similar **industry information**, such as a comparison of the client's ratio of sales to trade accounts receivable with industry averages, or with the ratios relating to other entities of comparable size in the same industry

(b) Analytical procedures also include consideration of relationships, for example:

- Among elements of financial information that would be expected to conform to a predictable pattern based on the entity's experience, such as gross margin percentages
- Between financial information and relevant non-financial information, such as payroll costs to number of employees

A variety of methods can be used to perform the procedures discussed above, ranging from **simple comparisons** to **complex analysis** using statistics, on a company level, branch level or individual account level. The choice of procedures is a matter for the auditors' professional judgement.

5.2.2 Analytical procedures as substantive procedures

> **FAST FORWARD**
>
> When using analytical procedures as **substantive procedures**, auditors should consider the information available, assessing its **availability, relevance** and **comparability**.

The auditors must decide whether using available analytical procedures as substantive procedures will be effective and efficient in **reducing audit risk** for specific financial statement assertions to an acceptably low level. Auditors may efficiently use analytical data produced by the entity itself, provided they are satisfied that it has been properly prepared.

When deciding whether to use analytical procedures as substantive procedures the auditors shall consider:

- Whether analytical procedures are suitable given the assessed risk of material misstatement
- Whether the data available for analytical procedures is reliable and relevant
- Whether the auditors' expected results are sufficiently precise to draw audit conclusions (for example, auditors normally expect greater consistency in comparing the relationship of gross profit to sales from one period to another than in comparing discretionary expenses, such as research or advertising)
- A level of variance from expectations that would necessitate further audit procedures to be carried out

Reliability factors	Example
Source	Information may be more reliable if its source is external to the entity (for example, industry averages).
Comparability	For example, broad industry averages may need adjusting to be truly relevant to a more specialised company within the industry.

Reliability factors	Example
Relevance	For example, a realistic budget will be more relevant for comparative purposes than a target budget.
The controls over the information	If controls are strong over comparative information then results of analytical procedures are more reliable.

Auditors will need to consider testing the controls, if any, over the **preparation** of **information** used in applying analytical procedures. When such controls are effective, the auditors will have greater confidence in the reliability of the information, and therefore in the results of analytical procedures.

The **controls** over **non-financial information** can often be tested in conjunction with tests of **accounting-related controls**. For example, in establishing controls over the processing of sales invoices, a business may include controls over unit sales recording. In these circumstances the auditors could test the controls over the recording of unit sales in conjunction with tests of the controls over the processing of sales invoices.

5.2.3 Investigating significant fluctuations or unexpected relationships

> **FAST FORWARD**
>
> Auditors must investigate **significant fluctuations** and **unexpected relationships**.

If analytical procedures performed in accordance with ISA 520 identify fluctuations or relationships that are inconsistent with other relevant information or that differ from expected values by a significant amount, the **auditor shall investigate such differences** by:

(a) Inquiring of management and obtaining appropriate audit evidence relevant to management's responses; and

(b) Performing other audit procedures as necessary in the circumstances.

Note. As stated earlier, the auditor should have determined an amount at which differences are significant.

5.2.4 Practical techniques

When carrying out analytical procedures, auditors should remember that every industry is different and each company within an industry differs in certain respects.

Ratio analysis can be a useful technique. However, ratios mean very little when used in isolation. They should be calculated for previous periods and for comparable companies. This may involve a certain amount of initial research, but subsequently it is just a matter of adding new statistics to the existing information each year. The permanent file should contain a section with summarised accounts and the chosen ratios for prior years.

In addition to looking at the more usual ratios the auditors should consider examining other ratios that may be relevant to the particular clients' business, such as revenue per passenger mile for an airline operator client, or fees per partner for a professional office.

Other analytical techniques include:

(a) **Examining related accounts** in conjunction with each other. Often revenue and expense accounts are related to balance sheet accounts and comparisons should be made to ensure relationships are reasonable.

(b) **Trend analysis**. Sophisticated statistical techniques (beyond the scope of this paper) can be used to compare this period with previous periods.

(c) **Reasonableness test (proof in total)**. This involves calculating the **expected value** of an item and comparing it with its actual value, for example, for the straight-line depreciation:

(Cost + Additions − Disposals) × Depreciation % = Charge in Statement of profit or loss and other comprehensive income

Important accounting ratios	• Gross profit margins, in total and by product, area and months/quarter (if possible) • Receivables collection period • Inventory turnover ratio (turnover divided into cost of sales) • Current ratio (current assets to current liabilities) • Quick or acid test ratio (liquid assets to current liabilities) • Gearing ratio (debt capital to equity capital) • Return on capital employed (profit before tax to total assets less current liabilities)
Related items	• Payables and purchases • Inventories and cost of sales • Non-current assets and depreciation, repairs and maintenance expense • Intangible assets and amortisation • Loans and interest expense • Investments and investment income • Receivables and irrecoverable debt expense • Receivables and revenue

Other areas for consideration

- **Examine changes** in **products, customers and levels** of **returns**.
- **Assess** the effect of **price and mix changes** on the cost of sales.
- **Consider** the effect of **inflation, industrial disputes, changes in production methods** and **changes in activity** on the charge for wages.
- **Obtain explanations** for all **major variances** analysed using a standard costing system. Particular attention should be paid to those relating to the over or under absorption of overheads since these may, inter alia, affect inventory valuations.
- **Compare trends in production and sales** and assess the effect on any provisions for obsolete inventories.
- **Ensure** that **changes in the percentage labour or overhead content** of production costs are also reflected in the inventory valuation.
- **Review other expenditure**, comparing:
  - Rent with annual rent per rental agreement
  - Rates with previous year and known rates increases
  - Interest payable on loans with outstanding balance and interest rate per loan agreement
  - Hire or leasing charges with annual rate per agreements
  - Vehicle running expenses to vehicles
  - Other items related to activity level with general price increase and change in relevant level of activity (for example telephone expenditure will increase disproportionately if export or import business increases)
  - Other items not related to activity level with general price increases (or specific increases if known)
- **Review** statement of profit or loss and other comprehensive income for **items** which may have been **omitted** (eg scrap sales, training levy, special contributions to pension fund, provisions for dilapidation etc).

> **Other areas for consideration**
> - **Ensure expected variations** arising from the following have occurred:
>   - Industry or local trends
>   - Known disturbances of the trading pattern (for example strikes, depot closures, failure of suppliers)

Certain of the comparisons and ratios measuring liquidity and longer-term capital structure will assist in evaluating whether the company is a going concern, in addition to contributing to the overall view of the accounts. We shall see in Chapter 17 however, that there are factors other than declining ratios that may indicate going concern problems.

The working papers must contain the completed results of analytical procedures. They should include:

- The outline **programme** of the work
- The summary of **significant figures** and relationships for the period
- A summary of **comparisons** made with budgets and with previous years
- Details of all **significant fluctuations** or **unexpected relationships** considered
- Details of the **results of investigations** into such fluctuations/relationships
- The audit **conclusions** reached
- **Information considered** necessary for assisting in the **planning** of subsequent audits

Exam focus point

> In the exam you may be given a set of figures and:
>
> (a) Asked to calculate changes, key ratios etc and hence identify significant areas of the accounts
> (b) Asked what audit work will be required on these significant areas
>
> When analysing figures, make sure that the points which you make are consistent with each other. Factors that indicate possible going concern problems are particularly important.

Mention of analytical procedures will generally be worth a couple of marks in any question on substantive testing. However you will not get any marks just for saying 'perform analytical procedures'; you will need to give details of the procedures that should be performed.

6 Automated tools and techniques (ATTs)

Exam focus point

> Use of computers on audits is now common practice. The examiner expects you to consider the computer aspects of auditing as a matter of course. Therefore in answering questions on obtaining evidence, remember to include reference to ATTs if they are relevant.

The overall objectives and scope of an audit do not change when an audit is conducted in a computerised environment. However, the application of auditing procedures may require auditors to consider techniques that use the computer as an audit tool. These uses of the computer for audit work are known as automated tools and techniques (ATTs).

(a) The absence of input documents or the lack of a visible audit trail may require the use of ATTs in the application of tests of control and substantive procedures.

(b) The effectiveness and efficiency of auditing procedures may be improved through the use of ATTs.

Computers can be used to perform either substantive audit procedures or tests of controls. There are two particularly common types of ATTs: **audit software** and **test data**.

Audit software is used to perform substantive procedures, including:

- **Tests of details of transactions and balances**, for example the use of audit software to test all (or a sample) of the transactions in a computer file
- **Analytical procedures**, for example the use of audit software to identify unusual fluctuations or items

Test data is used to perform tests of controls, including:

- **Tests of computer information system controls**, for example the use of test data to test access procedures to the program libraries, or the functioning of a programmed procedure

The **advantages** of using ATTs are:

- Auditors can test programme controls as well as general internal controls associated with computers.
- Auditors can test a greater number of items more quickly and accurately than would be the case otherwise.
- Auditors test transactions rather than paper records of transactions that could be incorrect.
- Once set up, ATTs are cost-effective in the long-term if the client does not change its systems.
- Results from ATTs can be compared with results from traditional testing – if the results correlate, overall confidence is increased.

Next we will explore the two common types of ATT, **audit software** and **test data**.

6.1 Audit software

Audit software consists of computer programs used by the auditors, as part of their substantive auditing procedures, to process data of audit significance from the entity's accounting system. Regardless of the source of the programs, the auditor should substantiate their validity for audit purposes prior to use. Audit software may consist of the **generalised audit software** or **custom audit software**.

(a) **Generalised audit software** allows auditors to perform tests on computer files and databases, such as:

- Reading and extracting data from a client's systems for further testing;
- Selecting data that meets certain criteria;
- Performing arithmetic calculations on data;
- Facilitating audit sampling; and
- Producing documents and reports.

Examples of generalised audit software are ACT and IDEA.

(b) **Custom audit software** is written by auditors for specific tasks when generalised audit software cannot be used.

Examples of uses of audit software are:

- Interrogation software, which accesses the client's data files
- Comparison programs which compare versions of a program
- Interactive software for interrogation of online systems
- Resident code software to review transactions as they are processed

There are a number of **difficulties** using audit software, such as:

- High set-up costs due to the detailed knowledge of the client's systems and files required before audit software can be used.
- Audit software may not be available for the client's specific systems, particularly if they are bespoke.
- The audit software may produce too much output if faulty and waste auditor time.
- Checking client records in a 'live' situation may cause corruption and, therefore, disruption to the client.

6.2 Test data

Test data techniques are used in **conducting tests of controls** by entering data (eg a sample of transactions) into an entity's computer system, and comparing the results obtained with predetermined results. Examples include:

(a) Test data used to test **specific controls** in computer programs.

For example, an auditor could try to access data or areas of a computer system which are password protected in order to determine whether the control is operating effectively.

(b) Test transactions

Here the auditor selects from previously processed transactions or transactions created by the auditors to test **specific processing characteristics** of an entity's computer system. Such transactions are generally processed separately from the entity's normal processing. Test data can for example be used to check the controls that prevent the processing of **invalid data** by entering data with say a non-existent customer code or worth an unreasonable amount, or a transaction which may if processed break customer credit limits.

(c) Test transactions used in an **embedded test facility**. This is where a 'dummy' unit (eg a department or employee) is established, and to which test transactions are posted during the normal processing cycle.

A significant problem with test data is that any resulting corruption of data files has to be corrected. This is difficult with modern real-time systems, which often have built-in (and highly desirable) controls to ensure that data entered **cannot** be easily removed without leaving a mark.

Other problems with **test data** are that it only tests the operation of the system at a **single point of time**, and auditors are only testing controls in the programs being run and controls which they know about. The problems involved mean that test data is being used less as an ATT.

Question
Invisible evidence

Try to think of examples of where visible evidence may be lacking in the accounting process.

Answer

(a) **Input documents** may be non-existent where sales orders are entered on-line. In addition, accounting transactions, such as discounts and interest calculations, may be generated by computer programs with no visible authorisation of individual transactions.

(b) The system may not produce a visible audit trail of **transactions processed** through the computer. Delivery notes and suppliers' invoices may be matched by a computer program. In addition, programmed control procedures, such as checking customer credit limits, may provide visible evidence only on an exception basis. In such cases, there may be no visible evidence that all transactions have been processed.

(c) **Output reports** may not be produced by the system. In addition, a printed report may only contain summary totals while supporting details are kept in computer files.

The major steps to be undertaken by the auditors in the application of ATTs are as follows.

- **Set the objective** of the ATT application
- **Determine** the **content** and **accessibility** of the entity's **files**
- **Define** the **transaction types** to be tested
- **Define the procedures** to be performed on the data
- **Define** the **output requirements**
- **Identify** the audit and computer **personnel** who may participate in the design and application of the ATT
- **Refine** the estimates of **costs** and **benefits**
- Ensure that the **use of the ATT is properly controlled** and **documented**
- Arrange the **administrative activities**, including the necessary skills and computer facilities
- Execute the **ATT application**
- **Evaluate the results**

Question — CAATs

(a) Outline the major types of ATTs and describe the potential benefits that might be derived from using them.
(b) Explain what is meant by a 'test pack'.
(c) Briefly explain the use that the auditors could make of such a test pack when examining a sales ledger system maintained on a computer system.
(d) Briefly outline the main practical problems encountered when using a test pack.

Answer

(a) Audit techniques that involve, directly or indirectly, the use of a client's computer are referred to as ATTs, of which the following are the two principal categories.

(i) **Audit software**: computer programs used for audit purposes to examine the contents of the client's computer files

(ii) **Test data**: data used by the auditors for computer processing to test the operation of the enterprise's computer programs

The benefits of using ATTs are as follows.

(i) By using computer audit programs, the auditors can scrutinise large volumes of data and concentrate skilled manual resources on the investigation of results, rather than on the extraction of information.

(ii) Once the programs have been written and tested, the costs of operation are relatively low, indeed the auditors do not necessarily have to be present during its use (though there are frequently practical advantages in the auditors attending).

(b) A 'test pack' consists of input data submitted by the auditors for processing by the enterprise's computer based accounting system. It may be processed during a normal production run ('live') or during a special run at a point in time outside the normal cycle ('dead').

The primary use of the test pack is in testing of application controls. The data used in the test pack will often contain items which should appear in exception reports produced by the system. The results of the processed test pack will be compared with the expected results.

(c) The auditors could use a test pack to test the receivables ledger system by including data in the pack which would normally be processed through the system, such as:

(i) Sales
(ii) Credits allowed
(iii) Cash receipts
(iv) Discounts allowed

The processing of the input would involve:

(i) Production of sales invoices (with correct discounts)
(ii) Production of credit notes
(iii) Posting of cash received, invoices and credit notes to individual receivable's accounts to appear on statements
(iv) Posting all transactions to the receivables ledger control account and producing balances

The result produced would be compared with those predicted in the test pack. Errors should appear on exception reports produced by the computer, for example, a customer credit limit being breached.

Note that where an entity has an integrated sales module the sales invoice, credit note, and monies received would be posted within the module and would automatically update the individual receivables account as well as the total receivables. Therefore, a receivables control account would not be used.

(d) The practical problems involved in using a test pack are as follows:

(i) In using 'live' processing there will be problems removing or reversing the test data, which might corrupt master file information.
(ii) In using 'dead' processing the auditors do not test the system actually used by the client.
(iii) The system will be checked by the test pack, but not the year-end balances, which will still require sufficient audit work. Costs may therefore be high.
(iv) Any auditors who wish to design a test pack must have sufficient skill in computing, and also a thorough knowledge of the client's system.
(v) Any changes in the client's system will mean that the test pack will have to be rewritten which will be costly and time-consuming.

7 Audit sampling

FAST FORWARD

Auditors usually seek evidence from **less than 100%** of items of the balance or transaction being tested.

7.1 Introduction to audit sampling

Auditors do not normally examine all the information available to them; it would be impractical to do so and using audit sampling will produce valid conclusions.

Some testing procedures do **not** involve sampling, such as:

- **Testing 100%** of items in a population (this should be obvious)
- Testing all items with a **certain characteristic** as selection is not representative

Auditors are unlikely to test 100% of items when carrying out tests of control, but 100% testing may be appropriate for certain substantive procedures. For example if the population is made up of a small number of high value items, there is a high risk of material misstatement and other means do not provide sufficient appropriate audit evidence, 100% examination may be appropriate.

ISA 530 *Audit Sampling* gives guidance when using samples.

Key terms

> **Audit sampling** involves the application of audit procedures to less than 100% of the items within an account balance or class of transactions such that all sampling units have a chance of selection. This will enable the auditor to obtain and evaluate audit evidence about some characteristic of the items selected in order to form or assist in forming a conclusion concerning the population.
>
> **Population** is the entire set of data from which a sample is selected and about which an auditor wishes to draw conclusions.

The auditors may use judgemental or statistical methods of sampling.

Key term

> **Statistical sampling** is any approach to sampling that involves random selection of a sample, and use of probability theory to evaluate sample results, including measurement of sampling risk.

7.2 Design and size of the sample

When designing the sample, the ISA requires the auditor to 'consider the **purpose** of the audit procedure and the **characteristics of the population** from which the sample will be drawn'.

Auditors must consider the specific audit objectives to be achieved and the audit procedures which are most likely to achieve them. The auditors also need to consider the nature and characteristics of the audit evidence sought.

The population may be divided into sampling units in a variety of ways, eg an individual accounts receivable balance or, in monetary unit sampling, $1 of the total accounts receivable balance. Auditors must **define** the **sampling unit** in order to obtain an efficient and effective sample to achieve the particular audit objectives.

Key term

> **Sampling units** are the individual items constituting a population.

The ISA requires that the auditor 'shall select items for the sample in such a way that each sampling unit in the population has a chance of selection'. This requires that **all items** in the population have an opportunity be selected.

There are a number of selection methods available.

(a) **Random selection** ensures that all items in the population have an equal chance of selection, eg by use of random number tables or computerised generator.

(b) **Systematic selection** involves selecting items using a constant interval between selections, the first interval having a random start. When using systematic selection auditors must ensure that the

population is not structured in such a manner that the sampling interval corresponds with a particular pattern in the population.

(c) **Haphazard selection** may be an alternative to random selection provided auditors are satisfied that the sample is representative of the entire population. This method requires care to guard against making a selection which is biased, for example towards items which are easily located, as they may not be representative. It should not be used if auditors are carrying out statistical sampling.

(d) **Sequence or block selection**. Sequence sampling may be used to check whether certain items have particular characteristics. For example an auditor may use a sample of 50 consecutive cheques to check whether cheques are signed by authorised signatories rather than picking 50 single cheques throughout the year. Sequence sampling may however produce samples that are not representative of the population as a whole, particularly if misstatements only occurred during a certain part of the period, and hence the misstatements found cannot be projected onto the rest of the population.

(e) **Monetary Unit Sampling (MUS)**. This is a selection method which ensures that every $1 in a population has an equal chance of being selected for testing. How MUS works is shown in the example below. The advantages of this selection method are that it is easy when computers are used, and that every material item will automatically be sampled. Disadvantages include the fact that if computers are not used, it can be time consuming to pick the sample, and that MUS does not cope well with misstatements of understatement of negative balances.

7.2.1 Example: MUS

You are auditing trade accounts payable. Trade account payables total $500,000 and materiality is $50,000. You will select the balances containing the 50,000th $1 from the ledger below.

Payable	Balance	Cumulative total	Selected
A	30,000	30,000	
B	35,000	65,000	Yes
C	45,000	110,000	Yes
D	**52,000**	162,000	Yes
E	13,000	175,000	
F	**50,000**	225,000	Yes
G	23,000	248,000	
H	500	248,500	
I	42,000	290,000	Yes
J	47,000	337,000	Yes
K	**54,000**	391,000	Yes
L	17,000	408,000	Yes
M	**80,000**	488,000	Yes
N	12,000	500,000	Yes
	500,000		

Material items are shown in bold and have all been selected. The cumulative column shows you when the next 50,000th $1 has been reached.

Stratification may be appropriate. Stratification is the process of dividing a population into subpopulations, each of which is a group of sampling units, which have similar characteristics (often in monetary value). Each sampling unit can only belong to one, specifically designed stratum, thus reducing the variability within each stratum. This enables the auditors to direct audit effort towards items which, for example, contain the greatest potential monetary misstatement. Ways of dividing items into strata include by age or by amount.

7.2.2 Risk

As we shall see in the next chapter, in obtaining evidence, the auditor should use professional judgement to assess audit risk and design audit procedures to ensure this risk is reduced to an acceptably low level. In determining the sample size, the auditor should consider whether sampling risk is reduced to an acceptably low level.

Key terms

> **Sampling risk** arises from the possibility that the auditor's conclusion, based on a sample of a certain size, may be different from the conclusion that would be reached if the entire population were subjected to the same audit procedure.
>
> **Non-sampling risk** arises from factors that cause the auditor to reach an erroneous conclusion for any reason not related to the size of the sample. For example, most audit evidence is persuasive rather than conclusive, the auditor might use inappropriate procedures, or the auditor might misinterpret evidence and fail to recognise an error.

The auditors are faced with sampling risk in both tests of control and substantive procedures, as follows.

(a) **Tests of controls**

　(i) **Risk of under-reliance.** The risk that, although the sample result does not support the auditor's assessment of control risk, the actual compliance rate would support such an assessment

　(ii) **Risk of over-reliance.** The risk that, although the sample result supports the auditor's assessment of control risk, the actual compliance rate would not support such an assessment

(b) **Substantive procedures**

　(i) **Risk of incorrect rejection.** The risk that, although the sample result supports the conclusion that a recorded account balance or class of transactions is materially misstated, in fact it is not materially misstated

　(ii) **Risk of incorrect acceptance.** The risk that, although the sample result supports the conclusion that a recorded account balance or class of transactions is not materially misstated, in fact it is materially misstated

The **greater** their reliance on the results of the procedure in question, the **lower** the sampling risk auditors will be willing to accept and the **larger** the sample size will be.

Key terms

> **Tolerable misstatement** is the maximum misstatement in the population that the auditor would be willing to accept so as to ensure that any total misstatement in the population does not exceed materiality.
>
> **Tolerable rate of deviation** is the maximum rate of deviation from an internal control that the auditors will accept.

These tolerable levels are considered during the planning stage and, for substantive procedures, is related to the auditor's judgement about materiality. We shall look at these matters in the next chapter. The smaller the tolerable misstatement or rate of deviation, the greater the sample size will need to be.

Larger samples will be required when misstatements are expected than would be required if none were expected, in order to conclude that the actual misstatement is less than the tolerable misstatement or rate of deviation. The size and frequency of misstatements is important when assessing the sample size; for the same overall misstatement, larger fewer misstatements will mean a bigger sample size than for smaller more frequent misstatements. If the expected misstatement rate is high then sampling may not be appropriate. When considering expected misstatement, the auditors should consider:

- **Misstatements identified in previous audits**

- **Changes in the entity's procedures**
- **Evidence available from other procedures**

Most auditing firms use computer programmes to set sample sizes, based on risk assessments and materiality.

7.3 Evaluation of sample results

7.3.1 Analysis of misstatements and deviations in the sample

To begin with, the auditors must consider whether the items in question are true misstatements, as they defined them before the test, eg a misposting between customer accounts will not affect the total accounts receivable.

When the expected audit evidence regarding a specific sample item cannot be found, the auditors must obtain sufficient appropriate audit evidence by performing the procedure on a **replacement item**. In such cases, the item is not treated as a misstatement.

The **qualitative** aspects of misstatements should also be considered, including the **nature and cause** of the misstatement. Auditors should also consider any possible effects the misstatement might have on **other parts of the audit** including the general effect on the financial statements and on the auditors' assessment of the accounting and internal control systems.

Where common features are discovered in misstatements, the auditors may decide to identify all items in the population which possess the common feature (eg location), thereby producing a sub-population. Audit procedures could then be extended in this area.

On some occasions the auditor may decide that the misstatements are **anomalies**. To be considered anomalous, the auditors have to be certain that the misstatements are not representative of the population. Extra work will be required to prove that a misstatement is anomalous.

Key term

> **Anomaly** means a misstatement that arises from an isolated event that has not recurred other than on specifically identifiable occasions and is therefore not representative of misstatements in the population.

7.3.2 Projection of misstatements

The auditors are required to project the misstatement results from the sample on to the relevant population. The auditors will **estimate the probable misstatement** in the population by extrapolating the misstatements found in the sample. This may be done by using:

(a) The ratio method

$$\text{Misstatement in sample} \times \frac{\text{population value}}{\text{sample value}}$$

(b) The difference method

$$\text{Misstatement in sample} \times \frac{\text{number of items in population (eg invoices)}}{\text{number of items in sample (eg invoices)}}$$

For substantive procedures, auditors will then **estimate any further misstatement** that might not have been detected because of the imprecision of the technique (in addition to consideration of the qualitative aspects of the misstatements).

Auditors should also consider the effect of the projected misstatement on other areas of the audit. The auditors should compare the projected population misstatement (net of adjustments made by the entity in the case of substantive procedures) to the tolerable misstatement or rate of deviation, taking account of other relevant audit procedures.

7.3.3 Reassessing sampling risk

If the projected misstatement **exceeds** or is close to tolerable misstatement, then the auditors should re-assess sampling risk. If it is unacceptable, they should consider extending auditing procedures or performing alternative procedures. However if after alternative procedures the auditors still believe the actual misstatement rate is higher than the tolerable misstatement or deviation rate, they should re-assess control risk if the test is a test of controls; if the test is a substantive test, they should consider whether the accounts need to be adjusted.

7.4 Summary

Key stages in the sampling process are as follows.

- Determining objectives and population
- Determining sample size
- Choosing method of sample selection
- Analysing the results and projecting misstatements

Question — Statistical sampling

Present the arguments for and against the use of statistical sampling in auditing and reach a conclusion.

Answer

An inevitable characteristic of audit testing is that a sample only of transactions or items can be examined. The auditors examine a sample of items and thereby seek to obtain assurance that the whole group is acceptable.

Provided that conditions are appropriate for its use, a statistical approach to sampling is likely to have many advantages over the alternative of judgement sampling.

Conditions favouring the use of statistical sampling are:

(a) Existence of large and homogeneous groups of items
(b) Low expected misstatement rate and clear definition of misstatement
(c) Reasonable ease of identifying and obtaining access to items selected

If these conditions are present, statistical sampling is likely to have the following advantages.

(a) At the conclusion of a test the auditors are able to state a definite level of confidence they may have that the whole population conforms to the sample result, within a stated precision limit.

(b) Sample size is objectively determined, having regard to the degree of risk the auditors are prepared to accept for each application.

(c) It may be possible to use smaller sample sizes, thus saving time and money.

(d) The process of fixing required precision and confidence levels compels the auditors to consider and clarify their audit objectives.

(e) The results of tests can be expressed in precise mathematical terms.

(f) Bias is eliminated.

Statistical sampling is not without disadvantages.

(a) The technique may be applied blindly without prior consideration of the suitability of the statistical sampling for the audit task to be performed. This disadvantage may be overcome by establishing

soundly-based procedures for use in the firm, incorporating standards on sampling in the firm's audit manual, instituting training programmes for audit staff and proper supervision.

(b) Unsuspected patterns or bias in sample selection may invalidate the conclusions. The probability of these factors arising must be carefully judged by the auditor before they decide to adopt statistical sampling.

(c) It frequently needs back-up by further tests within the population reviewed: large items, non-routine items, sensitive items like directors' transactions.

(d) At the conclusion of a statistical sampling-based test the auditors may fail to appreciate the further action necessary based on the results obtained. This potential disadvantage may be overcome by adequate training and supervision, and by requiring careful evaluation of all statistical sampling tests.

(e) Statistical sampling may be applied carelessly, without due confirmation that the sample selected is acceptably random.

(f) The selection exercise can be time-consuming.

(g) The degree of tolerance of acceptable misstatement must be predetermined.

The disadvantages listed above can all be overcome if the technique is applied sensibly and competently.

Provided that the conditions favouring its use are present, statistical sampling is a useful technique for several auditing tasks.

(a) Tests of controls
(b) Substantive procedures
(c) Direct confirmation of accounts receivable and payable
(d) Fraud investigation using discovery sampling

Statistical techniques should be used when they are convenient and of positive use to the auditors in achieving a level of reliability in their results. If they are used selectively, in cases where their advantages are conspicuous and their disadvantages can be reduced to a minimum, they can make a significant contribution towards greater quality control on an audit. But it is hard to resist the argument that properly devised and controlled 'judgemental methods' can achieve the same high standards with fewer administrative or technical problems.

Exam focus point

In the exam, you may be asked to describe sampling in general terms or how it will be used in a specific situation.

8 Documenting audit evidence

FAST FORWARD

It is important to document audit work performed in **working papers** to:

- Enable reporting partner to ensure all planned work has been completed adequately
- Provide details of work done for future reference
- Assist in planning and control of future audits
- Encourage a methodical approach and therefore quality

8.1 Working papers

All audit work must be documented: the working papers are the tangible evidence of the work done in support of the audit opinion. ISA 230 *Audit Documentation* states that 'auditors shall prepare audit documentation on a timely basis.'

Audit documentation is necessary for the following reasons:

- It provides **evidence of the auditor's basis for a conclusion** about the achievement of the overall objective.
- It provides **evidence that the audit was planned and performed** in accordance with ISAs and other legal and regulatory requirements.
- It assists the engagement team to plan and perform the audit.
- It assists team members responsible for supervision to direct, supervise and review audit work.
- It enables the team to be accountable for its work.
- It allows a **record of matters of continuing significance** to be retained.
- It enables the conduct of **quality control reviews** and inspections (both internal and external).

8.2 Form and content of working papers

FAST FORWARD — Working papers should be headed in a certain way and contain certain information. They may be automated.

The ISA requires working papers to be sufficiently complete and detailed to provide an overall understanding of the audit. Auditors cannot record everything they consider. Therefore judgement must be used as to the extent of working papers, based on the following general rule:

> What would be sufficient to enable an experienced auditor, having no previous connection with the audit, to understand the nature, timing and extent and the results of audit procedures, audit evidence obtained, significant matters arising during the audit and conclusions reached, and significant professional judgements made in reaching those conclusions.

The form and content of working papers are affected by matters such as:

- The **size and complexity** of the entity
- The **nature** of the audit procedures to be performed
- The **identified risks** of material misstatement
- The **significance** of the audit evidence obtained
- The nature and extent of **exceptions** identified

(ISA 230: para. A2)

8.2.1 Examples of working papers

- Information obtained in understanding the entity and its environment, including its internal control, such as the following:
    - Information concerning the legal documents, agreements and minutes
    - Extracts or copies of important legal documents, agreements and minutes
    - Information concerning the industry, economic environment and legislative environment within which the entity operates.
    - Extracts from the entity's internal control manual

- Evidence of the planning process including audit programs and any changes thereto
- Evidence of the auditor's consideration of the work of the internal audit function and conclusions reached
- Analyses of transactions and balances
- Analyses of significant ratios and trends
- The identified and assessed risks of material misstatements at the financial statement and the assertion level
- A record of the nature, timing, extent and results of auditing procedures
- Evidence that the work performed by assistants was supervised and reviewed
- An indication as to who performed the audit procedures and when they were performed
- Details of audit procedures applied regarding components whose financial statements are audited by another auditor
- Copies of communications with other auditors, experts and other third parties
- Copies of letters or notes concerning audit matters communicated to or discussed with management or those charged with governance, including the terms of the engagement and material weaknesses in internal control
- Letters of representation received from the entity
- Conclusions reached by the auditor concerning significant aspects of the audit, including how exceptions and unusual matters, if any, disclosed by the auditor's procedures were resolved or treated.
- Copies of the financial statements and auditors' reports
- Notes of discussions about significant matters with management and others
- In exceptional circumstances, the reasons for departing from a basic principle or essential procedure of an ISA and how the alternative procedure performed achieve the audit objective

The following is an illustration of a typical audit working paper.

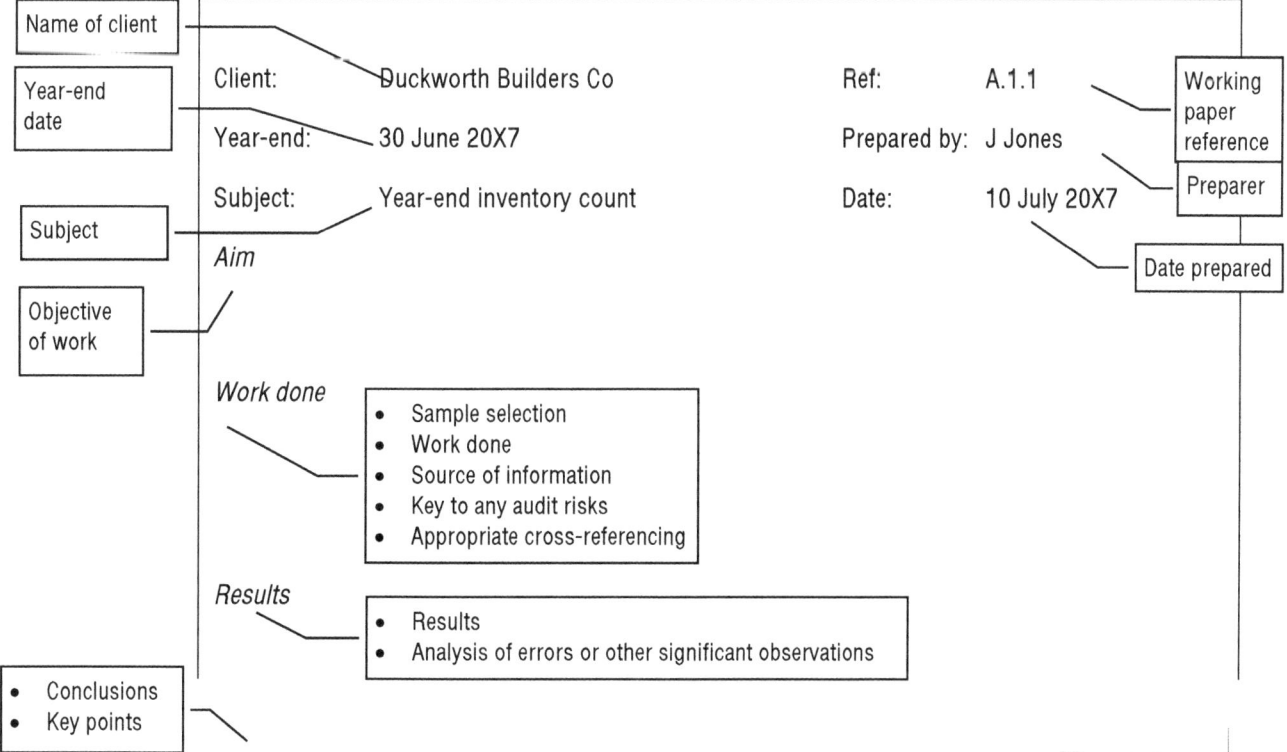

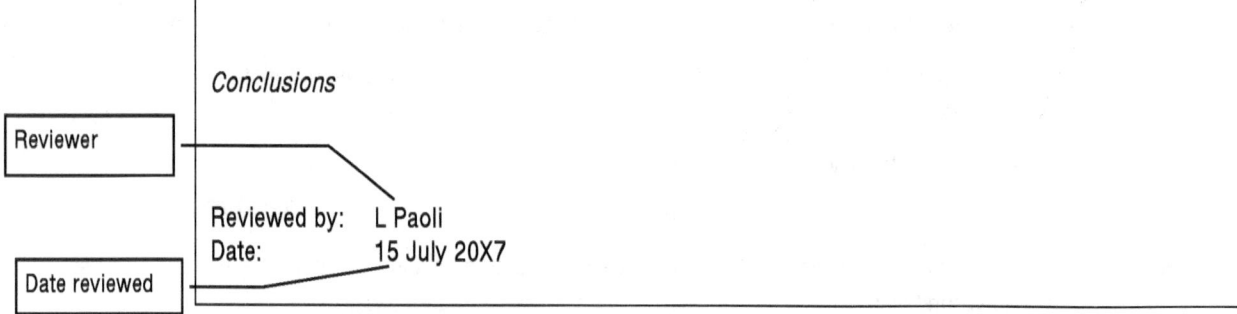

The auditor should record the identifying characteristics of specific items or matters being tested. Firms should have standard **referencing** and **filing** procedures for working papers, to facilitate their review.

8.2.2 Audit files

For recurring audits, working papers may be split between:

Permanent audit files (containing information of **continuing importance** to the audit). These contain:

- Engagement letters
- New client questionnaire
- The memorandum and articles
- Other legal documents such as prospectuses, leases, sales agreement
- Details of the history of the client's business
- Board minutes of continuing relevance
- Previous years' signed accounts, analytical review and management letters
- Accounting systems notes, previous years' control questionnaires

Current audit files (containing information of relevance to the current year's audit). These should be compiled on a timely basis after the completion of the audit and should contain:

- Financial statements
- Accounts checklists
- Management accounts details
- Reconciliations of management and financial account
- A summary of unadjusted misstatements
- Report to partner including details of significant events and misstatements
- Review notes
- Audit planning memorandum
- Time budgets and summaries
- Letter of representation
- Management letter
- Notes of board minutes
- Communications with third parties such as experts or other auditors

They also contain working papers covering each audit area. These should include the following:

- A lead schedule including details of the figures to be included in the accounts
- Problems encountered and conclusions drawn
- Audit programmes
- Risk assessments
- Sampling plans
- Analytical review
- Details of substantive tests and tests of control

If it is necessary to modify/add new audit documentation to a file after it has been assembled, the auditor should document:

- Who made the changes, and when, and by whom they were reviewed
- The reasons for making changes
- The effect of changes on the auditors' conclusions

If, in exceptional circumstances, changes are made to an audit file after the audit report has been signed, the auditor should document:

- The circumstances
- The audit procedures performed, evidence obtained, conclusions drawn
- When and by whom changes to audit documents were made and reviewed

8.3 Standardised and automated working papers

The use of **standardised** working papers, for example, checklists, specimen letters, may improve the efficiency of audit work but they can be dangerous because they may lead to auditors mechanically following an approach without using audit judgement.

Automated working paper packages have been developed which can make the documenting of audit work much easier. Such programs aid preparation of working papers, lead schedules, trial balance and the financial statements themselves. These are automatically cross-referenced, adjusted and balanced by the computer.

The **advantages** of automated working papers are as follows.

- The risk of misstatements is reduced.
- The working papers will be neater and easier to review.
- The time saved will be substantial as adjustments can be made easily to all working papers, including working papers summarising the key analytical information.
- Standard forms do not have to be carried to audit locations.
- Audit working papers can be transmitted for review via a modem, or fax facilities (if both the sending and receiving computers have fax boards and fax software).

Question — Working papers

'Auditors base their judgement as to the extent of working papers upon what would be necessary to provide an experienced auditor, with no previous connection with the audit, with an understanding of the work performed, the results of audit procedures, audit evidence obtained, significant matters arising during the audit and conclusions reached.'

Describe four benefits that auditors will obtain from working papers that meet the above requirement.

Answer

- The reporting partner can be satisfied that work delegated by him has been completed adequately.
- Working papers are a record of work performed and conclusions drawn which might be necessary in the future, for example, in litigation.
- Good working papers and the planning and control of future audits.
- Preparing working papers encourages auditors to adopt a methodical approach. This is likely to improve quality.

8.4 Retention of working papers

Judgement may have to be used in deciding the length of holding working papers, and further consideration should be given to the matter before their destruction. The AIA recommends **seven years as a minimum period**.

Working papers are the property of the auditors. They are not a substitute for, nor part of, the entity's accounting records.

Auditors must follow ethical guidance on the confidentiality of audit working papers. They may, at their discretion, release parts of or whole working papers to the entity, as long as disclosure does not undermine 'the independence or validity of the audit process'. Information should not be made available to third parties without the permission of the entity.

Chapter roundup

- Auditors must obtain **sufficient appropriate** audit evidence.
- Sufficiency relates to the **quantity** of evidence required which depends on the level of audit risk and the strength of the evidence.
- To be **appropriate**, evidence must be **relevant to the financial statement assertions** being tested and **reliable** (this depends on the source and format of the evidence).
- Audit procedures can be in the form of **tests of controls** or **substantive procedures** and are designed to obtain evidence about the financial statement assertions. Such procedures can be performed manually or using automated tools and techniques (ATTs).
- Audit evidence can be obtained by **inspection, observation, inquiry and confirmation, recalculation, reperformance and analytical procedures**.
- There are two types of **ATTs**: **audit software** (used to perform substantive procedures) and **test data** (used to perform tests of controls).
- Auditors usually perform **audit sampling** and seek evidence from **less than 100% of items** of the balance or transaction being tested.
- It is important to **document audit work performed** in working papers to:
  - Enable reporting partner to ensure all planned work has been completed adequately
  - Provide details of work done for future reference
  - Assist in planning and control of future audits
  - Encourage a methodical approach and therefore quality
- **Working papers** should be headed in a certain way and contain certain information. They may be automated.

Quick quiz

1. Explain the meaning of the phrase 'sufficient appropriate' audit evidence.
2. Name seven financial statement assertions.
3. Fill in the blanks.

   Audit evidence from external sources is .... than that obtained from the entity's records.

   Evidence obtained directly .... is more .... than that obtained by or from the entity.

4. Link the type of account with the purpose of the primary test in directional testing.

   (a) Assets   (i) Overstatement
   (b) Liabilities   (ii) Overstatement
   (c) Income   (iii) Understatement
   (d) Expense   (iv) Understatement

5. Identify the significant relationships in the list of items below.

   (a) Payables   (b) Interest   (c) Purchases   (d) Sales
   (e) Amortisation   (f) Loans   (g) Receivables   (h) Intangibles

6   Name two types of audit software.

    (1) ....

    (2) ....

7   Match the definitions to the terms.

    (a) Sampling risk

    (b) Non-sampling risk

    (i) The risk that the auditors' conclusion, based on a sample, may be different from the conclusions that would be reached if the entire population was subject to the same audit procedure.

    (ii) The risk that the auditors might use inappropriate procedures or might misinterpret evidence and thus fail to recognise an error.

8   Name three methods of sample selection.

    (1) ....

    (2) ....

    (3) ....

9   What is the general rule for documenting the audit process?

10 Give two advantages and one disadvantage of standardised working papers.

    Advantages   **Disadvantage**

    (1) ....   (1) ....

    (2) ....

11 Correct the table, putting the working papers under the correct heading.

Current audit file	Permanent audit file
Engagement letters	New client questionnaire
Financial statements	Management letter
Accounts checklists	Audit planning memo
Board minutes of continuing relevance	Accounting systems notes

Answers to quick quiz

1. **Sufficiency** is the measure of the quantity of audit evidence.

   Appropriateness is the measure of the quality (relevance and reliability) of audit evidence.

2. From: existence, rights and obligations, occurrence, completeness, accuracy, classification, cut-off, presentation, accuracy, valuation and allocation.

3. More reliable
   By auditors, reliable

4. (a) (i)
   (b) (iii)
   (c) (ii)
   (d) (iv)

5. (a) (c)
   (b) (f)
   (d) (g)
   (e) (h)

6. From:

   (1) Generalised audit software
   (2) Custom audit software

7. (a) (i)
   (b) (ii)

8. (1) Random
   (2) Haphazard
   (3) Systematic

9. What would be sufficient to enable an experienced auditor, having no previous connection with the audit, to understand the nature, timing and extent and results of audit procedures, audit evidence obtained, significant matters arising during the audit and conclusions reached, and significant professional judgements made in reaching conclusions

10. **Advantages**

    (1) Facilitate the delegation of work
    (2) Means to control quality

    Disadvantage

    (1) Detracts from proper exercise of professional judgement

11.

Current audit file	Permanent audit file
Financial statements	Engagement letters
Management letter	New client questionnaire
Accounts checklists	Board minutes of continuing relevance
Audit planning memo	Accounting systems notes

End of chapter question

Goreng Ltd (AIA May 2008)

Camilla Lee is the audit senior on the audit of Goreng Ltd. She has just completed the detailed audit testing on the sales cycle. As part of her testing, she used statistical sampling techniques to choose a sample of sales invoices. She checked this sample to ensure that the total value of each sales invoice agreed with the total that had been entered in the sales day book.

An extract from her audit working papers reveals the following information:

Total value of sales invoices = $1,560,400
Total number of sales invoices = 253
Number of items in sample = 11
Tolerable misstatement = $30,000

Invoice number	Total per invoice $	Total per sales day book $	Difference $
003	3,486	3,486	0
056	588	588	0
115	10,060	10,600	540
119	24,003	34,003	10,000
186	120	120	0
194	3,999	3,999	0
203	46	46	0
211	80,050	80,050	0
238	206	206	0
251	160	160	0
260	10,000	10,000	0
Total	132,718	143,258	10,540

Required

(a) Describe the main advantages for the auditor of using statistical sampling techniques rather than non-statistical (judgement) sampling. **(4 marks)**

(b) Describe the factors the auditor should have taken into account when determining the size of the sample to be tested. **(8 marks)**

(c) Evaluate the results of the testing of Goreng Ltd's sales invoices. **(10 marks)**

(d) Describe the auditor's possible courses of action if the tolerable misstatement has been exceeded. **(4 marks)**

(e) Explain why the use of sampling may not always be appropriate for carrying out audit testing. **(4 marks)**

(Total = 30 marks)

Sparks Ltd (AIA May 2006)

Sparks Ltd is a company that manufactures electrical goods, which it sells to retail shops. You are about to undertake the audit work for the year ended 31 January 20X6. The draft statement of financial position for the year is set out below, together with the statement of financial position for the year ended 31 January 20X5.

	31 January 20X6		31 January 20X5	
	$'000	$'000	$'000	$'000
Non-current assets				
Property, plant and equipment		40		42
Investments		4		4
		44		46
Current assets				
Inventory	104		358	
Trade receivables	156		272	
Cash	26		70	
	286		700	
Current liabilities				
Trade payables	242		266	
Bank loan	10		10	
	252		276	
Net current assets		34		424
Long term liabilities				
Bank loan		(40)		(50)
Provision for warranties		(40)		
Total (liabilities)/assets		(2)		420
Capital and reserves				
Share capital		4		4
Retained earnings		(6)		416
		(2)		420

Required

(a) Explain the concept of audit risk, and describe the separate components of the audit risk model. **(9 marks)**

(b) Explain the importance of analytical procedures as a tool for the auditor. **(6 marks)**

(c) Review the statements of financial position for Sparks Ltd, and set out the areas on which audit work should be concentrated, giving reasons in each case. **(10 marks)**

(Total = 25 marks)

Using the work of others

Topic list	Syllabus reference
1 Using the work of internal audit	3.4
2 Using the work of an auditor's expert	3.4

Introduction

In this chapter, we explore the options open to the auditor in terms of making use of other people and their work in contributing to the audit opinion.

Internal auditors can, and often do, carry out similar audit tests to external auditors. The external auditors will sometimes seek to use the work of internal audit. Section 1 of this chapter looks at the extent to which external auditors can use and rely on the work of internal auditors. It outlines the guidance in this matter, which is found in ISA 610 (Revised) *Using the Work of Internal Auditors*.

While auditors are highly trained individuals, it is possible that when conducting an audit they encounter issues which are outside the scope of their expertise, for example, valuation of buildings. In such circumstances an auditor will have to consult an auditor's expert. ISA 620 *Using the Work of an Auditor's Expert*, outlines the factors an auditor should bear in mind, as we see in Section 2.

1 Using the work of internal audit

FAST FORWARD

External auditors may make use of the work of the internal audit function when carrying out external audit procedures.

Key term

Internal audit function is 'a function of an entity that performs assurance and consulting activities designed to evaluate and improve the effectiveness of an entity's governance, risk management and internal control processes'.

ISA 610 (Revised) *Using the Work of Internal Auditors* is relevant where the audited entity has an internal audit (IA) function, and the external auditor expects to make use of the work of that function in carrying out the external audit. It **does not require** an external auditor to make use of the work of an internal audit function.

Note that ISA 315 (Revised) requires that, where there is an internal audit function, the external auditor obtains an understanding of that function. As a result of this assessment, the auditor may develop an expectation that the work of the internal auditor can be used to modify the nature or timing, or reduce the extent of audit procedures which need to be performed.

The objectives of external auditors who **intend** to use the work of internal audit are to:

- To determine whether the work of the internal audit function or direct assistance from internal auditors can be used, and if so, in which areas and to what extent;
- If using the work of the internal audit function, to determine whether that work is appropriate for the purposes of the audit; and
- If using internal auditors to provide direct assistance, to appropriately direct, supervise and review their work.

(ISA 610 (Revised): para. 13)

The **external auditor has sole responsibility for the opinion** expressed, but may use internal audit work in obtaining audit evidence to form a decision on the truth and fairness of the financial statements.

As we discussed in Chapter 3, the scope and objectives of the internal audit function vary widely but internal audit often reviews accounting and internal control systems, examine financial and operating information and monitor compliance with laws and regulations. An external auditor may be able to make use of some of this work rather than, in effect, doing the same work again.

An effective IA function may reduce, modify or alter the timing of external audit procedures, but it can **never** eliminate them entirely.

Even where the IA function is deemed ineffective, it may still be useful to be aware of the IA conclusions. The effectiveness of IA will have a great impact on how the external auditors assess the whole control system and the assessment of audit risk.

1.1 Whether the work of internal audit can be used

1.1.1 Evaluating the internal audit function

The following criteria will be evaluated by the external auditors in determining whether the work of internal audit can be used (ISA 610 (Revised): para. 15):

Evaluation of internal audit	
The extent to which its **objectivity** is supported by its organisational status, relevant policies and procedures	Consider the **status** of the internal audit function within the entity, **to whom** it **reports** (should be the board), whether the internal audit function has any **conflicting responsibilities** and **constraints or restrictions** on it, whether those charged with governance oversee **employment decisions** regarding internal auditors, whether **management acts** on recommendations made, whether internal auditors are members of professional bodies and obligated to comply with their requirements for objectivity. (ISA 610 (Revised): paras. A5-A7)
The level of **competence** of the function	Consider whether the internal auditor function is **adequately resourced**, whether internal auditors are **members of relevant professional bodies**, have adequate **technical training** and **proficiency**, whether there are established policies for hiring and training, whether internal auditors possess the **required knowledge** of financial reporting/the applicable financial reporting framework (ISA 610 (Revised): para. A8).
Whether the internal audit applies a **systematic and disciplined approach** (including quality control)	Consider whether internal audit activities include a systematic and disciplined approach to **planning, supervising, reviewing** and **documenting** assignments, whether the function has **appropriate quality control procedures**, the existence of **audit manuals, work programmes** and **internal audit documentation** (ISA 610 (Revised): para. A11).

The ISA states that if these determinations conclude that:

- IA's organisational status does not support the objectivity of the function
- IA is not sufficiently competent
- There is not a systematic and disciplined approach including quality control

Then the external auditor should not use the work of the internal audit function.

1.1.2 Nature and extent of work that can be used

The auditor should consider the nature and scope of specific work that has been or will be performed by IA.

Examples of **types of work that the external auditor might use** are:

- Testing of the operating effectiveness of controls
- Substantive procedures involving limited judgment
- Observations of inventory counts
- Tracing transactions through the information system relevant to financial reporting
- Testing of compliance with regulatory requirements

The auditor must also consider assessed audit risks of material misstatement for relevant classes of transaction/balances/disclosures (as the greater the risk, the less the external auditor should rely on IA work and the more directly involved in the audit work the external auditors should be)

If the external auditors are planning to use the work of the internal auditors, there are certain things that can be usefully agreed in advance, such as timing, extent of testing, materiality, sampling methods, documentation and reporting methods.

The external auditor needs to communicate with those charged with governance how the external auditor has planned to use the work of the internal audit function.

1.2 Using the work of the internal audit function

The external auditor shall:

- Discuss the planned use of IA's with IA to coordinate their work (this will involve discussion of matters such as timing, materiality, sample sizes)
- Read IA reports relating to the work to be used to obtain an understanding of the nature and extent of procedures and the related findings
- Perform audit procedures on the work to assess its adequacy
- Evaluate the work carried out
- Evaluate whether the preliminary conclusions about whether the work of IA can be used are still valid
- Reperform some of the work

1.2.1 Audit procedures

The external auditor's audit procedures must include some reperformance of IA work. Examples of other audit tests might be:

- Examining other similar items for the purpose of comparison
- Observing internal audit carrying out their work

1.2.2 Evaluating internal audit work

Relevant questions for the external auditors to ask are:

- Is the work properly supervised, reviewed and documented?
- Has sufficient, appropriate audit evidence been obtained to afford a reasonable basis for the conclusions reached?
- Are the conclusions reached appropriate given the circumstances?
- Are the reports produce consistent with the result of work performed?
- Have any unusual matters or exceptions arising and disclosed by internal audit been resolved properly?

1.3 Direct assistance

Key term

> **Direct assistance** is the use of the internal auditors to perform audit procedures under the direction, supervision and review of the external auditor.

The guidance states that the external auditor may use the internal auditor to provide direct assistance provided it is not prohibited by law. However the external auditor must evaluate the existence and significance of threats to objectivity and the level of competence of the internal auditors.

If there are significant threats to the objectivity of the internal auditor or the internal auditor lacks sufficient competence they should not provide direct assistance.

In addition the internal auditors **should not be used** to perform procedures that:

- Involve making significant **judgements**
- Relate to **higher assessed risks of material misstatement** where the judgement required is more than limited
- Relate to work which the **internal auditors have been involved** with and which has already been, or will be, reported to management or those charged with governance by the internal audit function
- Relate to **decisions** the external auditor makes in accordance with ISA 610 (Revised) **regarding the internal audit function** and the use of its work or direct assistance.

Prior to using internal auditors to provide direct assistance for purposes of the audit the external auditor is required to obtain written agreement:

- From the entity that the internal auditors will be allowed to follow their instruction and that the entity will not intervene
- From the internal auditors that they will keep matters confidential as instructed by the external auditors and disclose any threats to their objectivity.

The external auditor is required to direct, supervise and review the work performed by the internal auditors. In doing so the nature, timing and extent of this must be responsive to the fact that the internal auditors are not independent of the entity. In particular, review procedures must include some checking back to the underlying audit evidence by the external auditor.

> **Exam focus point**
>
> RPQ students: In accordance with ISA (UK) 610 (Revised) the use of internal auditors to provide direct assistance is **prohibited**.

1.4 Impact on auditor's report

If the external auditors feel that their own work and the work of the internal audit function gives them sufficient audit evidence to draw audit conclusions, they should draw those conclusions (if not, they should extend their tests). The auditors' responsibility for the audit opinion is their own, and they should not refer to the fact that they have used the work of the internal audit function in their report.

Question — Reliance on the work of the internal auditor

HABZ Co is a listed company with a year end of 30 April. HABZ Co's main activity is selling home improvement or 'Do-It-Yourself' (DIY) products to the public. Products sold range from nails, paint and tools to doors and showers; some stores also sell garden tools and furniture. Products are purchased from approximately 200 different suppliers. HABZ Co has 102 stores in eight different countries.

HABZ Co has a well-staffed internal audit department, which reports on a regular basis to the audit committee. Areas where the internal and external auditors may carry out work include:

(i) Attending the year-end inventory count in 34 stores annually. All stores are visited every three years on a rotational basis.

(ii) Checking the internal controls over the procurement systems (eg ensuring a liability is only recorded when the inventory has been received).

Required

For each of the above two areas, discuss whether the external auditor can rely on the work of the internal auditor and, if reliance is planned, the extent of that reliance.

Answer

(i) **Year-end inventory count**

HABZ Co has over a hundred stores in various countries, making it impossible for the external auditors to attend the inventory count in every store. The external auditors can place reliance on the work of the internal auditors, in addition to their own attendance at a small sample of inventory counts. The external auditors will need to review the work of internal audit to ensure that they can rely on the work undertaken. They should also compare their own results with those obtained by internal audit.

(ii) **Procurement system**

The external auditors may be able to rely on the work performed by internal audit on the controls over the procurement system, as these are relevant to financial statement assertions such as completeness of liabilities. The external auditors will still have to carry out their own work on the system, although it will be reduced if they can place reliance on any of the work done by the internal auditors.

2 Using the work of an auditor's expert

FAST FORWARD

External auditors may make use of the work of an auditor's expert when carrying out audit procedures.

2.1 Auditor's Experts

Key terms

An **auditor's expert** is 'an individual or organisation possessing expertise in a field other than accounting or auditing, whose work in that field is used by the auditor to assist the auditor in obtaining sufficient appropriate audit evidence. An auditor's expert may be either an auditor's internal expert (who is a partner or staff, including temporary staff, of the auditor's firm or a network firm) or an auditor's external expert' (ISA 620: para. 6(a)).

Management's expert is 'an individual or organisation possessing expertise in a field other than accounting or auditing, whose work in that field is used by the entity to assist the entity in preparing the financial statements' (ISA 620: para. 6(c)).

Professional audit staff are highly trained and educated, but their experience and training is limited to accountancy and audit matters. In certain situations it will therefore be necessary to employ someone else with different auditor's expert knowledge.

Auditors have **sole responsibility** for the audit opinion, but may use the work of an auditor's expert if they deem it necessary to obtain sufficient appropriate audit evidence.

Examples of areas in which an auditor's expert may be needed to help gain audit evidence include:

(a) **Valuations** of land and buildings

(b) **Valuation** of inventory or work in progress, including the determination of the physical condition of inventory

(c) **Legal opinions**, including expert opinions on the possible outcomes of litigation or disputes

Guidance on this area is provided by ISA 620 *Using the Work of an Auditor's Expert* (para. A4). An **auditor's expert** could be employed by the auditor **to assist in**:

(a) Obtaining an understanding of the entity and its environment, including its internal control
(b) Identifying and assessing the risks of material misstatement
(c) Determining and implementing overall responses to assessed risks at the financial statement level
(d) Designing and performing further audit procedures to respond to assessed risks at the assertion level
(e) Evaluating the sufficiency and appropriateness of audit evidence obtained in forming an opinion on the financial statements

ISA 620 *Using the Work of an Auditor's Expert* does not deal with situations where the engagement team includes a member, or consults an individual or organisation, with expertise in a specialised area of accounting or auditing, (which are dealt with in ISA 220 (Revised) *Quality Management for an Audit of Financial Statements*); or the auditor's use of the work of an individual or organisation possessing expertise in a field other than accounting or auditing, whose work in that field is used by the entity to assist the entity in preparing the financial statements (ie a management's expert, which is dealt with in ISA 500 *Audit Evidence*).

ISA 620 states that the auditor needs to determine whether it is necessary to obtain the work of an auditor's expert to obtain sufficient appropriate audit evidence, and then to determine whether that auditor's expert's work is appropriate for audit purposes.

2.2 Determining the need to use the work of an auditor's expert

When **considering whether to use the work of an auditor's expert**, the auditors should review:

- Whether management has used a management's expert in preparing the financial statements
- The nature and significance of the matter, including its complexity
- The risks of material misstatement in the matter
- The expected nature of procedures to respond to identified risks, including: the auditor's knowledge of and experience with the work of experts in relation to such matters; and the availability of alternative sources of audit evidence

2.3 Nature, extent and timing of audit procedures

The auditor will use his audit judgement to determine the level of audit procedures required on the auditor's expert's work in order to draw audit conclusions. Relevant factors will be:

- The nature of the matter concerning which the auditor's expert is providing expertise
- The risk of material misstatement
- The significance of the auditor's expert's work in the context of the audit
- The auditor's knowledge of an experience with previous work by the auditor's expert
- Whether the auditor's expert is subject to the same quality control requirements as the audit team

The auditor has to assess the competence of the auditor's expert, understand his field of work, agree the scope of the work for the purposes of audit and evaluate the adequacy of that work when it has been completed.

2.3.1 Competence and objectivity of the auditor's expert

The auditor shall **evaluate** whether the **auditor's expert** has the necessary **competence, capabilities and objectivity** for the auditor's purposes. Information regarding the competence, capabilities and objectivity of an auditor's expert may come from a variety of sources, such as:

- **Personal experience** with previous work of that auditor's expert
- **Discussions with that auditor's expert**
- **Discussions with other auditors or others** who are familiar with that auditor's expert's work
- Knowledge of that **auditor's expert's qualifications, membership of a professional body or industry association, license to practice**, or other forms of external recognition
- Published papers or books written by that auditor's expert
- The auditor's firm's **quality control policies and procedures**

The risk that an auditor's expert's objectivity is impaired increases when the auditor's expert is:

- **Employed** by the entity
- **Related** in some other manner to the entity, for example, by being financially dependent upon, or having an investment in, the entity

> **Exam focus point**
>
> If the auditors have **reservations** about the competence or objectivity of the auditor's expert they may need to carry out other procedures or obtain evidence from another auditor's expert.

2.3.2 Obtaining an understanding of the field of expertise of the auditor's expert

The auditor needs to understand this enough to determine the nature, scope and objectives of the work he wants the auditor's expert to do for the purposes of the audit and to be able to evaluate whether the work is adequate for audit purposes.

2.3.3 Agreement of terms

Written instructions usually cover the auditor's expert's terms of reference and such instructions may cover such matters as follows.

- Nature, scope and objectives of the auditor's expert's work
- The respective roles and responsibilities of the auditor and the auditor's expert
- Communications and reporting (eg nature and timing of auditor's expert's report)
- Confidentiality

2.3.4 Assessing the work of the auditor's expert

Auditors shall assess the relevance and reasonableness of:

- The results of auditor's expert's work (including **consistency** with other audit evidence)
- The significant **assumptions** made
- The **source data**

Example

An auditor's expert valuation of a commercial building could be compared to the value of other, similar commercial building in estate agent's windows or on the web.

The auditors do **not** have the expertise to judge the assumptions and methods used; these are the responsibility of the auditor's expert. However, the auditors should seek to obtain an understanding of these assumptions etc, to consider their reasonableness based on other audit evidence, knowledge of the business and so on.

2.4 Reporting

The auditor shall not refer to the work of the auditor's expert in the auditor's report unless required to do so by law or regulation. The auditor must be clear that he retains responsibility for the audit opinion.

Question — Using the work of an auditor's expert

ISA 620 *Using the Work of an Auditor's Expert* provides guidance to auditors on relying on work carried out by an auditor's expert.

Required

(a) List four examples of audit evidence that might be obtained from the use of an auditor's expert.

(b) Describe the factors that should be considered by the auditor when evaluating the work carried out by the expert.

(c) Explain the actions the auditor should take if they conclude that the results of the expert's work do not provide sufficient appropriate audit evidence or if the results are inconsistent with other audit evidence.

Answer

(a) Any four from:

  (1) Valuations of assets, such as land and buildings, plant and machinery, works of art, precious stones
  (2) Determination of quantities or physical condition of assets
  (3) Determination of amounts using specialised techniques or methods, such as an actuarial valuation
  (4) Measurement of work completed and to be completed on contracts in progress
  (5) Legal opinions concerning interpretations of agreements, statutes and regulations

(b) Factors to consider when evaluating the work carried out by an auditor's expert

When evaluating the expert's work the auditor should consider how relevant the work is, the standard of the work and its consistency with other audit evidence.

The auditor should also consider the relevance and reasonableness of any assumptions and methods used, along with the relevance, completeness and accuracy of any source data used.

(c) Actions to take if evidence is not sufficient or results are inconsistent

If the results of the expert's work do not provide sufficient appropriate audit evidence or are inconsistent with other audit evidence, the auditor needs to resolve the matter.

This could be done through discussions with the entity and the expert or applying additional audit procedures, including engaging another expert.

The auditor may need to consider whether the auditor's opinion should be modified if the issues are still unresolved after all the other avenues have been explored.

Chapter roundup

- External auditors may make use of the work of the internal audit function when carrying out external audit procedures.
- Under certain circumstances the external auditor may also request that the internal auditors provide direct assistance to them.
- External auditors may make use of the work of an auditor's expert when carrying out audit procedures.

Quick quiz

1. An effective internal audit function may eliminate the need for external audit procedures.

   True ☐

   False ☐

2. Name **four** factors the external audit function may consider when evaluating work carried out by the internal audit function.

   (1) ....

   (2) ....

   (3) ....

   (4) ....

3. Name two criteria for evaluating the internal audit function.

   (1) ....

   (2) ....

4. Complete the definitions using the words given below.

   An .... is a person or firm possessing ...., knowledge and .... in a particular field other than auditing.

   | special, auditor's expert, experience, skills |

5. The auditor may not use the work of an auditor's expert employed by the organisation being audited.

   True ☐

   False ☐

6. If the auditor relies on the work of an auditor's expert, he may refer to that person in his report and share responsibility with him.

   True ☐

   False ☐

Answers to quick quiz

1. False
2. From:
   - Is the work properly supervised, reviewed and documented?
   - Has sufficient, appropriate audit evidence been obtained to afford a reasonable basis for the conclusions reached?
   - Are the conclusions reached appropriate, given the circumstances?
   - Are any reports produced by internal audit consistent with the result of the work performed?
   - Have any unusual matters or exceptions arising and disclosed by internal audit been resolved properly?
3. From:
   (1) Objectivity
   (2) Technical competence
   (3) Systematic and disciplined approach
4. auditor's expert, special skill, experience
5. False
6. False

9: USING THE WORK OF OTHERS

End of chapter question

Cinders Ltd (AIA Nov 2007)

You are a manager in an audit firm, and you are about to commence the audit planning for a new client, Cinders Ltd. The finance director has told you that the company has an extremely efficient internal audit function, and that you will be able to reduce your audit work by using the internal auditors.

Required

Describe the factors you will take into account when deciding whether or not to place any reliance on the work of Cinders Ltd internal audit function. **(15 marks)**

Tests of controls: sales, purchases and wages

Topic list	Syllabus reference
1 Manual and computer based systems and controls	5.5
2 The sales system	5.5
3 The purchases and expenses system	5.5
4 The wages system	5.5
5 Smaller entities	5.5

Introduction

We have mentioned tests of controls in chapter 6. In this chapter we will look at **how tests of controls** might be **applied in practice**. We will examine each major component of an average accounting system.

In Chapter 6, we stated that the external auditors must ascertain the accounting system and the system of internal control. The auditors will then decide which controls, if any, they wish to rely on and plan **tests of controls** to obtain the audit evidence as to whether such reliance can be warranted. For each of the systems listed above we will look at the system **objectives** the auditors will bear in mind while assessing the internal controls and give examples of common controls. We shall then go on to look at a 'standard' programme of tests of controls.

In this chapter we deal with **sales, purchases** and **wages and salaries**. These areas are the areas that are most commonly tested in auditing exams.

1 Manual and computer based systems and controls

For each system we cover in this chapter, starting with the sales system, we look at objectives, controls and tests of controls. As you review these please bear in mind that controls may be either carried out **manually** or, in a computerised system, **electronically**. This also means tests of control could require a review or inspection of printed documents or electronic documents on screen.

For example:

(a) Where recording transactions is mentioned, these could be manually inputted transactions or they could be imported or automatically posted from integrated systems.

(b) Where authorisation of documents is discussed approval could be in the form of a written signature on a printed document, or it could be an electronic/digital signature to approve electronic files or entries. This means the auditor may be reviewing a physical signature or software audit logs to see if a document is approved and who it was approved by.

(c) References to numerical sequencing or matching of documents could relate to manual numbering or matching, but there could instead be auto generated sequential numbering or electronic (or even automatic) matching of related documents (orders, GRNs and Invoices for example).

(d) Sending of invoices, statements and other documents could be by post, by email or other electronic means (such as a customer portal).

It is not practical to duplicate every control and test of control in the sections throughout the chapter to cater for systems of varying levels of technology and automation. However, please note that where there are references to physical documents, authorisations or processes they could equally be electronic documents, authorisations or processes.

2 The sales system

> **FAST FORWARD**
>
> The tests of controls in the **sales system** will be based around:
> - **Selling** (authorisation)
> - **Goods outwards** (custody)
> - **Accounting** (recording)

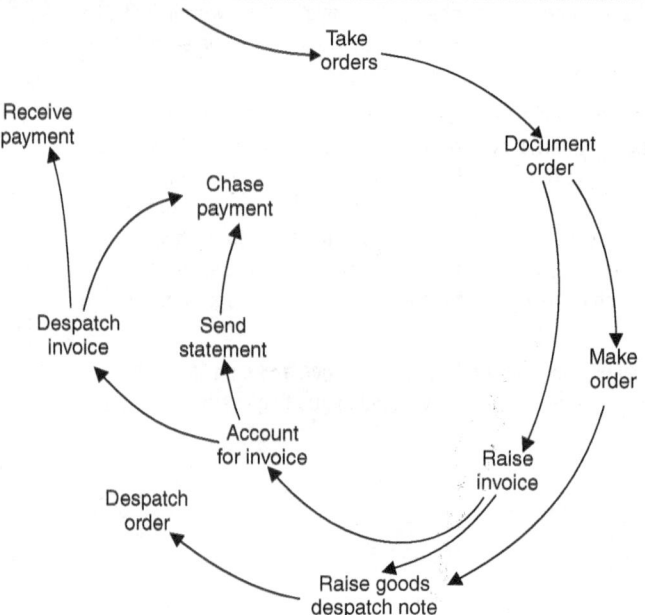

2.1 Control objectives

Area	Objectives
Ordering and granting of credit	- **Goods** and **services** are **only supplied** to **customers** with **good credit ratings**. - **Customers** are encouraged to **pay promptly**. - **Orders** are **recorded correctly**. - **Orders** are **fulfilled**.
Dispatch and invoicing	- All **dispatches** of goods are **recorded**. - All **goods and services** sold are **correctly invoiced**. - All **invoices** raised **relate to goods and services supplied** by the business. - **Credit notes** are only given for **valid reasons**.
Recording, accounting and credit control	- All sales that have been **invoiced** are **recorded** in the general and receivables ledgers. - All **credit notes** that have been **issued** are **recorded** in the general and receivables ledgers. - All **entries** in the receivables ledger are **made** to the **correct** receivables ledger **accounts**. - **Cut-off** is applied correctly to the receivables ledger. - Potentially **doubtful debts** are **identified**.

2.2 Controls

Area	Controls

Ordering and credit approval process	- **Segregation** of duties; credit control, invoicing and inventory dispatch
	- **Authorisation** of **credit terms** to customers
	   - References/credit checks obtained
	   - Authorisation by senior staff
	   - Regular review
	- **Authorisation** (signature or online/electronic approval) for changes in **other customer data**
	   - Change of address supported by letterhead
	   - Deletion requests supported by evidence balances cleared/customer in liquidation
	- **Orders** only **accepted** from **customers** who have no credit problems
	- **Sequential numbering** of blank pre-printed order documents
	- **Correct prices quoted** to **customers**
	- **Matching** of **customer orders** with production orders and dispatch notes and querying of orders not matched
	- **Dealing** with **customer queries**

Dispatches and invoice preparation	- **Authorisation** (signature or online/electronic approval) of **dispatch** of **goods**
	   - Dispatch only on sales order
	   - Dispatch only to authorised customers
	   - Special authorisation of dispatches of goods free of charge or on special terms
	- **Examination** of **goods outwards** as to quantity, quality and condition

Area	Controls
	• **Recording** of goods outwards
	• **Agreement** of goods outwards records to **customer orders, dispatch notes** and **invoices**
	• **Prenumbering** of dispatch notes and delivery notes and regular checks on sequence
	• **Condition** of **returns checked**
	• Recording of goods returned on **goods returned notes**
	• **Signature** (on paper/electronic handset) of **delivery notes** by customers

	• Preparation of invoices and credit notes
	  – **Authorisation** (signature or online/electronic approval) of **selling prices**/use of **price lists**
	  – **Authorisation** (signature or online/electronic approval) of **credit notes**
	  – **Checks on prices, quantities, extensions** and totals on invoices and credit notes
	  – **Sequential numbering** of blank invoices/credit notes and regular sequence checks

	• **Inventory records updated**
	• **Matching** of sales **invoices** with **dispatch** and **delivery notes** and sales orders
	• **Regular review** for **dispatch notes** not matched by invoices
Recording and credit problems	• **Segregation of duties:** recording sales, maintaining customer accounts and preparing statements
	• **Recording** of **sales invoices** sequence and **control** over **spoilt invoices**
	• **Matching** of **cash receipts** with **invoices**
	• **Retention** of **customer remittance advices**
	• **Separate recording** of **sales returns, price adjustments** etc
	• **Cut-off procedures** to ensure goods dispatched and not invoiced (or vice versa) are properly dealt with the correct period
	• Regular **preparation** of **trade accounts receivable statements**
	• **Checking** of **trade accounts' receivables statements**
	• **Safeguarding** of **trade accounts' receivables statements** so that they cannot be altered before dispatch
	• **Review** and **follow-up** of **overdue accounts**
	• **Authorisation** of **writing off** of **irrecoverable debts**
	• **Reconciliation** of **receivables ledger control account** (except where there is an integrated accounting system/sales module)
	• **Analytical review** of receivables ledger and profit margins

2.3 Tests of controls

Area	Test of controls
Ordering and granting of credit	• **Inspect all files of new customers** to ensure that references are being obtained for all new customers.

Area	Test of controls
	• Inspect all **new accounts** on the receivables ledger to ensure that they have been **authorised** by senior staff (signature or online/electronic approval). • **Review a sample of orders** to ensure that orders are only **accepted** from customers who are **within** their **credit terms** and **credit limits**. • Observe whether **customer orders** are being **matched** with **production orders** and **dispatch notes**.

Dispatches and invoices	• Verify details of **trade sales** or goods dispatched notes with **sales invoices**, checking
	   – **Quantities**
	   – **Prices** charged with official price lists
	   – **Trade discounts** have been properly dealt with
	   – **Calculations** and **additions**
	   – **Entries** in sales day book are correctly **analysed**
	   – **Sales tax**, where chargeable, has been properly **dealt with**
	   – **Postings** to receivables ledger
	• Verify details of trade sales with **entries in inventory records.**
	• Verify **non-routine** sales (scrap, non-current assets etc) with:
	   – **Appropriate supporting evidence**
	   – **Approval** by authorised officials
	   – **Entries** in **plant register**
	• Verify **credit notes** with:
	   – **Correspondence** or other supporting evidence
	   – **Approval** by authorised officials
	   – **Entries** in **inventory records**
	   – **Entries** in **goods returned records**
	   – **Calculations** and **additions**
	   – **Entries** in **day book**, checking these are correctly analysed
	   – **Postings** to **receivables ledger**
	• **Test numerical sequence** of **dispatch notes** and **enquire** into **missing numbers.**
	• **Test numerical sequence** of **invoices** and **credit notes, enquire** into **missing numbers** and **inspect copies** of those cancelled.
	• **Test numerical sequence** of **order forms** and enquire into missing numbers.
	• **Vouch** that **dispatches** of **goods free of charge** or on **special terms** have been **authorised** by management by inspection of documentation.

Area	Test of controls
Recording of and accounting for sales	**Sales day book** • **Match entries** with **invoices** and **credit notes** respectively. • **Re-cast additions** and **cross casts**. • **Review postings** to **receivables ledger control account**. • **Review postings** to **receivables ledger**. **Receivables ledger** • **Vouch** entries in a **sample of accounts** to sales day book. • **Re-cast additions** and **balances** carried down. • **Note** and **enquire of management** about **contra entries**. • **Inspect control account reconciliations** to ensure they have been **regularly reconciled** to total of receivables ledger balances. • **Scrutinise accounts** to see if credit limits have been observed. • **Inspect customer files** to ascertain whether **trade accounts' receivables statements** are **prepared** and **sent out regularly**. • **Determine** whether **overdue accounts** have been **followed up** by inspecting customer files for evidence of chasing letters. • **Vouch** that **all irrecoverable debts written off** have been **authorised** by management.

Exam focus point

In the exam you may be asked:

(a) What controls are appropriate for a specific situation?
(b) What are the major deficiencies in the system given in the question?
(c) What are the consequences of the failure or non-existence of controls?
(d) What tests would auditors use on the controls given in the question?

If you are asked about appropriate controls or deficiencies, remember the **objectives** for the accounting area. Controls should be in place to **fulfil** the **objectives** given, deficiencies will mean that the objectives are not fulfilled. You should also consider the **documentation** and **staff** involved in each area.

Exam focus point (cont'd)

You should give enough detail about the controls you suggest to enable a non-accountant to implement the controls.

You should use a similar thought process when deciding how to test the controls. Think of the **objectives** of the system; assess how the controls given **fulfil** those **objectives**; and set out tests which demonstrate whether the controls are working. Remember that different types of test can be used to test different controls. For example, inspection can be used to test whether different documents are being compared or documents are being properly authorised. Computation can be used to check invoices have been properly completed or reconciliations correctly made.

The examiner may ask you to describe or compile:

- An internal control questionnaire/checklist
- A work plan relating to internal control.

10: TESTS OF CONTROLS: SALES, PURCHASES AND WAGES

Question
Complete recording

What tests of controls can give auditors assurance that the company's system of control ensures that sales are completely recorded?

Answer

Tests of controls over completeness of recording of sales include:

(a) Sequence tests on sales orders, dispatch notes, invoices and credit notes to ensure that there are no missing numbers or two documents with the same number

(b) Comparisons of dispatch notes with order and invoices, checking documents are cross-referenced to each other

(c) Checking posting of sales day book to receivables ledger control account and receivables ledger

(d) Checking control account reconciliations have been carried out and have been reviewed by senior staff

(e) Controls over computerised input including:

    (i) Control totals
    (ii) Checking of output to source documents
    (iii) Procedure over resubmisson of rejected inputs

Question
Deficiencies and tests of controls

You are the auditor of Arcidiacono Stationery, and you have been asked to suggest how audit work should be carried out on the sales system.

Arcidiacono Stationery Ltd sells stationery to shops. Most sales are to small customers who do not have a receivables ledger account. They can collect their purchases and pay by cash. For cash sales:

(a) The customer orders the stationery from the sales department, which raises a pre-numbered multi-copy order form.

(b) The dispatch department make up the order and give it to the customer with a copy of the order form.

(c) The customer gives the order form to the cashier who prepares a hand-written sales invoice.

(d) The customer pays the cashier for the goods by cheque or in cash.

(e) The cashier records and banks the cash.

Required

(a) State the deficiencies in the cash sales system.
(b) Describe the systems-based tests you would carry out to check the controls over the system.

Answer

(a) **Deficiencies in the cash system**

(i) The physical location of the dispatch department and the cashier are not mentioned here, but there is a risk of the customer taking the goods without paying. The customer should pay the cashier on the advice note and return for the goods, which should only be released on sight of the paid invoice.

(ii) There is a failure in segregation of duties in allowing the cashier to both complete the sales invoice and receive the cash as he could perpetrate a fraud by replacing the original invoice with one of lower value and keeping the difference.

(iii) No-one checks the invoices to make sure that the cashier has completed them correctly, for example by using the correct prices and performing calculations correctly.

(iv) The completeness of the sequence of sales invoices cannot be checked unless they are pre-numbered sequentially and the presence of all the invoices is checked by another person. The order forms should also be pre-numbered sequentially.

(v) There is also no check that the cashier banks all cash received, ie this is a further failure of segregation of duties.

If the sales department prepared and posted the invoices and also posted the cash for cash sales to a sundry sales account, this would solve some of the internal control problems mentioned above. In addition, the sales department could run a weekly check on the account to look for invoices for which no cash had been received. These could then be investigated.

All of these deficiencies, and possible remedies, should be reported to management.

(b) **Tests**

(i) Select a sample of order forms issued to customers during the year. Trace the related sales invoice and check that the details correlate (date, unit amounts etc). The customer should have signed for the goods and this copy should be retained by the dispatch department.

(ii) For the sales invoices discovered in the above test, I would check that the correct order form number is recorded on the invoice, that the prices used are correct (by reference to the prevailing price list) and that the castings and cross-castings (ie arithmetic) is correct.

(iii) I will then trace the value of the sales invoices to the cash book and from the cash book that the total receipts for the day have been banked and appear promptly on the bank statement.

(iv) I would check that the sales invoices have been correctly posted to a cash or sundry sales account. For any sales invoices missing from this account (assuming they are sequentially numbered), I will trace the cancelled invoice and check that the cancelled invoice was initialled by the customer and replaced by the next invoice in sequence.

(v) Because of the deficiencies in the system I would carry out the following sequence checks on large blocks of order forms/invoices, eg four blocks of 100 order forms/invoices.

(1) Check all order forms present; investigate those missing.
(2) Check sales invoices raised for all order forms.
(3) Check all sales invoices in a sequence have been used; investigate any missing.
(4) Cash for each sales invoice has been entered into the cash book.

Using the results of the above tests I would decide whether the system for cash sales has operated without material fraud or error. If I am not satisfied that it has then I will consider the implications for the auditor's report on the financial statements.

3 The purchases and expenses system

FAST FORWARD

The tests of controls in the **purchases system** will be based around:

- **Buying** (authorisation)
- **Goods** inwards (custody)
- **Accounting** (recording)

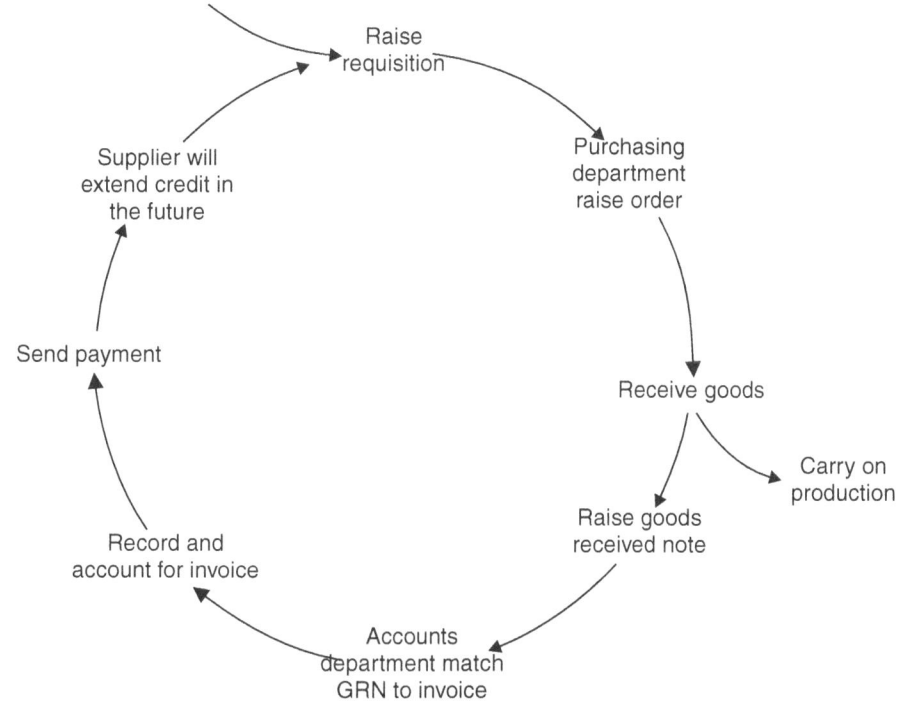

3.1 Control objectives

Area	Aims
Ordering	• All **orders for goods and services** are properly **authorised** (signature or online/electronic approval), and are for **goods and services** that are actually **received** and are for the company. • Orders are only made to **authorised suppliers**. • Orders are made at **competitive prices**.
Receipt and invoices	• All goods and services received are used for the **organisation's purposes**, and not private purposes. • Goods and services are **only accepted if** they have been **ordered**, and the **order** has been **authorised** (signature or online/electronic approval). • All **goods** and **services received** are accurately **recorded**. • **Liabilities** are **recognised** for all **goods and services** that have been **received**. • All **credits** to which business is due are **claimed** and **received**. • **Receipt** of **goods** and **services** is **necessary** to establish a **liability to be recorded**.
Accounting	• All **expenditure** is for goods that are **received**. • All **expenditure** is **authorised**. • All **expenditure** that is made is **recorded** correctly in the general and payables

Area	Aims
	ledger. • All **credit notes** that are received are **recorded** in the general and payables ledger. • All **entries** in the **payables ledger** are **made** to the **correct payables ledger accounts**. • **Cut-off** is **applied correctly** to the payables ledger.

3.2 Controls

Area	Controls
Ordering	• **Segregation** of duties; requisition and ordering • **Central policy** for choice of suppliers • Evidence required of **requirements** for purchase before purchase authorised (re-order quantities and re-order levels) • **Order forms** prepared only when a **pre-numbered purchase requisition** has been **received** • **Authorisation** (signature or online/electronic approval) of order forms • **Prenumbered order forms** • **Safeguarding** of **blank order forms** • **Review** for **orders not received** or invoiced • **Monitoring** of **supplier terms** and taking advantage of favourable conditions (bulk order, discount)

Goods and invoices received	• **Examination** of goods inwards
	  – Quality
	  – Quantity
	  – Condition
	• **Recording arrival** and **acceptance** of goods (prenumbered goods received notes)
	• **Comparison** of **goods received notes** with **purchase orders**
	• **Referencing** of supplier invoices; numerical sequence and supplier reference
	• **Checking** of **suppliers' invoices**
	  – Prices, quantities, accuracy of calculation
	  – Comparison with order and goods received note
	• **Recording return of goods** (pre-numbered goods returned notes)
	• Procedures for **obtaining credit notes** from suppliers

Area	Controls

Accounting for purchases	• **Segregation** of **duties:** accounting and checking functions
	• Prompt **recording of purchases** and **purchase returns** in day books and ledgers
	• **Regular maintenance** of **payables ledger**
	• **Comparison** of **supplier statements** with **payables ledger balances**
	• **Authorisation** of **payments**
	  – Authority limits
	  – Confirmation that goods have been received, accord with purchase order, and are properly priced and invoiced
	• **Review** of **allocation** of expenditure
	• **Reconciliation** of **payables ledger** control account to total of payables ledger balances (except where accounting system/purchases module is integrated)
	• **Cut-off** accrual of goods received notes not matched by purchases at year-end

3.3 Tests of controls

A most important test of controls is for auditors to **inspect invoices** to ensure that they are **supported** by authorised **purchase invoices** and **purchase orders**. The officials who approve the invoices should be operating within laid-down **authority limits**.

Area	Tests of controls

Receipts of goods and invoices	• Inspect invoices for goods, raw materials to ensure they are:
	  – **Supported** by **goods received notes and inspection notes**
	  – **Entered** in **inventory records**
	  – **Priced** correctly by checking to **quotations**, **price lists** to see the price is in order
	  – **Properly referenced** with a number and supplier code
	  – **Correctly coded** by type of expenditure
	• **Trace entry** in **record of goods returned** etc and see credit note duly received from the supplier, for invoices not passed due to defects or discrepancy.
	• For invoices of all types:
	  – **Re-cast calculations** and **additions**.
	  – **Vouch entries in purchase day book** and verify that they are correctly **analysed**.
	  – **Agree posting** to **payables ledger**.
	• For credit notes:
	  – **Verify** the **correctness** of credit received with correspondence.
	  – **Vouch entries** in **inventory records**.
	  – **Vouch entries** in **record of returns**.
	  – **Vouch entries** in **purchase day book** and verify that they are correctly analysed.
	  – **Agree postings** to **payables ledger**.

Area	Tests of controls

Receipts of goods and invoices *continued*	• Check for **returns** that **credit notes** are duly **received** from the suppliers.
	• Test **numerical sequence** and enquire into missing numbers of:
	  – Purchase requisitions
	  – Purchase orders
	  – Goods received notes
	  – Goods returned notes
	  – Suppliers' invoices
	• **Obtain explanations** for **items** which have been **outstanding** for a long time:
	  – Unmatched purchase requisitions
	  – Purchase orders
	  – Goods received notes (if invoices not received)
	  – Unprocessed invoices

Recording of purchases	• Verify that invoices and credit notes recorded in the purchase day book are:
	  – **Initialled** for prices, calculations and extensions
	  – **Cross-referenced** to purchase orders, goods received notes etc
	  – **Authorised** for payment
	• **Re-cast additions**.
	• **Agree postings** to general ledger accounts and control account.
	• **Agree postings** of entries to payables ledger.
	Payables ledger
	• For a sample of accounts recorded in the payables ledger:
	  – **Test check entries** back into books of prime entry.
	  – **Test check additions** and **balances** forward.
	  – **Note** and **enquire** into all contra entries.
	• Confirm **control account balancing** has been regularly carried out during the year.
	• **Examine control account** for unusual entries.

 Question   Purchase controls

Derek, a limited liability company, operates a computerised purchase system. Invoices and credit notes are posted to the bought ledger by the bought ledger department. The computer subsequently raises a cheque when the invoice has to be paid.

Required

List the controls that should be in operation:

(a) Over the addition, amendment and deletion of suppliers, ensuring that the standing data only includes suppliers from the company's list of authorised suppliers

(b) Over purchase invoices and credit notes, to ensure only authorised purchase invoices and credit notes are posted to the payables ledger

10: TESTS OF CONTROLS: SALES, PURCHASES AND WAGES

Answer

(a) Controls over the standing data file containing suppliers' details will include the following. These should prevent fraud by the creation of a fictitious supplier.

   (i) All amendments/additions/deletions to the data should be authorised by a responsible official. A standard form should be used for such changes.

   (ii) The amendment forms should be input in batches (with different types of change in different batches), sequentially numbered and recorded in a batch control book so that any gaps in the batch numbers can be investigated. The output produced by the computer should be checked to the input.

   (iii) A listing of all such adjustments should automatically be produced by the computer and reviewed by a responsible official, who should also check authorisation.

   (iv) A listing of suppliers' accounts on which there has been no movement for a specified period (6 months, 12 months) should be produced to allow decisions to be made about possible deletions, thus ensuring that the standing data is current. The buying department manager might also recommend account closures on a periodic basis.

   (v) Users should be controlled by use of passwords. This can also be used as a method of controlling those who can amend data.

   (vi) Periodic listings of standing data should be produced in order to verify details (eg addresses) with suppliers' documents (invoices/ statements).

(b) The input of authorised purchase invoices and credit notes should be controlled in the following ways:

   (i) Authorisation should be evidenced by the signature of the responsible official (say the Chief Accountant). In addition, the invoice or credit note should show initials to demonstrate that the details have been agreed: to a signed GRN; to a purchase order; to a price list; for additions and extensions.

   (ii) There should be adequate segregation of responsibilities between the posting function, inventory custody and receipt, payment of suppliers and changes to standing data.

   (iii) Input should be restricted by use of passwords linked to the relevant site number.

   (iv) A batch control book should be maintained, recording batches in number sequence. Invoices should be input in batches using pre-numbered batch control sheets. The manually produced invoice total on the batch control sheet should be agreed to the computer generated total. Credit notes and invoices should be input in separate batches to avoid one being posted as the other.

   (v) A program should check calculation of sales tax at standard rate and total (net + sales tax = gross) of invoice. Non-standard sales tax rates should be highlighted.

   (vi) The input of the supplier code should bring up the supplier name for checking by the operator against the invoice.

   (vii) Invoices for suppliers which do not have an account should be prevented from being input. Any sundry suppliers account should be very tightly controlled and all entries reviewed in full each month.

   (viii) An exception report showing unusual expense allocation (by size or account) should be produced and reviewed by a responsible official. Expenses should be compared to budget and previous years.

   (ix) There should be monthly reconciliations of payables ledger balances to suppliers' statements by someone outside the purchasing (accounting) function.

Question — Tests of controls

You have recently been appointed auditor of Dryden Manufacturing, a limited liability company, and are commencing the audit of the purchases system for the year ended 31 December 20X6. The company has about 200 employees and generally has sufficient staff for there to be a proper division of duties for internal control purposes.

Required

For the audit of the company's purchases system:

(a) Describe how you would evaluate the controls, and how your audit tests would be affected by the results of this evaluation;

(b) Describe the general form of your conclusions on the results of testing the purchase system and how these conclusions may influence your work at the final audit.

Answer

(a) Many large audit firms now use a standard method of internal control evaluation questionnaire (ICEQ) based on key control questions. The characteristics of this system are usually as follows.

   (i) It is concerned only with the primary or key controls.

   (ii) The format of the questionnaires leads to a detailed assessment of each of the primary control areas.

   (iii) The ICEQ schedules can normally be linked and cross-referenced to the flowcharts, ICQs or other systems records.

   (iv) It encourages the audit staff to design their tests to suit the particular needs of each client's systems. In other words, it ensures that time is not wasted in performing 'standard' audit programme tests that are not relevant to the circumstances, and that there is a direct link between the evaluation of the system of internal control and the tests carried out.

   One method of constructing an ICEQ could be by listing under each major control question the answers of the detailed questions relating to that control which appear in the ICQ and then answering the major question on the basis of the subsidiary questions.

   It is also important that against each major control question in the ICEQ there should be space for the auditors to cross-reference their answer to the action they have taken (eg modifying the audit programme or advising the client of deficiencies). An ICEQ will be useless unless the appropriate action is taken as a result of the evaluation.

(b) If the results of the auditors' tests on the purchases system are satisfactory they may conclude that it will produce reliable accounting records and this in turn will mean that they may keep substantive testing at the year end to a minimum. If, however, the tests of control reveal deficiencies in the system then at the final audit, the auditors will have to carry out a more extensive programme of substantive tests.

4 The wages system

> **FAST FORWARD**
>
> Key controls over **wages** cover:
>
> - **Documentation** and **authorisation** of staff changes
> - **Calculation** of wages and salaries
> - **Payment** of wages
> - **Authorisation** of deductions

4.1 Control objectives

Area	Objectives
Setting of wages and salaries	- **Employees** are **only paid** for **work** that they have **done**. - **Gross pay** has been **calculated correctly** and **authorised** (signature or online/electronic approval).
Recording of wages and salaries	- **Gross** and **net pay** and **deductions** are **accurately recorded** on the payroll. - **Wages and salaries paid** are **recorded correctly** in the **bank** and **cash records**. - **Wages and salaries** are **correctly recorded** in the **general ledger**.
Payment of wages and salaries	- The **correct employees** are **paid**.
Deductions	- All **deductions** have been **calculated correctly** and are **authorised**. - The **correct amounts** are **paid** to the **taxation authorities**.

4.2 Controls

While in practice separate arrangements are generally made for dealing with wages and salaries, the considerations involved are broadly similar and for convenience the two aspects are here treated together.

Area	Controls
General arrangements	Responsibility for the preparation of pay sheets should be delegated to a suitable person, and adequate staff appointed to assist him. The extent to which the staff responsible for preparing wages and salaries may perform other duties should be clearly defined. In this connection full advantage should be taken where possible of the division of duties, and checks available where automatic wage-accounting systems are in use.

Setting of wages and salaries	- **Staffing** and **segregation of duties**
	- **Maintenance of personnel records** and regular checking of wages and salaries to details in personnel records
	- **Authorisation** (signature or online/electronic approval)
	   – Engagement and discharge of employees
	   – Changes in pay rates
	   – Overtime
	   – Non-statutory deductions (for example pension contributions)
	   – Advances of pay
	- **Recording** of **changes** in **personnel** and **pay rates**
	- **Recording** of hours worked by **timesheets, clocking** in and out arrangements
	- **Review** of hours worked

Area	Controls
	• **Recording** of **advances** of **pay** • **Holiday pay** arrangements • **Answering queries** • **Review** of **wages** against **budget**

Payment of cash wages	• **Segregation of duties**
	  – Cash sheet preparation
	  – Filling of pay packets
	  – Distribution of wages
	• **Authorisation** of **wage cheque** cashed
	• **Custody** of cash
	  – Encashment of cheque
	  – Security of pay packets
	  – Security of transit
	  – Security and prompt banking of unclaimed wages
	• **Verification of identity**
	• **Recording** of distribution

Payment of salaries	• **Preparation** and **authorisation** of cheques and bank transfer lists • Comparison of **cheques** and **bank transfer list** with **payroll** • **Maintenance** and **reconciliation** of wages and salaries bank account
Wages and salaries	• **Bases** for **compilation** of payroll • **Preparation, checking** and **approval** of payroll • Dealing with **non-routine matters**
Deductions from pay	• **Maintenance** of **separate employees' records**, with which pay lists may be compared as necessary • **Reconciliation** of **total pay** and **deductions** between one pay day and the next • **Surprise cash counts** • **Comparison** of actual pay totals with **budget estimates** or standard costs and the investigation of variances • **Agreement** of **gross earnings** and **total tax deducted** with taxation returns

4.3 Tests of controls

Appropriate arrangements should be made for dealing with statutory and other authorised deductions from pay, such as taxation, pension fund contributions, and savings held in trust. A primary consideration is the establishment of adequate controls over the **records** and **authorising** deductions.

Area	Tests of controls
Setting of wages and salaries	Auditors should inspect whether the **wages** and **salary summary** is approved for payment. They should confirm that procedures are operating for **authorising changes** in **rates of pay**, overtime, and holiday pay. A particular concern will be joiners and leavers. Auditors will need to obtain evidence that staff only start being paid when they join the company, and are removed from the payroll when they leave the company. They should check that the **engagement** of **new employees** and **discharges** have been **confirmed in writing by inspecting** the

Area	Tests of controls
Setting of wages and salaries *continued*	HR files for individuals who have joined and left the organisation during the financial year. Auditors will also wish to recalculate a sample of calculations of wages and salaries. This test should be designed to verify whether the client is carrying out **checks** on **calculations** and also to provide substantive assurance that **wages** and **salaries** are being **calculated correctly**. For wages, this will involve checking **calculation** of **gross pay** with: • Authorised rates of pay • Production records. See that production bonuses have been authorised and properly calculated • Clock cards, time sheets or other evidence of hours worked. Verify that overtime has been authorised For salaries, auditors should **verify that gross salaries and bonuses are in accordance with personnel records, letters of engagement** etc and that increases in pay have been properly authorised.
Payment of wages and salaries	**If wages are paid in cash** • **Arrange to attend** the **pay-out** of wages to confirm that the official procedures are being followed. • Before the wages are paid **compare payroll** with **wage packets** to ensure all employees have a wage packet. • **Examine receipts** given by employees; **check unclaimed wages** are recorded in unclaimed wages book. • **Observe** wages being paid out to ensure that **no employee receives more than one wage packet.** • **Agree entries** in the **unclaimed wages book** with the entries on the payroll. • **Vouch that unclaimed wages** are **banked regularly.** • **Check** that unclaimed wages books shows **reasons** why wages are unclaimed. • **Review pattern** of **unclaimed wages** in unclaimed wages book; variations may indicate failure to record. **Holiday pay** • **Verify** a sample of **payments** with the **underlying records** and **check** the **calculation** of the amounts paid. For salaries, auditors should check that comparisons are being made between payment records and they should themselves **examine paid cheques** or a **certified copy** of the **bank list** for employees paid by cheque of banks transfer.
Recording of wages and salaries	A key control auditors will be concerned with will be the reconciliation of wages and salaries. For wages, there should have been reconciliations with: • The **previous week's payroll** • **Clock cards/time sheets/job cards** • **Costing analyses, production budgets** The total of **salaries** should be **reconciled** with the **previous week/month** or the **standard payroll.** In addition auditors should confirm that important calculations have been checked by

Area	Tests of controls
	the clients and re-perform those calculations. These include checking for wages for a number of weeks: • **Additions** of **payroll sheets** • **Totals** of **wages sheets** selected to summary • **Additions** and **cross-casts** of summary • **Postings** of **summary** to **general ledger** (including control accounts) • **Casts** of **net cash column** to cash book For salaries they include checking for a number of weeks/months: • **Additions of payroll sheets** • **Totals of salaries sheets** to **summary** • **Additions** and **cross-casts** of **summary** • **Postings** of **summary** to **general ledger** (including control accounts) • **Total** of **net pay column** to cash book
Deductions	Auditors should **confirm by recalculation** the **calculations** of **taxation** and **non-statutory deductions**. For income tax they should carry out the following tests: • **Scrutinise** the **control accounts** maintained to see **appropriate deductions** have been **made**. • **Agree** that the **payments** to the **taxation** bodies are **correct**. They should check other deductions to appropriate records. For voluntary deductions, they should see the authority completed by the relevant employees.

Question — Wages – control objectives and tests

The following questions have been selected from an internal control questionnaire for wages and salaries.

Internal control questionnaire – wages and salaries

                                                                                                       Yes   No

1   Does an appropriate official authorise rates of pay?

2   Are written notices required for employing and terminating employment?

3   Are formal records such as time cards used for time keeping?

4   Does anyone verify rates of pay, overtime hours and computations of gross pay before the wage payments are made?

5   Does the accounting system ensure the proper recording of payroll costs in the financial records?

Required

(a)   Describe the internal control objectives being fulfilled if the controls set out in the above questions are in place.

(b)   Describe the audit tests which would test the effectiveness of each control and help determine any potential material misstatement.

(c)   Identify the potential consequences for the company if the above controls were not in place.

You may answer in columnar form under the headings:

ICQ question	Internal control objective	Audit tests	Consequences

Answer

	ICQ question	Internal control objective	Audit tests	Consequences
1	Does an appropriate official authorise rates of pay?	Employees are paid amounts authorised	Test rates of pay from payroll to schedule of authorised pay rates (personnel files, board minutes etc)	Incorrect rates of pay could lead to over/under statement of profit
2	Are written notices required for employing and terminating employment?	All employees paid through payroll exist	Vouch a sample of employees from payroll files for authorisation of employment or termination Agree details for cheque or credit transfer salary payments to personnel files	Payroll may include fictitious employees
3	Are formal records such as time cards used for time keeping?	Employees are only paid for work done	Review time records to ensure they are properly completed and controlled Observe procedures for time recording Vouch time records where absences are recorded to payroll to ensure they have been accounted for Review the wages account and investigate any large or unusual amounts	Overstatement of payroll costs Employees over/under paid
4	Does anyone verify rates of pay, overtime hours and computation of gross pay before wage payments are made?	Employees are paid the correct amount	Examine payroll for evidence of verification Recompute gross pay (including overtime) Agree wage rates to authorised schedule	Misstatement of payroll costs
5	Does the accounting system ensure the proper recording of payroll costs in the financial records?	Payroll costs are properly recorded.	Agree posting of payroll costs to the nominal ledger.	Misstatement of payroll costs

5 Smaller entities

FAST FORWARD — Segregation of duties is a particularly important control in smaller entities.

5.1 Minimum business controls

The control systems in smaller entities are often not as sophisticated as those in larger entities. The particular area that can be a concern for smaller entities with few staff is **segregation of duties**. It can be impossible to adequately share duties between staff when there are only one or two staff.

Having established in Chapter 6 that proprietor involvement is the key to internal control in the small enterprise, we need next to be rather more precise and identify the types of control relevant to each principal accounting area. These controls can be referred to as **'minimum business controls'**.

It is important to appreciate that such controls will not, and **cannot, be evaluated and relied on** by the auditors as in a 'systems' audit approach, but they do **provide overall comfort** to the auditors, particularly when determining whether to seek to rely on management assurances as to the completeness of the accounting records.

The following checklist provides illustrative examples of minimum control standards.

Area and objectives	Question
Mail (Cash receipts are complete)	• Is all mail received and opened by the proprietor? • If the proprietor does not himself open the mail, is it opened by a person not connected with the accounts and read by him before it is distributed to the staff?
Receipts (Cash receipts are complete)	• Are all cheques and postal orders received by post counted by the proprietor before they are passed to the cashier? • Are all cheques and postal orders crossed to the company's branch of its bankers 'Not negotiable – account payee only'. • Are cash sales and credit sale receipts over the counter controlled by locked cash register tapes which only the proprietor can open? • Does the proprietor reconcile the cash register totals with the cash sales receipts daily? • Is the person performing the duties of cashier barred any responsibility concerning the sales, purchase or nominal ledgers?
Banking (Cash payments are complete)	• Is all cash received banked intact at intervals of not more than three days? • Does the proprietor reconcile all monies received with the copy paying-in slips at regular intervals?

Area and objectives	Question

Payments
 	
(Cash payments are complete)
	• Are all payments except sundry expenses made by cheques?
	• Does the proprietor sign all cheques?
	• Are cheques signed by the proprietor only after he has satisfied himself that:
	  – He has approved and cancelled all vouchers supporting the payment?
	  – All cheques are crossed not negotiable and account payee only?
	  – All cheque numbers are accounted for?
	• Are petty cash expenses controlled by the imprest system?
	• Does the proprietor review all expenses and initial the petty cash book before reimbursing the cashier?

Bank statements
 	
(Cash/cheques safeguarded against theft and liabilities not paid twice)
	• Are bank statements and paid cheques sent direct to the proprietor and opened only by him?
	• Does the proprietor scrutinise all paid cheques to ensure that he has signed them all before he passes them to the cashier?
	• Does the proprietor:
	  – Prepare a bank reconciliation each month? or
	  – Review in detail a reconciliation produced by the cashier?

Orders
 	
(Purchases are for the business only)
	• Are all purchase orders issued:
	  – Serially numbered by the printer?
	  – Pre-printed duplicate order forms?
	• Does the proprietor approve all orders?

Receipt of goods (Only ordered goods are accepted)	Are delivery notes: • Checked with goods? • Compared with the copy order? • Compared with the invoice?
Wages (Wages are paid to appropriate employee in correct amount)	• Is a separate cheque drawn for the exact amount to pay wages and tax? • Does the proprietor either prepare or examine the wages records before signing the cheque? • Does the proprietor initial the wages records after his examination? • Does the proprietor oversee the distribution of the wages packets or does he distribute them himself?

Receivables
 	
(Credit is extended to credit worthy customers and debt is chased)
	• If credit is granted to customers does the proprietor:
	  – Authorise every extension of credit to a customer?
	  – Approve credit limits for each customer?
	• Does the proprietor authorise all:
	  – Write offs of irrecoverable debts?
	  – Sales returns and allowances?
	  – Discounts other than routine cash discounts?
	• Does the proprietor receive a monthly list of **trade accounts receivable**, showing the age of the debts?
	• Are all authorisations by the proprietor evidenced by his initials?

Goods outwards	• Are pre-numbered dispatch notes prepared for all goods leaving the premises?

Area and objectives	Question

(Dispatches are recorded, invoiced and accounted for)	• Are all dispatch notes:
	  – Accounted for?
	  – Cross referenced with invoices and credit notes?
	• Is the proprietor satisfied that all goods leaving the premises have been accounted for?

Inventory **(Inventory is kept secure and valued properly)**	Does the proprietor scrutinise inventory regularly to: • Keep abreast of what is in inventory? • Discover obsolete items? • Discover damaged articles? • Ensure that inventory levels are kept under control?

Although the above types of control are desirable and feasible, they are nevertheless relatively informal. Consequently evidence of their performance tends to be lacking and they may indeed be overridden as there is no check on the proprietor himself.

Exam focus point

In the exam, run the following checklist through your mind when approaching questions about controls in smaller entities.

Are you being logical?

- Consider the number of staff the entity is likely to employ.
- Remember, top management or the owners are likely to be involved on a day to day level.
- Bear in mind a general rule: the smaller the entity, the fewer the day books and ledgers.

Chapter roundup

- The tests of controls in the **sales system** will be based around:
  - **Selling** (authorisation)
  - **Goods outwards** (custody)
  - **Accounting** (recording)

- The tests of controls in the **purchases system** will be based around:
  - **Buying** (authorisation)
  - **Goods inwards** (custody)
  - **Accounting** (recording)

- Key controls over **wages** cover:
  - **Documentation** and **authorisation** of staff changes
  - **Calculation** of wages and salaries
  - **Payment** of wages
  - **Authorisation** of **deductions**

- Segregation of duties is a particularly important control in smaller entities.

Quick quiz

1 Complete the table, putting the sales system control considerations under the correct headings.

Ordering/credit approval	Dispatch/invoicing	Recording/accounting

(a) All sales that have been invoiced have been put in the general ledger.
(b) Orders are fulfilled.
(c) Cut-off is correct.
(d) Goods are only supplied to good credit risks.
(e) Goods are correctly invoiced.
(f) Customers are encouraged to pay promptly.

2 State five controls relating to the ordering and granting of credit process.

(1) ………………………………………………………..
(2) ………………………………………………………..
(3) ………………………………………………………..
(4) ………………………………………………………..
(5) ………………………………………………………..

3 When checking sales invoicing the auditor should verify ……………………….., ………………….., ……………… and …………………………….., ……………………….., correct analysis in the receivables ledger and correct posting and that sales tax has been dealt with.

4 Complete the table, putting the purchase system control considerations under the correct headings.

Ordering	Receipts/invoices	Accounting

(a) Orders are only made to authorised suppliers.
(b) Liabilities are recognised for all goods and services received.
(c) Orders made at competitive prices.
(d) All expenditure is authorised.
(e) Cut-off is correctly applied.
(f) Goods and services are only accepted if there is an authorised order.

5   (a) State four examples of purchase documentation on which numerical sequence should be checked.

   (1) ....
   (2) ....
   (3) ....
   (4) ....

   (b) Why is numerical sequence checked?

6   List six procedures auditors should carry out if wages are paid in cash.

   (1) ....
   (2) ....
   (3) ....
   (4) ....
   (5) ....
   (6) ....

Answers to quick quiz

1

Ordering/credit approval	Dispatch/invoicing	Recording/accounting
(b) (d) (f)	(e)	(a) (c)

2   From:

- **Segregation** of duties; credit control, invoicing and inventory dispatch
- **Authorisation** of **credit terms** to customers
    - References/credit checks obtained
    - Authorisation by senior staff
    - Regular review
- **Authorisation** for changes in **other customer data**
    - Change of address supported by letterhead
    - Deletion requests supported by evidence balances cleared/customer in liquidation
- **Orders** only **accepted** from **customers** who have no credit problems
- **Sequential numbering** of blank pre-printed order documents
- **Correct prices quoted** to **customers**
- **Matching** of **customer orders** with production orders and dispatch notes and querying of orders not matched
- **Dealing** with **customer queries**

3   quantities, prices, calculations, additions, discounts

4

Ordering	Receipts/invoices	Accounting
(a) (c)	(b) (f)	(d) (e)

5   (a)   From:

- purchase requisitions
- purchase orders
- goods received notes
- goods returned notes
- suppliers invoices

(b)   Sequence provides a control that sales are complete. Missing documents should be explained, or cancelled copies available.

6   From:

- **Arrange to attend** the **pay-out** of wages to confirm that the official procedures are being followed.
- Before the wages are paid **compare payroll** with **wage packets** to ensure all employees have a wage packet.
- **Examine receipts** given by employees; **check unclaimed wages** are recorded in unclaimed wages book.
- **Observe** wages being paid out to ensure that **no employee receives more than one wage packet**.
- **Vouch entries in the unclaimed wages book with the entries on the payroll.**

- **Check that unclaimed wages** are **banked regularly.**
- **Check** that unclaimed wages books shows **reasons** why wages are unclaimed.
- **Review pattern** of **unclaimed wages** in unclaimed wages book; variations may indicate failure to record.
- **Verify** a sample of holiday pay **payments** with the **underlying records** and **check** the **calculation** of the amounts paid.

End of chapter question

Ocean Ltd (AIA Nov 2006)

You are the internal auditor of Ocean Ltd, a manufacturing company. The finance director has asked your advice on controls in the company's purchasing system. You have been asked to prepare a report outlining the procedures that should be in place over purchasing activities.

Ocean has separate departments for accounting, purchasing, and goods received. Most purchases are required by the production department, but other departments are able to raise their own requisitions for goods. The purchasing department is responsible for ordering high quality goods for the company at the lowest price, and for ensuring prompt delivery.

The accounts department is responsible for obtaining authorisation of purchase invoices before they are input into the computer, posting them to the payables ledger and the nominal ledger.

Required

(a) State the objective of an internal control system. **(3 marks)**

(b) Write a report to the finance director of Ocean, identifying the procedures that should be in place for:

    (i) controlling the purchase and receipt of goods; and **(11 marks)**
    (ii) controlling the recording of purchase invoices. **(6 marks)**

(Total = 20 marks)

Tests of controls: cash, inventory and non-current assets

Topic list	Syllabus reference
1 The cash system	5.5
2 The inventory system	5.5
3 Non-current assets	5.5
4 Internal audit: relevant cycles	5.5
5 Reporting to those charged with governance	6.3

Introduction

This chapter completes the tests of controls topic begun in Chapter 10. Other 'specialised' companies may have different systems, for example a share dealing system in a bank.

Controls over **cash and bank balances** cannot be seen in complete isolation from controls over the sales, purchases and wages cycle. In this chapter we concentrate on controls over and testing of the safe **custody and recording** of cash. You should note in particular the emphasis on prompt recording of receipts and payments, and prompt banking of cash and cheques received. Bear in mind also when you work through the section on bank and cash that controlling cheque receipts and payments is significantly easier than controlling cash receipts and payments.

For **inventory**, there should be **proper security arrangements** and **prompt recording**. You should note however the other aspects of control of inventory, particularly reviews of the condition of inventory, and inventory holding policies designed to ensure that the business is not holding too much or too little inventory. These controls interest auditors since they may impact upon how inventory is valued.

For **non-current assets,** it is vital that there are controls in place to ensure that capital items are capitalised as assets and revenue items are charged to the statement of profit or loss and other comprehensive income.

We also look at some of the wider **operational cycles** of interest to internal auditors, which were touched on in Chapter 3, and the aims and operations of controls in these cycles. We shall also consider tests of control which **internal auditors** might carry out on them.

Finally we will learn how auditors are required to communicate significant deficiencies in internal control with those charged with governance by ISA 265 *Communicating Deficiencies in Internal Control to those Charged with Governance and Management*. In addition, ISA 260 (Revised) *Communication with those Charged with Governance* sets out a number of matters that auditors must also communicate with those charged with governance.

1 The cash system

> **FAST FORWARD**
>
> Controls over cash receipts and payments should prevent fraud or theft.

1.1 Control objectives

- **All monies received** are **recorded**
- **All monies received** are **banked**
- **Cash and cheques** are **safeguarded** against loss or theft
- **All payments** are **authorised**, **made** to the **correct payees** and **recorded**
- **Payments** are **not made twice** for the same liability

1.2 Controls

> **FAST FORWARD**
>
> - Key controls over **receipts** include:
>   - Proper **post-opening** arrangements
>   - **Prompt recording**
>   - **Prompt banking**
>   - **Reconciliation** of records of cash received and banked
> - A further important control is **regular independent bank reconciliations.**
> - Key controls over **payments** include:
>   - **Restriction of access** to cash and cheques
>   - Procedures for **preparation and authorisation** of payments

Controls over the **completeness** of **recording** of cash receipts are particularly important. If these controls are inadequate, there may be insufficient audit evidence available when the auditor carries out substantive procedures.

Segregation of duties is also important. The person responsible for receiving and recording cash when it arrives in the post should not be the same as the person responsible for banking it. Ideally the cash book should be written up by a further staff member, and a fourth staff member should reconcile the various records of amounts received.

Controls: Cash at bank and in hand – receipts	
Segregation of duties between the various functions listed below is particularly important.	
Recording of receipts by post	• **Safeguards** to **prevent interception of mail** between receipt and opening • Appointment of **responsible person** to supervise mail • **Protection** of **cash and cheques** (restrictive crossing) • **Amounts received listed** when post opened • **Post stamped** with date of receipt

Recording of cash sales and collections	• **Restrictions** on **receipt of cash** (by cashiers only, or by sales staff etc)
	• **Evidencing** of receipt of cash
	   – Serially numbered receipt forms
	   – Cash registers incorporating sealed till rolls
	• **Clearance** of cash offices and registers
	• **Agreement of cash collections with till rolls**
	• **Agreement of cash collections with bankings and** cash and sales **records**
	• **Investigation** of cash shortages and surpluses

11: TESTS OF CONTROLS: CASH, INVENTORY AND NON-CURRENT ASSETS

Controls: Cash at bank and in hand – receipts	

General controls over recording	- Prompt **maintenance of records** (cash book, ledger accounts)
	- **Limitation** of **duties** of receiving cashiers
	- **Holiday arrangements**
	- **Giving** and **recording** of **receipts**
	  – Retained copies
	  – Serially numbered receipts books
	  – Custody of receipt books
	  – Comparisons with cash records and bank paying in slips

Banking	- **Daily bankings** - **Make-up** and **comparison** of **paying-in** slips against initial receipt records and cash book - **Banking** of receipts **intact**/control of disbursements

Safeguarding of cash and bank accounts	- **Restrictions** on **opening new bank accounts**
	- **Limitations** on **cash floats** held
	- **Restrictions** on **payments** out of **cash received**
	- **Restrictions** on **access** to cash registers and offices
	- **Independent checks** on cash floats
	- **Surprise cash counts**
	- **Custody** of **cash** outside **office hours**
	- **Custody** over **supply** and issue of cheques
	- **Preparation** of **cheques** restricted
	- **Safeguards** over **mechanically signed cheques**/cheques carrying printed signatures
	- **Restrictions** on issue of **blank** or **bearer** cheques
	- **Safeguarding** of **IOUs**, cash in transit
	- **Insurance arrangements**
	- **Control of funds** held in trust for employees
	- **Bank reconciliations**
	  – Issue of bank statements
	  – Frequency of reconciliations by independent person
	  – Reconciliation procedures
	  – Treatment of longstanding unpresented cheques
	  – Stop payment notice
	  – Sequence of cheque numbers
	  – Comparison with cash books
	- Key controls over **payments** include:
	  – **Restriction of access** to cash and cheques
	  – Procedures for **preparation and authorisation** of payments

Controls: Cash at bank and in hand – payments	
The arrangements for controlling payments will depend to a great extent on the nature of business transacted, the volume of payments involved and the size of the company.	
Cheque and cash payments generally	The cashier should generally not be concerned with keeping or writing-up books of account other than those recording disbursements nor should he have access to, or be responsible for the custody of, securities, title deeds or negotiable instruments belonging to the company. The person responsible for preparing cheques or traders' credit lists should not himself be a cheque signatory. Cheque signatories in turn should not be responsible for recording payments.

Cheque payments	• **Cheque requisitions**
	  – Appropriate supporting documentation
	  – Approval by appropriate staff
	  – Presentation to cheque signatories
	  – Cancellation (crossing/recording cheque number on requisition)
	• **Authority** to sign cheques
	  – Signatories should not also approve cheque requisitions
	  – Limitations on authority to specific amounts
	  – Number of signatories
	  – Prohibitions over signing of blank cheques
	• **Prompt dispatch** of signed **cheques**
	• **Obtaining** of paid **cheques** from **banks**
	• Payments **recorded promptly** in **cash book** and **general** and **purchase ledger**

Cash payments	• **Authorisation** (signature or online/electronic approval) of **expenditure** • **Cancellation** of **vouchers** to ensure they cannot be paid • **Limits** on **disbursements** • **Rules** on **cash advances** to employees, IOUs and cheque cashing

1.3 Tests of controls

Note that as well as testing controls over receipts, auditors are also obtaining evidence to support the assertion that sales and receipts are **completely recorded**.

Area	Tests of control

Receipts received by post	• **Observe procedures** for **post opening** are being followed.
	• **Observe** that **cheques** received by post are immediately **crossed** in the company's favour of the company.
	• For items entered in the rough cash book (or other record of cash, cheques etc received by post), **trace entries** to:
	  – **Cash book**
	  – **Paying-in book**
	  – **Counterfoil** or carbon copy receipts
	• **Verify amounts entered** as **received** with remittance advices or other supporting evidence.

11: TESTS OF CONTROLS: CASH, INVENTORY AND NON-CURRENT ASSETS

Area	Tests of control

Cash sales, branch takings	• For a sample of cash sales summaries/branch summaries from different locations:
	   – **Verify with till rolls** or copy cash sale notes
	   – **Agree to paying-in slip** date-stamped and initialled by the bank
	   – **Verify that takings** are banked intact daily
	   – **Vouch expenditure** out of takings

Collections	• For a sample of items from the original collection records:
	   – **Trace amounts** to **cash book** via collectors' cash sheets or other collection records.
	   – **Agree entries** on **cash sheets** or collection records with collectors' receipt books.
	   – **Verify** that **goods delivered** to travellers/salesmen have been regularly **reconciled** with sales and inventories in hand.
	   – **Vouch that the numerical sequence** of collection records is complete.

Receipts cash book	• For cash receipts for several days throughout the period:
	   – **Agree to entries in rough cash book**, receipts, branch returns or other records.
	   – **Vouch to paying-in slips** obtained direct from the bank, observing that there is no delay in banking monies received.
	   – **Re-cast additions** of **paying-in slips.**
	   – **Re-cast additions** of **cash book.**
	   – **Trace postings to the receivables ledger.**
	   – **Trace postings** to the **general ledger**, including control accounts.
	• **Scrutinise the cash book** and **investigate items** of a **special** or **unusual nature**.

Payments cash book (authorisation)	• For a sample of payments:
	   – **Compare** with paid cheques to ensure payee agrees.
	   – **Note** whether **cheques** are **signed** by the **persons authorised** to do so within their authority limits.
	   – **Vouch** to **suppliers' invoices** for goods and services. Verify that supporting documents are signed as having been **checked** and **passed for payment** and have been stamped 'paid'.
	   – **Agree** to **suppliers' statements.**
	   – **Check** to **other documentary evidence**, as appropriate (agreements, authorised expense vouchers, wages/salaries records, petty cash books etc).

Payments cash book (recording)	• For a sample of weeks:
	   – **Confirm the sequence of cheque numbers** and enquire into missing numbers.
	   – **Trace transfers** to other bank accounts, petty cash books or other records, as appropriate.
	   – **Vouch additions**, including extensions, and balances forward at the beginning and end of the months covering the periods chosen.
	   – **Agree postings** to the **payables ledger.**
	   – **Agree postings** to the **general ledger**, including the control accounts.

When vouching that bank and cash are **secure**, auditors should consider the security arrangements over blank cheques. Bank reconciliations are also a very important control and auditors should carry out the following tests on these.

Area	Tests of control
Bank reconciliations	• **Verify** that **reconciliations have been prepared** at **regular intervals** throughout the year. • **Scrutinise reconciliations for unusual items.**

Petty cash	• For a sample of payments:
	  – **Agree** to supporting vouchers.
	  – **Determine** whether they are properly **approved**.
	  – Inspect whether **vouchers** have been **marked and initialled** by the cashier to prevent their re-use.
	• For a sample of weeks:
	  – **Trace amounts** received to **cash books**.
	  – **Re-cast additions** and **balances carried** forward.
	  – **Agree postings** to the **nominal ledger**.

Exam focus point

Questions about the sales or purchases systems may also require consideration of controls over receipts or payments.

2 The inventory system

FAST FORWARD

Inventory controls are designed to ensure safe custody.

The inventory system can be very important in an audit because of the high value of inventory or the complexity of its audit. It is closely connected with the sales and purchases systems covered in Chapter 10.

2.1 Control objectives

Area	Aim
Recording	• All **inventory movements** are **authorised** and **recorded**. • **Inventory records** only **include items** that **belong** to the client. • **Inventory records include inventory** that **exists** and is **held** by the client. • **Inventory quantities** have been **recorded correctly**. • **Cut-off procedures** are **properly applied** to inventory.
Protection of inventory	• **Inventory** is **safeguarded** against loss, pilferage or damage.
Valuation of inventory	• The **costing system values inventory correctly**. • **Allowance** is **made** for **slow-moving, obsolete** or **damaged inventory**.
Inventory-holding	• **Levels of inventory held** are **reasonable**.

2.2 Controls

> **FAST FORWARD**
>
> Important controls over inventory include restriction of access, documentation and authorisation of movements, regular **independent inventory counting** and **review of inventory condition**.

Area	Controls

Recording of inventory	• **Segregation** of duties; custody and recording of inventories
	• **Reception, checking** and **recording** of goods inwards
	• **Inventory issues supported** by **appropriate documentation**
	• **Maintenance** of **inventory records**
	   – Inventory ledgers
	   – Bin cards
	   – Transfer records

Protection of inventory	• **Precautions** against **theft, misuse** and **deterioration**
	   – Restriction of access to stores
	   – Controls on stores environment (right temperature, precautions against damp etc).
	• **Security** over **inventory** held by third parties, and third party inventory held by entity
	• **Inventory counts** (see also Chapter 14).
	   – Regular inventory counts
	   – Fair coverage so that all inventory is counted at least once a year
	   – Counts by independent persons
	   – Recording
	   – Cut-off for goods in transit and time differences
	   – Reconciliation of inventory count to book records and control accounts

Valuation of inventory	• **Computation** of **inventory valuation**
	   – Accords with IAS 2 *Inventories*
	   – Reperformance of calculations
	• **Review** of **condition** of Inventory
	   – Treatment of slow-moving, damaged and obsolete inventory
	   – Authorisation of write-offs
	• **Accounting** for **scrap** and **waste**

Inventory holding	• **Control** of **inventory levels**
	   – Maximum inventory limits
	   – Minimum inventory limits
	   – Re-order quantities and levels
	• Arrangements for dealing with **returnable containers**

2.3 Tests of controls

Most of the testing relating to inventory has been covered in the purchase and sales testing outlined in Chapter 10. Auditors will primarily be concerned at this stage with ensuring that the business keeps track of inventory. To confirm this, checks must be made on how inventory **movements** are **recorded** and how **inventory** is **secured**.

Area	Tests of control
Inventory movements	• **Select** a sample of **inventory movements records** and **agree** to **goods received** and **goods dispatched notes**. • **Confirm** that **movements** have been **authorised** as **appropriate**. • **Select** a sample of **goods received** and **goods dispatched** notes and agree to **inventory movement records**. • **Perform a sequence check** of inventory records.
Other tests that auditors are likely to perform	• **Test** check **inventory counts** carried out from time to time (eg monthly) during the period and confirm: 　– **All discrepancies** between **book** and **actual** figures have been fully investigated. 　– **All discrepancies** have been **signed off** by a senior manager. 　– **Obsolete, damaged or slow-moving goods** have been **marked accordingly** and written down to net realisable value. • **Observe security arrangements** for inventories. • **Consider environment** in which inventories are held.

Auditors will carry out extensive tests on the **valuation** of inventory at the substantive testing stage (see Chapter 14).

Question — Cash control weaknesses

Jonathan is the sole shareholder of Furry Lion Stores, a company which owns five stores in the west of England. The stores mainly stock food and groceries, and four of the stores have an off-licence as well.

Each store is run by a full-time manager and three or four part-time assistants. Jonathan spends on average ½ a day a week at each store, and spends the rest of his time at home, dealing with his other business interests.

All sales are for cash and are recorded on till rolls which the manager retains. Shop manager wages are paid monthly by cheque by Jonathan. Wages of shop assistants are paid in cash out of the takings.

Most purchases are made from local wholesalers and are paid for in cash out of the takings. Large purchases (over $250) must be made by cheques signed by the shop manager and countersigned by Jonathan.

Shop managers bank surplus cash once a week, apart from a float in the till.

All accounting records including the cash book, wages and sales tax records are maintained by the manager. Jonathan reviews the weekly bank statements when he visits the shops. He also has a look at inventories to see if inventory levels appear to be about right. All invoices are also kept in a drawer by a manager and marked with a cash book reference, and where appropriate a cheque number when paid.

Required

Discuss the deficiencies in the control systems of Furry Lion Stores, and how the deficiencies can be remedied.

Answer

Deficiencies in the system, and their remedies, are as follows.

Inventory

The shops do not appear to have any inventory movement records. Jonathan has also only a very approximate indication of inventory levels. Hence it will be difficult to detect whether inventory levels are too high, or too low with a risk of running out of inventory. Theft of inventory would also be difficult to detect. The company should therefore introduce inventory movement records, detailing values and volumes.

In addition regular inventory counts should be made either by Jonathan or by staff from another shop. Discrepancies between the inventory records and the actual inventory counted should be investigated.

Cash controls

Too much cash appears to be held on site. In addition, the fact that most payments appear to be for cash may mean inadequate documentation is kept. The level of cash on site can be decreased by daily rather than weekly bankings. In addition the need for cash on site can be decreased by paying wages by cheque, and by paying all but the smallest payments by cheque.

The cash book should obviously still be maintained but cheque stubs should also show details of amounts paid. The cash book should be supported by invoices and other supporting documentation, and should be cross-referenced to the general ledger (see below).

Cash reconciliations

There is no indication of the till-rolls that are kept being reconciled to cash takings.

There should be a daily reconciliation of cash takings and till rolls; this should be reviewed if not performed by the shop manager.

Bank reconciliations

There is no mention of bank reconciliations taking place.

Bank reconciliations should be carried out at least monthly by the shop manager, and reviewed by the owner.

Purchases

There is no formal system for recording purchases. Invoices do not appear to be filed in any particular way. It would be difficult to see whether accounting records were complete, and hence it would be difficult to prepare a set of accounts from the accounting records available.

In addition the way records are maintained means that accounts would have to be prepared on a cash basis, and not on an accruals basis.

A purchase day book should be introduced. Invoices should be recorded in the purchase day book, and filed in a logical order, either by date received or by supplier.

General ledger

There is no general ledger, and again this means that annual accounts cannot easily be prepared (and also management accounts).

A general ledger should be maintained with entries made from the cash book, wages records and purchase day book. This will enable accounts to be prepared on an accruals basis.

Supervision

Jonathan does not take a very active part in the business, only signing cheques over $250, and visiting the shops only half a day each week. This may mean that assets can easily go missing, and Jonathan cannot readily see whether the business is performing as he would wish.

Jonathan should review wage/sales tax/cash book reconciliations. Management accounts should also be prepared by shop managers for Jonathan.

Tutorial note. This question deals with controls that are possible given the circumstances of the business. Greater segregation of duties does not appear to be possible as the shops are small, and Jonathan cannot spend more time at the shops (although he can use his time more productively by reviewing reconciliations).

3 Non-current assets

> **FAST FORWARD**
>
> Most of the key controls over non-current assets are the general purchase controls, covered in Chapter 10. One important distinction to make is the difference between capital and revenue expenditure.

The nature of financial statements means that it is important to classify capital and revenue expenditure correctly, or profit will be over or understated.

The controls and tests outlined below are often considered and performed during the audit of non-current assets as this is where the main issue of capitalisation occurs.

3.1 Control objectives

Area	Aim
Authorisation	• All expenditure is authorised (signature or online/electronic approval).
Recording	• All expenditure is classified correctly in the financial statements as capital or revenue expenditure.

3.2 Controls

> **FAST FORWARD**
>
> It is important that expenditure is recorded correctly, so that profit/loss and assets/liabilities are not misstated.

Area	Controls
Ordering	• Orders for capital items should be authorised. • Order should be requisitioned on appropriate (different from general purchases) documentation.
Invoices	• Invoices should be approved by the person who authorised the order. • They should be marked with the appropriate general ledger code.
Recording	• All the standard controls over purchases are relevant here. • Capital items should be written up in the non-current asset register. • The non-current asset register should be reconciled regularly to the general ledger.

3.3 Tests of controls

> **FAST FORWARD**
>
> It may not be cost-effective to test controls over non-current assets.

If the ordering documentation is different for capital purchases, all the standard purchase control tests should be carried out. If the documentation is not different, the auditor should enquire as to the client's system for recording and filing capital invoices.

It is likely that capital purchases in the year will be fewer than standard purchases in the year and if the invoices are not segregated it may not be cost-efficient to test the controls over this area. Substantive procedures would therefore be performed.

Alternative **substantive procedures** include:

Procedure	Description
Analytical procedures	• General comparison between current and prior year figures to ascertain any unexplained differences • Review of sensitive codes in the general ledger such as repairs or maintenance • Review of the movements on the non-current asset codes • Compare budgeted capital purchases with actual capital purchases
Enquiry and review	• Discuss the level of capital purchases in the year with the purchasing manager • Review the board minutes for authorisation of capital purchases

These substantive tests are often carried out as part of the substantive audit of non-current assets.

The auditor should be aware of the risks attaching to the audit of this area. As tests of controls might be cost-ineffective, control risk in this area is higher than would have been if they were tested.

Inherent risk can also be high in this area. Capital and revenue expenditure is treated differently for the purposes of tax, and if the client is sensitive to its tax bill, there may be motivation to account creatively.

4 Internal audit: relevant cycles

> **FAST FORWARD**
>
> The **internal auditors are interested in the risks arising to the company in certain cycles,** not simply the risks of misstatements arising in the financial statements.

In Chapter 3 we discussed some of the operational cycles that internal auditors might be interested in. These are likely to be of lesser interest to the external auditor, particularly where the cycle does not directly impact on the financial statements.

In this section we shall consider some of the matters which will affect the work of the internal auditors, in particular, aims of controls in the cycles, the controls themselves, and how the auditor will test those controls.

4.1 Procurement

We have already noted that many of the controls in this cycle will be the same as in the purchases cycle which the external auditor is interested in. However, as the scope of the internal auditor goes beyond the financial statements, consider these additional factors which he will be interested in.

A procurement system is likely to have many systems within it (for example, tendering, placing orders, checking goods inwards), which the internal auditor would probably approach separately.

Procurement system	
Control objectives	- The business has goods and services when it needs them.
- The business does not pay too much for those goods and services.
- The business does not make short-term savings on goods and services which lead to longer term inflated costs.
- Employees or suppliers do not defraud the company.
Controls	- The business always invites tenders for goods and services.
- Research is conducted on potential suppliers before they are invited to tender.
- Requirements for goods and services are always put in writing.
- Use is made of discounting and calculations of long-term costs where service is for a prolonged period.
- No transaction carried out with employees and connected persons.
Tests of controls	- A sample of contracts can be reviewed to confirm research and tender process.
- A sample of invoices agreed back to written requisition.
- For a sample of construction contracts, check long-term calculations exist and are correct.
- Review central database of suppliers to ensure that none are connected parties.

Exam focus point

As usual, there could be various tests of these controls. If required in an exam to suggest tests of controls, you should consider what the objective of the control is, and how you could prove that that objective is being met.

Remember however, that only internal audit would be interested in some of these controls features. In principle, for example, the external auditors are not too concerned if the company pays more than it should do for its goods and services, so long as what it does pay is recorded properly in the financial statements.

4.2 Marketing

Similarly to procurement, 'marketing' covers a wide range of systems, including research, advertising, promotions, sales, and after-sales.

Marketing system	
Control objectives	- Customer demand should be understood and met.
- Customers should be made aware of products.
- Products are competitive, not hampered by pricing or promotion tactics.
- Goods are sold for valuable consideration.
Controls	Some of the controls will be similar to those discussed in the sales cycle in Chapter 10. However, think again that the internal auditor is interested in objectives beyond the scope of the financial systems. The following controls might be used to meet the above objectives:
- Market research should be commissioned or carried out.
- Actual sales should be compared to budgets.
- Advertising is targeted.
- Promotions are timed to coincide with periods historically linked with sales, eg Christmas.
- Competitor prices are monitored.
- Terms and conditions are made known to customers.
- Credit checks are made.
Tests of controls	Some of the tests, particularly those in relation to credit, will be the same as those discussed in the sales system in Chapter 10.

11: TESTS OF CONTROLS: CASH, INVENTORY AND NON-CURRENT ASSETS

Question — Marketing – tests of controls

Try to think up some ways of testing the controls listed above.

Answer

Potential tests of controls include:

- Review company policy on commissioning market research.
- For a sample of major promotions, check that research was commissioned and used.
- Check that actual sales are compared to budget sales and that variances are investigated.
- For a sample of major promotions, ensure that timing has been considered and documented.
- Ensure that records are maintained of competitor pricing policy.
- Review terms and conditions to ensure that they comply with company policy.
- Check a sample of contracts/sales to ensure terms and conditions were highlighted.

You may have thought of other tests of controls, this list is not definitive. Check that your answers prove that the objective you had in mind is being tested.

4.3 Treasury

Treasury system	
Control objectives	• Money is available to the company when it is required. • Risks in relation to foreign currency and interest rates are managed effectively. • Transactions do not lose the company money over time. • Exposures are highlighted and reported on, on a timely basis.
Controls	• Cash flow forecasting • Arrangements with the bank in the event of cash emergencies • Contingency plans available • Clear policy on tolerated risk • Regular review of investment • Frequent two-way communication
Tests of controls	• Reviewing cash flow forecasts • Reading correspondence with the bank • Reading contingency plans and assessing them for realism • Discuss review of investments with investment managers • Seek evidence of such reviews being made (reports, memos) • Seek evidence of communication

4.4 Human resources

Human resources system	
Control objectives	- Sufficiently qualified and capable staff are available when required. - There is no significant over-reliance on key personnel. - Staff are paid the correct remuneration on a timely basis. - Staff are contented and not prone to industrial action or seeking alternative employment. - Employment laws are complied with. - The human resource is handled considerately.
Controls	- The business has a long-term human requirement plan. - Salary is benchmarked against the market. - Performance of staff is regularly and formally appraised. - Staff are given adequate training. - Key personnel are not put at risk together. - Long-term succession planning is undertaken. - Payroll controls as discussed in Chapter 10. - Relationships with trade unions are well maintained. - Human resources managers receive training in employment law.
Tests of controls	- Obtain a copy of the long term human resource plan and review it. - Obtain evidence that the HR department monitors pay levels in the market. - Review of appraisal procedure, check that a sample of employees have had appraisals. - Review training records to ensure that training is in accordance with company policy. - Review long-term succession plan and any 'apprenticing' schemes are in operation. - Review training procedures within department by discussion with staff.

Exam focus point

As you considered each of these cycles more carefully, you will have seen the strong links that they have with the income and asset cycles that the external auditor is interested in. You will also have seen that the internal auditor is interested in risks arising to the company, whereas the external auditor is more interested in risks of misstatements in the financial statements.

In the exam, you could be asked the difference between the internal and external auditors' interest in internal controls. Remember that the difference is in the objectives each is interested in, and the controls and the tests follow on from that. You might want to re-read the following sections in conjunction with one another, to see how the objectives of the internal auditors (or the company) extend further than the external auditors in each case:

- Cash/treasury
- Payroll/human resources
- Purchases/procurement
- Sales/marketing

5 Reporting to those charged with governance

In Chapters 10 and 11 we have considered the typical internal controls that management will implement in relation to sales, purchases, wages, cash, inventory and non-current assets.

The external auditor needs to consider internal controls as part of identifying and assessing risks that the financial statements will be misstated and should document their understanding of internal controls.

Where the auditor believes that internal controls are strong, they may decide to perform tests of controls to gather evidence to support their initial assumptions. During this process, the auditor may identify deficiencies in internal control and they should report significant deficiencies to those charged with governance.

This section explains the considerations the auditor should undertake in deciding whether to report deficiencies in internal control and also the main contents of the report.

5.1 Significant deficiencies

FAST FORWARD

> The auditor communicates **significant deficiencies** in internal control to management and those charged with governance in writing.

ISA 265 *Communicating Deficiencies in Internal Control to those Charged with Governance and Management* states that the objective of the auditor is 'to communicate appropriately to those charged with governance and management deficiencies in internal control that the auditor has identified during the audit and that, in the auditor's professional judgement, are of sufficient importance to merit their respective attentions'.

Key term

> It gives two key definitions for the auditor in making those judgements. A **deficiency in internal control** exists when:
>
> (a) A control is designed, implemented or operated in such a way that it is unable to prevent, or detect and correct, misstatements in the financial statements on a timely basis; or
>
> (b) A control necessary to prevent, or detect and correct, misstatements in the financial statements on a timely basis is missing.
>
> A **significant deficiency in internal control** is a deficiency or combination of deficiencies in internal control that, in the auditor's professional judgement, is of sufficient importance to merit the attention of those charged with governance.

The auditor must determine if he has identified significant deficiencies in internal control while obtaining an understanding of the system and testing it, and if he has done so, he must communicate these with management and those charged with governance **in writing**. The auditor must also communicate less significant deficiencies with management.

The auditor should consider the following matters when determining whether a deficiency in internal control is a significant deficiency:

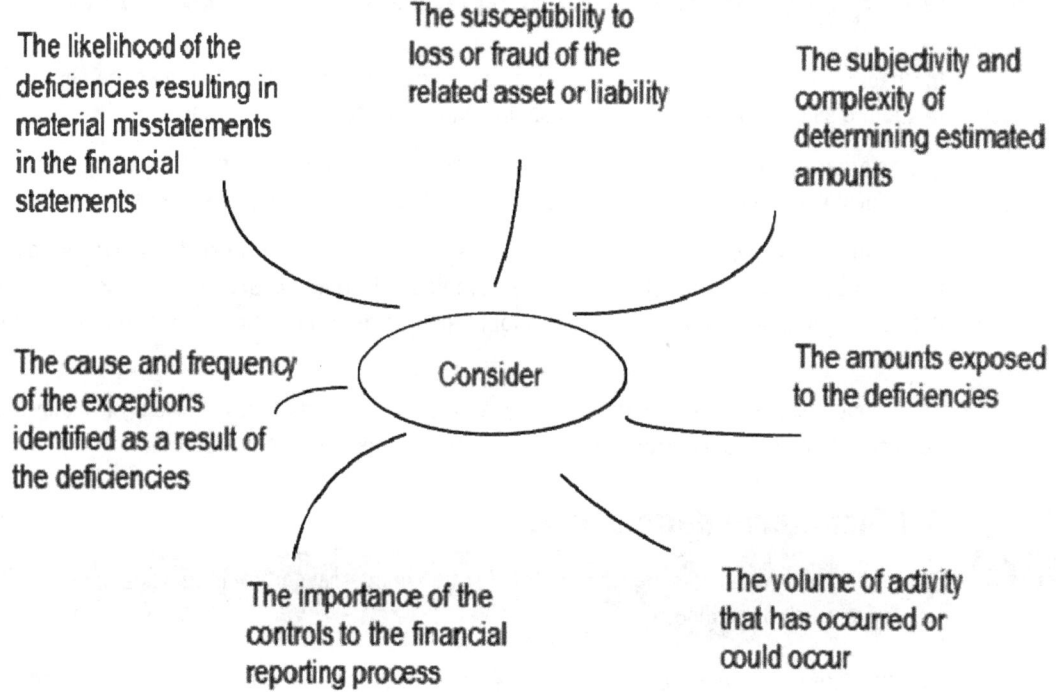

The communication must include a **description of the deficiency and its potential effect**.

In addition, the communication must make clear that it relates to deficiencies discovered while carrying out audit work, that it therefore does not necessarily include all existing deficiencies and that the purpose of the work was not to report on deficiencies in the system.

5.2 Communication of audit matters with those charged with governance

> **FAST FORWARD**
>
> The **auditor must also communicate prescribed audit matters** with those charged with governance.

ISA 260 (Revised) *Communication with those Charged with Governance* applies here. It sets out the **objectives of the auditor** in communicating with those charged with governance at the entity:

(a) To communicate clearly with those charged with governance **the responsibilities of the auditor in relation to the financial statement audit**, and **an overview of the planned scope and timing of the audit**;

(b) To **obtain** from those charged with governance **information** relevant to the audit;

(c) To **provide** those charged with governance with **timely observations** arising from the audit that are **significant and relevant** to their responsibility to oversee the financial reporting process; and

(d) To **promote effective two-way communication** between the auditor and those charged with governance.

(ISA 260 (Revised): para. 9)

Key term

> **Those charged with governance** is the term used to describe the role of persons entrusted with the responsibility for overseeing the strategic direction of the entity and obligations related to the accountability of the entity. This includes overseeing the financial reporting process.

The scope of the ISA is limited to matters that come to the auditors' attention as a result of the audit; the auditors are not required to design procedures to identify matters of governance interest. It says 'The auditor shall determine the appropriate person(s) within the entity's governance structure with whom to communicate'.

The auditors may communicate with the whole board, the supervisory board or the audit committee depending on the governance structure of the organisation. To avoid misunderstandings, the engagement letter shall explain that auditors will only **communicate matters** that come to their attention as a **result** of the **performance** of the audit. It shall state that the auditors are **not required** to **design procedures** for the purpose of identifying matters of governance interest.

The letter may also:

- **Describe** the **form** which any **communications** on governance matters will take
- **Identify** the **relevant persons** with whom such communications will be made
- **Identify** any **specific matters** of **governance** interest which it has agreed are to be communicated

5.3 Matters to communicate

ISA 260 (Revised) sets out the matters that shall be communicated under four key headings:

- *The Auditor's Responsibilities in Relation to the Financial Statement Audit*

    The auditor communicates their responsibility for forming and expressing an opinion on the financial statements and the fact that the audit does not relieve those charged with governance of their responsibilities.

- *Planned Scope and Timing of the Audit*

- *Significant Findings from the Audit*

    ISA 260 (Revised) provides a list of those matters under this heading:

    – The auditor's views about significant qualitative aspects of the entity's accounting practices, including accounting policies, accounting estimates and financial statement disclosures.

    – Significant difficulties, if any, encountered during the audit.

    – Unless all of those charged with governance are involved in managing the entity:

    (i) Significant matters, if any, arising from the audit that were discussed, or subject to correspondence with management; and

    (ii) Written representations the auditor is requesting;

    – Other matters, if any, arising from the audit that, in the auditor's professional judgement, are significant to the oversight of the financial reporting process.

- *Auditor Independence*

    In the case of listed entities, the auditor communicates that the engagement team (and others in the firm as appropriate) and the firm have complied with relevant ethical requirements regarding independence.

With regards to the method of communication, ISA 260 (Revised) says 'The auditor shall communicate in writing with those charged with governance regarding significant findings from the audit if, in the auditor's professional judgement, oral communication would not be adequate.' Reporting should take place on a timely basis.

Auditors should have regard to local laws and regulations, and local guidance on confidentiality when communicating with management.

Chapter roundup

- Controls over cash receipts and payments should prevent fraud or theft.
- Key controls over **receipts** include:
  - Proper **post-opening** arrangements
  - **Prompt recording**
  - **Prompt banking**
  - **Reconciliation** of records of cash received and banked
- A further important control is **regular independent bank reconciliations.**
- Key controls over **payments** include:
  - **Restriction of access** to cash and cheques
  - Procedures for **preparation and authorisation** of payments
- **Inventory controls** are designed to ensure safe custody.
- Important controls over inventory include restriction of access, documentation and authorisation of movements, regular **independent inventory counting** and **review of inventory condition**.
- Most of the key controls over capital and revenue expenditure are the general purchase controls, covered in Chapter 10.
- It is important that expenditure is recorded correctly, so that profit/loss and assets/liabilities are not misstated.
- It may not be cost-effective to test controls over revenue and capital expenditure.
- The **internal auditors are interested in the risks arising to the company in certain cycles,** not simply the risks of misstatements arising in the financial statements.
- The auditor must communicate **significant deficiencies** in internal control in writing to those charged with governance.
- The auditor should also communicate **the auditor's responsibilities in relation to the financial statement audit, the planned scope and timing of the audit, significant findings from the audit** and confirmation as to the **auditor's independence**.

Quick quiz

1. Name the five key aims of controls of the cash system.

2. Give five examples of tests to be performed on the cash payments book.

3. Three important controls over the protection of inventories are:

    - Restriction of access to stores
    - Regular inventory counts
    - Reconciliation of book inventory to physical inventory

    True ☐

    False ☐

4. Give two examples of **substantive procedures** that can be used to test capital and revenue expenditure.

5. Describe two of the four objectives of the auditor in communicating with those charged with governance at the entity.

Answers to quick quiz

1. (1) **All monies received** are **recorded.**
   (2) **All monies received** are **banked.**
   (3) **Cash and cheques** are **safeguarded** against loss or theft.
   (4) **All payments** are **authorised, made** to the **correct payees** and **recorded.**
   (5) **Payments** are **not made twice** for the same liability.

2. For a sample of payments:

   (1) **Compare** with paid cheques to ensure payee agrees.

   (2) **Note** that **cheques** are **signed** by the **persons authorised** to do so within their authority limits.

   (3) **Check** to **suppliers' invoices** for goods and services. Verify that supporting documents are signed as having been **reviewed** and **passed for payment** and have been stamped 'paid'.

   (4) **Check** to **suppliers' statements.**

   (5) **Check** to **other documentary evidence**, as appropriate (agreements, authorised expense vouchers, wages/salaries records, petty cash books etc).

3. True

4. **Analytical procedures**

   - General comparison between current and prior year figures to ascertain any unexplained differences.
   - Review of sensitive codes in the general ledger such as repairs or maintenance.
   - Review of the movements on the non-current asset codes.
   - Compare budgeted capital purchases with actual capital purchases.

   Enquiry and review

   - Discuss the level of capital purchases in the year with the purchasing manager.
   - Review the board minutes for authorisation of capital purchases.

5. Any two from:

   (a) To communicate clearly with those charged with governance the responsibilities of the auditor in relation to the financial statement audit, and an overview of the planned scope and timing of the audit;

   (b) To obtain from those charged with governance information relevant to the audit;

   (c) To provide those charged with governance with timely observations arising from the audit that are significant and relevant to their responsibility to oversee the financial reporting process; and

   (d) To promote effective two-way communication between the auditor and those charged with governance.

End of chapter question

Razorlight Ltd (AIA May 2008)

Razorlight Ltd is a manufacturer of high quality electrical goods. The directors of the company were concerned that the company's internal control systems were not as effective as they should be, and so decided to set up an internal audit function. They appointed you as head of this new department.

After an initial review of the company's internal controls, you have concluded that the two most urgent areas for attention are the control of raw materials, and the control of credit sales. The following are extracts from the notes you made during your initial review of internal controls:

Raw materials

Raw materials are kept in a locked storeroom. Storeroom staff comprise a supervisor and three clerks. Raw materials can be removed from the store only upon written or verbal authorisation from one of the production foremen.

There are no perpetual inventory records, so the storeroom does not keep a record of goods received or issued. Instead, a physical inventory count is taken monthly by the storeroom clerks.

After each count, the storeroom supervisor matches quantities counted against predetermined re-order levels. If a count for a given part is below the re-order level, the supervisor completes a materials requisition form, and sends this to the accounts payables clerk.

The accounts payables clerk prepares a purchase order for a predetermined reorder quantity, and sends the order to the supplier from whom the part was last purchased.

When ordered raw materials are delivered, they are signed for by the storeroom clerks.

They count the goods, and agree this to the suppliers' delivery note, which is then filed in the storeroom.

When the accounts payable clerk receives the invoice from the supplier, he agrees the details to the purchase order, and if all is correct, he sends a cheque to the supplier.

Credit sales

The company recently set up a new computerised system to process delivery, invoicing and accounts receivable records. Each of these three functions is permanently assigned to a specific computer operator, who is also responsible for making programme changes, running the programme, and reconciling the computer log. All of the computer operators have access to the computer room.

Razorlight delivers its products directly from its warehouse, which forwards goods despatched notes (GDNs) to the accounting department. There, the sales clerk enters the price of the item, and checks the numerical sequence of the GDNs. The GDNs are then sent to the computer department for processing.

The computer department generates a three-copy invoice that is forwarded to the sales clerk, and a daily sales register showing the total amount of sales.

The sales clerk posts two copies of each invoice to the customer, and retains the third copy in an open invoice file that provides a record of accounts receivable.

Required

(a) Identify the deficiencies in Razorlight's internal controls over raw materials and credit sales, and for each deficiency identified, suggest how it might be improved. **(20 marks)**

(b) Describe the main causes of the limitations of internal controls. **(5 marks)**

(Total = 25 marks)

Bank and cash

Topic list	Syllabus reference
1 Bank	5.7
2 Cash	5.7

Introduction

Work on bank and cash will concentrate on completeness and accuracy of balances. The audit of the bank reconciliation, bank confirmation letter and counting of cash are key audit procedures. The audit of cash book transactions has been considered in the chapters on sales, purchases and wages cycles, and non-current asset additions and disposals.

1 Bank

> **FAST FORWARD**
>
> **Bank balances** are usually **confirmed directly with the bank** in question via a bank confirmation letter.

1.1 Bank confirmation procedures

The audit of bank balances will need to cover **completeness, existence, rights and obligations and accuracy, valuation and allocation**. All of these assertions can be audited directly through the procedure of obtaining **third party confirmations** from the client's banks and reconciling these with the accounting records, having regard to cut-off.

The audit objectives linking these assertions are as follows:

- Recorded cash balances exist at the year end **(existence)**.
- Recorded cash balances include the effects of all transactions that occurred **(completeness)**.
- Year-end transfers are recorded in the correct period **(cut-off)**.
- Recorded balances are realisable at the amounts stated **(accuracy, valuation and allocation)**.
- The entity has legal title to all cash balances shown at the year end **(rights and obligations)**.

The auditors should obtain up to date details of bank accounts held by their audit client.

This type of audit evidence is valuable because it comes directly from an **independent source** and, therefore, provides greater assurance of reliability than that obtained solely from the bank's own records. The bank letter is mentioned as a source of external third party evidence in ISA 505 *External Confirmations* (para. A1).

1.2 Confirmation requests

> **FAST FORWARD**
>
> The **bank confirmation letter** can be used to ask a variety of questions, including queries about outstanding interest, contingent liabilities and guarantees.

The auditors should decide from which bank or banks to request confirmation, have regard to such matters as **size of balance**, **volume of activity**, **degree of reliance** on **internal control**, and **materiality** within the context of the financial statements.

The auditors should determine which of the following approaches is the most appropriate in seeking confirmation of balances or other information from the bank:

- **Listing balances** and other information, and requesting confirmation of their accuracy and completeness; or
- **Requesting details of balances** and other information, which can then be compared with the requesting bank's records

In determining which of the above approaches is the most appropriate, the auditors should weigh the **quality** of **audit evidence** they require in the particular circumstances against the **practicality** of obtaining a reply from the confirming bank.

Difficulty may be encountered in obtaining a satisfactory response even where the client company submits information for confirmation to the confirming bank. It is important that a response be sought for **all** confirmation requests. Auditors should not usually request a response only if the information submitted is incorrect or incomplete.

1.2.1 Preparation and dispatch of requests and receipt of replies

Control over the content and dispatch of confirmation requests is the responsibility of the auditors. However, it will be necessary for the request to be **authorised** by the client entity. Replies should be returned **directly to the auditors** and to facilitate such a reply, a pre-addressed envelope should be enclosed with the request.

1.2.2 Content of confirmation requests

The form and content of a confirmation request letter will depend on the purpose for which it is required and on local practices.

The most commonly requested information is in respect of balances due to or from the client entity on **current, deposit, loan and other accounts**. The request letter should provide the account description number and the type of currency for the account.

It may also be advisable to request information about **nil balances** on accounts, and accounts which were **closed** in the 12 months prior to the chosen confirmation date. The client entity may ask for confirmation not only of the balances on accounts but also, where it may be helpful, other information, such as maturity dates and interest terms on loans and overdrafts, unused facilities, lines of credit/standby facilities, any offset or other rights or encumbrances, and details of any collateral given or received.

The client entity and its auditors are likely to request confirmation of **contingent liabilities**, such as those arising on guarantees, comfort letters, bills and so on.

Banks often hold **securities** and other items in safe custody on behalf of customers. A request letter may thus ask for confirmation of such items held by the confirming bank.

1.2.3 The procedure

The procedure is simple but important.

(a) The banks will require **explicit written authority** from their client to disclose the information requested.

(b) The **auditors' request** must **refer** to the **client's letter** of authority and the date thereof. Alternatively it may be countersigned by the client or it may be accompanied by a specific letter of authority.

(c) In the case of joint accounts, **letters of authority** signed by all **parties** will be necessary.

(d) Such letters of authority may either give **permission** to the bank to disclose information for a **specific request** or grant permission for an **indeterminate length of time.**

(e) The request should **reach** the **branch manager** at least **one month in advance** of the client's **year-end** and should state both that year-end date and the previous year-end date.

(f) The **auditors** should themselves **check** that the bank **answers all the questions** and, where the reply is not received direct from the bank, be responsible for establishing the authenticity of the reply.

(g) The **standard letter** should always be used in its **complete form**. Where further information is required a separate letter specifying the additional information should be sent. Note that the letter should only be used for audit purposes and not for the routine preparation of accounts.

(h) Note from the **principal headings** of the letter that the confirmations sought cover more than just the bank account; information is also requested concerning:

- Customer's assets held as security
- Customer's other assets held (as custodian)
- Contingent liabilities
- Other banks and branches that the respondent bank is aware have a relationship with the client

All points disclosed in the bank's reply should be followed up.

1.3 Cut-off

Care must be taken to ensure that there is no **window dressing**, by checking **cut-off** carefully. Window dressing in this context is usually manifested as an attempt to overstate the liquidity of the company by:

(a) Keeping the cash book open to take credit for **remittances actually received** after the year end, thus enhancing the balance at bank and reducing receivables

(b) **Recording cheques paid in** the period under review which are not actually despatched until after the year end, thus decreasing the balance at bank and reducing liabilities

A combination of (a) and (b) can contrive to present an artificially healthy looking **current ratio**.

With the possibility of (a) above in mind, where lodgements have not been cleared by the bank until the new period the auditors should **examine the paying-in slip** to ensure that the amounts were actually paid into the bank **on or before** the date of the statement of financial position.

As regards (b) above, where there appears to be a particularly **large number of outstanding cheques** at the year-end, the auditors should check whether these were **cleared within** a **reasonable time** in the new period. If not, this may indicate that dispatch occurred after the year-end.

Performing cut-off testing for transactions at the end of the reporting period gives assurance over the **completeness** and **existence** of cash balances at that date.

1.4 Audit procedures relating to bank

AUDIT PLAN: BANK

- **Obtain standard bank confirmations** from each bank with which the client conducted business during the audit period.
- **Reperform arithmetic** of bank reconciliation.
- **Trace cheques shown as outstanding** from the bank reconciliation to the cash book prior to the year-end and to the **after date bank statements** and **obtain explanations** for any **large or unusual items** not cleared at the time of the audit.
- **Compare cash book(s)** and **bank statements** in detail for the last month of the year, and **check items outstanding** at the reconciliation date to bank reconciliations.
- **Review bank reconciliation** previous to the year-end bank reconciliation and check that **all items** are **cleared** in the last period or **taken forward** to the year-end bank reconciliation.
- **Obtain satisfactory explanations** for **all items** in the **cash book** for which there are **no corresponding entries** in the **bank statement** and vice versa.
- **Verify contra items** appearing in the cash books or bank statements with original entry.

AUDIT PLAN: BANK

- **Verify** by inspecting pay-in slips that **uncleared bankings** are **paid in** prior to the year-end.
- **Examine all lodgements** in respect of which payment has been refused by the bank; ensure that they are cleared on representation or that other appropriate steps have been taken to effect recovery of the amount due.
- **Verify balances** per the **cash book** according to the **bank reconciliation** with **cash book, bank statements and general ledger.**
- **Verify** the **bank balances** with reply to **standard bank letter** and with the **bank statements**.
- **Inspect** the cash book and bank statements before and after the end of the reporting period for **exceptional entries** or **transfers** which have a material effect on the balance shown to be in hand.
- **Identify** whether any **accounts** are **secured** on the **assets** of the company.
- **Consider** whether there is a **legal right** of **set-off** of overdrafts against positive bank balances.
- **Determine** whether the **bank accounts** are **subject** to any **restrictions**.

Note. Auditors should ensure that all cheques are dispatched immediately after signature and entry in the cash book. Examine the interval between dates of certain of the larger cheques in the cash book and payment by the bank since this may indicate that cheques were dispatched after the year-end (window dressing).

Exam focus point

Remember that the bank confirmation letter contains the balance held by the client at the bank **per the bank's records**. This must be reconciled to the balance held with the bank **per the client's records**.

Question — Bank letter

(a) Explain the importance of the bank confirmation letter and describe the process used to obtain confirmations from the bank.

(b) Describe the audit procedures you would perform on the bank reconciliation shown below.

ANOTHER CO
BANK RECONCILIATION 31 DECEMBER 20X1

	$	$
Balance per bank statement 31 December 20X1		35,111.91
Add: deposits outstanding		
30 December (ref 1122)	10,222.00	
31 December (ref 1123)	25,000.00	35,222.00
		70,333.91
Less: outstanding cheques		
2411	10,250.00	
2721	2,300.40	
2722	5,000.00	
2723	1,345.25	
2724	1,900.00	
2726	2,200.00	
2728	1,005.50	
2729	1,576.75	
2730	1,255.65	26,833.55
Balance per bank in the general ledger 31 December 20X1		43,500.36

(c) Describe other audit procedures that should be carried out in respect of bank balances shown in the financial statements.

> **Answer**

(a) The bank confirmation letter is important because it is independent confirmation of a number of significant matters in the client's financial statements. It confirms cash and bank balances which may well be a significant asset. It also provides confirmation of customers' assets held as security, customers' other assets held (as custodian) and contingent liabilities. Auditors also ask the bank to give details of other banks and branches that the respondent bank is aware of having a relationship with the client.

Process

(i) Obtain written authority from the client to the bank to disclose the necessary information.

(ii) Send a bank confirmation letter in standard form to the bank in sufficient time for it to arrive at least a month before the year end. The letter should state both the year-end date and the previous year-end date, and should refer to the client's granting of authority.

(iii) If additional information over and above what is in the standard letter is requested, send a separate letter requesting that information.

(iv) When confirmation is received from the bank, check that the bank has answered all the questions in the letter.

(v) Follow up all points disclosed in the bank confirmation letter.

(b) The following audit procedures should be carried out on the bank reconciliation:

(i) Agree the balance per bank statement at 31 December 20X1 as shown on the reconciliation ($35,111.91) to the bank statement and to the amount for that account shown on the bank confirmation letter.

(ii) Test arithmetic of bank reconciliation by recasting it.

(iii) Review the bank reconciliation previous to the year-end bank reconciliation (30 November reconciliation if carried out monthly) and test whether items shown on it cleared in the last period or have been taken forward to the bank reconciliation at 31 December.

(iv) Trace the cheques shown as outstanding on the bank reconciliation to the cash book prior to the year end and ensure they have cleared the bank by looking at the after-date bank statements. Obtain explanations for any that have not cleared at the time of the audit. In particular the outstanding cheque for $10,250 has a reference (2411) which appears to suggest it was raised much earlier in the year than the others and the fact it has not cleared is unusual. Enquiries should be made in respect of this outstanding cheque.

(v) Verify by checking paying-in slips that the uncleared bankings (deposits outstanding – ref 1122 and 1123) were paid in prior to the year end, and review whether they cleared quickly after the year end. Any that have not cleared soon after the year end should be investigated.

(vi) Verify that the year-end balance per the general ledger according to the reconciliation ($43,500.36) agrees with the general ledger account balance at 31 December 20X1 and that this has been properly reflected in the financial statements.

(c) Other audit procedures that should be carried out in respect of bank balances shown in the financial statements include:

  (i) Obtain standard bank confirmation letters from each bank with which the client conducted business during the period.

  (ii) Verify the bank balances with reply to standard bank confirmation letter and with the bank statements.

  (iii) Scrutinise the cash book and bank statements before and after the period end for exceptional entries or transfers which have a material effect on the balance shown to be in hand.

  (iv) Identify whether any accounts are secured on the assets of the company.

  (v) Consider whether there is a legal right to set-off overdrafts against positive bank balances.

  (vi) Determine whether the bank accounts are subject to any restrictions.

  (vii) Review disclosures related to the cash at bank figure included in the financial statements and ensure they are in accordance with International Financial Reporting Standards.

2 Cash

FAST FORWARD

Cash balances should be **verified** if they are **material** or **irregularities are suspected.**

Cash balances/floats are often individually immaterial but they may require some audit emphasis because of the opportunities for fraud that could exist where internal control is weak and because in total they may be material.

However in enterprises such as hotels, the amount of cash in hand at the end of the reporting period could be considerable; the same goes for retail organisations. Cash counts may be important for internal auditors, who have a role in **fraud prevention**.

Auditors will be concerned that the cash **exists**, is **complete** and belongs to the company (**rights and obligations**).

Where the auditors determine that cash balances are potentially material they may conduct a cash count, ideally at the end of the reporting period. Rather like attendance at an inventory count, the conduct of the count falls into three phases: planning, the count itself and follow-up procedures.

2.1 Planning

Planning is an essential element, for it is an important principle that all cash balances are counted at the same time as far as possible. Cash in this context may include unbanked cheques received, IOUs and credit card slips, in addition to notes and coins.

As part of their planning procedures the auditors will hence need to determine the **locations** where cash is held and which of these locations warrant a count.

Planning decisions will need to be recorded on the current audit file including:

- The **precise time** of the count(s) and location(s)
- The **names** of the **audit staff** conducting the counts
- The **names** of the **client staff** intending to be present at each location

Where a location is not visited it may be expedient to obtain a letter from the client confirming the balance.

2.2 Cash count

The following matters apply to the count itself.

- All cash/petty **cash books** should be **written up** to date in ink (or other permanent form at the time of the count).
- All **balances** must be **counted** at the **same time**.
- All **negotiable securities** must be **available** and **counted** at the time the cash balances are counted.
- At **no time** should the **auditors** be left **alone** with the cash and negotiable securities.
- **All cash** and securities **counted** must be **recorded** on working papers subsequently filed on the current audit file. Reconciliations should be prepared where applicable (for example imprest petty cash float).

2.3 Audit procedures relating to cash

Audit plan: cash

- **Count cash balances** held and agree to petty cash book or other record:
    - Count all balances simultaneously
    - All counting to be done in the presence of the individuals responsible
    - Enquire into any IOUs or cashed cheques outstanding for unreasonable periods of time
- **Obtain certificates** of cash in hand from responsible officials.
- **Confirm** that bank and cash **balances** as reconciled above are **correctly stated** in the accounts.

Follow-up

- Ensure **certificates of cash-in-hand** are **obtained** as appropriate.
- Verify **unbanked cheques/cash receipts** have subsequently been **paid in** and agree to the bank reconciliation.
- Ensure **IOUs** and cheques cashed for employees have been **reimbursed.**
- Check **IOUs or cashed cheques outstanding** for **unreasonable periods** of time have been provided for.
- Verify the **balances** as **counted** are **reflected** in the **accounts** (subject to any agreed amendments because of shortages and so on).

Question

Auditing bank and cash

(a) Explain the term window dressing.
(b) Explain why an auditor might test cash balances even if they are not material.

Answer

(a) Window dressing is the practice of manipulating when cash receipts and payments are recorded and sent out to manipulate the assets and liabilities shown in the statement of financial position at the year end.

For example, if a company wanted liabilities to look lower than they were then it might record a number of payments but not physically send those cheques out until after the year end. Such cheques would appear as unpresented cheques on the bank reconciliation (reducing the bank

balance), so that in practice, the bank balance is higher than it appears to be in the financial statements, as is the payables balance.

(b) Auditors will commonly test cash balances even if they are not material because cash is highly susceptible to fraud.

As a minimum audit procedures may involve performing analytical procedures on the cash balance year on year, however the auditor may also attend and observe the cash count at the year end as they would for the inventory count.

Chapter roundup

- **Bank balances** are usually **confirmed directly with the bank** in question via a bank confirmation letter.
- The bank confirmation letter can be used to ask a variety of questions, including queries about outstanding interests, contingent liabilities and guarantees.
- **Cash balances** should be **verified** if they are material or irregularities are suspected.

Quick quiz

1. Summarise the procedure for obtaining confirmation from a client's bank of the year end bank balance.

    (1) ....
    (2) ....
    (3) ....
    (4) ....
    (5) ....
    (6) ....

2. Complete the following audit procedures that would be performed to verify the bank reconciliation.

    (a) Trace cheques shown as outstanding on the .... to the .... prior to the year end and ....

    (b) Obtain satisfactory explanations for all items in the .... for which there is no corresponding entry in the .... and ....

3. State whether the following statements are true or false in respect of bank confirmation letter requests:

    (a) Bank confirmation letter requests are sent out by the auditor directly to the bank
    (b) Bank confirmation letter requests should be made at the year end date.

4. What are the relevant financial statement assertions for cash in the statement of financial position?

5. Give two examples of business where cash floats could be considerable.

    (1) ....
    (2) ....

6. What planning matters relating to a cash count should be recorded in the current audit file?

    (1) ....
    (2) ....
    (3) ....

Answers to quick quiz

1. (1) The banks will require **explicit written authority** from their client to disclose the information requested.

   (2) The **auditors' request** must **refer** to the **client's letter** of authority and the date thereof. Alternatively it may be countersigned by the client or it may be accompanied by a specific letter of authority.

   (3) In the case of joint accounts, **letters of authority** signed by all **parties** will be necessary.

   (4) Such letters of authority may either give **permission** to the bank to disclose information for a **specific request** or grant permission for an **indeterminate length of time.**

   (5) The request should **reach** the **branch manager** at least **two weeks in advance** of the client's **year-end** and should state both that year-end date and the previous year-end date.

   (6) The **auditors** should themselves **check** that the bank **answers all the questions** and, where the reply is not received direct from the bank, be responsible for establishing the authenticity of the reply.

2. Bank reconciliation, cash book, after date bank statements, bank statements, cash book, bank reconciliation

3. (a) True, although the bank will only respond to the request if the client has given them permission to.

   (b) False, requests should normally be made at least one month in advance of the year end to allow the bank time to process the letter.

4. Existence, completeness, valuation and allocation

5. (1) Hotels
   (2) Retail operations

6. (1) Time of count
   (2) Names of client staff attending
   (3) Names of audit staff attending

End of chapter question

Newpiece Textiles

Your firm is the auditor of Newpiece Textiles, a privately owned incorporated business, and you are auditing the financial statements for the year ended 31 October 20X7. The company has a revenue of $2.5 million and a profit before tax of $150,000.

(a) The company has supplied you with the following bank reconciliation at the year-end. You have entered the 'date cleared' on the bank reconciliation, which is the date the cheques and deposits appeared on November's bank statement.

				$	$
Balance per bank statement at 31 October 20X7					(9,865)
Add: deposits not credited					
CB date		Type	Date cleared		
31 Oct		SL	3 Nov	11,364	
24 Oct		CS	3 Nov	653	
27 Oct		CS	4 Nov	235	
28 Oct		CS	5 Nov	315	
29 Oct		CS	6 Nov	426	
30 Oct		CS	7 Nov	714	
31 Oct		CS	10 Nov	362	
					14,069

Less: uncleared cheques

CB date	Cheque no	Type	Date cleared	$	$
30 Oct	2163	CP	3 Nov	1,216	
31 Oct	2164	PL	18 Nov	10,312	
31 Oct	2165	PL	19 Nov	11,264	
31 Oct	2166	PL	18 Nov	9,732	
31 Oct	2167	PL	20 Nov	15,311	
31 Oct	2168	PL	21 Nov	8,671	
31 Oct	2169	PL	19 Nov	12,869	
31 Oct	2170	PL	21 Nov	9,342	
31 Oct	2171	CP	3 Nov	964	
					(79,681)
Balance per cash book at 31 October 20X7					(75,477)

Notes

1. 'CB date' is the date the transaction was entered in the cash book.

2. Type of transaction:

   SL sales ledger receipt
   CS receipt from cash sales
   PL purchase ledger payment
   CP cheque payment (for other expenses)

3. All cheques for purchase ledger payments are written out at the end of the month.

12: BANK AND CASH

Required

(i) Describe the matters which cause you concern from your scrutiny of the bank reconciliation.

(ii) Describe the investigations you will carry out on the items in the bank reconciliation which cause you concern.

(iii) Describe the adjustments you will probably require to be made to the financial statements if your investigations confirm the problems you have highlighted in (i) above. **(10 marks)**

(b) The manager in charge of the audit has asked you to consider the petty cash system and recommend what audit work may be necessary. You have found that petty cash is recorded in a hand written analysed petty cash book and it is not kept on an imprest system. From the petty cash book you have recorded the petty cash expenditure for each month.

	$
20X6	
November	855
December	6,243
20X7	
January	972
February	796
March	893
April	751
May	986
June	695
July	749
August	8,634
September	948
October	849
Total	23,371

Required

(i) Advise the audit manager as to the desirability of performing further substantive procedures on petty cash. You should consider materiality and audit risk in relation to the petty cash system.

(4 marks)

(ii) Assuming the audit manager decides that further audit work is necessary, describe the detailed substantive tests of transactions and balances you should carry out on the petty cash system.

(6 marks)
(Total = 20 marks)

Non-current assets

Topic list	Syllabus reference
1 Tangible non-current assets	5.7
2 Intangible non-current assets	5.7

Introduction

This chapter covers the audit of non-current assets, a key balance in the statement of financial position and highlights the key objectives for each major component of non-current assets.

You must understand what **objectives** the various audit procedures are designed to achieve. Objectives of particular significance for **tangible non-current assets** are **rights and obligations**, **existence** and **accuracy, valuation and allocation**. You should note it is generally necessary to carry out different procedures on rights and obligations and existence. The auditors will concentrate on testing any valuations (internal or external) made during the year, and also whether other values appear reasonable given asset usage and condition. A very important aspect of testing this assertion is reviewing depreciation rates.

Objectives of particular significance for **intangible non-current assets** are **existence** and **valuation**. The auditor will need to perform procedures to determine whether an intangible is a genuine asset and whether it is appropriately valued.

A topic we covered in Chapter 9, using the work of an auditor's expert, may well be important in the audit of non-current assets.

1 Tangible non-current assets

FAST FORWARD

Key areas when testing **tangible non-current assets** are:
- **Confirmation** of ownership
- **Valuation** by third parties
- **Inspection** of non-current assets
- **Adequacy** of depreciation rates

1.1 Audit objectives for tangible non-current assets

Financial statement assertion	Audit objective
Existence	• Additions represent assets acquired in the year and disposal represents assets sold or scrapped in the year • Recorded assets represent those in use at the year end
Completeness	• All additions and disposals that occurred in the year have been recorded • Balances represent assets in use at the year end
Rights and obligations	• The entity has rights to the assets purchased and those recorded at the year end
Accuracy, valuation and allocation	• Non-current assets are correctly stated at cost less accumulated depreciation • Additions and disposals are correctly recorded
Classification	• Tangible assets have been recorded in the correct accounts, and expenses which are not of a capital nature are taken to profit or loss

1.2 Internal control considerations

The **non-current asset register** is a very important aspect of the internal control system. It enables assets to be identified, and comparisons between the general ledger, non-current asset register and the assets themselves provide **evidence** that the assets are **completely recorded**.

Another significant control is procedures over acquisitions and disposals, that acquisitions are properly **authorised**, and **disposals** are **authorised** and **proceeds accounted for**. Other aspects are:

- **Security arrangements** over non-current assets are **sufficient**.
- **Non-current assets** are **maintained properly**.
- **Depreciation** is **reviewed every year**.
- **All income** is **collected** from **income-yielding assets**.

1.3 Audit procedures relating to tangible non-current assets

Audit plan: tangible non-current assets	

Completeness	• **Obtain** or **prepare** a **summary** of tangible non-current assets showing how:
	  – **Cost/valuation**
	  – **Accumulated depreciation**
	  – **Carrying amount**
	reconcile with the **opening position**.
	• **Compare non-current assets** in the general ledger with the **non-current assets register** and **obtain explanations** for **differences**.
	• For a sample of assets which **physically exist**, vouch that they are **recorded** in **non-current asset register** by **inspection** of the register.
	• If a non-current asset register is not kept, **obtain** a **schedule** showing the original costs and present depreciated value of major non-current assets.
	• **Reconcile** the **schedule** of non-current assets with the **general ledger.**

Existence	• **Confirm** that the **company physically inspects** all items in the non-current asset register each year.
	• **Inspect assets,** concentrating on high value items and additions in year. Confirm items inspected:
	  – Exist
	  – Are in use
	  – Are in good condition
	  – Have correct serial numbers
	• **Review records** of **income yielding assets.**
	• **Reconcile** opening and closing **vehicles** by numbers as well as amounts.

Accuracy, valuation and allocation	• **Verify valuation** to valuation certificate.
	• **Consider reasonableness** of **valuation**, reviewing:
	  – Experience of valuer
	  – Scope of work
	  – Methods and assumptions used
	  – Valuation bases are in line with accounting standards
	• **Check revaluation** surplus has been **correctly calculated.**
	• Check valuations of all assets that have been revalued have been **updated regularly**.
	• Check that client has **recognised** revaluation losses in the **statement of profit or loss and other comprehensive income** unless there is a credit balance in respect of that asset in equity, in which case it should be debited to equity to cancel the credit. All revaluation gains should be credited to equity.

Audit plan: tangible non-current assets	

Accuracy, valuation and allocation (Depreciation)	• **Review depreciation** rates applied in relation to:
	  – Asset lives
	  – Residual values
	  – Replacement policy
	  – Past experience of gains and losses on disposal
	  – Consistency with prior years and accounting policy
	  – Possible obsolescence
	• **Check depreciation** has been **charged on all assets** with a limited useful life.
	• For **revalued assets**, ensure that the charge for **depreciation** is **based** on the **revalued amount.**
	• Check **calculation** of depreciation rates by **reperforming** calculations on a sample of assets in the register.
	• **Compare ratios** of depreciation to non-current assets (by category) with:
	  – Previous years
	  – Depreciation policy rates
	• **Ensure no further depreciation** provided on **fully depreciated assets.**
	• Check that **depreciation policies and rates are disclosed** in the accounts by reviewing the draft financial statements.

Accuracy, valuation and allocation (Insurance)	• **Review insurance policies** in force for all categories of tangible non-current assets and consider the adequacy of their insured values and check expiry dates.

Rights and obligations	• **Verify title** to land and buildings by inspection of:
	  – Title deeds
	  – Land registry certificates
	  – Leases
	• Obtain a certificate from solicitors/bankers:
	  – **Stating purpose** for which the deeds are being held (custody only)
	  – **Stating deeds** are **free** from **mortgage** or **lien**
	• **Inspect registration documents** for vehicles held, checking that they are in client's name.
	• **Confirm** all vehicles used for the **client's business.**
	• **Examine documents** of **title** for other assets (including purchase invoices, architects' certificates, contracts, hire purchase or lease agreements).

Rights and obligations (Charges and commitments)	• **Review for evidence** of charges in statutory books and by company search. • **Review leases** of leasehold properties to ensure that company has fulfilled covenants therein. • **Examine invoices received after year-end, orders and minutes** for evidence of capital commitments.

13: NON-CURRENT ASSETS

Audit plan: tangible non-current assets	

Additions	These tests are to confirm **rights and obligations, accuracy, valuation and allocation** and **completeness**.
	
	• **Verify additions** by inspection of architects' certificates, solicitors' completion statements, suppliers' invoices etc.
	• **Determine** whether **capitalisation** of **expenditure** is correct by considering for non-current assets additions and items in relevant expense categories (repairs, motor expenses, sundry expenses) whether:
	   – Capital/revenue distinction is correctly drawn
	   – Capitalisation is in line with consistently applied company policy
	• **Vouch** that **purchases** have been **properly allocated** to correct non-current asset accounts.
	• **Determine** whether **purchases** have been **authorised** by directors/senior management by reviewing board minutes.
	• **Ensure** that appropriate **claims** have been made for **grants**, and grants received and receivable have been received.
	• **Trace additions** to ensure that they have been **recorded** in non-current asset register and general ledger.

Self-constructed assets	These tests are to confirm **accuracy, valuation and allocation** and **completeness**.
	
	• **Verify material** and **labour** costs and **overheads** to invoices, wage records etc.
	• **Ensure expenditure** has been **analysed correctly** and **properly charged** to capital.
	• Expenditure should be capitalised if it:
	   – **Enhances** the **economic benefits** of the asset in excess of its previously assessed standard of performance
	   – **Replaces or restores a component** of the assets that has been treated separately for depreciation purposes, and depreciated over its useful economic life
	   – Relates to a **major inspection** or **overhaul** that restores the economic benefits of the assets that have been consumed by the entity, and have already been reflected in depreciation
	• **Review costs** to ensure that **no profit element** has been included in costs.
	• **Review accounts** to ensure that **finance costs** have been **capitalised** or not capitalised on a consistent basis, and costs capitalised in period do not exceed total finance costs for period.

Disposals	These tests are to confirm **rights and obligations, completeness, occurrence** and **accuracy**. • **Verify disposals** with supporting documentation, checking transfer of title, sales price and dates of completion and payment. • **Check calculation** of profit or loss. • Check that **disposals** have been **authorised** by **reviewing** minutes of board meetings.

Audit plan: tangible non-current assets	
	• **Consider** whether **proceeds** are **reasonable**. • If the asset was **used as security**, ensure **release from security** has been correctly made.
Presentation	• Review non-current asset disclosures in the financial statements to ensure they meet IAS 16 *Property, Plant and Equipment* criteria. • For a sample of **fully depreciated assets**, inspect the non-current asset register to ensure no further depreciation is charged.

Question

Tangible non-current assets

You are the manager in charge of the audit of Puppy, a building and construction company, and you are reviewing the tangible non-current asset section of the current audit file for the year ended 30 September 20X5. You find the following five matters which the audit senior has identified as problem areas. She is reviewing the company's proposed treatment of the five transactions in the accounts and is not sure that she has yet carried out sufficient audit work.

The five matters are as follows.

(i) During the year Puppy built a new canteen for its own staff at a cost of $450,000. This amount has been included in buildings as at 30 September 20X5.

(ii) Loose tools included in the financial statements at a total cost of $166,000 are tools used on two of the construction sites on which Puppy operates. They are classified as non-current assets and depreciated over two years.

(iii) A dumper truck, previously written off in the company's accounting records has been refurbished at a cost of $46,000 and this amount included in plant and machinery as at 30 September 20X5.

(iv) The company's main office block has been revalued from $216,000 to $266,000 and this amount included in the statement of financial position as at 30 September 20X5.

(v) A deposit of $20,000 for new equipment has been included under the heading plant and machinery although the final instalment of $35,000 was not paid over until 31 October 20X5 which was the date of delivery of the plant.

You are required, for each of the above matters to:

(a) Comment on the acceptability of the accounting treatment and disclosure as indicated above.
(b) Outline the audit work and evidence required to substantiate the assets.

Answer

(a) **Acceptability of accounting treatment and disclosure**

(i) **New staff canteen**. The costs of building a new staff canteen can quite properly be capitalised and treated as part of buildings in the statement of financial position as work has produced future economic benefits (IAS 16). The company's normal depreciation policy should be applied, subject only to the canteen being completed and in use at the year end.

(ii) **Loose tools**. Loose tools tend to have a very limited life and individually not to be material in value. For these reasons any capitalisation policy must be extremely prudent. The acceptability of this accounting treatment would depend on the policy in previous years and normal practice within the industry.

(iii) **Dumper truck.** The refurbishment costs have obviously extended the useful life of this asset and it therefore seems reasonable to capitalise the expenditure. Depreciation should be charged on the refurbishment costs over the estimated remaining useful life.

(iv) **Revaluation of office block.** The revaluation of property is acceptable, but the auditors will need to ensure that the company complies with a number of disclosure requirements.
A note to the accounts should give details of the revaluation and the name of the valuer. The surplus on revaluation should be transferred to a separate non-distributable reserve in the statement of financial position as part of shareholders' funds. In addition any other assets of a similar nature to this should also be revalued.

(v) **Deposit for new equipment.** As the equipment was not actually in the company's possession and use at the year-end, the deposit should not have been shown as plant and machinery, but rather as a payment on account. If the amount was considered to be material a note to the accounts should give details of this prepayment.

(b) The audit work and evidence required to substantiate each of the assets referred to in (a) above would be as follows.

(i) **New staff canteen**

(1) Physically confirm existence of the asset.

(2) Confirm title to building by reference to central registry certificate.

(3) Ascertain and confirm the details of any security granted over the asset, ensuring that this is properly recorded and disclosed.

(4) Test the detailed costings of the building and obtain explanations for any material variances from the original budget. Particular care should be taken in assessing the reasonableness of any overheads included as an element of cost.

(5) Review the depreciation policy for adequacy and consistency.

(ii) **Loose tools**

(1) Visit the two sites where the loose tools are used to confirm the existence and condition of a sample of them.

(2) Vouch the cost and ownership of the loose tools to purchase invoices and the company's asset register.

(3) Confirm the company's estimate of a two year life for these assets.

(4) Review control procedures for safe custody of the loose tools.

(5) Review the company's policy with regard to scrapping and/or sale of tools no longer required to ensure that any proceeds are properly recorded and the assets register appropriately updated and tools are completely recorded.

(iii) **Dumper truck**

(1) Inspect the truck to confirm its existence and to gain evidence of its valuation by reviewing its condition and the fact that it is still being used.

(2) If the vehicle is used at all on public roads then the vehicle registration document should be inspected as some evidence of title.

(3) Inspect the insurance policy for the truck as evidence of valuation.

(4) Vouch the expenditure on refurbishment to suppliers' invoices or company's payroll records where any of the work has been done by the client's own staff.

(5) Review the depreciation policy and assess for reasonableness by discussion with management and past experience of similar vehicles.

(iv) **Revaluation of office block**

(1) Inspect the building to confirm its existence and state of repair.

(2) Examine documents of title to confirm ownership.

(3) Enquire about any charges on the building and confirm that these have been properly recorded and disclosed.

(4) Review the valuer's certificate and agree to the amount used in the financial statements, with consideration also being given to his qualifications, experience and reputation.

(5) Assess the reasonableness of the valuation by comparison with any similar properties which may have recently changed hands on the open market.

(v) **Deposit for new equipment**

(1) Agree the payment of the deposit to the contract for purchase of the equipment.

(2) Agree the payment of the deposit to the cashbook and bank statement.

(3) Confirm the existence of the plant following its delivery on 31 October 20X5 as it is unlikely that the audit work will have been completed by that date.

1.4 Leases

An entity may decide to lease an asset rather than purchase it. In this case the auditor must ensure that the entity has accounted for the lease in accordance with IFRS 16 *Leases*.

Key terms

IFRS 16 *Leases* defines a lease as a **contract** that 'conveys the right to control the use of an identified asset for a period of time in exchange for consideration' (IFRS 16: para. 9).

For **lessees**, this includes an assessment of whether the contract allows both of the following:

- The right to obtain substantially all the economic benefits from use of the identified asset
- The right to direct the use of the identified asset (known as a '**right-of-use asset**')

For a right-of-use asset (and hence lease) to be recognised, the asset should:

- Not be easily substituted by lessors; and
- Not be an exempt item, such as some intellectual property, assets related to mineral extraction, agricultural items or service contracts.

Revenue and liabilities from maintenance elements for assets must be shown separately from the lease liability within the lessee's financial statements.

A **right-of-use asset is recognised at cost**, including any fees and dismantling costs at the end of the lease term.

Depreciation is on a **straight-line basis**. Leases can be revalued if market conditions (including impairment reviews) support this.

A **lease liability** is created for all right-of-use assets – this includes all relevant financial commitments, eg the present value of lease payments not yet paid and any purchase options.

Some leased assets can be **exempt** from this accounting treatment: short-term leases (less than 12 months) and low-value assets (likely to be <$5,000) can be expensed instead.

IFRS 16 requires right-of-use assets and lease liabilities to be shown separately, either on the face of the statement of financial position (SoFP) or within the notes.

Disclosure includes:

- Depreciation charges and carrying amounts for any right-of-use assets held at the reporting date
- Interest expenses on lease liabilities
- Gains and losses from sale and leaseback transactions
- Expenses incurred on short-term and low-value leases
- Total cash outflow for leases

Disclosure is not required for leases where the information is deemed to be non-material.

Lessors follow a different approach under IFRS 16 *Leases* must be differentiated between 'finance leases' (where substantially all the risks and rewards of ownership are passed to the lessee, and the asset is derecognised in the lessor's financial statements once the lease terminates) and 'operating leases' (basically any other lease where the asset is held on the lessor's SoFP while income is received from the lessee) in their financial statements.

Question

Leases

Required

What would you consider to be the most significant audit risks when auditing an entity which leases property, plant and equipment and how would the auditor respond to some of these risks?

Answer

Leases may be inappropriately recognised as leases (or not recognised when they should be) because one or more of the necessary conditions under **IFRS 16 *Leases*** has not been observed:

- The lessor does not have the right to substantially all the economic benefits of an identified asset.
- The asset may be easily substituted by the lessor so cannot be part of a lease agreement.
- The lessor does not have the right to direct or control the asset included in the lease.
- The conditions for recognising a 'right-of-use asset' may apply but have been ignored.

A combined contract to provide both a leased asset and servicing of the asset may not have been split into its constituent parts which could lead to incorrect recognition of the service element.

Initial recognition of the lease liability may be either incomplete or inaccurate due to some/all of the constituent elements being missed/misstated:

- The present value of the lease payments not yet paid and the discount factor used
- Any penalties for relevant early termination
- Uncertainty over any options to purchase the asset at the end of the lease term
- The agreed or implied lease term

Similarly, lease assets may be misstated due to failure to correctly account for any of the following:

- Initial fees and other charges which may have been ignored.

- Failure to account for any impairments or revaluations that have occurred during the lease term.

- Failure to account for dismantling and restoration provisions that might be required at the end of the lease term.

Assets may be treated as either short-term leases or low-value assets when they are neither (so would need to have assets and liabilities recognised on the statement of financial position).

Disclosures may be inadequate or incomplete for either lessees or lessors based on what IFRS 16 requires in each case.

2 Intangible non-current assets

FAST FORWARD

Key assertions for intangible non-current assets are **existence** and **accuracy, valuation and allocation**.

Key term

An **intangible asset** is an identifiable non-monetary asset without physical substance. It may be used in the production and supply of goods and services, or for rental to others, or for administrative purposes. The asset must be controlled by the entity as a result of past events, capable of generating future economic benefits, and be identifiable.

The accounting treatment for intangible assets is governed by IAS 38 *Intangible Assets*. Intangible assets cover a range of assets such as computer software, patents, goodwill, copyrights, investments and licences, to name a few.

The key assertions relating to intangibles are **existence** (not so much 'do they exist?', but 'are they genuinely assets?') and **valuation**. They will therefore be audited with reference to criteria laid down in the financial reporting standards. As only purchased goodwill or intangibles with a readily ascertainable market value can be capitalised, **audit evidence should be available** (purchase invoices or specialist valuations). Audit of **amortisation** will be similar to the audit of depreciation.

2.1 Audit procedures relating to intangible non-current assets

Audit plan: Intangible non-current assets	
Goodwill	• Agree the consideration to sales agreement by **inspection**.
	• Consider whether the asset valuation is reasonable by comparison to the prior year and through discussion with management.
	• Agree that the calculation of purchased goodwill is correct by **recalculation**.
	• Ensure non-purchased goodwill is not included in the total of goodwill.
	• Review amortisation charge for goodwill by **recalculating** the charge and assessing whether the rate appears reasonable.
	• If the useful life of goodwill is judged to be indefinite, confirm that an **impairment review** has been carried out. Review the conclusions reached review discuss the assumptions made with management.
	• Ensure valuation of goodwill is reasonable and that any required goodwill impairment has been recognised by **discussions** with appropriate management.
Research and Development (R&D) costs	• Assess whether capitalised development costs conform to IAS 38 *Intangible Assets* **criteria** by **inspecting details** of projects and expenditure invoices and though **discussions** with technical managers.
	• Inspect invoices relating to expenditure incurred on research and development projects to confirm that such expenditure has correctly been capitalised or has been written off to the statement of profit or loss and other comprehensive income.

13: NON-CURRENT ASSETS

Audit plan: Intangible non-current assets	
	• Check amortisation calculation for a sample of costs by recalculating the charge, ensuring it commences with production and appears reasonable. • Inspect accounting records to confirm that projects are **clearly defined** (separate cost centre or general ledger codes) and that related expenditure can be separately identified and certified to invoices and timesheets. • **Confirm feasibility and viability** of projects by examining market research reports, feasibility studies, budgets and forecasts, and discussions th technical project managers. • Review budgeted costs and revenues by examining results to date, production forecasts, advance orders and discussions with management. • Review calculations of future cash flows to ensure resources exist to complete the projects. • **Review previously deferred expenditure** to ensure IAS 38 criteria are still justified.
Other intangibles (for example: licences, franchises and lists of customer data)	• Agree newly purchased intangibles by **inspection** of purchase documentation (agreements, assignments and supporting documentation). • Confirm purchases in the period have been **authorised by inspection** of minutes of board meetings. • Verify amounts capitalised of any patents developed by the entity with supporting costing records. • **Review specialist valuations** of intangibles and ensure they are reasonable, considering also the qualifications of the valuer, scope of work performed and assumptions and methods used. • Review amortisation calculations and ensure they are correct by **recalculation** based on the entity's accounting policy for other intangibles. • Assess whether amortisation rates used appear reasonable.

Exam focus point

Although you are more likely to have a question on tangible assets, do not neglect intangibles to your detriment if they come up. A previous exam question on the audit of investments asked students to explain the audit objectives for investments and to devise audit procedures to verify the financial statement assertion of valuation.

Question — Intangible non-current assets

You are the audit manager of ARPT, a packaging company which has been in operation for 30 years. The company has been developing a new form of packaging for fruits and vegetables as an alternative to the plastics commonly used in supermarkets. Several large supermarket chains have expressed an interest in using the packaging when it becomes available. ARPT expects the packaging will be available for sale in one year.

Required

Explain the substantive procedures that should be performed in relation to the above matter in order to be able to reach a conclusion as to the appropriate treatment of the packaging costs.

Answer

The substantive procedures the auditors need to perform are as follows:

- Review the accounting records to ensure that the expenditure can be readily measured, eg separate cost centre or nominal ledger code.
- Review invoices to verify expenditure by ARPT on the project.
- Verify wages costs to supporting documentation such as timesheets.
- Discuss the stage of development of the new packaging with ARPT's directors.
- Discuss the technical feasibility of the project with ARPT's technical staff.
- Consider probability of future economic benefits (ie commercial viability) and ability to sell or use the packaging in relation to market research results, advance orders, budgets and forecasts.
- Review budgeted revenues and costs. Ensure that they are reasonable based on results to date, discussion with directors, production forecasts and advance orders.
- Review cash flow forecasts to ensure that adequate resources exist to complete the project. Discuss any shortfalls ARPT's directors.
- Obtain written representations from management of their intention to complete the packaging and either use or sell it.
- Ensure any development costs capitalised are disclosed and presented in line with the requirements of IAS 38 *Intangible Assets*

Chapter roundup

- Key areas when testing **tangible non-current assets** are:
  - **Confirmation** of ownership
  - **Valuation** by third parties
  - **Inspection** of non-current assets
  - **Adequacy** of **depreciation** rates
- Key assertions for intangible non-current assets are **existence** and **accuracy, valuation and allocation**.

Quick quiz

1   Complete the control procedures.

   (a)   Acquisitions are properly ....

   (b)   Disposals are .... and proceeds ....

   (c)   Security .... over non-current assets are ....

   (d)   .... is reviewed ....

2   Complete the table using options (a) to (h) below, to show which procedures are designed to provide evidence about which financial statement assertion.

Completeness	Existence
Accuracy, valuation and allocation	Rights and obligations

   (a)   Inspect assets
   (b)   Verify to valuation certificate
   (c)   Inspect title deeds
   (d)   Compare assets in ledger to non-current asset register
   (e)   Review depreciation rates
   (f)   Verify material on self-constructed assets to invoices
   (g)   Examine invoices after the year-end
   (h)   Review repairs in general ledger

3   Name two audit procedures to confirm rights and obligations concerning charges and commitments.

   (1)   ....
   (2)   ....

4   Which of the following audit procedures would provide audit evidence as to the existence of a tangible non-current asset?

    (a)   Inspecting board minutes approving authorisation of the purchase of the asset
    (b)   Physically inspecting the asset
    (c)   Reviewing the non-current asset register for inclusion of the asset
    (d)   Inspecting the invoice and purchase order documentation of the asset

5   Inspecting the title deeds of a building provides audit evidence concerning which one of the following financial statement assertions?

    (a)   Existence
    (b)   Valuation
    (c)   Rights and obligations
    (d)   Completeness

6   What are the key financial statement assertions for intangible non-current assets?

Answers to quick quiz

1. (a) authorised
   (b) authorised, accounted for
   (c) arrangements, sufficient
   (d) depreciation, every year

2. **Completeness**
   (d) Compare assets in ledger to register
   (h) Review repairs in general ledger

   Accuracy, valuation and allocation
   (b) Verify to valuation certificate
   (e) Review depreciation rates
   (f) Verify material on self-constructed assets to invoice

   Existence
   (a) Inspect assets

   Rights and obligations
   (c) Inspect title deeds
   (g) Examine invoices after the year-end

3. From:
   - **Review for evidence** of charges in statutory books and by company search.
   - **Review leases** of leasehold properties to ensure that company has fulfilled covenants therein.
   - **Examine invoices received after year-end, orders and minutes** for evidence of capital commitments.

4. (b) Physically inspecting the asset

5. (c) Rights and obligations

6. Existence and valuation

End of chapter question

Boston Manufacturing

You are the audit assistant assigned to the audit of Boston Manufacturing. The audit senior has asked you to plan the audit of tangible non-current assets. He has provisionally assessed materiality at $72,000.

Boston Manufacturing maintains a register of tangible non-current assets. The management accountant reconciles a sample of entries to physical assets and vice versa on a three-monthly basis. Authorisation is required for all capital purchases. Items valued less than $10,000 can be authorised by the production manager, items costing more than $10,000 must be authorised by the Managing Director. The purchasing department will not place an order for capital goods unless it has been duly signed.

The company has invested in a large amount of new plant this year in connection with an 8 year project for a government department.

The management accountant has provided you with the following schedule of non-current assets:

	Land and buildings $	Plant and equipment $	Computers $	Motor vehicles $	Total $
Cost					
At 31 March 20X6	500,000*	75,034	30,207	54,723	659,964
Additions		250,729	1,154		251,883
At 31 March 20X7	500,000	325,763	31,361	54,723	911,847
Accumulated depreciation					
At 31 March 20X6	128,000	45,354	21,893	25,937	221,184
Charge for the year	8,000	28,340	2,367	13,081	51,788
At 31 March 20X7	136,000	73,694	24,260	39,018	272,972
Carrying amount					
At 31 March 20X7	364,000	252,069	7,101	15,705	638,875
At 31 March 20X6	372,000	29,680	8,314	28,786	438,780

*Of which, $100,000 relates to land.

Required

(a) Without undertaking any calculations, assess the level of audit risk associated with the audit of the tangible non-current assets of Boston Manufacturing making reference to the components of audit risk.

(6 marks)

(b) State the audit procedures you would undertake on non-current assets in respect of the following assertions:

    (i) Existence **(3 marks)**
    (ii) Accuracy, valuation and allocation (excluding depreciation) **(4 marks)**
    (iii) Completeness **(3 marks)**

(c) Describe how you would assess the appropriateness of the depreciation rates. **(4 marks)**

(Total = 20 marks)

Inventory

Topic list	Syllabus reference
1 Inventory in the financial statements	5.7
2 Inventory quantity	5.7
3 Inventory cut-off	5.7
4 Inventory valuation	5.7

Introduction

No area of the statement of financial position creates more potential problems for the auditors than that of inventory.

Closing inventory does not always form an integrated part of the double entry bookkeeping system and hence a misstatement (under or overstatement) may not be detected from procedures in other audit areas.

The key assertions relating to the substantive audit of inventory (completeness, existence, rights and obligations, cut-off and accuracy, valuation and allocation) require careful consideration.

The auditor's attendance at the inventory count is a particularly important part of the audit of inventory. This is because the inventory count gives evidence about the **existence** and **completeness** of inventory and a review of the condition of the inventory at the inventory count is also an important part of assessing whether inventory has been correctly **valued**.

1 Inventory in the financial statements

1.1 Calculating inventory

The inventory figure in the financial statements comprises the inventory **quantity multiplied** by its **valuation**.

In this chapter, we will consider how the inventory quantity is determined by the company and how it is audited, as well as the considerations that should be made in determining the valuation of inventory.

The auditing requirements in relation to inventory are set out in ISA 501 *Audit Evidence – Specific Considerations for Selected Items*. Auditors must attend the inventory count where possible and then carry out follow-up tests. All the necessary audit procedures relating to inventory are set out in detail in the rest of this chapter.

1.2 Key assertions

FAST FORWARD

The key assertions relating to inventory are:
- Existence
- Completeness
- Rights and obligations
- Valuation
- Cut-off

The audit of inventory can pose problems for auditors as a result of its nature and potential material value on the statement of financial position. The audit approach taken depends on the auditor's assessment of the controls in place. In this chapter we focus on the **substantive** audit of inventory.

The following table demonstrates the audit objectives for inventory and the related financial statement assertions. The audit procedures described in the remainder of this chapter are undertaken to provide audit evidence to support these assertions.

Financial statement assertion	Audit objective
Existence and occurrence	• Recorded purchases and sales represent inventories bought and sold. • Inventory on the statement of financial position physically exists.
Completeness	• All purchases and sales are recorded. • All inventory at year end is included on the statement of financial position.
Rights and obligations	• The entity has rights to inventory recorded in the period and at the year-end.
Accuracy, valuation and allocation	• Costs are accurately determined in accordance with accounting standards. • Inventory is recorded at year end at the lower of cost and net realisable value (NRV) (IAS 2: para. 9).

Financial statement assertion	Audit objective
Classification	• Inventory is recorded in the proper accounts
Cut-off	• All purchases and sales of inventories are recorded in the correct period.
Presentation	• Inventory is properly classified in the accounts. • Disclosures relating to classification and valuation are adequate and in accordance with accounting standards.

2 Inventory quantity

FAST FORWARD

> It is management's responsibility to determine the quantity of inventory held at the year end. This can be done by a full inventory count or by continuous (or perpetual) inventory counting.
>
> Physical inventory count procedures are vital as they provide evidence which cannot be obtained elsewhere or at any other time about the quantities and conditions of inventories and work in progress.

Exam focus point

> You **must** have a thorough knowledge of audit procedures before, during and after the physical inventory count.

A business may count inventory by one or a combination of the following methods.

(a) **Physical inventory count at the year-end**

From the viewpoint of the auditor this is often the best method.

(b) **Physical inventory count before or after the year-end**

This will provide audit evidence of varying reliability depending on:

(i) The **length of time** between the physical inventory count and the year-end; the greater the time period, the less the value of audit evidence

(ii) The **business's system** of **internal controls**

(iii) The **quality of records** of **inventory movements** in the period between the physical inventory count and the year-end

(c) **Continuous (or perpetual) inventory counting** where management has a programme of inventory-counting throughout the year

2.1 The physical inventory count

The inventory count performed by management is an **internal control** which management use to confirm the completeness and accuracy of the quantity of inventory held.

The external auditor will typically attend at least one inventory count per year. The auditor's attendance at the inventory count serves as a **test of control** as they observe whether management's inventory count procedures are being adhered to.

The auditor will also perform **substantive audit procedures** at the inventory count to obtain audit evidence concerning the existence, completeness and valuation of inventory.

Responsibilities in relation to inventory	
Management	Ensure inventory figure in accounts • Represents inventory that **exists** • Includes all inventory **owned** Ensure accounting records include **statements of physical inventory count.**
Auditors	**Obtain sufficient audit evidence** about inventory figure from • Inventory records • Inventory control systems • Results of physical inventory counts • Test counts by auditors **Attend physical inventory count** if inventory is material and evidence of existence is provided by management inventory counts.

2.2 Planning attendance at inventory count

FAST FORWARD

> Before the physical inventory count the auditors should ensure audit **coverage** of the **count** is **appropriate**, and that the client's **count instructions** have been reviewed.

Planning inventory count	
Gain knowledge	• **Review** previous year's **arrangements.** • **Discuss** with **management inventory count arrangements** and **significant changes.**
Assess key factors	• The **nature** and **volume** of the **inventory** • **Risks** relating to inventory • The **identification** of **high value items** • **Method of accounting for inventory** • **Location** of inventory and how it affects inventory control and recording • **Internal control** and **accounting systems** to identify potential areas of difficulty
Plan procedures	• Ensure a **representative selection** of **locations**, **inventory** and **procedures** are covered. • Ensure sufficient attention is given to **high value items.** • **Arrange to obtain** from **third parties confirmation** of inventory they hold. • Consider the need for **expert help.**
Review of inventory count instructions	
Organisation of count	• **Supervision** by senior staff including senior staff not normally involved with inventory • **Tidying** and **marking** inventory to help counting • **Restriction** and **control** of the production process and inventory movements during the count • **Identification of damaged, obsolete, slow-moving, third party** and **returnable** inventory

Counting	• **Systematic counting** to ensure all inventory is counted
	• Teams of **two counters,** with one counting and the other checking or two **independent counts**
Recording	• **Serial numbering, control** and **return** of all inventory sheets
	• Inventory sheets being **completed** in **ink** and **signed**
	• **Information** to be recorded on the **count records** (location and identity, count nits, quantity counted, conditions of items, stage reached in production process)
	• Recording of **quantity, conditions** and **stage of production** of **work-in-progress**
	• Recording of last numbers of **goods inwards** and **outwards** records and of internal transfer records
	• **Reconciliation** with **inventory records** and **investigation** and correction of any **differences**

2.3 Attendance at inventory count

During the count the auditors should **check the count** is being carried out according to instructions, carry out **test counts**, and watch for **third party** and **slow-moving inventories** and **cut-off problems.**

Audit plan: attendance at inventory count

- **Observe** whether the **client's staff** are following instructions as this will help to ensure the count is complete and accurate.
- **Perform test counts** to ensure procedures and internal controls are working properly.
- **Observe** whether the **procedures** for **identifying damaged, obsolete** and **slow-moving** inventory operate properly; the auditors should obtain information about the inventories' condition, age, usage and in the case of work in progress, its stage of completion to ensure that it is later valued appropriately.
- **Confirm** that **inventory held** on behalf of **third parties** is separately identified and accounted for so that inventory is not overstated.
- **Conclude** whether the **count** has been **properly carried out** and is sufficiently reliable as a basis for determining the existence of inventories.
- **Consider** whether any **amendment** is necessary to subsequent **audit procedures.**
- **Gain** an **overall impression** of the levels and values of inventories held so that the auditors may, in due course, judge whether the figure for inventories appearing in the financial statements is reasonable.

When carrying out test counts the auditors should select items from the count records and from the physical inventories and check one to the other, to confirm the accuracy of the count records. The auditors should concentrate on high value inventory. If the results of the test counts are not satisfactory, the auditors may request inventory be recounted.

The auditors' working papers should include:

- Details of their **observations** and **tests**
- The manner in which **points** that are **relevant** and **material** to the inventories being counted or measured have been dealt with by the client
- Instances where the **client's procedures** have **not been satisfactorily carried out**
- **Items for subsequent testing**, such as photocopies of (or extracts from) rough inventory sheets

- **Details** of the **sequence** of **inventory sheets**
- The **auditors' conclusions**

2.4 After the inventory count

> **FAST FORWARD**
>
> After the count the auditors should check that **final inventory sheets** have been **properly compiled** from count records and that **book inventory** has been **appropriately adjusted**.

After the count, the matters recorded in the auditors' working papers at the time of the count or measurement should be followed up. Key procedures include the following:

Audit plan: following up the inventory count

- **Trace items** that were **test counted** to final inventory sheets.
- **Check all count** records have been **included** in final inventory sheets.
- **Inspect final inventory sheets** to assess whether they are **supported by** count records.
- **Ensure** that **continuous inventory records** have been **adjusted** to the amounts physically counted or measured, and that differences have been investigated.
- **Confirm cut-off** by using details of the last serial number of goods inward and outwards notes; and of movements during the count.
- **Review replies** from **third parties** about inventories held by or for them.
- **Confirm** the client's final **valuation** of inventory has been calculated correctly.
- **Follow up queries** and **notify any problems** to management.

Question — Inventory count

In connection with your examination of the financial statements of Camry Products, a limited liability company, for the year ended 31 March 20X9, you are reviewing the plans for a physical inventory count at the company's warehouse on 31 March 20X9. The company assembles domestic appliances, and inventories of finished appliances, unassembled parts and sundry inventories are stored in the warehouse which is adjacent to the company's assembly plant. The plant will continue to produce goods during the inventory count until 5pm on 31 March 20X9. On 30 March 20X9, the warehouse staff will deliver the estimated quantities of unassembled parts and sundry inventories which will be required for production for 31 March 20X9; however, emergency requisitions by the factory will be filled on 31 March. During the inventory count, the warehouse staff will continue to receive parts and sundry inventories, and to dispatch finished appliances. Appliances which are completed on 31 March 20X9 will remain in the assembly plant until after the count has been completed.

Required

(a) List the principal procedures which the auditors should carry out when planning attendance at a company's physical inventory count.

(b) Describe the procedures which Camry Products should establish in order to ensure that all inventory items are counted and that no item is counted twice.

Answer

(a) In planning attendance at a physical inventory count the auditors should:

(i) Review previous year's audit working papers and discuss any developments in the year with management.

(ii) Obtain and review a copy of the company's count instructions.

(iii) Arrange attendance at count planning meetings, with the consent of management.

(iv) Gain an understanding of the nature of the inventory and of any special problems this is likely to present, for example liquid in tanks, scrap in piles.

(v) Consider whether expert involvement is likely to be required as a result of any circumstances noted in (iv) above.

(vi) Obtain a full list of all locations at which inventories are held, including an estimate of the amount and value of inventories held at different locations.

(vii) Using the results of the above steps, plan for audit attendance by appropriately experienced audit staff at all locations where material inventories are held, subject to other factors (for example rotational auditing, reliance on internal controls).

(viii) Consider the impact of internal controls upon the nature and timing of attendance at the count.

(ix) Ascertain whether inventories are held by third parties and if so make arrangements to obtain written confirmation of them or, if necessary, to attend the count.

(b) Procedures to ensure a complete count and to prevent double-counting are particularly important in this case because movements will continue throughout the count.

(i) Clear instructions should be given as to procedures, and an official, preferably not someone normally responsible for inventories, should be given responsibility for organising the count and dealing with queries.

(ii) Before the count, all locations should be tidied and inventories should be laid out in an orderly manner.

(iii) All inventories should be clearly identified and should be marked after being counted by a tag or indelible mark, so that it is evident that it has been counted.

(iv) Pre-numbered sheets should be issued to counters and should be accounted for at the end of the count.

(v) Counters should be given responsibility for specific areas of the warehouse. Each area should be subject to a recount.

(vi) A separate record should be kept of all goods received or issued during the day (for example by noting the GRN or dispatch note numbers involved).

(vii) Goods received on the day should be physically segregated until the count has been completed.

(viii) Similarly, goods due to be dispatched on the day should be identified in advance and moved to a special area or clearly marked so that they are not inadvertently counted in inventory as well as being included in sales.

2.5 Continuous (or perpetual) inventory counting

If perpetual inventory is used, auditors will check that management:

(a) Ensures that all inventory lines are counted at least once a year.

(b) Maintains **adequate inventory records** that are kept up-to-date. Auditors may compare sales and purchase transactions with inventory movements, and carry out other tests on the inventory records, for example checking casts and classification of inventory.

(c) Has **satisfactory procedures** for **inventory counts** and **test-counting**. Auditors should confirm the inventory count arrangements and instructions are as rigorous as those for a year-end inventory count by reviewing instructions and observing counts. Auditors will be particularly concerned with **cut-off**, that there are no inventory movements whilst the count is taking place, and inventory records are updated up until the time of the inventory counts.

(d) **Investigates** and **corrects** all **material differences**. Reasons for differences should be recorded and any necessary corrective action taken. All corrections to inventory movements should be **authorised** by a manager who has not been involved in the detailed work; these procedures are necessary to guard against the possibility that inventory records may be adjusted to conceal shortages. Auditors should assess whether the procedures are being operated.

> **AUDIT PLAN: PERPETUAL INVENTORY COUNT**
>
> - Attend one of the inventory counts (to observe and confirm that instructions are being adhered to).
> - **Follow up** the **inventory counts attended** to compare quantities counted by the auditors with the inventory records, obtaining and verifying explanations for any differences, and checking that the client has reconciled count records with book inventory records.
> - **Review** the **year's inventory counts** to confirm the extent of counting, the treatment of discrepancies and the overall accuracy of records (if matters are not satisfactory, auditors will only be able to gain sufficient assurance by a full count at the year-end).
> - Assuming a full count is not necessary at the year-end, **compare** the **listing of inventory with the detailed inventory records**, and carry out other procedures (**cut-off, analytical review**) to gain further comfort.

Attendance at an inventory count gives evidence of the **existence** and apparent **ownership** of inventory (**rights and obligations**). It also gives evidence of the **completeness** of inventory, as do the follow-up tests to ensure all inventory sheets were included in the final count.

3 Inventory cut-off

FAST FORWARD

> Auditors should test **cut-off** by noting the **serial numbers** of items received and dispatched just before and after the year-end, and subsequently checking that they have been included in the **correct period**.

3.1 The importance of cut-off

Cut-off is most critical to the accurate recording of transactions in a manufacturing enterprise at particular points in the accounting cycle as follows:

- The **point** of **purchase** and **receipt** of **goods** and **services**
- The **requisitioning** of **raw materials** for production
- The **transfer** of **completed work-in-progress** to finished goods
- The **sale** and **dispatch** of **finished goods**

3.2 Audit procedures

The auditors should consider whether management has instituted adequate cut-off procedures: procedures intended to ensure that movements into, within and out of inventories are properly identified and reflected in the accounting records.

Purchase invoices should be recorded as liabilities only if the goods were received prior to the count. A schedule of 'goods received not invoiced' should be prepared, and items on the list should be accrued for in the accounts.

Sales cut-off is generally more straightforward to achieve correctly than purchases cut-off. Invoices for goods dispatched after the count should not appear in the statement of profit or loss and other comprehensive income for the period.

Prior to the physical inventory count management should make arrangements for cut-off to be properly applied.

(a) Appropriate systems of recording of receipts and dispatches of goods are in place, and also a system for documenting materials requisitions. Goods received notes (GRNs) and goods dispatched notes (GDNs) should be sequentially pre-numbered.

(b) Final GRN and GDN and materials requisition numbers are noted. These numbers can then be used to check subsequently that purchases and sales have been recorded in the current period.

(c) Arrangements should be made to ensure that the cut-off arrangement for inventories held by third parties are satisfactory.

There should ideally be no movement of inventories during the count. Preferably, receipts and dispatches should be suspended for the full period of the count. It may not be practicable to suspend all deliveries, in which case any deliveries which are received during the count should be segregated from other inventory and carefully documented.

Audit plan: cut-off	

Inventory count	• Record **all movement notes** relating to the period, including:
	  – All interdepartmental requisition numbers
	  – The last goods received notes(s) and dispatch note(s) prior to the count
	  – The first goods received notes(s) and dispatch note(s) after the count
	• **Observe** whether **correct cut-off procedures** are being **followed** in the dispatch and receiving areas.
	• **Discuss procedures** with **company staff performing** the **count** to ensure they are understood.
	• **Ensure** that **no goods finished** on the day of the count are **transferred** to the warehouse.

Final audit	• **Match up** the **goods received notes** with **purchase invoices** and ensure the **liability** has been **recorded** in the **correct period** (only goods received before the year-end should be recorded as purchases). • **Match up** the **goods dispatched notes** to **sales invoices** and ensure the **income** has been **recorded** in the **correct period** (only goods dispatched before the year-end should be recorded as sales). • **Match up** the **requisition notes** to the **work in progress** figures for the receiving department to ensure correctly recorded.

Question: Cut-off

Using the information in the last question above, describe the audit procedures you would carry out at the time of the physical inventory count in order to ensure that cut-off is correct.

Answer

In order to ensure that cut-off of inventory is correct, the following procedures should be carried out.

(a) Make a record during the count attendance of all movement notes relating to the period, including:

　(i) All interdepartmental requisition numbers

　(ii) The last goods received note and dispatch note prior to the count

　(iii) The first goods received note and dispatch note after the count. This information can be used for subsequent cut-off tests.

(b) Observe whether correct cut-off procedures are being followed in the dispatch and receiving areas. Discuss procedures with company staff performing the count to ensure they are understood.

(c) Ensure that no goods finished on the day of the count are transferred to the warehouse.

4 Inventory valuation

FAST FORWARD

The **valuation** and **disclosure** rules for inventory are laid down in IAS 2 *Inventories*. Inventory should be valued at the **lower of cost and net realisable value**.

4.1 IAS 2 *Inventories*

Key terms

Cost is defined by IAS 2 *Inventories* as comprising all costs of purchase and other costs incurred in bringing inventories to their present location and condition.

Net realisable value is the estimated selling price in the ordinary course of business, less the estimated costs of completion and the estimated costs necessary to make the sale.

IAS 2 *Inventories* requires inventory to be stated at the **lower** of **cost** and **net realisable value** (IAS 2: para. 9). Broadly speaking, this means that inventory should be stated at cost, because companies tend to sell inventory for more than its cost. It is possible, however, that the inventory is not worth what it cost – perhaps because it is damaged or obsolete – in which case it should be stated at what it is worth, ie its net realisable value.

In most cases inventory will be stated at **cost**, but what 'cost' means is not always simple or obvious; for one thing, costs fluctuate, and moreover one item of inventory might have several different costs associated with it. IAS 2 advocates measuring cost by adding together three things:

- Costs of purchase, net of trade discounts received
- Costs of conversion – ie materials and labour absorbed in the item, including fixed and variable overheads
- Other costs incurred in bringing the inventories to their present location and condition

(IAS 2: para. 10)

IAS 2 allows entities to use **standard costing**. This means that instead of working out exactly how much of each input – cost, labour, materials – relates to each individual item of inventory, the entity can just assign a 'standard cost' for that **type of inventory**, and use this as its cost. IAS 2 permits standard costing to be used, provided that it **approximates** actual cost (IAS 2: paras. 21-22).

> **FAST FORWARD**
>
> Auditing the valuation of inventories includes:
>
> - Checking the **allocation of overheads** is appropriate
> - Confirming inventories are carried at the **lower** of **cost** and **net realisable value**

4.2 Assessment of cost and net realisable value

Exam focus point

> Valuation of inventory is a very popular exam topic in auditing exams. You must know the audit work needed to confirm valuation of inventory when overheads have been absorbed, and to confirm inventory is stated at the lower of cost and net realisable value.
>
> Knowledge of the requirements of IAS 2 *Inventories* is essential.

Auditors must understand how the company determines the cost of an item for inventory valuation purposes. Cost should include an appropriate proportion of overheads, in accordance with IAS 2.

There are several ways of determining cost. Auditors must ensure that the company is **applying** the method **consistently** and that each year the method used **gives** a **fair approximation** to cost. They may need to support this by additional procedures:

- **Reviewing price** changes near the year-end
- **Ageing the inventory** held
- **Checking gross profit** margins to reliable management accounts

4.2.1 Valuation of raw materials and bought-in components

The auditors should check that the correct prices have been used to value raw materials and bought-in components valued at actual costs by **referring** to **suppliers' invoices**. The valuation may include unrealised profit if inventory valued at the latest invoice price. Reference to suppliers' invoice will also provide the auditors with assurance as regards ownership.

If standard costs are used, auditors should **check** the **basis** of the **standards**, **compare standard costs** with **actual costs** and **confirm** that **variances** are being **treated appropriately**.

4.2.2 Valuation of work in progress and finished goods

'Cost' comprises the cost of purchase plus the costs of conversion. The cost of conversion comprises:

- Costs specifically attributable to units of production
- Production overheads
- Other overheads attributable to bringing the product or service to its present location and condition

4.3 Audit procedures

The audit procedures will depend on the methods used by the client to value work in progress and finished goods, and on the adequacy of the system of internal control.

The auditors should consider what tests they can carry out to check the reasonableness of the valuation of finished goods and work in progress. **Analytical procedures** may assist comparisons being made with items and categories from the previous year's summaries. If the client has a computerised accounting system, the auditors may be able to request an exception report listing, for example, all items whose value has changed by more than a specified amount. A reasonableness check will also provide the auditors with assurance regarding completeness.

4.3.1 Cost

Audit plan: inventory production costs	
For materials:	• **Check** the **valuation** of raw materials to **invoices** and **price lists**. • **Confirm appropriate basis** of **valuation** (eg FIFO) is being used. • **Confirm correct quantities** are being used when calculating raw material value in work in progress and finished goods.
For labour costs:	• **Check labour costs** to **wage records**. • **Review standard labour costs** in the light of actual costs and production. • **Check labour hours** to **time summaries**.

The auditors should ensure that the client includes a proportion of overheads **appropriate** to **bringing** the **inventory** to its **present location and condition**. The basis of overhead allocation should be:

- Consistent with prior years
- Calculated on the normal level of production activity

Thus, overheads arising from **reduced levels of activity**, **idle time** or **inefficient production** should be written off to the statement of profit or loss and other comprehensive income, rather than being included in inventory.

(a) All **abnormal conversion** costs (such as idle capacity) must be **excluded**.

(b) Where firm sales contracts have been entered into for the provision of goods or services to customer's specification, design, marketing and selling costs incurred before manufacture may be included.

(c) Overheads are **classified by function** when being allocated (eg whether they are a function of production, marketing, selling or administration).

(d) The costs of **general management**, as distinct from functional management, are not directly related to current production and are, therefore, **excluded**.

(e) The allocation of costs of **central service departments** should depend on the function or functions that the department is serving. **Only** those costs that can reasonably be allocated to the **production function** should be **included**.

(f) In determining what constitutes **'normal' activity** the following factors need to be considered:

    (i) The volume of production which the production facilities are **designed to achieve**

    (ii) The **budgeted level of activity** for the year under review and for the ensuing year

    (iii) The **level of activity achieved** both in the **year under review** and in **previous years**

Although temporary changes in the load of activity may be ignored, persistent variation should lead to revision of the previous norm.

Difficulty may be experienced if the client operates a system of total overhead absorption. It will be necessary for those overheads that are of a general, non-productive nature to be identified and excluded from the valuation.

4.3.2 Cost v NRV

Auditors should **compare cost and net realisable value** for each item of inventory. Where this is impracticable, the comparison may be done by group or category.

Net realisable value is likely to be less than cost when there has been:

- An **increase in costs** or a fall in selling price
- **Physical deterioration**
- **Obsolescence** of products
- A **marketing decision** to manufacture and sell products at a loss
- **Errors in production or purchasing**

> **Audit plan: inventory – cost v NRV**
>
> - **Review and test the client's system** for **identifying slow-moving**, obsolete or damaged inventory.
> - **Follow-up** any **such items** that were **identified** at the **inventory count**, ensuring that the client has made adequate provision to write-down the items to net realisable value.
> - **Examine inventory records** to identify slow-moving items (it may be possible to incorporate into a computer audit program certain tests and checks such as listing items whose value or quantity has not moved over the previous year).
> - **Examine the prices** (per sales invoices) at which finished goods have been sold after the year-end and ascertain whether any finished goods items need to be reduced below cost.
> - **Review quantities of goods sold after the year end** to determine that year-end inventory has, or will be, realised.
> - If significant quantities of finished goods inventory remain unsold for an unusual time after the year-end, **consider the need to make appropriate provision.**

For work in progress, the **ultimate selling price** should be **compared** with the **carrying amount** at the year end plus **costs** to be **incurred** after the year-end to bring work in progress to a finished state.

Question — Cost v NRV

Your firm is the auditor of Arnold Electrical, a limited liability company, and you have been asked to audit the valuation of the company's inventory at 31 May 20X1 in accordance with IAS 2 *Inventories*. Arnold Electrical operates from a single store and purchases domestic electrical equipment from wholesalers and manufacturers and sells them to the general public. These products include video and audio equipment, washing machines, refrigerators and freezers. In addition, it sells small items such as electrical plugs, records and compact discs.

A full physical inventory count was carried out at the year-end, and you are satisfied that the inventory was counted accurately and there are no cut-off errors. Because of the limited time available between the year-end and the completion of the audit, the company has valued the inventory at cost by recording the selling price and deducting the normal gross profit margin. Inventory which the company believes to be worth less than cost has been valued at net realisable value. The selling price used is that on the item in the store when it was counted.

The inventory has been divided into three categories.

(a) Video and audio equipment: televisions, blu-ray players, video cameras and audio equipment
(b) Domestic equipment: washing machines, refrigerators and freezers
(c) Sundry inventory: electrical plugs, records and compact discs

The normal gross profit margin for each of these categories has been determined and this figure has been used to calculate the cost of the inventory (by deducting the gross profit margin from the selling price). In answering the question you should assume there are no sales taxes.

Required

(a) List and describe the audit work you will carry out to check that inventory has been correctly valued at cost.

(b) List and describe the audit work you will carry out to:

    (i) Find inventory which should be valued at net realisable value
    (ii) Check that net realisable value is correct

(c) List and describe the other work you will perform to check that the inventory value is accurate.

Note. In answering the question you are only required to check that the price per unit of the inventories is correct. You should assume that the inventory quantities are accurate and there are no purchases or sales cut-off errors.

Answer

(a) This method of valuation at cost is permitted by IAS 2, but it is usually applied to large retail concerns which stock thousands of low value items, for example supermarket chains. This method is only permitted when it can be shown that it gives a reasonable approximation of the actual cost.

The following tests should be performed to ensure that the inventory is correctly valued at cost.

    (i) Obtain a schedule of the client calculations of the gross profit margins. Check the mathematical accuracy and consider the reliability of all sources of information used in the calculation.

    (ii) Where the normal overall gross margin has been used, check the reasonableness of the figure by comparing it to the monthly management accounts for the year and last year's published accounts.

    Test a sample of items to make sure that gross profit does not vary too much across all items of inventory (which is unlikely for Arnold Electrical). The test will compare selling price to purchase price.

    (iii) If a weighted average gross margin has been used, check that the weighting is correct in terms of the proportion of each type of product in closing inventory.

    (iv) Select a sample of high value lines and check the reasonableness of the gross profit estimate by calculating the gross profit for each of those lines. Sales price will be compared to inventory sheets and to sales prices in the shop at the year end. Cost will be checked by examining purchase invoices. The weighted average profit margin for the selected lines can then be calculated and compared to the gross margin applied to the whole inventory. (**Note.** High value lines may consist of individual items with a high selling price, or a large number of low value items.)

    (v) Overvaluation of slow-moving inventories is possible when the prices of those items are affected by inflation. To test this, examine the inventory sheets for any slow moving items (or ask the management of the company or use my own observation). Compare the value of the inventories at the end of the accounting period to cost according to purchase invoices. If an overvaluation has occurred it should be quantified.

(vi) Check whether any goods were being offered for sale at reduced prices at the year-end. If the reduced price is greater than cost, the use of an average gross profit percentage will cause inventory to be undervalued. This undervaluation must be quantified. If full selling price was used in the calculation then the problem will not arise. Check a sample of inventory items to sales invoices issued around the year-end to make sure that the correct price was used in the costing calculation.

(b) (i) Inventories which may be worth less than cost will include:

    (1) Slow moving inventories
    (2) Obsolete or superseded inventories
    (3) Seconds and items that have been damaged
    (4) Inventories which are being, or are soon likely to be, sold at reduced prices
    (5) Discontinued lines

Finished goods where the selling price is less than cost will be valued at net realisable value. This is defined as the actual or estimated selling price less costs to completion and marketing, selling and distribution expenses.

To identify inventories which may be worth less than cost the following work will be carried out.

(1) Examine the computerised inventory control system and list items showing an unacceptably low turnover rate. An unacceptable rate of turnover may be different for different items, but inventory representing more than six months' sales is likely to qualify.

(2) Check the inventory printout for items already described as seconds or recorded as damaged.

(3) Discuss with management the current position regarding slow-moving inventories and their plans and expectations in respect of products that may be discontinued. The standard system must be carefully considered and estimates obtained of the likely selling price of existing inventories. The most likely outcome regarding the use and value of discontinued components must be decided.

(4) At the physical inventory count, look for inventory which is dusty, inaccessible and in general not moving and mark on the inventory sheets.

(5) Find out whether any lines are unreliable and therefore frequently returned for repairs as these may be unpopular.

(6) Check with the trade press or other sources to see whether any of the equipment is out of date.

(ii) Determining the net realisable value of inventories is a difficult task and involves management judging how much inventory can be sold and at what price, together with deciding whether to sell off raw materials and components separately or to assemble them into finished products. Each separate type of inventory item should be considered separately in deciding on the level of prudent provision.

To determine the net realisable value of the inventories the following tests should be carried out.

(1) Find the actual selling prices from the latest sales invoice. For items still selling, invoices will be very recent, but for slow moving and obsolete items the invoiced prices will be out of date and allowance will have to be made for this (probably a reduction in estimating the most likely sale price of the inventory concerned).

(2) Estimate the value of marketing, selling and distribution expenses using past figures for the types of finished goods concerned as a base. I would update and check for reasonableness against the most recent accounting records.

(3) Discuss with management what selling prices are likely to be where there is little past evidence. Costs to completion will be questioned where these are difficult to estimate and where there are any unusual assembly, selling or distribution problems.

(c) The following procedures would also be performed to check the value of inventory at the year end.

(i) Compare current results with prior year(s). This would include gross profit margins, sales and turnover. Marked variations from the current year's results should be investigated.

(ii) Consider the effects of new technology and new fashions. The electrical appliance business will be exposed to obsolescence problems. Quantify any necessary write down.

(iii) Compare selling prices to those charged elsewhere. If the prices elsewhere are lower, than the distortion in selling price might affect the value of the inventory of Arnold Electrical. Alternatively, if prices elsewhere are higher, then the company's prices may occasionally fall below cost. Again, any adjustment discovered to be necessary must be quantified.

(iv) Compare the valuation of inventory this year to that at the end of last year. This will be particularly useful for lines held at both dates. If the values are comparable, taking account of inflation, then the current valuation is more likely to be correct.

(v) Sale prices should be checked as long after the year end as possible, to make sure that prices were not kept artificially high over the year end and then reduced at a later date. Inventory turnover should also be examined on this same basis.

4.4 Summary audit procedures for inventory

Audit plan: inventory	
Completeness	• **Trace** test counts to the detailed inventory listing. • Where inventory is held in **third-party locations**, **physically inspect** this inventory or **review confirmations** received from the third party and match to the general ledger. • **Compare** the gross profit percentage to the previous year or industry data.
Existence	• Observe the **physical inventory count** (see Section 4 for details of attendance at the inventory count).
Rights and obligations	• Verify that any **inventory held for third parties** is not included in the year-end inventory figure by being appropriately segregated during the inventory count. • For any **'bill and hold' inventory** (ie where the inventory has been sold but is being held by the entity until the customer requires it), identify such inventory and ensure that it is segregated during the inventory count so that it is not included in the year-end inventory figure. • Confirm that any inventory held at **third-party locations** is included in the year-end inventory figure by reviewing the inventory listing.

Audit plan: inventory	
Accuracy, valuation and allocation	<ul><li>Obtain a copy of the inventory listing and **agree** the totals to the general ledger.</li><li>**Cast** the inventory listing to ensure it is mathematically correct.</li><li>**Vouch** a sample of inventory items to suppliers' invoices to ensure it is correctly valued.</li><li>Where **standard costing** is used, test a sample of inventory to ensure it is correctly valued.</li><li>For **materials**, agree the valuation of raw materials to invoices and price lists.</li><li>Confirm that an appropriate **basis of valuation** (eg FIFO) is being used by discussing with management.</li><li>For **labour** costs, agree costs to wage records.</li><li>**Review** standard labour costs in the light of actual costs and production.</li><li>**Reconcile** labour hours to time summaries.</li><li>Make **enquiries of management** to ascertain any slow-moving or obsolete inventory that should be written down.</li><li>**Examine prices** at which finished goods have been sold after the year end to ascertain whether any finished goods need to be written down.</li><li>If significant levels of finished goods remain unsold for an unusual period of time, **discuss** with management and consider the need to make allowance.</li><li>**Compare** the gross profit percentage to the previous year or industry data.</li><li>**Compare** raw material, finished goods and inventory collection period to the previous year and industry averages.</li><li>**Compare** inventory holding period with the previous year and industry average.</li><li>**Compare** the current year standard costs to the previous year after considering current conditions.</li><li>**Compare** actual manufacturing overhead costs with budgeted or standard manufacturing overhead costs.</li><li>Obtain a copy of the inventory listing and **cast** it, and test the mathematical extensions of quantity multiplied by price.</li><li>**Trace** test counts back to the inventory listing.</li><li>If the entity has adjusted the general ledger to agree with the physical inventory count amounts, **agree** the two amounts.</li><li>Where a **continuous (perpetual) inventory system** is maintained, agree the total on the inventory listing to the continuous inventory records, using ATTs.</li></ul>
Cut-off	<ul><li>Note the numbers of the **last GDNs and GRNs** before the year end and the **first GDNs and GRNs** after the year end and check that these have been included in the correct financial year.</li></ul>
Occurrence and rights and obligations	<ul><li>**Enquire** of management and **review** any loan agreements and board minutes for evidence that inventory has been pledged or assigned.</li><li>Enquire of management about warranty obligation issues.</li></ul>

Audit plan: inventory	
Classification	• **Review** the inventory listing to ensure that inventory has been properly classified between raw materials, work-in-progress and finished goods. • **Read** the notes to the accounts relating to inventory to ensure they are understandable.
Presentation	• **Review** the financial statements to confirm whether the cost method used to value inventory is accurately disclosed. • **Read** the notes to the financial statements to ensure that the information is accurate and properly presented at the appropriate amounts. • Complete the **disclosure checklist** to ensure that all the disclosures relevant to inventory have been made.

Chapter roundup

- The inventory figure in the financial statements comprises the quantity of inventory multiplied by its valuation.
- It is management's responsibility to determine the quantity of inventory held and this can be done by a physical inventory count at the year-end, a physical inventory count before or after the year-end or by continuous (or perpetual) inventory counting.
- Physical inventory count procedures are vital as they provide evidence which cannot be obtained elsewhere or at any other time about the quantities and conditions of inventories and work in progress.
- Before the physical inventory count the auditors should ensure audit **coverage** of the **count** is **appropriate**, and that the client's **count instructions** have been reviewed.
- During the count the auditors should **check the count** is being carried out according to instructions, carry out **test counts**, and watch for **third party** and **slow-moving inventories** and **cut-off problems**.
- After the count the auditors should check that **final inventory sheets** have been **properly compiled** from count records and that **book inventory** has been **appropriately adjusted**.
- Auditors should test **cut-off** by noting the **serial numbers** of items received and dispatched just before and after the year-end, and subsequently checking that they have been included in the **correct period**.
- The **valuation** and **disclosure** rules for inventory are laid down in IAS 2 *Inventories* which states that inventory should be valued at the **lower of cost and net realisable value**.
- **Cost** comprises: purchase costs, conversion costs and other costs incurred in bringing the inventories to their present location and condition.
- **Net realisable value** is the estimated selling price in the ordinary course of business, less the estimated cost of completion and the estimated costs necessary to make the sale.
- Inventory may be valued using **standard costing** as long as this approximates to actual cost.
- Auditing the valuation of inventories includes:
  - Checking the **allocation of overheads** is appropriate
  - Confirming inventories are carried at the lower of **cost** and **net realisable value**
- Where inventory comprises **work in progress** the auditor should consider management's assessment of the percentage completion at the year end.

Quick quiz

1. Complete the definition, using the words given below.

   .... is defined by IAS ...... comprising all costs of .... and other costs incurred in bringing the inventories to their .... and ....

   > 2, purchase, condition, present, cost, location

2. Name three methods of inventory counting.

   (1) ....
   (2) ....
   (3) ....

3. When should the following inventory counting tests take place?

   (a) Observe whether client staff are following instructions.
   (b) Review previous year's inventory count arrangements.
   (c) Assess method of accounting for inventories.
   (d) Trace counted items to final inventory sheets.
   (e) Inspect replies from third parties about inventory held for them.
   (f) Gain an overall impression of levels and values of inventories.
   (g) Consider the need for expert help.

BEFORE	DURING	AFTER

4. Name four points in the accounting cycle when cut-off is critical.

   (1) ....
   (2) ....
   (3) ....
   (4) ....

5. Give four occasions when the net realisable value of inventory is likely to fall below cost.

   (1) ....
   (2) ....
   (3) ....
   (4) ....

6   Consider each of the following audit procedures plus results from the audit file recording attendance at the year-end inventory count of Glad Rags, a clothing manufacturer. From the list of assertions supplied, select the most appropriate assertion for that procedure.

	Assertion
Audit procedure Form an opinion of the condition of inventory and record any instances of damage or obsolescence. **Result** There were 15 × 10 metre rolls of fabric stored near the roof of the warehouse where birds had nested, making the fabric unusable.	
Audit procedure Trace 10 × 10 metre rolls of fabric from the inventory sheets to the relevant shelves of the warehouse. **Result** All 10 rolls were found on the shelves in the locations specified by the main accounting system.	
Audit procedure Trace 10 × 10 metre rolls of fabric from the relevant shelves of the warehouse to the inventory sheets. **Result** All 10 rolls were traced back to the list generated by the main accounting system.	
Audit procedure Confirm that the fabric and garments held in the secure off-site storage facility are to be included in Glad Rags' inventory balance by verifying them to supporting documentation and invoices. **Result** All rolls of fabric and garments were traced back to storage invoices and haulage records, confirming that they belong to Glad Rags.	

COMPLETENESS   EXISTENCE   RIGHTS AND OBLIGATIONS   VALUATION

Answers to quick quiz

1 Cost, 2, purchase, present location, condition

2 (1) Year-end
  (2) Pre/post year-end
  (3) Continuous (or perpetual)

3 (a) DURING
  (b) BEFORE
  (c) BEFORE
  (d) AFTER
  (e) AFTER
  (f) DURING
  (g) BEFORE

4 (1) The **point** of **purchase** and **receipt** of **goods** and **services**
  (2) The **requisitioning** of **raw materials** for production
  (3) The **transfer** of **completed work-in-progress** to finished goods
  (4) The **sale** and **dispatch** of **finished goods**

5 From:
  (1) An **increase in costs** or a fall in selling price
  (2) **Physical deterioration**
  (3) **Obsolescence** of products
  (4) A **marketing decision** to manufacture and sell products at a loss
  (5) **Errors in production or purchasing**

6

	Assertion
Audit procedure Form an opinion of the condition of inventory and record any instances of damage or obsolescence. **Result** There were 15 × 10 metre rolls of fabric stored near the roof of the warehouse where birds had nested, making the fabric unusable.	Valuation
Audit procedure Trace 10 × 10 metre rolls of fabric from the inventory sheets to the relevant shelves of the warehouse. **Result** All 10 rolls were found on the shelves in the locations specified by the main accounting system.	Existence
Audit procedure Trace 10 × 10 metre rolls of fabric from the relevant shelves of the warehouse to the inventory sheets. **Result** All 10 rolls were traced back to the list generated by the main accounting system.	Completeness
Audit procedure Confirm that the fabric and garments held in the secure off-site storage facility are to be included in Glad Rags' inventory balance by verifying them to supporting documentation and invoices. **Result** All rolls of fabric and garments were traced back to storage invoices and haulage records, confirming that they belong to Glad Rags.	Rights and obligations

End of chapter question

Inventory count (AIA Nov 2004)

You are an audit partner. One of your clients is a small company, which manufactures kitchen equipment. This company is about to undertake its year-end inventory count. Counting will take place at the company's factory and at the nearby warehouse. You have asked one of your trainee audit assistants to attend. Outline the procedures that the assistant should carry out before and during the inventory count. **(15 marks)**

Receivables and revenue

Topic list	Syllabus reference
1 Introduction	5.7
2 Receivables	5.7
3 Revenue	5.7
4 Prepayments	5.7

Introduction

Receivables will generally be a material figure on a company's statement of financial position.

You must ensure that you are fully conversant with the 'standard' procedures, such as the confirmation of receivables. The receivables confirmation is primarily designed to test the audit client's entitlement to receive the debt (existence and rights and obligations), not the customer's ability to pay (valuation).

Auditors also need to consider cut-off for receivables. Revenue testing is often carried out in conjunction with the audit of receivables, as the two are linked. We also briefly consider the audit of prepayments which is normally carried out using analytical procedures.

1 Introduction

1.1 Key assertions: revenue and receivables

The following table sets out the assertions that apply to revenue and receivables. The audit procedures in the remainder of this chapter are used to provide evidence for these assertions.

Assertions about classes of transactions and related disclosures	<ul><li>All revenue transactions recorded have occurred and relate to the entity (**occurrence**)</li><li>All revenue transactions that should have been recorded have been recorded (**completeness**)</li><li>Amounts relating to transactions have been recorded appropriately (**accuracy**)</li><li>All transactions have been recorded in the correct period (**cut-off**)</li><li>All transactions are recorded properly (**classification**)</li><li>All disclosed events and transactions relating to receivables have occurred and pertain to the entity (**occurrence, rights and obligations**)</li><li>All disclosures required have been included (**completeness**)</li><li>Financial information is appropriately presented and described and disclosures clearly expressed (**presentation**)</li><li>Financial and other information is disclosed fairly and at appropriate amounts (**presentation**)</li></ul>
Assertions about account balances at the period end and related disclosures	<ul><li>Recorded receivables exist (**existence**)</li><li>The entity controls the rights to receivables and related accounts (**rights and obligations**)</li><li>All receivables that should have been recorded have been recorded (**completeness**)</li><li>Receivables are included in the accounts at the correct amounts (**accuracy, valuation and allocation**)</li><li>All disclosures required have been included (**presentation**)</li><li>Financial information is appropriately presented and described and disclosures clearly expressed (**presentation**)</li><li>Financial and other information is disclosed fairly and at appropriate amounts (**presentation**)</li></ul>

2 Receivables

2.1 Audit procedures relating to receivables

FAST FORWARD

Existence, completeness and valuation are key assertions relating to the audit of receivables.

Audit procedures for receivables are set out in the table below which also covers the audit of revenue and prepayments. Receivables are often tested in conjunction with revenue. The key assertions for revenue are occurrence, completeness and accuracy.

The receivables confirmation is used as an audit procedure in the table below and is described in more detail later in this section.

Audit plan: receivables	
Completeness	• **Agree** the balance from the individual receivables ledger accounts to the aged receivables' listing and vice versa. • **Match** the total of the aged receivables' listing to the receivables ledger control account. • **Cast and cross-cast** the aged trial balance before selecting any samples to test. • **Trace** a sample of shipping documentation to sales invoices and into the receivables ledger. • Complete the **disclosure checklist** to ensure that all the disclosures relevant to receivables have been made. • **Compare** the gross profit percentage by product line with the previous year and industry data. • **Compare** the level of prepayments to the previous year to ensure the figure is materially correct and complete. • **Review detailed statement of financial position** to ensure all likely prepayments have been included.

Existence	• Perform a **receivables circularisation** on a sample of year-end trade receivables.
	• **Follow up** all balance disagreements and non-replies to the receivables confirmation.
	• **Perform alternative procedures** for any exceptions and non-replies to the receivables confirmation, such as:
	  – **Review after-date cash receipts** by inspecting bank statements and cash receipts documentation.
	  – Examine the **customer's account and customer correspondence** to assess whether the balance outstanding represents specific invoices and confirm their validity.
	  – Examine the **underlying documentation** (purchase order, despatch documentation, duplicate sales invoice etc).
	  – **Enquire from management** explanations for invoices remaining unpaid after subsequent ones have been paid.
	  – **Observe** whether the balance on the account is growing and, if so, find out why by discussing with management.

Audit plan: receivables	
Rights and obligations	• Review **bank confirmation** for any liens on receivables. • Make **enquiries of management, review** loan agreements and review board minutes for any evidence of receivables being sold (eg to factors).
Accuracy, valuation and allocation	• **Compare** receivables turnover and receivables collection period with the previous year and/or with industry data, and investigate any significant differences. • **Compare** the aged analysis of receivables from the aged trial balance with the previous year. • **Review** the adequacy of the allowance for uncollectable accounts through discussion with management. • **Compare** the irrecoverable debt expense as a percentage of sales with the previous year and/or with industry data. • **Compare** the allowance for receivables as a percentage of receivables or credit sales with the previous year and/or with industry data. • Confirm adequacy of allowance by **reviewing correspondence** with customers and solicitors. • **Examine credit notes** issued after year end for allowances that should be made against current period balances. • **Examine** large customer accounts individually and compare with the previous year's balances. • For a sample of old debts on the aged trial balance, obtain further information regarding their recoverability by **discussions** with management and **review** of customer correspondence. • **Review after-date cash receipts** by inspecting bank statements and cash receipts documentation. • For a sample of prepayments from the prepayments' listing, **recalculate** the amount prepaid to ensure that it has been accurately calculated.
Cut-off	• For a sample of sales invoices around the year end, **inspect the dates** and compare with the dates of despatch and the dates recorded in the ledger for application of correct cut-off. • For **sales returns**, select a sample of returns documentation around the year end and trace to the related credit entries. • Perform **analytical procedures** on sales returns, comparing the ratio of sales returns to sales. • **Review material** after-date invoices, credit notes and adjustments and ensure that they are recorded correctly in the relevant financial period. • For a sample of sales invoices, **compare** the prices and terms to the authorised price list and terms of trade documentation. • Test whether **discounts** have been properly applied by recalculating them for a sample of invoices. • Test the correct calculation of **tax** on a sample of invoices.
Classification	• Take a sample of sales invoices and examine for proper **classification** into revenue accounts.
Occurrence	• For a sample of sales transactions recorded in the ledger, **vouch** the sales invoice back to customer orders and despatch documentation.

Audit plan: receivables	
Occurrence and rights and obligations	• Determine, through **discussion** with management, whether any receivables have been pledged, assigned or discounted and whether such items require disclosure in the financial statements.
Classification	• **Review** the aged analysis of receivables for any large credits, non-trade receivables and long-term receivables and consider whether such items require separate disclosure. • **Read** the disclosure notes relevant to receivables in the draft financial statements and review for understandability.
Presentation	• **Read** the disclosure notes to ensure the information is accurate and properly presented at the appropriate amounts.

It is worth noting that some of the audit procedures above test for **more than one assertion**. For example:

(a) Reviewing after-date cash receipts is an excellent test for both **valuation** and **existence**

(b) Comparing the gross profit per product line with the previous year tests for the existence and completeness of receivables, as well as the occurrence and accuracy of revenue and the completeness, occurrence, accuracy and classification of cost of sales

2.2 Receivables listing and aged receivables analysis

Much of the auditors' detailed work will be based on a selection of receivables' balances chosen from a listing of receivables ledger balances, prepared by the client or auditors. Ideally the list should be aged, showing the period or periods of time money has been owed. The following substantive procedures test the **completeness** and **accuracy** of a client-prepared list.

- **Check** the **balances** from the **individual receivables ledger accounts** to the **list of balances** and *vice versa*.
- **Check** the **total** of the **list** to the **receivables ledger control account**.
- **Cast** the **list of balances** and the **receivables ledger control account**.
- **Confirm** whether **list of balances reconciles** with the **receivables ledger control account**.

2.3 The receivables confirmation

FAST FORWARD

A **confirmation of receivables** is a major procedure, usually achieved by **direct contact** with customers. There are two methods of confirmation: **positive** and **negative**.

2.3.1 Objectives of the confirmation

Key term

External confirmations are audit evidence obtained as a direct written response to the auditor from a third party (the confirming party), in paper form, or by electronic or other medium.

ISA 505 *External Confirmations* covers the confirmation of amounts by third parties, including the confirmation of amounts by receivables.

The verification of trade receivables by direct confirmation is the normal means of providing audit evidence to satisfy the objective of testing whether customers exist and owe *bona fide* amounts to the company (**existence** and **rights and obligations**).

Confirmation will produce for the current audit file a written statement from each respondent that the amount owed at the date of the confirmation is correct. This is, *prima facie*, reliable audit evidence, being from an **independent source** and in **documentary** form. The confirmation of receivables on a test basis should not be regarded as replacing other normal audit tests, such as the in-depth testing of sales transactions, but the results may influence the scope of such tests.

2.3.2 Client's mandate

Confirmation is essentially an act of the **client**, who alone can authorise third parties to divulge information to the auditors.

The ISA 505 (para. 8) outlines what the auditors' response should be when management refuses permission for the auditors to contact third parties for evidence. If management asks the auditor not to seek the confirmation, the auditor shall enquire about management's reasons for the refusal and seek audit evidence regarding the validity and reasonableness of the reasons. They shall also evaluate the implications of the refusal on the assessment of the risk of material misstatement and on the nature, timing and extent of other audit procedures. The auditor shall perform alternative audit procedures to obtain relevant and reliable audit evidence. If the auditor concludes that the refusal is unreasonable, or the auditor cannot obtain relevant and reliable audit evidence elsewhere, the auditor shall communicate with those charged with governance in accordance with ISA 260 (Revised) and consider the implications for the auditor's report (ISA 505: para. 9).

2.3.3 Positive vs negative confirmation

Key terms

> A **positive confirmation request** is 'a request that the confirming party respond directly to the auditor indicating whether the confirming party agrees or disagrees with the information in the request, or providing the requested information' (ISA 505: para. 6(b)).
>
> A **negative confirmation request** is 'a request that the confirming party respond directly to the auditor only if the confirming party disagrees with the information provided in the request' (ISA 505: para. 6(c)).

When confirmation is undertaken, the method of requesting information from the customer may be either **positive** or **negative**.

- Under the **positive** method, the customer is requested to confirm the accuracy of the balance shown or state in what respect they are in disagreement.
- Under the **negative** method, the customer is requested to reply only if the amount stated is disputed.

The positive method is generally preferable, as it is designed to encourage definite replies from those contacted.

The negative method provides less persuasive audit evidence and **shall not be used as the sole substantive procedure** to audit receivables unless all of the following are present:

(a) The **risk** of material misstatement has been assessed as **low**.

(b) The auditor has obtained sufficient appropriate audit evidence on the operating effectiveness of relevant **controls**.

(c) The population consists of a **large number of small, homogeneous account balances**.

(d) A **very low exception rate** is expected.

(e) The auditor is not aware of circumstances or conditions that would cause customers to **disregard the requests**.

(ISA 505: para. 15)

Exam focus point

RPQ candidates should be aware that the use of **negative confirmations** is **prohibited** in an audit conducted in accordance with **ISAs (UK)** (ISA (UK) 505 (Revised October 2023): para. 6c).

Accordingly, RPQ candidates should note that the study material relating to negative confirmations is not applicable to their exam.

A specimen 'positive' confirmation letter is shown below.

The statements will normally be prepared by the client's staff, from which point the auditors, as a safeguard against the possibility of fraudulent manipulation, must maintain **strict control** over the preparation and despatch of the statements.

Precautions must also be taken to ensure that undelivered items are returned, not to the client, but to the auditors' own office for follow-up by them.

MANUFACTURING CO LIMITED
15 South Street
London

Date

Messrs   (customer)

In accordance with the request of our auditors, ABC Co, we ask that you kindly confirm to them directly your indebtedness to us at [insert date] which, according to our records, amounted to $.......... as shown by the enclosed statement.

If the above amount is in agreement with your records, please sign in the space provided below and return this letter direct to our auditors in the enclosed stamped addressed envelope.

If the amount is not in agreement with your records, please notify our auditors directly of the amount shown by your records, and if possible detail on the reverse of this letter full particulars of the difference.

Yours faithfully,

For Manufacturing Co Limited

Reference No: ....

....

(Tear-off slip)

The amount shown above is/is not* in agreement with our records as at

Account No   ....   Signature   ....
Date   ....   Title or position   ....

* The position according to our records is shown overleaf.

Notes

- The letter is on the client's paper, signed by the client.
- A copy of the statement is attached.
- The reply is sent directly to the auditor in a prepaid envelope.

2.3.4 Sample selection

Auditors will normally only contact a **sample** of receivables. If this sample is to yield a meaningful result it must be based on a **complete list** of all receivables. In addition, when constructing the sample, the following classes of account should receive special attention:

- **Old, unpaid** accounts
- Accounts **written-off** during the period under review
- Accounts with **credit balances**
- Accounts settled by **round sum payments**
- Accounts with **large balances**
- Accounts with **nil balances**

2.3.5 Follow-up procedures

ISA 505 (para. A7) states that the auditor may send an additional confirmation request when a reply to a previous request has not been received within a **reasonable time**. For example, the auditor may send an additional or follow-up request having rechecked the accuracy of the original address. Also, with the client's permission, the auditor can phone the customer to request a reply to the original request.

2.3.6 Exceptions and non-responses

Key terms

> An **exception** is 'a response that indicates a difference between information requested to be confirmed, or contained in the entity's records, and information provided by the confirming party' (ISA 505: para. 6(e)).
>
> A **non-response** is 'a failure of the confirming party to respond, or fully respond, to a positive confirmation request, or a confirmation request returned undelivered' (ISA 505: para. 6d)).

Auditors will have to carry out further work in relation to those receivables who:

- **Disagree** with the **balance stated** (positive and negative confirmation), resulting in **exceptions**
- **Do not respond**, resulting in **non-responses**

In the case of disagreements, the customer response should have identified specific amounts which are disputed. These give rise to exceptions and may indicate misstatements or potential misstatements in the financial statements. When a misstatement is identified, the auditor must evaluate whether this is indicative of fraud (in accordance with ISA 240). Exceptions might also indicate a deficiency in internal control. Some exceptions of course do not represent misstatements, as they may be due to timing, measurement or clerical errors in the confirmation procedures. The table below outlines some reasons for exceptions occurring.

Reasons for exceptions
There is a **dispute** between the client and the customer. The reasons for the dispute would have to be identified, and provision made if appropriate against the debt.
Cut-off problems exist, because the client records the following year's sales in the current year or because goods returned by the customer in the current year are not recorded in the current year. Cut-off testing may have to be extended (see below).
The customer may have sent the **monies before** the year end, but the monies were **not recorded** by the client as receipts until **after** the year end. Detailed cut-off work may be required on receipts.
Monies received may have been posted to the **wrong account** or a cash-in-transit account. Auditors should check if there is evidence of other mis-posting. If the monies have been posted to a cash-in-transit account, auditors should ensure this account has been cleared promptly.

15: RECEIVABLES AND REVENUE

> **Reasons for exceptions**
>
> Customers who are also suppliers may **net-off balances** owed and owing. Auditors should check that this is allowed.
>
> **Teeming and lading, stealing monies** and **incorrectly posting** other receipts so that no particular customer is seriously in debt is a **fraud** that can arise in this area. Teeming and lading involves an employee first stealing the cash receipts from a receivable (receivable 1) and not recording the receipt against the customer account. Then the employee receives more cash from another receivable (receivable 2) and allocates it against receivable 1 in order to conceal the stolen funds. Similarly, they then allocate monies from receivable 3 against amounts owed from receivable 2, and so on. By allocating the funds in this way, there is only an apparent time lag on posting the receipt of cash, rather than an obvious uncollected debt. If auditors suspect teeming and lading has occurred, detailed testing will be required on cash receipts, particularly on prompt posting of cash receipts.

(ISA 505: paras. A21–A22)

In the case of **non-responses**, the ISA states that the auditor shall perform **alternative audit procedures** to obtain relevant and reliable audit evidence. These could include reviewing subsequent cash receipts, shipping documentation and sales near the period end.

2.3.7 Reliability of responses

The ISA 505 (para. 10) states that the auditor shall obtain further audit evidence to resolve any **doubts about the reliability** of a response to a confirmation request. This could include contacting the confirming party.

If the auditor concludes that a response to a request is **not reliable**, they shall evaluate the impact of this on the assessment of the risk of material misstatement (including the risk of fraud) and on the related nature, timing and extent of other audit procedures (ISA 505: para. 11).

Question

Auditing receivables

Sherwood Textiles, a listed company, manufactures knitted clothes and dyes these clothes and other textiles. You are carrying out the audit of the financial statements of the company for the year ended 30 September 20X6 which show revenue of approximately $10 million, and a profit before tax of circa $800,000.

You are attending the final audit in December 20X6 and are commencing the audit of trade receivables, which are shown in the draft financial statements at $2,060,000.

Tests of controls were carried out during the interim audit in July 20X6 and it showed that there was a good system of internal control in the sales system and no serious errors were found in the audit procedures. The company's receivables ledger is maintained on a computer, which produces at the end of each month:

(i) A list of transactions for the month
(ii) An aged list of balances
(iii) Open item statements which are sent to customers (these are statements that show all items which are outstanding on each account, irrespective of their age).

Required

(a) List and briefly describe the audit procedures you would carry out to verify trade receivables at the year-end. You are not required to describe how you would carry out a direct confirmation of receivables.

(b) Describe the audit work you would carry out on the following replies to a receivables' confirmation:

(i) Balance agreed by customer
(ii) Balance not agreed by customer
(iii) Customer is unable to confirm the balance because of the form of records kept by the customer
(iv) Customer does not reply to the confirmation letter

Answer

(a) The auditors will carry out the following audit procedures on the list of balances.

(i) Agree the balances from the individual receivables ledger accounts to the list of balances and vice versa.

(ii) Agree the total of the list to the receivables ledger control account.

(iii) Re-cast the list of balances and the receivables ledger control account.

Other general procedures auditors will carry out will be to:

(i) Agree the opening balance on the receivables ledger control account to ensure that last year's audit adjustments were recorded.

(ii) Scrutinise ledger balances for unusual entries.

(iii) Carry out analytical procedures considering particularly changes in receivables' collection period and in age profile of receivables.

The determination of whether the company has made reasonable allowance for receivables, will be facilitated as the company produces an aged listing of balances.

Auditors will carry out the following procedures to test irrecoverable debts.

(i) Debts against which an allowance has been made (and debts written off) should be examined in conjunction with correspondence, lawyers'/debt collection agencies' letters, liquidators' statements and so on, and their necessity or adequacy confirmed.

(ii) A general review of relevant correspondence may reveal debts where an allowance is warranted, but has not been made.

(iii) Where allowances have been determined using the aged analysis, the auditors should ensure that the analysis has been properly prepared by comparing the analysis with the dates on invoices and matching cash receipts against outstanding invoices. They should assess the reasonableness and consistency of any formula used to calculate allowances.

(iv) Additional tests that should be carried out on individual balances will include the ascertainment of the subsequent receipt of cash, paying particular attention to round sum payments on account, examination of specific invoices and, where appropriate, goods received notes, and enquiry into any invoices that have not been paid when subsequent invoices have been paid.

(v) Excessive discounts should be examined, as should journal entries transferring balances from one account to another and journal entries that clear customer balances after the year-end.

(vi) Credit notes issued after the year-end should be reviewed and allowances checked where they refer to current period sales.

In order to verify cut-off and hence completeness, the auditors should, during the physical inventory count, have obtained details of the last serial numbers of goods outwards issued before the commencement of the count. The following substantive procedures are designed to test that goods taken into inventory are not also treated as sales in the year under review and, conversely, goods despatched are treated as sales in the year under review and not also treated as inventory.

(i) Check goods outwards and returns inwards notes around year end to ensure that:

    (1) Invoices and credit notes are dated in the correct period; and

    (2) Invoices and credit notes are posted to the receivables ledger and nominal ledger in the correct period.

(ii) Reconcile entries in the receivables ledger control around the year-end to daily batch invoice totals ensuring batches are posted in correct year.

(iii) Review receivables ledger control account around year-end for unusual items.

(iv) Review material after date invoices and ensure that they are properly treated as following year sales.

(b) The verification of trade receivables by direct confirmation is the normal means of providing audit evidence to prove that trade receivables represent *bona fide* amounts due to the company, existence and rights and obligations.

The audit work required on the various replies to a receivables' confirmation would be as follows.

(i) **Balances agreed by customer**

Where the balance has been agreed by the customer all that is required would be to ensure that the debt does appear to be collectable. This would be achieved by reviewing cash received after date or considering the adequacy of any allowance made for a long outstanding debt.

(ii) **Balances not agreed by customer**

All balance disagreements must be followed up and their effect on total trade receivables evaluated. Differences arising that merely represent invoices or cash in-transit (which are normal timing differences) generally do not require adjustment, but disputed amounts, and errors by the client, may indicate that further substantive work is necessary to determine whether material adjustments are required.

(iii) **Customer is unable to confirm the balance because of the form of records he or she maintains**

Certain companies, often computerised, operate systems which make it impossible for them to confirm the balance on their account. Typically in these circumstances their payables ledger is merely a list of unpaid invoices. However, given sufficient information the customer will be able to confirm that any given invoice is outstanding. Hence the auditors can undertake external confirmations of such enterprises successfully, but they will need to break down the total on the account into its constituent outstanding invoices.

(iv) **Customer does not reply to confirmation letter**

When the positive request method is used the auditors must follow up by all practicable means those customers who fail to respond. Second requests should be sent out in the event of no reply being received within two or three weeks and if necessary this may be followed by telephoning the customer with the client's permission.

After two, or even three attempts to obtain confirmation, a list of the outstanding items will normally be passed to a responsible company official, preferably independent of the sales department, who will arrange for them to be investigated.

Alternative audit procedures might include the following.

(1) Confirm receipt of cash after date.

(2) Verify valid sales orders, if any.

(3) Examine the account to see if the balance represents specific outstanding invoices.

(4) Obtain explanations for invoices remaining unpaid after subsequent ones have been paid.

(5) See if the balance on the account is growing, and if so, why.

(6) Test the company's control over the issue of credit notes and the write-off of irrecoverable debts.

3 Revenue

FAST FORWARD

Revenue is a material figure often audited by analytical procedures as it should have predictable relationships with other figures in the financial statements.

Receivables will often be tested in conjunction with revenue. Auditors will seek to obtain evidence that revenue pertains to the entity (**occurrence**) are **completely** and **accurately recorded**. This will involve carrying out certain procedures to test for **completeness** of revenue and also testing **cut-off.**

3.1 Revenue from contracts with customers

FAST FORWARD

Revenue recognition is an extremely important issue, with both the completeness and occurrence assertions being equally important.

IFRS 15 *Revenue from Contracts with Customers* provides guidance regarding the accounting treatment of sales and related issues. The standard defines a contract as a series of 'performance obligations' which are then transferred to the customer (whether goods or services). The transfer of goods and services is understood in terms of the transfer of **control**. **Control of an asset** is described in the standard as the ability to direct the use of, and obtain substantially all the remaining benefits from, the asset.

For straightforward retail transactions IFRS 15 will have little, if any, effect on the amount and timing of revenue recognition. For contracts such as long-term service contracts and multi-element arrangements, however, it could result in changes either to the amount or to the timing of revenue recognised.

The main requirements of IFRS 15 are as follows.

3.1.1 Definitions

Key terms

Contract. An agreement between two or more parties that creates enforceable rights and obligations.

Customer. A party that has contracted with an entity to obtain goods or services that are an output of the entity's ordinary activities in exchange for consideration.

Income. Increases in economic benefits during the accounting period in the form of inflows or enhancements of assets or decreases of liabilities that result in an increase in equity, other than those relating to contributions from equity participants.

> **Performance obligation.** A promise in a contract with a customer to transfer to the customer either:
> - A good or service (or a bundle of goods or services) that is distinct; or
> - A series of distinct goods or services that are substantially the same and that have the same pattern of transfer to the customer.
>
> **Revenue.** Income arising in the course of an entity's ordinary activities.
>
> **Transaction price.** The amount of consideration to which an entity expects to be entitled in exchange for transferring promised goods or services to a customer, excluding amounts collected on behalf of third parties.

3.1.2 Steps in recognising revenue

Step 1 Identify the contract(s) with a customer

A contract with a customer is within the **scope** of IFRS 15 only when:

(a) The parties have approved the contract and are committed to carrying it out

(b) Each party's rights regarding the goods and services to be transferred can be identified

(c) The payment terms for the goods and services can be identified

(d) The contract has commercial substance

(e) It is probable that the entity will collect the consideration to which it will be entitled

The contract can be written, verbal or implied.

Contracts should be combined when the following criteria are met.

(a) The contracts are negotiated as a package with a single commercial objective.

(b) The amount of consideration to be paid in one contract depends on the price or performance of the other contract.

(c) The goods or services promised in the contracts are a single performance obligation.

Step 2 Identify the performance obligations in the contract

The key point is distinct goods or services. A contract includes promises to provide goods or services to a customer. Those promises are called performance obligations. A company would account for a performance obligation separately only if the promised good or service is distinct.

A good or service is distinct if:

- The customer can benefit from the good or services on its own or in conjunction with other readily available resources
- The entity's promise to transfer the good or service to the customer is separately identifiable from other promises in the contract

Step 3 Determine the transaction price

The transaction price is the amount of consideration a company expects to be entitled to from the customer, in exchange for transferring goods or services. The transaction price would reflect the company's probability-weighted estimate of variable consideration (including reasonable estimates of contingent amounts) in addition to the effects of the customer's credit risk and the time value of money (if material). Variable contingent amounts are only included where it is highly probable that there will not be a reversal of revenue when any uncertainty associated with the variable consideration is resolved.

Step 4   **Allocate the transaction price to the performance obligations in the contract**

Where a contract contains more than one distinct performance obligation a company allocates the transaction price to all separate performance obligations in proportion to the standalone selling price of the good or service underlying each performance obligation. If the good or service is not sold separately, the company would estimate its standalone selling price.

So, if any entity sells a bundle of goods and/or services which it also supplies unbundled, the separate performance obligations in the contract should be priced in the same proportion as the unbundled prices. This would apply to mobile phone contracts where the handset is supplied 'free'. The entity must look at the standalone price of such a handset and some of the consideration for the contract should be allocated to the handset.

Step 5   **Recognise revenue when (or as) the entity satisfies a performance obligation**

The entity satisfies a performance obligation by transferring control of a promised good or service to the customer. A performance obligation can be satisfied at a point in time, such as when goods are delivered to the customer, or over time. An obligation satisfied over time will meet one of the following criteria.

- The customer simultaneously receives and consumes the benefits as the performance takes place.
- The entity's performance creates or enhances an asset that the customer controls as the asset is created or enhanced.
- The entity's performance does not create an asset with an alternative use to the entity and the entity has an enforceable right to payment for performance completed to date.

The amount of revenue recognised is the amount allocated to that performance obligation in Step 4.

An entity must be able to reasonably measure the outcome of a performance obligation before the related revenue can be recognised. In some circumstances, such as in the early stages of a contract, it may not be possible to reasonably measure the outcome of a performance obligation, but the entity expects to recover the costs incurred. In these circumstances, revenue is recognised only to the extent of costs incurred.

We shall briefly look at the substantive procedures around sales and receivables in the following sections.

3.2 Completeness and occurrence of sales

Analytical procedures are likely to be important when testing completeness. A client is likely to have a great deal of information about company sales and should be able to explain any functions or variances. Auditors should consider the following.

- The **level of sales** over the year, compared on a month-by-month basis with the previous year
- The effect on sales value of **changes in quantities** sold
- The effect on sales value of **changes in products** or **prices**
- The level of **goods returned, sales allowances** and **discounts**
- The **efficiency of labour** as expressed in sales or profit per tax per employee

In addition auditors must record reasons for changes in the **gross profit margin**. Analysis of the gross profit margin should be as detailed as possible, ideally broken down by **product area** and **month or quarter**.

As well as analytical procedures, auditors may feel that they need to carry out a test of detail on **completeness of recording** of individual sales in the accounting records. To do this, auditors should start with the documents that first record sales (**goods dispatched notes** or **till rolls** for example), and trace sales recorded in these through intermediate documents such as sales summaries to the **receivables ledger**.

Auditors must ensure that the population of documents from which the sample is originally taken is itself complete, by checking for example the **completeness** of the **sequence** of goods dispatched notes.

> **Exam focus point**
>
> You must remember the **direction** of this test. Since we are checking the completeness of recording of sales in the receivables ledger, we cannot take a sample from the ledger since the sample cannot include what has not been recorded.

3.3 Other audit procedures relating to revenue

Audit Plan: Revenue – accuracy

- For a sample of invoices, agree the **pricing calculations** to the client's price list and re-cast the invoice totals to ensure invoices are accurate.
- Recalculate **discounts** to ensure they have been **properly calculated**.
- **Inspect** invoices to determine whether **sales tax** has been **added appropriately**.

Other audit procedures that may be carried out on revenue include:

- **Trace debits** in the **revenue account** to credit notes.
- **Re-casting** of **receivables ledger accounts** and **receivables ledger control account**.
- **Review reconciliations** of receivables ledger control account and other relevant reconciliations (for example till rolls) and investigate unusual items.

If the auditors suspect that sales may have been **invalidly** recorded, and have not **occurred**, then the sample will be taken from the **receivables ledger** and **confirmed** to **supporting documentation** (orders, dispatch notes etc).

3.4 Revenue cut-off

We can now turn to the requirement to confirm that cut-off of revenue is satisfactory and hence revenue is complete. During the Inventory count the auditors will have obtained details of the last serial numbers of goods dispatch notes issued before the commencement of the inventory count.

Audit plan: Revenue cut-off

- **Vouch goods dispatched** and **returns inwards** notes around year-end to ensure:
  - **Invoices** and **credit notes** are **dated** in the **correct period**
  - **Invoices** and **credit notes** are **posted** to the **sales ledger** and **general ledger** in the correct period
- **Reconcile entries** in the **receivables ledger control account** around the **year-end** to daily batch invoice totals ensuring batches are posted in correct year.
- **Review receivables ledger control account** around year-end for **unusual items**.
- **Review material after-date invoices, credit notes** and **adjustments** and ensure that they are properly treated as following year sales.

3.5 Goods on sale or return

Care should be exercised to ensure that goods on sale or return are properly treated in the accounts. Except where the client has been notified of the sale of the goods they should be reflected in the accounts as **inventory** at cost and not as receivables, otherwise profits may be incorrectly anticipated.

Question — Auditing revenue

You are an audit senior conducting the audit of WSIT Co for the year ended 30 September 20X6, a wholesale seller of printers and photocopiers.

WSIT Co has the following revenue figures:

	20X6 (draft) $	20X5 (actual) $
Revenue	3,040,000	2,600,000

You have performed analytical procedures on the revenue figure for the year and have noted that, on average, sales grew by between four and five percent from 20X5 to 20X6. However, on obtaining a breakdown of revenue on a month by month basis, you have identified that recognised within revenue are a series of credit sales of inventory totalling $300,000 which took place close to the year end.

Required

Explain the issue you should consider and describe the audit procedures you would perform in order to determine whether revenue is fairly stated for the year ended 30 September 20X6.

Answer

Issue:

If WSIT Co has experienced growth at a rate of 4% - 5% during the year, then revenue for the year ended 30 September 20X6 would be expected to be between $2,704,000 and $2,730,000 ($2,600,000 × 1.04/1.05). Actual revenue is reported to be $3,040,000 and the unexpected increase appears to be due to the $300,000 of credit sales made just prior to the year end.

The auditor's key concern is therefore that the credit sales of $300,000 are not *bona fide* sales or have been recognised in the wrong accounting period.

Audit procedures:

- Trace the sales invoices relating to the $300,000 credit sales to the related goods despatched notes (GDNs).
- Vouch the date on the GDNs to determine whether the date of despatch was before the year end.

4 Prepayments

FAST FORWARD — Prepayments may also be tested by analytical procedures.

The auditors will be concerned primarily that prepayments **exist** and have been **completely** and **accurately** included on the statement of financial position at the appropriate **value**.

4.1 Audit procedures relating to prepayments

Audit plan: Prepayments

- **Verify prepayments** by reference to the cash book, expense invoices, correspondence and so on (existence and rights and obligations).
- **Reperform calculations** of prepayments (accuracy, valuation and allocation).
- **Review** the **detailed statement of financial position** to ensure that all likely prepayments have been provided for (completeness).
- **Review** the **prepayments** for **reasonableness** by comparing with prior year's and using analytical procedures where applicable.

Question

Auditing revenue

You are an audit senior conducting the audit of prepayments of PUSR Co for the year ended 31 December 20X6.

You have been provided with the following information:

	20X6 (draft) $	20X5 (actual) $
Prepayments:		
Photocopier rental cost	1,260	1,200
Head office: premises rates	3,200	3,000
Warehouse: insurance premium	4,500	0
Total	8,960	4,200

You have been told that during the year PUSR Co changed the way in which it paid its insurance premiums. Previously these had been paid monthly but this year PUSR Co paid insurance for the year ended 31 December 20X7 on 23 December 20X6 in order to save costs.

Required

Describe the audit procedures you would perform in order to determine whether prepayments are fairly stated for the year ended 31 December 20X6.

Answer

Audit procedures:

- Perform analytical procedures on the prepayments relating to the photocopier rental cost and head office premises rates in order to determine whether the increases (5% and 6.6% respectively) are reasonable in comparison with current price increases.

- Obtain a copy of the invoices relating to the photocopier rental cost and head office premises rates and recalculate the value of the prepayments by reference to the period prepaid.

- Obtain a copy of the warehouse insurance premium paid on 23 December 20X6 in order to confirm that the payment relates to the year ended 31 December 20X7. Vouch the payment to the cash book and bank statement.

- Recalculate the value of the warehouse insure premium to ensure that it is accurate.

Chapter roundup

- Receivables are usually audited using a combination of **tests of details** and **analytical procedures**.
- Key assertions relating to the audit of receivables are **existence, completeness** and **valuation**.
- A **receivables confirmation** is a key audit procedure used to gather evidence over the **existence** and **rights and obligations** of receivables. It involves a sample of receivables (chosen by the auditor) confirming, in writing and directly to the auditor, the balance owed to the audit client at the year end. There are two methods of confirmation: **positive** and **negative**.
- Auditors must follow up **customer disagreements** and **failure by customers** to respond.
- Revenue is a material figure often audited by analytical procedures as it should have predictable relationships with other figures in the financial statements.
- Prepayments may also be tested using analytical procedures.

Quick quiz

1. The negative method of the receivables confirmation should only be used if permitted by ISA 505 *External Confirmations* and if the client has a good internal control and a small number of large receivables accounts.

    True ☐
    False ☐

2. Name four types of account which should receive special attention when picking a sample for a receivables confirmation.

    (1) ……………………………………………..
    (2) ……………………………………………..
    (3) ……………………………………………..
    (4) ……………………………………………..

3. Complete the following procedures which aim to confirm the valuation of an allowance for receivables.

    (a) Confirm adequacy of allowance by reviewing correspondence with
    …………………………………….. or ……………………………………………..

    (b) Examine …………………………………….. issued after the year-end for allowances that should be made against current period balances.

4. Name three things that can be considered when undertaking analytical procedures on revenue.

    (1) ……………………………………………..
    (2) ……………………………………………..
    (3) ……………………………………………..

5. Give two examples of audit procedures to verify prepayments.

    (1) ……………………………………………..
    (2) ……………………………………………..

6   State whether the following statement is true or false:

    'Auditors may test understatement of sales revenue by tracing a sale from the general ledger back through the system to the sales order'.

    True   ☐
    False   ☐

Answers to quick quiz

1. False

2. Any four from:
   - **Old unpaid accounts**
   - **Accounts written off** during the period under review
   - **Accounts with credit balances**
   - **Accounts settled by round sum payments**
   - **Accounts with nil balances**
   - **Accounts which** appear to have been **paid** by the date of the examination

3. (a) customers, solicitors
   (b) credit notes

4. (1) Level of sales, month by month
   (2) Price
   (3) Goods returned

5. Any two from:
   (1) Verify by reference to invoices, cash book correspondence
   (2) Check calculations by reperformance
   (3) Review detailed statement of financial position to ensure that all likely prepayments have been included
   (4) Use analytical procedures to review reasonableness

6. False.

   Understatement is tested by starting with source documents (for example, sales orders).

End of chapter question

Ridesafe Ltd (AIA May 2007)

You are the audit senior on the audit of Ridesafe Ltd for the year to 30 April 20X7. Ridesafe manufactures three types of safety car seats for children:

(1) Model A – a car seat for babies (up to 3 years).
(2) Model B – a car seat for children aged 3–12.
(3) Model C – a car seat that converts from a baby seat into a seat for older children.

Revenue has increased from $135,510 for the year to 30 April 20X6, to $208,760 for the year ended 30 April 20X7. The net profit before tax increased from $25,485 last year, to $45,620 for the year to 30 April 20X7. These increases are almost entirely due to the introduction of the new Model C. This new model has proved very popular with customers, and Ridesafe has a large order book for future supplies of this type of seat.

At the year-end, the figure for accounts receivable was $62,360 (20X6: $28,225). Details of the receivables ledger balances analysed by age are:

	20X7 $	20X6 $
0-30 days	20,390	15,800
31-60 days	14,555	9,029
61-90 days	10,235	2,265
91-120 days	9,537	987
121 days or more	7,643	144
Total receivables ledger balances	**62,360**	**28,225**

A receivables confirmation was performed by a junior member of the audit team, who selected 10 receivable balances from the receivables listing. The confirmation requests were sent out just after the year-end, and second requests were sent to non-replies. The receivables confirmation control schedule is:

Name	Balance per listing ($)	Comments on reply to receivables' confirmation
Abacus Ltd	567	No reply to 1st request. No reply to 2nd request.
Borus	1,120	Balance of $1,120 confirmed.
Findlay Ltd	163	Unable to confirm – the company does not operate a purchase ledger.
Granta Stores	356	Balance confirmed as nil. $156 paid by cheque dated 30 April 20X7, and an invoice for $200 does not relate to Granta Stores.
Hamelaw Group	4,540	Hamelaw Group will not pay because the balance relates to a consignment of Model C seats. Hamelaw are being sued by a customer who used one of the seats. A ragged edge on the seat caused injury to a child.
Malton plc	3,400	Balance of $3,400 confirmed.

Name	Balance per listing ($)	Comments on reply to receivables' confirmation
Orkney Ltd	1,690	Orkney returned a consignment of Model C seats on 14 May 20X7 because they had ragged edges. A credit note was issued for $1,690 on 30 May.
Pansy Ltd	446	Balance of $446 confirmed.
Total Trading	355	Request returned marked 'gone away'.
Vanguard Ltd	1,105	Balance of $600 confirmed. Vanguard have no knowledge of goods referred to in a Ridesafe invoice for 505, dated 20 January 20X7.

The client has supplied you with the following irrecoverable debts' allowance calculation:

	20X7 $	20X6 $
Specific allowance		
Ashley Ltd	250	
Shona Ltd	135	
Jules Ltd	215	
	600	500
General allowance	1,500	1,500
Total allowance for receivables	2,100	2,000

You have discussed the confirmation and the irrecoverable debt allowance with the audit manager. She has asked you to prepare notes detailing, for each type of difference in the confirmation, the additional audit work that will be required to determine the extent of any misstatement in the sales ledger. She has also asked you to review the irrecoverable debt allowance, and to provide her with notes in respect of any matters which you have found which have implications for other areas of the audit.

Required

(a) Describe the procedures that should be followed when carrying out a receivables confirmation.

(7 marks)

(b) Prepare notes for the audit manager detailing for each type of receivables balance difference identified, the additional audit work which will be required to be carried out. **(10 marks)**

(c) Prepare notes for the audit manager detailing the further work required on the allowance for receivables.

(6 marks)

(d) Explain whether or not you think the current allowance for receivables is adequate. **(6 marks)**

(e) Prepare notes for the audit manager identifying any other issues arising from the work on accounts receivable, which may have a wider impact on the audit of Ridesafe. **(6 marks)**

(Total = 35 marks)

Liabilities, expenses and capital

Topic list	Syllabus reference
1 Introduction	5.7
2 Payables	5.7
3 Purchases and other expenses	5.7
4 Wages and salaries	5.7
5 Accruals	5.7
6 Non-current liabilities	5.7
7 Provisions, contingent liabilities and contingent assets	5.7
8 Share capital, reserves and directors' emoluments	5.7

Introduction

In this chapter, we examine the audit of liabilities, including payables and accruals, provisions and non-current liabilities as well as purchases and other expenses.

When auditing payables, the auditor must test for understatement (ie completeness). Rather than sending a payables confirmation letter, it is more common to obtain audit evidence from suppliers' statement reconciliations.

Testing of purchases and other expenses is often carried out in conjunction with the audit of payables, as the two are linked. We also briefly consider the audit of accruals which is normally carried out using analytical procedures.

Auditing non-current liabilities can be a sensitive area of the audit as it affects the company's liquidity and gearing ratios and these may be closely related to bank borrowing covenants or debenture agreements. Testing for **understatement** and **completeness** is particularly important.

The audit of provisions can be particularly complex due to the accounting treatment and the degree of judgement involved in calculating the provision.

Section 8 discusses share capital, reserves and directors' emoluments. The audit objectives are to ascertain that:

(a) **Share capital** has been **properly classified** and **disclosed** in the financial statements and **changes** properly **authorised**.

(b) **Movements** on reserves have been properly **authorised** and, in the case of statutory reserves, **only used** for **permitted purposes**.

(c) **Statutory records** have been **properly maintained** and returns properly and expeditiously dealt with.

1 Introduction

1.1 Key assertions: purchases and payables

In this chapter we will examine the substantive audit of trade payables, purchases, accruals, non-current liabilities and provisions and end with a look at share capital, reserves and directors' emoluments.

The following table sets out the financial statement assertions to which audit testing is directed.

Assertions about classes of transactions and related disclosures	<ul><li>All purchase transactions recorded have occurred and relate to the entity (**occurrence**).</li><li>All purchase transactions that should have been recorded have been recorded (**completeness**).</li><li>Amounts relating to transactions have been recorded appropriately (**accuracy**).</li><li>Purchase transactions have been recorded in the correct period (**cut-off**).</li><li>Purchase transactions are recorded properly in the accounts (**classification**).</li><li>All disclosed events and transactions relating to liabilities have occurred and relate to the entity (**presentation**).</li><li>All disclosures required have been included (**presentation**).</li><li>Financial information is appropriately presented and described and disclosures clearly expressed (**presentation**).</li><li>Financial information is disclosed fairly and at appropriate amounts (**presentation**).</li></ul>
Assertions about period-end account balances and related disclosures	<ul><li>Trade payables and accrued expenses are valid liabilities (**existence**).</li><li>Trade payables and accrued expenses are the obligations of the entity (**rights and obligations**).</li><li>All liabilities have been recorded (**completeness**).</li><li>All liabilities are included in the accounts at appropriate amounts (**valuation and allocation**).</li><li>All disclosures required have been included (**presentation**).</li><li>Financial information is appropriately presented and described and disclosures clearly expressed (**presentation**).</li><li>Financial information is disclosed fairly and at appropriate amounts (**presentation**).</li></ul>

2 Payables

The largest figure in **current liabilities** will normally be **trade payables**, which is generally tested by comparison of **suppliers' statements** with **payables ledger accounts**.

2.1 Completeness

As with trade receivables, the trade payables figure is likely to be a material figure in the statement of financial position of most businesses. The purchases cycle tests of controls will have provided the auditors with some assurance as to the completeness of liabilities.

Auditors should however be particularly aware, when conducting their tests of detail, of the possibility of **understatement** of **liabilities** to improve liquidity and profits (by understating the corresponding purchases). The primary objective of their procedures will be to ascertain whether **liabilities** existing at the year-end have been **completely** and **accurately recorded**.

As regards **trade payables**, this primary objective can be subdivided into two detailed objectives.

- Is there a **satisfactory cut-off** between goods received and invoices received, so that purchases and trade payables are recognised in the correct year?
- Do trade payables represent the *bona fide* amounts due by the company?

2.2 Audit procedures relating to payables

Audit procedures for payables are set out in the table below which also covers the audit of purchases and accruals. Payables are often tested in conjunction with purchases.

Supplier statement reconciliations are used as an audit procedure in the table below and are described in more detail later in this section.

Audit plan: payables	
Completeness	<ul><li>Obtain a listing of trade payables and **agree** the total to the general ledger by casting and cross-casting.</li><li>Test for unrecorded liabilities by **enquiries of management** on how unrecorded liabilities and accruals are identified and examining post year end transactions.</li><li>Obtain selected suppliers' statements and **reconcile** these to the relevant suppliers' accounts.</li><li>Examine files of unmatched purchase orders and supplier invoices for any **unrecorded liabilities**.</li><li>Perform a **payables confirmation** for a sample of suppliers.</li><li>Complete the **disclosure checklist** to ensure that all the disclosures relevant to liabilities have been made.</li><li>**Compare** the current year balances for trade payables and accruals with the previous year.</li><li>**Compare** the amounts owed to a sample of individual suppliers in the trade payables listing with amounts owed to these suppliers in the previous year.</li><li>**Compare** the payables turnover and payables payment period to the previous year and industry data.</li><li>**Reperform casts** of **payroll records** to confirm completeness and accuracy.</li><li>**Confirm** payment of net pay per payroll records to cheque or bank transfer summary.</li></ul>

Audit plan: payables	
	• **Agree** net pay per cash book to payroll. • **Inspect** payroll for **unusual items** and **investigate** them further by **discussion** with management. • Perform **proof-in-total (analytical procedures)** on payroll and compare to figure in draft financial statements to assess reasonableness.
Existence	• **Vouch** selected amounts from the trade payables listing and accruals listing to supporting documentation, such as purchase orders and suppliers' invoices. • Obtain selected suppliers' statements and **reconcile** these to the relevant suppliers' accounts. • Perform a **payables confirmation** for a sample of suppliers. • Perform **analytical procedures** comparing current year balances with the previous year to confirm reasonableness, and also calculating payables' turnover and comparing with the previous year.
Rights and obligations	• **Vouch** a sample of balances to supporting documentation, such as purchase orders and suppliers' invoices, to obtain audit evidence regarding rights and obligations.
Accuracy, valuation and allocation	• **Trace** selected samples from the trade payables listing and accruals listing to the supporting documentation (purchase orders, minutes authorising expenditure, suppliers' invoices etc). • Obtain selected suppliers' statements and **reconcile** these to the relevant suppliers' accounts. • For a sample of **accruals, recalculate** the amount of the accrual to ensure the amount accrued is correct. • **Compare** the current year balances for trade payables and accruals with the previous year. • **Compare** the amounts owed to a sample of individual suppliers in the trade payables listing with amounts owed to these suppliers in the previous year. • **Compare** the payables turnover and payables payment period with the previous year and industry data, and investigate any significant differences. • **Recalculate** the mathematical accuracy of a sample of suppliers' invoices to confirm the amounts are correct. • **Recast** calculation of **remuneration**. • **Reperform** calculation of **statutory deductions** to confirm whether correct. • Confirm validity of **other deductions** by **agreeing** to supporting documentation. • **Recast** calculation of **other deductions**.
Cut-off	• For a sample of vouchers, **compare the dates** with the dates they were recorded in the ledger for application of correct cut-off. • **Test transactions** around the year end to determine whether amounts have been recognised in the correct financial period. • **Perform analytical procedures** on purchase returns, comparing the purchase returns as a percentage of sales or cost of sales to the previous year.

16: LIABILITIES, EXPENSES AND CAPITAL

Audit plan: payables	
Occurrence	• For a sample of vouchers, **inspect** supporting documentation, such as authorised purchase orders. • **Agree individual remuneration** per payroll to personnel records, records of hours worked, salary agreements etc. • Confirm **existence** of employees on payroll by meeting them, attending wages payout, inspecting personnel and tax records, and confirmation from managers. • **Agree benefits** on payroll to supporting correspondence.
Classification	• **Review** the trade payables listing to identify any large debits (which should be reclassified as receivables or deposits) or non-current liabilities which should be disclosed separately. • **Read** the disclosure notes relevant to liabilities in the draft financial statements and review for understandability.
Presentation	• **Read** the disclosure notes to ensure the information is accurate and properly presented at the appropriate amounts.

Question — Post year end payments

You are an audit senior responsible for testing completeness of payables at Dress You Like Co which has a year end of 30 September 20X6. You have decided to review payments made post year end in order to determine whether there are any unrecorded liabilities.

The following schedule shows the work performed on post year end payments, the work covers the period immediately after the year end:

Date of payment	Amount paid ($'000)	Included in payables ledger or accruals?	Explanation
1/10/20X6	25	Yes	
1/10/20X6	36	No	Payment for invoice to Freda's Fabrics dated 12/09/20X6
2/10/20X6	44	Yes	
2/10/20X6	21	Yes	
3/10/20X6	15	Yes	
3/10/20X6	98	Yes	
4/10/20X6	63	Yes	
4/10/20X6	51	Yes	
5/10/20X6	35	No	Payment for invoice to Three Linens Ltd dated 29/09/20X6
5/10/20X6	79	No	Payment for invoice to Fabricated dated 1/10/20X6

Date of payment	Amount paid ($'000)	Included in payables ledger or accruals?	Explanation
6/10/20X6	20	Yes	
6/10/20X6	75	Yes	
7/10/20X6	65	Yes	
7/10/20X6	8	No	Payment for internet – July to September 20X6

Required

(a) Consider the information in the schedule above. Explain the matters that you should consider relating to the payables balance at the year end.

(b) Describe the audit procedure that you have conducted in part (a) documenting the reason for the audit procedure.

Answer

(a) Matters to consider are:

(i) The payments to Freda's Fabrics and Three Linens Ltd both relate to invoices that were dated before the year end but have not been included in the year end purchase ledger. This means the purchase ledger is **understated** by $71,000 ($36,000 + $35,000) and purchases are understated by the same amount. An adjustment should be proposed to include the $71,000 in payables and purchases.

(ii) The payment to Fabricated is **correctly excluded** from the purchases ledger at year end since it relates to an invoice received after the year end.

(iii) The $8,000 payment for internet has not been included in the accruals listing. Since it relates to the provision of internet during the year ending 30 September 20X6, this indicates an understatement of accruals. An adjustment to include the $8,000 in accruals and expenses should be proposed.

(b) For a sample of post year end payments in the cash book, vouch the payment to supporting documentation (for example invoices, GRNs) to determine whether the payments relate to the year ending 30 September 20X6. If they do, vouch these amounts have been included in the purchases ledger or accruals listing to ensure completeness of payables and accruals. This test looks for unrecorded liabilities.

2.3 Trade payables listing

The list of balances will be one of the principal sources from which the auditors will select their samples for testing. The listing should be extracted from the payables ledger by the client. The auditors will carry out the following substantive tests to verify that the extraction has been properly performed.

- **Check** from the **payables ledger accounts** to the **list of balances** and *vice versa*.
- **Reconcile** the **total** of the list with the **payables ledger control account.**
- **Cast** the **list** of balances and the payables ledger control account.

The client should also prepare a detailed schedule of trade and sundry accrued expenses.

2.4 Confirmation of trade payables

We have already discussed the receivables confirmation procedure in Chapter 15. It is also possible to undertake confirmation of trade payables, although this is not used a great deal in practice because the auditor can test trade payables by examining **reliable, independent evidence** in the form of suppliers' invoices and suppliers' statements. However, where an entity's internal controls are assessed as deficient, suppliers' statements may not be available, and, in this situation, it may be relevant to undertake confirmation procedures. Confirmation of trade payables provides evidence primarily for the **completeness** assertion.

Where the entity has **strong controls** in place to ensure that all liabilities are recorded, the confirmation will focus on **large balances**.

Where the auditor is **concerned** about the presence of **unrecorded liabilities**, regular suppliers with **small or zero balances** on their accounts and a sample of **other accounts** will be confirmed as well as **large balances**.

Auditors use a **positive confirmation**, referred to as a **blank or zero-balance confirmation**. This confirmation **does not state** the balance owed but requires the supplier to declare the amount owed at the year end and to provide a detailed statement of the account. When the confirmation is received back, the amount must be **reconciled** with the entity's records. Differences between the balance confirmed and that on the payables ledger are likely to be for reasons that are similar to those for the receivables confirmation, ie goods in transit, cash in transit, or disputed invoices. Any differences should be investigated and reconciled.

The selection and sending out of payables' confirmations should be controlled using the same procedures as for the receivables' confirmation that we discussed in Chapter 15.

2.5 Reconciliations of payables with suppliers' statements

Many suppliers provide **monthly statements** to their customers. These may therefore be available in the entity for examination. Because they are a source of documentary evidence originating outside of the entity, they are a **reliable** source of evidence to support suppliers' balances and provide evidence as to the **existence, completeness** and **valuation** of balances.

Having said this, auditors do still need to be **cautious** when using them, as they may have been **tampered** with by the entity. The auditor should not rely on **photocopies or faxed statements**. If there is any doubt, the auditor should request a copy **directly** from the supplier or confirm the balance with the supplier (see above).

When selecting accounts for testing, the auditor should consider the **volume of business** during the year, not the balance outstanding at the year end, because the risk is understatement of balances. Most differences between balances on suppliers' statements and the year-end accounts payables' listing are likely to be due to goods and cash-in-transit and disputed amounts; however, all differences need to be investigated thoroughly.

Exam focus point | Testing suppliers' statements is frequently examined in auditing exams.

3 Purchases and other expenses

3.1 Purchases and expenses

When testing purchases and expenses, auditors are testing whether they are for **valid** reasons, that goods and services purchased have provided benefits to the company. They are also checking for **accuracy of recording** so again **cut-off** procedures will be important.

3.1.1 Occurrence and completeness of purchases

As with revenue, **analytical procedures** will be important. Auditors should consider:

- The **level of purchases and expenses** over the year, compared on a month-by-month basis with the previous year
- The effect on value of purchases of **changes in quantities purchased**
- The effect on purchases value of changes in **products** purchased (for example a change in ingredients), or **prices of products**
- How the **ratio of trade payables to purchases** compares with previous figures
- How the **ratio of trade payables to inventory** compares with previous years' figures

Audit plan: purchases – completeness and occurrence

- Agree **purchases and other expenses recorded** in the **payables or general ledger or cash book** to supporting documentation (books of prime entry, invoices, delivery notes) considering whether:
  - **Purchases and expenses are valid** (invoices addressed to the client, for goods and services ordered by the client, for the purposes of the business)
  - **Purchases** and expenses have been **allocated** to the correct **payables or general ledger** account
- Consider **reasonableness of deductions** from purchases or expenses by reference to subsequent events.
- Check whether **valid debts** are **recorded** in **payables ledger** by inspecting **credit notes.**

3.1.2 Purchases cut-off

The procedures applied by the auditors will be designed to ascertain whether:

- **Goods received** for which **no invoice** has been **received** are **accrued**
- **Goods received** which have been **invoiced** but **not yet posted** are **accrued**.
- **Goods returned** to suppliers **prior** to the **year-end** are **excluded** from **inventory** and **trade payables**

At the year-end inventory count the auditors will have made a note of the last serial numbers of goods received notes. Suggested substantive procedures are as follows.

Audit plan: purchases cut-off

- **Check from goods received notes** with serial numbers before the year-end to ensure that invoices are either:
  - Posted to payables ledger prior to the year-end, or
  - Included on the schedule of accruals
- **Review the schedule of accruals** to ensure that goods received after the year-end are not accrued.
- **Check from goods returned notes prior to year-end** to ensure that **credit notes** have been **posted** to the payables ledger prior to the year-end or accrued.
- **Review large invoices** and **credit notes** included after the year-end to ensure that they refer to the following year.
- **Review outstanding purchase orders** for indications of any purchases completed but not invoiced.
- **Reconcile daily batch invoice totals** around the year-end to payables ledger control ensuring batches are posted in the correct year.
- **Review** the **control account** around the year-end for **any unusual items**

Question — Analytical procedures: purchases

You have prepared the following schedule which compares the purchases of Dress You Like Co, a clothing manufacturer, for the year ending 30 September 20X6 with the purchases for the year ending 30 September 20X5.

Purchase	30/09/20X6 $'000	30/09/20X5 $'000	Difference $'000	Change %
Fabric	45,276	37,912	7,364	19%
Buckles, hooks and clips	75	75	–	0%
Thread	185	180	5	3%
Buttons	89	89	–	0%
Zips	50	75	(25)	–33%
Beads and sequins	102	66	36	55%
Payroll	12,677	11,721	956	8%
Telephone and internet	50	49	1	2%
Electricity	85	82	3	4%
Insurance	33	32	1	3%
Equipment maintenance	39	25	14	56%
Transportation costs	145	189	(44)	–23%
Other purchases	469	485	(16)	–3%
Total cost of sales	59,275	50,980	8,295	16%

Required

Use the analytical procedures performed on the schedule to explain the matters you should consider and further audit work that may be required for the audit of purchases for the year ended 30 September 20X6.

Note: exclude payroll costs.

Answer

(1) The largest purchase for Dress You Like Co is fabric which has increased by 19% compared to the prior year.

(2) We will need to ascertain why this is and should discuss with the production manager to determine whether the cost of fabrics has increased or whether Dress You Like Co is manufacturing more products and extra fabric is required.

(3) Alternatively, there may have been a misstatement and the figure for purchases of fabric is too high, due to an issue, for example, with cut-off of purchases. We need to obtain evidence that the increase is genuine.

(4) We can see that the purchases of zips have fallen by 33% which is unusual and transportation costs have fallen by 23% which seems strange. Both these variances will need further investigation, there may be some costs missing or costs may have been allocated incorrectly.

(5) The figure for equipment maintenance has increased by 56% year on year. This may be a legitimate increase as the company's equipment ages over time. However the increase might be due to a misclassification of costs from another area that should not be included in cost of sales. The same applies to the 55% increase in the cost of beads and sequins. We will need to look into both these increases.

3.1.3 Purchase of goods subject to reservation of title clauses

Under certain transactions, the seller may retain legal ownership of goods passed to a 'purchaser'. The requirements are known as 'reservation of title'.

In UK cases, particularly the *Romalpa* case, it is suggested that a reservation of title clause will only be upheld if it states that the seller has a charge over the goods and the goods, any products made from them and any sale proceeds are kept separately and are readily identifiable.

> **Audit plan purchases (reservation of title)**
>
> - **Ascertain** how the **client identifies suppliers selling** on terms which **reserve title** by enquiry of those responsible for purchasing and the board.
> - **Review** and test the **procedures** for **quantifying** or **estimating** the **liabilities**.
> - **Consider** whether **disclosure** is **sufficient** by itself if the directors have decided quantification is impractical.
> - **Consider** the adequacy of the **disclosures** in the accounts.
> - **Review the terms of sale** of **major suppliers** to confirm that liabilities not provided for do not exist or are immaterial.

Question — Trade payables and purchases

You have been assigned to the audit of Carter Brandon Co (CBC), and you are drafting the audit programme for payables and purchases for the year ended 31 December 20X7.

The company operates from a site in West Wendon. All raw materials are received in the stores and all deliveries are checked to the delivery note and purchase order. The stores supervisor raises a goods received note and is also responsible for raising credit requests if there are any problems with the raw materials delivered.

When the payables ledger department staff receive the purchase invoices, they match them to the relevant goods received notes and purchase orders, and post them to the computerised payables ledger. Suppliers are paid on the last day of each month.

Required

Describe the audit work you will carry out:

(a) To compare suppliers' statements with balances recorded on the payables ledger
(b) To check that purchases cut-off has been applied correctly.

Answer

(a) The audit work to compare suppliers' statements to the balances on the payables ledger is as follows.

Select a sample of balances and **compare suppliers' statements with payables ledger balances**. The extent of the sample will depend on the results of tests of controls and assessment of the effectiveness of controls within the purchases system (ie if the system of control is strong I will check fewer items).

Select the **sample on a random basis**. Selection of only large balances or those with many transactions will not yield an appropriate sample as I am looking for understatement of liabilities. Nil and negative balances will also need to be included in the sample.

If **no statement** was **available** for the supplier, I would ask for **confirmation** of the balance **from the supplier**.

If the balance **agrees exactly**, no further work needs to be carried out.

Where differences arise these need to be categorised as either in-transit items or other (including disputed) items.

In-transit items

In-transit items will be either goods or cash.

If the difference relates to goods in transit, I would **ascertain** whether the **goods** were **received** before the year-end by reference to the GRN and that they are included in year end inventory and purchase accruals. If not, a cut-off error has occurred and should be investigated.

If the goods were received after the year-end, the difference with the suppliers' accounts is correct.

Similarly, cash in-transit would arise where the payment to the supplier was made by cheque before the year-end but was not received by him until after the year-end. The **date** the **cheque** was **raised** and its subsequent **clearing** through the bank account after the year-end should be **verified by checking the cash book** and the post year-end bank statements.

However, if the cheque clears after the year-end date, it may indicate that the cheque, though raised before the year-end was not sent to the supplier until after the year-end. The relevant amount should be added back to year-end payables and to the end of year bank balance.

Other items

Differences which do not arise from in-transit items need to be investigated and **appropriate adjustments** made where necessary.

These differences may have arisen due to **disputed invoices**, where for example the client is demanding credit against an invoice which the supplier is not willing to agree. The client may decide not to post the invoice to the supplier account as he does not consider it to be a liability of the company. However, differences may also arise because **invoices** have been **held back** in order to reduce the level of year-end payables.

If significant unexplained differences are discovered it may be necessary to **extend** my **testing**. There may also be a problem if sufficient suppliers' statements are not available. Alternative procedures, eg an external confirmation may then be required.

(b) The audit work to verify that purchases cut-off has been correctly carried out at the year end is as follows.

   (i) From my notes taken at the inventory count I will have the **number** of the **last GRN** that was issued before the year-end.

   (ii) **Select a sample** of **GRNs** issued in the period immediately before and immediately after the year-end. The period to be covered would be at least two weeks either side of the year-end.

   (iii) **Concentrate** my sample on **high value items**, and more on those GRNs from before the year end as these represent the greatest risk of cut-off error.

   (iv) **Check** that the **GRNs** have a **correct number**, according to the last GRN issued in the year and whether the **goods** were **received before or after the year-end**.

   (v) For **GRNs** issued **before the year-end**, check whether the **inventory** has been included in the year-end **inventory** total. In addition, I will check whether that the **payable** is either **included** in **trade payables** or **purchase accruals**.

(vi) For **GRNs** issued **after the year-end**, to ensure that the **inventory** is **included** in the inventory records **after the year-end**. In addition, I will need to **check** to the **payables ledger** to ensure that the relevant **invoice** has been **posted** to the supplier account after the year-end.

4 Wages and salaries

4.1 Wages and salaries

Although auditors may test other expenses solely by analytical procedures, they may carry out more detailed testing on wages and salaries, partly because of the consequences of failure to deduct income tax correctly.

Analytical procedures will nonetheless be used to give some assurance on wages and salaries.

Auditors should consider:

- **Wages and salaries levels** month-by-month with **previous years**
- **Effect on wages and salaries of rate changes** during the year
- **Average wage** per month **over the year**
- **Sales/profits** per **employee**
- **Payroll proof in total** (pay rise × staff changes × staff mix)

Audit plan: wages and salaries payable	
Occurrence	• **Check individual remuneration** per payroll to **personnel records, records of hours** worked, **salary agreements** etc.
	• **Confirm existence** of **employees** on payroll by meeting them, attending wages payout, inspecting personnel and tax records, and confirmation from managers.
	• **Check benefits** (pensions) on payroll to **supporting documentation.**
Accuracy	• **Check accuracy of calculation of remuneration.**
	• **Check** whether **calculation** of **statutory deductions is correct.**
	• Check **validity** of **other deductions** (pension contributions, share save etc) by agreement to supporting documentation (personnel files, conditions of pension scheme) and **check accuracy** of **calculation** of other deductions.
Completeness	• **Check casts** of **payroll records.**
	• **Confirm** payment of **net pay** per payroll records to **cheque** or **bank transfer** summary.
	• **Agree net pay** per cash book to **payroll.**
	• **Scrutinise payroll** and **investigate unusual items.**

Question
Analytical procedures: purchases

The management accounts of Dress You Like Co contain the following schedule which compares the payroll expense for the years ending 30 September 20X6 and 30 September 20X5:

Month	Year ended 20X6 ($'000)	Year ended 20X5 ($'000)
October	980	933
November	1,254	1,165
December	1,508	1,180
January	990	936
February	995	937
March	989	937
April	988	937
May	991	937
June	992	937
July	993	940
August	999	942
September	998	940
Total	12,677	11,721

Required

(a) Consider the information in the above schedule. Explain any matters that might require investigation.

(b) What audit procedures you would perform on this schedule?

Answer

(a) The payroll expense for November and December is significantly higher than the other months in both periods and will need investigation to ensure there is not a misstatement of the expense in these months. The increase could have a legitimate explanation such as the payment of bonuses, overtime or hiring of temporary staff for a busy period.

The payroll expense for December 20X5 is $1,508,000 and seems particularly high being 28% higher than the expense in December 20X4. This will need investigation to determine whether the increase is genuine or a potential material misstatement.

Excluding November and December, the total payroll expense has increased by 6%. The reason for this needs to be investigated to ensure it is for a genuine reason (eg annual salary increases, increased number of staff) rather than a material misstatement.

(b) Audit procedures:

- Perform analytical procedures on the monthly payroll expense, comparing to the prior year and investigate any significant differences.
- Cast the figures in the payroll expense schedule to ensure its accuracy
- Agree the total payroll figure in the schedule to the trial balance.
- Agree the 20X4-20X5 payroll figure to the prior year financial statements and audit documentation.
- Agree the total payroll expense for all months in the schedule to the computerised wages system at Dress You Like Co.

- Agree the total payroll expense for all months in the schedule to the bank statements and cash book of Dress You Like Co
- Compare the 20X5-20X6 monthly payroll expense to budgeted figures and enquire of management the reason for any significant differences.

5 Accruals

FAST FORWARD

Auditors should review **after-date invoices and payments**, and consider whether anything else that would have been expected has not been accrued.

5.1 Sundry accruals

Checking the completeness and valuation of sundry accruals is an area that lends itself to **analytical procedures** and reconciliation techniques.

A variety of sources can indicate possible accruals. These include **last year's accruals**, **expense items** where an accrual would be expected, and **invoices received** and **cash paid** after the year-end.

Auditors should also use their **knowledge of the business** to consider whether there are accruals which they would expect to be there, but which may not be invoiced or paid until long after the year-end.

Audit plan: purchases accruals

- Check that **accruals** are **fairly calculated** and **verify** by reference to **subsequent payments** and **supporting documentation**.
- **Review the statement of profit or loss and other comprehensive income** and **prior years' figures** and consider liabilities inherent in the trade to **ensure** that all **likely accruals have been provided**.
- **Scrutinise payments** made **after year-end** to ascertain whether any payments made should be accrued.
- **Consider basis** for **round sum accruals** and ensure it is consistent with prior years.
- **Ascertain** why any **payments on account** are being **made** and **ensure** that the **full liability is provided**.
- **Income tax**; Normally this should represent one month's deductions. Check amount paid to taxation authorities by inspecting receipted annual declaration of tax paid over, or returned cheque.
- **Sales tax**: Check reasonableness to next return. **Verify last amount paid in year** per cash book to return.

Question — Accruals

Continuing the audit of Carter Brandon Co (CBC) for the year ended 31 December 20X7, you are now reviewing accruals.

You have been provided with a schedule of accruals and note that they relate to time-apportioned expenses such as electricity and telephone.

Required

Describe the audit work you will carry out to confirm that accruals are complete and have been accurately stated.

Answer

The audit work will include:

(i) **Assess the system of control** instituted by management to identify and quantify accruals and other liabilities.

(ii) Using the client's accruals listing, **recalculate accruals** to determine whether they have been **calculated correctly** and verify them by reference to subsequent payments. **Check** that **all time apportionments** have been made correctly (for example, for electricity).

(iii) **Review the statement of profit or loss and other comprehensive income** and **prior year figures** (for any accruals which have not appeared this year or which did not appear last year) and consider liabilities inherent in the trade (eg weekly wages) to ensure that all likely accruals have been provided.

(iv) **Scrutinise payments** made after the year-end to ascertain whether any payments made should be accrued. This will include consideration of any payments relating to the current year which are made a long time after the year-end.

(v) **Consider and document** the basis for **round sum accruals** and ensure it is consistent with prior years.

6 Non-current liabilities

FAST FORWARD

Non-current liabilities are usually **authorised** by the **board** and should be **well documented**.

We are concerned here with long-term liabilities comprising debentures, loan stock and other loans **repayable** at a date **more than one year after the year-end**.

Auditors will primarily try and determine:

- **Completeness:** whether all long-term liabilities have been disclosed
- **Accuracy:** whether interest payable has been calculated correctly and included in the correct accounting period
- **Classification:** whether long-term loans and interest have been correctly disclosed in the financial statements

The major complication for the auditors is that debenture and loan agreements frequently contain conditions with which the company must comply, including restrictions on the company's total borrowings and adherence to specific borrowing ratios.

6.1 Audit procedures relating to non-current liabilities

The audit procedures below relate to both non-current liabilities in the statement of financial position and the related finance charge in the statement of profit or loss.

Audit plan: non-current liabilities

- **Obtain/prepare schedule of loans** outstanding at the end of the reporting period showing, for each loan: name of lender, date of loan, maturity date, interest date, interest rate, balance at the end of the period and security.
- **Compare opening balances** to previous year's audited financial statements.
- **Test the clerical accuracy** of the analysis.

Audit plan: non-current liabilities

- **Compare balances** to the **general ledger**.
- **Agree name** of **lender** etc, to **register** of **debenture holders** or equivalent (if kept).
- **Trace additions** and **repayments** to **entries** in the **cash book**.
- **Confirm repayments** are in accordance with **loan agreement**.
- **Examine cancelled cheques** and **memoranda of satisfaction** for **loans repaid**.
- **Verify** that **borrowing limits** imposed either by Articles or by other agreements are **not exceeded**.
- **Examine signed Board minutes** relating to **new borrowings/repayments**.
- **Obtain direct confirmation** from **lenders** of the amounts outstanding, accrued interest and what security they hold.
- **Verify** that **interest charged** for the period is in accordance with known interest rates and **consider** the adequacy of accrued interest.
- **Confirm assets charged** have been **entered** in the **register of charges** and **notified** to the **Registrar**.
- **Review restrictive covenants** and provisions relating to default:
  - **Review** any **correspondence** relating to the loan
  - **Review confirmation** replies for non-compliance
  - If a **default appears** to exist, **determine** its **effect**, and schedule findings
- **Review minutes, cash book** to **check** if all **loans have been recorded**.
- **Review draft financial statements** to ensure that **disclosures** for non-current liabilities are in accordance with accounting standards/legal requirements. Verify that any element repayable within one year is classified under current liabilities.

Question

Non-current liabilities

You are responsible for the audit of non-current liabilities of HEC Ltd. You have reviewed the response to the bank confirmation letter and have noted that your client has a mortgage (a loan secured on property) which is repayable over 20 years.

Required

Describe audit procedures that should be conducted in relation to the mortgage.

Answer

The following audit procedures should be carried out:

- Vouch the total mortgage outstanding at the year end to the bank confirmation letter.
- Obtain a copy of the mortgage repayment schedule, agree the repayments to the mortgage documentation and recalculate the amounts which are due for repayment within the next 12 months and after more than one year. Vouch that the disclosure in the financial statements agrees to this schedule.
- Review the disclosure made in the financial statements in order to determine whether the fact that the property is pledged as security for the loan has been disclosed.
- Recalculate the finance charge in the statement of profit or loss by reference to the interest rate charged on the mortgage. Discuss any significant differences between the expected and actual finance charge with management.

7 Provisions, contingent liabilities and contingent assets

FAST FORWARD

The accounting rules governing provisions and contingencies are complex and that can make them difficult to audit.

7.1 Accounting issues

Key terms

A **provision** is a liability of uncertain timing or amount.

A **liability** is a present obligation of the entity arising from past events, the settlement of which is expected to result in an outflow from the entity of resources embodying economic benefits.

An **obligating event** is an event that creates a legal or constructive obligation that results in an entity having no realistic alternative to settling that obligation.

A **legal obligation** is an obligation that derives from:

(a) A contract (through its explicit or implicit terms);
(b) Legislation; or
(c) Other operation of law.

A **constructive obligation** is an obligation that derives from an entity's actions where:

(a) By an established pattern of past practice, published policies and sufficiently specific current statement, the entity has indicated to other parties that it will accept certain responsibilities, and

(b) As a result, the entity has created a valid expectation on the part of those other parties that it will discharge those responsibilities.

A **contingent liability** is:

(a) A possible obligation that arises from past events and whose existence will be confirmed only by the occurrence or non-occurrence of one or more uncertain future events not wholly within the control of the entity; or

(b) A present obligation that arises from past events but is not recognised because:

   (i) It is not probable that an outflow of resources embodying economic benefits will be required to settle the obligation; or

   (ii) The amount of the obligation cannot be measured with sufficient reliability.

A **contingent asset** is a possible asset that arises from past events and whose existence will be confirmed only by the occurrence or non-occurrence of one or more uncertain future events not wholly within the control of the entity.

Under IAS 37 *Provisions, Contingent Liabilities and Contingent Assets*, an entity should not recognise a **contingent asset** or a **contingent liability**. However if it becomes probable that an outflow of future economic benefits will be required for a previous contingent liability, a provision should be recognised (IAS 37: para. 30).

A contingent asset should not be accounted for unless its realisation is virtually certain; if an inflow of economic benefits has become probable, the asset should be disclosed (IAS 37: paras. 33 and 34).

The standard provides a table summarising when contingent assets and liabilities are to be recognised.

Provisions and contingent liabilities		
Where, as a result of past events, there may be a outflow of resources embodying future economic benefits in settlement of (a) a present obligation or (b) a possible obligation whose existence will be confirmed by the occurrence or non-occurrence of one or more uncertain future events not wholly within the enterprise's control, and		
There is a present obligation that probably requires an outflow of resources.	There is a possible obligation or a present obligation that may, but probably will not, require an outflow of resources.	There is a possible obligation or a present obligation where the likelihood of an outflow of resources is remote.
A provision is recognised and disclosures are required for the provision.	No provision is recognised but disclosures are required for the contingent liability.	No provision is recognised and no disclosure is required.

A contingent liability also arises in the extremely rare case **where there is a liability** that cannot be recognised because it cannot be **measured reliably**. Disclosures are required for the contingent liability.

Contingent assets		
Where, as a result of past events, there is a possible asset whose existence will be confirmed by the occurrence or non-occurrence of one or more uncertain future events not wholly within the enterprise's control, and		
The inflow of economic benefits is virtually certain.	The inflow of economic benefits is probable but not virtually certain.	The inflow is not probable.
The asset is not contingent.	No asset is recognised but disclosures are required.	No asset is recognised and no disclosure is required.

Examples of the principal types of contingencies disclosed by companies are:

- **Guarantees**
    - For other group companies
    - Of staff pension schemes
    - Of completion of contracts
- **Discounted bills of exchange**
- **Uncalled liabilities** on shares or loan stock
- **Lawsuits** or claims pending
- **Options** to purchase assets

7.2 Obtaining audit evidence of contingencies

Part of ISA 501 *Audit Evidence – Specific Considerations for Selected Items* covers contingencies relating to litigation and legal claims, which will represent the major part of audit work on contingencies. Litigation and claims involving the entity may have a material effect on the financial statements, and so will require adjustment to/disclosure in those financial statements. The auditor needs to carry out procedures designed to identify litigation and claims that might be materially misstated in the financial statements.

Such procedures would include the following.

16: LIABILITIES, EXPENSES AND CAPITAL

Audit plan: provisions/contingencies

- Make appropriate **inquiries of management** regarding provisions and contingencies, including obtaining written representations.
- Review minutes of meetings of those charged with governance and correspondence between the entity and its external legal counsel.
- **Review legal expense** account.

When audit procedures indicate that material litigation or claims may exist, or the auditor has assessed a risk of material misstatement relating to litigation, the auditor shall, seek direct communication with the entity's external legal counsel. This will help to obtain sufficient appropriate audit evidence as to whether potential material litigation and claims are known and management's estimates of the financial implications, including costs, are reliable.

This communication should be prepared by management, requesting the counsel to communicate directly with the auditor. If it is thought unlikely that the lawyer will respond to a general enquiry, the letter should specify the following.

(a) A list of **litigation and claims**

(b) **Management's assessment** of the outcome of the litigation or claim and its estimate of the financial implications, including costs involved

(c) A request that the **lawyer confirm the reasonableness** of management's assessments and provide the auditor with further information if the list is considered by the lawyer to be incomplete or incorrect

The auditors must consider these matters up to the date of their report and so a further, updating letter may be necessary.

A meeting between the auditors and the lawyer may be required, for example where a complex matter arises, or where there is a disagreement between management and the lawyer. Such meetings should take place only with the permission of management, and preferably with a management representative present.

ISA 501 states that:

> 'If management refuses to give the auditor permission to communicate or meet with the entity's external legal counsel, or the entity's external legal counsel refuses to respond appropriately to the letter of inquiry, or is prohibited from responding; and the auditor is unable to obtain sufficient appropriate audit evidence by performing alternative audit procedures, the auditor shall modify the opinion in the auditor's report in accordance with ISA 705 (Revised).'

7.3 Audit procedures relating to provisions and contingencies

The audit procedures below relate to both provisions and contingencies.

Audit plan: provisions/contingencies

- **Obtain details** of all **provisions** which have been included in the accounts and all **contingencies** that have been disclosed.
- **Obtain** a **detailed analysis** of all **provisions** showing opening balances, movements and closing balances.
- **Determine** for each material provision **whether** the **company** has a **present obligation** as a result of past events by:
    - **Review** of **correspondence** relating to the item

Audit plan: provisions/contingencies

- **Discussion** with the **directors**. Have they created a valid expectation in other parties that they will discharge the obligation?
- **Determine** for each material provision **whether** it is **probable** that a **transfer of economic benefits** will be required to settle the obligation by:
  - **Checking** whether any **payments** have been **made** after the end of the reporting period in respect of the item
  - **Review of correspondence** with solicitors, banks, customers, insurance company and suppliers both pre and post year-end
  - **Sending** a **letter** to the **solicitor** to obtain their views (where relevant)
  - **Discussing** the **position** of similar **past provisions** with the directors. Were these provisions eventually settled?
  - **Considering** the **likelihood** of **reimbursement**
- **Recalculate** all **provisions** made.
- **Compare** the **amount provided** with any post year-end payments and with any amount paid in the past for similar items.
- In the event that it is not possible to estimate the amount of the **provision**, check that this **contingent liability** is **disclosed** in the accounts.
- **Consider** the **nature** of the **client's business**. Would you expect to see any other provisions eg warranties?
- Consider adequacy of disclosure of **provisions, contingent assets** and **contingent liabilities**.

Exam focus point

You should appreciate that the problems of accounting for provisions and contingencies makes auditing them difficult.

Question — Provisions

You are auditor of WSD Co, a company that designs and installs audio and lightning equipment into public buildings (theatres, museums etc). WSD Co is being sued by one of its customers for breach of contract.

Required

(a) State the three criteria which must be satisfied in order for the directors of WSD Co to be required to make a provision in the financial statements; and

(b) Describe THREE audit procedures you would perform in this area.

Answer

(a) The three criteria from IAS 37 are:

- WSD Co must have a present obligation at the year-end as a result of a past event;
- It must be probable that an outflow of economic resources will be required to settle the obligation and
- It must be possible to make a best estimate of the amount.

(b) Audit procedures include:

- Discuss the nature of the claim with the management and review the customer contract to determine the nature of the breach of contract.
- Review any legal correspondence and determine WSD Co's solicitor's opinion as to whether the claim will be successful or not.
- Review the outcome of the claim in the post year-end period in terms of whether the case has gone to court or whether any amounts have been paid in settlement of the claim.

8 Share capital, reserves and directors' emoluments

FAST FORWARD

The main concern with **share capital** and **reserves** and **company books** is that the company has complied with the law.

8.1 Share (equity) capital, reserves and distributions

The issued share capital as stated in the accounts must be **agreed** in total with the **share register**. An examination of transfers on a test basis should be made in those cases where a company handles its own registration work. Where the registration work is dealt with by independent registrars, auditors will normally examine the reports submitted by them to the company, and obtain from them at the year-end a certificate of the share capital in issue.

Auditors should check carefully whether clients have complied with local legislation about share issues or purchase of own shares. Auditors should take particular care if there are any movements in reserves that cannot be distributed, and should **confirm** that these movements are **valid**.

8.2 Audit procedures relating to share capital and related issues

Audit plan: capital and related issues	
Share equity capital	• **Agree** the **authorised share capital** with the statutory documents governing the company's constitution. • **Agree changes** to **authorised share capital** with **properly authorised resolutions**.
Issue of shares	• **Verify any issue** of share capital or other changes during the year with general and board **minutes**. • **Ensure issue or change** is within the **terms** of the **constitution**, and directors possess appropriate authority to issue shares. • **Confirm** that **cash** or **other consideration** has been **received** or **receivable(s) is included** as called up share capital not paid.

Transfer of shares	• **Verify transfers of shares** by reference to:
	    – Correspondence
	    – Completed and stamped transfer forms
	    – Cancelled share certificates
	    – Minutes of directors' meeting
	• **Check the balances** on **shareholders' accounts** in the register of members and the total list with the amount of issued share capital in the general ledger.

Audit plan: capital and related issues	
Dividends	• **Agree dividends** paid and proposed to **authority** in minute books and **check calculation** with **total share capital** issued to ascertain whether there are any outstanding or unclaimed dividends. • **Check dividend payments** with **documentary evidence** (say, the returned dividend warrants). • **Check** that **dividends do not contravene** the distribution provisions of the legislation. • Check that **imputed tax** has been accounted for to the taxation authorities and correctly treated in the accounts.
Reserves	• **Check movements on reserves** to **supporting authority**. • **Ensure that movements on reserves do not contravene** the **legislation** and the company's constitution. • **Confirm** that the **company** can **distinguish** those reserves at the end of the reporting period that are **distributable** from those that are **non-distributable**. • **Ensure appropriate disclosures** of movements on reserves are made in the company's accounts.

8.3 Statutory books

Incorporated entities in all countries will be governed by some kind of local or national company legislation. Certain minimum standards of record-keeping will be normally required. In particular legislation may require specific records to be kept of share movements, minutes of management meetings, directors'/management shareholdings in the company and so on.

Audit plan: statutory books	
Register of members of governing board/ committee	• **Update permanent file** giving details of **board members.** • **Verify** any **changes** with the **minutes** and ensure that the necessary details have been filed at any central registry (if required by local legislation). • **Verify** that the **number of directors complies** with the **company's constitution.**
Register of managers'/directors' interests in shares and debentures	• **Ensure** that **managers'/directors' interests** are **noted** on the permanent file for cross-referencing to accounts. • **Ensure** that **shareholdings comply** with the **company's constitution.**
Minute books	• **Obtain photocopies** or **prepare extracts** from the **minute books** of meetings concerning financial matters, cross-referencing them to appropriate working papers. • **Ensure** that **extracts** of **agreements** referred to in the minutes are **prepared** for the permanent file. • **Note the date** of the last **minute reviewed.** • **Check** that **meetings** have been **properly convened** and that quorums attended them.

Audit plan: statutory books	
Register of interests in shares (if applicable)	• **Scrutinise register** and verify that *prima facie* it appears to be in order. • **Ensure** that **significant interests** are **noted on** the permanent file.
Register of charges	• **Update permanent file schedule** from the register. • **Ensure** that **any assets** which are **charged** as security for loans from third parties are **disclosed** in the accounts. • **Obtain confirmation** that there are **no charges** to be recorded if no entries are recorded in the register. • **Consider carrying out company search** at Central Registry to verify the accuracy of the register.

Accounting records	• Consider whether the accounting records are adequate to:
	  – **Show** and **explain** the **company's transactions**
	  – **Disclose** with **reasonable accuracy**, at any time, the **financial position** of the **company**
	  – **Comply** with **local legislation** by recording money received and expended, assets and liabilities, year-end inventory and physical inventory count, sales and purchases
	  – **Enable** the **managers/directors** to ensure that the **accounts give a true and fair view** or **present fairly**

General ledger and journals	• **Check opening balances** in general ledger to **previous year's audited** accounts. • **Check additions** of **general ledger accounts**. • **Review general ledger accounts** and ensure significant transfers and unusual items are *bona fide*. • **Review the journal** and ensure that significant entries are **authorised** and properly **recorded**. • **Check extraction** and **addition** of **trial balance** (if prepared by the client).
Returns	• **Check that regulatory returns** have been **filed** properly.
Managers'/ directors' service contracts	• **Inspect copies** of directors' service contracts or memoranda. • **Verify** that **long-term service contracts** have been **approved in general meeting**.

8.4 Directors' emoluments

The auditors may have a duty to include in their report the required disclosure particulars of directors' emoluments and transactions with directors, if these requirements have not been complied with in the accounts.

The auditors will have carried out an evaluation of salaries payroll procedures, including the system in operation for directors' salaries, earlier in the audit. At the year end, they can probably concentrate on limited substantive work designed to ensure that the final **figures** in the **accounting records** are **complete** and the disclosure requirements in respect of directors have been complied with.

8.5 Audit procedures relating to directors' emoluments

Audit plan: directors' emoluments

- **Ascertain** whether **monies payable or benefits** in kind provided have been **properly approved** in accordance with the company's memorandum and articles of association and that they are not prohibited by legislation.
- **Confirm** that all **monies payable** and **benefits receivable** in relation to the current accounting period have been **properly accounted for**, unless the right to any of these has been waived by inspecting:
    - Salary records
    - Service contracts
    - Board minutes
    - Other relevant records
- **Consider** whether the **most common types of benefit** (company cars or cheap loans) may have been **omitted**.
- **Review directors' service contracts.**
- **Review** the **company's procedures** to ensure that **all directors advise** the board of all disclosable **emoluments.**
- **Review** the **procedures** for ensuring that any **payments made to former directors** of the company are **identified** and **properly disclosed.**
- **Consider** the **need** for any **amounts** included in directors' remuneration to be **further disclosed** in accordance with legislation.

Question — Directors' emoluments

You are responsible for auditing the directors' emoluments of Dress You Like Co for the year ending 30 September 20X6 and have been provided with the information below:

	Fixed remuneration		Variable remuneration		
	Salary $	Pension $	Bonuses $	Incentive payments $	Total $
Gary Lewis (Chairman)	120,000	40,000	90,000	–	250,000
Katie Escombe (Chief Finance Officer)	80,000	32,000	50,000	–	162,000
Fred Gurth (CEO)	75,000	15,000	–	–	90,000
Mary Batter (CEO)	20,000	6,500	5,000	10,000	41,500
	295,000	93,500	145,000	10,000	543,500

During the year Fred Gurth resigned as CEO and left the company on 31 July 20X6, Mary Batter was appointed CEO on 1 August 20X6.

Required

Describe the substantive procedures you should perform on each element of the schedule to obtain sufficient and appropriate evidence in relation to director's emoluments.

Answer

Salary:

- Vouch salary amounts to monthly payroll records and bank statements to ensure the amounts are accurate.
- For Fred Gurth, vouch his leaving date to HR records and board meeting minutes. Recalculate his salary on a pro-rata basis to ensure it is accurately recorded.
- For Mary Batter, obtain her start date from the HR department and vouch this to board meeting minutes. Recalculate her salary on a pro-rata basis to ensure it is accurately recorded.

Pension:

- Vouch the pension amounts to monthly payroll records and bank statements to ensure the amounts are accurate

Bonuses:

- Vouch the level of bonuses awarded to board meeting minutes, payroll records and bank statements to ensure they have been authorised and are accurately recorded.

Incentive payments:

- Review the employment contract for Mary Batter to verify that there is a clause outlining that this payment is applicable.
- Vouch the level of this payment to board meeting minutes, payroll records and bank statements.

General:

- Recast the schedule to ensure the note is accurate.
- Review the disclosure to ensure that it is in accordance with applicable law and accounting standards.

Chapter roundup

- The largest figure within **current liabilities** will normally be **trade payables**, this is generally audited by comparison of **suppliers' statements** with **payables ledger accounts.**

- Auditors should also review **after-date invoices received** and **payments made**, in order to consider whether there are any liabilities or accruals which have not been recognised at the year end.

- **Purchases and other expenses** are often tested alongside trade payables although **analytical procedures** may also be conducted.

- **Wages and salaries** are also tested using **analytical procedures** although payments may also be vouched to payroll records and employment contracts (particularly for directors' emoluments).

- **Non-current liabilities** are usually **authorised** by the board and should be well documented.

- The accounting rules governing provisions and contingencies are complex and that can make them difficult to audit.

- The main concern with **share capital, reserves** and **company books** is that the company has complied with the law.

Quick quiz

1. What are the two primary objectives of work on liabilities?

    (1) ....

    (2) ....

2. Nil balances should not be included in a supplier statement test.

    True ☐

    False ☐

3. Give two instances where a trade payable confirmation may be required.

    (1) ....

    (2) ....

4. Give four factors auditors should consider when carrying out analytical procedures on wages and salaries.

    (1) ....

    (2) ....

    (3) ....

    (4) ....

5. Complete the definition:

    Non-current liabilities comprise ...., ...-.................... and other loans .... at a date .... a year .... the year-end.

6. What are the audit objectives relating to share capital?

    (1) ....

    (2) ....

    (3) ....

7. Name three audit procedures in relation to minutes of directors' meetings.

    (1) ....

    (2) ....

    (3) ....

8. Name three sources of information on directors' emoluments.

    (1) ....

    (2) ....

    (3) ....

Answers to quick quiz

1. To ensure (1) completely and (2) accurately recorded

2. False

3. (1) Supplier statements are unavailable
   (2) Weak internal controls

4. (1) Salary rate changes
   (2) Average wage by month over the year
   (3) Salary/employee
   (4) Payroll proof in total

5. debentures, loan-stock, repayable, more than, after.

6. Share capital has been (1) properly classified and (2) disclosed in the financial statements and changes are (3) properly authorised.

7. Any three from:
   (1) Obtain photocopies of minutes relating to FS items.
   (2) Ensure that extracts of agreements in minutes are copied to permanent audit file.
   (3) Note the date of the last minute reviewed.
   (4) Check that meetings have been properly convened/attended.

8. (1) Salary records
   (2) Service contracts
   (3) Board minutes

End of chapter question

Olorosa Ltd (AIA May 2005)

You are the auditor of Olorosa Ltd. The company's draft statement of financial position for the year shows the following amounts under 'share capital and reserves':

	$'000
Ordinary share capital	550
Share premium account	75
Revaluation reserve	120
Retained earnings	85
	830

The company paid a dividend of $25,000 during the year, and the directors are proposing a final dividend of $15,000.

Required

(a) Describe the general audit objectives for share capital, reserves and dividends. **(10 marks)**

(b) Describe the specific audit tests that you would carry out to verify the revaluation reserve. **(5 marks)**

(Total = 15 marks)

Audit completion and review

Topic list	Syllabus reference
1 Going concern	6
2 Subsequent events	6.5
3 Written representations	6.4
4 Overall review of financial statements	6.6
5 Final completion issues	6.7, 6.8, 6.9, 6.10

Introduction

This chapter will consider the reviews that take place to complete the audit.

There are two key reviews:

- Going concern
- Subsequent events

These are both important disclosure issues in the financial statements. If the disclosures are not appropriate, this will impact on the **auditors' report**.

Certain matters must be confirmed in writing by management in written representations before the audit report can be signed.

The auditor will carry out an **overall review of the financial statements** and the uncorrected misstatements that have been detected during the audit are analysed to determine their impact on the auditor's report.

These procedures are extremely important; failure to carry them out can lead to the gravest consequences for the auditors. Given this fact, they tend to be fairly standard in most audit approaches.

1 Going concern

FAST FORWARD

Auditors must consider the **future plans** of directors and any signs of **going concern problems** which may be noted throughout the audit.

1.1 The going concern basis of accounting

Key term

Under the '**going concern basis of accounting**' an entity is ordinarily viewed as continuing its operations for the **foreseeable future**. When the use of the going concern basis of accounting is appropriate, assets and liabilities are recorded on the basis that the entity will be able to realise its assets and discharge its liabilities in the normal course of business.

ISA 570 (Revised) *Going Concern* states that 'The objectives of the auditor are:

(a) To **obtain sufficient appropriate audit evidence** regarding, and conclude on, the **appropriateness** of management's use of the **going concern basis of accounting** in the preparation of the financial statements;

(b) To **conclude**, based on the audit evidence obtained, **whether a material uncertainty exists** related to events or conditions that may cast significant doubt on the entity's ability to continue as a going concern; and

(c) To **report in accordance with ISA 570 (Revised)**.

When preparing accounts, **management** shall make a specific **assessment** of the entity's ability to continue as a going concern. Most financial reporting frameworks, for example that provided by IAS 1 *Presentation of Financial Statements*, require management to do so.

When management are making the assessment, the following factors should be considered.

(a) The **degree of uncertainty** about the events or conditions being assessed increases significantly the further into the future the assessment is made.

(b) Judgements are made on the basis of the **information available** at the time.

(c) Judgements are affected by the **size** and **complexity** of the entity, the **nature** and **condition** of the business and the **degree** to which it is **affected** by **external factors**.

ISA 570 (Revised) includes examples of events or conditions that may cast doubt about the going concern basis of accounting. These fall under three headings: 'financial', 'operating' and 'other', and are shown in the table below.

Events or conditions that may cast doubt about the entity's ability to continue as a going concern	
Financial	• Net liability or net current liability position
	• Fixed-term borrowings approaching maturity without realistic prospects of renewal or repayment
	• Excessive reliance on short-term borrowings to finance long-term assets
	• Withdrawal of financial support by creditors
	• Negative operating cash flows
	• Adverse key financial ratios
	• Substantial operating losses or significant deterioration in the value of assets used to generate cash flows
	• Arrears or discontinuance of dividends
	• Inability to pay creditors on due dates
	• Inability to comply with terms of loan agreements

17: AUDIT COMPLETION AND REVIEW

Events or conditions that may cast doubt about the entity's ability to continue as a going concern	
	• Change from credit to cash on delivery transactions with suppliers • Inability to obtain financing for essential new product development or other essential investments
Operating	• Management intentions to liquidate or cease operations • Loss of key management without replacement • Loss of a major market, key customers, licence, or principal suppliers • Labour difficulties • Shortages of important supplies • Emergence of a highly successful competitor
Other	• Non-compliance with capital or other statutory requirements • Pending legal or regulatory proceedings against the entity • Changes in law or regulations that may adversely affect the entity • Uninsured or under-insured catastrophes when they occur

Exam focus point

A question on going concern might ask you to identify signs that a particular client may not be a going concern.

The significance of such indications can often be **mitigated** by other factors.

(a) The effect of an entity being unable to make its normal debt repayments may be counterbalanced by management's plans to maintain **adequate cash flows** by alternative means, such as by disposal of assets, rescheduling of loan repayments, or obtaining additional capital.

(b) The loss of a principal supplier may be mitigated by the availability of a suitable alternative source of supply.

1.2 Management's responsibilities for going concern

Management has specific responsibilities relating to going concern that may be set out in law or regulation and in the financial reporting framework. IAS 1 *Presentation of Financial Statements* contains a specific requirement that management makes an assessment of an entity's ability to continue as a going concern.

Because general purpose financial statements are prepared on a going concern basis, the going concern basis of accounting is a **fundamental principle** in the preparation of financial statements. Therefore management's responsibility for the preparation and presentation of the financial statements also encompasses a responsibility to assess the entity's ability to continue as a going concern even if there is no explicit requirement to do so in the financial reporting framework.

Management's assessment involves making a **judgement** about inherently uncertain future outcomes of events or conditions. This judgement is affected by the following:

- **Degree of uncertainty** which increases the further into the future an event/condition/outcome occurs
- **Size and complexity** of the entity
- **Nature and condition** of the business
- Judgement about the future is based on **information available** at the time the judgement is made but **subsequent events** may result in **inconsistent outcomes**

This section highlights why audit work on going concern is crucial – because of the **judgements** used by management in making its assessment of going concern.

1.3 Management's assessment

Management may have performed a **preliminary assessment** of whether the entity can continue as a going concern. If it has, the auditor shall discuss it with management. If the assessment has not been performed, the auditor shall discuss with management the basis for the intended use of the going concern assumption.

The auditor shall **remain alert** throughout the audit for evidence of events or conditions that may cast significant doubt on the entity's ability to continue as a going concern.

The auditor shall **evaluate** management's assessment of the entity's ability to continue as a going concern. However, if this assessment covers less than 12 months from the date of the financial statements, the auditor shall ask management to extend its assessment period to **at least 12 months** from that date.

The auditor shall also inquire of management its knowledge of events or conditions beyond the period of the assessment that may cast significant doubt on the entity's ability to continue as a going concern.

1.4 Auditors' responsibilities

FAST FORWARD

> When reporting on the accounts, auditors shall consider whether the going concern basis is **appropriate**, and whether **disclosure** of going concern problems is **sufficient**.

1.4.1 Events or conditions identified

If events or conditions are identified that may cast significant doubt on the entity's ability to continue as a going concern, the auditor shall obtain sufficient appropriate audit evidence to determine whether a material uncertainty exists by:

- Requesting management to make its **assessment** where this has not been done
- Evaluating management's **plans for future action**
- Evaluating the **reliability of underlying data** used to prepare a cash flow forecast and considering the **assumptions** used to make the forecast
- Considering whether any **additional facts or information** have become available since the date management made its assessment
- Requesting **written representations** from management and those charged with governance about plans for future action and the feasibility of these plans

Specific audit procedures the auditor might carry out could include the following:

- **Analyse and discuss cash flow**, profit and other relevant forecasts with management
- **Analyse and discuss** the entity's latest available **interim financial statements** (or management accounts)
- **Review the terms of debentures and loan agreements** and determine whether they have been breached
- **Read minutes** of the meetings of shareholders, the board of directors and important committees for reference to financing difficulties
- **Inquire** of the entity's lawyer regarding **litigation and claims**
- **Confirm the existence, legality and enforceability** of arrangements to provide or maintain financial support with related and third parties
- **Assess** the **financial ability** of such parties to **provide additional funds**

- **Consider the entity's position** concerning unfulfilled customer orders
- **Review events after the period-end** for items affecting the entity's ability to continue as a going concern

1.5 Audit reporting

The auditor shall consider whether a **material uncertainty** exists related to events or conditions which may cast doubt on the entity's ability to continue as a going concern, as this will have an impact on the opinion issued in the auditor's report because the uncertainty must be disclosed.

A material uncertainty relating to going concern is a **key audit matter** as defined by ISA 701 *Communicating Key Audit Matters in the Independent Auditor's Report*. However, it would not be reported as one due to other reporting requirements.

Key term

> A **material uncertainty** exists when the magnitude of its potential impact and likelihood of occurrence is such that, in the auditor's judgement, appropriate disclosure of the nature and implications of the uncertainty is necessary for the fair presentation of the financial statements (for a fair presentation financial reporting framework) or for the financial statements not to be misleading (for a compliance framework).

The following table summarises the possible scenarios that could arise following the auditor's review of going concern. We discuss audit reporting in the next chapter, so you may wish to revisit this section again after having studied that material. ISA 570 (Revised) does provide example extracts in respect of the following scenarios and these are presented in the following table.

Scenario	Impact on auditor's report
1 Going concern basis of accounting appropriate but material uncertainty exists which is adequately disclosed (Scenario 1)	**Unmodified opinion** and explanatory paragraph titled **'Material Uncertainty Related to Going Concern'**
2 Going concern basis of accounting appropriate but material uncertainty exists which is not adequately disclosed (Scenario 2)	**Qualified opinion** or **adverse opinion** (ie modified opinion)
3 Use of going concern basis of accounting inappropriate (Scenario 3)	**Adverse opinion** (ie modified opinion)
4 Management unwilling to make or extend its assessment (Scenario 4)	**Qualified opinion** or **disclaimer of opinion** (ie modified opinion)

Scenario 1: Going concern assumption appropriate but material uncertainty exists which is adequately disclosed

In this situation, the **opinion** on the financial statements will be **unmodified** but the auditor's report will include an explanatory paragraph immediately below the Basis for Opinion paragraph, headed 'Material Uncertainty Related to Going Concern' detailing the uncertainty. The ISA contains an example of such an extract from the auditor's report:

> **Opinion**
>
> We have audited the financial statements of ABC Company ('the Company'), which comprise the statement of financial position as at December 31, 20X1, and the statement of comprehensive income, statement of changes in equity and statement of cash flows for the year then ended, and notes to the financial statements, including a summary of significant accounting policies. In our opinion, the accompanying financial statements present fairly, in all material respects, (or give a true and fair view of) the financial position of the Company as at December 31, 20X1, and (of) its financial performance and its cash flows for the year then ended in accordance with International Financial Reporting Standards (IFRSs).

Basis for Opinion

We conducted our audit in accordance with International Standards on Auditing (ISAs). Our responsibilities under those standards are further described in the Auditor's Responsibilities for the Audit of the Financial Statements section of our report. We are independent of the Company in accordance with the ethical requirements that are relevant to our audit of the financial statements in [jurisdiction], and we have fulfilled our other ethical responsibilities in accordance with these requirements. We believe that the audit evidence we have obtained is sufficient and appropriate to provide a basis for our opinion.

Material Uncertainty Related to Going Concern

We draw attention to Note 6 in the financial statements, which indicates that the Company incurred a net loss of ZZZ during the year ended December 31, 20X1 and, as of that date, the Company's current liabilities exceeded its total assets by YYY. As stated in Note 6, these events or conditions, along with other matters as set forth in Note 6, indicate that a material uncertainty exists that may cast significant doubt on the Company's ability to continue as a going concern. Our opinion is not modified in respect of this matter.

Key Audit Matters

Key audit matters are those matters that, in our professional judgment, were of most significance in our audit of the financial statements of the current period. These matters were addressed in the context of our audit of the financial statements as a whole, and in forming our opinion thereon, and we do not provide a separate opinion on these matters. In addition to the matter described in the Material Uncertainty Related to Going Concern section, we have determined the matters described below to be the key audit matters to be communicated in our report.

[Description of each key audit matter in accordance with ISA 701.]

Scenario 2: Going concern assumption appropriate but material uncertainty exists which is not adequately disclosed

In this situation, as inadequate disclosure has been made of the material uncertainty, the auditor's opinion will be modified – either a qualified or adverse opinion will be issued depending on the magnitude of the failure to disclosure. An extract from the auditor's report where a qualified opinion is issued is provided by the ISA and set out below:

Qualified Opinion

In our opinion, except for the incomplete disclosure of the information referred to in the Basis for Qualified Opinion paragraph, the accompanying financial statements present fairly, in all material respects (or 'give a true and fair view of') the financial position of the Company as at December 31, 20X0, and (of) its financial performance and its cash flows for the year then ended in accordance with International Financial Reporting Standards.

Basis for Qualified Opinion

As discussed in Note X, The Company's financing arrangements expire and amounts outstanding are payable on March 19, 20X1. The Company has been unable to conclude re-negotiations or obtain replacement financing. This situation indicates that a material uncertainty exists that may cast significant doubt on the Company's ability to continue as a going concern. The financial statements do not adequately disclose this matter.

> **Key Audit Matters**
>
> Key audit matters are those matters that, in our professional judgment, were of most significance in our audit of the financial statements of the current period. These matters were addressed in the context of our audit of the financial statements as a whole, and in forming our opinion thereon, and we do not provide a separate opinion on these matters. In addition to the matter described in the Basis for Qualified Opinion section, we have determined the matters described below to be the key audit matters to be communicated in our report.
>
> [Descriptions of each key audit matter in accordance with ISA 701.]

Scenario 3: Use of going concern assumption inappropriate

When the going concern assumption has been used but this is considered inappropriate by the auditor, an adverse opinion must be issued, regardless of whether or not the financial statements include disclosure of the inappropriateness of management's use of the going concern assumption. We will look at adverse opinions in more detail in the next chapter.

Scenario 4: Management unwilling to make or extend its assessment

In some circumstances, the auditor may ask management to make or extend its assessment. If management does not do this, a qualified opinion or a disclaimer of opinion in the auditor's report may be appropriate, because it may not be possible for the auditor to obtain **sufficient appropriate audit evidence** regarding the use of the going concern basis of accounting in the preparation of the financial statements. Examples of auditor's reports with a disclaimer of opinion are provided in the next chapter, when we look at modifications to the auditor's opinion in detail.

1.6 Communicating to those charged with governance

The auditor shall **communicate with those charged with governance** events or conditions that may cast doubt on the entity's ability to continue as a going concern. This will include:

- Whether the events or conditions constitute a material uncertainty
- Whether the use of the going concern basis of accounting is appropriate in the preparation and presentation of the financial statements
- The adequacy of related disclosures
- Implications for the auditor's report, if necessary

Question — Going concern

During the course of your audit of a client, you have discovered that the company is having cash flow problems, and has breached its covenants with its bank.

Required

(a) Describe the responsibilities of the directors and of the auditors in respect of the going concern status of a company.

(b) Explain how the audit report may be affected where there is uncertainty about the going concern status of a company.

Answer

(a) Going concern is a fundamental principle in the preparation of financial statements. It is the responsibility of the directors preparing the financial statements to make an assessment of whether or not the entity is a going concern and to prepare the financial statements accordingly.

ISA 570 (Revised) *Going Concern* requires the auditor to evaluate the directors' assessment of the entity's ability to continue as a going concern. In order to do this, there are some specific procedures the auditor shall perform such as making enquiries of the directors, as well as a requirement by the ISA to remain alert to any events or circumstances discovered during the course of the audit that may influence the going concern assessment. The evaluation should begin at the planning stages and continue throughout the audit.

If the auditor becomes aware of a situation or event that does cast into doubt the ability of the entity to continue as a going concern, then ISA 570 (Revised) requires the auditor to gather further evidence to confirm or dispel the doubt. Any concerns that the auditors have regarding going concern shall be fully documented and researched. If the auditor is able to obtain sufficient appropriate evidence to enable them to conclude that the entity is a going concern then they will be able to conclude that the financial statements do show a true and fair view.

(b) ISA 570 (Revised) defines a material uncertainty as existing when the magnitude of the potential impact of an event is such that, in the auditor's judgement, clear disclosure of the nature and implications of the uncertainty is necessary for the presentation of the financial statements not to be misleading.

An example of this would be a court case, the decision of which is vital to the continuation of the business, but the result of which is unknown at the year-end. Where there is material uncertainty over going concern, but the auditors do not disagree with the use of the going concern basis of accounting and disclosure is adequate, then a 'material uncertainty related to going concern' section shall be included in the auditor's report. The content of this section will be determined by the extent of the auditors' concerns. If disclosure is not adequate, the auditor will not be able to conclude that the accounts give a true and fair view, and so will express a qualified opinion.

If the auditors are not satisfied that the directors made or extended (if required) their assessment of the going concern basis of accounting, the audit opinion shall disclaim the opinion.

An adverse audit opinion shall be expressed where the auditors disagree with preparation using the going concern basis of accounting.

2 Subsequent events

> **FAST FORWARD**
>
> Auditors should consider the effect of **subsequent events** (after the end of the reporting period) on the accounts.

'Subsequent events' include:

- Events occurring between the period end and the date of the auditor's report
- Facts discovered after the date of the auditor's report

You should remember from your accounting studies that IAS 10 *Events After the Reporting Period* deals with the treatment in the financial statements of events, both favourable and unfavourable, occurring after the period end. It identifies two types of event:

- Those that provide further evidence of conditions that existed at the period end (adjusting events)
- Those that are indicative of conditions that arose subsequent to the period end (non-adjusting events)

17: AUDIT COMPLETION AND REVIEW

ISA 560 *Subsequent Events* states that 'the **objectives** of the auditor are:

(a) To obtain sufficient appropriate audit evidence about whether events occurring between the date of the financial statements and the date of the auditor's report that require adjustment of, or disclosure in, the financial statements are appropriately reflected in those financial statements in accordance with the applicable financial reporting framework; and

(b) To respond appropriately to facts that become known to the auditor after the date of the auditor's report, that, had they been known to the auditor at that date, may have caused the auditor to amend the auditor's report.'

2.1 Procedures

FAST FORWARD

Auditors have a responsibility to **review subsequent events** before they sign their audit report, and may have to take action if they become aware of subsequent events between the date they sign their audit report and the date the financial statements are laid before members.

The following time line is helpful when considering subsequent events and the auditor's responsibilities concerning them.

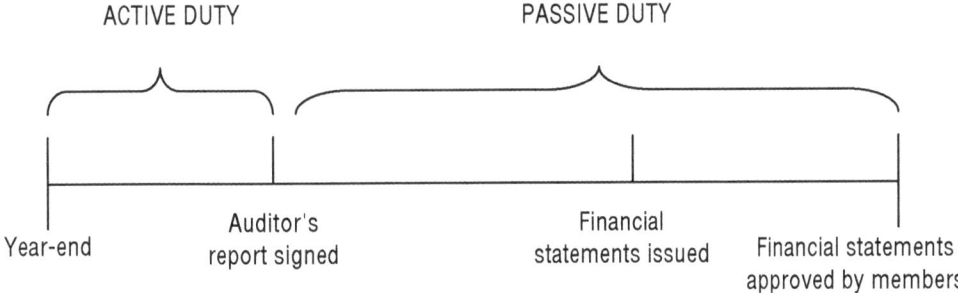

2.1.1 Events occurring between the date of the financial statements and the date of the auditor's report

'The auditor shall perform audit procedures designed to obtain sufficient appropriate audit evidence that all events occurring between the date of the financial statements and the date of the auditor's report that require adjustment of, or disclosure in, the financial statements have been identified.'

These procedures should be applied to any matters examined during the audit which may be susceptible to change after the year end. They are in addition to tests on specific transactions after the period end, eg cut-off tests. The ISA lists procedures to identify subsequent events which may require adjustment or disclosure. They should be performed as near as possible to the date of the auditors' report.

	Procedures testing subsequent events
Enquiries of management	Inquiring of management and, where appropriate, those charged with governance as to whether any subsequent events have occurred which might affect the financial statements.
	Status of items involving **subjective judgement**/accounted for using preliminary data
	Specific inquiry relating to:
	• Whether new commitments, borrowings or guarantees have been entered into.
	• Whether sales or acquisitions of assets have occurred or are planned.
	• Whether there have been increases in capital or issuance of debt instruments, such as the issue of new shares or debentures, or an agreement to merge or liquidate has been made or is planned.

	Procedures testing subsequent events
	• Whether any assets have been appropriated by government or destroyed, for example, by fire or flood. • Whether there have been any developments regarding contingencies. • Whether any unusual accounting adjustments have been made or are contemplated. • Whether any events have occurred or are likely to occur that will bring into question the appropriateness of accounting policies used in the financial statements, as would be the case, for example, if such events call into question the validity of the going concern assumption. • Whether any events have occurred that are relevant to the measurement of estimates or provisions made in the financial statements. • Whether any events have occurred relevant to the recoverability of assets.
Other procedures	Obtaining an understanding of any **procedures management has established** to ensure that subsequent events are identified. **Reading minutes**, if any, of the meetings, of the entity's owners, management and those charged with governance, that have been held after the date of the financial statements. Reading the entity's latest subsequent **interim financial statements**, if any. Obtain evidence concerning any **litigation or claims** from the company's solicitors (only with client permission)

Reviews and updates of these procedures may be required, depending on the length of the time between the procedures and the signing of the auditors' report and the susceptibility of the items to change over time. 'When the auditor becomes aware of events which materially affect the financial statements, the auditor should consider whether such events are properly accounted for and adequately disclosed in the financial statements.'

2.1.2 Facts discovered after the date of the auditor's report but before the financial statements are issued

The financial statements are the management's responsibility. They should therefore inform the auditors of any material subsequent events between the date of the auditors' report and the date the financial statements are issued. The auditors do **not** have any obligation to perform procedures, or make enquires regarding the financial statements **after** the date of their report.

'.... if, after the date of the auditor's report but before the date the financial statements are issued, a fact becomes known to the auditor that, had it been known to the auditor at the date of the auditor's report, may have caused the auditor to amend the auditor's report, the auditor shall:

(a) Discuss the matter with management and, where appropriate, those charged with governance;
(b) Determine whether the financial statements need amendment and, if so;
(c) Inquire how management intends to address the matter in the financial statements.'

When the financial statements are amended, the auditors should **extend the procedures** discussed above to the **date of their new report**, carry out any other appropriate procedures and issue a new audit report dated the day it is signed.

The situation may arise where the statements are not amended but the auditors feel that they should be. The ISA says '...if management does not amend the financial statements in circumstances where the auditor believes they need to be amended, then:

(a) If the auditor's report has not yet been provided to the entity, the auditor shall modify the opinion as required by ISA 705 (Revised) and then provide the auditor's report; or

(b) If the auditor's report has already been provided to the entity, the auditor shall notify management and, unless all of those charged with governance are involved in managing the entity, those charged with governance, not to issue the financial statements to third parties before the necessary

amendments have been made. If the financial statements are nevertheless subsequently issued without the necessary amendments, the auditor shall take appropriate action, to seek to prevent reliance on the auditor's report.'

The action taken will depend on the auditors' legal rights and obligations and the advice of the auditors' lawyer.

2.1.3 Facts discovered after the financial statements have been issued

Auditors have no obligations to perform procedures or make enquiries regarding the financial statements **after** they have been issued. '...if, after the financial statements have been issued, a fact becomes known to the auditor that, had it been known to the auditor at the date of the auditor's report, may have caused the auditor to amend the auditor's report, the auditor shall:

(a) Discuss the matter with management and, where appropriate, those charged with governance;
(b) Determine whether the financial statements need amendment and, if so;
(c) Inquire how management intends to address the matter in the financial statements.

The ISA gives the appropriate procedures which the auditors should undertake when management revises the financial statements.

(a) **Carry out the audit procedures** necessary in the circumstances.

(b) **Review the steps taken by management** to ensure that anyone in receipt of the previously issued financial statements together with the auditors' report thereon is informed of the situation.

(c) **Extend the audit procedures**....to the date of the new auditor's report and **issue a new report** on the revised financial statements.

'The auditor shall include in the new or amended auditor's report an Emphasis of Matter paragraph or Other Matter(s) paragraph referring to a note to the financial statements that more extensively discusses the reason for the amendment of the previously issued financial statements and to the earlier report provided by the auditor.'

Where local regulations allow the auditor to restrict the audit procedures on the financial statements to the effects of the subsequent event which caused the revision, the new auditor's report should contain a statement to that effect.

Where the management does **not** revise the financial statements but the auditors feel they should be revised, or if the management does not intend to take steps to ensure anyone in receipt of the previously issued financial statements is informed of the situation, then the auditors shall consider steps to take, on a timely basis, to prevent reliance on their report. The actions taken will depend on the auditors' legal rights and obligations (eg to contact the shareholders directly) and legal advice received.

2.2 Significant delay in the approval of the financial statements

If there is a significant delay in the approval of the financial statements, the auditors must ask the reason for the delay. If the auditor thinks the reason may be due to events or conditions relating to the going concern assessment, the auditor must carry out additional procedures as we set out in Section 1.4 above and consider the effect on the auditor's conclusion regarding the possible existence of a material uncertainty.

Question — Subsequent events

You are the audit senior finalising the audit of Dress You Like Co for the year ending 30 September 20X6. Revenue is $51,895,000 and profit before tax is $1,025,000.

During the audit you learned that the finance director left the company in March 20X6 and was suing Dress You Like Co for constructive dismissal. After much discussion between the audit partner and directors of Dress You Like Co, the company agreed to make a provision of $100,000 in relation to this claim.

It is now 18 November 20X6 and the auditor's report has not yet been signed. As part of your finalisation procedures you have spoken to Dress You Like Co's legal counsel and they have informed you that the finance director won their case for constructive dismissal. Dress You Like have been ordered to pay damages of $500,000 by the court.

Required

Explain whether the financial statements of Dress You Like Co for the year ending 30 September 20X6 will need amending in relation to the result of the court case with the legal director.

Answer

Dress You Like Co have made a provision of $100,000 for a court case but the settlement was for $500,000 and so the provision is understated by $400,000 on the statement of financial position. Correspondingly, profit in the statement of profit and loss is overstated by the same amount and expenses are understated by $400,000.

The amount of the misstatement is 0.8% ($400,000/$51,895,000) of revenue and 39% ($400,000/$1,025,000) of profit before tax. It is therefore borderline material to revenue but material to profit before tax.

The settlement of a court case between the year-end date and the date the financial statements are signed is an adjusting event.

The financial statements of Dress You Like Co for the year ending 30 September 20X6 will need to be adjusted before the auditor's report is signed.

3 Written representations

FAST FORWARD

> The auditor obtains **written representations** from management concerning its responsibilities and to support other audit evidence where necessary.

Key term

> **Written representations** are written statements by management provided to the auditor to confirm certain matters or to support other audit evidence. They do not include the financial statements, assertions or supporting books and records.

ISA 580 *Written Representations* provides guidance to auditors in this area. The objectives of the auditor are:

- To obtain written representations that management believes that it has fulfilled the fundamental responsibilities that constitute the premise on which an audit is conducted

- To support other audit evidence relevant to the financial statements if determined by the auditor or required by other ISAs

- To respond appropriately to written representations or if management does not provide written representations requested by the auditor

3.1 Written representations about management's responsibilities

The auditor shall request management to provide written general representations on the following matters:

- That management has fulfilled its responsibility for the **preparation and presentation of the financial statements** as set out in the terms of the audit engagement and whether the financial statements are prepared and presented in accordance with the applicable financial reporting framework
- That management has provided the auditor with all **relevant information** agreed in the terms of the audit engagement and that all transactions have been recorded and are reflected in the financial statements
- A description of management's responsibilities

3.2 Other written representations

Other ISAs require written representations but if the auditor considers it necessary to obtain specific representations in order to support other audit evidence, the auditor shall request these other written specific representations.

The following table includes examples of other written representations.

Other written representations
Whether the selection and application of accounting policies are appropriate
Plans or intentions that may affect the carrying value or classification of assets and liabilities
Liabilities, both actual and contingent
Title to, or control over, assets, liens or encumbrances on assets and assets pledged as collateral
Aspects of laws, regulations and contractual agreements that may affect the financial statements, including non-compliance
All deficiencies in internal control that management is aware of have been communicated to the auditor
Written representations about specific assertions in the financial statements
Significant assumptions used in making accounting estimates are reasonable
All subsequent events requiring adjustment or disclosure have been adjusted or disclosed
The effects of uncorrected misstatements are immaterial, both individually and in aggregate
Disclosed the results of management's assessment of the risk that the financial statements may be materially misstated as a result of fraud
Disclosed all information in relation to fraud or suspected fraud involving management, employees with significant roles in internal control, and others where fraud could have a material effect on the financial statements
Disclosed all information in relation to allegations of fraud or suspected fraud communicated by employees, former employees, analysts, regulators or others
Disclosed all instances of non-compliance or suspected non-compliance with laws or regulations

3.3 Form of written representations

The written representations shall be in the form of a representation **letter** addressed to the auditor.
ISA 580 includes an example representation letter in an appendix.

3.4 Doubt about the reliability of written representations

Written representations are more reliable than oral representations, since oral representations can be retracted.

However, although written representations are a form of audit evidence, they are from an internal source and **on their own** they **do not provide sufficient appropriate audit evidence** about the issues they relate to.

If written representations are **inconsistent** with other audit evidence, the auditor shall perform audit procedures to try to resolve the matter. If the matter cannot be resolved, the auditor shall reconsider the assessment of the competence, integrity and ethical values of management, and the effect this may have on the reliability of representations and audit evidence in general.

If the auditor concludes that written representations are not reliable, the auditor shall take appropriate actions, including determining the impact on the auditor's report.

3.5 Written representations not provided

If management does not provide one or more requested written representations, the auditor shall:

- **Discuss** the matter with management.
- **Re-evaluate** the integrity of management and evaluate the effect this may have on the reliability of representations and audit evidence in general.
- Take **appropriate actions**, including determining the **impact** on the auditor's report.

Question — Written representations

Required

Explain, with reasons, whether or not the auditor should request a written representation in relation to following scenarios:

(a) To confirm that management has adjusted or disclosed all events subsequent to the date of the financial statements where adjustment or disclosure is required.

(b) To confirm that management has disclosed any fraud affecting the company under audit during the year.

(c) To confirm the disposal of delivery vans with a material value.

Answer

(a) The auditor should request a written representation. Confirming that management has adjusted or disclosed all events subsequent to the date of the financial statements where adjustment or disclosure is required is a requirement of ISA 560 *Subsequent Events*.

(b) The auditor should request a written representation. ISA 240 *The Auditors' Responsibilities Relating to Fraud in an Audit of Financial Statements* requires a written representation from management which, amongst other things, requires management to confirm that they disclosed any fraud or suspected fraud affecting the entity.

(c) The auditor should not request a written representation. Sufficient appropriate audit evidence should be available via other means (eg inspecting sales contracts, cash received in bank statements etc) and would not need to be supported by a written representation.

4 Overall review of financial statements

> **FAST FORWARD**
>
> The auditors must perform and document an **overall review** of the financial statements by undertaking **analytical procedures** before they can reach an opinion.

Once most of the substantive procedures have been carried out, the auditors will have a draft set of financial statements which should be supported by appropriate and sufficient audit evidence. As the beginning of the end of the audit process, it is usual for the auditors to undertake an **overall review** of the financial statements.

This review of the financial statements, in conjunction with the conclusions drawn from the other audit evidence obtained, gives the auditors a reasonable basis for their opinion on the financial statements. It should be carried out by a senior member of the audit team, with appropriate skills and experience.

4.1 Compliance with accounting regulations

The auditors should consider whether:

(a) The information presented in the financial statements is in accordance with local/national statutory requirements.

(b) The accounting policies employed are in accordance with accounting standards, properly disclosed, consistently applied and appropriate to the entity. For the purposes of this international paper, the main concern will be IFRS Accounting Standards.

When examining the **accounting policies**, auditors should consider:

(a) Policies **commonly adopted in particular industries**

(b) Policies for which there is **substantial authoritative support**

(c) Whether any **departures from applicable accounting standards** are necessary for the financial statements to give a true and fair view

(d) Whether the **financial statements reflect the substance** of the underlying transactions and not merely their form

When compliance with local/national statutory requirements and accounting standards is considered, the auditors may find it useful to use a **checklist**.

4.2 Review for consistency and reasonableness

The auditors should consider whether the financial statements are consistent with their knowledge of the entity's business and with the results of other audit procedures, and the manner of disclosure is fair.

The principal considerations are as follows.

(a) Whether the financial statements adequately reflect the **information** and **explanations** previously obtained and conclusions previously reached during the course of the audit

(b) Whether it reveals any **new factors** which may affect the presentation of, or disclosure in, the financial statements

(c) Whether **analytical procedures** applied when completing the audit, such as comparing the information in the financial statements with other pertinent data, **produce results** which assist in arriving at the overall conclusion as to whether the financial statements as a whole are consistent with their knowledge of the entity's business)

(d) Whether the **presentation** adopted in the financial statements may have been unduly influenced by the **directors' desire** to present matters in a favourable or unfavourable light

(e) The potential impact on the financial statements of the **aggregate of uncorrected misstatements** (including those arising from bias in making accounting estimates) identified during the course of the audit and the preceding period's audit, if any

Analytical procedures at the final stage should cover the following:

- Important accounting ratios
- Related items
- Changes in products/customers
- Price and mix changes
- Wages changes
- Variances
- Trends in production and sales
- Changes in material and labour content of production
- Other expenditure in the statement of profit or loss
- Variations caused by industry or economy factors

As at other stages, significant fluctuations and unexpected relationships must be investigated by **enquiries of management** and obtaining appropriate audit evidence relevant to **management's responses**, and **performing other audit procedures** considered necessary.

4.3 Problems of accounting treatment

As noted in the previous section auditors review the financial statements to assess whether the **accounting policies are consistently applied**. Auditors should therefore consider whether new accounting policies are appropriate, whether matters in the financial statements are consistent with each other, and whether financial statements give a true and fair view.

4.4 Alternative treatments

From your accounting studies, you should also be aware that there are some accounting standards which allow a choice of treatments. As always, when reviewing the accounting treatment used, the auditors should consider whether they provide a true and fair view.

5 Final completion issues

FAST FORWARD

> As part of their completion procedures, auditors should consider whether the **aggregate of uncorrected misstatements** is material.

5.1 Misstatements

Key terms

A **misstatement** is a difference between the amount, classification, presentation, or disclosure of a reported financial statement item and the amount, classification, presentation, or disclosure that is required for the item to be in accordance with the applicable financial reporting framework. It can arise from error or fraud.

An **uncorrected misstatement** is a misstatement accumulated during the audit by the auditor which has not been corrected.

ISA 450 *Evaluation of Misstatements Identified During the Audit* requires the auditor to accumulate misstatements identified during the audit, other than those that are clearly trivial. The ISA distinguishes between **factual misstatements** (misstatements about which there is no doubt), **judgemental misstatements** (misstatements arising from management's judgement concerning accounting estimates or accounting policies) and **projected misstatements** (the auditor's best estimate of misstatements arising from sampling populations).

ISA 450 requires the auditor to **communicate all misstatements** accumulated during the audit with the appropriate level of management on a timely basis and to request management to correct those misstatements. If management refuses, the auditor must establish the reasons why and consider this when evaluating whether the financial statements as a whole are free from material misstatement.

As part of their completion procedures, auditors shall consider whether the **aggregate of uncorrected misstatements** in the financial statements is **material**, having first reassessed materiality in accordance with ISA 320 *Materiality in Planning and Performing an Audit* to confirm that it is still appropriate. When determining whether uncorrected misstatements are material (individually or in aggregate), the auditor shall consider the size and nature of the misstatements and the effect of uncorrected misstatements related to prior periods on the financial statements as a whole.

5.2 Summarising misstatements

Whilst many misstatements will be corrected during the audit, some misstatements may still be outstanding at the end of the audit and the auditors will summarise these **uncorrected misstatements**.

The summary of misstatements will not only list misstatements from the current year, but also those in the previous year(s). This will allow misstatements to be highlighted which are reversals of misstatements in the previous year, such as in the valuation of closing/opening inventory. Cumulative misstatements may also be shown, which have increased from year to year. It is normal to show both the statement of financial position and the statement of profit or loss and other comprehensive income, as in the example given here.

SCHEDULE OF UNCORRECTED MISSTATEMENTS

		20X2				20X1			
		Statement of profit or loss and other comprehensive income		Statement of financial position		Statement of profit or loss and other comprehensive income		Statement of financial position	
		Dr $	Cr $	Dr $	Cr $	Dr $	Cr $	Dr $	Cr $
(a)	ABC Co debt unprovided	10,470			10,470	4,523			4,523
(b)	Opening / closing inventory undervalued*		21,540		21,540		21,540	21,540	
(c)	Closing inventory undervalued		34,105	34,105					
(d)	Opening unaccrued expenses								
	Telephone*		453	453			453		453
	Electricity*		905	905			905		905
(e)	Closing unaccrued expenses								
	Telephone	427			427				
	Electricity	1,128			1,128				
(f)	Obsolete inventory write off	2,528			2,528	3,211			3,211
	Total	36,093	35,463	35,463	36,093	9,092	21,540	21,540	9,092
	*Cancelling items	21,540			21,540				
			453	453					
			905	905					
		14,553	34,105	34,105	14,553				

5.3 Evaluating the effect of uncorrected misstatements

ISA 450 states that when evaluating the effect of uncorrected misstatements 'The auditor shall determine whether uncorrected misstatements are **material, individually or in aggregate**'.

The aggregate of uncorrected misstatements comprises:

(a) **Specific misstatements** identified by the auditors, including the net effect of uncorrected misstatements identified during the audit of the previous period

(b) Their **best estimate of other misstatements** which cannot be quantified specifically (ie projected misstatements)

If the auditors consider that the aggregate of misstatements may be material, they must consider reducing audit risk by extending audit procedures or requesting management to adjust the financial statements (which management may wish to do anyway).

If management refuses to adjust the financial statements and the results of extended audit procedures do not enable the auditor to conclude that the aggregate of uncorrected misstatements is not material, the auditor should consider the appropriate modification to the auditor's report.

If the aggregate of the uncorrected misstatements that the auditors have identified approaches the materiality level, the auditors should consider whether it is likely that undetected misstatements, when taken with aggregated uncorrected misstatements, could exceed the materiality level. Thus, as aggregate uncorrected misstatements approach the materiality level the auditors should consider reducing the risk by:

(a) **Performing additional audit procedures or**
(b) By **requesting management** to adjust the financial statements for identified misstatements

The schedule will be used by the audit manager and partner to decide whether the client should be requested to make adjustments to the financial statements to correct the misstatements.

5.4 Documenting misstatements

ISA 450 (para. 15) requires the auditor to document the following information:

- The amount below which misstatements would be regarded as clearly trivial
- All misstatements accumulated during the audit and whether they have been corrected
- The auditor's conclusion as to whether uncorrected misstatements are material and the basis for that conclusion

5.5 Completion checklists

Audit firms frequently use **checklists** which must be signed off to ensure that all final procedures have been carried out and that all material amounts are supported by sufficient appropriate audit evidence.

5.6 Disclosure checklists

The auditor provides an opinion not just on the amounts in the financial statements but also in relation to presentation (disclosure). As such it is imperative that the auditor is satisfied that the presentation within the financial statements conforms to accounting standards as well as any relevant legal requirements. Audit firms will tend to complete a **disclosure checklist** in order to determine whether the presentation of items in the financial statements is appropriate.

5.7 Final meeting with clients

At the end of the audit, but **before the auditor's report is signed**, senior members of the audit team (such as the audit partner and audit manager) should hold a meeting with the client. Ideally this should be with the audit committee (if one exists), if not then with those charged with governance at the entity.

The primary purpose of the meeting is to present the audit findings and conclusions, to ensure a clear understanding of the results, and agree on the timeframe for any corrective action that needs to be taken.

If the auditor plans to modify their auditor's report in any way, this should also be discussed as should any findings during the current year audit that may impact on the following year's audit.

5.8 Points for future audits

During the course of the current year audit, the audit team will maintain a record of any information that may affect the audit for the following year. These may include:

- Difficulties encountered during the current year audit that make require extra audit time the following year
- Subsequent events that are likely to have an impact on the audit for the following year
- Future planned changes in accounting or internal control systems
- Proposed changes to the client's business/operations

5.9 Quality management

Quality management procedures should be implemented throughout the audit process from planning the audit, to conducting it and through to the final review stage.

At the **final review stage**, the auditor should consider whether:

- The work has been performed in accordance with the firm's policies or procedures, professional standards and applicable legal and regulatory requirements
- Significant matters have been raised for further consideration
- Appropriate **consultations** have taken place and the resulting **conclusions** have been **documented** and implemented
- There is a need to revise the nature, timing and extent of work performed
- The **work performed supports the conclusions reached** and is appropriately documented
- The evidence obtained is sufficient and appropriate to provide a basis for the auditor's opinion
- The objectives of the audit procedures have been achieved

(ISA 220 (Revised): para. A88)

Before the auditor's report is issued, the engagement partner must be sure that sufficient and appropriate audit evidence has been obtained to support the audit opinion. Reviews should be carried out at the appropriate stage of the audit, in order to ensure that any significant matters are resolved on a timely basis.

The audit engagement partner need not review all audit documentation, but may do so. They should review significant matters, significant judgements and other important matters (ISA 220 (Revised): para. 31).

Chapter roundup

- Auditors must consider the **future plans** of directors and any signs of **going concern problems** which may be noted throughout the audit.
- When reporting on the financial statements, auditors should consider whether the going concern basis of accounting is **appropriate**, and whether **disclosure** of any going concern problems is **sufficient**.
- Auditors should consider the effect of **subsequent events** (after the end of the reporting period) on the financial statements.
- Auditors have a responsibility to **review subsequent events** before they sign their audit report, and may have to take action if they become aware of subsequent events between the date they sign their audit report and the date the financial statements are laid before members.
- The auditor obtains **written representations** from management concerning its responsibilities and to support other audit evidence where necessary.
- The auditors must perform and document an **overall review** of the financial statements before they can reach an opinion.
- As part of their completion procedures, auditors should consider whether the **aggregate of uncorrected misstatements** is material, they should also hold a final meeting with the audit client which presents the audit findings and conclusions.

Quick quiz

1. Complete the definition, using the words given below.

   The .... basis of accounting: the entity is viewed as .... its operations for the ....

intention, future, going, necessity, continuing, foreseeable, trading, concern

2. Complete the table putting the indicators of an entity's inability to continue as a going concern under the correct headings.

Financial	**Operating**	**Other**
(a) Legal proceedings	(c) Loss of key market	(e) Withdrawal of financial support by creditors
(b) Inability to pay creditors	(d) Loss of key licence	
		(f) Loss of key management

3. The directors must satisfy themselves that the going concern basis of accounting in the financial statements is appropriate.

   True ☐
   False ☐

4. Name three enquiries that should be made of management to test subsequent events.

   (1) ....
   (2) ....
   (3) ....

5. Name two written representations that the auditor would always be expected to obtain.

   (1) ....
   (2) ....

6. Name four factors which the auditors should consider when examining accounting policies.

   (1) ....
   (2) ....
   (3) ....
   (4) ....

7. Give five examples of what areas analytical procedures at the final stage should cover.

   (1) ....
   (2) ....
   (3) ....
   (4) ....
   (5) ....

8. In evaluating whether the financial statement give a true and fair view, auditors should assess the materiality of the aggregate of uncorrected misstatements.

   True ☐
   False ☐

Answers to quick quiz

1. going concern, continuing, foreseeable future

2.
Financial	Operating	Other
(b) (e)	(c) (d) (f)	(a)

3. True

4. From:
   - What the status is of items involving subjective judgement
   - Whether there are any new commitments, borrowings or guarantees
   - Whether any assets have been sold or destroyed
   - Whether any new shares/debentures have been issued
   - Whether there have been any developments in risk areas
   - Any unusual accounting adjustments
   - Any major events

5. (1) Acknowledgement of management's responsibilities for preparation of the financial statements
   (2) All transactions have been recorded and are reflected in the financial statements.

6. (1) Policies **commonly adopted in particular industries**
   (2) Policies for which there is **substantial authoritative support**
   (3) Whether any **departures from applicable accounting standards** are necessary for the financial statements to give a true and fair view
   (4) Whether the **financial statements reflect the substance** of the underlying transactions and not merely their form

7. From:
   - Important accounting ratios
   - Related items
   - Changes in products/customers
   - Price and mix changes
   - Wages changes
   - Variances
   - Trends in production and sales
   - Changes in material and labour content of production
   - Other expenditure in the statement of profit or loss and other comprehensive income
   - Variations caused by industry or economy factors

8. True

End of chapter question

Subsequent events and going concern (AIA Nov 2009) (amended)

You are the auditor of Serif Ltd, a paper-making business, and you are nearing the end of the audit for the year ended 31 January 20X9. You are considering the form of the audit report which you are about to issue.

You have become aware of one matter which is causing you some concern. In February 20X9, the directors of Serif Ltd decided to sell one of their four paper mills. The decision was made because the company is seriously short of cash and needed the money from the sale. The paper mill which was sold was the most profitable mill owned by the company. Of the remaining three, two made losses in the last financial year, and the other mill just managed to breakeven.

Required

(a) Explain why the auditor should be concerned about events such as the sale of the mill, since it was a transaction which took place after the year end. **(5 marks)**

(b) Outline the auditor's responsibilities in respect of the going concern status of Serif Ltd, as described in ISA 570 (Revised) *Going Concern*. **(7 marks)**

(c) Discuss how Serif's going concern status might have an impact in the audit opinion in the audit report. **(8 marks)**

(Total = 20 marks)

Audit reports

Topic list	Syllabus reference
1 The auditors' report on financial statements	7.1
2 Unmodified opinions in the auditor's report	7.2
3 Modified opinions in the auditor's report	7.2
4 Changes to the auditor's report	7.3
5 Other reporting responsibilities	7.3

Introduction

The **auditor's report** is the means by which the external auditors express their opinion on the **truth and fairness** of a company's financial statements. This is principally for the benefit of the shareholders, but also for other users as the auditor's report is usually kept on public record, with the filed financial statements.

Many of the contents of the auditor's report are prescribed by statute (for example, the *UK Companies Act 2006*), they are also subject to the professional requirements in the form of ISA 700 (Revised) *Forming an Opinion and Reporting on Financial Statements*.

The auditor's report may contain an unmodified or a modified opinion. The different types of modified opinion are considered in detail in this chapter. Sometimes it is necessary to bring matters to the user's attention without modifying the audit opinion. We will see how key audit matters, emphasis of matter and other matter paragraphs can be used to do just that.

1 The auditors' report on financial statements

FAST FORWARD

The auditor is required to produce an **auditor's report** at the end of the audit which sets out their opinion on the **truth and fairness** of the financial statements. The report contains a number of consistent **elements** so that users know the audit has been conducted according to **recognised standards**.

Point to note

> **RPQ Students**
> The UK has adopted ISA 700 (Revised) *Forming an Opinion and Reporting on Financial Statements*. The FRC revised several ISAs (UK) in June 2016 and again in November 2019 and updated ISA (UK) 700 (Revised) in May 2022. These can be found on the FRC website in the standards and guidance section.

Auditor's reports are covered by the following ISAs:

- ISA 700 (Revised) *Forming an Opinion and Reporting on Financial Statements*
- ISA 701 *Communicating Key Audit Matters in the Independent Auditor's Report*
- ISA 705 (Revised) *Modifications to the Opinion in the Independent Auditor's Report*
- ISA 706 (Revised) *Emphasis of Matter Paragraphs and Other Matter Paragraphs in the Independent Auditor's Report*

ISA 700 (Revised) *Forming an Opinion and Reporting on Financial Statements* establishes standards and provides guidance on the form and content of the auditor's report issued as a result of an audit performed by an independent auditor of the financial statements of an entity.

It states that 'The auditor shall form an opinion on whether the financial statements are prepared, in all material respects, in accordance with the **applicable financial reporting framework**' (ISA 700 (Revised): para. 10).

In forming an opinion the auditor needs to consider whether **sufficient, appropriate audit evidence** has been obtained, and whether **uncorrected misstatements are material** (either individually or in aggregate).

Furthermore the auditor will need to evaluate:

- Whether the financial statements are **prepared**, in all material respects, in accordance with the requirements of the **applicable financial reporting framework**.
- Whether in view of the requirements of the applicable financial reporting framework:
  - The financial statements **adequately disclose** the **significant accounting policies** selected and applied;
  - The **accounting policies** selected and applied are **consistent** with the applicable financial reporting framework and are appropriate;
  - The **accounting estimates** made by management are **reasonable**;
  - The **information** presented in the financial statements is **relevant, reliable, comparable and understandable**;
  - The financial statements provide **adequate disclosures** to enable the intended users to understand the effect of material transactions and events on the information conveyed in the financial statements; and
  - The **terminology** used in the financial statements, including the title of each financial statement, is **appropriate**.
- Whether the financial statements adequately refer to or describe the applicable financial reporting framework.

(ISA 700 (Revised): para. 11-15)

2 Unmodified opinions in the auditor's report

Key term

> An **unmodified opinion** is the opinion expressed by the auditor when the auditor concludes that the financial statements give a true and fair view (or are presented fairly) and are prepared, in all material respects, in accordance with the applicable financial reporting framework (ISA 700 (Revised): para. 16).

An example auditor's report with an **unmodified opinion** is given in ISA 700 (Revised) *Forming an Opinion and Reporting on Financial Statements* (Appendix Illustration 1).

INDEPENDENT AUDITOR'S REPORT

To the Shareholders of ABC Company [or Other Appropriate Addressee]

Report on the Audit of the Financial Statements

Opinion

We have audited the financial statements of ABC Company (the Company), which comprise the statement of financial position as at December 31, 20X1, and the statement of comprehensive income, statement of changes in equity and statement of cash flows for the year then ended, and notes to the financial statements, including a summary of significant accounting policies.

In our opinion, the accompanying financial statements present fairly, in all material respects, (or give a true and fair view of) the financial position of the Company as at December 31, 20X1, and (of) its financial performance and its cash flows for the year then ended in accordance with International Financial Reporting Standards (IFRS Accounting Standards).

Basis for Opinion

We conducted our audit in accordance with International Standards on Auditing (ISAs). Our responsibilities under those standards are further described in the *Auditor's Responsibilities for the Audit of the Financial Statements* section of our report. We are independent of the Company in accordance with the International Ethics Standards Board for Accountants' *Code of Ethics for Professional Accountants* (IESBA Code) together with the ethical requirements that are relevant to our audit of the financial statements in [jurisdiction], and we have fulfilled our other ethical responsibilities in accordance with these requirements and the IESBA Code. We believe that the audit evidence we have obtained is sufficient and appropriate to provide a basis for our opinion.

Key Audit Matters

Key audit matters are those matters that, in our professional judgment, were of most significance in our audit of the financial statements of the current period. These matters were addressed in the context of our audit of the financial statements as a whole, and in forming our opinion thereon, and we do not provide a separate opinion on these matters.

[Description of each key audit matter in accordance with ISA 701.]

Other Information

Management is responsible for the other information. The other information comprises the [information included in the X report, but does not include the financial statements and our auditor's report thereon.]

Our opinion on the financial statements does not cover the other information and we do not express any form of assurance conclusion thereon.

In connection with our audit of the financial statements, our responsibility is to read the other information and, in doing so, consider whether the other information is materially inconsistent with the financial statements or our knowledge obtained in the audit or otherwise appears to be materially misstated. If, based on the work we have performed, we conclude that there is a material misstatement of this other information, we are required to report that fact. We have nothing to report in this regard.

Responsibilities of Management and Those Charged with Governance for the Financial Statements

Management is responsible for the preparation and fair presentation of the financial statements in accordance with IFRSs and for such internal control as management determines is necessary to enable the preparation of financial statements that are free from material misstatement, whether due to fraud or error.

In preparing the financial statements, management is responsible for assessing the Company's ability to continue as a going concern, disclosing, as applicable, matters related to going concern and using the going concern basis of accounting unless management either intends to liquidate the Company or to cease operations, or has no realistic alternative but to do so.

Those charged with governance are responsible for overseeing the Company's financial reporting process.

Auditor's Responsibilities for the Audit of the Financial Statements

Our objectives are to obtain reasonable assurance about whether the financial statements as a whole are free from material misstatement, whether due to fraud or error, and to issue an auditor's report that includes our opinion. Reasonable assurance is a high level of assurance, but is not a guarantee that an audit conducted in accordance with ISAs will always detect a material misstatement when it exists. Misstatements can arise from fraud or error and are considered material if, individually or in the aggregate, they could reasonably be expected to influence the economic decisions of users taken on the basis of these financial statements.

As part of an audit in accordance with ISAs, we exercise professional judgment and maintain professional scepticism throughout the audit. We also:

- Identify and assess the risks of material misstatement of the financial statements, whether due to fraud or error, design and perform audit procedures responsive to those risks, and obtain audit evidence that is sufficient and appropriate to provide a basis for our opinion. The risk of not detecting a material misstatement resulting from fraud is higher than for one resulting from error, as fraud may involve collusion, forgery, intentional omissions, misrepresentations, or the override of internal control.

- Obtain an understanding of internal control relevant to the audit in order to design audit procedures that are appropriate in the circumstances, but not for the purpose of expressing an opinion on the effectiveness of the Company's internal control.

- Evaluate the appropriateness of accounting policies used and the reasonableness of accounting estimates and related disclosures made by management.

- Conclude on the appropriateness of management's use of the going concern basis of accounting and, based on the audit evidence obtained, whether a material uncertainty exists related to events or conditions that may cast significant doubt on the Company's ability to continue as a going concern. If we conclude that a material uncertainty exists, we are required to draw attention in our auditor's report to the related disclosures in the financial statements or, if such disclosures are inadequate, to modify our opinion. Our conclusions are based on the audit evidence obtained up to the date of our auditor's report. However, future events or conditions may cause the Company to cease to continue as a going concern.

- Evaluate the overall presentation, structure and content of the financial statements, including the disclosures, and whether the financial statements represent the underlying transactions and events in a manner that achieves fair presentation.

We communicate with those charged with governance regarding, among other matters, the planned scope and timing of the audit and significant audit findings, including any significant deficiencies in internal control that we identify during our audit.

We also provide those charged with governance with a statement that we have complied with relevant ethical requirements regarding independence, and to communicate with them all relationships and other matters that may reasonably be thought to bear on our independence, and where applicable, related safeguards.

From the matters communicated with those charged with governance, we determine those matters that were of most significance in the audit of the financial statements of the current period and are therefore the key audit matters. We describe these matters in our auditor's report unless law or regulation precludes public disclosure about the matter or when, in extremely rare circumstances, we determine that a matter should not be communicated in our report because the adverse consequences of doing so would reasonably be expected to outweigh the public interest benefits of such communication.

Report on Other Legal and Regulatory Requirements

'The form and content of this section of the auditor's report would vary depending on the nature of the auditor's other reporting responsibilities prescribed by local law, regulation, or national auditing standards. The matters addressed by other law, regulation or national auditing standards (referred to as "other reporting responsibilities") shall be addressed within this section unless the other reporting responsibilities address the same topics as those presented under the reporting responsibilities required by the ISAs as part of the Report on the Audit of the Financial Statements section. The reporting of other reporting responsibilities that address the same topics as those required by the ISAs may be combined (ie, included in the Report on the Audit of the Financial Statements section under the appropriate subheadings) provided that the wording in the auditor's report clearly differentiates the other reporting responsibilities from the reporting that is required by the ISAs where such a difference exists.'

The engagement partner on the audit resulting in this independent auditor's report is [name].

[Signature in the name of the audit firm, the personal name of the auditor, or both, as appropriate for the particular jurisdiction]

[Auditor Address]

[Date]

2.1 Basic elements of the auditor's report

The auditor's report includes the following basic **elements**, usually in the following layout.

Basic elements of audit report	Explanation
Title	The auditor's report must have a title that clearly indicates that it is the report of the independent auditor. This signifies that the auditor has met all the ethical requirements concerning independence and therefore distinguishes the auditor's report from other reports.
Addressee	The addressee will be determined by law or regulation, but is likely to be the shareholders or those charged with governance.
Opinion paragraph	The opinion paragraph must identify the entity being audited, state that the financial statements have been audited, identify the title of each statement that comprises the financial statements being audited, refer to the summary of significant accounting policies and other explanatory notes, and specify the date or period covered by each statement comprising the financial statements.

Basic elements of audit report	Explanation
	If the auditor expresses an **unmodified opinion** on financial statements prepared in accordance with a fair presentation framework, the opinion shall use one of the following equivalent phrases: • The financial statements present fairly, in all material respects, …in accordance with [the applicable financial reporting framework]; or • The financial statements give a true and fair view of … in accordance with [the applicable financial reporting framework].
Basis for opinion	The basis for opinion paragraph must state that the audit was conducted in accordance with the ISAs, and refer to the 'Auditor's responsibilities for the audit of the financial statements' section which describes the auditor's responsibilities under the ISAs. The auditor must also state that they are independent of the audited entity, in accordance with the relevant ethical requirements relating to the audit. Finally, the auditor must state that they believe the audit evidence obtained is sufficient and appropriate to provide a basis for the audit opinion.
Material uncertainty relating to going concern	Where the auditor considers a material uncertainty related to going concern exists, this should be described in a separate paragraph headed 'Material uncertainty related to going concern.'
Key audit matters	For the audit of **listed** entities, or where required by law or regulation, the auditor should include a 'Key audit matters' paragraph. This paragraph describes the matters that, in the auditor's professional judgement, are most significant to the audit. (See section below.)
Other information	For the audit of listed entities or any other entity where the auditor has obtained other information, an 'Other information' section should be included in the auditor's report. This section should include: • A statement that management is responsible for the other information • An identification of the other information obtained before the date of the auditor's report (for listed entities, also the other information expected to be obtained after the date of the auditor's report) • A statement that the auditor's opinion does not cover the other information • A description of the auditor's responsibilities for reading, considering and reporting on other information, and Where other information has been obtained, either a statement that the auditor has nothing to report, or a description of any uncorrected material misstatement

Basic elements of audit report	Explanation
Responsibilities for the financial statements	This part of the report describes the responsibilities of those who are responsible for the preparation of the financial statements. This section should describe management's responsibility including the following: • The preparation of the financial statements in accordance with the applicable financial reporting framework; • The implementation of such internal control as are necessary to enable the preparation of financial statements that are free from material misstatement, whether due to error or fraud. • The assessment of the entity's ability to continue as a going concern, the appropriateness of the going concern basis of accounting and adequacy of related disclosures; Reference shall be made to 'the preparation and fair presentation of these financial statements' (or 'the preparation of financial statements that give a true and fair view') where the financial statements are prepared in accordance with a fair presentation framework.
Auditor's responsibilities for the audit of the financial statements	The report must state that the auditor's objectives are to obtain reasonable assurance whether the financial statements as a whole are free from material misstatement, whether from fraud or error, and to issue an auditor's report that includes the auditor's opinion. The auditor must state that reasonable assurance is a high level of assurance, but is not a guarantee that an audit conducted in accordance with the ISAs will always detect a material misstatement when it exists. Further, the auditor must explain that misstatements can arise from fraud or error, and describe the meaning of materiality. The report must explain that the auditor exercises professional judgement and maintains professional scepticism throughout the audit, and describe the auditor's responsibilities in an audit. The description of the auditor's responsibilities must either be set out in the body of the auditor's report, in an appendix to the auditor's report or by including a specific reference in the body of the auditor's report to such a description on the website of an appropriate authority, where this is permitted by law and regulation.
Other reporting responsibilities	If the auditor is required by law to report on any other matters, this must be done in an additional paragraph below the opinion paragraph which is titled 'Report on other legal and regulatory requirements' or otherwise as appropriate.
Name of the engagement partner	The name of the engagement partner should be identified for the audit of **listed** entities, unless such a disclosure is reasonably expected to lead to a significant personal security threat.
Auditor's signature	The report must contain the auditor's signature, whether this is the auditor's own name or the audit firm's name or both.
Auditor's address	The location where the auditor practises must be included.
Date of the report	The report must be dated no earlier than the date on which the auditor has obtained sufficient appropriate audit evidence on which to base the auditor's opinion on the financial statements.

(ISA 700 (Revised): para. 21-49)

A measure of uniformity in the form and content of the auditor's report is desirable because it helps to promote the reader's understanding and to identify unusual circumstances when they occur.

> **Exam focus point**
>
> You should be able to list the elements of an unmodified audit report and explain the purpose of each element.

2.2 UK Companies Act 2006

In the UK, where the auditor's report includes an unmodified opinion, the auditors state expressly that the financial statements give a **true and fair** view, or **present fairly**. The audit opinion may also **imply** certain things are true, because otherwise the audit report would have mentioned them. In the UK, such implications include:

- **Adequate accounting** have been kept.
- **Proper returns** adequate for the audit have been received from branches not visited.
- The **accounts agree** with the **accounting records** and **returns**.
- **All information and explanations** have been **received** as the auditors think necessary and they have had access at all times to the company's books, accounts and vouchers.
- **Details** of **directors' emoluments** and **other benefits** have been correctly **disclosed** in the financial statements.
- Particulars of **loans** and **other transactions** in favour of **directors** and others have been correctly disclosed in the financial statements.

Question — Auditor's report

The following is a summarised auditor's report which has been signed by the auditors of Kiln, a limited liability company. The auditor's opinion is unmodified.

INDEPENDENT AUDITOR'S REPORT

To the shareholders of Kiln Company

Report on the audit of the financial statements

Opinion

We have audited the accompanying financial statements of Kiln Company, which comprise the statement of financial position as at December 31, 20X1, and the statement of profit or loss and other comprehensive income, statement of changes in equity and statement of cash flows for the year then ended, and a summary of significant accounting policies and other explanatory notes.

In our opinion, the financial statements give a true and fair view of (or 'present fairly, in all material respects,') the financial position of Kiln Company as of December 31, 20X1, and of its financial performance and its cash flows for the year ended in accordance with International Financial Reporting Standards.

Responsibilities of management and those charged with governance for the financial statements

Management is responsible for the preparation and fair presentation of these financial statements in accordance with International Financial Reporting Standards. This responsibility includes: designing, implementing and maintaining internal control relevant to the preparation and fair representation of financial statements that are free from material misstatement, whether due to fraud or error; selecting and applying appropriate accounting policies; and making accounting estimates that are reasonable in the circumstances.

Auditor's responsibilities for the audit of the financial statements

Our responsibility is to express an opinion on these financial statements based on our audit. We conducted our audit in accordance with International Standards on Auditing. Those standards require that we comply with ethical requirements and plan and perform the audit to obtain reasonable assurance whether the financial statements are free from material misstatement.

An audit involves performing procedures to obtain audit evidence about the amounts and disclosures in the financial statements. The procedures selected depend on the auditor's judgement, including the assessment of the risks of material misstatement of the financial statements, whether due to fraud or error. In making those risk assessments, the auditor considers internal control relevant to the entity's preparation and fair presentation of the financial statements in order to design audit procedures that are appropriate in the circumstances, but not for the purpose of expressing an opinion on the effectiveness of the entity's internal control. An audit also includes evaluating the appropriateness of accounting policies used and the reasonableness of accounting estimates made by management, as well as evaluating the overall presentation of the financial statements.

We believe that the audit evidence we have obtained is sufficient and appropriate to provide a basis for our audit opinion.

Auditor

6 March 20X2

Required

Explain the purpose and meaning of the following phrases taken from the above extracts of an unqualified audit report.

(a) '... which comprise the statement of financial position ... and other explanatory notes.'
(b) '... in accordance with International Standards on Auditing.'
(c) 'In our opinion ...'

Answer

(a) *'...which comprise the statement of financial position ... and other explanatory notes.'*

   Purpose

   The purpose of this phrase is to make it clear to the reader of an audit report the part of a company's annual report upon which the auditors are reporting their opinion.

   Meaning

   An annual report may include documents such as a five year summary and other voluntary information. However, only the statement of profit or loss and other comprehensive income, statement of financial position and associated notes are required to be audited in true and fair terms. IAS 7 *Statements of Cash Flows* also requires a statement of cash flows for the financial statements to show a true and fair view. Page references (for instance, 8 to 20) may be used instead to cover the statement of profit or loss and other comprehensive income, statement of financial position, notes to the accounts and statement of cash flows. The **directors' report**, or any equivalent, is **not** included in these references.

(b) *'...in accordance with International Standards on Auditing ....'*

   Purpose

   This phrase is included in order to confirm to the reader that best practice, as laid down in ISAs, has been adopted by the auditors in both carrying out their audit and in drafting their audit opinion. This means that the reader can be assured that the audit has been properly conducted, and that

should he or she wish to discover what such standards are, or what certain key phrases mean, he or she can have recourse to ISAs to explain such matters.

Meaning

Auditing Standards are those auditing standards prepared by the International Auditing and Assurance Standards Board.

These prescribe the principles and practices to be followed by auditors in the planning, designing and carrying out various aspects of their audit work, the content of audit reports, both qualified and unqualified and so on. Members are expected to follow all of these standards.

(c) *'In our opinion ...'*

Purpose

Auditors are required to report on every statement of financial position, income and statement of cash flows laid before shareholders. In reporting, they are required to state their opinion on those accounts. Thus, the purpose of this phrase is to comply with the requirement to report an opinion.

Meaning

An audit report is an expression of opinion by suitably qualified auditors as to whether the financial statements give a true and fair view, and have been properly prepared in accordance with any relevant local legislation. It is not a certificate; rather it is a statement of whether or not, in the professional judgement of the auditors, the financial statements give a true and fair view.

2.3 Key audit matters

> **FAST FORWARD** **Listed** company auditor's reports include a description of the key audit matters.

ISA 701 *Communicating Key Audit Matters in the Independent Auditor's Report* applies to **listed entity** audits and sets out the auditor's responsibility to communicate key audit matters (KAMs). Let's start with the definition:

Key term

> **Key audit matters**: 'Those matters that, in the auditor's professional judgment, were of most significance in the audit of the financial statements of the current period. Key audit matters are selected from matters communicated with those charged with governance' (ISA 701: para. 8).

Reporting on KAMs aims to improve **transparency** by helping users to understand the most significant issues the auditor faced. This should enhance the **communicative value** of the auditor's report.

KAMs are part of every listed company auditor's report, and can be included by other auditors if needed (ISA 701: para. 5).

KAMs do not constitute a modification of the report or of the opinion. They are a part of the standard report which must be tailored to each company's circumstances. KAMs are not a substitute for disclosures, for emphasis of matter (EoM) or other matter (OM) paragraphs, nor for modified opinions.

Matters which the auditor may determine to be KAMs include:

- Areas of **higher risk** of material misstatement, or 'significant risks' identified in line with ISA 315 (Revised) (eg at the planning stage)
- **Significant judgements** in relation to areas where management made judgements
- The effect of **significant events or transactions**

(ISA 701: para. 9)

The key part of the definition of KAMs above is that these are the **most significant matters**. Identifying the most significant matters involves using the auditor's **professional judgement**.

Other factors to consider when determining KAMs include:

- The importance of the matter to intended **users' understanding**, including **materiality**
- The nature of the underlying accounting policy relating to the matter or the **complexity** or **subjectivity** involved
- Any **misstatements** related to the matter
- The nature and extent of **audit effort** needed to address the matter
- The nature and severity of **difficulties** in applying audit procedures, obtaining evidence or forming conclusions, including **more subjective judgements**
- The severity of any **control deficiencies**
- Whether **several separate issues** interacted, eg if a long-term contract had repercussions in several areas (revenue recognition, litigation or contingencies).

(ISA 701: para. A29)

KAMs are communicated in a separate paragraph of the auditor's report. The description of each KAM says **two main things**:

ISA 701: para. 13

The description of each key audit matter in the Key Audit Matters section of the auditor's report shall include a reference to the related disclosure(s), if any, in the financial statements and shall address:

(a) Why the matter was considered to be one of most significance in the audit and therefore determined to be a key audit matter; and

(b) How the matter was addressed in the audit.

Here is an example of how KAMs could appear, taken from the IAASB's guidance publication *Auditor Reporting – Illustrative Key Audit Matters*:

Key Audit Matters

Key audit matters are those matters that, in our professional judgment, were of most significance in our audit of the financial statements of the current period. These matters were addressed in the context of our audit of the financial statements as a whole, and in forming our opinion thereon, and we do not provide a separate opinion on these matters

Goodwill

Under IFRSs, the Group is required to annually test the amount of goodwill for impairment. This annual impairment test was significant to our audit because the balance of XX as of December 31, 20X1 is material to the financial statements. In addition, management's assessment process is complex and highly judgmental and is based on assumptions, specifically [describe certain assumptions], which are affected by expected future market or economic conditions, particularly those in [name of country or geographic area].

Our audit procedures included, among others, using a valuation expert to assist us in evaluating the assumptions and methodologies used by the Group, in particular those relating to the forecasted revenue growth and profit margins for [name of business line]. We also focused on the adequacy of the Group's disclosures about those assumptions to which the outcome of the impairment test is most sensitive, that is, those that have the most significant effect on the determination of the recoverable amount of goodwill.

The Company's disclosures about goodwill are included in Note 3, which specifically explains that small changes in the key assumptions used could give rise to an impairment of the goodwill balance in the future.

> **Revenue Recognition**
>
> The amount of revenue and profit recognised in the year on the sale of [name of product] and aftermarket services is dependent on the appropriate assessment of whether or not each long-term aftermarket contract for services is linked to or separate from the contract for sale of [name of product]. As the commercial arrangements can be complex, significant judgment is applied in selecting the accounting basis in each case. In our view, revenue recognition is significant to our audit as the Group might inappropriately account for sales of [name of product] and long-term service agreements as a single arrangement for accounting purposes and this would usually lead to revenue and profit being recognised too early because the margin in the long-term service agreement is usually higher than the margin in the [name of product] sale agreement.
>
> Our audit procedures to address the risk of material misstatement relating to revenue recognition, which was considered to be a significant risk, included:
>
> - Testing of controls, assisted by our own IT specialists, including, among others, those over: input of individual advertising campaigns' terms and pricing; comparison of those terms and pricing data against the related overarching contracts with advertising agencies; and linkage to viewer data; and
> - Detailed analysis of revenue and the timing of its recognition based on expectations derived from our industry knowledge and external market data, following up variances from our expectations.
>
> (IFAC, 2015)

2.3.1 Relationship with the auditor's opinion

The KAMs are the key matters for the audit of the whole financial statements. They are **not** separate auditor's opinions for each part of the financial statements, but merely **further information** on the process that led up to the opinion on the financial statements as a whole. Likewise, the auditor's opinion refers to the financial statements as a whole: as a whole they might give a true and fair view, or as a whole they might be true and fair 'except for' one area (and so on).

If a **modified opinion** is expressed, the matter that gives rise to the modified opinion will be described in the 'basis for modified opinion' paragraph, so it **must not be included as a KAM** (although the KAM section will include a reference to the 'basis for modified opinion paragraph') (ISA 701: para. 15). ISA 701 (para. 12) emphasises this:

> The auditor shall not communicate a matter in the Key Audit Matters section of the auditor's report when the auditor would be required to modify the opinion in accordance with ISA 705 (Revised) as a result of the matter.

Note that where the auditor **disclaims an opinion** on the financial statements, a Key Audit Matters section must **not** be included in the auditor's report (ISA 705 (Revised): para. 29).

ISA 701 (para. 15) also makes special mention of **going concern** problems, which we have covered in Chapter 17. Where there is a material uncertainty in relation to going concern, this is described in the 'Material uncertainty related to going concern' section. **Going concern issues should not be included as a KAM** (although the KAM section will include a reference to the 'Material uncertainty related to going concern section).

This section has introduced you to the unmodified opinion. The next section looks at modified opinions.

3 Modified opinions in the auditor's report

FAST FORWARD

> The auditor will express a modified opinion in the auditor's report when they believe that they cannot express an unmodified opinion.

Exam focus point

> Modified opinions are very important in this syllabus and you must be comfortable with stating what type of modified opinion you would issue in a given situation. The exam may give several separate issues and require candidates to comment as to the type of audit opinion would be given. You need to know whether an opinion will be modified, and if so, exactly how it would be modified. You must work through the questions in the Exam Question Bank to practise this skill.

3.1 Modified opinions

ISA 705 (Revised) *Modifications to the Opinion in the Independent Auditor's Report* sets out the different types of modified opinions that can result. It identifies **three possible types of modifications**:

- A **qualified** opinion
- An **adverse** opinion
- A **disclaimer** of opinion

3.1.1 Types of modifications

The type of modification issued depends on the following:

- The **nature of the matter** giving rise to the modifications (ie whether the financial statements **are materially misstated** or whether they may be misstated when **the auditor cannot obtain sufficient appropriate audit evidence**)
- The auditor's judgement about the **pervasiveness** of the effects/possible effects of the matter on the financial statements

A modified opinion is required when:

- The auditor concludes that the financial statements as a whole are not free from material misstatements or
- The auditor cannot obtain sufficient appropriate audit evidence to conclude that the financial statements as a whole are free from material misstatement.

(ISA 705 (Revised): para. 6)

Key term

> **Pervasiveness** is a term used to describe the effects or possible effects on the financial statements of misstatements or undetected misstatements (due to an inability to obtain sufficient appropriate audit evidence). There are three types of pervasive effect:
>
> – Those that are not confined to specific elements, accounts or items in the financial statements
> – Those that are confined to specific elements, accounts or items in the financial statements and represent or could represent a substantial portion of the financial statements
> – Those that relate to disclosures which are fundamental to users' understanding of the financial statements

The following table summarises the different types of modified opinion:

Nature of Matter Giving Rise to the Modification	Auditor's Judgement about the Pervasiveness of the Effects or Possible Effects on the Financial Statements	
	Material but not Pervasive	**Material and Pervasive**
Financial statements are materially misstated	Qualified opinion	Adverse opinion
Inability to obtain sufficient appropriate audit evidence	Qualified opinion	Disclaimer of opinion

3.1.2 Qualified opinions

A **qualified opinion** must be expressed in the auditor's report in the following two situations:

(1) **The auditor concludes that misstatements are material, but not pervasive, to the financial statements.**

   Material misstatements could arise in respect of:

   - The appropriateness of selected accounting policies
   - The application of selected accounting policies
   - The appropriateness or adequacy of disclosures in the financial statements

(2) **The auditor cannot obtain sufficient appropriate audit evidence on which to base the opinion but concludes that the possible effects of undetected misstatements, if any, could be material but not pervasive.**

   The auditor's inability to obtain sufficient appropriate audit evidence could arise from:

   - Circumstances beyond the entity's control (eg accounting records destroyed)
   - Circumstances relating to the nature or timing of the auditor's work (eg the timing of the auditor's appointment prevents the observation of the physical inventory count)
   - Limitations imposed by management (eg management prevents the auditor from requesting external confirmation of specific account balances)

Where the auditor has to modify their opinion due to the circumstances above, the opinion paragraph in the auditor's report becomes a **qualified opinion** paragraph and the basis for opinion paragraph becomes a '**Basis for qualified opinion**' paragraph. The 'Basis for qualified opinion' paragraph provides a description of the matter giving rise to the qualified opinion.

Example 1: Qualified opinion due to material misstatement

In this example, inventories are materially misstated but the effect is not pervasive.

Qualified opinion

We have audited the financial statements of ABC Company ('the Company'), which comprise the statement of financial position as at December 31, 20X1, and the statement of comprehensive income, statement of changes in equity and statement of cash flows for the year then ended, and notes to the financial statements, including a summary of significant accounting policies.

In our opinion, **except for** the effects of the matter described in the Basis for Qualified Opinion section of our report, the accompanying financial statements present fairly, in all material respects, (or give a true and fair view of) the financial position of the Company as at December 31, 20X1, and (of) its financial performance and its cash flows for the year then ended in accordance with International Financial Reporting Standards (IFRSs).

Basis for Qualified Opinion

The Company's inventories are carried in the statement of financial position at xxx. Management has not stated the inventories at the lower of cost and net realizable value but has stated them solely at cost, which constitutes a departure from IFRSs. The Company's records indicate that, had management stated the inventories at the lower of cost and net realizable value, an amount of xxx would have been required to write the inventories down to their net realisable value. Accordingly, cost of sales would have been increased by xxx, and income tax, net income and shareholders' equity would have been reduced by xxx, xxx and xxx, respectively.

> We conducted our audit in accordance with International Standards on Auditing (ISAs). Our responsibilities under those standards are further described in the Auditor's Responsibilities for the Audit of the Financial Statements section of our report. We are independent of the Company in accordance with the ethical requirements that are relevant to our audit of the financial statements in [jurisdiction], and we have fulfilled our other ethical responsibilities in accordance with these requirements. We believe that the audit evidence we have obtained is sufficient and appropriate to provide a basis for our qualified opinion.

Example 2: Qualified opinion due to inability to obtain sufficient appropriate audit evidence

In this example, the inventory count was not attended by the auditor, but in the context of the financial statements, even though inventory could be materially misstated (which the auditor cannot conclude on – so the phrase 'possible effects' is used), the effects would not be pervasive.

> **Qualified opinion**
>
> We have audited the consolidated financial statements of ABC Company and its subsidiaries ('the Group'), which comprise the consolidated statement of financial position as at December 31, 20X1, and the consolidated statement of comprehensive income, consolidated statement of changes in equity and consolidated statement of cash flows for the year then ended, and notes to the consolidated financial statements, including a summary of significant accounting policies.
>
> In our opinion, **except for** the possible effects of the matter described in the Basis for Qualified Opinion section of our report, the accompanying consolidated financial statements present fairly, in all material respects, (or give a true and fair view of) the financial position of the Group as at December 31, 20X1, and (of) its consolidated financial performance and its consolidated cash flows for the year then ended in accordance with International Financial Reporting Standards (IFRSs).
>
> **Basis for Qualified Opinion**
>
> The Group's investment in XYZ Company, a foreign associate acquired during the year and accounted for by the equity method, is carried at xxx on the consolidated statement of financial position as at December 31, 20X1, and ABC's share of XYZ's net income of xxx is included in ABC's income for the year then ended. We were unable to obtain sufficient appropriate audit evidence about the carrying amount of ABC's investment in XYZ as at December 31, 20X1 and ABC's share of XYZ's net income for the year because we were denied access to the financial information, management, and the auditors of XYZ. Consequently, we were unable to determine whether any adjustments to these amounts were necessary.
>
> We conducted our audit in accordance with International Standards on Auditing (ISAs). Our responsibilities under those standards are further described in the Auditor's Responsibilities for the Audit of the Consolidated Financial Statements section of our report. We are independent of the Group in accordance with the ethical requirements that are relevant to our audit of the consolidated financial statements in [jurisdiction], and we have fulfilled our other ethical responsibilities in accordance with these requirements. We believe that the audit evidence we have obtained is sufficient and appropriate to provide a basis for our qualified opinion.

3.1.3 Adverse opinions

An adverse opinion is expressed when the auditor, having obtained sufficient appropriate audit evidence, concludes that **misstatements** are both **material and pervasive** to the financial statements. The table below gives one example of why an adverse opinion might be expressed for each of the three possible reasons for misstatements being determined as pervasive.

Reason deemed pervasive	Example
Misstatements are not confined to specific elements, accounts or items in the financial statements.	No depreciation has been provided on plant and equipment, a receivable balance consisting half of total receivables is irrecoverable and has not been provided and trade payables have been significantly understated, All misstatements are material and these balances are significant on the SOFP.
Misstatements are confined to specific elements, accounts or items in the financial statements and represent a substantial portion of the financial statements.	A house building company has included all the houses it has constructed in the year as non-current assets rather than inventory. The value of these houses constitutes 90% of the total asset value on the SOFP.
Misstatements relate to disclosures which are fundamental to users' understanding of the financial statements.	There is a material uncertainty in respect of going concern which has not been adequately disclosed.

Sometimes it is easier to think in more general terms when deciding whether an adverse opinion is warranted (apart from specific instances where reasons for adverse opinions are specified by ISAs, such as in relation to going concern).

The question to ask yourself is this: Am I significantly diverted from the real financial position of the company as a result of the misstatement(s)?

In the house builder example above, the financial statements presented would suggest that the company was holding no property for sale but had significant company property that was being utilised by the business. The effects of the misstatement are clearly pervasive.

Where the auditor has to express an adverse opinion, the opinion paragraph in the auditor's report becomes an **adverse opinion** paragraph and the basis for opinion paragraph becomes a '**Basis for adverse opinion**' paragraph. The 'Basis for adverse opinion' paragraph provides a description of the matter giving rise to the adverse opinion.

Example 3: Adverse opinion due to material misstatement with a pervasive effect

This example is an adverse opinion for the house building company we looked at in Section 3.1.3, which included inventory as depreciated non-current assets.

Adverse Opinion

We have audited the consolidated financial statements of ABC Company and its subsidiaries ('the Group'), which comprise the consolidated statement of financial position as at December 31, 20X1, and the consolidated statement of comprehensive income, consolidated statement of changes in equity and consolidated statement of cash flows for the year then ended, and notes to the consolidated financial statements, including a summary of significant accounting policies.

In our opinion, because of the significance of the matter discussed in the Basis for Adverse Opinion section of our report, the accompanying consolidated financial statements do not present fairly (or do not give a true and fair view of) the consolidated financial position of the Group as at December 31, 20X1, and (of) its consolidated financial performance and its consolidated cash flows for the year then ended in accordance with International Financial Reporting Standards (IFRSs).

> **Basis for Adverse Opinion**
>
> As explained in Note X, the Group has not consolidated subsidiary XYZ Company that the Group acquired during 20X1 because it has not yet been able to determine the fair values of certain of the subsidiary's material assets and liabilities at the acquisition date. This investment is therefore accounted for on a cost basis. Under IFRSs, the Company should have consolidated this subsidiary and accounted for the acquisition based on provisional amounts. Had XYZ Company been consolidated, many elements in the accompanying consolidated financial statements would have been materially affected. The effects on the consolidated financial statements of the failure to consolidate have not been determined.
>
> We conducted our audit in accordance with International Standards on Auditing (ISAs). Our responsibilities under those standards are further described in the Auditor's Responsibilities for the Audit of the Consolidated Financial Statements section of our report. We are independent of the Group in accordance with the ethical requirements that are relevant to our audit of the consolidated financial statements in [jurisdiction], and we have fulfilled our other ethical responsibilities in accordance with these requirements. We believe that the audit evidence we have obtained is sufficient and appropriate to provide a basis for our adverse opinion.

3.1.4 Disclaimers of opinion

An opinion must be disclaimed when the auditor **cannot obtain sufficient appropriate audit evidence** on which to base the opinion and concludes that the **possible effects** on the financial statements of undetected misstatements, if any, **could be both material and pervasive**.

The opinion must also be disclaimed in situations involving **multiple uncertainties** when the auditor concludes that, despite having obtained sufficient appropriate audit evidence for the individual uncertainties, it is not possible to form an opinion on the financial statements due to the **potential interaction of the uncertainties and their possible cumulative effect** on the financial statements.

One example of when a disclaimer of opinion is used was given in Chapter 17 where, in relation to going concern, management is unwilling to make or extend its assessment. Another example might be where the auditor is unable to attend the inventory count and unable to request receivable confirmations, and there is no other realistic means of gathering evidence on these two areas. If these two areas form a significant element of the total assets value, a disclaimer may be appropriate.

Where the auditor has to disclaim their opinion, the opinion paragraph in the auditor's report becomes a **disclaimer of opinion** paragraph and the basis for opinion paragraph becomes a '**Basis for disclaimer of opinion**' paragraph. The 'Basis for disclaimer of opinion' paragraph provides a description of the circumstances which meant that the auditor had to disclaim their opinion.

Example 4: Disclaimer of opinion due to inability to obtain sufficient appropriate audit evidence about multiple elements of the financial statements

In this example, the auditor has not only been unable to attend the inventory count, but has also been unable to gain evidence over other areas. As a result the auditor has concluded the effects of the possible misstatements could be material and pervasive.

> **Disclaimer of opinion**
>
> We were engaged to audit the consolidated financial statements of ABC Company and its subsidiaries ('the Group'), which comprise the consolidated statement of financial position as at December 31, 20X1, and the consolidated statement of comprehensive income, consolidated statement of changes in equity and consolidated statement of cash flows for the year then ended, and notes to the consolidated financial statements, including a summary of significant accounting policies.
>
> We do not express an opinion on the accompanying consolidated financial statements of the Group. Because of the significance of the matter described in the Basis for Disclaimer of Opinion section of our report, we have not been able to obtain sufficient appropriate audit evidence to provide a basis for an audit opinion on these consolidated financial statements.
>
> **Basis for Disclaimer of Opinion**
>
> The Group's investment in its joint venture XYZ Company is carried at xxx on the Group's consolidated statement of financial position, which represents over 90% of the Group's net assets as at December 31, 20X1. We were not allowed access to the management and the auditors of XYZ Company, including XYZ Company's auditors' audit documentation. As a result, we were unable to determine whether any adjustments were necessary in respect of the Group's proportional share of XYZ Company's assets that it controls jointly, its proportional share of XYZ Company's liabilities for which it is jointly responsible, its proportional share of XYZ's income and expenses for the year, and the elements making up the consolidated statement of changes in equity and the consolidated cash flow statement.

3.1.5 Impact on the auditor's report

We have seen that when the auditor has had to modify their opinion, the auditor's report must amend the paragraph after the opinion paragraph, which provides a description of the matter giving rise to the modification. This paragraph will be entitled 'Basis for qualified opinion' or 'Basis for adverse opinion' or 'Basis for disclaimer of opinion' depending on the type of modification.

The section of the auditor's report containing the opinion will be headed either 'Qualified opinion', 'Adverse opinion' or 'Disclaimer of opinion', again depending on the type of modification.

When the auditor expresses a qualified or adverse opinion, the section of the report on the auditor's responsibilities must be amended to state that the auditor believes that the audit evidence obtained is sufficient and appropriate to provide a basis for the auditor's modified audit opinion.

When the auditor disclaims an opinion due to being unable to obtain sufficient appropriate audit evidence, the section on the auditor's responsibilities must be amended to include the following: 'Because of the matter(s) described in the Basis for Disclaimer of Opinion paragraph, however, we were not able to obtain sufficient appropriate audit evidence to provide a basis for an audit opinion'.

3.1.6 Communication with those charged with governance

ISA 705 (Revised) (para. 30) states that when the auditor expects to express a modified opinion, the auditor must **communicate with those charged with governance** the circumstances leading to the expected modification and the proposed wording of the modification in the auditor's report.

This allows the auditor to give **notice** to those charged with governance of the intended modification and the reasons for it, to **seek agreement or confirm disagreement** with those charged with governance with respect to the modification, and to give those charged with governance an **opportunity to provide further information and explanations** on the matter giving rise to the expected modification. (ISA 705 (Revised): para. A27)

18: AUDIT REPORTS

Exam focus point

> Exam questions on the auditor's report are often about possible modifications in specific situations.

Question — Modified opinions

During the course of your audit of the non-current assets of Eastern Engineering, a listed company, at 31 March 20X4, two problems have arisen.

(a) The calculations of the cost of direct labour incurred on assets in the course of construction by the company's employees have been accidentally destroyed for the early part of the year. The direct labour cost involved is $10,000.

(b) The company incurred development expenditure of $25,000 spent on a viable new product which will go into production next year and which is expected to last for ten years. The expenditure has been debited in full to the statement of profit or loss.

(c) Other relevant financial information is as follows.

	$
Profit before tax	100,000
Non-current asset additions	133,000
Assets constructed by company	34,000
Carrying amount of non-current assets	666,667

Required

(a) List the general forms of modified audit opinions available to auditors in drafting their report and state the circumstances in which each is appropriate.

(b) State whether you feel that a modified audit opinion should be given for each of the two circumstances outlined above, giving reasons in each case.

(c) On the assumption that you decide that a modified audit opinion is necessary with respect to the treatment of the development expenditure, draft the section of the report describing the matter (the whole report is not required).

Answer

(a) ISA 705 (Revised) *Modifications to the Opinion in the Independent Auditor's Report* states that the auditors may need to modify their audit opinion under one of two main circumstances:

   (i) The financial statements are materially misstated.

   (ii) The auditors have been unable to obtain sufficient appropriate audit evidence to conclude that the financial statements are not materially misstated.

   For both circumstances there can be two 'levels' of modified opinion:

   (i) A **qualified opinion** where the issue is **material but not pervasive**, resulting from either a material misstatement or the inability to obtain sufficient appropriate audit evidence to conclude that the financial statements are not materially misstated.

   (ii) An **adverse opinion** (where the financial statements contain misstatements that are **material and pervasive**) or a **disclaimer of opinion** (where the auditor has been unable to obtain sufficient appropriate audit evidence and the effects of undetected misstatements could be **material and pervasive**).

(b) Whether a modification of the audit opinion would be required in relation to either of the two circumstances described in the question would depend on whether or not the auditors considered either of them to be material. An item is likely to be considered as material in the context of a company's financial statements if its omission, misstatement or non-disclosure would prevent a proper understanding of those statements on the part of a potential user. Whilst for some audit purposes materiality will be considered in absolute terms, more often than not it will be considered as a relative term.

(i) **Loss of records relating to direct labour costs for assets in the course of construction**

The loss of records supporting one of the asset figures in the statement of financial position would result in the auditor being unable to obtain sufficient appropriate audit evidence. The $10,000, which is the value covered by the lost records, represents 29.4% of the expenditure incurred during the year on assets in the course of construction but only 6% of total additions to non-current assets during the year and 1.5% of the year-end carrying amount of non-current assets. The total amount of $10,000 represents 10% of pre-tax profit but, as in relation to asset values, the real consideration by the auditors shall be the materiality of any over- or under-statement of assets resulting from error in arriving at the $10,000 rather than the total figure itself.

Provided there are no suspicious circumstances surrounding the loss of these records and the total figure for additions to assets in the course of construction seems reasonable in the light of other audit evidence obtained, then it is unlikely that this matter would be seen as sufficiently material to merit any modification of the audit opinion. If other records have been lost as well, however, it may be necessary for the auditors to comment on the management's failure to maintain adequate books and records.

(ii) **Development costs debited to the statement of profit or loss**

The situation here is one of disagreement, since best accounting practice, as laid down by IAS 38 *Intangible Assets*, requires that development costs should be taken to profit or loss over the useful life of the product to which they relate.

This departure from IAS 38 does not seem to be justifiable and would be material to the reported pre-tax profits for the year, representing 22.5% of that figure.

While this understatement of profit would be material to the financial statements, it is not likely to be seen as pervasive and therefore a qualified opinion on the basis of a material misstatement would be appropriate.

(c) **Qualified audit opinion extract**

Qualified opinion

We have audited the financial statements of Eastern Engineering, which comprise the statement of financial position as at March 31, 20X4, and the statement of comprehensive income, statement of changes in equity and statement of cash flows for the year then ended, and notes to the consolidated financial statements, including a summary of significant accounting policies.

In our opinion, **except for** the effects of the matter described in the Basis for Qualified Opinion section of our report, the financial statements present fairly, in all material respects, (or give a true and fair view of) the financial position of Eastern Engineering as at March 31, 20X4, and (of) its financial performance and its cash flows for the year then ended in accordance with International Financial Reporting Standards.

Basis for qualified opinion

As explained in note ... development costs in respect of a potential new product have been deducted in full against profit instead of being spread over the life of the relevant product as required by IAS 38 *Intangible assets*; the effect of so doing has been to decrease profits before and after tax for the year by $25,000.

We conducted our audit in accordance with International Standards on Auditing (ISAs). Our responsibilities under those standards are further described in the Auditor's Responsibilities for the Audit of the Financial Statements section of our report. We are independent of the Company in accordance with the ethical requirements that are relevant to our audit of the financial statements in [jurisdiction], and we have fulfilled our other ethical responsibilities in accordance with these requirements. We believe that the audit evidence we have obtained is sufficient and appropriate to provide a basis for our qualified opinion.

4 Changes to the auditor's report

Having considered modified audit opinions we will now consider two ways in which the auditor's report can change **without** auditor expressing a modified audit opinion: emphasis of matter (EoM) and other matters (OM).

4.1 Emphasis of matter paragraphs and other matter paragraphs in the auditor's report

FAST FORWARD

Emphasis of matter paragraphs and **other matter paragraphs** can be included in the auditor's report under certain circumstances. Their use **does not modify the auditor's opinion** on the financial statements.

ISA 706 (Revised) *Emphasis of Matter Paragraphs and Other Matter Paragraphs in the Independent Auditor's Report* provides guidance to auditors on the inclusion of paragraphs in the auditor's report that either **draw users' attention to a matter** that is of such importance that it is **fundamental** to their understanding or that is **relevant** to their understanding of the audit, the auditor's responsibilities or the auditor's report.

4.1.1 Emphasis of matter paragraphs

Key term

An **emphasis of matter paragraph** is a paragraph included in the auditor's report that refers to a matter **appropriately presented or disclosed** in the financial statements that, in the auditor's judgement, is of such importance that it is **fundamental to users' understanding** of the financial statements (ISA 706 (Revised): para. 7(a)).

Emphasis of matter paragraphs are used to draw readers' attention to a matter **already presented or disclosed** in the financial statements that the auditor feels is **fundamental** to their understanding, provided that the auditor has obtained sufficient appropriate audit evidence that the matter is **not materially misstated**.

Note that an emphasis of matter paragraph is **not used** when the issue has been covered as a **key audit matter**.

ISA 706 (Revised) calls on the auditor to exercise judgement in deciding where to place the emphasis of matter paragraph in the auditor's report. This decision depends on the nature of the information to be communicated in the emphasis of matter paragraph, and the relative significance of this information to the intended users of the financial statements.

Where there is a Key Audit Matters section, the emphasis of matter paragraph can come either before or after the KAMs, depending on how significant the matters discussed is (ISA 706 (Revised): para. A16).

The paragraph must contain a **clear reference** to the matter being emphasised and to where relevant disclosures that fully describe it can be found in the financial statements. The paragraph must state that

the auditor's opinion is not modified in respect of the matter emphasised. In addition, the paragraph must clearly state that the audit opinion is not modified (ISA 706 (Revised): para. 9).

The following are examples of situations in which the auditor might include an emphasis of matter paragraph in the auditor's report.

- An uncertainty relating to the future outcome of **exceptional litigation or regulatory action**
- A significant subsequent event which occurs between the date of the financial statements and the date of the auditor's report
- **Early application of a new accounting standard** that has a **pervasive effect** on the financial statements
- A **major catastrophe** that has had, or continues to have, **a significant effect** on the entity's financial position

(ISA 706 (Revised): para. A5)

ISA 706 (Revised) (Appendix 3) contains an example auditor's report that contains an emphasis of matter paragraph, relevant extracts of which are shown below.

> **'Emphasis of Matter**
>
> We draw attention to Note X of the financial statements, which describes the effects of a fire in the Company's production facilities. Our opinion is not modified in respect of this matter.'

Exam focus point

> Candidates can often struggle to distinguish between a modified audit opinion and a modified auditor's report. It is crucial to understand that where an Emphasis of Matter paragraph is included, the report is modified, but the audit opinion remains unmodified.

4.1.2 Other matter paragraphs

Key term

> An **other matter paragraph** is a paragraph included in the auditor's report that refers to **a matter other than those presented or disclosed in the financial statements** that, in the auditor's judgement, is **relevant to users' understanding** of the audit, the auditor's responsibilities or the auditor's report (ISA 706 (Revised): para. 7(b)).

Other matter paragraphs are used where the auditor considers it necessary to draw readers' attention to a matter that is relevant to their understanding of the audit, the auditor's responsibilities or the auditor's report (ISA 706 (Revised): para. 10).

The other matter paragraph can be used whenever the auditor judges the matter to be relevant to users' understanding of the audit. **Examples** include:

- The auditor is unable to withdraw from the engagement and yet is unable to obtain sufficient appropriate audit evidence;
- The auditor has been requested to report on other matters or to provide more clarifications in line with the legal jurisdiction of the country.

(ISA 706 (Revised): paras. A10–A11)

An other matter paragraph must **not** refer to something that has been included as a key audit matter (ISA 706 (Revised): para. 10).

The following is an example of an Other Matter paragraph, taken from the appendix to ISA 706 (Revised).

> **Other Matter**
>
> The financial statements of ABC Company for the year ended December 31, 20X0, were audited by another auditor who expressed an unmodified opinion on those statements on March 31, 20X1.

Again, the auditor must exercise judgement in deciding where to place the other matter paragraph. ISA 706 (Revised): para. A16 states:

(a) When an 'Other Matter' paragraph is included to draw users' attention to a matter relating to Other Reporting Responsibilities addressed in the auditor's report, the paragraph may be included in the Report on Other Legal and Regulatory Requirements section.

(b) When relevant to all the auditor's responsibilities or users' understanding of the auditor's report, the 'Other Matter' paragraph may be included as a separate section following the Report on the Audit of the Financial Statements and the Report on Other Legal and Regulatory Requirements.

The content of the other matter paragraph must reflect clearly that the other matter is not required to be presented and disclosed in the financial statements, and does not include information that the auditor is prohibited from providing by law and regulations or other standards, or information that is required to be provided by management.

4.1.3 Communication with those charged with governance

ISA 706 (Revised) (para. 12) states that when the auditor expects to include an emphasis of matter paragraph or an other matter paragraph, the auditor must communicate with those charged with governance the circumstances and the proposed wording of the paragraph in the auditor's report.

4.1.4 Relationship with Emphasis of Matter (EoM) and Other Matter paragraphs

There is potentially some degree of overlap between matters which could be disclosed as KAMs or in an EoM paragraph. Where ISA 701 applies, ISA 706 (Revised) (para. A1) states that the use of an EoM is not a substitute for a description of individual key audit matters. In other words if the matter meets the definition of a KAM it should be disclosed as such. Where a KAM is also judged to be fundamental to the users' understanding of the financial statements the auditor may wish to highlight its relative importance. This could be done, for example, by presenting the matter as the first matter in the KAM section (ISA 706 (Revised): para. A2). If a matter is not determined to be a KAM but is fundamental to the users' understanding and the auditor wishes to draw attention to the matter it should be disclosed in the EoM paragraph (ISA 706 (Revised): para. A3).

A similar principle applies to the potential overlap between matters that may be included as 'Other Matters'. ISA 706 (Revised) (para. 10) states that the matter must be included in an 'Other Matter' paragraph provided, where ISA 701 applies, the matter has not been determined to be a KAM.

Point to note

> **RPQ Students**
>
> The UK has also issued ISA (UK) 701 (Revised) in November 2019 and updated in May 2022, which is aligned with ISA 701, and can be found on the FRC website.

Auditor's reports

You are the audit manager of Check & Co and are reviewing the key issues identified in the audit files of four audit clients, each of which has a year end of 30 September 20X2.

(1) The first audit client is Little Bees Co (LB). The fieldwork stage for this audit has been completed and the draft financial statements show a profit before tax of $175,000.

(2) LB has valued a certain inventory line at its total cost price of $17,000. These inventory items have not been sold for a number of years and it is unlikely that they can be sold in the future unless the price is reduced to $3,000. The finance director is confident that the issue will be resolved and no write down was made with regards to this balance.

(3) The second audit client is Hayden Co (Hayden). On 1 January 20X2 Hayden implemented a new accounting system; this was generally a success, with the exception of February 20X2 when one month of Hayden's inventory records were lost. Despite several attempts the audit team was unable to perform alternative audit procedures to verify material inventory transactions in February 20X2, although the year-end inventory count went smoothly.

(4) The third audit client is Maker Co (Maker), a listed construction company which specialises in residential housebuilding. One of Maker's construction workers, Edward Shift, was dismissed in August 20X2 after turning up for work under the influence of alcohol. In September 20X2, Mr Shift began a case against Maker for unfair dismissal. Mr Shift has sent a huge amount of paperwork to Maker detailing the extent of his claim along with supporting medical documentation and character references that the audit team has had to devote a significant amount of audit attention to this area of the audit. The directors have not made any reference to the claim in the financial statements and you agree with Maker's lawyers' indication that it is highly unlikely that Mr Shift will be successful in his claim.

(5) The fourth audit client is TH Co (TH). The audit fieldwork is complete; however, your audit senior has raised an outstanding issue. The directors of TH have made appropriate disclosures relating to worries over going concern in the financial statements. Your audit senior has a significant level of concern regarding the going concern basis but feels the disclosure is appropriate and agrees with the use of the going concern basis. You concur with the audit senior's conclusions.

Required

(1) Explain, with reasons, the impact the inventory issue will have on LB's auditor's report if it remains unresolved?

(2) Explain, with reasons, the impact the loss of inventory records will have on Hayden's auditor's report if it remains unresolved?

(3) Based on the above information explain whether the audit opinion on Maker's financial statements should be modified or unmodified and whether any additional disclosure should be made in the auditor's report.

(4) Based on the above information explain whether the audit opinion on TH's financial statements should be modified or unmodified and whether any additional disclosure should be made in the auditor's report.

Answer

(1) LB has not valued inventory at the lower of cost and net realisable value on a line by line basis, which is contrary to the accounting standard IAS 2 *Inventories*.

If it had, then the inventory line would have been written down by $14,000 ($17,000 cost less $3,000 NRV).

The error is material as it represents 8% of profit before tax ($14,000/$175,000), so management should correct this error in the financial statements.

As the finance director has refused to amend this error then the auditor's opinion will need to be modified. As management has not complied with IAS 2 and the error is material but not pervasive, a **qualified opinion** 'except for' would be necessary.

The auditor's report would include a qualified opinion section, together with a basis for qualified opinion section explaining both the material misstatement in relation to the inappropriate valuation of inventory, and quantifying its effect on the financial statements.

(2) Check & Co has been unable to gather sufficient appropriate audit evidence over the inventory transactions which occurred in February 20X2, and these are considered to be material as they represent one twelfth of the year's transactions.

It has, however, been able to gather sufficient appropriate audit evidence over the year-end inventory balance and so this issue is considered to be material but not pervasive.

As such a **qualified opinion** 'except for' would be expressed, and a basis for qualified opinion section would be included to explain the potential impact of the loss of inventory records.

Note: an emphasis of matter paragraph would not be issued as the issue is not believed to be fundamental to the financial statements.

(3) The directors of Maker have not made any reference to the claim in the financial statements. This seems appropriate as the scenario states that you agree with the lawyer's indication that the claim will not be successful. Therefore an **unmodified audit opinion** would be issued.

However, Maker is a **listed** entity and the claim has taken up a significant amount of audit time and so this would be included within a **key audit matters** paragraph.

Note: the issue would not be included as an emphasis of matter (since it has been dealt with as a key audit matter) and there is no indication that it impacts Maker's ability to continue as a going concern.

(4) TH's directors have made **appropriate disclosures** of worries over going concern in the financial statements, and the auditor feels that the disclosure is appropriate. The audit opinion will therefore be **unmodified**.

However, significant concern over going concern still exists and so the auditor will include a '**material uncertainty relating to going concern**' section in their report.

Note: the emphasis of matter paragraph is used to highlight matters which are fundamental to users' understanding of the financial statements, with the exception of matters relating to going concern.

5 Other reporting responsibilities

FAST FORWARD

The auditor may have other reporting responsibilities.

In certain circumstances, an auditor may be required to audit and report on a single financial statement, or a specific element, account or item of the financial statements. Guidance is provided in ISA 805 (Revised) *Special Considerations – Audits of Single Financial Statements and Specific Elements, Accounts or Items of a Financial Statement*.

Appendix 1 of ISA 805 (Revised) includes the following examples:

- Accounts receivable, allowances for accounts receivable, inventory, the liability for accrued benefits of a private pension plan, the recorded value of identified intangible assets, or the liability for 'incurred but not reported' claims in an insurance portfolio, including related notes.
- A schedule of externally managed assets and income of a private pension plan, including related notes
- A schedule of net tangible assets, including related notes

This ISA explains how other ISAs are applied in these circumstances. In particular, special considerations are required in relation to acceptance of the engagement, planning and performance and forming an opinion.

Point to note

> **RPQ Students**
>
> The UK has now adopted ISA 805 (Revised) and ISA (UK) 805 can be found on the FRC website.

5.1 Acceptance

The key issue to consider on acceptance is the acceptability of the financial reporting framework. The auditor must consider whether this will 'result in a presentation that provides adequate disclosures to enable the intended users to understand the information conveyed in the financial statements or the element, and the effect of material transactions and events on the information conveyed in the financial statements or the element.'

The auditor must also consider whether the expected form of opinion is appropriate in the circumstances.

5.2 Planning and performing the audit

The auditor is required to consider the relevance of each ISA to the particular circumstances. Where the auditor is also auditing the entity's complete set of financial statements the auditor may be able to use audit evidence obtained as part of this work in the audit of the single financial statement or element.

The auditor also needs to consider the interrelated nature of financial statements and elements. Audit procedures may have to be performed on other items in order to meet the objectives of the audit.

5.3 Forming an opinion

The reporting considerations can be summarised as follows:

Auditor reports on the complete set of financial statements and on a single financial statement or specific element	A separate opinion must be expressed for each engagement. The auditor must consider whether the presentation of the single statement or specific element is sufficiently differentiating it from the complete set of financial statements. Where this is not the case the auditor must ask management to do so.
The auditor's report on the entity's complete set of financial statements is modified, or includes an Emphasis of Matter paragraph or Other Matter paragraph	The auditor must determine whether this has an effect on the report on the single statement or the specific element.
The auditor has expressed an adverse opinion or a disclaimer of opinion on the entity's complete set of financial statements	The auditor must not include in the same auditor's report an unmodified opinion on a single financial statement or specific element that forms part of those financial statements as this would contradict the adverse opinion or disclaimer of opinion on the complete set of financial statements. If not prohibited by law the auditor may express an unmodified opinion on a specific element where an adverse opinion or disclaimer of opinion has been expressed on the complete set of financial statements provided that: - This opinion is not published together with the auditor's report containing the adverse opinion or disclaimer of opinion - The specific element does not constitute a major portion of the entity's complete set of financial statements

Chapter roundup

- The auditor is required to produce an auditor's report containing a number of consistent **elements** so that users know the audit has been conducted according to recognised standards.
- An unmodified opinion may be expressed only when the auditor is able to conclude that the financial statements give a true and fair view in accordance with **the identified financial reporting framework**.
- Modified audit opinions arise when auditors believe that they cannot express an unmodified audit opinion.
- The auditor's opinion may be modified due to material misstatement or because of insufficient inappropriate evidence.
- A qualified opinion will be issued where the matter is material but not pervasive, whilst an adverse opinion or disclaimer of opinion will be issued if the matter is material and pervasive.
- In certain circumstances it may be necessary for the auditor to add a key audit matter (KAM), emphasis of matter (EoM) or other matter(s) (OM) paragraph to the audit report.
- KAMs are required to be disclosed for **listed** company audits to describe significant audit matters and how they were addressed.
- EoM paragraphs refer to matters which are appropriately presented or disclosed in the financial statements but which are fundamental to users' understanding.
- OM paragraphs refer to matters other than those presented or disclosed in the financial statements which are relevant to users' understanding.
- The auditor must also communicate prescribed audit matters with those charged with governance.
- The auditor may have other reporting responsibilities.

Quick quiz

1. Complete the opinion paragraph that would feature in an unmodified auditor's report.

    In our opinion the .... give a ....
    .... of (or .... , in all ....
    respects) the financial position of the company as of December 31 20XX, and of the .... of its operations and its cash flows for the year then ended in accordance with IFRS or relevant
    ....] and comply with [relevant .... or
    ....].

2. The statement of management' responsibilities for the financial statements is always included in the auditors' report.

    True ☐
    False ☐

3. Draw a table that summarises the different modified opinions that can arise in the auditor's report.

4. The inclusion of an emphasis of matter paragraph in the auditor's report does not affect the auditor's opinion on the financial statements.

    True ☐
    False ☐

5. Which of the following are examples of amounts or other items that may be included in other information?

    Explanations of critical accounting estimates ☐
    Information contained on the entity's website ☐
    Written representations ☐
    Financial ratios ☐
    Overview of strategy ☐

Answers to quick quiz

1. financial statements, true and fair view, present fairly, material, results, national standards, statute, law.
2. True
3. Modification table

Nature of circumstances	Material but not pervasive	Material and pervasive
Financial statements are materially misstated	Qualified opinion	Adverse opinion
Auditor unable to obtain sufficient appropriate audit evidence	Qualified opinion	Disclaimer of opinion

4. True
5. Explanations of critical accounting estimates, financial ratios and the overview of strategy are all examples of amounts or other items that may be included in other information.

18: AUDIT REPORTS

End of chapter questions

Samson Inc (AIA Nov 2008) (amended)

You are the auditor of Samson Inc, and are about to complete the audit for the company for the year ended 30 April 20X8. The draft accounts for the company show revenue of $13.6m and profit before tax of $3.4m. The net assets of the company are $126m. During the audit of the company for the year ended, several problems have arisen:

(i) One of Samson's customers, Blakemore Ltd, is in serious financial difficulty. Through your contacts in the financial community, you are aware that Blakemore is about to go into liquidation. It is extremely unlikely that Samson will receive any of the outstanding debt due from Blakemore, which amounted to $335,000 at the year-end. The directors of Blakemore are refusing to write-off the debt on the grounds that doing so might signal to Blakemore that they are no longer interested in pursuing the debt.

(ii) The company's statement of financial position includes several properties under non-current assets. The company purchased these for $400,000, when property prices were relatively low. The directors have now decided to include the properties in the statement of financial position at the revalued amount of $4.5m. The directors are unwilling to obtain an independent valuer's report to support this valuation.

(iii) More than 60% of Samson's revenue is derived from one customer, DDC Ltd, with whom it has a three-year renewable contract. This contract is due for renewal in October 20X8, and it is not clear at this stage whether or not negotiations to renew it will be successful. The directors have included a note to the accounts explaining the situation in full. The directors of Samson require you to sign the audit report by the end of July 20X8.

(iv) Samson is involved in a major court case, which, if the company loses, will result in the loss of their trading licence, and the inability to continue trading. Samson's lawyers have estimated that the company has a 50% chance of winning the case. Because of the sensitivity of the case, the directors of Samson do not want to draw attention to it by referring to it anywhere in the financial statements.

Required

(a) ISA 705 (Revised) *Modifications to the Opinion in the Independent Auditor's Report* provides guidance on the circumstances when the independent auditor's opinion in the auditor's report should be modified.

Explain what is meant by a modified audit opinion, and explain when it might be necessary for an auditor to issue such an opinion. **(8 marks)**

(b) For each of the items (i) to (iv), state whether you think a modified audit opinion would be necessary, giving your reasons in each case. Where appropriate, you should also indicate what type of modified report you would give. **(12 marks)**

(Total = 20 marks)

Answers to end of chapter questions

ANSWERS TO END OF CHAPTER QUESTIONS

Chapter 1 Development

This question assesses students' knowledge of the historical development of the external company audit.

There is evidence that auditing procedures existed in the economic activities of many of the earliest civilisations, including those of Rome and ancient Egypt. Sometimes property owners who wanted to verify the activities of their employees undertook the task. In Britain in medieval times independent auditors who were employed by landowners carried out the job. The objective was to verify that the landowners were receiving the correct returns from the tenant farmers who worked on the estates. Early auditing also existed in government, usually related to the collection of taxation revenues.

In the nineteenth century, the evolution of corporate organisations significantly separated ownership from management. This brought about the need to account to the shareholders of companies by means of published accounts, as well as the corresponding need to verify the quality of the content of the statements.

The Joint Stock Companies Act of 1844 was the first enactment to require all incorporated companies to have their annual financial statements audited. In most cases, the auditor was one of the shareholders, elected by them. The audit report was to state whether the statement of financial position gave a 'full and fair view' of its state of affairs. In addition there was another major audit objective – to detect fraud and error in the company's accounting records.

The Companies Act 1856 removed the requirement for a statutory audit, but audits continued to be conducted on a voluntary basis. The government also retained the requirement for audit for industries with particularly bad records of dishonest managerial practices, such as the railways and banks.

In 1900 the requirement for an audit was restored for every company. The auditor was still not required to be a professional accountant, although he could not be a director of officer of the company being audited. However, as transactions became more complex, there grew a need for auditors with an accounting expertise sufficient to cope with the increasing complexity of accounting record keeping.

Until the 1920s, fraud and error detection continued to be the dominating factor in company audits. Gradually, however, there was a growing awareness of the usefulness of accounting information to investors, and more emphasis than before was placed on the information content of company accounts. The role of the auditor began to be viewed in terms of lending credibility to the financial statements, rather than certifying that they are free from fraud and error.

Along with this change in audit emphasis came the emergence of a self-regulated accountancy profession, whose members were educated and trained sufficiently to take responsibility for the corporate audit. These changes were formally recognised in the Companies Act 1948, which introduced for the first time the requirement that the auditor was to express an opinion as to the truth and fairness of the statement of profit or loss and other comprehensive income as well as the statement of financial position. In addition, the auditor was required to possess a recognised professional qualification, and detailed provisions were included regarding their duties, powers and responsibilities. This Act has been amended by subsequent Companies Acts, but its main requirements remain substantially unchanged.

In the late 1940s, the first UK accounting practice guidelines began to be issued by the Institute of Chartered Accountants of England and Wales. In 1961 the first formal guidance for auditors was issued. For the first time, audit practice was no longer a matter for individual auditors' professional judgement. In 1980, the main accounting bodies introduced a new series of Auditing Standards and Guidelines intended to set out the basic principles and practices which auditors were expected to follow.

The emphasis of today's company audit has switched from the detailed checking of individual transactions, to an overall review of the systems in operation, followed by an examination of the records and the financial statements. The detection of fraud is no longer the main objective of the audit, although material discrepancies should be picked up as a result of normal audit procedures.

Chapter 2 Larch Ltd

This question tests students' understanding of the regulatory safeguards designed to ensure the auditor cannot be removed without the approval of the shareholders, and requires the student to critically appraise these measures.

(a) Statutory legislation should ensure that in cases such as this, the directors would find it very difficult to dismiss the auditor. The rules should ensure that the auditor is protected from unjustified attempts to remove her from office, (while allowing a company to replace their auditor in a situation where another audit firm can offer a more efficient or effective service).

If the shareholders wish to remove the auditor, they should be able to do so at any time, simply by voting at a general meeting. A reasonable notice period is required when the auditor is being removed before the expiration of the normal term of office. Several safeguards should be in place to protect the auditor from unwarranted dismissal.

- On the receipt of the notice, the company should send a copy to the existing auditor.

- The auditor should have the right to make representations in writing, not exceeding a reasonable length, and may request that these be notified to the members.

- Upon receipt of such representations, the company should circularise copies of the representations to everyone who is entitled to receive notice of the meeting. If this is not done, then the auditor should have a right to have them read out at the meeting itself.

- The auditor should have the right to attend and be heard at the general meeting.

Any auditor who ceases to hold office should deliver a statement to the company. This must either state that there are no circumstances connected with the resignation that the auditor considers should be brought to the attention of the members and creditors of the company, or include a statement outlining such circumstances. This requirement is designed to thwart anyone's attempt to remove the auditor in order to suppress some damaging information. This provision should apply to all changes of auditor, even where the auditor is resigning from office. This prevents the auditor from quietly resigning instead of reporting some embarrassing facts.

These measures are all designed to prevent the directors in a situation such as Larch Ltd 'getting rid of' the auditor without the shareholders' knowledge.

(b) The rules do go some way to help protect the auditor's independence from the directors. In particular, they are geared towards ensuring that the auditor has the ability to communicate directly with the shareholders. However, one of the problems is that, in practice, the shareholders are likely to be strongly influenced by the directors. It is very rare for shareholders to vote against the proposals about the removal and replacement of the auditor. Directors who wish to remove an auditor will be able to invent a reason to offer to the shareholders, such as the fees being too high, or poor quality audit work. It is unlikely that the auditor will wish to engage in a public 'showdown' with the directors and the real reasons for the change in appointment may never become known.

ANSWERS TO END OF CHAPTER QUESTIONS

Chapter 2 Watkins Ltd

This question assesses students' knowledge of the auditor's rights and duties in respect of independence in reporting, resignation and removal.

There are three alternative actions that the auditor could take in this situation:

(a) The auditor could bow down to the pressure from the directors. As a result, the draft accounts would not be amended and the auditor would issue an unmodified report. This action is not a satisfactory one for the auditor to take as it compromises the auditor's professional standards because of the fear of losing audit fees

(b) The auditor could resign from office and issue no report on the financial statements in question. In order to resign the auditor should proceed as follows:

   (i) The auditor should deposit a written notice at the registered office of the company to take effect on the date specified in the notice.

   (ii) In order to be effective, such notice should contain a statement to the effect that there are no circumstances surrounding the resignation that must be brought to the attention of members or creditors of the company, or if there are circumstances details should be given. In this latter case, the auditor may also requisition the directors to call an extraordinary general meeting to consider the resignation circumstances.

   (iii) The company should send a copy to the registrar of companies and also a copy to each person entitled to receive a copy of the annual financial statements.

(c) The auditor could insist on the issuing of a modified audit report on the annual financial statements if the directors of Watkins Ltd do not agree to the amendments. If this takes place and the directors wish to remove the auditor, they must give special notice to the company and this notice must be sent immediately to the retiring auditor.

The auditor then has the right to make written representations and can request that these are sent to the company's shareholders. Any notice of the proposed resolution to remove the retiring auditor should state the fact that representations have been made and a copy of these should be sent to each shareholder, unless they were received too late. If received too late or because of the company's default, they must be read out at the meeting.

The auditor also has the right to attend the AGM and to receive all notices in relation to the meeting and to speak at the meeting on all matters affecting him or her as auditor.

In choosing which of the above courses of action to take, the auditor should remember that he or she must in no way compromise his or her position of independence or fall short of the requirements of the professional bodies.

Alternative (a) above is clearly unacceptable. With regard to the alternative actions (b) and (c) it is quite likely that, despite the problems, the auditor does not wish to lose this client because of the substantial audit fees entailed. If this is the case, the auditor should take action (c) and fight the dismissal. However, it may be that, because of all the problems both past and present, the auditor does not wish to continue in office. In these circumstances it would appear that action (b) would be most suitable.

ANSWERS TO END OF CHAPTER QUESTIONS

Chapter 3 Sparky

MEMORANDUM

From: The auditor of Sparky Ltd
To: The directors of Sparky Ltd

(a) The audit committee has a particular role, acting independently from the executive directors, to ensure the interests of shareholders are properly protected in relation to financial reporting and internal control. It provides a point of reference for the external auditors and adds to the objectivity of the internal audit function by allowing that function to report to independent non-executive directors rather than the main board.

The audit committee's precise remit will be agreed at board level, but its main responsibilities will normally include:

- Monitoring the integrity of the financial statements.
- Reviewing the company's internal financial controls and its internal control and risk management systems.
- Monitoring the effectiveness of the internal audit function. If there is no internal audit function, the committee should regularly consider the need to establish one.
- Making recommendations to the board on the appointment/removal of the external auditor, and to approve their terms of engagement and remuneration.
- Monitoring the external auditor's independence and objectivity, and the effectiveness of the audit process.
- Developing and implementing policy on the engagement of the external auditor to supply non-audit services.
- Reviewing arrangements by which staff may raise concerns about possible improprieties ('whistleblowing').

(b) The main advantages of having an audit committee are:

- Increasing shareholders' confidence in the credibility and objectivity of the company's financial statements.
- Assisting directors in meeting their responsibilities in respect of financial reporting and corporate governance.
- Strengthening the independence of the company's external auditor.
- Improving communication between the directors and external auditor.

Possible disadvantages of having an audit committee are:

- Additional costs arising because of the additional time involved.
- Non-executive directors being forced to become over-involved in the detail of the finances and financial systems of the company.
- The board of directors becoming split between those on the committee, and those not on the committee.

(c) Ideally, the audit committee should be made up of at least three independent non-executive directors (at least two for smaller companies). At least one member of the committee should have recent and relevant financial experience. When deciding which of the non-executive directors to appoint to the committee, the board should ensure that appointees have appropriate personal skills such as the ability to ask challenging questions and to arrive at balanced judgements in complex situations.

Chapter 3 Mendelson Ltd

The internal audit function is an independent appraisal function that is established by the management of an organisation to examine and evaluate its activities. The objective of internal auditing is to assist management to effectively and efficiently discharge its responsibilities.

The internal audit function gives directors assurance on the internal controls within an organisation. It provides an independent appraisal of measures taken to address areas of potential deficiency. It advises, evaluates and reports to management on the adequacy and effectiveness of the systems.

The emphasis placed on different goals can vary from company to company. The directors of Mendelson Ltd may initially want to ensure that the internal audit function provides them with reliable information, and that fraud and theft are prevented. Once established, they may ask the internal audit function to focus on procedures which monitor the company's efficiency in the use of resources.

Specifically, the internal audit function can assist management by any of the following:

- Carrying out systems audits
- Providing professional guidance on best practice
- Carrying out consultancy work for management
- Carrying out value for money studies
- Carrying out fraud investigations
- Advising on systems development
- Making recommendations to the audit committee
- Liaising with external audit and providing assurance to external audit.

The internal auditors can be used to advise management as to whether or not they are meeting their current (and forthcoming) obligations under specific legislation, such as the Companies Act 2006 and the Financial Services Act 2012. They can also provide reassurance to management on whether they are meeting their more general legal obligations, such as those relating to fraud, health and safety, data protection, corporate governance and tax and national insurance.

Chapter 4 – Independence

(a) If an auditor is to have credibility then it is vital that they are seen to be independent of any concern on which they are required to report. However, independence is but one of a number of qualities which the modern auditor must possess if they are to be accepted as suitable for their role.

Outside of independence, perhaps the two most important qualities required of an auditor are:

(i) **Integrity**

The auditor must be seen as honest. Having formed their opinion, based on the audit evidence they have collected, they will not allow others to sway their judgement to suit their own ends. It is the auditor's integrity which will allow interested parties to place reliance on their reports.

IFAC and national supervisory bodies do a great deal to try and ensure that the integrity of the profession as a whole, as well as that of individual members, is maintained. This is done by laying down ethical guidelines which all members are required to follow (disciplinary proceedings are taken against any member known to have breached such guidelines). The accounting bodies also assist in this area by providing a broad framework for the training and examination of prospective new members.

(ii) **Professional competence**

Clearly the auditor must be in possession of certain technical skills. This fact is clearly recognised so far as statutory audits are concerned, as only suitable qualified accountants are recognised as being competent to hold office as auditor. Examples of some of the skills required of the modern auditor are that they must be:

- Aware of and understand audit objectives
- Able to interpret systems
- Able to communicate well with others
- Conversant with required techniques such as sampling
- Able to cope with the impact of modern technology on accounting and internal control systems

The accounting profession is only too well aware of the need to maintain and improve standards of professional competence and for this reason has issued and recently revised a number of International Standards on Auditing. In addition the accounting bodies are heavily involved in running courses to assist members in maintaining and improving their technical skills.

(b) Independence on the part of the auditor as a reporting accountant is seen by many to be a fundamental concept of auditing. It has been said that it would never be sufficient for an auditor to claim that they were independent. In fact, they must always be clearly seen to be independent in practice. Given this situation, it would be almost impossible to draw up a set of rules to cover every conceivable situation where an auditor's independence might be called into question.

While not able to provide an exhaustive list of recommendations, the main principles which should be applied when considering the question of independence may be found in the relevant section of the IESBA *Code of Ethics for Professional Accountants* (*Code*). With this in mind, the following comments could be made in relation to the situations specified in the question:

(i) The audit partner has no shareholdings in the client company and so, all other things being equal, they could be seen as giving an objective audit opinion. However, the audit manager does have a shareholding in the client company which, while not material to the company (at 1% of issued share capital), could be material to the audit manager. This is a self-interest threat as it might be seen to influence their ability to give an impartial opinion in relation to the company's affairs. As the partner will inevitably have to rely upon the work completed and controlled by the audit manager it is clearly undesirable for the manager to have such a financial involvement in the client's affairs.

(ii) The *Code* suggests that when the total fees from an audit client represent a large proportion of the total fees of the firm, a self-interest or intimidation threat is created (IESBA *Code*: para. 410.14 A1). The reason for this is that the fear of losing a major client, and thus a substantial proportion of fee income, could prejudice the auditor's objectivity and make them more likely to bow to pressures from the client. In such a situation, the significance of the threat must be evaluated and safeguards applied where necessary to eliminate the threat or reduce it to an acceptable level.

The audit fee from Janet Co contributes some 14.3% of the total fees income of the practice. Janet Co is a private company.

The significance of 14.3% as a percentage depends on factors such as the operating structure of the audit firm, whether the audit firm is newly established and the significance of Janet Co as a client (IESBA *Code*: para. 410.14 A3).

ANSWERS TO END OF CHAPTER QUESTIONS

If the threat to objectivity is found to be significant, the audit firm must apply safeguards. These could include but are not limited to reducing dependency on Janet Co by taking on other clients, asking an external party to carry out a quality review and consulting a professional third party on any key audit judgements.

> **RPQ students**
>
> Under the FRC's *Ethical Standard* Part B2, for audits of private companies whose total fees are expected to exceed 15% of a firm's income regularly, the auditor is required to resign from the audit. Given that the income percentage at Janet Co is close to this mark, it is worth making this point, and stating that the firm needs to monitor this, particularly if it loses other clients or if the fees for Janet Co rise.

(iii) As another instance of where financial involvement in a client's affairs could be seen to impair an auditor's objectivity, the *Code* states that there should be no loans or guarantees in respect of loans between an auditor and a client (IESBA *Code*: para. R511.4). Any such financial involvement could be seen to impair the auditor's judgement either because of a client putting pressure on the auditor or because of the auditor's own fear of suffering some financial loss.

However, the *Code* does allow for one exception in making the above recommendation and that is where the client is a bank or other similar institution, and the loan is made under 'normal lending procedures, terms and conditions' (IESBA *Code*: para. R511.5). It is part of a bank's normal business to make personal loans and if the rate of interest being paid by the audit senior is the normal commercial rate of interest, this transaction is unlikely to be seen as impairing the auditor's independence.

(iv) The *Code* also considers the problems that can be created when conflicts of interest arise between different clients and between clients and the auditor's own business interests. It concludes that every effort must be made to avoid conflicts of interest arising and that it would be unethical for an accountant to act in a situation where they knew that a conflict of interest existed (IESBA *Code*: para. R310.4).

The situation described in the question is a good example of the type of conflict of interest with which the *Code* is concerned. The audit partner should not advise Jean Co with regard to the contract tender received from Harry Co. The auditor should explain the professional reasons why they are unable to act on this occasion and suggest that Jean Co seek advice from another firm of accountants.

Chapter 5 – PLD Associates

(a) PLD Associates is a high risk client on two counts:

(i) The **nature of its business is property development**, a high risk activity
(ii) The **deficiencies of the company's internal control system**

With such a potential client, the auditors must ensure that there are no independence or other ethical problems likely to cause conflict with the ethical code before accepting the appointment.

The procedures which an audit firm should carry out before accepting a potentially high audit risk client are as follows.

(i) **Request** the prospective clients' **permission to communicate** with the **previous auditors**. If such permission is refused the appointment should be declined.

(ii) On receipt of permission the prospective auditors should **request** in writing of the previous auditors all **information** which ought to be made available to them to enable them to decide whether they are prepared to accept nomination.

The information requested from the old auditors could go as far as asking about the integrity of the management of PLD Associates.

(iii) Ensure that the firm's **existing resources are adequate** to service the needs of the new client. This will raise questions of staff and time availability and the firm's technical expertise. This will be important in the case of PLD Associates as property development is a specialist area.

(iv) **Seek references** in respect of the new client company; it may be, as is often the case, that the directors of the company are already personally known to the firm; if not, independent enquiries should be made concerning the status of the company and its directors. Agencies such as Dun & Bradstreet might be of assistance. It will be necessary to find out whether any regulatory authority has disciplined the company.

(v) A **preliminary assessment of audit risk** should be made. This will involve discussions with the management of the client and assessing the internal control structure (which in the case of the PLD Associates is obviously poor).

(vi) The **costs and benefits** of accepting the client should be estimated; this appointment may be considered too costly in terms of potential liability (or raised insurance premiums) and bad publicity.

(b) The measures that audit firms might introduce to try to minimise the practice of 'opinion shopping' by prospective audit clients are as follows.

(i) To **establish why the question is being asked**. Is the prospective client looking for auditors who will confirm his views on the treatment of a particular transaction? He may be trying to use this against his current auditors with whom he is in dispute.

(ii) No **opinion** should be **given** until the **present auditors** have been **informed**. This is not only a matter of courtesy but may reveal other aspects to the problem which had not been forthcoming from the prospective client.

(iii) If an audit firm decides to give an opinion it should do so **in writing** giving the facts of the problem as it has been presented to them. This will protect the audit firm against the situation where an incorrect opinion is given because the facts have been misrepresented by the prospective client to order to get the opinion which concurred with their own.

Chapter 6 Internal control

(a) **Objectives of a system of internal control**

ISA 315 (Revised) states that the objective of a system of internal control is to provide reasonable assurance about the achievement of an entity's objectives with regard to:

- The reliability of financial reporting
- The effectiveness and efficiency of operations
- Compliance with applicable laws and regulations

(b) **Review of a system of internal control**

External auditor

As part of their audit, the external auditor is required to **ascertain the system and controls**. Once the system has been ascertained, the external auditor will walkthrough the systems to ensure that they operate as they have been led to believe that they do.

The auditor will then determine their **audit approach**. If they are planning to rely on the controls in the system, they have to evaluate the controls first to assess whether they are **reliable enough to** produce financial records which are free of material misstatement. In other words, they are assessing whether the systems achieve the fourth objective given above.

They will conduct tests of controls to ensure that the controls have operated properly in the year. If these tests produce good results, the auditor can rely on the systems and undertake reduced substantive testing on the financial statements.

The auditor will decide not to undertake tests of controls if the controls do not appear effective, or it is more cost-effective to undertake detailed substantive procedures, unless it is an area where substantive procedures alone are not effective (for example, a highly automated system).

Internal auditor

Internal audit function is an appraisal or monitoring activity established by the directors. It functions, amongst other things, by **examining and evaluating the adequacy and effectiveness of components of the accounting and internal control systems**.

Internal audit function therefore reviews and tests internal control systems to assess whether the systems are **achieving the four objectives** stated above.

Conclusion

The external auditor is interested in the components of the system of internal control which help to produce the financial statements which they are auditing. Internal auditors are interested more generally in internal controls to ensure that they meet their objectives of helping the business to operate effectively and reduce risks.

Chapter 7 Kudos Ltd

This question assesses students' knowledge of the importance of audit planning, and the risk-based approach to auditing, in particular the identification of high risk areas, using analytical review.

(a) The annual audit is intended to provide shareholders with reasonable assurance that the financial statements are free from material misstatements. It would always be possible to gather more evidence, but that would be at the expense of a higher audit fee, and also a delay in the completion of the audit.

The shape of statistical distributions usually means that each additional percentage point of assurance costs more than the last. It would be relatively expensive to move from 95% to 96%, and even more expensive to go higher.

The norms that prevail throughout the accountancy profession suggest that 95% certainty is an acceptable goal. The figure is set on the basis of compromise between a variety of conflicting objectives, such as assurance, value for money, and speedy reporting.

There would always be a risk that the auditor would miss something. The risk based approach makes it possible for the auditor to manage this risk, and to quantify it.

(b) The following are key risk areas for the audit of Kudos Ltd for the year to 30 September 20X6.

Drop in sales

Sales have fallen this year, with this year's projected sales estimated to be $74m, down from last year's $82m. This will have a material effect on gross profit and may increase pressure on the company to include sales from next year to boost the figures.

Accuracy of accounting for expenses

Cost of sales is lower than expected. Last year's gross margin was 14.6% whereas this year it is 17.8%. Administration expenses are forecast to be more than $7m – much higher than last year

ANSWERS TO END OF CHAPTER QUESTIONS

and higher than budget. It may be that expenses have been wrongly classified as administrative expenses rather than cost of sales.

Potential management manipulation of results

Overall the results are not encouraging for the company. The company has recently taken on significant new borrowings, with conditions that certain profit targets are met for the duration of the loans. Although the company's anticipated profit before tax for the year, at $822,000 is within the profit target of $800,000, the directors will be under considerable pressure to ensure the target is met.

Deferred development costs

This is the first time the company has incurred such expenditure, so there is a risk that they will not account for it correctly in accordance with IAS 38 *Intangible Assets*. The classification of expenditure should be reviewed, particularly because of the poor results and the pressure on management. Costs to date are in excess of the total forecast costs, so it should be ensured that these will be recovered.

Valuation of new factory

Valuations of self-built assets may not be accurate. The company may have capitalised employees' wages as part of the cost of the factory, when in fact they should be treated as an expense in the statement of profit or loss.

Depreciation policies

Disposals of non-current assets have caused large losses during the year. There is a risk that depreciation policies are not appropriate, and write-downs are not being applied when necessary.

Manufacturing plant and equipment

Despite the check only being half finished, it has yielded large differences. There is therefore a risk that non-current assets as a whole are overstated. It also indicates that there is a control deficiency over the monitoring of non-current assets, which is a concern due to the large size of the balances.

Investment in Ace Ltd

The value of the investment in Ace Ltd may have fallen as a result of the drop in trading due to the alleged infringement of patent rights. The directors may be reluctant to recognise a fall in value due to the pressure on the results. Group accounts will have to be prepared for the first time, and careful consideration must be given to the accounting for goodwill. Internal audit function therefore reviews and tests internal control systems to assess whether the systems are **achieving the four objectives** stated above.

Chapter 8 Goreng Ltd

This question assesses students' knowledge of the theory and application of sampling techniques as part of the audit.

(a) The main advantages for the auditor of using statistical sampling techniques rather than non-statistical sampling techniques are:

- Because the sample is chosen randomly, there is less scope for bias.
- It allows the auditor to draw precise conclusions about the nature of a population, and is clear about the degree of risk attached to these conclusions.
- It allows the auditor to know in advance the size of the sample required, rather than the sample sizes being determined arbitrarily.

ANSWERS TO END OF CHAPTER QUESTIONS

- It allows the auditor to justify the sample size, and the conclusions drawn, if anyone subsequently claims that the amount of testing was inadequate.

(b) When determining the sample size, the auditor should consider audit risk, tolerable misstatement, and expected misstatement.

Audit risk

There are various components of audit risk. Inherent risk is the risk that a material misstatement will occur before the internal controls set up by management can prevent or detect it. If the auditor thinks that inherent risk is high, the sample will have to be larger to provide the required level of assurance that there are no material misstatements in the population.

Control risk is the risk that internal controls fail to prevent or detect material misstatements. If the auditor is satisfied, based on compliance testing, that reliance can be placed on an internal control, the amount of substantive testing may be reduced and a smaller sample can be selected.

Detection risk is the risk that audit tests may fail to detect a material misstatement. One aspect of this is sampling risk, which is the risk that the conclusion drawn from testing a sample of the population is different from the conclusion that would be drawn if the population as a whole had been tested. If the auditor has judged inherent risk and control risk to be high, the auditor can reduce the overall audit risk by increasing the sample size to be tested. Similarly, If the auditor has judged inherent and control risk to be low, the sample size may be reduced.

Tolerable misstatement

This is the maximum misstatement that the auditor is prepared to tolerate, and still be able to conclude that the audit objective has been achieved. This means that the auditor may accept a certain number of instances of a failure to operate a control properly, but still conclude that the procedure is operating properly. Or the auditor may accept a certain number or amount of substantive misstatements in the sample, but still conclude that the population it is drawn from is not materially misstated.

If the test is looking at low value items, the sample need not be large because even a large misstatement may be immaterial in the context of the financial statements. On the other hand, some items may be of such high value that the population as a whole must be tested, rather than only a sample.

Expected misstatement

The sample must be increased where the auditor expects a high misstatement rate, either because of the results of the work on controls, or because of experience in prior years.

This is because sampling becomes more imprecise as the misstatement rate increases. Low sample sizes are only acceptable when the misstatement rate is expected to be low. In cases of a very high expected misstatement rate, sampling is likely to be inappropriate.

(c) Before quantifying the possible effect of the misstatements found in the sample, the auditor should consider the underlying causes of the misstatements. If there is any suspicion that the misstatements have been caused intentionally, or deliberately concealed, then the possibility of fraud should be considered. In this case, one of the misstatements appears to be a simple transposition misstatement, with the person recording the transaction having recorded two digits in the wrong order. The other misstatement overstating an invoice by $10,000 may be deliberate, or may simply be another straightforward misstatement.

The invoice numbers relating to both misstatements are very close, showing that they were issued and recorded during the same period. The auditor should investigate the possibility of breakdown of internal controls at that time, perhaps during staff illness or a holiday period. If this is the case, the auditor should extend audit testing to all of the invoices and postings created during this particular period.

If there is no reason to suspect that the misstatements are isolated, the auditor should project the misstatement results from the sample onto the relevant population. The auditor will estimate the probable misstatement in the population by extrapolating the misstatements found in the population. This can be done in two ways:

The ratio method

Here, the projected misstatement is found by the formula:

$$\text{Most likely misstatement in population} = \text{Misstatement found in sample} \times \frac{\text{Population value}}{\text{Sample value}}$$

Total value of invoices	$1,560,400
Sample value of invoices	$132,718
Value of misstatements found in sample	$10,540

$$\text{Most likely misstatement in population} = \$10,540 \times \frac{\$1,560,400}{\$132,718}$$

$$= \underline{\$123,922}$$

The difference method

Here, the most likely misstatement is found by the formula:

Most likely misstatement in population = Misstatement found in sample × $\frac{\text{Number of items in population}}{\text{Number of items in sample}}$

Total number of invoices	253
Sample number of invoices	11
Value of misstatements found in sample	$10,540

$$\text{Most likely misstatement in population} = \$10,540 \times \frac{253}{11}$$

$$= \underline{\$242,420}$$

Of these two methods, the ratio method is most appropriate in this case. This is because as the monetary value of the invoice increases, so does the potential monetary value of any misstatement. The difference method is more appropriate when the misstatement does not have a direct relationship to the monetary value of the item.

In both cases, however, the projected population misstatement is much greater than the tolerable misstatement of $30,000. The auditor cannot therefore conclude with reasonable assurance, and without undertaking further audit work, that the financial statements are not materially misstated.

(d) If the auditor concludes that tolerable misstatement has been exceeded, there are various possible courses of action.

The auditor should first establish whether the sample results were unrepresentative of the population as a whole. This will usually involve extended audit testing. By extending the sample size, the auditor can check whether there was an unintentional bias towards incorrect items in the original sample.

The auditor could also ask the client to conduct a detailed investigation of the transactions or balances in question, in order to assure the auditor that there is not a major problem. In this case, the population of invoices is relatively low in number at 253, so it should be possible for either the client or the auditor to check each one to the sales day book, as an added reassurance to the auditor.

If the results of this work suggest that there are indeed material misstatements in the value of sales as a result of numerous mispostings, the auditor should ask the directors to adjust the accounts. In the unlikely event they refuse to do so, the auditor will be forced to publish a qualified audit report.

(e) Sampling is not appropriate to all situations. For example, sampling is not suitable where:
- The auditor anticipates that there are likely to be a large number of misstatements in a population, or has been alerted to the possibility of irregularities.
- Populations are too small for valid conclusions to be drawn.
- It may be quicker to test all transactions rather than constructing a sample.
- All the transactions in a population are material.
- The data may require detailed and accurate disclosure in the financial statements, regardless of value (for example, director's salaries).

Chapter 8 Sparks Ltd

This question assesses the students' understanding of the theory behind the audit risk approach and the reasons for undertaking analytical review. It also tests their ability to make judgements as to what areas to focus on during audit testing, as a result of a practical example of analytical procedures.

(a) Audit risk is the risk that the auditor will give an inappropriate opinion when the financial statements are materially misstated. It is made up of three different elements:

Inherent risk

These are the risks that occur naturally in a business. There is always a risk that the statements are incorrect. There are, however, circumstances which can increase this risk considerably. The auditor must investigate the business' environment, its financial position, and the motives of its management, and consider whether the directors are under undue pressure to distort the truth and fairness of the financial statements.

Inherent risk may arise at the entity level – for example, the business may operate in a very volatile market. It may exist at the account balance level, as some accounts are more prone to errors than others (inventory, for example compared to cash at bank). It may also exist at the transaction level – the journal entry for the year end position on a long term contract is more complicated than accounting for a cash sale.

Control risk

Management will usually introduce controls into the environment so that any fraud or error can be either prevented or detected. These controls include segregation of duties, authorisation controls, physical controls, performance of reconciliations, and other management controls. Control risk is the risk that a material misstatement would not be prevented, or detected and corrected by the accounting and internal control systems.

Detection risk

Detection risk is the risk that the auditor's procedures do not detect a material misstatement that exists in the financial statements. It comprises two elements: sampling risk and non-sampling risk. Sampling risk is the risk that the auditor's conclusion drawn from a sample is different to what it would have been had the whole population been tested. Non-sampling risk is that the auditor uses inappropriate procedures or misinterprets audit evidence.

(b) Analytical procedures are used to identify anomalies in financial statements. Analytical procedures involve analysing the relationships existing over time and between items to obtain an understanding of relationships and trends, and to help direct audit effort. It is used during planning, overall review, and as a substantive procedure. When analytical procedures are used effectively, they are an efficient means of collecting audit evidence.

If a relationship or trend is identified which is significantly different from expectations, the auditor will seek an explanation from management. If a plausible explanation is obtained, the auditor will seek evidence to substantiate it. In the absence of an explanation, the auditor will be forced to conduct more detailed substantive procedures.

If the relationship or trend identified is in line with expectations, the auditor should be able to cut down on the other types of substantive procedures to be conducted. This saves time and costs, and allows the auditor to focus the audit effort on more risky aspects of the financial statements.

(c) **Going concern**

The two statements of financial position reveal several indicators of going concern issues for Sparky Ltd. The statement of financial position has reduced considerably in value since the previous year. Net current assets have fallen from $424,000 to $34,000, and the company has overall net liabilities this year. The retained earnings reserve has moved from $416,000 to -$6,000, revealing that the company has made a retained loss for the year of $422,000.

Net assets show a reduction in both inventory and trade receivables, which suggests a decrease in activity, although trade payables have not shown a corresponding fall. However, this could be explained by Sparks Ltd not paying its suppliers as quickly as in the previous year. It will be necessary to review the statement of profit or loss and other comprehensive income to determine whether there has been a reduction in trading.

The cash position has also worsened, with cash falling by $44,000. The cash flow statement will reveal more information about this fall. However, the company has paid off $10,000 of its bank loan, reducing overall debt.

Inventory

The inventory value has fallen considerably, from $358,000 to $104,000, which is an unusual trend for a manufacturing company. There is no indication from the statement of financial position why this should be so. For example, if trade receivables were correspondingly high, that could indicate high sales volume just prior to the year end, or if trade payables were correspondingly low it could suggest low pre-year end purchases.

Investigation should be made to ensure that all items of inventory were included in the year end count. Alternatively, it could simply confirm a fall in activity. Manufacturing activity during the year should be investigated, and enquiry made about employees possibly having been laid off in the period.

Warranty provision

A provision of $40,000 has been included this year, although there was no similar provision last year. The reasons for this must be investigated, and the auditor must check that it has been properly accounted for, in accordance with accounting standards.

The sudden appearance of a warranty provision in the statement of financial position suggests a change in the terms of the contracts given to customers. Alternatively, it suggests that accounting standards had been wrongly applied in the current year, or should have been applied in the previous year.

Chapter 9 Cinders Ltd

This question tests students' knowledge of the relationship between the internal and the external auditor.

Viewed from the perspective of the external auditor, an internal audit function can be an important part of a client's internal control. It can provide assurance to management that the accounting systems, internal accounting controls and management review procedures are operating effectively and that reliable financial information is generated. Internal audit function may also provide assurance as to the effectiveness of operating controls exercised by management.

The auditor should assess the effectiveness of Cinders' internal audit function as part of the assessment of the control environment and take the conclusions into account when determining the audit strategy and the substantive testing plan. Effective co-operation with a properly organised internal audit function can often result in significant reductions in the extent of the audit work as well as improving client service.

Guidance in this area is set out in ISA 610 (Revised) *Using the Work of Internal Auditors*. As required by ISA 315 (Revised) external auditors should obtain a sufficient understanding of internal audit function activities to assist in planning the audit and developing an effective audit approach. When determining whether to use the work of internal auditors, the auditor should assess the following factors that contribute to its overall quality:

- **The internal auditors' independence and objectivity**

    The level within the organisation to which the internal auditors report the results of their work, and the level to which they report administratively, are indications of the importance the client attaches to the internal audit function. For maximum effectiveness, the internal audit function should have direct access to, and freedom to report to, senior management, including the chief executive, the board of directors and, where one exists, the audit committee.

    The auditor should ascertain the extent to which the internal auditors have the authority to carry out such work as they consider necessary (with access to all relevant records) without first obtaining the permission of senior management.

    Internal audit function reports should be sent to managers who have a direct responsibility for the function being audited and who have the authority to take action on internal audit function recommendations. The auditor should carefully consider Cinders' management's attitude to internal audit function reports, including whether the action taken in response to those reports is both timely and appropriate.

- **Technical knowledge and professional competence**

    The auditor should determine whether there are sufficient suitably qualified and experienced auditors to meet the objectives of the internal audit function. The auditor should consider matters such as: the level of education attained; relevant work experience; specialised skills (eg computer auditing or industry expertise); participation in training programmes; and professional qualifications.

    The auditor should review Cinders' company policy and procedures manuals, internal audit function manuals and other technical guidance, and assess the internal auditors' awareness of such material. This awareness might be obtained through training programmes and by attendance at regular staff meetings. The internal auditors' knowledge of the systems of control and the business generally will be indicative of their knowledge and competence.

- **The professional standards, including quality control procedures, applied in their work**

  The auditor should review the scope and objectives of Cinders' internal auditors' work, and consider whether it is carried out with due professional care (eg whether it is subjected to adequate standards of planning, control, recording and review). The auditor might obtain further evidence of appropriate standards from, for example, the existence of internal audit function manuals, internal audit function plans, quality control reviews and follow-up arrangements.

Chapter 10 Ocean Ltd

This question assesses students' knowledge of internal controls, requiring them to apply general controls over purchases into a specific company scenario.

(a) **Objective of internal control system**

The objective of an internal control system is to provide reasonable assurance about the achievement of an entity's objectives with regard to:

- The reliability of financial reporting
- The effectiveness and efficiency of operations
- Compliance with applicable laws and regulations

(b) **Report**

To: Finance Director
From: Internal auditor

The following procedures should be in operation over the purchasing activities of Ocean Ltd:

(i) **Purchase and receipt of goods**

- The only suppliers that should be used are those on a list that has been approved by a senior purchasing department official.
- The terms that potential suppliers offer should be reviewed whenever a new supplier is chosen, and the best deal obtained. Records of the reasons for the decision should be retained.
- The performance of the suppliers should be regularly reviewed, and details retained of problems such as short orders. The terms major suppliers offer should be periodically compared with terms offered by alternative suppliers.
- The purchasing department should only accept purchase requisitions if the goods are for purchases that the requisitioning department is allowed to purchase, and there is evidence of need (eg inventory is less than the re-order levels).
- Order forms should only be prepared on receipt of an authorised requisition from the department that needs the goods.
- The purchasing department should not be allowed to authorise requisitions for its own requirements. These should be authorised by a different department.
- Order forms should be authorised by a senior purchasing department official.
- Copies of order forms should be sent to the supplier and each of the requisitioning, goods received and accounts department.
- Blank order forms should be pre-numbered, and held securely.

- Goods received notes should be raised when goods are received, and copies sent to the purchasing department. Copies of invoices received by the accounts department should also be sent to the purchasing department.

- The purchasing department should match goods received notes and invoices with purchase orders. The purchase department should investigate unmatched purchase orders, or orders where details do not agree with goods received notes or invoices, or goods received notes for which there is no purchase order.

(ii) **Recording of purchase invoices**

- Invoices received should be promptly recorded.

- Invoices should be referenced in a numerical sequence, with the appropriate supplier and expense reference.

- A list of staff who can authorise invoices for payment should be approved by senior management. These staff should be different from those who can authorise purchase orders or requisitions.

- Each individual should be given a maximum monetary limit for authorisation of invoices. Invoices above that limit should need additional authorisation by a second signatory, or only be authorised by a more senior member of staff.

- Invoices should only be authorised if:
    - The prices on the invoice have been checked
    - The calculation of the invoice has been checked
    - The quantity and description of the goods has been checked by matching the goods received notes with the purchase orders.

- Invoices that have been queried should be filed separately by the accounts department until the matter is resolved.

- When approved, invoices should be posted to the purchase and general ledgers.

ANSWERS TO END OF CHAPTER QUESTIONS

Chapter 11 Razorlight Ltd

This question tests students' knowledge and understanding of the nature of internal controls, and requires them to apply this knowledge to a particular situation. It also requires them to show an appreciation of the limitations of internal controls.

(a) **Raw materials**

Internal control deficiency	Improvement
Raw materials may be removed from the storeroom upon verbal authorisation from one of the production foremen.	Removal should only be allowed upon written authorisation. The authorisation form should be pre-numbered, signed and dated.
There is no perpetual inventory system. Quantities in inventory at the end of one month may not be sufficient to last until the next month's count.	A perpetual inventory system should be established under the control of someone other than the storekeepers. When physical counts are taken these should be matched to the perpetual records, and any differences investigated.
Raw materials are always purchased from the same supplier.	The company should obtain competitive bids on all purchases over a certain amount.
There is no separate receiving department.	A receiving department should be established separate from the storeroom staff, which should count and check all goods received and prepare a receiving report.
The accounts payable clerk is responsible for handling both the purchasing function and payment of invoices.	The purchasing function should be handled by someone separate from the person making payments.
Invoices are paid without confirming that goods have actually been received.	The accounts payable clerk should check each invoice against the supplier's delivery note as well as the purchase order.

Credit sales

Internal control deficiency	Improvement
The functions of computer programming and computer operating are not adequately separated.	The computer operations should be carried out by different employees to those who are responsible for programming the system.
The computer operator should not reconcile the computer log.	The computer log should be reconciled by the computer operator supervisor, or some other independent employee.
Programmers' access to the computers is not properly limited.	Only the computer operators should be allowed free access to the computers. Programmers' access should be limited to testing and debugging.
Batch totals are not developed for later comparison with output.	Batch totals should be used to ensure that data has been properly recorded and not lost or improperly changed.
Processing controls, such as limit tests, reasonableness tests and validity tests are lacking.	Processing controls should be put in place to ensure that errors in the input records will be detected.
The sales clerk should not be responsible for maintaining the accounts receivable records.	An individual who is independent from sales should maintain the accounts receivable records.

(b) The main limitations of internal controls are problems caused by:

Collusion: Controls such as segregation of duties may be nullified by two or more employees who join forces to perpetuate a fraud.

Abuse of authority: A senior official in a position of trust may abuse his or her position in such a way that controls will not prevent or detect the abuse.

Over-ride of controls: Management may be in a position to over-ride controls to hide their misconduct or incompetence.

Pressure on staff: Staff with personal or work-related pressures may act out of character and make simple errors or commit fraud.

Human error: No system is fool-proof; tiredness or carelessness can allow mistakes to get through.

Sophistication in fraudsters: With networked computer systems accessible from outside the organisation, professional fraudsters are constantly developing increasingly sophisticated devices to break down control systems.

Chapter 12 Newpiece Textiles

(a) (i) The matters that are of concern in the bank reconciliation are as follows.

(1) **Delay in banking cash sales**. Cash received does not appear to have been banked until a week after the cash was received. A **teeming** and **lading fraud** could have occurred, where an embezzlement of receipts is covered up by an apparent delay in banking subsequent receipts.

(2) **Delay in presentation of cheques by suppliers.** Most suppliers would bank cheques within seven to ten days. However payments to the majority of suppliers entered on October 31 have not been cleared for over two weeks. Cheques, although entered prior to the year-end, may not therefore have been sent to suppliers until some time after the year-end. The reason for doing this would be to **improve** the appearance of the company's **liquidity** in its accounts, by decreasing cash and payables, and hence improving the company's current and acid test ratios.

(ii) **Cash sales**

The following tests should be carried out.

(1) Compare the date on the bank statement with the date stamped on the paying-in slip. If the dates are the same or a day apart, then that is strong evidence of when the cheques were actually banked.

(2) Compare amounts banked with cash records for the day (invoices or the till roll).

(3) Compare receivable ledger cash received per cash book with daily listing of cash received.

(4) Carry out further investigations if there does appear to be a significant delay between collecting and banking cash. Investigations should cover other periods of the year and the situation at the date of the audit.

(5) If there is unbanked cash at the date of the audit, inspect this cash. Failure to produce this cash would be strong evidence of fraud.

ANSWERS TO END OF CHAPTER QUESTIONS

Uncleared payments

The following tests should be carried out.

(1) Ask cashiers and others involved in sending cheques out when the cheques were actually sent.

(2) Obtain suppliers' statements after the year-end, and check the date the cash is shown as received. If this date is similar to the date shown on the bank statement, the cheques would probably have been sent out after the year-end.

(iii) (1) If the cash receipts represent monies that have been embezzled, these receipts should be excluded from the cash balances at the year-end ($2,705). If the money is irrecoverable, it should be charged as an expense to profit or loss; if it appears to be recoverable, it should be charged as an amount owing.

(2) Cash and payables should be increased as it appears that the true date of the cheques, the date that the cheques were sent to suppliers, was after the year-end. Thus the bank balance and current liabilities should be increased by $77,501, the total of cheques 2164 to 2170.

Thus the true cash book balance will be $681 overdrawn.

(b) (i) **Materiality**

Two commonly used measures of materiality are 1% of revenue and 5% of profit before tax. For Newpiece these two measures would suggest materiality levels of $25,000 and $7,500 respectively. Total petty cash expenditure is well over the profit measure and slightly under the revenue measure, and this indicates that on balance it should be audited. However about $15,000 of total expenditure occurred in two months. This suggests that testing should be concentrated on these months, with a briefer review taking place of other months, since material fraud and error is unlikely to occur during those months.

Audit risk

Petty cash is a high risk audit area for the following reasons.

(1) Cash is the most liquid asset, and hence there is a high risk of defalcation.

(2) Supporting documentation for payments may be limited.

(3) The failure to keep petty cash on an imprest system means that it may not be subject to regular management review.

(4) Risk would be increased by a large petty cash balance (say over $1,000), as this would offer greater opportunity for fraud.

(ii) The audit tests that will be carried out are as follows.

Initial procedures

(1) Agree opening balances to working papers for last year
(2) Cast additions in petty cash book
(3) Agree petty cash book totals to the general ledger

Review of unusual items and analytical review

(1) Review cash payments in the general ledger and investigate unusual transactions

(2) Carry out analytical procedures on balances by comparing amounts with cash flow forecasts

Transactions (to test existence, completeness and rights and obligations)

(1) Verify individual payments in petty cash book (concentrating on the larger items) to supporting documentation and check that employee has acknowledged receipt of cash

(2) Check cash cut-off procedures have been performed by reviewing reconciliation at the year-end, and checking that all reconciling items can be satisfactorily explained and have subsequently been cleared

Cash counts (to verify existence, completeness, rights and obligations and accuracy, valuation and allocation)

(1) Count all balances simultaneously and agree to petty cash book or other record.

(2) All counting should be done in the presence of the individuals responsible and they should sign at the end of the count to acknowledge funds returned are complete.

(3) Enquire into any IOUs or cashed cheques outstanding for unreasonable periods of time.

(4) Confirm that bank and cash balances as reconciled above are correctly stated in the accounts.

Follow-up procedures should include the following tests

(1) Check unbanked cheques/cash receipts have subsequently been paid in and agree to the bank reconciliation.

(2) Check IOUs and cheques cashed for employees have been reimbursed.

(3) Check IOUs or cashed cheques outstanding for unreasonable periods of time have been provided for.

Presentation and classification

Check presentation of cash balances in the accounts is correct.

Chapter 13 Boston Manufacturing

(a) **Audit risk in the tangible non-current asset audit**

Control risk

The controls over non-current assets at Boston Manufacturing appear to be strong. The company maintains and reconciles a non-current asset register and there are authorisation procedures in operation. These controls should be tested, and if they prove effective, control risk could be assessed low.

Inherent risk

The tangible non-current assets are material on the basis of the proposed materiality level. There has been a substantial movement on the plant and equipment account this year, but this appears to be supported by the information given by the management accountant. There appear to be no disposals in the year, which may indicate that they have been omitted, or that obsolete items are included in the register. It is also unclear whether land is being depreciated. It would be inappropriate if it was being depreciated. Overall, the inherent risk seems to be medium.

Detection risk

Given that inherent risk has been assessed as medium and control risk has been assessed as low, detection risk will be assessed as higher. However, there is usually good evidence in relation to the existence and valuation of non-current assets and these are the key assertions which the auditors are interested in. There will also be scope to carry out good analytical procedures, such as proof-in-total of depreciation.

Conclusion

The audit of non-current assets appears to be medium to low risk.

(b) **Audit procedures**

(i) **Existence**

In many cases it is self-evident that land and buildings exist. However, it is important for the auditors to verify all components of land and buildings contained within the statement of financial position, if they are on a site different to the one which the auditors are primarily attending, for example. Land and buildings should also be verified to **title deeds** to ensure that they **not only exist**, but that **they are owned** by the client.

The other classes of asset should be **inspected**. A sample of assets from the **register should be agreed to the physical asset**. There may be scope to rely on the work that the management accountant has undertaken here. The auditor should check a reconciliation which the accountant has undertaken. The auditors should make use of any identification marks on assets recorded in the register, for example, security tags or bar codes which are kept on assets to distinguish them. The auditor should inspect the **condition** of the assets and ensure that they are **in use**.

The motor vehicles should be **reconciled in terms of number of vehicles existing at the opening and closing positions**. Again, to ensure that they not only exist, but are owned by the company, the auditors should check the **registration documents** to ensure that the company is the registered owner.

For all the above assets, the external auditor should also review the insurance provision for the assets. This gives **third party evidence** of the existence of assets as the insurer would not insure an asset which did not exist.

(ii) **Accuracy, valuation and allocation (excluding depreciation)**

Land and buildings appear to be stated at historic **cost** as the schedule does not contain the words 'at valuation'. The auditors should **confirm** that this is the case with the management accountant. The cost can then be **agreed to brought forward figures** as there have been no additions in the year. These figures will have been audited in the previous year. If the assets are held at valuation, the auditors must ensure that the requirements of IAS 16 in relation to revaluations are being complied with.

Similarly, as there have been no movements in the year, **motor vehicles** can be agreed to the **opening position**.

To audit the valuation of **plant and computers**, the auditors should **agree the opening position**. They should then **obtain a schedule of additions** to non-current assets, which can be **agreed to purchase invoices** to verify valuation.

Lastly, the auditors should investigate whether the cost figures include any **fully-written down assets**. This is implied by the fact that the depreciation charge on plant excluding additions is low. If so, the auditor should find out whether these assets **are still in use**, and if not, consider whether they **should be excluded** from the cost and accumulated depreciation figures contained within the notes to the accounts. Excluding them would have a net effect on the reported figure of $0.

(iii) **Completeness**

The schedule of non-current assets prepared should be reconciled to:

- The **opening position** (that is, the previous statement of financial position)
- The **closing position** (what is disclosed in the financial statements)
- The **underlying records** (the nominal ledger)

If the non-current asset register contains details of the cost and accumulated depreciation of each asset, the **register should also be reconciled to the schedule**. Explanations should be sought for any differences.

The additions of the schedule should also be checked to ensure that the opening and closing positions reconcile within the schedule.

The auditors should also carry out a test on some of the **individual additions**, tracing the transaction through the system, from purchase orders to delivery notes and invoices and through the ledgers to the financial statements to ensure that additions have been included completely.

(c) **Depreciation**

(i) **Appropriateness**

The appropriateness of the rates should be considered and discussed with management. **Relevant factors** to consider are matters such as:

- The **replacement policy** for the asset
- The pattern of **usage** in the business
- The **purpose of the asset** being owned

In this instance, the auditors should establish the rationale behind the depreciation rates applied, particularly in the case of plant. In the case of the plant purchased this year, the depreciation charged for the year appears to be lower than would be expected given that the plant is going to be used for an eight year project.

(ii) **Audit procedures**

Depreciation on **buildings** can be verified by agreeing the purchase date of the buildings to last year's file or historic invoices/purchase documents and the valuation applied to the building portion.

For the other classes of asset, depreciation should be agreed for individual assets, as it is not possible to agree them in total. The auditors should obtain a **breakdown of the charges** for the year. They should be able to **recalculate the depreciation** from details in the non-current asset register and compare the results.

Chapter 14 Inventory count

This question tests students' knowledge of the auditor's role at an inventory count.

Before the count starts the audit assistant should:

- Note the nature, location and layout of the inventories to be counted;
- Establish that any weighbridge or weighing machine to be used in the count gives accurate results;
- Determine whether inventories are marked, labelled or otherwise described so that they can be identified by the count team(s);
- Review the adequacy of the client's inventory count instructions and procedures.

The assistant should attend the start of the count (and any briefing by the client) to ensure that it is orderly, well controlled and methodical from the outset.

During the count, the assistant should carry out the following procedures:

- Observe and enquire whether inventories are adequately safeguarded and protected against deterioration.

- Confirm that the procedures for segregating inventory not owned by the client, or to be otherwise excluded from the count, have been followed.
- In the case of work-in-progress, ensure by observation that each production stage has been segregated and the stage of completion has been identified.
- Test counts should be carried out. To obtain evidence in respect of both completeness and existence (as well as accuracy), the assistant should select items for testing from two sources:
    - The count records, verifying the existence and quantity of the inventories (existence and accuracy).
    - The physical inventories, ensuring that the amounts are accurately included in the count records (completeness and accuracy).
- Confirm, by touring the location and observing the work of the counting teams, that the instructions are carried out effectively so that:
    - All inventories owned by the client are counted
    - All other inventories are excluded from the results of the count (clients frequently count all inventories present in a particular location, identifying third party goods to ensure their subsequent exclusion)
    - Inventory sheets, tags or other means used to record quantities are adequately controlled
    - Movements of goods during the count are properly controlled to avoid double counting or omission
    - Slow-moving, obsolete or damaged inventories are clearly identified
- Record details of despatch and receipts records, for cut-off purposes. These might include the last prenumbered despatch notes or goods received notes issued prior to the inventory count date, and the last entries in goods inwards/outwards registers. Also for cut-off purposes, it is important to identify and note:
    - Items which appear to have been recently delivered (eg in the goods inwards bay but not unpacked); and
    - Items which appear ready for despatch (eg inventories in the despatch bay or packed and addressed).
- Obtain details, at the conclusion of the count, of all records used in the count, so that it is possible to check later for suppression, manipulation, addition or substitution of records after the count. If it is not practicable to retain copies of the count records, the assistant should note details of, and take extracts from, the records used. It may be necessary to authenticate the records by initialling them.

ANSWERS TO END OF CHAPTER QUESTIONS

Chapter 15 Ridesafe Ltd

This question tests students' knowledge and understanding of audit evidence, in the context of the audit of accounts receivable.

(a) The procedures for a receivables confirmation are as follows:

Select sample

Prepare letter. The request is normally typed on the client's letterhead and signed by a responsible official. A stamped addressed envelope addressed to the auditor's office should accompany the request. All requests should be sent by the audit staff and not left to the client staff. Control of the confirmation requests must remain with the audit staff at all times, from the moment of preparation up to and including the time of posting.

Follow-up any non-replies.

These include the following:

A follow-up letter and copy of the original request. This should be subject to the same control as the original.

With the client's permission, telephone the customer.

Perform alternative verification procedures. If it proves impossible to obtain confirmations from individual customers after the follow-up procedures, alternative methods of verifying those balances should be adopted.

Evaluate results. All differences and non-replies should be followed-up and their effect on the population as a whole should be evaluated. Differences due to acceptable timing differences and mistakes made by the customer are generally not a problem. Disputed amounts and mistakes made by the client are more cause for concern, eg unrecorded credit notes. These should be aggregated and extrapolated to the population to estimate the potential misstatement in the population as a whole

(b) Differences in receivable confirmations:

Non-replies

There were two non-replies, and further work must be carried out on these balances. This will involve vouching back from the invoice to the despatch notes to ensure that the invoice was sent to the recipient of the goods. The cashbook should also be checked to establish if any cash has been received after the year-end.

Inability to confirm

One customer was unable to confirm the balance, because they did not operate a payables ledger. A further letter should be sent with the individual invoices separately itemised, as this may allow the customer to check against their records.

Posting errors

Two of the customers replied that part of the circularised balance did not relate to them. This would suggest invoices are being incorrectly posted. It must be established how many mispostings have occurred, as this might affect the recoverability of debts. It must also be established why those misposted invoices had not been picked up earlier by Ridesafe's control system.

Disputed balances

The confirmations identified a disputed account with Hamelaw Group, due to ragged edges on a seat. They are refusing to pay as they are being sued as a result of an injury. This must be discussed with the directors of Ridesafe, as another company, Orkney Ltd also returned seats and received a credit note as a result.

An allowance will be required for Hamelaw's balance, as it is unlikely that this will be received. In addition, the balance for Orkney Ltd should be written-off to correctly reflect the credit note issued after the year-end.

(c) Additional audit work required on the irrecoverable debt allowance relates to:

Discussion with client

All debts identified as irrecoverable will have to be discussed with Ridesafe's accountant. The accountant will have knowledge of the customers, and will also be aware of any action taken by Ridesafe to recover the debt.

Procedures for screening new customers

If comprehensive checks are carried out on prospective customers regarding liquidity and credit records, this will reduce the risk of irrecoverable debts as all the customers will be reputable and should be in a position to pay their debts. Consideration should be made of whether realistic credit limits are put in place, and whether any action is taken if these are exceeded.

Reviewing correspondence

Reviewing the correspondence with customers will give evidence as to the likelihood that the debt will be received. The correspondence will show if any legal action is taken against the client or if there are any problems preventing the customer paying.

Review past payment record

Reviewing the past payment record will show if the customer is normally a slow payer. If normally the balances are cleared quickly, but one item is outstanding for significantly longer, this could indicate a problem with the debt, which will require further investigation to its recoverability.

(d) The current allowance for receivables is inadequate. The 20X7 allowance is only $100 more than the previous year's allowance, although receivables have increased by over $34,000.

A review of the receivables/revenue ratio indicates that customers were taking approximately 109 days to pay in 20X7, compared to 76 days in 20X6. This points to a possible recoverability problem, which is strengthened by the fact that 28% of the receivable balances are greater than 90 days old, compared with 4% in 20X6.

Both the general allowance and the specific allowance appear to be inadequate. In 20X6, the general allowance was 5% of receivables, whereas this year it represents only 2% of receivables. It would be advisable to increase the allowance to 5%, in line with the previous year. The specific allowance at $600 is likely to be inadequate, especially when viewed in relation to receivables greater than 90 days of over $17,000.

(e) Wider implications for the audit are:

Inventory write-off

An inventory allowance will be needed against the Model C seats included in inventory at the year-end. Work will be needed to ascertain how many of the seats are affected, how easily the defect can be rectified, and what effect this will have on the value of the seats.

Going concern

Revenue has increased due to the high sales on Model C. If the model cannot be rectified and sales are discontinued, revenue would fall to such an extent that Ridesafe may be unable to continue trading. If so, the audit opinion may need to be modified in respect of going concern.

ANSWERS TO END OF CHAPTER QUESTIONS

Potential litigation

We should review all correspondence with Ridesafe's lawyers in relation to the potential claim by Hamelaw Group. If it seems likely that a claim will be made, we should consider the need to disclose a contingent liability in respect of the litigation.

Chapter 16 Olorosa Ltd

(a) The audit objectives for share capital, reserves and dividends are set out below. The auditor should obtain enough evidence to ensure that:

Completeness; accuracy; existence; accuracy, valuation and allocation	All changes in the authorised or allotted share capital have been properly accounted for.
	All movements on reserves have been properly accounted for and items which should be reserve movements have been included as such.
	All dividends have been approved and properly accounted for.
	The authorised share capital is in agreement with the Memorandum of Association, and the allotted share capital is in agreement with the share register.
	All dividends have been correctly calculated.
	Transfers to, and movements between, reserves have been correctly made in accordance with appropriate resolutions, minutes, or other authorisations.
	The amounts reported in the financial statements are in agreement with the accounting records.
	All amounts shown in respect of share capital and reserves have been correctly valued.
	Appropriate policies have been applied to account for the issue of shares at nominal or fair value.
Cut-off	Movements in share capital and reserves have been accounted for in the correct accounting period.
Rights and obligations	Rights and obligations relating to share capital, reserves and dividends have been correctly identified.
Presentation and Classification	Share capital, reserves and dividends have been properly classified, described and disclosed in the financial statements.

(b) The audit of the revaluation reserve will involve:

- Preparing a schedule showing movements in the year
- Assessment for the reason for any revaluation, the basis of the revaluation and its reasonableness in the light of the auditor's knowledge of the business and the property market
- Evaluation of the qualifications and experience of the valuer
- Checking that the correct entries for the revaluation have been made in the nominal ledger
- Ensuring that adequate disclosures have been made in the financial statements, including the qualifications of the valuer, and any difference between the recorded value and market value

ANSWERS TO END OF CHAPTER QUESTIONS

Chapter 17 Subsequent events and going concern

This question tests students' knowledge and understanding of audit completion procedures, particularly the subsequent events review and going concern considerations, and their effect on the auditor's report.

(a) Auditors have a responsibility to review events which occur after the year end, before they sign the audit report, and consider their effect on the financial statements, and on the audit report. ISA 560 *Subsequent Events* states that 'the auditor should perform procedures designed to obtain sufficient appropriate audit evidence that all events up to the date of the auditor's report that may require adjustment of, or disclosure in, the financial statements have been identified'.

Subsequent events might affect the amounts at which items are stated in the financial statements or they might require disclosure. It is therefore important to be alert to the possibility of such events at all stages of the audit. In addition, specific audit procedures should be carried out to ascertain whether such events have occurred. The objective of these procedures should be to provide reasonable assurance that all material subsequent events, including 'window dressing' transactions have been identified and, where appropriate, either disclosed or accounted for. Audit procedures should cover the period between the end of the reporting period and the date the audit report is signed.

(b) When preparing financial statements, the directors should satisfy themselves as to whether the going concern basis is appropriate. ISA 570 (Revised) *Going Concern* states that when planning and performing audit procedures and in evaluating the results, the auditor must consider the appropriateness of management's use of the going concern basis of accounting in the preparation of financial statements.

Audit procedures in relation to going concern are intended to provide assurance that:

- The going concern basis of accounting used in the preparation of the financial statements as a whole is appropriate; and
- The existence of material uncertainties about the going concern basis of accounting that need to be disclosed in the accounts.

The auditor should therefore consider:

- The process management used to assess going concern;
- The assumptions on which management's assessment is made;
- Management's plans for future action.

In the case of Serif Ltd, the sale of the company's only profitable paper mill has cast significant doubts over the company's ability to continue as a going concern. In these circumstances, ISA 570 (Revised) states that the auditor should:

- Review management's plans for future actions, based on its going concern assessment;
- Gather sufficient appropriate audit evidence to confirm or dispel whether or not a material uncertainty exists;
- Seek written representations from management regarding its plans for future actions.

This means that the auditor must actively seek evidence to determine whether or not the company will be able to continue for the foreseeable future. The auditor is likely to focus on future cash flows of the business, as it is unlikely to be able to carry on trading if it has insufficient funds.

Serif Ltd's auditor should discuss with management their plans for future action. Particularly, the auditor should find out what the directors plan to do with the money generated from the sale of the paper mill – for example, will this be used to pay off the company's existing debts, or to invest in new technology which may allow the remaining mills to become profitable.

(c) There are various options available to the auditor in respect of the audit report, depending on his or her assessment of the company's going concern status, and the treatment and disclosures made in the financial statements.

If the use of the going concern basis of accounting is appropriate but a material uncertainty exists, the auditor should consider whether the financial statements:

(i) Adequately describe the principal events or conditions that give rise to the significant doubt on the company's ability to continue in operation and management's plans to deal with these events or conditions; and

(ii) State clearly that there is a material uncertainty related to events or conditions which may cast significant doubt on the company's ability to continue as a going concern and, therefore, that it may be unable to realise its assets and discharge its liabilities in the normal course of business.

If adequate disclosure is made in the financial statements, the auditor should express an unqualified opinion but modify the auditor's report by adding an explanatory paragraph titled 'Material Uncertainty Related to Going Concern' that highlights the existence of a material uncertainty relating to the event or condition that may cast significant doubt on the company's ability to continue as a going concern and draws attention to the note in the financial statements that discloses the relevant matters.

In evaluating the adequacy of the financial statement disclosure, the auditor should consider whether the information explicitly draws the reader's attention to the possibility that the company may be unable to continue realising its assets and discharging its liabilities in the normal course of business.

If adequate disclosure is not made in the financial statements, the auditor should express a qualified or adverse opinion, as appropriate. The report should include specific reference to the fact that there is a material uncertainty that may cast significant doubt about the company's ability to continue as a going concern.

If, in the auditor's judgement, the company will not be able to continue as a going concern, the auditor should express an adverse opinion if the financial statements have been prepared on a going concern basis. If, on the basis of the additional audit procedures carried out and the information obtained, including the effect of management's plans, the auditor's judgment is that the company will not be able to continue as a going concern, the auditor should conclude, regardless of whether or not disclosure has been made, that the going concern basis of accounting used in the preparation of the financial statements is inappropriate and should express an adverse opinion.

When the company's management has concluded that the going concern basis of accounting used in the preparation of the financial statements is not appropriate, the financial statements need to be prepared on an alternative basis. If on the basis of the additional audit procedures carried out and the information obtained the auditor determines the alternative basis is appropriate, the auditor can issue an unqualified opinion if there is adequate disclosure but may require an emphasis of matter in the auditor's report to draw the user's attention to that basis.

ANSWERS TO END OF CHAPTER QUESTIONS

Chapter 18 Samson Inc

This question tests students' knowledge and understanding of the requirements of ISA 705 (Revised) regarding modified audit opinions, and requires them to apply this knowledge to the audit report in particular circumstances.

(a) There are two circumstances that could give rise to a modified audit opinion. These are:

(1) Where the auditor has been unable to obtain sufficient appropriate audit evidence which could have a material effect on the financial statements

(2) Where there is a material misstatement in the financial statements

There are three forms of the modified audit opinion, and the form of the modification will depend on the circumstances that the auditor has found. The following table summarises the possible modifications to the auditor's opinion:

Nature of Matter Giving Rise to the Modification	Auditor's Judgement about the Pervasiveness of the Effects or Possible Effects on the Financial Statements	
	Material but Not Pervasive	Material and Pervasive
Financial statements are materially misstated	Qualified opinion	Adverse opinion
Inability to obtain sufficient appropriate audit evidence	Qualified opinion	Disclaimer of opinion

To warrant modification, the matter must be material, however some matters may be so serious that they are considered to be not just material, but pervasive/significant to the financial statements. The auditor must use judgement when making the distinction between material and pervasive.

(b) (i) **Blakemore Ltd – irrecoverable debt**

This item is material, as it represents nearly 10% of Samson's profit before tax, and approximately 0.27% of the company's net assets. The matter is not pervasive, as it only affects a few account balances, and is unlikely to result in the financial statements being seriously misleading. The auditor should issue a qualified audit opinion on the grounds of a material misstatement, clearly setting out the reasons for the qualification and quantifying the effects on the financial statements. The audit opinion will state that in the auditor's opinion the financial statements give a true and fair view, except for this particular matter. The basis for qualified opinion paragraph will describe the reason for the qualified opinion.

(ii) **Revalued properties**

The increase in the valuation of the properties represents over 3% of the net assets of the company, and as such the revaluation is clearly material. The auditor may be able to obtain alternative audit evidence is respect of the value of the properties such as using an auditor's expert to provide an independent valuation. However, if this is not possible, this would represent a situation where the auditor has been unable to obtain sufficient appropriate audit evidence. Should this be the case, the auditor should therefore issue a qualified opinion. The basis for qualified opinion paragraph should clearly set out the reasons for the lack of sufficient appropriate audit evidence and quantify the effects on the financial statements. The audit opinion will state that in the auditor's opinion the financial statements give a true and fair view, except for this particular matter.

(iii) **Contract with DDC Ltd**

Samson is faced with a significant uncertainty concerning the outcome of its negotiations to renew this contract. The uncertainty is significant because it impacts on the going concern status of Samson, as if the contract is not renewed, it is likely that Samson will not remain a going concern. In forming an opinion on the financial statements, the auditor must take into account the adequacy of the treatment of the uncertainty. Assuming the auditor considers the directors' explanatory note to be adequate, the auditor should not modify the audit opinion. However, a material uncertainty relating to going concern paragraph which refers to the directors' disclosure should be included after the basis for opinion paragraph.

(iv) **Court case**

This court case is potentially very serious for the company – if Samson loses the case, which it has a 50% chance of doing, it will certainly go out of business, since it would lose its trading licence. This item therefore represents a fundamental uncertainty. If the directors were to make adequate disclosure of the fundamental uncertainty then the auditor should include an emphasis of matter paragraph to draw users' attention to the matter. However, because the directors are refusing to disclose the matter, the auditor should include an adverse opinion in the auditor's report. This will state that in the auditor's opinion the accounts do not give a true and fair view and the basis for adverse opinion paragraph should describe the reasons for the adverse opinion.

ANSWERS TO END OF CHAPTER QUESTIONS

Practice question bank

Question 1

International Standards on Auditing (ISAs) are issued by the International Auditing and Assurance Standards Board (IAASB).

One of these standards is ISA 700 (Revised) *Forming an Opinion and Reporting on Financial Statements*, which deals with the form and content of the auditor's report issued as a result of an audit of financial statements.

Required

(a) Discuss why the worldwide auditing profession is required to comply with ISAs. **(5 marks)**

(b) Explain the form and content of the basic elements of the auditor's report as required by ISA 700 (Revised).

(**Note.** You are not required to discuss the requirements of ISA 705 (Revised), which deals with auditor's reports with modified opinions.)

(10 marks)

(Total 15 marks)

Question 2

The following is an extract from a recent article in Views of Today's News, a newspaper with a worldwide readership. The author of the article clearly is of the opinion that auditors and the auditing profession are an unnecessary waste of time and money.

VIEWS OF TODAY'S NEWS

www.viewsoftodaysnews.com   THE WORLD'S FAVOURITE NEWSPAPER   - Since 1999

WHO AUDITS THE AUDITORS?

As a rule I'm usually tolerant, but some things make me very angry. One is a deep hatred of the proliferation in recent years of bureaucracies like the auditing profession. Auditors claim to ensure high standards in all sorts of organisations. In my opinion, the whole of the auditing profession should be abolished.

These busybodies have damaged our business communities and have made everyone's quality of life much worse, not better. The millions of hours and dollars spent making managers jump through their endless and ever-changing hoops distracts and detracts from actually doing their jobs. What a waste of time and money! No one would deny the principle of accountability, especially of taxpayers'

The auditors seem to have the mantra 'if it moves, audit What use is an audit, for example, to a small local voluntary group, run by its members, for its members? Even if we concede that large companies should have some accountability to their shareholders, surely the current audit goes way too far and the costs far outweigh any benefits?
It baffles me that the business community doesn't resist all this rubbish more. A good society runs on liberty and trust, not surveillance and audit. Auditing is a marginal, third-order activity that has accidentally become centre-stage by some fluke of history. Who needs it?

Required

(a) Identify and briefly discuss the historical factors that have created the demand for modern international auditing. **(10 marks)**

(b) Write a response to the editor of Views of Today's News explaining how the following organisations might benefit from having an audit carried out by an independent auditor:

- A large, multinational company such as Microsoft
- A large charity such as the Red Cross
- A country's central bank, such as the Bank of England
- A small family-run grocery store
- A local sports club

(15 marks)

(Total 25 marks)

Question 3

Consider the newspaper article below concerning the resignation of DQT Co:

AMP news Daily

3 September 2020

Surprise resignation of audit firm, DQT Co

In an unexpected move, audit firm DQT Co resigned as auditor of SAY Co last week stating that they were unable to reach a satisfactory conclusion in relation to the disclosure of financial instruments in SAY Co's financial statements.

In a short statement to the local stock exchange yesterday, SAY Co's CEO, Jeff Pryke, explained that SAY Co and DQT Co could not come to an agreement as to whether certain financial instruments required disclosure in the financial statements and that DQT Co also had concerns over some of SAY Co's corporate governance policies.

Jeff Pryke reported that the Board had sought professional advice relating to the required disclosures and that this was contrary to the opinions held by DQT Co's technical department. Mr Pryke noted that the resignation of DQT Co was a matter the Board would take seriously and that they would seek to appoint a replacement auditor at the earliest opportunity.

Required

(a) Discuss why an auditor may choose to resign from an audit assignment. **(12 marks)**

(b) Explain what procedures DQT Co should have undertaken on their resignation from the audit of SAY Co. **(13 marks)**

(Total 25 marks)

Question 4

(a) A recent business magazine included an article about the changing face of the auditing profession. The article argued that audit firms were having to adapt in response to various global trends.

Required

Discuss to what extent the following factors affect the demand for and the performance of auditing services:

(i) Economic expansion and development
(ii) Globalization and the internationalization of capital markets
(iii) The increasing complexity of financial operations
(iv) Information technology advances **(6 marks)**

(b) The International Federation of Accountants (IFAC) is an international accounting body. IFAC has set up, and supports, the International Auditing and Assurance Standards Board (IAASB), the independent standard-setting body for international auditing standards.

Required

Discuss the role of both IFAC and the IAASB, explaining how international auditing standards are set. **(7 marks)**

(c) Anders Torven is a registered independent auditor. He is concerned about the management structure of one of his new audit clients, GHL Ltd. The company's board of directors is dominated by the president, Jenny Styles. She makes most of the major operating and business decisions herself, and she has a reputation in the business community for making optimistic projections about future earnings and then putting considerable pressure on operating and accounting staff to make sure those projections are met. She has also been associated with other companies in the past that have gone bankrupt.

During the initial stages of the audit, Anders was surprised to discover that many of the internal controls over inventory, which Jenny had told him were operating efficiently, were in fact either absent, or being operated in a half-hearted and inadequate manner. Anders was also concerned that large quantities of inventory, which Jenny had told him were less than two months old, had in fact been purchased by GHL Ltd over six months previously.

Required

Discuss Anders responsibilities as auditor of GHL Ltd in respect of the detection of any fraud and/or error. **(7 marks)**

(Total 20 marks)

Question 5

You are an audit partner with a large accountancy firm. One of your clients, Magnum plc, is currently considering whether or not to obtain a listing on the London Stock Exchange. They have sought your advice on several matters which concern them. This is the latest email you have received from the company's finance director:

PRACTICE QUESTION BANK

> Subject: Internal audit
> From: JJones@magnum.co.uk
> To: S.Lee@RPG.co.uk
>
> Dear Sally,
>
> Thank you for all your helpful advice as our company moves towards obtaining a stock exchange listing.
>
> I have yet another question for you. As you know, if we become listed, we will need to comply with corporate governance best practice. As we recently discussed, it was important for the company to set up an audit committee. You will be pleased to know that this has now been done, and the committee met for the first time last week.
>
> You also mentioned that we should set up an internal audit department, but we have not yet got around to doing this.
>
> Before we commit to the expense involved in setting this up, I'd be grateful if you would explain how Magnum plc could benefit from having an internal audit function, and what the relationship should be between the internal audit department and the audit committee.
>
> Looking forward to hearing from you,
>
>
> Best regards,
>
> Joe

Required

Produce a reply to the finance director's email. **(20 marks)**

Question 6

You are Paul Winter, an audit partner with Chandavar Associates, an accountancy firm which provides audit services. Your firm has recently been appointed as auditors of Hawk plc. Although Hawk has been operating for many years, you are the first auditor to be appointed, since the company was previously able to take advantage of the small company audit exemption.

You are aware that the directors of Hawk have appointed your firm as auditor very reluctantly. They were forced to appoint an auditor because the company has grown, and no longer meets the size criteria for audit exemption.

You have just received the following letter from Avril Archibald, the company's finance director.

Avril has only recently been appointed as finance director. She previously worked for the company as financial controller, but was promoted following the sudden death of the previous finance director. Avril has no professional accountancy qualification, but has worked her way up the company since joining as a bookkeeping assistant when she left school.

Mr Paul Winter
Chandavar Associates
20 Main Street
Anytown

1 May 20X3

Dear Mr Winter,

As you are aware, your firm will be commencing the first audit of our company next month. As I know you are also aware, my fellow directors and I are somewhat unhappy that our company is now required to have an audit.

I have been asked by my board to write to you about three specific matters which are of concern to us.

Firstly, we still do not understand why we need to have an audit given that we have successfully managed without one since the company was started ten years ago. We cannot see any advantages, but do see it as an unnecessary expense which will add little, if any, value to the business.

Secondly, one of the other directors has told us that now we have an auditor, we will need to form an audit committee. Is this the case, and what is the purpose of such a committee?

Finally, as finance director, I am very anxious about what will happen if you find any errors in the draft accounts which I am in the process of preparing. If I make any mistakes and the audit report is modified as a result, this will put me in a very difficult position with my fellow directors, and my job may well be at risk.

I look forward to hearing from you.

Yours sincerely,

Avril Archibald
Finance director

Required

Prepare a letter replying to Avril Archibald. **(25 marks)**

Question 7

You are in charge of the internal audit department at Olorosa University. It is the university's policy to charge students for any large quantities of printed classroom materials, although smaller quantities are not normally charged. It is up to the individual lecturers to determine whether or not to make such a charge, and to collect the money from students.

You have received a copy of some correspondence between the university finance officer and a member of the teaching staff. The lecturer had collected some cash from a first-year class for the photocopying of notes. She had lodged most of this with the finance office, but had kept approximately $45 in respect of some expenses which she had incurred on university business. She had submitted a memo to say that she had done so, which was supported by valid receipts for the expenses. The receipts were signed by the lecturer's head of department to confirm that the expenditure had been authorised.

PRACTICE QUESTION BANK

The head of finance is unhappy that cash receipts are not being banked intact, and has asked you to investigate the matter.

Required

(a) Explain why the university's cash takings should always be banked promptly, and without any deductions, even if there is no intention to defraud. **(8 marks)**

(b) Explain how the auditor should audit the university's income from photocopying for completeness. **(6 marks)**

(Total 14 marks)

Question 8

You are Jo Jones, a qualified accountant with many years' experience who was recently appointed as the ethics partner with Samsons, a medium-sized accountancy firm. On your first day in the job, you are introduced to Sarah Chan, a less experienced accountant who will be your assistant.

Sarah has been in post for a month already, during which time she was approached by several members of staff asking questions about possible violations of the Code of Ethics for Professional Accountants. Sarah has collected the questions together and has produced the following memo for your attention:

From: Sarah Chan
To: Jo Jones
Date: 1 May 20X4

Several members of staff have been in touch with me in the last few weeks, asking for advice on the following matters. I would be grateful if you could give me your opinion, and I will get back to the staff concerned.

(i) Zeta Jason is a partner in Samsons' tax department in the Edinburgh office. She was required to prepare and submit a tax return to the tax authorities, based on information provided to her by Emporium Ltd one of the firm's non-audit clients. Zeta is concerned that the information she was given deliberately omitted some of the income the client received from cash sales.

(ii) Carlos Egea is a partner in our London office. This office was recently the subject of a review of its quality management procedures, carried out by the Financial Reporting Council, which is the firm's regulatory body. During this review, some of the audit staff were asked questions about their working papers, which resulted in them disclosing information which Carlos believes is confidential to the audit clients concerned. Carlos is furious, and is considering taking disciplinary action against the staff involved.

(iii) Pierre Volant is one of the managers in the firm's Cardiff office. He is concerned about whether or not he should agree to carry out additional work on behalf of a client. The client is Fedamax Ltd, a small company which is owned and run by a local couple. Samsons carried out the audit of the company last year, and had issued an unqualified audit report. The company's bookkeeper has recently had to retire due to ill health, and the directors have asked Pierre to help them out by keeping the company's books and records updated until they are able to appoint a new bookkeeper.

(iv) Maxine Stoppard is the senior partner in Samsons' Belfast office. She has recently gained a new audit client for the firm – WineWorld plc. Several other audit firms tendered for the audit, and Maxine and her team were delighted to beat the competition. The directors of WineWorld have invited Maxine and her team to join them for a long weekend break in the company's villa on the Spanish island of Ibiza. The villa is normally used only to entertain WineWorld's corporate clients. The directors have explained that the purpose of this visit will be two-fold – firstly, to congratulate Maxine and her colleagues on being awarded the contract, and also to allow the audit team to get to know WineWorld's directors and senior staff, and to learn more about their business. Maxine has asked whether it would be appropriate to accept the invitation.

Required

(a) Explain why there is a need for a Code of Ethics for Professional Accountants. **(3 marks)**

(b) Reply to Sarah's memo, identifying and discussing the ethical implications of each of the situations she has brought to your attention. **(12 marks)**

(Total 15 marks)

Question 9

Chris Jenkins is a recently qualified accountant working for Massy & Co, an accountancy firm. He was recently a member of the audit team carrying out the audit of Steffi Ltd. The audit had almost all been completed, and the team was finishing off the audit field work, making sure everything had been satisfactorily completed and signed off, and tying up any loose ends. Samira Darweesh, the audit partner, had indicated that she was under pressure from the client to sign the audit report by the end of the week, and had asked the team to try to finish off the work as quickly as possible.

Chris was finalising the audit work on purchases and trade payables. One of the junior audit staff had noticed a large invoice being received from a single supplier just before the year end, which was matched by a credit note issued by the supplier immediately after the year end. The credit note was unlike any normal credit note, being handwritten on a plain sheet of paper and the signature was illegible. The audit junior had flagged the transactions as unusual, and had wondered whether there was any irregularity about them.

Chris had mentioned the matter to Samira, who had told him that he should ask Joshua Chew, Steffi Ltd's finance director, about the transactions. Samira pointed out that Steffi Ltd had been one of her audit clients for many years, without any major audit issues, and it was highly unlikely that there was anything untoward about the transactions. Samira added that she had known Joshua for a long time, since they both studied accountancy together at the same college. 'I know him well, and he would never approve of anything unethical or illegal', she said. Chris was aware that Massy & Co also carried out lucrative consultancy work for Steffi Ltd from time to time, and suspected that Samira would not want him to upset Joshua.

When Chris spoke to Joshua about the matter, he told her that the credit note was legitimate, although he couldn't remember exactly why it had been received. He said he didn't want the supplier to be asked about it, since their business relationship was 'a bit fragile', the boss was away on a business trip, and anyway it would take far too long to investigate. He reminded Chris that as far as he was concerned, this was the final day of the audit, and he wanted to get everything signed off by Friday.

When Chris told Samira what Joshua had said, she agreed not to get the audit signed off until Chris had got to the bottom of the transactions with the supplier. Samira warned him, however, that he should be very sure that the irregularity was worth delaying the signing of the audit report.

PRACTICE QUESTION BANK

Required

(a) Accountants and other professionals often have a joint role, both as employee and as a member of their chosen profession.

    (i) Compare and contrast the duties and responsibilities of the two roles of employee and professional accountant, and explain why there may be ethical conflicts for an individual who is trying to fulfil both roles. **(5 marks)**

    (ii) Identify and discuss the ethical issues arising from this joint role which were raised for Chris in the scenario. **(5 marks)**

(b) Discuss three threats to auditor independence which are apparent in the scenario. **(6 marks)**

(Total 16 marks)

Question 10

Tina Barker and her husband James founded Sunshine Cabs, a charity with the purpose of providing specially adapted vehicles for the use of disabled children. The charity raised enough money over the years to purchase many hundreds of these vehicles, used by children and their carers throughout the country.

The Barkers paid themselves huge salaries and bonuses from the funds the charity raised, mainly from television appeals. The Barkers and other senior employees at the charity had flamboyant lifestyles, and the headquarters were decorated in opulent style, including gold plated bathroom taps and extravagant chandeliers. The Barkers used a fleet of luxury vehicles to travel on behalf of the charity, and stayed in several luxury houses owned by Sunshine Cabs.

The charity was a private organisation and, in the country where it was based, it was not subject to any regulatory oversight of its financial affairs or fund raising activities. Tina Barker attempted to enhance the credibility of Sunshine Cabs and deflect any criticism of her lifestyle by emphasising to potential donors and other third parties that the organisation had 'excellent accountants', and external audits performed by 'reputable firms of accountants'.

The charity was audited by Longmuir & Co, an independent audit firm. Longmuir & Co had accepted Sunshine Cabs as a client following the audit firm's adoption of an aggressive client development strategy. Since the firm adopted this policy, its fee income had increased by 300%, largely as a result of accepting high-risk audit clients. Sunshine Cabs was one of the largest clients which the accounting firm had on its books.

Sunshine Cabs had very lax financial and accounting controls. A secret executive payroll account was operated by the Barkers, which they used to pay themselves and their associates. The account was so secret that not even the charity's chief financial officer was aware of the nature of the expenses being paid through it, and members of the charity's Management Board were not aware of its existence. Surprisingly, this account was maintained by a partner of Longmuir & Co – the same partner responsible for supervising the audit engagement. One of the Barkers would telephone the partner whenever they wanted a cheque to be written on this account.

When eventually the fraud at Sunshine Cabs came to light, the Barkers were forced to resign and were each fined and sentenced to several years in prison for fraud, embezzlement and conspiracy. The charity itself collapsed, leaving behind a large number of disgruntled donors and millions of pounds in debt to suppliers and investors.

Longmuir & Co were criticised by the judge in the case, for allegedly aiding and abetting the Barkers, by misrepresenting the affairs of the charity, and being instrumental in enabling the fraud to take place. As a result, and because the Barkers were by now bankrupt and penniless and unable to repay any of the money they had stolen, the audit firm were sued for damages by several parties who had suffered financial loss due to their involvement with the charity, losing money which had been fraudulently embezzled by the Barkers.

Required

(a) Discuss the ethical questions raised by the maintenance of the secret payroll account for Sunshine Cabs by the Longmuir & Co partner. **(4 marks)**

(b) Discuss the procedures that Longmuir & Co should have performed prior to accepting Sunshine Cabs as an audit client. **(4 marks)**

(c) Discuss how it may be possible for Longmuir & Co to be successfully sued for the wrongdoing of the executives of Sunshine Cabs. **(4 marks)**

(d) Explain what measures Longmuir & Co should have taken to protect the firm against litigation of this kind. **(4 marks)**

(Total 16 marks)

Question 11

You are an audit partner with Olsen & Co, an accountancy firm. You have recently been approached by the board of directors of Meditec plc, with a view to your firm taking over as company auditor.

Meditec is a pharmaceutical company which has recently featured prominently in the press. The company has announced that it expects to make substantial losses in the current financial year. This is as a result of a decision to write off the costs of developing a new drug for treating cancer, called Avanti. Initially the company had high hopes for this new drug, which was seen as a potential miracle cure for the disease, but in tests it caused such serious side effects that Avanti is no longer considered viable.

The company has also been subjected to a great deal of negative publicity from animal rights activists, who object to the company's use of animals as part of the drug testing process.

The directors of Meditec have invited your firm to carry out an independent review of the company's accounting policies for revenue recognition and development costs. The directors have stated that following this review, it is proposed that your firm will be appointed as auditors.

This prospective appointment was discussed at a recent meeting of the partners of your firm. Your senior partner expressed concern that your firm knows relatively little about Meditec. If taken on, Meditec would become one of your firm's largest clients. It was agreed that rigorous client acceptance procedures should be carried out in order for the partners to consider the matter further at their next meeting.

Required

(a) Explain why an audit firm should have client acceptance procedures in place, rather than simply accepting any audit appointment which they are offered. **(3 marks)**

(b) Identify the client acceptance issues which should be considered by Olsen's partners in relation to the invitation to act for Meditec. **(12 marks)**

(Total 15 marks)

PRACTICE QUESTION BANK

Question 12

Ajani Kwaku is an audit partner working for an accountancy firm in Nigeria. He was recently approached by Sade Junala, a director of The Yoruba Corporation, a small but growing Nigerian manufacturing company. Ms Junala asked Mr Kwaku if his firm would be prepared to take over as auditor of Yoruba for the year ended 30 September 20X4, since the retirement due to ill health of the company's previous auditor.

Mr Kwaku has investigated the situation, and he is satisfied that his firm, AuditAfrica, has the resources to carry out this work, and that there are no professional reasons why the firm should not agree to the appointment. The only outstanding matter concerns the audit fee.

Ms Junala sent Mr Kwaku an email, pointing out that the previous auditor had charged a fixed fee for carrying out the audit, and that fee was determined and agreed before the audit work started. Ms Junala is most insistent that AuditAfrica should agree to accept the same audit fee as they had paid last year, plus a 2% increase to allow for inflation.

Mr Kwaku is keen to obtain the work, but he is not happy about accepting Ms Junala's payment terms.

Required

(a) Reply to Ms Junala's email, explaining how the audit fee should be calculated, according to the Code of Ethics for Professional Accountants. **(4 marks)**

(b) Assuming that Ms Junala agrees to AuditAfrica's proposal in respect of fees, draft the audit engagement letter which Mr Kwaku should send to the directors of Yoruba. **(12 marks)**

(Total 16 marks)

Question 13

You are Samira Swann, the newly appointed head of internal audit at Berwick Camera Manufacturing Ltd ('Berwick'). The company has only recently formed an internal audit department, as the directors were previously of the opinion that the company was small enough that it did not need to incur the extra costs associated with having an internal audit function.

The company has experienced growth in the last few years, and the directors have been told by the company's external auditor that the company's control environment is poor, and as a result there are deficiencies in the company's system of internal control. Although the directors are not really sure what a control environment is, they accepted the external auditor's advice, and have set up an internal audit department with you in charge.

One of the directors' main concerns is that the external auditor told them there are failings within the goods received department. They are worried that there could be inadequacies in the system, and have asked you to carry out an investigation and produce a report.

Berwick produces high quality, expensive precision digital cameras. The specifications of the cameras' component parts are vital to the success of the manufacturing process.

Berwick buys valuable camera lenses and large quantities of sheet metal and screws. The lenses and screws are ordered by Berwick and invoiced by the suppliers on a unit basis. Sheet metal is ordered by Berwick and is invoiced by the suppliers on the basis of weight.

The goods received clerk is responsible for documenting the quality and quantity of goods received. You have carried out a preliminary review of internal control structure, which has indicated that the following procedures are being followed:

Goods received report

Properly authorised purchase orders, which are prenumbered, are filed numerically. The copy sent to the goods received clerk is an exact duplicate of the copy sent to the supplier. Receipts of goods are recorded on the duplicate copy by the goods received clerk.

Sheet metal

The company receives deliveries of sheet metal by rail. The rail transport company independently weighs the sheet metal and reports the weight and date of receipt on a goods delivered note which accompanies each delivery. The goods received clerk then checks the weight on the goods delivered note to the original purchase order.

Screws

The goods received clerk opens the packages containing screws, then inspects and weighs the contents. The weight is converted to number of units by means of conversion charts. The goods received clerk then checks the calculated quantity to the purchase order.

Camera Lenses

Each camera lens is delivered in a separate box. The boxes are counted as they are received by the goods received clerk, and the number of boxes is checked to purchase orders.

Required

Write a memo to the Board of Directors explaining:

(a) What a control environment is, and why it is important to a company; **(7 marks)**

(b) Whether Berwick's internal controls over the receipt of sheet metal, screws and lenses, are adequate or inadequate; and **(13 marks)**

(c) What financial statement misstatements may arise because of any inadequacies in Berwick's control system. **(5 marks)**

(Total 25 marks)

Question 14

You are head of internal audit at Carron Ltd, a manufacturing company. The directors have asked you to review internal control over the purchase, receipt, storage and issue of raw materials. You have prepared the following notes that describe Carron's procedures:

Raw materials, which consist mainly of high-cost electronic components, are kept in a locked warehouse. Warehouse staff include a supervisor and four assistants. All are well trained and competent.

Raw materials are removed from the warehouse only upon written or oral authorisation of one of the production foremen.

There are no perpetual inventory records. The warehouse staff do not keep records of goods received or issued. To compensate, a physical inventory count is taken monthly by the warehouse assistants.

PRACTICE QUESTION BANK

> After the physical count, the warehouse supervisor matches quantities counted against predetermined reorder levels. If the count for a given part is below the reorder level, the supervisor enters the part number on a materials requisition list and sends this list to the accounts payable clerk.
>
> The accounts payable clerk, who is also responsible for paying suppliers on receipt of invoices, prepares a purchase order for a predetermined reorder quantity for each part, and sends the purchase order to the supplier from whom the part was last purchased.
>
> When ordered materials arrive at Carron, they are received by the warehouse assistants. The assistants count the goods and agree the counts to the suppliers' goods despatched notes (GDNs). All GDNs are initialled, dated and filed in the warehouse.

Required

Advise the directors of Carron as to the weaknesses in internal control, and recommend improvements in Carron's procedures for the purchase, receipt, storage and issue of raw materials. **(25 marks)**

Question 15

You are James Dodds, an audit senior with the accountancy firm of Casey & Co. You are currently involved in the audit of Country Kitchens Ltd. Country Kitchens is a retail company which specialises in kitchen appliances, such as cookers, fridges and washing machines, which it sells to kitchen installers as well as to the general public.

The company has a central head office and warehouse, and several shops throughout the country which sell the appliances. Appliances are received from manufacturers either at the individual shops, or at the central warehouse. Details of the goods received are entered into the company's computer system either by staff at the shops or at the central warehouse.

You have carried out a preliminary assessment of the computerised purchases system, and have made the following notes for the audit file:

> **Country Kitchens Ltd – Audit file note by James Dodds**
>
> **Purchases system**
>
> When goods are required to be purchased, the user department (ie the shop or central warehouse) issues a purchase requisition, which is sent to the buying department at head office.
>
> The buying department issues a purchase order (PO) which it sends to the supplier. This order is logged on the computer system.
>
> When the goods are received, they are checked and a goods received note (GRN) is raised by the goods received department in the shop or central warehouse. Details of the goods received are entered into the computer system, and are allocated against the purchase order.
>
> The accounts department at head office receives the purchase invoice. This is sent to the relevant user department, who authorise it and return it to the accounts department.
>
> The accounts department input the purchase order details into the computer, which automatically posts the details to the purchase ledger.
>
> The computer system only allows payment of the invoice if the system has recorded the purchase order, and the goods received note.
>
> When the purchase invoice is due for payment, the computer prints the cheques and remittance advices to the suppliers.

You have just received the following email from Karen Ling, the partner in charge of the audit, who has read your file note on the purchasing system.

From: K.Ling@Casey.com

To: J.Dodds@Casey.com

Thank you for your file note on Country Kitchens' purchasing system.

I know that you will be visiting the client next week to obtain more details about the internal controls which are in place in their purchasing system.

Before you undertake that visit, I should be grateful if you would send me a memo outlining the various internal controls you would expect to find in Country Kitchen's purchasing system. I can then review this and discuss it with you before your visit.

The two particular areas I am interested in are controls of individual purchases of appliances and controls over the computer system (including the terminals).

Required

Produce the memo that the audit partner has asked for.

You should discuss the controls you would expect to see in operation at Country Kitchens, from raising the purchase requisition to the computer accepting the purchase invoice. You should also discuss the general controls that should be in place within the company's computer system. **(25 marks)**

Question 16

Caledonian Rangers is a professional football team based in Scotland. Known as Caledonian to its fans, the team were once a poorly performing club but in recent years, under the influence of Jack Stein, the flamboyant owner of the club, the team has outperformed its rivals and has become very successful.

A recent newspaper article about the team discussed them in glowing terms:

Scottish Football World
For all the latest news about the beautiful game

Caledonian Rangers and the Man that Made Them
By Monty Rakesh, club correspondent

Since taking over at the troubled Caledonian Rangers Club, owner-manager Jack Stein has transformed the club from a loss-making third rate team languishing at the bottom of the minor football leagues, into one of the most successful teams in recent Scottish history.

In everything from profit generation to stadium maintenance, Caledonian has become the best example of how a football team should be run. Last year, the club, which is owned by the Stein family, was valued at an incredible $250 million. In the last decade, Caledonian has been the most profitable team in Scotland, with profit margins approaching 25% in many years.

Jack Stein attributes the success of his club to the experts he has retained to run the various functions. Although a great football fan, he recognises that he is no expert on running all aspects of the club:

'I don't have to be an expert on taxes, stadium design, scoring goals, or cleaning the players' dressing room. I have bought in the talent to cover all these areas.'

Eddie Campos, a long-time accountant for Caledonian, was apparently a perfect example of one of the experts employed by Stein. Campos started off as a junior trainee with the club, but after nearly twenty years, had worked his way up to become the supervisor in charge of the payroll department, a job with considerable prestige within the club.

After taking charge of the department, Campos designed and implemented a new payroll system, which only he fully understood. He personally completed the weekly payroll records for each of the four hundred employees at Caledonian. He was known for his work ethic, and his loyalty to the club. Even when he was on holiday, he still came back to calculate the payroll.

Unfortunately, the trust of Caledonian was misplaced. Over a period of several years, he embezzled many thousands of pounds from the club. He did this by adding several fictitious employees to various departments within the organisation. He also inflated the number of hours worked by several employees and shared the resulting overpayments with these individuals.

The fraudulent scheme was eventually discovered when Campos fell ill, and his job was taken over temporarily by the club's financial controller. When completing the payroll one week, she noticed that several employees were being paid unusual amounts. Following a criminal investigation, all the individuals involved in the payroll fraud confessed.

Required

(a) Explain the key control objectives in a payroll system, and explain how these should be met.

(6 marks)

(b) Explain what internal control weaknesses were evident in Caledonian's payroll system. **(3 marks)**

(c) Discuss three specific audit procedures might have led to the discovery of the fraudulent scheme devised by Campos.

(6 marks)

(Total 15 marks)

Question 17

You are the manager responsible for the audit of an Australian company, Wallaby Limited, which has a year end of 31 December 2013. This is the first year that your firm has undertaken the audit of Wallaby, having succeeded the previous auditor at the last annual general meeting of the company, following a successful tender for the audit.

Your firm, SDF, is a medium sized accountancy firm. It has an office in Sydney, the largest city in Australia, as well as offices in around twenty other locations throughout the country.

You have had preliminary discussions with the directors of Wallaby and have obtained some background information about the company. The company's head office is in Sydney. The company manufactures electrical components in a factory in Jakarta in Indonesia, which it imports back into Australia. There are several warehouses throughout the country which hold large inventories of these components so that local demand for its products can be met quickly. Inventory records are not maintained, and a full count is to be carried out at the year end.

The company has an internal audit function which is based at its head office. Internal auditors make regular visits to the warehouses. SDF's partner in charge of the audit has asked you to assess whether the internal audit function might be able to assist the external audit team in carrying out its work.

You are aware of recent newspaper reports in the Australian press that allege that one of Wallaby's most popular products is potentially dangerous. The newspapers report that the product is liable to overheat and can burst into flames causing injury or even death. An official enquiry has been set up to investigate the situation, but so far Wallaby Limited has made no comment.

Required

(a) Explain the objectives of audit planning. **(5 marks)**

(b) Identify the circumstances that should be taken into account when planning the audit of Wallaby Limited, and set out your outline audit approach in these areas. **(15 marks)**

(Total 20 marks)

Question 18

You are John Lumbus, a partner in the audit and accountancy firm of Ashka & Lumbus. Your firm is currently carrying out the audits of several clients for which you are responsible. During the course of these audits, the following (unrelated) matters were discovered:

(i) During the audit of Marlings Savings and Loans, a small rural bank, the audit team discovered a significant amount of loans to farmers which are secured by farmland. The price of farmland, as well as the price of farm produce, has experienced a sharp decline in the previous year.

(ii) Georgia Pacific Ltd is a client which manufactures metal parts for the car industry. The company normally sells the scrap metal left over from production. This year, analytical review shows that revenue from scrap sales has declined by almost 30%, despite production having increased from last year.

(iii) Coventry plc is a wholesale distributor of scientific instruments. During a tour of the warehouse, an audit assistant noticed a large section containing inventories of high-value barometers that the company had recently discontinued as a product line.

(iv) Charlaine Ltd is an audit client which has applied to its bank for an increase in its existing overdraft. The bank has agreed to this, provided the company can achieve a 10% increase in its current year's profits.

(v) When carrying out a month by month analytical procedures of the accounts for Happy Days Ltd, a company which sells school supplies, a member of the audit team noticed an abnormally high volume of sales in June. The company's year end is 30 June.

Required

(a) In each of the above cases, identify how audit risk has been increased by the condition identified. **(5 marks)**

(b) In each case, explain how the audit programme should be modified, given the circumstances. **(10 marks)**

(Total 15 marks)

PRACTICE QUESTION BANK

Question 19

Before performing substantive audit tests for Myst Ltd, a large company which manufactures farm machinery, Sinitta Cowell and her audit team conducted a survey of the business and industry and applied analytical procedures. They obtained an initial understanding of Myst Ltd's control structure, policies and procedures.

Profits in the industry had declined during 20X4 to the point where Myst Ltd was the only company which was reporting net profits. The six remaining companies which were identified as being broadly similar to Myst Ltd were all reporting losses ranging from minimal to substantial. One of the companies, Astro Farmers Ltd, was in receivership by the end of the year.

Analytical procedures revealed higher than normal sales in November, the last month of Myst Ltd's financial year. In addition, the gross profit ratio increased from 35% in 20X3 to 47% in 20X4.

The preliminary study of control structure in the areas of sales and dispatch of goods led Sinitta and her team to conclude that the controls were generally adequate to prevent unauthorised shipments or invoicing, and therefore should be further tested to allow the possibility of lowering the assessed control risk.

Required

(a) Identify and discuss the audit risk implications of the Myst Ltd audit. **(3 marks)**

(b) Explain how the possibility of Myst Ltd's management overriding controls will affect the auditor's assessment of detection risk. **(4 marks)**

(c) Discuss how the auditor should deal with inherent risk in the case of Myst Ltd. **(4 marks)**

(d) Explain why attribute sampling is appropriate for testing certain types of controls to assess control risk, but is not appropriate for testing others. **(6 marks)**

(e) Explain in what ways statistical sampling might assist Sinitta and her audit team to quantify the various audit risk factors confronting them in this audit engagement. **(8 marks)**

(Total 25 marks)

Question 20

Davies Partners are the independent auditors of Wheels Ltd, a large manufacturer of bicycles. The audit firm is conducting a test of control procedures over sales processing.

During the year to 31 October 20X5, Wheels had issued 11,400 pre-numbered sales invoices ranging from 22447 to 33847. Each sales invoice is accompanied by a Goods Despatched Note (GDN) signed by the carrier. These forms are also pre-numbered, and range from 44233 to 55833. The warehouse manager has explained to Gary Daker, the in-charge auditor on the assignment, that shipping orders are frequently voided, and this explains the overuse of these forms compared to the sales invoices.

Based on his initial understanding of Wheels' control structure, Gary believes that controls over initial sales processing, invoicing, and collection are adequate, but he now wants to confirm this by testing the controls for operating effectiveness. Specifically, he is concerned about the following attributes relating to sales to customers:

1. Proper approval of customer credit prior to shipping
2. A sales invoice exists for every shipment
3. The GDN is signed by the carrier
4. Prices on the invoice are in accordance with official price lists
5. The sale has been properly recorded and posted to the customer's account.

Gary has developed a sampling plan to determine whether the assessed level of control risk relating to sales can be reduced below maximum. Given an acceptable risk of underassessment of 5%, he has set the following percentages for expected occurrence rate and tolerable occurrence rate:

Attribute number	Expected occurrence rate (%)	Tolerable rate (%)
1	1	4
2	2	5
3	2	4
4	1	5
5	2	5

Required

(a) Identify the population and sampling unit for the purposes of the sampling plan, and explain why this is the case. **(5 marks)**

(b) Explain how the auditor should select the sample to be tested, in order to comply with random sampling rules. **(5 marks)**

(c) The auditor selected a random sample of 200 units to be tested. On carrying out the tests, he discovered the following errors:

Attribute number	Number of actual errors
1	2
2	11
3	3
4	3
5	3

Determine whether or not the actual error rate for each attribute is acceptable. **(5 marks)**

(d) Discuss to what extent, if any, the auditor can reduce the assessed level of control risk in Wheels' area of sales processing. **(10 marks)**

(Total 25 marks)

Question 21

You are an audit manager with Radial Accountants, in charge of the audit of Gold Coast Planters Pty (GCP), an Australian company which is a new client. You have just completed an initial analytical review of the company's draft financial statements, and have identified certain matters which you wish to investigate in the course of the audit.

The company's financial statements indicate that large amounts of bank loans were paid off during the period under audit. GCP had held the loans from Billabong Bank for between five and ten years.

You also noticed that one customer's account in the accounts receivable ledger, Queensland Trading Pty, is much larger than the other accounts.

PRACTICE QUESTION BANK

A review of GCP's accounting system has revealed that the following types of evidence will be available to you and your audit team when you visit the client's premises to carry out the main audit work:

Sources of evidence in relation to bank loans:

Debit entries in the loans payable account in the general ledger.

Entries in the cheque register.

Paid cheques.

Receipts from Billabong Bank stamped PAID, and the date of payment.

Statement by GCP's treasurer that the loans had been paid at maturity.

Letter received by Radial Accountants directly from Billabong Bank stating that no indebtedness on part of GCP existed at the period end date.

Sources of evidence in relation to customer accounts:

Computer printout from accounts receivable subsidiary ledger showing customer balances at the year end.

Copies of sales invoices.

Purchase order received from Queensland Trading.

Shipping document describing the articles sold to Queensland Trading.

Letter received by GCP from Queensland Trading acknowledging the correctness of the receivable of the amount shown in GCP's accounting records.

Letter received by Radial Accountants directly from Queensland Trading acknowledging the correctness of the amount shown as receivable in GCP's accounting records.

Required

(a) ISA 500 *Audit Evidence* requires auditors to obtain sufficient appropriate audit evidence on which to base the audit opinion.

Discuss how an auditor will decide whether sufficient audit evidence has been obtained, before signing the audit report. **(6 marks)**

(b) Evaluate the reliability of each of the types of evidence which will be available to Radial Accountants to support the transactions for bank loans and for customer accounts. **(19 marks)**

(Total 25 marks)

Question 22

You are Jenny Wren, an employee of the accountancy firm of Liffe & Co. You are currently the auditor in charge of the audit of the accounts of Playtime Ltd (known as Playtime), a company which manufactures children's toys. You and some of the more junior members of the audit team attended the inventory count at the year end, and you are satisfied that inventory quantities have been properly determined. You are now obtaining audit evidence to satisfy yourself that Playtime's stock of finished goods has been properly valued. You have discovered the following matters:

Production levels for the year to 31 October 20X3 show a downturn of approximately 30% compared to the year ended 31 October 20X2. As a result, the fixed cost overhead element per unit of production has increased. The effect is shown as follows on one of the company's most popular items, the Action Doll:

	Year to 31/10/X3 $	Year to 31/10/X2 $
Direct material cost	8.50	8.50
Direct labour cost	11.00	11.00
Overhead allocation	15.00	12.00
Total	34.50	31.50
Selling price	55.00	55.00

According to Playtime's directors, production is expected to return to previous levels in the year to 31 October 20X4.

Inventory levels of certain product lines have increased steadily throughout the year, and you are considering whether a provision for slow moving and obsolete inventory should be made.

Just before the end of October, Playtime sent goods to several retailers on a consignment basis. The agreements with the retailers state that when the goods are sold to retail customers, Playtime will issue an invoice which the retailers will immediately pay. These items were correctly counted as part of Playtime's inventory at the year end. Your review of costs reveals that the value of these goods include distribution costs (transportation to the retailers), and a proportion of selling expense overheads.

Required

(a) Describe the audit procedures you would carry out to obtain assurance that direct material cost and direct labour cost have been correctly determined. **(9 marks)**

(b) Explain how you would advise management on their accounting treatment of overhead expenditure, distribution cost and selling expense. **(9 marks)**

(c) Describe the audit procedures you would adopt in respect of the slow moving inventory items. **(7 marks)**

(Total 25 marks)

Question 23

Historic Spain is an organisation which was set up to encourage tourists to visit art galleries, museums and other places of historic interest in Spain. One of the properties which it owns is Castillo Aragon, an ancient castle which is open to the public.

On the days when the castle is open, two tour guides are positioned at the entrance. It is their job to answer any questions which visitors might have about the castle, and to collect an admission fee of €5 from each visitor. Members of Historic Spain are allowed to enter free of charge upon presentation of their membership cards.

At the end of each day, one of the guides hands over all the cash collected to the organisation's accounts assistant, who has an office in the castle. The accounts assistant counts the cash in the presence of the guide and places it in a safe. At the end of each week, the accounts assistant and one of the guides deliver all the cash held in the safe to the bank. The bank issues them with a deposit slip which provides the basis for the weekly entry in the cash receipts journal.

The Board of Trustees of Historic Spain has identified a need to improve the control procedures for cash admission fees. The Board commissioned a study which concluded that the cost of installing turnstiles and sales booths, or otherwise altering the physical layout of the castle, would exceed any benefits which might be derived. However, the Board has agreed that the sale of admission tickets must be an integral part of its improvement efforts.

Required

(a) ISA 315 (Revised) *Identifying and Assessing the Risks of Material Misstatement* requires that an auditor should obtain an understanding of the accounting and internal control systems sufficient to plan the audit and develop an effective audit approach.

    (i) Define the terms 'accounting system' and 'internal control'. **(4 marks)**

    (ii) Describe the procedures which an auditor should use to evaluate internal controls. **(3 marks)**

(b) Identify five weaknesses in Historic Spain's existing procedures for cash admission fees to Castillo Aragon, and recommend one improvement for each of the weaknesses you identify. **(8 marks)**

(Total 15 marks)

Question 24

You are currently working on the audit of the financial statements of Sanjay Ltd for the year ended 31 December 20X2. Sanjay is involved in the manufacture of components used by motor vehicle manufacturers.

The schedule below shows the movement in the non-current assets of the company for the year.

	Buildings $	Vehicles $	Plant and machinery $
Cost			
As at 1 January 20X2	1,250,000	100,000	60,500
Additions in the year	400,000	12,000	20,000
Disposals	–	(15,000)	(10,000)
As at 31 December 20X2	1,650,000	97,000	70,500
Accumulated depreciation			
As at 1 January 20X2	55,000	45,000	6,700
Charge for the year	33,000	22,500	6,500
Disposals	–	(11,000)	(7,500)
As at 31 December 20X2	88,000	56,500	5,700

The company depreciates its non-current assets as follows:

Buildings   2% Straight line
Vehicles   30% Reducing balance
Plant and machinery   10% Straight line

Required

Prepare the programme of audit work which you would undertake for the substantive testing of Sanjay Ltd's non-current assets. **(15 marks)**

Question 25

Jaffrey, Ismail and Howarth (JIH) is an accountancy firm which offers audit and assurance services. One of the firm's major audit clients is Gleeson Manufacturing Ltd (Gleeson), a pharmaceutical company which develops and produces vaccines, used by health professionals throughout the world to protect people from a range of diseases.

Gleeson carries an inventory of finished products consisting of 50 different types of items valued at approximately $40 million. Because of the unstable nature of the vaccines, they must be held in sterile conditions at a specific temperature. About $15 million of the inventory value represents inventory produced by the company and billed to customers prior to the audit date. This inventory is being held for the customers at a monthly rental charge until they request shipment, and is not held separately from the company's own inventory.

The permanent audit file contains the following notes about Gleeson's inventory system:

Jaffrey, Ismail and Howarth	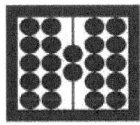

Client: Gleeson Manufacturing Ltd (Gleeson)

Subject: Finished goods inventory

Date: 21.10.X4

Prepared by: *Jack Strachan*

The company maintains separate perpetual ledgers at the factory office for both inventory owned and inventory being held for customers. The cost department also maintains a perpetual record of inventory owned. The perpetual records reflect quantities only.

The company does not take a complete physical inventory at any time during the year, since the temperatures and the sterile conditions in the storage facilities would not allow anyone to spend more than a few minutes inside. A glass window all around the storage areas means it is possible to obtain a broad idea of the quantities of inventory being held in different areas according to type. It would not be practical to move items outside the storage facilities for the purpose of taking a physical inventory. Because of these circumstances, it is impractical to test count quantities to the extent of completely counting specific items.

The company considers as its inventory valuation at year-end the aggregate of the quantities reflected by the perpetual record of inventory owned, maintained at the plant office, priced at the lower of cost or market value.

Required

(a) Identify the two principal problems facing JIH in the audit of Gleeson's inventory, and discuss the general approach that the auditor should take to enable them to reach an opinion about the accuracy of inventory. **(10 marks)**

(b) Identify the specific audit tests that JIH should carry out in order to assess the accuracy of the inventory owned by the company, and that held on behalf of customers. **(15 marks)**

(Total 25 marks)

Question 26

You are Stefan Jasinski, the audit senior in charge of the trade payables section of the audit of Lightning Ltd, a chain of high street shops selling electrical goods. The company's next year end date is 30 November 20X2.

During a discussion a few months ago with Tony Lee, the company's financial controller, he indicated that there had been a few changes in the system for recording purchases this year. In response to requests from several suppliers, Lightning now allows suppliers who deliver goods directly to the individual stores, to send the purchase invoices directly to Lightning's head office. Most of these purchase invoices relate to deliveries sent to several different stores. Previously all invoices were sent to whichever store the goods were delivered to, before being forwarded to head office with the Goods Received Note (GRN) attached. According to the financial controller, the system has improved because the invoicing is now under central control and therefore more easily managed.

The change has also had the added advantage of allowing Lightning to reduce the number of accounting staff at head office. Previously, they had needed three people to check all the invoices coming from the various stores, but now they were able to manage with only one member of staff who can deal with the whole system of accounting for purchases, from recording the invoices on receipt from the suppliers to reconciling the purchase ledger and the nominal ledger. The financial controller told you that the savings for the company as a result of a reduced wages bill have been considerable.

According to your notes from that meeting, the procedures currently adopted by the company include the following:

> Each retail outlet maintains a goods received book
>
> For each delivery, a pre-numbered GRN is prepared and sent to head office
>
> Invoices are entered into the invoice register at head office on receipt
>
> The invoice is agreed to the GRN, then posted to the purchase ledger
>
> Purchase ledger balances are reconciled to supplier statements
>
> The purchase ledger total is reconciled to the nominal ledger control account
>
> Accruals are made monthly for estimated goods received but not invoiced

You have just received the following email from Jane Johnston, the audit partner:

> From: j.johnston@WLB.com
>
> To: s.jasinski@WLB.com
>
> Hope this finds you well and enthusiastic about starting the audit of Lightning.
>
> I just wanted to emphasise to you that the completeness of trade payables is a key audit objective on this audit. With this in mind, could you please draft a note for the audit planning section of the file, explaining the audit tests which will be included in the audit programme to test for completeness of trade payables.
>
> Could you please include in your note an explanation of the approach which will be taken when selecting a sample of suppliers' balances for testing during the final audit work.
>
> Regards,
>
> Jane

Required

Produce the audit file note for the audit partner,

(a) describing the audit approach for testing for completeness of trade payables; and **(17 marks)**

(b) explaining the basis of selection for trade payables for testing at the year end. **(8 marks)**

(Total 25 marks)

Question 27

You are audit partner in charge of the audit of the financial statements of Marshall plc for the year ended 31 January 20X3. The board of directors approved the financial statements for the year ended 31 January 20X3 on 25 April 20X3.

You have set the materiality level for this audit assignment at $50,000.

Prior to signing your audit report, you had a meeting with the finance director, who brought two matters to your attention. Firstly, the company experienced a fire in its warehouse on 2 May 20X3. There was not much damage to the warehouse itself, but inventory amounting to approximately $35,000 was destroyed.

On a happier note, the finance director told you that at their board meeting last week, Marshall's directors had agreed to a merger with Solent Ltd, one of the company's major competitors. Although the details have still to be finalised, it is hoped that the combined entity will become a leading company in their particular industrial sector.

You completed your audit work on 14 May 20X3 and signed the audit report on that date. The report includes an unmodified audit opinion. The financial statements and audit report are to be issued to the members of the company on 1 June 20X3.

On 18 May 20X3 you become aware that Pike Ltd, a major customer of Marshall, has ceased to trade, and that the courts have appointed a liquidator to the company. Marshall is owed $200,000 by the customer and $160,000 of this amount was due as at 31 January 20X3. It is not expected that the unsecured creditors will receive any payment on completion of the liquidation.

Required

(a) It is the responsibility of the auditor to review subsequent events before they sign the audit report.

Explain what procedures the auditor should undertake to review subsequent events. **(6 marks)**

(b) Explain how the directors of Marshall should reflect the fire at the warehouse and the merger with Solent, in the financial statements, and explain what action, if any, the auditor should take if he or she disagrees with this treatment. **(6 marks)**

(c) Discuss the responsibility of Marshall's auditor when informed of the liquidation of Pike and what action the auditor should take. **(7 marks)**

(d) Explain how your answer to (c) would differ if the auditor became aware of the liquidation of Pike on 10 June 20X3. **(6 marks)**

(Total 25 marks)

Question 28

Your client, Safari Ltd, operates a chain of hotels in Kenya, an African country. Safari was established in 20X4 and grew quickly through the acquisition of hotels throughout the country. The acquisitions were largely financed by bank borrowing and retained profits. In the year 20X8 the company incurred a significant loss due a downturn in the tourism industry. The company had severe cash flow problems in

20X8 and at that time the company's bank had considered appointing a receiver to the company. Due to an improved tourist season in 20X9 and cost reductions the company's financial position improved in 20X9. The Managing Director of the company has informed you that he believes the company is now on a sound financial footing and that no threat exists to the future viability of the business.

Required

(a) The auditor's responsibility is to consider the appropriateness of management's use of the going concern basis of accounting in the presentation of the financial statements. Set out the programme of work the auditor should undertake to fulfil this responsibility in the audit of Safari Ltd for the year ended 31 December 20X9. **(9 marks)**

(b) Discuss the possible impact (if any) that the going concern issue may have on the final auditor's report issued on the financial statements of Safari Ltd for the year ended 31 December 20X9 based on the following two assumptions:

   (i) that adequate disclosure is made in notes to the financial statements of uncertainty relating to the ability of the company to continue to trade in the future.

   (ii) that inadequate disclosure is made in notes to the financial statements of uncertainty relating to the ability of the company to continue to trade in the future. **(6 marks)**

(Total 15 marks)

Question 29

Sally Chan is a registered auditor. She has just completed field work for her examination of Comelybank plc, a manufacturing company, for the year ended 31 December 20X4, and she is now is in the process of determining whether to modify her report. Presented below are two independent, unrelated situations which arose during the course of the audit work.

In September 20X4, a lawsuit was filed against Comelybank to have the court order it to install pollution-control equipment in one of its older plants. Comelybank's legal counsel has informed Sally that it is not possible to forecast the outcome of this litigation. However, Comelybank's management has told Sally that the cost of the pollution control equipment is not economically feasible and that the plant will be closed if the case is lost. In addition, Sally was told by management that the plant and its production equipment would have only minimal resale values and that the production that would be lost could not be recovered at other plants.

The other situation that arose relates to a franchise which Comelybank purchased during 20X4. It paid an amount equal to approximately 20% of the company's assets in return for the exclusive right to produce and sell a newly patented product in the US. There has been no production in marketable quantities of the product anywhere to date, and neither the franchiser nor any franchisee had conducted any market research with respect to the product.

Adapted from Hayes, Dassen, Schilder & Wallage, 2005, p. 538.

Required

Discuss the factors which Sally Chan should consider when deciding on which type of audit report she should issue, indicating which would be most appropriate for each situation outlined above. Assume that in both cases the matter is adequately disclosed in the financial statements. **(20 marks)**

Question 30

You are Jay Rayner, an audit partner with Abacus, an accounting firm which offers clients a range of services, including audit. The company's next year end is 30 April 20X4.

On 23 April 20X4, you received a letter from Tommy Lee, the finance director of one of your clients, Hing Sing Ltd. Mr Lee's letter informed you that the company has a serious shortage of working capital because of heavy operating losses incurred since 1 January 20X4. Mr Lee requested a meeting with you to discuss this and other matters relevant to the audit.

At the meeting with Mr Lee, you made the following notes:

Meeting notes

Client: Hing Sing Ltd

Date: 28.4.X4

Present: Tommy Lee (Hing Sing), Jay Rayner (Abacus)

(1) As a result of the financial difficulties facing Hing Sing Ltd, the company has applied for a bank loan. The bank's loan officer has requested audited financial statements in order to consider whether or not to provide the loan. Mr Lee has asked that we save time by auditing the financial statements prepared by Hing Sing's chief accountant as of 31 January 20X4. Mr Lee offered assurances that the scope of our audit would not be limited by the company in any way.

(2) If we are not prepared to carry out our audit based on financial statements for the period ended on 31 January, Mr Lee agreed that we could conduct an audit of the financial statements for the year ended 30 April 20X4. Mr Lee pointed out that we would need to produce our audit report by 15 May to meet the deadline from the bank for obtaining the loan. To save time and reduce the cost of the audit, Mr Lee requested that our audit should not include confirmation of accounts receivable or observation of the taking of inventory.

(3) During last year's audit, Abacus audited Hing Sing Ltd's earthquake insurance policies. We were concerned that the company's insurance coverage against loss by earthquake was inadequate, and mentioned the matter in the management letter at the end of the audit. Given the company's current circumstances, it is clear that, if a loss occurs, the company may have insufficient assets to liquidate its debts. After a discussion with Mr Lee, he stated that the board of directors have refused to increase the amount of insurance coverage.

(4) During a discussion of Hing Sing Ltd's accounting policies, Mr Lee let me know that the company has changed the accounting method it uses to depreciate non-current assets from straight-line to reducing balance. As the change was made towards the end of the financial year, the effect on this year's financial statements will be immaterial. However, the effect in future years is likely to be material. Mr Lee provided assurances that the relevant details will be fully disclosed in the footnotes to the financial statements.

(5) Finally, Mr Lee told me that during the year, Hing Sing Ltd built a new factory. It used its own staff to carry out the construction. In accordance with International Accounting Standards, the company correctly capitalised the direct costs associated with constructing the building. However, the company also capitalised administration and general overhead costs, which is not allowed by International Accounting Standards. Mr Lee is determined that Hing Sing Ltd will not adjust its accounts, saying that to do so would be too time consuming and expensive. The effect of this departure from International Accounting Standards on Hing Sing Ltd's accounts is highly significant.

PRACTICE QUESTION BANK

Required

Discuss the type of audit opinion you would give under each of above set of circumstances, giving reasons for your decision. **(20 marks)**

Question 31

You are an audit partner with a medium sized accountancy firm. You are about to finalise and sign the audit report for four of your clients. In each case, there has been a significant audit issue brought to your attention.

Middleton Ltd

In carrying out the audit of inventory the audit team determined that for a number of products the net realisable value is less than cost. They have estimated that the downward adjustment required to the inventory to state the figures at the lower of cost and net realisable value would be $350,000. The company's profit for the year ended 30 August 20X3 is approximately $800,000. The directors of Middleton Ltd have refused to adjust the accounts to correct for this overstatement of inventory on the basis that they disagree with the accounting principle of reducing inventory value to the lower of cost and net realisable value.

Windsor Ltd

Windsor Ltd is currently involved in a legal dispute with Buckingham Ltd. Buckingham Ltd is claiming that Windsor has infringed certain patent rights that Buckingham Ltd owns. Buckingham Ltd has instituted court proceedings against Windsor Ltd claiming royalties and punitive damages. Windsor Ltd denies any wrongdoing or liability and is mounting a robust defence.

The matter is likely to be the subject of a full high court hearing at some time in the future. Windsor Ltd has a number of legal opinions from senior lawyers that supports the company's view that they are not liable for royalties or damages. Based on these opinions and the directors' strongly held view that the company has no liability in respect of this matter no provision has been made in the financial statements for royalties and/or damages.

The financial statements have fully disclosed by way of a note the full details of the claim and the fact that the matter is likely to proceed to a full court hearing at which point the uncertainty relating to this matter will be resolved. As auditor to Windsor Ltd, you have considered the adequacy of the disclosures made in relation to this matter in the financial statements, and are of the opinion that the financial statements show a true and fair view.

Holyrood Ltd

You were appointed auditor to Holyrood Ltd in October 20X3. You are auditing the financial statements for the year ended 30 September 20X3. As you were not auditor at the date of the annual inventory count you did not attend the count. Inventories represent 65% of the company's net assets at 30 September 20X3.

Essex Ltd

Essex Ltd has an excess of liabilities over assets of $500,000. The company continues to trade because the principal shareholder and director Charles Cornwall has provided a financing facility to the company in the form of a shareholder's loan of $800,000. He has confirmed to you in writing that it is his intention to continue to support the company in the future by the provision of this facility and additional facilities if required. The financial statements contain a note that fully explains the basis on which the accounts have been prepared on a going concern basis and details of the director's/shareholder's intentions in relation to the continued provision of finance to the company.

Required

In respect of each of the above situations, you are required to state the audit report modification (if any) or emphasis of matter paragraph (if any) that would be appropriate in the circumstances outlined, and draft the text of the qualification/explanatory paragraph where appropriate. **(20 marks)**

Practice answer bank

Question 1

(a) Several decades ago, many accountancy professional bodies throughout the world realised that there was a need to introduce auditing standards, just as there was a need for accounting standards. This was in response to a number of audit failures caused by a lack of objectivity, or technical incompetence. These had led to a great deal of adverse publicity, and had created a lack of confidence in the auditing profession.

More recently, it has been recognised that a set of international auditing standards would be even more useful than a series of standards for individual countries. And so many countries are choosing to adopt ISAs, albeit sometimes adapted slightly to suit their particular circumstances. UK auditors, for example, are required to comply with ISAs.

The adoption of international standards provides users of financial statements with assurance, when making comparisons between companies around the world, that the reliability of financial information does not vary from company to company. This assurance arises through knowing that each set of financial statements has been audited to the same common standards.

The IAASB's goal is 'to enhance the quality and uniformity of practice throughout the world and strengthen public confidence in the global auditing and assurance profession.'

(b) The format of the auditor's report is governed by ISA 700 (Revised) *Forming an Opinion and Reporting on Financial Statements*. The basic auditor's report contains the following main elements:

The title

The title must clearly indicate that it is the report of an independent auditor.

The addressee

The report should be addressed as appropriate to the circumstances of the engagement, but in most cases this will be to the shareholders of the company being audited.

An opinion paragraph

This contains an expression of opinion on the financial statements. When expressing an unmodified opinion on financial statements prepared in accordance with a fair presentation framework, the auditor's opinion should, unless otherwise required by law or regulation, use one of the following phrases:

(a) The financial statements present fairly, in all material respects, ... in accordance with [the applicable financial reporting framework]; or

(b) The financial statements give a true and fair view of ... in accordance with [the applicable financial reporting framework].

Basis for Opinion

The basis for opinion paragraph must state that the audit was conducted in accordance with the ISAs, and refer to the 'Auditor's responsibilities for the audit of the financial statements' section which describes the auditor's responsibilities under the ISAs.

The auditor must also state that they are independent of the audited entity, in accordance with the relevant ethical requirements relating to the audit.

Finally, the auditor must state that they believe the audit evidence obtained is sufficient and appropriate to provide a basis for the audit opinion.

PRACTICE ANSWER BANK

A statement of the management's responsibility for the financial statements

This section of the auditor's report describes the responsibilities of those in the company that are responsible for the preparation of the financial statements.

The description shall include an explanation that management is responsible for the preparation of the financial statements in accordance with the applicable financial reporting framework, and for such internal control as it determines is necessary to enable the preparation of financial statements that are free from material misstatement, whether due to fraud or error.

A statement of the auditor's responsibility

The report should state that the responsibility of the auditor is to express an opinion on the financial statements based on the audit. It should also state that the audit was conducted in accordance with International Standards on Auditing and explain that those standards require that the auditor comply with ethical requirements, and that the auditor plan and perform the audit to obtain reasonable assurance about whether the financial statements are free from material misstatement.

This section should also briefly describe the audit process, for example by pointing out that an audit involves performing procedures to obtain audit evidence about the amounts and disclosures in the financial statements, and includes evaluation of the appropriateness of the accounting policies used.

Any other reporting responsibilities

This paragraph is only required where the auditor is required by law to report on any additional matters.

Auditor's signature

This signature can be the auditor's own name, or the audit firm's name.

The date of the auditor's report

The report should be dated no earlier than the date on which the auditor has obtained sufficient appropriate audit evidence on which to base their opinion on the financial statements.

Auditor's address

The location of the audit firm must be included.

Question 2

(a) The practice of modern auditing dates back to the beginning of the modern corporation at the start of the industrial revolution. Previously, auditing existed primarily as a method to maintain governmental accountancy, and record-keeping was its mainstay. With the industrial revolution, the growth of technology along with improvements in communications and transport allowed companies access to expanding worldwide markets.

As a result, the demands of owner-managed enterprises for capital rapidly exceeded the combined resources of the owners' savings and the wealth-creating potential of the businesses themselves. Businesses had to turn to the wider community to provide funding to grow. The result was the growth of sophisticated securities markets and credit-granting institutions which serve the financial needs of large national and international corporations.

An important characteristic of the modern corporation is the fact that ownership is almost totally divorced from management. Generally, the directors manage a company on behalf of the shareholders who own the company. As companies grew in size, the separation of the ownership and management functions became more evident. In order to ensure that funds continued to flow from investors to companies, and the financial markets functioned smoothly, there was a need to convince the participants in the financial markets that the company's financial statement provided a true and fair portrayal of its financial position and performance.

Management has control over the accounting systems of these enterprises. Management is not only responsible for the financial reports to investors; it also has the authority to determine the precise nature of the information that goes into those reports. To reduce the investor's potential lack of confidence about management's reports a demand for independent assurance has arisen, which is called auditing. Today, the main audit function is to provide credibility to the financial statements prepared by company managers for their shareholders.

(b) Dear Sir,

I am writing in response to the recent article in your newspaper, 'Who Audits the Auditors'. The author of the article clearly feels very strongly about the topic, but I believe their views are based on a lack of understanding of the nature of the auditing profession and what it does.

I would be grateful for the opportunity to bring to your readership's attention the following examples of a variety of organisations each of which could benefit from having an independent audit.

Large companies like Microsoft have investors and run operations all over the world. A financial statement audit is useful to provide consistent information to prospective investors. Present shareholders need a report that monitors the company because they have limited control. Stakeholders are concerned that the company complies with relevant regulations and statutory requirements and that there is adequate disclosure of information.

Large charities such as the Red Cross are not for profit organisations which raise funds internationally and must comply with certain regulations to retain a tax-free status. A financial audit will be important to people who contribute to the organisation in order to get an accurate picture of how their donations are spent. An audit of how effectively they meet their goals will be helpful to give credibility to the organisation.

The financial statements of a country's **central bank**, such as the Bank of England, should show a true and fair view for its users. An operational audit could show how efficient and effective the organisation is, especially the bank's control procedures. An audit would determine compliance with the laws, statutes, policies and procedures of the relevant government. An audit of such a sensitive organization might help protect the government against large banking disasters.

In most countries, a **small grocery store** will not be required by legislation to have an independent audit. However, the bank which makes loans to the grocery store or the partners of the enterprise may require audited financial statements. A small company can benefit from an operational audit, for instance, to see if they have proper controls and if the inventory is handled effectively. The audit will also help ensure the company pays the correct amount of income tax.

A **local sports club** would benefit from a compliance audit to determine if the club is fulfilling the criteria of a non-profit organisation, which might be helpful to tax authorities and members who make contributions. Traditionally, clubs have little in the way of controls, and an operational audit of controls would probably be helpful in tightening procedures relating to cash receipts and payments. A compliance audit would help determine if the club is using the membership fees for the requirements of its members.

I hope that these illustrative examples might convince both the author of the article and your readership that the auditing profession is necessary for the effective functioning of business and the community.

Yours faithfully,

A N Auditor

PRACTICE ANSWER BANK

Question 3

(a) There are a number of reasons why an auditor may want to, or may have to, resign from an audit engagement. These reasons may include:

Threats to audit independence becoming known only after commencement of the engagement, and they are unable to be reduced to an acceptable level through the application of appropriate and effective safeguards.

The auditor is unable to obtain sufficient appropriate audit evidence, and the possible effects on the financial statements of undetected misstatements could be both material and pervasive.

The auditor is unable to agree to a change of the terms of the audit engagement, that effectively limits the scope of the audit subsequent to accepting the engagement.

As a result of a misstatement resulting from fraud or suspected fraud, the auditor encounters exceptional circumstances that bring into question the auditor's ability to continue performing the audit. This would generally be because:

- If an occurrence was identified, those charged with governance not taking appropriate remedial action; or
- A significant risk of material and pervasive fraud is considered to exist.

Management or those charged with governance do not take corrective action that the auditor considers appropriate for non-compliance with laws and regulations.

If the two-way communication between the auditor and those charged with governance is not adequate and the situation cannot be resolved.

Concerns about the competence, integrity or ethical values of those charged with governance, or about their commitment to or enforcement of these, emerge during the course of the audit which cause the auditor to conclude that the risk of misrepresentation in the financial statements is such that an audit cannot be conducted.

Revision of the other information (financial and non-financial) included in the document containing the financial statements and audit report is necessary, and those charged with governance refuse to make the revision.

(b) When DQT Co decided to resign, they should have given notice to SAY Co. The notice should have been accompanied by a statement of the circumstances connected with the firm ceasing to hold office unless the firm considered that there were no circumstances in connection with it ceasing to hold office that needed to be brought to the attention of members or creditors of the company.

If DQT Co considered that there were no circumstances in connection with it ceasing to hold office that needed to be brought to the attention of members or creditors of the company, DQT Co should have deposited at the company's registered office a statement to that effect. SAY Co must send a copy of the auditor's resignation notice to the relevant regulatory authority.

In this case, DQT Co has resigned from the audit of SAY Co for reasons which should be brought to the attention of the company's shareholders. DQT Co should therefore have supplied a statement of the circumstances connected with the firm's resignation. DQT Co has the right to deposit a signed requisition with the notice calling on the directors of the company to convene a general meeting of the shareholders of the company at once to receive and consider the firm's explanation of the circumstances connected with the firm's resignation.

DQT Co could request the company to circulate to SAY Co's shareholders a statement in writing of the circumstances connected with the firm's resignation either before the meeting, or before any general meeting at which the firm's term of office would have expired (had the firm not resigned) or at a general meeting at which it is proposed to fill the vacancy caused by DQT Co's resignation.

The directors of SAY Co must proceed to convene a general meeting. Unless the statement is received by it too late, the company must state the fact that a statement has been made in any notice of the resolution given to the shareholders and send a copy of the statement to every shareholder of SAY Co to whom notice of the meeting is or has been sent. If a copy of the statement is not sent out as required because it was received too late or because of the company's default, DQT Co may (without affecting the firm's right to be heard orally) require that the statement is read out at the general meeting.

If DQT Co supplies a statement of the circumstances connected with their resignation, SAY Co must either send a copy of it to every person who is entitled to be sent copies of the accounts or apply to the court. If the company applies to the court, the company must notify DQT Co of the application. If the court decides that the auditor is trying to secure needless publicity for a defamatory matter, they may direct that copies of the statement need not be sent out and order the auditor to pay the company's court costs in full or in part.

Question 4

(a) All these environmental factors affect the demand for and the performance of external auditors.

  (i) Economic developments affect the demand for audit as a result of an increasing number of companies and a higher volume of business activities. As a result, there is a higher demand placed on the audit market.

  (ii) Globalisation and internationalisation of the capital market affect competition among audit firms and may create a higher concentration in the audit market. It may result in a higher quality of audit if the auditors acquire the necessary competency, training and specialisation. However, the concentrated audit market may also impair the auditor's independence and performance.

  (iii) The increasing number of financial instruments and financial operations which require more sophisticated accounting standards and auditing techniques significantly affect the audit scope and auditor performance. These also create the demand for specialised audit and high level of competency and training.

  (iv) The rapid advance of online technologies and other forms of IT systems considerably affect the auditor's performance and demand for audit. As part of the audit process, the auditor should make an assessment of a company's information system and different types of risks, and obtain an understanding of the extent to which they influence the company's financial reporting and the quality of information produced. The auditor may seek to use audit data analytics in their testing.

(b) The International Federation of Accountants is the global organisation for the accountancy profession dedicated to serving the public interest by strengthening the profession and contributing to the development of strong international economies. It tries to serve the public interest by contributing to the development of high-quality standards and guidance and contributing to the development of strong professional accountancy organisations and accounting firms and to high-quality practices by professional accountants, thus promoting the value of professional accountants worldwide, as well as speaking out on public interest issues.

One of IFAC's main tasks is to develop, promote, and enforce high-quality, internationally recognised standards for auditing and assurance, education, ethics, and public sector accounting. In its view, these standards and related regulation are essential to ensuring the credibility of information upon which investors and other stakeholders depend and to achieving sustainable global economic development. As a result, IFAC has set up the International Auditing and Assurance Standards Board (IAASB) an independent standard-setting body that serves the public interest by setting high-quality international standards for auditing, quality management, review, other assurance, and related services, and by facilitating the convergence of international and national standards. The IAASB enhances the quality and uniformity of practice throughout the world and strengthens public confidence in the global auditing and assurance profession.

The IAASB's efforts are focused on development, adoption and implementation of international standards addressing audit, quality management, review, other assurance, and related services engagements. The IAASB's attempts to serve the public interest, by supporting global financial stability; enhancing the role, relevance and quality of assurance and related services in an evolving world; and facilitating the adoption and implementation of the standards.

The IAASB follows a rigorous due process in developing its pronouncements. Input is obtained from a wide range of stakeholders including the IAASB's Consultative Advisory Group, national auditing standard setters, IFAC member bodies and their members, regulatory and oversight bodies, firms, governmental agencies, investors, preparers, and the general public. Exposure drafts of proposed pronouncements are posted on the website and comments are invited; final pronouncements are accompanied by a basis of conclusions with respect to comments received. The Public Interest Oversight Board (PIOB) oversees the work of the IAASB to ensure that the activities of the IAASB follow due process and are responsive to the public interest.

(c) Auditors are responsible for obtaining reasonable assurance that material misstatements included in the financial statements are detected, whether those misstatements are due to fraud or error. Professional standards acknowledge that it is often more difficult to detect fraud than errors because management or employees perpetrating the fraud attempt to conceal the fraud. That difficulty, however, does not change the auditor's responsibility to properly plan and perform the audit. Auditors are required to specifically assess the risk of material misstatement due to fraud and should consider that assessment in designing the audit procedures to be performed.

There has been increased emphasis on auditors' responsibility to evaluate factors that may indicate an increased likelihood that fraud may be occurring. In the case of GHL Ltd, the domination and reputation of Jenny Styles, considered together, should cause Anders to conclude that the likelihood of fraud is fairly high. In such a circumstance, he should put increased emphasis on searching for material misstatements due to fraud.

The auditor may also uncover circumstances during the audit that may cause suspicions of fraudulent financial reporting. In this case, Anders is suspicious that he has been misled by Jenny about the age of certain inventory items. In these circumstances, Anders must evaluate their implications and consider the need to modify audit evidence.

Adequate internal control should be the principal means of thwarting and detecting misappropriation of assets. To rely entirely on an independent audit for the detection of misappropriation of assets would require expanding the auditor's work to the extent that the cost might be prohibitive. The auditor normally assesses the likelihood of material misappropriation of assets as a part of understanding the entity's internal control and assessing control risk. In this case, Anders has found an absence of adequate controls and a failure to follow prescribed procedures, thus he should look for further audit evidence if he believes a material fraud could result.

Question 5

From: S.Lee@RPG.co.uk
To: JJones@magnum.co.uk

Dear Joe,

Thank you for your email. I was very pleased to hear that Magnum now has an audit committee in place, and I am delighted to be able to clarify how Magnum would also benefit from setting up an internal audit department.

Internal auditing is a cornerstone of strong governance. It bridges the gap between management and the board, assesses the ethical climate and the effectiveness and efficiency of operations, and serves as a company's safety net for compliance with rules, regulations, and overall best business practices.

Magnum's directors are responsible for establishing and maintaining a system of internal controls within the company on behalf of the company's shareholders. Currently Magnum has no internal audit department, and is running the risk of relying on management who may not be in the best position to provide skilled, independent, and objective opinions on internal controls. As things currently stand, Magnum is missing out on the valuable benefits that professional internal auditors provide.

A primary lesson from the financial failure and collapse of many high-profile company collapses in recent years is that good governance, risk management, and internal controls are essential to corporate success and longevity.

Because of its unique and objective perspective, in-depth organisational knowledge, and application of sound audit and consulting principles, a well-functioning, fully resourced and independent internal audit activity would be well positioned to provide the directors of Magnum with valuable support and assurance.

Magnum's audit committee and the internal auditors will be interdependent and should be mutually accessible, with the internal auditors providing objective opinions, information, support, and education to the audit committee, and the audit committee providing validation and oversight to the internal auditors.

The audit committee and the internal auditors will have interlocking goals. A strong working relationship is essential for each to fulfil its responsibilities to the board of directors, shareholders, and other stakeholders. Appropriate reporting lines for the internal auditors are critical if they are to achieve their requisite independence, objectivity, and organisational stature needed to effectively assess the organisation's internal control, risk management, and governance processes. Best practice recommends that, to achieve necessary independence, the internal auditors should report directly to the audit committee.

A direct channel of communication between the internal auditor and Magnum's audit committee will be essential. The internal auditor should have access to the audit committee chair and be able to attend audit committee meetings to present the audit plan, report on the results of major audits and key audit findings or other matters, and discuss their observations on risk and internal controls within the company.

Question 6

Ms Avril Archibald
Finance Director
Hawk PLC
97 High Street
Anytown

8 May 20X3

Dear Ms Archibald,

Thank you for your letter of 1 May. I hope I will be able to address the concerns which you have about the forthcoming audit of Hawk plc.

The need for an audit

Like you, many company directors see the annual visit of the external auditor as little more than a nuisance – they view it as disruptive, taking up management time, and adding little value to the business. The auditor's role is defined by legislation, and yet from the perspective of many directors, the auditor produces nothing of interest.

This view is unfortunate, since with a bit of effort and an improved understanding of the nature of an audit, it is possible for managers and directors to minimise the disruptive aspects of the annual audit, and to appreciate the many benefits the auditor can provide to the business as a whole.

Auditing is no different from any other industry in that a key measure of its output is the added value it brings to clients and to the wider business community. Auditing is not a commodity to be traded but a complex service which needs to be carefully tailored to the needs of the business. Although the audit fee is undoubtedly an important consideration to many clients, it will not necessarily be the only consideration.

Part of the audit process involves analysing business processes and examining risks and controls, which enables the audit team to spot both weaknesses and possibilities for improvement in the various parts of the company. The audit thereby serves as a tool with added value for our clients.

As you are aware, financial statements are used for a variety of purposes and decisions. For example, shareholders use them to evaluate how well the directors are performing as stewards of their assets. Investors use them for deciding whether to buy or sell shares. Credit rating agencies use them in making decisions about a company's credit worthiness, and banks will use them in reaching lending decisions. By having an independent audit report, all the users of financial statements should have increased confidence in the quality of the published information.

We recognise that the annual audit can be an expensive undertaking, in terms of both the company's time and money. However, the audit can be more of an investment than an expense if we have time to analyse and evaluate accounts and procedures, rather than preparing accounting-type schedules. We will communicate with you prior to the visit, providing you with a listing of information we require to conduct the audit. By making sure we have the information we need, disruption and cost can be kept to a minimum.

Audit committees

Many companies have set up an audit committee in order to assist the directors to comply with their legal duty to publish financial statements which give a true and fair view. The precise role of the committee will be a matter for the board to decide, although its principal duty would normally be to strengthen the role of both the internal and the external auditors.

In some countries, such as the UK, it is a requirement that listed companies should have an audit committee, consisting of at least three independent non-executive directors, or two for smaller companies.

Most small companies do not have an audit committee. In the absence of an audit committee, the auditors would be expected to report to the board through the finance director which may be a less independent platform. Having an audit committee opens up a direct channel of communication between the auditors and the board, and is something even smaller companies should consider.

The audit committee should consider significant accounting policies, any changes to them and any significant estimates and judgements. The management should inform the audit committee of the methods used to account for significant or unusual transactions where the accounting treatment is open to different approaches. Taking into account the external auditor's view, the audit committee should consider whether the company has adopted appropriate accounting policies and, where necessary, made appropriate estimates and judgements.

Avoiding audit modifications

For the directors of a company, producing draft accounts should not be seen as some sort of test or examination of their financial skills. Some companies have a great deal of resources available, in the form of sophisticated accounting software and many well-qualified accounting personnel, while smaller businesses have far fewer resources. It is the directors' duty to ensure that accounts are produced to the best of their abilities, but nobody, including the auditor, expects the directors to always get it right first time.

The auditor will try to take steps to avoid modifying the audit report, usually by discussing any problem areas with the directors, before finalising the report.

In general, the auditor will be as reluctant to modify the audit report as the directors will be to incur a modification. A modified report suggests that the auditor has been unable to convince the directors to change the financial statements.

Many disagreements over accounting policies can be resolved by discussion between the auditor and the directors. While the auditor will not be prepared to condone any deliberate manipulation of the accounts, the company's accounting policies could be amended in a way that is satisfactory to both the directors and the auditor.

Potential modifications over uncertainty might also be avoided by identifying the source of the auditor's doubts, and addressing the issues raised. For example, it may be possible to postpone the date of publication of the financial statements in order to allow some uncertainty to be resolved. Similarly, missing records could perhaps be recreated in order to allow an important audit test to be carried out, and in this way avoid a modified audit report.

I hope that this letter has reassured you, but if you would like to discuss any matters further, please do get in touch.

Yours sincerely,

Paul Winter
Chandavar Associates

PRACTICE ANSWER BANK

Question 7

(a) Cash takings are notoriously vulnerable to fraud, and the slightest weakness in controls may lead to theft. Even when there is no intention to defraud, it is essential that all such takings be banked promptly and without deductions.

This is partly to minimise the risk of theft, but also to ensure that the university's records are complete and up to date. Although the amounts involved are likely to be relatively small, it is important that the university finance department is aware not only of the cash recovered from students, but also of any allowable expenses incurred by staff.

By deducting the expenses from the cash receipts, it is possible that the university's accounting system will fail to treat the items correctly, resulting in overstated photocopying costs, and understated lecturers' expenses. Whereas this particular case may have caused no damage, it is important to ensure that where the university has rules and procedures, these are not circumvented.

(b) Income from photocopying is unlikely to form a large part of the university's income. However, to ensure that it is complete, the following procedures should be adopted by the auditor:

- Identify those departments where photocopying costs are high.
- Compare photocopying costs with amounts received from students.
- Investigate all those departments where there is a discrepancy between the two amounts.
- Obtain explanations for any shortfall, such as a departmental policy of not reclaiming photocopying costs from students.
- Select a sample of courses within these departments, and calculate the money which should have been received (cost per student multiplied by number of students).
- Compare the anticipated income with the actual money received.
- Seek explanations from individual lecturers for any discrepancies.

Note: only six procedures were required.

Question 8

(a) Accountants throughout the world have a duty to observe the highest standards of conduct and integrity, and to uphold the good standing and reputation of the profession. They must also refrain from any conduct which might discredit the profession. Auditors are representatives of the shareholders and the public, and therefore the standards of the profession are greatly determined by the public interest.

Members must avoid actions or situations which are inconsistent with their professional obligations. The Code of Ethics provides guidelines for maintaining a professional attitude and acting in a manner that will enhance the image of the profession, and allows accountants to strive for the highest standards of professionalism. The Code also helps ensure that all accountants act in a consistent manner, regardless of where in the world they are working.

(b) (i) If Zeta Jason believes her client omits income, she should first of all confront the directors of Emporium Ltd. If the directors maintain that all revenue is declared and can satisfy Jones that there is no misstatement, there is no violation and Jones need not take any further action.

If information has been withheld from the tax authorities, Zeta should advise the directors to immediately inform the tax authorities. If they ignore the advice to disclose, Zeta should stress to the client that failure to disclose increases the likelihood of prosecution. If the directors continue to refuse to notify the authorities, Samsons should cease to act for Emporium Ltd, and should inform the tax authorities that they are doing this because accounts which the accountant signed as being accurate cannot be relied upon.

(ii) Carlos Egea would be wrong to discipline the staff who disclosed audit client information to the FRC. The IESBA *Code of Ethics* states that all accountants have a duty to keep client information confidential:

'A professional accountant shall comply with the principle of confidentiality, which requires an accountant to respect the confidentiality of information acquired as a result of professional and business relationships. An accountant shall: […] Not disclose confidential information acquired as a result of professional and business relationships outside the firm or employing organization without proper and specific authority, unless there is a legal or professional duty or right to disclose.' (IESBA *Code of Ethics*: para. R114.1(d))

However, the auditor is allowed to disclose information for a quality review. There is a professional duty for an auditor to comply with technical standards and ethics requirements. As such, Samsons' staff should comply with the quality review of the FRC, and should respond to any inquiries or investigations by the regulatory body.

(iii) The ethical issue involved in this situation is that of independence. Independence in auditing means having a position to take an unbiased viewpoint in the performance of audit tests, analysis of results, and attestation in the auditor's report. It is essential that the auditor be independent and is perceived as such by the users of audited financial statements.

If Pierre decides to update the books and records for Fedamax, that would not be a violation of ethical conduct in respect of last year's audit. Samsons has completed the audit of the company's financial statements for last year, and updating the books now will not have an effect on last year's audit.

The *Code of Ethics* states that an audit firm may provide audit clients that are not listed with accounting and bookkeeping services, provided the services are of a routine or mechanical nature and any self-review threat created is reduced to an acceptable level. (IESBA *Code of Ethics*: para. R601.5)

If Samsons continue to act as Fedamax's auditor this year, the firm will therefore have to ensure that safeguards are in place to reduce the threat to an acceptable level. Such safeguards are likely to include Samsons making arrangements to ensure that the bookkeeping services are not performed by staff members who are also part of the of the audit team.

(iv) Maxine should refuse the offer to stay at the villa in Ibiza because the gift is not 'trivial and inconsequential' and therefore would interfere with the firm's independence. The *Code of Ethics* points out that gifts and hospitality from a client can give rise to threats to compliance with the rules on independence. In particular, self-interest threats to objectivity may be created if a gift from a client is accepted where the value is not 'trivial and inconsequential'.

The significance of such threats will depend on the nature, value and intent behind the offer. An auditor may accept a small gift that is usually given to everyone at the company such as a bottle of wine. However, staying at a villa, which is only normally used by clients, would be deemed questionable, and should certainly be refused.

Question 9

(a) (i) The nature of a profession involves members having a duty to serve the public interest above all else. Many professions such as lawyers and doctors involve joint professional and organisational responsibilities, where the individual has a responsibility to their employer, but also to the profession to which they belong. Usually there is no conflict between the two roles. Where any conflict does arise, it is usually assumed that the professional's duty to the public interest should take precedence over their responsibilities to the organisation which employs them.

As a member of the staff of Massy & Co, Chris is part of the organisation and answerable to his employers, who pay his salary. As an employee, Chris is accountable to the principals of the organisation – in this case, the partners in the accountancy firm. He therefore has a contractual duty to comply with the requirements of his employers. There is a reasonable expectation that he will conform to the business practices of the firm, and that he will work efficiently to the best of his abilities.

As a professional accountant, Chris has a duty to maintain the professional and ethical standards of his profession. Many professions, including the accountancy profession, have adopted codes of ethics, and so Chris will need to comply with that. He is accountable to his professional body in terms of continued registration and professional behaviour. In most cases of conflict, this responsibility will be more important than that to an employer.

(ii) On the one hand, Chris needs to carefully manage his relationship with Samira, his employer, who seems convinced that Steffi Ltd, and Joshua in particular, are incapable of doing any wrong. Samira is showing signs of poor judgment and it may well be that her independence is compromised. Chris is in the difficult situation of having to decide how to deal with Samira's poor professionalism, which may involve approaching one or more of the other partners in the firm.

The other side of this is that Chris has a duty to both the public interest and the shareholders of Steffi Ltd to ensure that the financial statements do contain a 'true and fair view'. The inadequate explanation from Joshua about the transactions in question should be of concern to Chris as a professional accountant, although he may decide in the end that the invoice and related credit note in question do not require any delay in signing the audit report.

(b) Independence requires integrity and an objective approach to the audit process. The concept requires the auditor to carry out the audit work freely and in an objective manner. The auditor must be independent of the client for several reasons. It increases credibility and underpins confidence in the audit process, which is primarily for the benefit of the shareholders, who appoint the auditor. Independence also helps to ensure the reliability of the audit report, since any evidence of lack of independence has the potential to undermine the audit report, making the audit process itself pointless. An audit is only effective if the parties are independent of each other.

There are several threats to independence described in the case of Steffi Ltd. Firstly, Samira has been the audit partner for 'many years'. This is a familiarity threat and is in contravention of the corporate governance codes operating in many countries. For example, The UK Corporate Governance Code specifies that auditors should be rotated periodically to avoid the familiarity threat in relation to audit clients.

Massy & Co provides more than one service to Steffi Ltd. One of the threats to independence is an over-dependence on any particular client arising from the provision of several services to the same client. Good practice is not to offer additional services to audit clients to avoid the appearance of compromised independence.

Samira is an old friend of Joshua, the finance director of Steffi Ltd. This is another example of a familiarity threat which Samira should have disclosed to Massey & Co at the outset, as it should almost certainly disqualify her from acting as audit partner on the Steffi Ltd account.

Note: only three threats were required.

Question 10

(a) The partner's involvement in the secret payroll is illegal and questions their integrity.

Another ethical situation raised by the case is whether or not the independence of Longmuir & Co was impaired in fact. Once it was publicly known that the Longmuir & Co partner had maintained the secret payroll account for Sunshine Cabs, the apparent independence of the audit firm was questioned as well.

If Sunshine Cabs had been subject to regulation by an oversight body (such as the Securities and Exchange Commission (SEC) in the US), the maintenance of the secret payroll account by the Longmuir & Co partner would have been a violation of that agency's auditor independence rules. Some regulatory bodies, have extremely strict independence rules, and include a prohibition on the provision of bookkeeping services and other accounting work by auditors to their clients.

When auditors are allowed to provide bookkeeping services to clients, they must take special precautions to ensure that their objectivity and independence is not threatened. For example, when an auditor does carry out bookkeeping services for a client, they should ensure that they do not assume a role equivalent to that of an employee of that client.

Likewise, the auditor should impress upon management that the latter has the ultimate responsibility for the client's financial records and financial statements, even though the auditors may have been involved in the recording and compilation of the client's financial data.

(b) The quality management standards for audit firms require them to establish policies and procedures to minimise the likelihood of association with a client whose management lacks integrity. The specific procedures which Longmuir & Co should have used in connection with the acceptance of Sunshine Cabs as a client include:

Communication with the Sunshine Cabs' predecessor audit firm. Longmuir & Co should have asked their predecessors if there was any reason that the firm might have to question the integrity of the prospective client's management.

Inquiry of the business associates of Sunshine Cabs, including the charity's bankers, legal counsel, underwriters, and executives of competing companies, regarding the competence and trustworthiness of the prospective client's key personnel.

Contact regulatory authorities (such as a Charities Commission) that have any oversight responsibilities for Sunshine Cab's industry to determine whether disciplinary or legal measures have been taken in the past against the company's key executives.

Commission an investigative agency to perform background checks on all key executives of the potential new client.

(c) Investors and creditors (or in this case charity donors) who suffer financial losses as a result of the demise or near demise of a business entity often seek to recover those losses from the entity's accounting firm, whether or not the firm is actually culpable. The significant capital resources of most large accounting firms make them prime targets for disgruntled parties who have made poor investment or lending decisions.

In the case of Sunshine Cabs, the executives were bankrupt and not in a position to make financial redress for their fraudulent activity which had led to the collapse of the charity. Recognising this, the lawyers who represented the parties who had made losses would have realised that, even if they could obtain a court judgement against the Barkers, it would be a pointless exercise as they would not be in a position to repay any of the debt.

The lawyers attempted to obtain redress from Longmuir & Co, probably in the hope that the firm would make a sizeable out-of-court settlement, and avoid the financial costs of a prolonged legal battle. Longmuir & Co might well prefer to avoid the damage to their firm's reputation which would no doubt be caused by a lawsuit, even if it was ultimately resolved in their favour.

(d) The key preventative measure that Longmuir & Co should have taken to protect itself from being sued by third parties is to ensure that the firm follows generally accepted auditing standards on all of their audit engagements. This was clearly not the case with the audit of Sunshine Cabs, given the accounting role of the audit partner.

However, even if Longmuir & Co had complied with auditing standards, it may have found itself involved in this costly litigation, and should have taken the following steps to protect the firm:

- Establish quality management procedures, quality reviews and practice standards which meet (or even exceed) those established by the profession.

- Adopt rigorous client acceptance procedures – this was evidently not the case when taking on Sunshine Cabs.

- Adopt a policy of refusing to make out-of-court settlements. This would have discouraged any of Sunshine Cabs investors from making speculative, nuisance lawsuits, and discourage potential plaintiffs from suing the firm.

- Carry adequate professional indemnity insurance.

Question 11

(a) Whilst it may seem common sense to accept all audit engagements so that the firm can increase profitability and increase its client base, all engagements expose the audit firm to a degree of risk. In order to decide whether or not to take on a new audit engagement or to continue with an existing engagement, audit firms need to have an understanding of the risk profile of their clients and the potential impact on the audit firm. Client acceptance procedures form an integral part of an audit firm's risk management system.

(b) Issues for Olsen's partners to consider prior to acceptance of Meditec include:

Previous auditors ceasing to hold office

Olsen will need to obtain the 'Statement of Circumstances filed' by the previous auditors, ask permission to contact the previous auditors, and discuss the reasons for the previous auditors removal or resignation with the directors of Meditec. Olsen needs to establish whether there are any reasons why it should not accept the appointment.

Pharmaceutical company

Meditec is a high profile company that has recently featured prominently in the press. As it is potentially engaged in ethically, morally and socially questionable activities, any adverse public reaction to its products or activities could have an impact on Olsen as auditors. Furthermore, companies in this section are subject to stringent regulatory issues which increases audit risk.

Competence, and knowledge of the business

Prior to accepting Meditec, the partners must carefully review whether the firm has the technical competencies required, and thorough understanding of the pharmaceutical industry in order to act as auditors. Unless the firm has the ability to understand the potentially complicated transactions and processes, it should not accept the appointment.

Losses

Meditec is expecting to make substantial losses this year. Its new cancer drug, Avanti, is no longer considered viable. This places concern over Meditec's ability to continue as a going concern.

If Meditec were not to be a going concern, there would be a risk that the audit fees would not be paid, and also the collapse of such a high profile company could affect Olsen's reputation as auditors and business advisors.

Given the substantial losses, there is also the risk that the directors of Meditec may be encouraged to use creative accounting techniques to manipulate the accounts and cover up their current weak performance. Olsen must be alert to this risk if they agree to act as auditor.

Potential 'opinion shopping'

Olsen has been asked to undertake an independent review of Meditec's accounting policies, prior to being appointed as auditor. There is a risk that Meditec is attempting to establish which audit firm will agree with potentially inappropriate accounting policies prior to appointing an audit firm. It will also be difficult for Olsen to subsequently question the accounting policies as external auditors, if they have already agreed that they were reasonable as part of their independent review.

Size of Meditec

If accepted as an audit client, Meditec would become one of Olsen's largest clients. The firm must ensure that they have adequate resources to staff this significant assignment.

Level of fee income

Olsen must be careful to ensure that the firm is not, and is not seen to be, financially dependent on Meditec. The firm must review the likely recurring fee income that will be gained from Meditec, and ensure that it does not bring into question the firm's independence and objectivity.

Independence issues

As with all audit engagements, Olsen will need to undertake the usual acceptance procedures, including business and family connections, beneficial interests and conflicts of interest.

Question 12

(a) From: A.Kwaku@AuditAfrica.com

To: junala@yoruba.com

Thank you for your email. I was very pleased to hear that Yoruba is still keen to appoint AuditAfrica this year.

I note that you are concerned about the audit fee. I would make the following points in this respect:

According to international ethics, the fee we charge for our audit services should be a fair reflection of effort. This should take the following conditions into account:

- The skill and knowledge required for the type of professional services involved
- The level of training and experience of the persons necessarily engaged in performing the professional services

- The time necessarily occupied by each person engaged in performing the professional services
- The degree of responsibility that performing those services entails

The fee should be calculated on the basis of appropriate rates per hour or per day for the time of each person engaged in performing professional services. These rates should be based on the premise that the audit is well planned, controlled and managed. Out-of-pocket expenses, in particular travelling expenses, attributable directly to the professional services performed for your company's audit would normally be charged to you in addition to professional fees.

I hope this clarifies our position on the matter, and I look forward to hearing from you.

(b)

AuditAfrica

International Accountants

743 Queen Street, Lagos

The Board of Directors
The Yoruba Corporation
400 Danube Street
Benin City

1 June 20X4

Dear Sirs,

You have requested that we audit the statement of financial position of The Yoruba Corporation (Yoruba) as of 31 September 20X4, and the related statements of profit or loss and cash flows for the year then ending. We are pleased to confirm our acceptance and our understanding of this engagement by means of this letter. Our audit will be made with the objective of our expressing an opinion on the financial statements.

We will conduct our audit of Yoruba in accordance with International Standards on Auditing. These ISAs require that we plan and perform the audit to obtain reasonable assurance about whether the Yoruba financial statements are free of material misstatements. An audit includes examining, on a test basis, evidence supporting the amounts and disclosures in the Yoruba financial statements. Our audit will also include assessing the accounting principles used and significant estimates made by the directors and management of Yoruba, as well as evaluating the overall financial statement presentation.

Because of the test nature and other inherent limitations of an audit, together with the inherent limitations of any accounting and internal control systems, there is an unavoidable risk that even some material misstatement may remain undiscovered.

In addition to our report on Yoruba's financial statements, we expect to provide you with a separate letter concerning any material deficiencies in Yoruba's accounting and internal control systems which come to our notice.

We remind you that the responsibility for the preparation of financial statements including adequate disclosure is that of the management Yoruba. This includes the maintenance of adequate accounting records and internal controls, the selection and application of accounting policies, and the safeguarding of the assets of the company. As part of our audit process, we will request from management of Yoruba written confirmation concerning representations made to us in connection with the audit.

We look forward to full cooperation with Yoruba's staff and we trust that they will make available to use whatever records, documentation, and other information requested in connection with our audit.

Our fees are based on standard hourly rates, which we estimate will take 125 hours, plus direct out-of-pocket expenses. Individual hourly rates vary between $50 and $350 according to the degree of responsibility involved and the experience and skill required. The payment will be 33% at the beginning of the audit with the balance at the end of the audit. Should we find any conditions that could significantly affect our initial estimate, we will notify you immediately.

This letter will be effective for future years unless it is terminated, amended or superseded.

Please sign and return the attached copy of this letter to indicate that it is in accordance with your understanding of the arrangements for our audit of Yoruba's financial statements.

Yours faithfully,

Ajani Kwaku

Ajani Kwaku

Partner

Acknowledged on behalf of The Yoruba Corporation by

(signed) _____

Name and Title

Question 13

> **MEMO**
>
> **From:** Samira Swann, Head of Internal Audit
> **To:** The Board of Directors
> **Date:** 1 June 20X4
>
> **Subject:** The control environment, and internal controls in the goods received department.
>
> **The control environment**
>
> Control environment means the overall attitude, awareness, and actions of directors and management regarding the system of internal control and its importance in the company. Control environment factors include integrity, ethical values and competence of the company's staff; management's philosophy and operating style; the way management assigns authority and responsibility, and organises and develops its staff; and the attention and direction provided by the board of directors.
>
> The control environment is important because it is the foundation for all other components of internal control, providing discipline and structure. Furthermore, the control environment has a pervasive influence on the way business activities are structured, the way objectives are established and the way risks are assessed.
>
> The control environment influences the control consciousness of its people. Effectively controlled companies set a positive 'tone at the top' and establish appropriate policies and procedures.

The control environment and 'tone at the top' are influenced significantly by the company's board of directors. An active and involved board of directors possessing an appropriate degree of management, technical and other expertise coupled with the necessary stature and mind set so that it can adequately perform the necessary governance, guidance and oversight responsibilities is critical to effective internal control.

The adequacy of internal controls in the goods received department

The adequacy of controls in this area is questionable because the goods received clerk does not receive a copy of the purchase order which has the quantity blocked out (concealed). This practice may cause the goods received clerk to bypass the counting and inspection procedures.

The goods received clerk may only compare the purchase order and goods delivery note when preparing a goods received report. As a result of this weakness, incorrect quantities of goods, or inferior quality goods, may be received and accepted. However, in the case of Berwick, certain areas have compensating controls.

Receipt of sheet metal

Although the goods received clerk may only compare quantities on the purchase order and the goods received note, there is a compensating control over the quantity of sheet metal received.

This compensating control is the independent verification of weights received and date of receipt, which are provided in the goods delivered note. However, sheet metal with unacceptable quality specifications may still be delivered and accepted.

Receipt of screws

Since the goods received clerk weighs the screws upon receipt, and the weight is converted into units, controls over quantity received is adequate. Furthermore, screws of an unacceptable specification may be expected to be detected during the weighing and inspection process.

Receipt of camera lenses

Because there are no controls that compensate for the weaknesses in checking the actual receipt of camera lenses, there is inadequate control over the quantity and quality of lenses received.

Financial statement misstatements that may result from inadequacies

The inadequacies identified in the internal control system over receipt of goods means that there could be several misstatements and inaccuracies in Berwick's financial statements.

Firstly, inventory may be overstated because additions to inventory may be based on suppliers' invoices, which may include non-usable items, or items that were not received. If inventory is overstated, the assets in the statement of financial position will be overstated by a corresponding amount.

Because the value of inventory forms part of the calculation of cost of goods sold, any overvaluation will have an effect on the statement of profit or loss and other comprehensive income too. Profit will be overstated by the same amount of overstatement of inventory.

Finally, because the company may have erroneously accrued the cost of non-usable items or items not received, accounts payable may be overstated.

Question 14

Weakness	Recommend improvement
Raw materials may be removed from the warehouse upon oral authorisation from one of the production foremen.	Raw material should be removed from the warehouse only upon written authorisation from a production foreman. The authorisation forms should be prenumbered and accounted for, list quantities and job or production number, and be signed and dated.
Carron's practice of monthly physical inventory counts does not compensate for the lack of a perpetual inventory system. Quantities on hand at the end of the month may not be sufficient to last until the next month's count.	A perpetual inventory system should be established under the control of someone other than the warehouse staff. The system should include quantities and values for each item of raw material. Total inventory value per the perpetual records should be agreed to the general ledger at reasonable intervals. When physical counts are taken they should be compared to the perpetual records. Where differences occur, they should be investigated, and if the perpetual records are in error they should be adjusted.
Raw materials are purchased at a predetermined reorder level and in predetermined quantities. Since production levels may vary during the year, quantities ordered may be either too small or too great for the current production demands.	Requests for purchases of raw materials should come from the production department management, and be based on current production schedules and quantities on hand per the perpetual records.
The accounts payable clerk handles both the purchasing function and payment of invoices. This is not a satisfactory segregation of duties.	The purchasing function should be centralised in a separate department. Prenumbered purchase orders should originate from and be controlled by this department. A copy of the purchase order should be sent to the accounting and receiving departments.
Raw materials are always purchased from the same supplier.	The purchasing department should be required to obtain competitive bids on all purchases over a specified amount.

Weakness	Recommend improvement
There is no receiving department or receiving report. For proper segregation of duties, the individuals responsible for receiving should be separate from the warehouse staff.	A receiving department should be established. Staff in this department should count or weigh all goods received and prepare a prenumbered receiving report. These reports should be signed, dated, and controlled, and a copy should be sent to the accounting department, purchasing department, and warehouse.
There is no inspection department. Since high-cost electronic components are required to meet certain specifications, they should be tested for these requirements when received.	An inspection department should be established to inspect goods as they are received. Prenumbered inspection reports should be prepared and accounted for, and a copy of the reports should be sent to the accounting department.

Question 15

MEMO

To: Karen Ling
From: James Dodds
Re: Country Kitchens Ltd – purchases system controls

Controls over individual purchases

Goods should only be purchased from approved suppliers. The list of approved suppliers should be regularly reviewed to ensure the company is obtaining the best possible terms.

When the buying department receives a request from a user department to raise a purchase order (PO), it should consider whether the user department is authorised to purchase the goods and services.

Once the PO has been entered into the computer, the buying department should retain a copy of the order, send the order itself to the supplier, and a copy to the user department.

The goods received departments should check the quality and quantity of the goods which have been received, and check on the computer that the goods received agree with the purchase order. The goods received department should then enter details into the computer, and raise a GRN, a copy of which should be sent to the user department.

When the accounts department receives the purchase invoice, a note should be made that it has been received and the invoice sent to the user department.

The user department should check that the invoice details agree with the purchase order details, authorise the invoice, and send it to the accounting department.

The accounting department should check that the user department has carried out the checks, and has authorised the invoice.

The accounting department should post the invoice to the purchase ledger. The computer system should reject the invoice if the supplier is not on the standing data file, and should not make payment on the invoice if no PO has been received, or no GRN recorded. Any invoice that is not supported by a PO or GRN should be investigated.

The accounting department should carry out regular checks on POs where goods have not been received, GRNs where no invoice has been received, and invoices which have been with user departments for a long time. The accounting department should also investigate gaps in the sequential numbering of POs or GRNs.

Controls over computer system terminals

Access to the main computer should be restricted to the usual working hours of the company. Any person requiring access out-with these hours would require special authorisation.

The computer should log terminals and users, and this log should be regularly reviewed for unusual access times.

Each terminal should be set up to provide only these services which the users of that terminal need to use. For example, the terminals in the goods received departments should not have access to the payroll, sales, or nominal ledger systems.

Individual users should be restricted to accessing only those facilities which they need to use in the course of their normal job. This can be implemented by the use of passwords. The system should note any instance of an invalid password being used, and terminals should be disabled if invalid passwords are used three times in a row.

Passwords should be unique to the individual, and should be changed periodically. Computer users should be instructed to memorise their passwords, rather than write them down. Passwords should not be displayed on screen when they are being keyed in by users.

An alternative to passwords is that users could be issued with plastic cards or infrared keys to allow them to access the terminal, but there is a danger that these could be lost or stolen.

The main computer should be able to check whether the terminal that is contacting it is authorised to do so.

Controls over the programs used to process accounting data should be very strict. Amendments should only be allowed when authorised by a senior official.

Question 16

(a) The objectives of internal controls for payroll are to ensure that payroll disbursements are made only upon proper authorisation to *bona fide* employees, that payroll disbursements are properly recorded and that related legal requirements (such as payroll tax deposits) are complied with.

Each employee should have a payroll/personnel file, containing updated salary, benefits, employment status, and withholding information, as well as beginning date of employment and termination date, when applicable.

A personnel manual should describe the organisation's policies, established by the board, regarding vacations, holidays and sick leave. Records should be kept for each employee to ensure that these policies are being followed.

The time sheet is the most common tool used to document employee hours (including overtime) and authorise payments to employees. Time sheets can be designed to incorporate information regarding vacation, sick leave, and holidays. Time sheets are usually submitted by the employee to his or her immediate supervisor for signature, and may also be reviewed periodically by senior management. Ideally, the person authorising an employee's hours does not also prepare the payments.

Payroll payments should be made in keeping with the procedures for all other cash disbursements. Additional segregation of duties related to the payroll function include having someone other than the payroll clerk hold unclaimed pay cheques and review the payroll register and post payroll to the general ledger.

Many organisations choose to have a separate bank account for payroll that is used for issuing payments. A payroll register, listing who was paid, how much, and cheque number is maintained, either as a subsidiary journal if there is a separate payroll account, or as part of the cash disbursements journal when payroll is integrated with other cash disbursements in a manual system. Some organisations require that employees sign the employee register to acknowledge receipt of their payment.

(b) The following internal control weaknesses were apparent in Caledonian's payroll system:

- The extent of control that Eddie Campos had over the payroll system, which began with his design of the system, and included his involvement in the detailed operations of that system.
- The lack of enforced vacations for key personnel. All officials should be made to take mandatory, regular holidays in order to avoid them being able to cover up fraudulent activity on a continuous basis.
- An apparent lack of the periodic testing of the payroll transactions cycle by internal auditors or a similar control group. Such testing should have resulted in the discovery of Campos' fraudulent scheme.

(c) The following are example of specific audit procedures which might have led to the discovery of Campos' embezzlement scheme:

- A surprise distribution of payroll cheques for selected departments might have resulted in unclaimed cheques and thus eventual discovery of Campos' fraud.
- Manual or computer-based 'limit tests' should have disclosed instances of employees being paid for an excessive number of hours.
- Analytical procedures to assess the reasonableness of Caledonian's periodic payroll expenses by department may have indicated that certain departments' payrolls were out of line with expectations.

Question 17

(a) The objectives of audit planning are as follows:

- To ensure that appropriate attention is devoted to important areas of the audit
- To help the auditor identify and resolve potential problems on a timely basis
- To ensure that the audit is organised, managed, and performed effectively
- To assist in the proper assignment of work between team members
- To facilitate the direction, supervision and review of work

(b)

Circumstances	Outline audit approach
This is the first year that SDF has undertaken the audit of Wallaby Limited	In order to be satisfied about the previous financial statements, the auditor should: (i) Hold consultations with management (ii) Review Wallaby's records, working papers and accounting and control procedures for the previous period (iii) Communicate with the previous auditor (iv) Become familiar with the nature of the business and the accounting systems, through discussions with management (v) Review interim and management accounts
Wallaby has a head office in Sydney, a factory in Indonesia, and several warehouses throughout Australia	The audit staff must be planned to carry out the audit from SDF's offices throughout the country. Provision should be made for visiting the factory in Indonesia, or arranging for this to be done by another audit firm associated with SDF. Staff must be adequately briefed and provided with the audit plan detailing their specific tasks and deadlines.
No inventory records have been kept, but a full inventory count is to be carried out at the year end	It is very important that the auditors are satisfied with the inventory count. The written count instruction must be reviewed well in advance of the year end, so that any improvements can be suggested by SDF and incorporated into the client's instructions. The auditors should ensure that sufficient staff with the necessary experience is available to attend the count at all material locations.
SDF is considering relying on the work of Wallaby's internal auditors	The external auditor must consider the following when deciding whether to rely on the work of Wallaby's internal audit function: The organisational status and reporting responsibilities on the internal auditors Internal auditors formal terms of reference Internal audit documentation such as an audit manual and audit plans Professional membership and practical experience Internal audit reports generated and feedback from management

Circumstances	Outline audit approach
One of Wallaby's major products has been identified as being potentially dangerous	The auditor must ascertain: For how long has Wallaby been selling this component, and in what quantity? How much of this component the company currently holds in inventory The auditor must keep up to date with the findings of the official enquiry. The auditor should consider what provision should be made in the financial statements for any compensation due.

Question 18

(a) Increased audit risk	(b) Audit approach
(i) Marlings Savings and Loans Loans due from farmers may be difficult to collect and there may be inadequate security to claim upon and farmers may be unable to service the interest payments. This may mean that receivables are overstated and could lead to potential cash flow and going concern problems.	Increase extent of vouching of loan repayments Review surveyors' reports for value of farmland of loans in default Evaluate in detail the loan loss reserve
(ii) Georgia Pacific Ltd Possible unrecorded revenue; possible stealing of scrap; possible fraud involving collusion with scrap dealers which may lead to incomplete balances in the financial statements, for example revenue.	Ask production staff for explanations (possible improved production process) Consider confirming scrap sales volume by contacting scrap dealers sold to in previous years Ascertain security of storage for scrap metal inventory
(iii) Coventry plc Possible obsolete inventory leading to possible overstatement of profits and current assets	Ask client about likely destination for the barometers Examine sales subsequent to year end to ensure barometers are not included in inventory at more than net realisable value

(a) Increased audit risk	(b) Audit approach
(iv) Charlaine Ltd Pressure to increase profits could lead to deliberate profit overstatement	Increase professional scepticism and extent of audit testing in areas where this could be achieved, such as: • Non-current asset additions (capitalisation of repairs) • Sales, purchases and inventory cut-off • Confirmation of trade receivables • Search for unrecorded liabilities
(v) Happy Days Ltd Possibility of July sales recorded in June leading to overstatement of revenue and profit.	Increase sales cut-off tests Increase trade receivables confirmations Examine goods despatched notes in support of year-end sales Consider confirming material year-end sales with customer

Question 19

(a) The major audit risk factor in the audit of Myst Ltd appears to be the company's apparent profit buoyancy in the face of a severe industry decline. An attitude of professional scepticism should lead the auditor to suspect possible profit inflation.

This is particularly important given the reported losses from other similar companies, and the fact that one other company had been forced into receivership.

Particular attention needs to be directed towards the November sales increase and the significant rise in the current year's gross profit rate.

(b) Notwithstanding effective internal control procedures, if the control environment suggests the possibility of management override, control risk will be assessed at or near maximum.

Moreover, the results of analytical procedures in the planning stages of the Myst Ltd audit, if not adequately explained by other conditions, should prompt the auditors to set the inherent risk at 100%.

High control risk, coupled with high internal risk, will require a low detection risk in order to achieve the desired overall risk level. Low detection risk, in turn, will lead to increased substantive audit testing in the Myst Ltd engagement, particularly in the areas of sales, accounts receivable, and inventories.

(c) Given the results of analytical procedures, ie the high gross profit rate and unusually high November sales, inherent risk should probably remain at 100%.

In designing substantive audit procedures, Sinitta should consider expanding year-end sales cut-off tests, confirming a larger proportion of year end accounts receivable, and planning to devote more time to observing Myst Ltd's physical inventory taking.

PRACTICE ANSWER BANK

(d) Control testing may be appropriate in three different ways, depending on the nature of the controls.

If a visible audit trail exists in the form of documentation, the auditor can examine the documents as appropriate to verify the operating effectiveness of internal control procedures. Evidence as to whether transactions have been executed in accordance with management's authorisation and recorded correctly is gathered through such examination.

In the absence of a visible audit trail, the auditor can test controls through observation. The auditor observes the control procedures, such as asset safeguards, and the control environment. In the presence of complex processing systems, the auditor may find transaction reprocessing the most effective means for testing selected controls.

Statistical sampling methods, involving attribute sampling, are commonly applied in the first form of controls testing. Observation and reprocessing ordinarily do not require the use of statistical sampling, although reprocessing usually involves judgement sampling in developing test transactions to process through the accounting system.

(e) Statistical sampling for attributes may be considered by Sinitta and her audit team as a means for quantifying control risk. It could also assist in determining detection risk for substantive audit testing purposes.

For the purpose of quantifying control risk, Sinitta needs to follow through on her initial control structure assessment. She has determined that control procedures in the area of sales and shipments appear to be adequate, but that the business environment suggests the possibility of management override.

Attribute sampling, by calculating an upper occurrence limit, will assist in either confirming or denying Sinitta's initial assessment of control effectiveness.

A low observed error rate would be indicative of the absence of management override; a high rate, especially if it includes instances of document fabrication, or recording next year's sales in the current year, will confirm the existence of management override.

In any event, attribute sampling should help Sinitta in further assessing control risk and designing appropriate substantive audit programmes.

Question 20

(a) The sampling unit is the Goods Despatched Note (GDN), and the population is the total of the forms used during the period. This comprises 11,601 forms, ranging in number from 44223 to 55833.

The reason the sampling unit is the GDN rather than the sales invoice, is to satisfy the objective of attribute number 2. To determine that a sales invoice exists for a given shipment, the auditor must select a GDN and trace it to the sales invoice to verify that the shipment was billed to the customer.

(b) The auditor should first determine the sample size, which is done using statistical tables which take into account the tolerable error rate and required confidence levels. Once the sample size has been decided, the auditors will select the items to be tested.

From random number tables, the auditor will use a random start and a predetermined pattern for moving through the table, in order to select the required number of GDNs. This is most often carried out using statistical sampling software.

(c) With a sample size of 200, the following calculation shows the percentage of actual errors can be compared with the tolerable error rate as follows:

Attribute number	Tolerable error rate (%)	Number of actual errors	Percentage of actual errors
1	4%	2	1%
2	5%	11	5.5%
3	4%	3	1.5%
4	5%	3	1.5%
5	5%	3	1.5%

This indicates that for attributes 1, 3, 4 and 5 the tolerable error rate is higher than the actual error rate, but for attribute 2 the actual error rate exceeded the tolerable error rate.

(d) The results of the testing suggest that Wheels Ltd's system for sales ensures the proper approval of customer credit, authenticity of shipments as evidenced by signed GDNs, the agreement of invoice prices with official price lists, and proper recording of sales.

Selling only to customers with prior credit approval reduces the probability of bad debts, which in turn may permit reduced auditor attention to the allowance for bad debts. A low error incidence related to recording of sales and the correct pricing of invoices increases auditor confidence in the valuation of revenue accounts and suggests a reduction of testing in this area.

The results for attributes 2 however, suggest a higher probability of shipments not being billed to customers. In terms of impact on substantive audit programmes, this problem area may lead the auditor to devote increased attention to year-end inventory quantities, particularly if unbilled shipments are not credited to perpetual inventory records.

In terms of developing sampling plans for substantive testing purposes, the results will also impact sample sizes for inventory testing purposes and accounts receivable confirmation requests.

Question 21

(a) If the cost and time involved in collecting evidence are too high there will be no demand for audit. An auditor could spend a long time accumulating evidence which would give a high degree of certainty that the figures were correct, but the cost involved would be prohibitive. The auditor's task must be to accumulate evidence that is sufficiently (but not overly) persuasive to support the figures in the accounts, in as short a time scale as possible.

The auditor should examine the consistency of audit evidence from different sources. Where evidence from two independent sources is consistent, the sum of the assurance gained by the auditor is greater than the sum of the individual parts. For example, an auditor wishing to confirm the accuracy of a supplier's balance could examine client generated evidence and also external evidence. If they agree, the auditor can be reasonably satisfied that the figures are accurate.

The contrasting principle is that of diminishing marginal effect. Where evidence is obtained from one source only, further consistent evidence from the same source will increase the total audit assurance by less than the sum of the parts. For example, an auditor wishing to confirm that cheque payments are adequately supported will verify a sample of payments with the supporting documentation. Beyond a certain number the assurance he or she will obtain from checking additional items will be less than the effort involved in doing the work.

(b) **Bank loans**

Debit entries in the loans payable account in GCP's general ledger are definitely not conclusive evidence that the loans have been paid. The worth of this type of evidence would depend largely on the quality of GCP's internal control.

Entries in GCP's cheque register are also not conclusive evidence that the loans were paid. If the entries in the cheque register correspond to the debits in the loans payable account (after taking interest payments into consideration), and the cheque register and general ledger are maintained by different employees, the value of this evidence is increased.

Paid cheques constitute strong evidence, but the possibility remains that the cheques may have been issued for some purpose other than the payment of the loans to Billabong Bank.

Receipts from Billabong Bank stamped PAID, and the date of payment are the strongest kind of evidence that the loans have in fact been repaid. None of the items previously identified is as important as this type of evidence.

A statement by GCP's treasurer that the loans had been paid at maturity is not very dependable evidence. A company's treasurer may be in a position to falsify loan documents, and it is also possible that this statement, although made in good faith, is made without full knowledge of the facts.

A letter received by Radial Accountants directly from Billabong Bank stating that no indebtedness existed at the period end date is strong evidence similar in quality to the inspection of the paid receipts.

Customer account

Examination of the computer printout from GCP's accounts receivable subsidiary ledger showing customer balances at the year end would be merely a preliminary step in the gathering of evidence by the auditors. The reliability of this printout would depend a great deal upon the adequacy of GCP's internal controls; specifically upon such points as whether the person maintaining this subsidiary ledger for accounts receivable had access to cash receipts, and was also responsible for maintaining the general ledger.

Copies of the sales invoices would be dependable audit evidence only if the internal control structure was strong, so that the person maintaining the accounts receivable records had no opportunity to obtain or falsify invoices, and the invoices were carefully controlled using serial numbers.

A purchase order received from Queensland Trading constitutes somewhat stronger documentary evidence than invoices created within GCP, but could nevertheless be fraudulently created without too much difficulty. The purchase order would be of more significance if Queensland Trading and the nature of its operations were known to the auditors.

A shipping document describing the articles sold to Queensland Trading would be of considerable significance if prepared in the goods despatched department by persons having nothing to do with accounting records and if the document were serially numbered and properly controlled. This document is still, however, subject to the limitations of all documentary evidence prepared within the client company.

A letter received by GCP from Queensland Trading acknowledging the receivable is not of much value when it has passed through the client's hands prior to its inspection by the auditors. It is of the same general order of reliability as a purchase order from a customer.

A letter received by Radial Accountants directly from Queensland Trading acknowledging the correctness of the amount shown as a receivable in GCP's accounting records is excellent evidence. As a further precaution, as in this case where the receivable in question is large in relation to the other assets of the client, Radial Accountants may wish to verify the existence and the credit rating of Queensland Trading by reference to trade journals and directories and by inquiry of a credit rating agency.

Question 22

(a) **Direct material cost**

Carry out compliance tests on the system of recording all movements of direct materials, and substantive tests on the inventory movements.

Check stores requisition notes to ensure that each requisition has been properly charged to production or assembly batches, and has been costed using an acceptable basis such as FIFO or average cost.

Compare actual cost with budgeted cost and enquire into any material deviations.

Direct labour cost

Verify the time charged for a sample of production batches, using timesheets detailing which batches have been worked on and for how long.

Reconcile total time charged for all batches with total available time per employee.

Verify rate at which labour is charged to wage records.

Compare actual labour hours with estimations and enquire into material deviations.

(b) **Overhead expenditure**

IAS 2 *Inventories* states that the allocation of fixed production overheads to the costs of conversion should be based on the normal capacity of the production facilities. Normal capacity is the production expected to be achieved on average over a number of periods under normal circumstances. It appears that the year to 31 October 20X3 was not a 'normal' year, since production was considerably lower than usual during the year. The value of the inventory should therefore be reduced to a lower overhead allocation rate, reflecting normal activity levels.

Distribution costs and selling expenses

IAS 2 states that cost of conversion comprises:

- directly attributable costs
- production overheads, and
- other overheads attributable in the particular circumstances of the business to bringing the product or service to its present location and condition.

The distribution costs required to transfer the goods to the retailers (their present condition) therefore falls into the 'other overheads' category, and should consequently be included in inventory values.

The selling costs have yet to be incurred and hence should not be included in inventory values, since it is not appropriate to capitalise costs yet to be incurred.

(c) **Slow-moving inventory items**

The fact that levels of certain inventory items have been increasing steadily throughout the year is an indication that Playtime may be finding it difficult to sell those items. As a result, the realisable values of the old inventory may be less than cost. The auditor should consider the inventory turnover of all product lines, and for those which appear slow-moving, determine the relationship between inventory quantities and annual sales in order to determine how long it would take to sell those items.

Production and sales plans should be discussed with management in order to determine what future plans they have to sell the inventory (eg reduced selling price or increased sales effort). A review of events since the year end should provide additional audit evidence.

Obsolete inventory should have been deducted from the price lists, and the auditor should check whether sufficient provision has already been made, or whether additional provisions are required.

Question 23

(a) (i) **Accounting system** means the series of tasks and records of an entity by which transactions are processed as a means of maintaining financial records. Such systems identify, assemble, analyse, calculate, classify, record, summarize and report transactions and other events.

Internal control is a process designed to provide reasonable assurance regarding the achievement of an entity's objectives in respect of the effectiveness and efficiency of operations, the reliability of financial reporting, and compliance with applicable laws and regulations.

(ii) The following procedures should be used by an auditor to evaluate internal control:

Inquiries of appropriate management, supervisory and other personnel at various organisational levels within the entity, together with reference to documentation, such as procedures manuals, job descriptions and flow charts.

Inspection of documents and records produced by the accounting and internal control systems such as journals or internal control reports.

Observation of the entity's activities and operations, including observation of the organisation of computer operations, management personnel and the nature of transaction processing.

(b) Castillo Aragon – income system weaknesses and recommendations for improvement:

Weakness	Recommendation
There is no basis for establishing the documentation of the number of paying visitors	Prenumbered admission tickets should be issued upon payment of the admission fee
There is no segregation of duties between the person responsible for collecting admission fees and the person responsible for authorising admission	One guide should collect admission fees and issue prenumbered tickets. The other guide should authorise admission upon receipt of the ticket or proof of membership
An independent count of paying visitors is not made	The admission guides should retain a portion of the prenumbered admission ticket (admission ticket stub)
There is no proof of the accuracy of amounts collected by the guides	Admission ticket stubs should be reconciled with cash collected by the accounts assistant each day

Weakness	Recommendation
Cash receipts records are not promptly prepared	The cash receipts should be recorded by the guides daily on a permanent record that will serve as the first record of accountability
Cash receipts are not promptly deposited. Cash is left undeposited for up to a week	Cash should be deposited at least once each day
There is no proof of the accuracy of amounts deposited	Deposit slips should be compared with the daily cash receipts records. Discrepancies should be promptly investigated and resolved

Question 24

Carry out analytical procedures relevant to non-current assets. Procedures that should be undertaken include:

- Review depreciation charge for year for reasonableness.
- Review the list of additions and assess if the additions are in line with the knowledge of business gathered in the planning of the audit, paying particular attention to the $400,000 buildings additions.
- Compare capital expenditure to budget and investigate deviations.
- Compare knowledge of business activities to repairs expensed and investigate unusual fluctuations.
- Compare capital commitments disclosed to auditor's knowledge of business.

Where a non-current asset register is maintained agree the accounts figures for non-current assets to the register.

Trace the opening cost figures and accumulated depreciation figures in the schedule provided by the client to the prior year audited accounts.

Obtain a list of additions and agree this to the asset schedule.

Consider the nature of the additions and identify any items on the list that are revenue items. In particular, confirm the buildings additions all relate to purchase of new property and should not be reclassified as repairs to existing buildings. Similarly, confirm the plant and machinery additions of $20,000 relate to purchase of new plant and machinery, and are not repairs to existing assets.

Agree $12,000 paid for new vehicles to the invoice and cash book and vouch that the invoice is in the company name.

Select a representative sample of the additions and vouch these sample items to purchase invoices. In particular agree:

- The asset is invoiced to the company
- The asset is recorded at the cost price
- The description of the assets on the invoice is in agreement with the books and records of the company

In the case of the buildings additions, agree details to title deeds and correspondence with the company's solicitor.

PRACTICE ANSWER BANK

Investigate disposals of vehicles and plant and machinery, and trace proceeds of sale to books and records. Check entries in disposal account for accuracy. In checking disposal consider what evidence is available that all disposals are recorded. An assets inspection and enquiry from staff are two possible tests that will provide evidence in this regard.

Confirm that the company has good and valid title to the property owned, including the additions during the year.

Determine if the property is pledged as security for bank borrowings and if so disclose in a note to the accounts details of the security held by the financial institution. Written confirmation from the company's solicitor that the company has good and valid title to the property may be the most practical way that the auditor can satisfy himself that the company has good and valid title to the property recorded in the books of the company.

Obtain a schedule to support the depreciation figures in the accounts and agree the schedule to the non-current asset note. Carry out a review of the depreciation calculations to determine the accuracy of the calculations.

Consider if the depreciation rates charged are appropriate and adequate to charge the cost of the asset to income over the life of the assets. In particular, review whether 30% reducing balance is appropriate for the vehicles, looking at how long the company normally uses them, and also whether the 10% straight-line method is appropriate for plant and machinery.

Carry out a physical asset inspection. In undertaking the inspection trace both from records to the physical assets and from the physical assets to the records.

Identify capital commitments identifying which are contracted for but not provided for in the financial statements and which are authorised but not contracted. Check if disclosure of such commitments in the financial statements are adequate.

Question 25

(a) The two principal problems facing the auditor are (i) the impracticability of observing a physical inventory to make test counts of the inventory quantities, and (ii) the auditor's responsibility with regard to the inventory being held for customers.

Since it is impractical to make test counts of the inventory quantities, the auditor must place primary emphasis upon reviewing the inventory for reasonableness and obtaining an understanding of the internal control structure for the book quantities and assessing control risk.

The auditor would determine the latter by a careful review of:

- Internal control structure for shipments
- Method of handling production reports
- Sales invoices and related shipping documents
- Proof of production records and sales
- An actual testing of recorded entries
- The consistency of results between the two independent perpetual records maintained on inventory owned by the company.

If the internal control structure and accounting and control procedures were determined to be deficient, the auditor could not express an unmodified opinion.

The auditor's responsibility with regard to the inventory held for customers pertains to the possibility of customers' accounts being understated by improper sales by the company, and the possibility of the company's inventory being inflated or deflated by improper book transfers to and from the inventory being held for customers.

In dealing with these possibilities, the auditor must again direct attention to the internal control structure for this inventory and the procedures used to account for it. The auditor's responsibility in connection with the customer's inventory would include obtaining direct confirmation from a substantial number of customers and comparing the replies with the balances reflected by the perpetual record maintained on inventory owned by customers.

(b) The specific tests which the auditor should carry out are as follows:

Company inventory

(i) At year-end, obtain a listing of the quantities of items reflected on the perpetual ledger and sight-test items having material quantities, giving special attention to the reasonableness of such quantities in view of the inventory seen.

(ii) Select a representative number of items from the floor and determine that they are being reflected in the inventory.

(iii) Support entries to the perpetual ledger maintained at the plant office with production reports and sales invoices for a sample of entries.

(iv) Prove the production records by comparing output to production expected from purchasing of produce.

(v) Review the accounts for unusual entries.

(vi) Review the perpetual record at the main office for required adjustments to reflect inventory reported by the factory office at year-end.

Customers' inventory

(i) At the year-end, obtain a complete listing of the quantities of items being held for customers as reflected by the perpetual ledger.

(ii) Sight-test items having material quantities, and give attention to the reasonableness of such quantities considering the inventory sighted.

(iii) Request direct confirmation from a substantial number of customers who normally store inventory with the client.

(iv) Compare the replies to these requests with the quantities at (1), and investigate material differences.

(v) Post second confirmations where necessary.

(vi) Make a test comparison of the customers' inventory ledgers to the record of monthly rental charges to determine that customers with inventory shown in storage are being charged in accordance with the terms of their contracts, and conversely, that no charges are recorded to customers for whom the ledgers show no inventory is being held.

(vii) If necessary, request direct confirmation from a representative number of customers of their monthly rental charges and payments in this connection.

(viii) Review the customers' ledgers for customers' accounts not frequently cleared (these are the accounts in which improper transfers are most likely), and reasonably large additions or deductions near the end of the year.

Question 26

Lightning Ltd
Year end 30.11.X2
Prepared by: Stefan Jasinski

Planning note for testing of completeness of trade payables

(a) **Audit approach:**

Systems testing

(i) Update systems notes from last year's file to reflect changes in purchases system and discuss whether there have been any subsequent changes with Tony Lee.

(ii) Document the changes in the system.

(iii) Perform a walkthrough of the system to confirm it operates as documented.

Tests of controls

Perform compliance tests to ensure that the controls operate adequately. In particular, in relation to the changes to the system:

(i) Test that GRNs recorded by the stores in the goods received book have been received by head office.

(ii) Test the file of GRNs to ensure that they are being regularly matched to invoices.

Assess the controls in the system for adequacy in ensuring that all transactions are captured. In particular, in relation to the changes to the system:

(i) Assess the level of segregation of duties which now exists within the accounting department for purchases. One person should not have responsibility for all of the tasks, and it is likely that this will require increased audit testing.

(ii) Assess the possibly unintended consequences of the changes from the previous system.

Substantive testing

(i) Analytical review of the level of trade payables as compared to last year, and review levels month on month. Obtain explanations for any deviations from expected trends

(ii) Analytical review of the level of trade payables by individual store, comparing levels between stores and also levels of previous years

(iii) Review key ratios such as gross margins and average settlement period for trade receivables to ensure figures appear reasonable at the year end and do not appear to be understated

(iv) Reconcile a sample of suppliers' statements to the purchase ledger, following up any reconciling items (the basis for selection of the balances is detailed below)

(v) Circularise a sample of suppliers if supplier statements are unavailable, following up all differences

(vi) Reconcile the purchase ledger to the nominal ledger, ensuring no balances have been omitted

(vii) Cut off testing: purchase transactions on either side of the year end should be tested to ensure that all transactions occurring before the year end are included in the accounts and those that occur after the year end are not

(viii) Review monthly accruals for estimated goods received but not invoiced

(ix) Review post year end invoices to check whether goods were delivered to any of the stores pre-year end, but not accrued

(x) Review the purchase ledger for any large and unusual items and obtain explanations

(b) **Selecting trade payables balances for testing at year end:**

Once we are satisfied from our systems work that the population forming the basis of our selection is complete, we can select a sample of balances for testing. A representative sample should be chosen as follows:

(i) Large balances at the year end (to cover a high proportion of the overall figure)

(ii) Large balances at other times of the year (to catch understatement of these at the year-end)

(iii) Major suppliers (as there is more activity on these accounts, more errors might occur)

(iv) Other smaller suppliers (as they may make up a large proportion of the purchase ledger)

(v) Any unusual balances (such as nil balances for regular suppliers, or debit balances where a credit note may have been processed but not the original invoice)

(vi) Balances which have been static for a certain length of time (perhaps not all transactions have been recorded)

(vii) Suppliers of non-current assets (these are non-standard and may be more prone to error)

(viii) Any balances under dispute (to ensure they are correctly treated)

Question 27

(a) Suggested audit procedures include:

(i) Reviewing the books and records of the company in the post year-end period.

(ii) Reading the company's board minutes

(iii) Obtaining evidence about any litigation from the company's solicitor

(iv) Reading the company's latest interim financial statements (if available)

(v) Obtaining a briefing from management on the affairs of the company, including

(vi) New capital commitments

(vii) Sales or acquisitions of assets

(viii) Changes in capital or debt

(ix) Planned mergers or acquisitions

(x) Validity of going concern qualification

(xi) Obtaining written representations from management that all potential matters arising were disclosed to the auditor.

(b) Both the fire at the warehouse and the proposed merger with Solent are non-adjusting events. They relate to conditions that arose after the year-end date.

IAS 10 *Events After the Reporting Period* states that if non-adjusting events after the end of the reporting period date are material, non-disclosure could influence the economic decisions of users taken on the basis of the financial statements.

In the case of the fire at the warehouse, the total value of the inventory which was destroyed amounted to $35,000. This is below the materiality level set by the auditor. The directors may choose to disclose the event in a note to the accounts, but if they do not do so there is no need for the auditor to qualify the audit report.

On the other hand, the merger with Solent, while it is also a non-adjusting event, is clearly material and should be brought to the attention of the shareholders of Marshall by disclosing it in a note to the accounts. Specifically, the note should give details of the nature of the event and an estimate of its financial effect, or, in this case, a statement that such an estimate cannot be made.

If the directors are not prepared to disclose the information about the merger, the auditor should issue a qualified audit report, on the grounds of material misstatement.

(c) The auditor became aware of the liquidation of Pike Ltd after signing off the audit report but before the issue of the financial statements to the members of the company.

In this time period ISA 560 *Subsequent Events* states that the auditor has no responsibility to perform audit procedures to identify subsequent events but if the auditor becomes aware of a fact that may materially affect the financial statements the auditor should consider whether the financial statements need amendment, discuss the issue with management and take appropriate action.

Marshall's auditor will therefore need to consider the implications for the financial statements of the liquidation of Pike, discuss this matter with Marshall's directors and establish how the directors intend to address the matter in the financial statements.

If Marshall's directors are prepared to amend the financial statements to write off Pike's irrecoverable debt from the figure for accounts receivable the financial statements may require further auditing and a new audit report. The auditor should extend the audit procedures testing subsequent events to the date of the new audit report.

If Marshall's directors will not comply, the auditor should seek legal advice and consider the implications for the audit report. The auditor may also consider speaking at the AGM.

The auditor must take all steps required to avoid reliance by third parties on the auditor's report. The auditor should also consider the need to resign from the audit.

(d) If the matter had taken place on 10 June 20X3 the financial statements would at that point be issued to the members. In that situation ISA 560 *Subsequent Events* states that the auditor has no obligation to make any inquiry regarding such financial statements.

However, it is then stated that if the auditor becomes aware of a relevant fact that would have caused a different audit report if known at the date of issue of the report, then they should discuss the issue with management and take the action appropriate. It is suggested that legal advice may be needed if management refuse to take any action in relation to the matter. The ISA also points to the rights of the auditor to address the AGM and suggest that this could be considered.

As the guidance provided by the ISA is slightly ambiguous the matter will ultimately be a matter of judgment for the auditor having taken advice.

Question 28

(a) The following is a proposed programme of work in respect of an examination of the appropriateness of management's use of the going concern basis of accounting in the preparation of the financial statements of Safari Ltd:

- Obtain copies of budgets and forecasts for the next 12 months and in particular the cash flow projections.
- Consider the adequacy of the evidence these documents provide in relation to the company's ability to continue as a going concern.
- Examine the management accounts prepared for the post year end period and consider the evidence provided by these accounts in relation to the future viability of the company.
- Meet with senior management to discuss the current trading prospects of the company.
- Consider the company's ability to raise additional bank finance. In particular consider what assets are available to provide as security for bank borrowings and the company's ability to demonstrate its capacity to repay new borrowings.
- Examine in detail the changes made by Safari Ltd in its cost structure in 20X8 and consider the adequacy of these changes in addressing the company's financial difficulties.
- Consider the external economic environment in which Safari Ltd operates. In particular, consider the strength of the Kenyan tourism industry and the projections for that industry in 20Y0.

The above information will allow the auditor to reach a conclusion on whether or not it is appropriate for management to prepare the financial statements for the year ended 31 December 20X9 on a going concern basis.

(b) (i) In order to decide on the impact on the auditor's report of a situation where adequate disclosure is made in notes to the financial statements of uncertainty relating to the ability of the company to continue to trade in the future, the auditor will first have to establish if there is one significant uncertainty or multiple uncertainties. On the basis that there is one uncertainty, then the auditor will have to consider does the disclosure in relation to this uncertainty given in the financial statements provide a true and fair view.

If the disclosures do provide a true and fair view, then an unmodified audit opinion will be given but consideration should be given to including a 'Material uncertainty related to going concern' section in the auditor's report. The inclusion of such a section would not constitute a modification of the opinion, but would draw the reader's attention to the going concern note in the financial statements.

(ii) If inadequate disclosure is made in notes to the financial statements of the uncertainty in relation to the company's ability to continue to trade in the future, then the auditor will have to give a modified opinion due to disagreement over inadequate disclosure. The opinion would be an 'except for' qualified opinion on the financial statements.

If the effect of the inadequate disclosure is so material and pervasive to the financial statements that the auditor concludes that an 'except for' qualification of the report is not adequate to disclose the misleading or incomplete nature of the financial statements, then an adverse opinion will be given instead.

PRACTICE ANSWER BANK

Question 29

Looking first at the lawsuit issue, in gathering her evidence Sally would have confirmed the uncertainty of the outcome of the lawsuit with Comelybank's independent legal counsel. With Comelybank's consent Sally might want to get an opinion of another independent legal counsel such as her own. If legal counsel cannot give an opinion on the outcome of the lawsuit, it would be unreasonable to assume Sally will have the expertise necessary to make this decision. But she should have the expertise to evaluate the effect on the financial statements if the lawsuit is lost. In this evaluation she should consider the impact of other ramifications such as existing commitments and union contracts at that plant.

The auditor's evaluation of the aggregate effect of an adverse decision will determine the type of report she will issue. If she concludes that the consequences of losing the lawsuit are of such a widespread nature as to have a pervasive impact on the financial statements and that the company cannot continue as a going concern, she will most likely issue a disclaimer of opinion because she does not have the expertise to evaluate the outcome of the case.

In reaching her decision, Sally must consider the validity of the statements made by management – namely, that the purchase of the required equipment is not economically feasible, that the plant would have to be closed, that the plant and its production equipment would have only minimal resale value, and that the production could not be recovered at other plants.

In this respect, Sally should consider any past experience of Comelybank or other similar companies. For example, if Comelybank had been required to install pollution control equipment in other plants and had done so economically, Sally may consider Comelybank's statement on the current situation as overreacting. If this were the case, Sally may need to re-evaluate the relative magnitude of the monetary impact of closing the plant in relation to an independent evaluation of the economic feasibility of installing the pollution-control equipment.

Sally must also consider how long it will take before there is an impact on the financial statements. There may be evidence that the case will be litigated for a number of years; or, if the case is lost, that the court may allow Comelybank an extended period of time to install the pollution control equipment. Under these circumstances Sally may consider the possible outcome to have little effect on decisions applicable to the current financial statements and would also give the company time to increase its ability to absorb the impact of an adverse decision. Thus, this exception may not be relevant to the current year's report.

In the second situation, Sally must again consider the relative magnitude of the monetary effect in relation to other items in the financial statements. Since the franchise amounts to 20% of Comelybank's assets, Sally should be most concerned over the probability and timing of Comelybank's recovering the franchise cost from future sales.

Her measure of this would most likely be based on two other considerations. First would be the past experience, if any, of Comelybank in similar ventures. If Comelybank has a good record of past performance in developing similar products, Sally may be satisfied that the probability of the recovery is high.

Second, Sally should consider if she, as an auditor, has the expertise to determine the probability of the recovery of the franchise cost. This consideration is necessary for Sally to determine if she can accept the responsibility for the evaluation of the item relative to fair presentation in the financial statements.

In reaching a decision, Sally must evaluate the underlying documentation and especially the thoroughness and objectivity with which Comelybank's management investigated the franchise and possibility of success before entering into the agreement. Sally should have studied minutes and notes of the negotiations leading to the purchase and financial projections of the overall effect on Comelybank's operations of adding the franchise.

In addition, while gathering evidence for reaching this decision, Sally might want to obtain, with Comelybank's consent, an independent expert's opinion on the marketing prospects of the newly patented product.

Sally should also consider the nature of the item – whether it relates to a specific matter or a general condition. Is the exception only a matter of realisation of a specific asset or is there a question of whether Comelybank can continue as a going concern if it cannot recover the cost of the franchise? In the latter case, the exception could permeate the financial statements and make a reader's appraisal of them virtually impossible.

Question 30

(1) Financial statements may properly be prepared as of any day of any month. In this situation Abacus may be able to carry out all required audit procedures, and therefore, an unmodified opinion could be issued for the 31 January 20X4 financial statements.

The audit must meet generally accepted auditing standards. For example, Abacus must be satisfied regarding the physical inventory, assuming it is material. To prevent the financial statements from being misleading, the heavy operating losses incurred by Hing Sing Ltd during the post balance-sheet period should be disclosed.

(2) The circumstances to be considered here are whether or not Abacus has the resources and the availability of these resources to carry out Hing Sing Ltd's audit at such short notice, and within such a short time-frame. Unless the audit firm is able to do so, it should decline Mr Lee's request.

A major consideration is the materiality of the receivables and inventory. If the amount of these assets is immaterial, the omission of International Auditing Standards procedures need not be mentioned.

If the amount is material and the auditor cannot obtain sufficient evidential matter then Abacus should issue an audit report containing a disclaimer of opinion. A qualified opinion may be rendered if the amount is not sufficiently large to preclude an expression of opinion on the statements as a whole but is large enough to deserve mention. Note that the qualified opinion is based on the degree of materiality.

(3) The auditor need make no mention of the adequacy or inadequacy of insurance in the standard audit report. The function of that report is to state whether the financial statements constitute a fair presentation in accordance with generally accepted accounting principles. International Accounting Standards do not require disclosure of remote contingencies. The insuring of assets is a matter of managerial choice and has nothing to do with accounting principles. It is not practicable or desirable to enumerate all the possible losses inherent in an uncertain future. Losses from flood or from acts of war are also contingencies faced by business concerns, but specific disclosure is not required.

Although disclosure of inadequate insurance coverage is not required in the audit report, the auditor may deem it advisable to bring the matter to the client's attention, but such a communication has nothing to do with the expression of an opinion on the financial statements.

(4) The change in the accounting method Hing Sing Ltd uses to depreciate non-current assets from straight-line to reducing balance is not a change in accounting policy but rather a change in estimation technique. As such it will not require the auditor to give anything other than a standard audit opinion, as the effect on this year's financial statements will be immaterial, and the relevant details will be fully disclosed in the footnotes to the financial statements. Were this to have a material effect then it could be referred to in an emphasis of matter paragraph.

In the financial statements for the next financial year, when the change in Hing Sing's accounting method will be material, the auditor will seek to ensure that he agrees with the treatment and disclosure in the accounts and an 'emphasis of matter' paragraph may be required.

(5) The company has chosen not to comply with international accounting standards in its treatment of self-constructed non-current assets. As the effect of this departure from generally accepted accounting principles is significant, the financial statements do not present fairly the financial position, the results of the operations and the cash flows of the company.

Abacus must decide whether the matter is simply material, in which case the audit report should be modified using an 'except for' audit opinion, or material and pervasive, in which case the auditor should issue an adverse opinion due to material misstatement.

Question 31

Middleton Ltd

In the situation outlined, the departure from accounting standards has caused the financial statements to contain a material misstatement and therefore either an adverse opinion or a qualified opinion is warranted.

At 44% of profit for the year the effect of the departure from accounting standards is material to the financial statements. The matter is unlikely to be pervasive given that this is one balance and the financial statements do not appear to be misleading. A qualified opinion is the appropriate opinion. A suggested modification is as follows:

Qualified opinion on financial statements

In our opinion, **except for** the effects of the matter described in the Basis for Qualified Opinion section of our report, the accompanying financial statements present fairly, in all material respects, (or give a true and fair view of) the financial position of the Company as at 31 August 20X3 and (of) its financial performance and its cash flows for the year then ended in accordance with International Financial Reporting Standards (IFRSs).

Basis for qualified opinion on financial statements

As more fully explained in Note X to the financial statements, the company has failed to reduce certain items of inventory to their net realisable amount in order to comply with the requirements of IAS 2. This has resulted in an overvaluation of inventory of $350,000 as at 31 August 20X3. If the inventory had been reduced to its net realisable amount, the effect would have been to reduce the carrying amount of inventory by $350,000, and reduce the profits for the year and retained profit by $350,000.

Windsor Ltd

In this situation, the financial statements are affected by significant uncertainties. As there is only one uncertainty and the financial statements, including disclosure notes about the uncertainty give a true and fair view, the appropriate audit report would be an unmodified audit report including an emphasis of matter paragraph. Suggested wording:

Emphasis of matter – possible outcome of lawsuit

In forming our opinion, which is not modified, we have considered the adequacy of the disclosure in Note X to the financial statements concerning the possible outcome of a lawsuit, alleging infringements of certain patent rights and claiming royalties and punitive damages where the company is the defendant. The ultimate outcome of the matter cannot presently be determined and no provision for any liability that may result has been made in the financial statements.

Holyrood Ltd

In this situation the auditor has not attended the inventory count and on the basis that they were not able to perform alternative audit procedures to gather sufficient and appropriate evidence in relation to the existence of inventory as at 30 September 20X3, the auditor should qualify the audit opinion based on an inability to obtain sufficient appropriate audit evidence:

Qualified opinion on financial statements

In our opinion, except for the possible effects of the matter described in the Basis for Qualified Opinion paragraph the financial statements show a true and fair view……

Basis for qualified opinion on financial statements

With respect to inventories having a carrying amount of $x the evidence available to us was limited because we did not observe the counting of the physical inventories as of 30 September 20X3, since that date was prior to our appointment as auditors of the company.

Owing to the nature of the company's records we were unable to obtain sufficient appropriate audit evidence regarding the inventory quantities by using other audit procedures.

Essex Ltd

In this situation, there is a significant level of concern about Essex Ltd's ability to continue as a going concern because the company is dependent on the continued provision of a financing facility by the principal shareholder.

As there is only one significant uncertainty and this uncertainty has been fully disclosed in the financial statements to allow the financial statements to show a true and fair view, an unmodified opinion can be given but consideration should be given to adding a material uncertainty relating to going concern paragraph to the report.

Material uncertainty relating to going concern

In forming our opinion, which is not modified, we have considered the adequacy of the disclosure made in Note X to the financial statements concerning the company's ability to continue as a going concern. The company is financed through the provision of a finance facility of $800,000 by Charles Cornwall, the principal shareholder of the company and a director of the company. Mr Cornwall has confirmed in writing that it is his intention to continue to support the company in the future by the provision of this facility and additional facilities if required. On this basis, the directors have prepared the financial statements on a going concern basis. This condition indicates the existence of a material uncertainty which may cast significant doubt about the company's ability to continue as a going concern. The financial statements do not include the adjustments that would result if the company was unable to continue as a going concern because of the withdrawal of this financial support.

Exam question bank

Question 1 [Hamilton and Harvey] [November 2021]

Hamilton & Harvey, a firm of Chartered Accountants, has been invited by two potential clients to consider accepting appointment as the company's auditor. The potential clients' details are as follows:

Company X: This is a medium sized public company which has grown rapidly in recent years. The Managing Director is worried that the company has outgrown its system of internal control; in each of the last two years the auditor has commented on significant weaknesses in the company's internal accounting systems. Hamilton & Harvey has another client in the same industry as Company X.

Company Y: This is not a public company and in the previous three years its income and assets were such that it was exempt from the requirement to appoint an auditor. Prior years' financial statements reveal that in each of the past two years the company made pre-tax losses, but they give little other information as they provide minimal disclosures. The major shareholder is considering a public share issue but he plans to retain a controlling shareholding.

Required

(a) Determine the factors an auditor should consider before accepting an audit engagement.

(10 marks)

(b) Prepare a brief report for Hamilton & Harvey advising whether they should accept Company X and/or Company Y, or neither, as an audit client. In your report, clearly identify and explain factors you considered in reaching your decision. **(10 marks)**

(Total 20 marks)

Question 2 [Internal Control] [November 2021]

An effective system of internal control (ISA 260 (Revised), 315 (Revised)) is essential for a company to operate successfully, assist with risk management, comply with reporting requirements, and allow for an efficient and effective external audit. However, all systems of internal control have inherent weaknesses which may interfere with and affect the application, quality and effectiveness of internal controls.

Required

Analyse the above statement focusing on:

(a) The components which constitute a system of internal control. **(5 marks)**

(b) The importance of effective controls for:

    (i)   The company, and
    (ii)   The external auditor.

(5 marks)

(c) The inherent weaknesses in any system of internal control. **(5 marks)**

(Total 15 marks)

Question 3 [Analytical Procedures] [November 2021]

Analyse the meaning, use and importance of analytical procedures (ISA 520) in a financial statement audit.

Required

(a) Determine what is meant by the term 'analytical procedures.' **(3 marks)**

(b) Answer the following:

(i) Determine the three stages in the audit process in which analytical procedures are used;

(ii) Demonstrate the purpose of using analytical procedures in each of these stages; and

(iii) Provide specific examples of the analytical procedures that might be used in each of the three stages of the audit where analytical procedures are used. **(8 marks)**

(c) Analyse the importance of analytical procedures in the audit process. **(4 marks)**

(Total 15 marks)

Question 4 [The Gym plc] [November 2021]

You are the engagement partner for the audit of The Gym plc. The company's financial year ended on 31 March 2021 and it is now 30 May 2021.

The Gym's draft financial statements show a net profit for the year of £94m and net assets of £378m. For the year ended 31 March 2020, net profit amounted to £176m and net assets totalled £274m. On 1 July 2020, The Gym purchased a new spa and fitness centre in the Cayman Islands. The purchase contract included an agreement to refurbish the spa and fitness centre to The Gym's specifications. The total contract was agreed at a price of £88 million. It was also agreed that the work would be completed by 31 December 2020. The Gym financed its purchase of this spa and fitness centre by issuing new shares.

The Managing Director of The Gym is anxious for the audit to be completed by mid-July 2021 as he is planning to launch another share issue in August 2021, in order to raise further equity finance for the purchase and refurbishment of another spa and fitness centre in Fiji.

Unlike previous years, this year's audit has been difficult. In October 2020, The Gym appointed a new Finance Director who you (as the audit engagement partner) have found to be aggressive and uncooperative. He has made the changes to the financial statements that you requested but did so reluctantly and with bad grace. Three issues remain unresolved. These are as follows:

(a) One of The Gym's complexes (Manilla Spa Ltd), 100 per cent of which is owned by The Gym, is in the Philippines. Manilla Spa Ltd's financial year ended on 30 September 2020 and its financial statements have been audited by a local Filipino auditing firm. You have received the audited financial statements, together with an unmodified (i.e. 'clean') audit report, but you have recently discovered that the auditing firm in question is facing court action as a result of alleged negligence in its audit of a large listed company in the Philippines. Over the past six weeks, you have repeatedly requested the audit firm to send you copies of their working papers for the audit of Manilla Spa Ltd. However, they have not returned your telephone calls or acknowledged your emails or letters – nor have they provided the requested working papers. In the 2021 financial year, Manilla Spa Ltd contributed £14m to The Gym's draft net profit of £94m and accounted for £58m of its £378m of net assets.

(b) The officers and employees of a major global IT company (Big Tech Ltd) routinely use the spa and fitness facilities of The Gym around the world. In the past, Big Tech has settled its account promptly when invoiced for use of The Gym's facilities. However, in recent months the company has not paid its account and, according to The Gym's records, on 31 March 2021, the company owed The Gym £1.2 million. Big Tech has acknowledged that it owes this amount but has indicated that it is currently experiencing cash flow difficulties. It has promised that it will settle the account once it has negotiated some bridging finance.

(c) Because of a hold-up in the supply of some of the fittings and furnishings required for The Gym's new spa and fitness centre in the Cayman Islands, instead of the facilities being ready for occupancy by 1 January 2021, the refurbishment will not be completed until 30 June 2021. The contract did not include a penalty clause for late completion of the contract. As the contract was

nearing completion on 31 March 2021, the new spa and fitness centre has been included in The Gym's financial statements at its total contract price of £88 million.

Required

(i) For each of the three issues (a-c) above, demonstrate the action you, as the audit engagement partner, would take. **(13 marks)**

(ii) Treating each issue (a-c) as if it is the only issue you have to resolve, and assuming that the directors of The Gym agree with its Finance Director that no change is to be made to the company's financial statements in respect of the item concerned, analyse what impact the issues would have on the opinion you express in your audit report. **(12 marks)**

(Total 25 marks)

Question 5 [Dreamland Ltd] [November 2021]

You are an audit senior who has been given responsibility for the audit of the current assets of Dreamland Ltd – a manufacturer and retailer of beds.

Under the heading 'Current Assets', the draft financial statements for the year ended 31 March 2021 show the following:

	£ million
Accounts Receivable	75.2
Inventory	70.1
Cash	6.4
	151.7

The trial balance shows the following entries:

	£ million
Raw materials	10.2
Manufacturing Work in Progress	24.6
Finished Goods Inventory	35.3
Accounts Receivable	78.2
Provision for Doubtful debts	3.0
Bad Debts	1.5

Your earlier work, carried out as part of an interim audit, has given you reasonable assurance that the controls over the sales-receivables-receipts accounting sub-system are working effectively. However, discussions with Dreamland personnel have brought the following matters to your attention:

(1) A major customer (Hotels Galore), owes Dreamland Ltd £5.2 million (because of purchasing beds when refurbishing its chain of hotels in December 2020), went into liquidation on 1 April 2021. It does not appear as if any of the £5.2 million owed by Hotels Galore will be recovered by Dreamland Ltd. Enquiry of the Finance Director has revealed that, as Hotels Galore did not go into liquidation until after the end of the financial year, no adjustment has been made to the Provision for Doubtful Debts.

(2) The Manufacturing Work in Progress includes £300,000 of administrative salaries which were erroneously recorded in Manufacturing Overhead.

(3) The Raw Materials were counted by Dreamland staff members who were assigned individually to different components of the raw materials. Each staff member counted their part of the inventory without assistance from any other staff member.

(4) Beds with a cost price of £300,000 and retail price of £400,000 were sold on credit on 31 March 2021 but were not delivered to the customers concerned until 2 April 2021. These beds were recorded as inventory at year end.

(5) Timber, springs and material required for manufacturing beds, valued at £865,000, were purchased from an overseas supplier on 30 March 2021. Under the terms of the contract, ownership passed to Dreamland as soon as they were despatched. They left the supplier's premises on 31 March 2021 and arrived at Dreamland on 30 April 2021.

(6) The Finance Director considers that, as Dreamland Ltd knows its customers well, it should select the customers whose account balances are to be confirmed and should also prepare and mail the confirmation requests. He further believes that, in order to minimise the inconvenience caused to customers whose account balances are to be confirmed, they should be asked to respond only if they believe that the amount stated in the confirmation request is incorrect.

Required

(a) Determine the action you would take in relation to each of the matters identified above. **(6 marks)**

(b) Advise on the audit tests you would perform in order to ascertain whether or not the amounts shown in the draft financial statements for the following accounts are fairly stated:

   (i) Accounts Receivable
   (ii) Inventory
   (iii) Cash

   Note. For accounts receivable and inventory, consider how you would verify the existence, value and ownership of the accounts receivable or inventory, as applicable.

(19 marks)

(Total 25 marks)

Question 6 [1] [May 2022]

(a) You are a partner with a smaller but reputable audit firm. Your firm has been asked to consider performing the audit for a mid-sized retailer of electronic consumer products who operates a number of branches across the country and wishes to significantly expand its network in the near future.

Required

Review the above scenario and:

   (i) Determine the key factors that your firm needs to consider in deciding whether to accept this appointment.

   (ii) Demonstrate the importance of these factors to an audit and the audit opinion. **(9 marks)**

(b) Assume that, after it reviewed the factors under 1 a), your firm agrees to act as the external auditor for this retailer. Your firm will start by performing the company's audit of the 2022 financial statement. As the firm begins the audit, it needs to perform a number of initial audit steps, including the following:

   (i) Gain a thorough understanding of the client's business.
   (ii) Evaluate the risk of material misstatements in the company's financial statements.
   (iii) Determine materiality limits appropriate to an audit of the company's financial statements.

Required

For each of the audit steps described in 1 (b) above, describe the importance of the step to the audit and demonstrate how each step is actually performed. **(11 marks)**

(Total 20 marks)

Question 7 [2] [May 2022]

"Auditor independence refers to the independence of the external auditor tasked with performing an entity's audit, and requires, among others, integrity, objectivity and the absence of conflicts of interests which could interfere with the performance of the auditor's duties." (Examiner quote)

Required

Analyse the statement set out above. Your answer should include, but is not limited to, a definition of independence in the context of external audit, a demonstration of the crucial importance of auditor independence to audit quality, and determining various threats to auditors' independence and how these might arise. Where appropriate, provide specific examples which can demonstrate a breach of auditors' independence. **(Total 15 marks)**

Question 8 [3] [May 2022]

"The auditor's report on the financial statements to shareholders is too technical, frequently limited by being binary in its expression of an opinion on key matters, and fails to reflect properly on much of the information present in an entity's annual report." (Examiner quote)

Required

Analyse the statement set out above. Your answer should include your interpretation of the nature and value of the auditor's communication with shareholders, and an elaboration on how the audit report might be further improved to make auditors' communication to shareholders more informative and valuable to these users of the financial statements. **(Total 15 marks)**

Question 9 [4] [May 2022]

Cablecard is a large listed fintech (financial technology) company. The company has grown very rapidly over the past ten years, has global operations, and frequently introduces new products and services. BigAudit, a large audit firm, has conducted the audit for the past ten years, and in each of these years has issued an unqualified audit opinion. The audit partner in charge regularly meets with executive management and the audit committee of the entity.

Recently, there have been a number of reports in a leading business newspaper which raised concerns about the reliance of Cablecard on a small number of overseas partner organisations for the generation of nearly 100 percent of the company's profits, opaque business practices, and allegations of fraud within the company.

Upon a number of such reports, BigAudit conducted an investigation into Cablecard's operations, with particular focus on the internal processes at the heart of the relationship with the overseas partner organisations responsible for the generation of most of Cablecard's profits. This internal audit provided a clean bill of health and BigAudit proceeds with the audit without further investigation or any concerns about its client.

However, a subsequent separate draft forensic audit conducted by a different large audit firm commissioned by Cablecard's board of directors, was unable to confirm the existence of the overseas operations, on which most of Cablecard's reported profits are based.

Very shortly afterwards, Cablecard enters insolvency and members of the executive management are under investigation for fraud.

Required

(a) In light of the case above:

    (i) Determine auditor's responsibilities relating to fraud in an audit of financial statements as per ISA 240. **(5 marks)**

    (ii) Advise on tests auditors could perform to establish whether there are any misstatements in the financial statements due to fraud. **(5 marks)**

(b) In light of the BigAudit's internal investigation which provided a clean bill of health, despite reports that indicate otherwise, demonstrate the action(s) you might have taken if you were the audit partner in charge of the audit of this company. **(5 marks)**

(c) Reflect on the assertion that "auditors have no responsibilities for detecting fraud, as primary responsibility for detecting fraud lies with the directors and management of the entity". Carefully support your answer with reference to ISAs you deem relevant in the circumstances. **(10 marks)**

(Total 25 marks)

Question 10 [5] [May 2022]

(a) In a number of different audit clients, you encountered the eight possible internal control deficiencies listed below.

    (1) All manufacturing staff have access to raw materials which are kept in a designated area of the client's premises.

    (2) Storeroom staff record goods received on sequentially numbered receiving reports. The receiving reports are used to update the inventory records and then filed in number order in a filing cabinet in the storeroom office. No further action is taken in respect of the receiving reports.

    (3) A large medical practice deposits all cash received once a week.

    (4) The mail is opened by a single employee who records any cash receipts.

    (5) The employee who opens the mail (see point 4.) takes any cash receipts to the bank and then updates the cash receipts journal. This employee is also responsible for completing the bank reconciliation at the end of each week.

    (6) The board of directors of a multi-national company delegates authorisation of capital budgeting expenditures of less than £50,000 to the manager of the manufacturing division.

    (7) The client's cheque books are kept in an unlocked drawer in the chief accountant's office.

    (8) The sales staff check the current price list before completing a sales invoice.

Required

For each of the eight possible control deficiencies listed above (1-8):

    (i) Determine whether it is, or is not, a deficiency, giving reasons to support your conclusion. **(8 marks)**

    (ii) For each deficiency you identified in (i) above, demonstrate how the deficiency may be overcome (i.e. may be rectified). **(8 marks)**

(b) Outline the meaning of the 'going concern' concept, and analyse its relevance to the financial statement auditor. Elaborate on the audit stages where the propriety of the directors adopting the going concern basis for preparing the company's financial statements might be reviewed.

(9 marks)

(Total 25 marks)

Question 11 [Audit of current assets] [November 2022]

Goodnight Ltd makes and sells mattresses, and you are the audit senior responsible for the audit of the company's current assets. The following current assets are shown in the draft financial statements for the year ended 31 March 2022:

	£ million
Accounts receivable	80.5
Inventory	75.3
Cash	9.3
	165.1

The trial balance shows the following entries:

	£ million
Finished goods inventory	40.2
Manufacturing work in progress	30.1
Raw materials	11.3
Accounts receivable	85.4
Provisions for doubtful debts	4.1
Bad debts	2.1

You gained reasonable assurance during an interim audit that the controls over the revenue cycle are working effectively, however, subsequent discussions with Goodnight Ltd's management have brought the following matters to your attention:

(a) BigHotel, a major customer who owes Goodnight Ltd £6.5 million after purchasing mattresses in December 2021, went into liquidation as of 1 April 2022, and it is highly unlikely that any of the £6.5 million will be recovered by Goodnight Ltd. No adjustments have been made by Goodnight Ltd to its provisions for doubtful debts, which the Finance Director explains is due to the fact that BigHotel went into liquidation after the end of the financial year.

(b) On 31 March 2022, mattresses with a cost price of £0.4 million and retail price of £0.5 million were sold on credit, but could not be delivered to the customers concerned (excluding BigHotel) until 2 April 2022.

(c) During the inventory count, individual Goodnight Ltd staff were assigned to total particular raw material lines. Each member of staff did this on their own, without assistance or oversight from any other staff member.

(d) The Finance Director suggests that, as Goodnight Ltd knows its customers extremely well and has built long term relationships with most of them, the company is best placed to select the customers whose account balances are to be confirmed and that Goodnight Ltd should draft and mail the confirmation requests directly, rather than asking the auditor to do this. She further believes that customers should be asked to respond only if they find a discrepancy between their records and the information provided in the confirmation request.

(e) Materials used in the manufacturing of the mattresses, valued at £1 million, were purchased from an overseas supplier on 30 March 2022. Under the terms of the contract, ownership of these materials passed to Goodnight Ltd as soon as they were despatched by the supplier. They left the supplier's premises on 31 March 2022 and arrived at Goodnight Ltd on 30 April 2022.

Required

Determine the actions you would take as audit senior with regard to each of the matters identified above (a-e). **(4 marks each (a-e))**

(Total 20 marks)

Question 12 [Auditor's communication with users of financial statements] [November 2022]

The external auditor's report is the final step in the audit process and typically the auditor's only communication with the company's shareholders and other external parties interested in the reporting entity.

Required

Advise on the opinion the auditor should express in the auditor's report in each of the following circumstances:

(a) The financial statements give a true and fair view of the company's financial position and performance and also comply with the applicable financial reporting framework and relevant legislation.

(b) The financial statements give a true and fair view of the company's financial position and performance and also comply with the applicable financial reporting framework and relevant legislation. However, a very significant contingent liability (which has arisen as a result of selling faulty, and potentially dangerous, products) seems likely and, if it does, puts in question the company's likelihood to survive financially. This is properly reported in a note in the financial statements.

(c) The auditor and the company's directors disagree about the value of the inventory. The company has valued a significant proportion of the inventory at cost, when in the auditor's opinion is should have been valued at net realisable value. The amount involved is substantial (it would result in a reduction in net profit of 20% and total assets of 15%), but the directors refuse to alter the financial statements.

(d) Two months into the financial year, some of the company's records were lost due to a fire at one of its fifteen warehouses. All of the warehouses are of approximately equal size in terms of volume of business, assets and financial results. The auditors have audited everything else and, apart from the matters they are unable to confirm (as a result of the lost records due to the warehouse fire) consider that the financial statements do not contain any material misstatements.

(e) The auditor has reviewed the 'other information' in the company's annual reports which contains the audited financial statements. They have found some information in the unaudited 'other information' which is inconsistent with the information in the audited financial statements. They have not found any material misstatements in the financial statements.

(3 marks each (a-e))

(Total 15 marks)

Question 13 [Audit evidence and sampling as an audit technique] [November 2022]

"In conducting an audit of financial statements, the overall objectives of the auditor include: To obtain reasonable assurance about whether the financial statements as a whole are free from material misstatement, whether due to fraud or error, thereby enabling the auditor to express an opinion on whether the financial statements are prepared, in all material respects, in accordance with an applicable financial reporting framework. Reasonable assurance … is obtained when the auditor has obtained sufficient appropriate audit evidence to reduce audit risk (that is, the risk that the auditor expresses an inappropriate opinion when the financial statements are materially misstated) to an acceptably low level" (ISA 200, *Overall Objectives of the Independent Auditor and the Conduct of an Audit in Accordance with International Standards on Auditing* paras 5 and 11 emphasis added).

Meanwhile, ISA 530 Audit Sampling: "…applies when the auditor has decided to use audit sampling in performing audit procedures." (ISA 530), para 1).

Required

(a) Determine the meaning of 'sufficient appropriate audit evidence'. In your answer you should explain the meaning of the terms: 'audit evidence', 'sufficient' and 'appropriate'. You should also determine how the concepts of sufficiency and appropriateness are related. **(6 marks)**

(b) Determine the meaning of 'sampling' in the context of a financial statement audit, and why sampling is essential in a modern financial statement audit. **(4 marks)**

(c) Demonstrate the difference between judgemental (selecting specific items) and statistical audit sampling, and determine the circumstances in which the auditor might decide it is more appropriate to use judgemental sampling and statistical sampling (explain using examples the circumstances for either approach). **(5 marks)**

(Total 15 marks)

Question 14 [Internal Controls] [November 2022]

Fab Fashions Ltd retails clothing and accessories and has had a period of rapid expansion. The company operates worldwide from its Head Quarters (HQ) in Europe, targeting 15 to 25 year olds, at the lower range of prices. The company's year-end is 30 September 2022. In the past, the company ordered the majority of its goods twice a year, which at times resulted in significant inventory write-downs if fashion trends were misjudged. In response, the company recently introduced an ordering system where smaller quantities are ordered at a time, but it does so 12 times a year. Fab Fashions Ltd uses internal audit, which currently is limited to performing inventory counts at stores.

A purchasing manager decides on initial store inventory levels for each country, with quantities directly being communicated to the central buying department at HQ, without feedback from stores. An ordering assistant combines country orders by continent, and passes these to a purchasing director for authorisation. As goods are sold, store managers are responsible for reordering through the purchasing manager. Store managers are prompted weekly to review inventory levels. The lead time for goods to be delivered to stores regularly exceeds one month. Individual store managers are not authorised to order goods in high demand from another store, even if other stores have excess supply, and customers are asked to check with other stores themselves.

Goods are distributed directly from suppliers to individual stores. Store assistants produce a goods received note (GRN) once they have verified the order quantity against a suppliers delivery note (SDN). GRNs are then sent to HQ to be matched manually against purchase invoices. Manually matching GRNs from individual stores can be a very time-consuming process given the large number of stores to which a supplier may distribute their goods. Once each individual invoice has been agreed, this is forwarded to the Purchasing Director for authorisation, and the relevant data is then entered onto the purchase ledger.

Required

(a) Analyse what issues the auditor should consider when determining whether a deficiency in internal controls is significant. If you were a more junior member of the auditing team, which colleagues would you seek advice from in relation to this, and what advice would you seek? **(10 marks)**

EXAM QUESTION BANK

(b) As the audit partner responsible for the external audit of Fab Fashions Ltd, draft a memorandum with a separate covering note to the company's management in relation to the purchasing system which:

(i) Demonstrates THREE deficiencies in that system
(ii) Analyses possible implication of each deficiency
(iii) Provides a recommendation to address each deficiency

(15 marks)

(Total 25 marks)

Question 15 [Planning] [November 2022]

You are an Audit Manager at Really Big Auditors (RBA), a registered audit firm with 300 offices around the world. RBA provides assurance, advisory and tax services and aims to adhere to the highest ethical standards. You have recently been assigned to assess whether or not to accept the audit of Squeaky Clean Plc ("SC Plc"), a company specialising in the treatment of hazardous waste. SC Plc has a year-end of 31 December 2021. The following working paper is pending review.

Working Paper:	A-100		
Client:	SC Plc	Year-end:	31 December 2021
Prepared By:	A Trainee	Date:	12 November 2021
Reviewed By:	A Manager	Date:	13 November 2021

Purpose of the working paper

Background information relevant to pre-engagement activities as part of determining whether or not to accept the client.

Information

Nature of business

SC Plc is in the waste disposal business, specializing in industrial waste, medical waste, radioactive waste, and other waste products. It has long-term contracts with various local and national governments, mines, refineries, two nuclear power plants and various hospital groups in the Peoples Republic of Freedonia (PR Freedonia) and other parts of the world.

Tom Bull (CEO) and his wife Jessica Bull (CFO) founded the company 40 years ago. The company was listed on the Freedonia Stock Exchange (FSE) 10 years after it was founded. Only 30% of the shares are publicly traded. 70% of the shares are held in a family trust. The company's operations are split as follows:

Subsidiary	Waste Type	Operational activity	Countries	Number of operational locations
Squeaky Clean Nuclear Waste	Nuclear	Waste storage	PR Fredonia, Country B	2
Squeaky Clean Medical Waste	Medical	Waste treatment	PR Freedonia	18
Squeaky Clean Governmental Waste	Municipal	Waste removal	PR Freedonia	252
Squeaky Clean Refinery Waste	Refinery run-off	Waste treatment	PR Freedonia	4
Squeaky Clean Mining Waste	Mining	Waste removal and treatment	PR Freedonia, Country C, D, E	55
Number of waste removal and treatment locations				**331**

Board of directors

The CEO is known to dislike any critique of his management style and decisions, and he was recently quoted in the news justifying the use of armed security guards to protect the firm's assets against peaceful protesters.

The CFO of the company, Jessica Bull, a Chartered Accountant, is currently under investigation for fraud and corruption. It is alleged that bribes were paid to foreign officials during the aggressive expansion campaign, to obtain the licenses needed for the construction of a new mine waste treatment plant in Country B. The CFO has not been suspended while a criminal investigation is on-going.

Financial position

More recently, the company started an aggressive expansion campaign in various overseas countries. Because of this rapid expansion, the company is at present experiencing liquidity problems and is heavily leveraged. The company recently applied for a loan from a major bank to finance its day-to-day activities, but the loan application was rejected, with reference to the company's risk profile.

Previous auditor

Until 31 October 2021, Another Big Auditor (ABA) was the previous auditor. According to Tom Bull, the previous auditors were fired because they reported the CFO's activities to the Freedonia Regulatory Board for Practicing Auditors. The decision was ratified by a Board resolution on 31 October 2021. Tom Bull gave the new audit team verbal permission to contact Sheila Old who had been the engagement leader responsible for SC Plc's audit for the previous 15 years.

During a conversation with the previous auditor, it was determined that Sheila Old had uncovered a series of related party transactions that she believes had been designed to conceal fraud perpetrated by Tom Bull. Sheila Old further noted that an outstanding audit fee had only been paid after she explained to Tom Bull that unless the outstanding fee is paid, she would send letters to SC Plc's bankers and creditors informing them of the related party transactions and warning them to exercise care in dealing with SC Plc.

Audit deadline

The deadline for the audit upon acceptance of the assurance engagement is 31 January 2022.

Proposed Fee

The proposed fee is £100,000 for the entire audit engagement, including all the subsidiaries. Tom Bull indicated that the fee was the lowest quote received during the tender process, with the next lowest fee being £500,000.

Audit team members available

The audit team is composed of 15 team members, made up as follows:

Trainees	11
Managers	3
Audit Partners	1
	15

Required

(a) Provide possible reasons for a client to change its external auditor. **(5 marks)**

(b) Analyse the factors which the RBA engagement partner should consider when evaluating whether or not to accept SC Plc as an audit client. **(5 marks)**

(c) Based on the information provided (including Working Paper A-100), provide 4 examples of business risks. **(4 marks)**

(d) Using the information provided in Working Paper A-100, analyse the risk of material misstatement at the overall/financial statement level for SC Plc. **(9 marks)**

(e) Determine (using appropriate examples) two fundamental principles of ethical behaviour. **(2 marks)**

(Total 25 marks)

Question 16 [Case Study] [May 2023]

You have been provided with the following working paper regarding the audit of Pepper Ltd ('Pepper'):

Working Paper:	B-2		
Client:	Pepper Ltd		
Prepared By:	A Trainee	Year-end:	31 December 2022
Reviewed By:	A Manager	Review Date:	Pending

Purpose of working paper

To provide an overview of the process followed to recognise expenses and pay creditors (payables).

Creation and addition of a new vendor

- Only approved suppliers can have goods or services ordered by Pepper on the system. The system has a drop-down list of vendors which Pepper may use to buy goods or services. This is known as the approved supplier list.

- The procurement clerk will identify the need for a new vendor to be added to the system due to a new service or goods request. The procurement clerk will complete a new supplier form outlining the type of product or service needed, the expected cost per month and when the product or service is needed.

- The procurement clerk will submit the new supplier form to the operations manager who will review it for completeness and then source three quotations from suppliers which match the request from the procurement clerk. The operations manager will then select the quotation with the lowest price and attach that to the new supplier form before submitting it to the finance manager for approval.

- The finance manager will review the new supplier form against the attached quotation to confirm the cost, type of product or service and expected timelines and then either approve or reject it. Approved supplier forms and quotations are sent to the financial accountant to upload the new supplier details onto the approved supplier list on the system.

- The finance manager will review the list of approved suppliers on a quarterly basis and request the financial accountant to remove any vendors no longer used by the entity. This request is performed via e-mail. Once removed, no orders may be processed to that vendor and the financial accountant will use the e-mail request as approval to remove the vendor from the supplier master file on the system.

Monthly payment of creditors(payables)

- Pepper's system generates a sequentially numbered purchase order each time a request for a product or service is made on the system. Anyone can generate a purchase order on the system.

- The creditors' clerk will identify the purchase orders on the system and contact a supplier (from the approved supplier list) to provide the ordered items. This task is performed daily. The creditors' clerk will load the quotation received from the supplier as well as the final invoice (once received) on the system and manually allocate it to the purchase order to indicate that the product or service has been received.

- On a monthly basis, the bank clerk receives an Excel printout from the creditors' clerk of all invoices for payment in that month and processes payment based on the approved supplier list bank details for the invoices received.

- On a monthly basis, Pepper's system generates an aging of all supplier balances based on the invoices and payments recorded for that month. This is based on the manually recorded invoices from the creditors' clerk as well as the manually recorded bank payments from the bank clerk.

- On a monthly basis, the creditors' clerk will receive statements from all the Pepper suppliers and perform a reconciliation between the balance on the Pepper system and the supplier statement. Any reconciling differences are followed up via e-mail.

- Each month the finance manager will review the creditor reconciliations for a sample of creditors selected judgementally. Any reconciling differences are discussed with the creditors and bank clerks.

- Each month the Chief Financial Officer (CFO) performs a review of the creditor aging to identify any long outstanding payables as well as any unusual movements in the balance owed. The CFO will discuss these balances with the finance manager and contact any suppliers where a renegotiation of credit terms may be needed.

Errors detected to date

- An invoice for US$150,000 dated 1 January 2022 in respect of rental expenditure for a pop-up shop (a temporary retail outlet) in the Kingdom of Atchoo from October-November 2021 was incorrectly recorded in the current period's expenditure.

- An invoice was incorrectly duplicated and paid to the value of US$1,200 for maintenance costs during the current financial period.

- Intercompany creditors were overstated by US$10,000 due to a payment to Pepper Logistics Ltd, a private company, not being recorded despite being made on 31 December 2022.

- Sales Tax was incorrectly recorded at 19% instead of 9% on an invoice from Pepper Farms Ltd (a private company). Total invoice amount, including the correct tax, was US$256,000.

End of working paper.

Required

(a) Determine 5 possible controls which Pepper Ltd can implement to limit duplicate creditor balances. **(5 marks)**

(b) Prepare a schedule of substantive procedures which can be performed on:

    (i) The completeness of trade creditors. **(8 marks)**
    (ii) The disclosure of trade creditors. **(3 marks)**

(c) Advise on the difference between a control deficiency and a misstatement. **(4 marks)**

(Total 20 marks)

Question 17 [Case Study: Audit evidence and ethics] [May 2023]

You have just been assigned as an audit engagement senior to Allgood Ltd ('Allgood'), an existing client of your firm. The audit for the year ended 30 September 2022 is scheduled to start in a few weeks' time. The audit manager and partner met with the Finance Director (FD) and Managing Director (MD) of Allgood on 19th September 2022 and the audit manager noted the following from this meeting:

(1) Allgood has experienced tough competition in the last 12 months. As a result it has relaxed its credit terms with customers to help to compete for new business.

(2) The debtor/receivables days have increased by 25%.

(3) There are significant accounts receivable balances in the 'over 90' days category and the following schedule was provided by Allgood's FD:

Accounts Receivable	Over 90 days (£000)	Client comments
Evenbetter Ltd	400	Payment due on 15th October 2022
Bale Ltd	150	There is a similar balance for Bale Ltd in Accounts Payable
Out Ltd	350	To be passed to a debt collection agency
In Ltd	150	Assurances have been received that the amount will be paid
Alsace Ltd	275	The outstanding amount is insured
Other small balances	255	Mostly small balances considered unrecoverable
Total	**1,580**	

At the end of the meeting the FD noted that the credit controller will soon go on a 12 month leave of absence. The FD asked if your firm could provide staff to provide interim cover for this position during this period. This person would also be required to update some account records from the fourth quarter, when the accounts payable clerk had been on holiday and had fallen behind in processing paperwork.

An audit senior from your firm recently left the firm and is providing financial accounting services to Allgood on a consultancy basis. The FD has been impressed by their work and is sure that one of your staff would be able to help with resolving the issues which she is facing in Accounts Receivable. Since the meeting the audit manager has identified that £10,000 of the prior year £60,000 audit fees have yet to be paid.

Required

(a) Using the schedule provided at the meeting, draft a memo to the audit team outlining the work to be done on the over 90 days accounts receivable balance. Your answer should cover the following two aspects:

    (i) general work on the accounts receivable ledger, and **(3 marks)**

    (ii) specific work on each balance. **(6 marks)**

(b) Determine any ethical issues from the case study and what considerations and decisions you think the audit partner should take. **(6 marks)**

(Total 15 marks)

Question 18 [Audit Risk] [May 2023]

ISA (UK) 200 *Overall Objectives of the Independent Auditor and the Conduct of an Audit in Accordance with International Standards on Auditing (UK)* (Revised June 2016, paragraph 13c) defines audit risk as: "The risk that the auditor expresses an inappropriate audit opinion when the financial statements are materially misstated. Audit risk is a function of the risks of material misstatement and detection risk". Meanwhile, ISA (UK) 330 *The Auditor's Responses to Assessed Risks* (Revised July 2017, paragraph 18), states that: "Irrespective of the assessed risks of material misstatement, the auditor shall design and perform substantive procedures for each material class of transactions, account balance, and disclosure". Finally, ISA (UK) 330 (Revised July 2017, paragraph 26) also requires the auditor to conclude whether sufficient appropriate audit evidence has been obtained.

Required

(a) In the above definition of audit risk, reference is made to the financial statements being 'materially misstated'.

    (i) Determine what is meant by 'material' in the auditing context.

    (ii) Analyse what is meant by 'planning (or overall) materiality' and 'tolerable error'.

    (iii) Estimate with examples how appropriate amounts may be arrived at for: 'planning (or overall) materiality' and 'tolerable error'.

(11 marks)

(b) Determine the components of audit risk. In your answer distinguish between those components of audit risk which are:

    (i) Directly controllable by the auditor.
    (ii) Not directly controllable by the auditor.

(4 marks)

(Total 15 marks)

Question 19 [Case Study: BlockRon Ltd - Planning] [May 2023]

You have recently completed your degree and have joined AA Auditors (AAA), a medium-size audit firm based in Rubber City, Freedonia. Your first assignment is to assist with the audit of BlockRon Ltd ('BlockRon'). The company is incorporated in Freedonia and is listed on the Freedonia Stock Exchange (FSE). The currency in Freedonia is the Freedonia Mark (FM). The financial year-end is 30 June 2022 and the audit deadline has been set as 31 July 2022.

Below is an extract of the audit file working papers. Working paper PLN-01 summarises information obtained from a meeting with BlockRon's Chief Financial Officer (CFO – Mr Aldous Bong) held on 1 March 2022 as part of the process of gaining an understanding of the client and assessing the risk of material misstatement.

Working Paper:	PLN-01		
Client:	BlockRon Ltd	Year-end:	30 June 2022
Prepared By:	Mr D Hill Berg	Date:	2 March 2022
Reviewed By:	Mrs A Serious - Manager	Date:	3 March 2022

Purpose of the working paper

To summarise information obtained from a meeting with the CFO, on 1 March 2022.

Information

- BlockRon is an online streaming service that gives on-demand access to films, documentaries and TV series to subscribed members. Members pay a once-off joining fee of FM200, as well as an annual subscription fee of FM100 to gain access to the content made available by BlockRon. Content can then be watched over the internet on any device with a screen.

- Mr Nicky Santoro, the Chief Executive Officer (CEO) of BlockRon, founded the company 10 years ago after his long and illustrious career in acting. He brought in his best friend, Mr Bong, to take care of the accounting side of things, while Mr Santoro focussed on growing the brand and managing its operations. The on-demand viewing model was an instant success. BlockRon grew rapidly and has recently listed on the Freedonia Stock Exchange (FSE) and Mr Santoro and Mr Bong both still hold significant equity interests in the company.

- In recent years, the competition against BlockRon has grown fierce, in Freedonia and abroad. Big Theatre, Ali Prime and Wisney are just some of the new companies that offer similar services to BlockRon. To remain competitive, BlockRon has had to create patents and copyrights over its business model and original content. It also carries out extensive customer research to ensure that it stays ahead of the game with online movie services.

- Management performance bonuses are based on the annual amount of joining fees earned, as well as the number of subscription renewals. Mr Santoro himself was closely involved in creating the remuneration policy of BlockRon and reviews it annually. He has always held customer satisfaction in the highest regard and wanted to incentivise his managers to work towards that goal.

- The rest of the Board of Directors is comprised of:
  - Mrs Rachel Blue, Chief Information Officer (CIO) and part-time waitress.
  - Mr Peter Greenstein, Finance Manager, PhD in palaeontology.
  - Mrs Ginger McKenna, Aesthetic Manager and part-time singer.
  - Mrs Monica Greenstein, independent non-executive director and sister of Mr Peter Greenstein.

All directors are very close friends of Mr Santoro and Mr Bong. They were chosen to serve on the Board of Directors because Mr Santoro knows he can trust them and they spend a lot of time together outside of business hours, which makes it easy to discuss pressing matters.

End of working paper.

After you met with Mr Bong, your audit manager asked you to meet with the Finance Manager, Mr Greenstein, to obtain an understanding of the revenue process. Working paper REV-01 summarises the information obtained from a meeting with Mr Greenstein held on 1 March 2022.

Working Paper:	REV-01		
Client:	BlockRon Ltd	Year-end:	30 June 2022
Prepared By:	Mr D Hill Berg	Date:	2 March 2022
Reviewed By:	Mrs A Serious - Manager	Date:	3 March 2022

Purpose of the working paper

To summarise information obtained from a meeting with Mr Peter Greenstein, the Finance Manager of BlockRon, on 1 March 2022 about the Revenue and Receivables Cycle of BlockRon.

Information

1 **Streams of Revenue.**

   1.1 **Revenue from subscription services.**

   - BlockRon follows a subscription-based model rather than generating revenue from selling or renting specific titles. Subscribers pay a once-off joining fee of FM200 and then an additional FM100 per annum to gain access to all the content available on BlockRon. A new subscriber must pay both upfront to join (i.e. a total of FM300). The joining-fee revenue is recognised at a point in time when the subscriber joins. The annual subscription fee, however, is recognised over time and not upon invoicing the customer.

   - All accounting and invoicing for subscriptions are automatically dealt with on the e-Portal. Mrs Blue used a widely available online accounting package to create this e-Portal.

   - The following journal entry is automatically processed as a subscriber joins:

DEBIT	Bank	FM300
CREDIT	Joining fee revenue	FM200
CREDIT	Content obligation	FM100

   - The annual fee is then automatically accounted by the following journal entry processed by the e-Portal:

DEBIT	Content Obligation	FM100
CREDIT	Annual fee revenue	FM100

   - At the end of every week, a reasonability test is automatically performed by the e-Portal system over annual fee revenue and reviewed by Mr Greenstein to ensure that actual revenue recorded is equal to expected revenue from subscribers.

   - BlockRon now has over 1 million subscribers to their online platform.

   1.2. **Revenue from the sale of merchandise**

   BlockRon provides access to a large range of original content, as well as many well-known series, movies and documentaries. Mr Santoro decided to expand his business model in September 2020 to include the sale of merchandise. BlockRon sells merchandise (such as T-shirts and novelties) on the e-Portal, which is then shipped free-of-charge to anywhere within Freedonia. One of the most successful items is their "BlockRon & Relax" line of merchandise. BlockRon also sells merchandise for well-known movies and series that they have acquired rights to, such as "When Bally met Belly" and "The Wheezing Dead". In total, more than 500,000 items have been sold since merchandise was put on offer.

> Business has been booming over the last three years. This is especially true when it comes to the last 6 months of the current financial year because people have been spending more time at home following pandemic lockdowns in Freedonia.

End of working paper.

Required

(a) In respect of the **working paper PLN-01**, identify and analyse the risk of material misstatement at the overall/financial statement and assertion-level. Indicate clearly if each risk is at the overall/financial statement or assertion-level. **(10 marks)**

(b) You have completed your risk assessment and understanding of the entity. AA Auditors must now formulate the audit approach. Determinate what is meant by an "audit approach" and outline the components that make up an audit approach. Detailed audit procedures are not required. **(5 marks)**

(c) Concerning **working paper REV-01**, analyse the nature, timing and extent of the audit procedures to be performed over revenue. Your answer must NOT include any substantive procedures or tests of controls. **(10 marks)**

(Total 25 marks)

Question 20 [BlockRon Ltd - Completion] [May 2023]

Please note: Students are advised not to attempt Q5 until they have attempted Q4.

The auditors are busy finalising the audit of BlockRon (see Question 4) for the 30 June 2022 Financial Year. Peter Harris, a third-year audit trainee on the audit team, received the following email from the audit manager (Don Belushi):

To:	PeterHarrisThirdYear@AAA.com
From:	DonBelushiAuditManager@AAA.com
Subject:	Preparation of the schedule of misstatements

Hi Peter

I trust you are well. Please see the attached working papers (WP – 027) detailing the misstatements identified in the audit fieldwork and testing. I need you to please prepare the schedule of misstatements that we need to communicate to the client as well as a report explaining each misstatement. Please contact me if you have any questions.

Kind regards

Don Belushi, Audit Manager

When Peter opens Attachment: WP – 027, he finds the following working paper:

Working Paper:	WP - 027		
Client:	BlockRon Ltd	Year-end:	30 June 2022
Prepared By:	Frank Marino - Third-Year	Date:	20 July 2022
Reviewed By:	Don Belushi - Audit Manager	Date:	22 July 2022

Purpose of the working paper

To document the misstatements that were identified during the execution of the audit.

Materiality levels for the audit:
Performance materiality – FM110,000
Clearly trivial – FM5,000

The following issues were identified in the execution and testing of the audit:

Issue 1: During the testing of Intangible Assets, an error in the amortisation was identified. An intangible asset, with a cost of FM720,000, was amortized under the cost model over 36 months instead of 24 months. This appears to be a once-off error and does not indicate any instance of fraud.

Issue 2: When testing the provision for bad debts the amount was recalculated by the audit team and amounted to FM260,000 using a percentage of 7.5% based on industry data and trends, economic climate and historic data. The client, however, recorded an amount of FM150,000.

Issue 3: During the testing of accounts receivable, it was noted that an invoice was recorded as FM4,008 instead of the amount on the invoice of FM4,080.

Issue 4: Research costs of FM300,000 were capitalised. These did not meet the recognition criteria in the Conceptual Framework and IAS 38 *Intangible Assets*. The financial manager provided a schedule of the breakdown of capitalised costs which reflected an amortisation charge of FM12,000.

Issue 5: The testing of expenses revealed that the insurance expense for the year was incorrect. A premium of FM40,000 was paid on 1 September 2021 and the full amount was expensed in the 2022 year.

End of working paper.

Additional information:

Management of BlockRon has refused to adjust the amounts in the financial statements as per your schedule of misstatements.

Required

(a) Demonstrate with examples the difference between a qualified audit opinion, a disclaimed audit opinion and an adverse audit opinion. **(5 marks)**

(b) Respond to the email sent by the Audit Manager using working paper WP – 027. Your answer should include the following:

   (i) A **schedule of unadjusted** differences which shows the proposed correcting entries and the effect on the audit client's assets, liabilities, equity and profit or loss. **(8 marks)**

   (ii) An analysis of each of the issues outlining:
   - The type of misstatement (i.e. factual or based on an estimate).
   - The materiality of the misstatement.
   - The overall effect on the audit opinion.

   (12 marks)

   (Total 25 marks)

Question 21 [Self-regulation] [November 2023]

Auditing is a long and well established profession. One of the hallmarks of a profession is that it is self-regulating. Self-regulation describes a situation when a profession has its own rules and regulations that it follows in its daily affairs and professional work which is not prescribed by the government.

However, since the early 1990s, the external audits of companies' financial statements and the professional conduct of external auditors in the United Kingdom (as in many other countries) have been increasingly subject to regulation, oversight, inspection, and periodic review by regulatory bodies.

Required

Giving specific examples to illustrate your answer, determine the role of each of the following in governing or regulating the audits of public companies' financial statements in the United Kingdom:

(a) The Companies Act 2006. **(7 marks)**

(b) Common (or case) law. **(6 marks)**

(c) Regulations and Standards – in particular, various Auditing and Ethical Standards and the Corporate Governance Code (UK). **(7 marks)**

(Total 20 marks)

Question 22 [Overall objective of the independent auditor] [November 2023]

International Standard on Auditing (UK) 200 (Revised June 2016) *Overall Objectives of the Independent Auditor and the Conduct of an Audit in Accordance with International Standards on Auditing (UK)* states:

The overall objectives of the auditor are: To obtain reasonable assurance about whether the financial statements as a whole are free from material misstatement, whether due to fraud or error, thereby enabling the auditor to express an opinion on whether the financial statements are prepared, in all material respects, in accordance with an applicable financial reporting framework (para 11). Reasonable assurance is a high level of assurance. It is obtained when the auditor has obtained sufficient appropriate audit evidence to reduce audit risk (that is, the risk that the auditor expresses an inappropriate opinion when the financial statements are materially misstated) to an acceptably low level (para 5).

Your mid-sized audit firm has recently won the bid to become external auditor for a new client. This client is a new company in business less than five years, recently listed on the main stock exchange, operates globally in the Fintech sector, and has been expanding rapidly through takeovers of existing local and international companies. However, some of these newly added companies are engaging in business areas other than those of your new client. Your firm has limited prior expertise in auditing companies in the Fintech sector. Finally, the new client has expressed that they are keen on quick completion of the audit and at a low cost.

Required

(a) There is usually a great amount of evidence available to the auditor. Determine the factors auditors should consider when deciding which evidence to gather. Reflect on the above case scenario to support your answer. **(5 marks)**

(b) Relating to the above case scenario for examples for your answer, demonstrate the difference between compliance and substantive procedures (or tests) and explain the importance of each of these types of procedures in the audit process. **(4 marks)**

(c) Auditing Standards require auditors to gain a thorough understanding of their client's industry, business and operations. In reflection on the above case scenario, analyse:

    (i) The importance of this step in the audit process, and **(3 marks)**

    (ii) How auditors may perform it. **(3 marks)**

(Total 15 marks)

Question 23 [Case study: ABC (I)] [November 2023]

Note. Questions 3 and 4 share the same case information. You can answer Q3 and Q4 in any order, but you must read the case information before attempting either question.

Both questions relate to the audit of the same private company 'ABC'.

Case Information

(Please note again that this information is shared with Q4, but only shown here. Hence, when you attempt Q4, please refer to the case information shown here).

ACME Auditors LLP (ACME) is a medium-sized audit firm that provides assurance and non-assurance services to its clients. Miss Cecile Speyer (Cecile) is one of the engagement partners at ACME and has extensive experience in the energy and renewables industry. During March 2022, the predecessor auditor of ABC Ltd (ABC) resigned with immediate effect. On 1 April 2022, Cecile successfully secured the external audit of ABC. ABC sells a variety of unusual sweets and chocolates. Cecile negotiated the appointment of ACME with Mr Fredrick Weasley (Fredrick), the Chief Executive Officer (CEO) of ABC.

Cecile and Fredrick informally agreed on the engagement and negotiated an audit fee of GBP 700,000 for the audit of ABC for the year ended 31 May 2022. The fee was 30% lower than that paid to the previous auditors. ABC agreed to provide a year's supply of their famous Every Flavour Jellybeans, to Cecile, free of charge. This is one of ABC's premium range of sweets. Furthermore, they offered to create a customised jellybean flavour and name it after ACME to help the firm attract potential clients. Cecile accepted the agreement at a lower fee knowing that ABC would be an important addition to ACME's diverse range of clients.

Miss Georgia Weasley (Georgia) is a Chartered Accountant, Fredrick's twin sister and the Chief Financial Officer (CFO) of ABC. Georgia stated that the resignation of the previous auditor was due to a difference in accounting treatment on certain matters. Georgia also mentioned that controls over inventory have been updated for deficiencies noted. The inventory controls have been reviewed by the internal audit function. Cecile promised that her audit team would assist the internal audit team in correcting and implementing new controls as well as monitoring the operating effectiveness of the controls. Georgia requested that Cecile and the external audit team focus on testing controls instead of substantive procedures because:

"Testing controls is far less time-consuming and onerous and will help meet the audit deadline of 31 July 2022 as we need an unqualified audit report by this date to apply for additional financing to expand our brand into other markets."

Georgia specifically requested that Cecile not speak to the previous auditors before accepting the engagement. Cecile agreed to these terms and assured Georgia that the audit opinion provided would enable ABC to apply for additional financing.

The following three working papers (WP-1, WP-2, WP-3) form part of the audit of ABC and are part of the information for the case.

EXAM QUESTION BANK

	WP-1		
Client	ABC		
Prepared by	ACME	Date	5 April 2022
Reviewed by	A Manager	Date	8 April 2022
Year-end	31 May 2022		
Title	Understanding the Entity		

ABC was established by the Weasley twins in 2015 with an individual store in Puddletown. They each hold 50% of the shares in ABC. Over the years, the company have expanded into the province around Puddletown and currently has 5 stores. Due to a major expansion in 2018, ABC entered into a 15-year lease agreement for a factory in Torville as it was no longer feasible to make the sweets in their kitchen at home.

The sweets and chocolates can be purchased by customers at the various stores or purchased online on ABC's newly launched application which can be downloaded onto any smartphone. ABC allows for both credit and cash purchases.

The IT systems and database are all located at their head office in Puddletown. The maintenance of the database and app is outsourced to a local IT firm.

As a result of the lockdown in 2020, ABC was not able to perform optimally and generated a net loss of GBP 200,000 during the 2022 financial year. Despite this, ABC is certain that it will recover from the loss due in part to:

- COVID-19 restrictions have been lifted leading to a significant increase in customer volumes, and
- During April 2022, ABC was offered an agreement with a popular supermarket, Pick and Buy, the terms of which mean that ABC will sell a quarter of all its inventory on a consignment basis. The contract has been set up for one year but Pick and Buy has indicated if product sales are successful, the contract will be extended for a further five years.

	WP-2		
Client	ABC		
Prepared by	ACME	Date	31 May 2022
Reviewed by	A Manager	Date	3 June 2022
Year-end	31 May 2022		
Title	Intangible Assets		

During the year, Mr Ronny Weasley (Ronny), the Weasley twin's younger brother, contracted COVID-19. Even after 10 days of isolation, Ronny struggled to taste anything. One day, when visiting the Torville Factory, a new brightly coloured jellybean of Every Flavour Jellybeans caught his eye. On trying the brightly coloured jellybean, Ronny was surprised to find his ability to taste returned. Further investigations revealed that the new jellybean flavour was successful in helping people suffering from the long-term effects of COVID to regain their sense of taste in 80% to 90% of cases. The jellybean was a result of experimenting with orange, ginger and turmeric.

Georgia suggested the recipe be patented. The patent was successfully registered on 1 January 2022 for the new jellybean flavour called "the taste tester". The patent has a useful life of 50 years and ABC selected to hold the intangible asset at cost.

	WP-3		
Client	ABC		
Prepared by	ACME	Date	31 May 2022
Reviewed by	A Manager	Date	3 June 2022
Year-end	31 May 2022		
Title	Change in accounting policy		

At the beginning of the year, ABC decided to change the accounting policy of their property, plant and equipment currently from the cost to the revaluation model. No other changes to the accounting policy were implemented.

Note. The materiality figure for the audit has been calculated as GBP 800,000.

Required

(a) Determine the objective of an audit and the benefits of a private company like ABC having its financial statements voluntarily audited. **(10 marks)**

(b) Identify and demonstrate the risks of material misstatement at the assertion level for ABC's new patent. **(5 marks)**

(Total 15 marks)

Question 24 [Case study: ABC (II)] [November 2023]

Note. Questions 3 and 4 share the same case information. You can answer Q3 and Q4 in any order, but you must read the case information shown in Q3 before attempting either question.

Both questions relate to the audit of the same private company 'ABC'.

Required

(a) Prepare a short report which:

    (i) Analyses any ethical concerns which Cecile should have considered before accepting ABC as an audit client; **(8 marks)**

    (ii) Demonstrates other considerations which should have been factored into the client acceptance process; and **(8 marks)**

    (iii) Concludes on whether or not the audit should have been accepted. **(1 mark)**

(b) Determine and demonstrate the risks of material misstatement at the overall level for ABC Ltd (ABC). **(8 marks)**

(Total 25 marks)

Question 25 [Lovely Toys] [November 2023]

You are a third-year trainee at Avenue Ltd (AVENUE), a medium-sized audit firm, and have been assigned to a new client Lovely Toys Ltd (TOYS). The audit is currently in the planning phase, and you are assisting in understanding the entity and its environment.

Background

TOYS was incorporated in Freedonia on 1 January 2005 and has a 31 December year-end. TOYS specialises in selling toys. TOYS has grown substantially since its incorporation and has stores in multiple provinces in Freedonia. TOYS has decided to rent stores in shopping centres. James Deane, the CEO, decided that TOYS should purchase the toys rather than manufacture them as the company does not have the necessary machinery and plant to do so. The suppliers of TOYS are both local and foreign entities.

Please carefully read the below working paper (A-1) for further details related to the audit of this company.

Working Paper:	A-1		
Client:	Lovely Toys Ltd		
Prepared By:	A Trainee	Year-end:	31 December 2022
Reviewed By:	A Manager	Review date	Pending

Purpose of working paper

To provide an overview of the process followed by the client to manage stock.

Acquisition of inventory

TOYS has recently implemented a new accounting software called "Lampoon" to assist with ordering, processing purchases and maintaining supplier information. Claudia Monroe (Claudia) is employed as the IT manager and is responsible for the implementation and maintenance of the system. Claudia has also implemented a new system called Quanty X which tracks the quantity of inventory and automatically sends an alert to the warehouse manager when reorder levels have been reached.

Addition of suppliers to the suppliers' list

To add a supplier to the suppliers' Masterfile, the supplier is required to submit prices of its toys and additional documentation to prove the supplier's authenticity. Examples include company registration documents and tax registration numbers. Order clerks are responsible for adding the approved suppliers to the suppliers' list using the Lampoon system.

Ordering process

If a reorder level is reached, the warehouse manager receives an alert from Quanty X. The warehouse manager then approves and sends a requisition to the ordering department. After receiving an approved requisition from the warehouse, the order clerks select a supplier from the approved suppliers' list and use Lampoon to capture and process the order of the toys. Before the order can be processed, the system indicates the availability of the products and current prices. Lampoon can provide this information because it interfaces with approved suppliers' stock systems. After the order clerks capture the order, Lampoon processes the order by sending the order to the supplier's system. After processing the purchases order, Lampoon automatically sends a notification regarding the purchases order to the receiving bay situated in the inventory warehouse of TOYS. TOYS' purchasing manager, Doug Stevens, oversees all purchases.

An electronic file of all the purchase orders is automatically kept by Lampoon. Upon the delivery of the toys by the supplier, the receiving bay clerks inspect if there is a corresponding purchase order. If there is one, the clerks accept the order, sign the supplier's delivery note and complete a goods received note based on the supplier's delivery note. The purchase orders are not marked as completed. The received toys are then sent to the warehouse from the receiving bay without the goods received note because the warehouse manager and the receiving bay manager believe that the goods received note should be retained by the receiving bay as proof of receipt of the toys, to avoid suppliers delivering duplicate orders. No other documentation is prepared when the toys are moved from the receiving bay. However, a copy of the goods received note is sent to the accounting department.

The toys are placed on their respective shelves based on their description by the warehouse clerks. The shelves are stocked in the presence of the warehouse manager to prevent theft. Quanty X is used to keep track of the availability of stock within the stores as well. As soon as the reorder level for the store is reached, Quanty X alerts the store manager. The store manager will prepare and send a requisition to the TOYS warehouse. The store manager checks that the particular toy is required and considers if the quantity ordered is reasonable based on current demand. If the quantity of toys per Quanty X is not ordered, the store manager must supply a reason which is reviewed by Head Office for reasonableness. A check is performed by the warehouse manager to confirm that the requisition was sent by an appropriate individual (the store manager). The warehouse clerks are responsible for selecting the toys based on the approved order. Once the toys for each store are packaged by the warehouse clerks, items are sent to the despatch bay. The delivery staff then collect the orders for each store.

Human resources

The delivery personnel are hired by the TOYS' HR department. All the delivery personnel are hired without background checks being performed because the HR department of TOYS operates under a tight budget and believes that every person deserves an opportunity.

Required

(a) Analyse the controls which should be in place over the addition of suppliers to the Masterfile.

Note. You do not need to deal with automated controls over data input and passwords. **(5 marks)**

(b) Assume that the Lampoon system operates effectively. Prepare a table which:

(i) Determines control weaknesses in the inventory acquisition process including stock despatch to the stores. **(10 marks)**

(ii) Provides a recommendation for improvement for each weakness. **(10 marks)**

(Total 25 marks)

Exam answer bank

Question 1

Hamilton & Harvey. This question is a case scenario and assesses the students' knowledge of factors to be considered by the auditor prior to accepting an audit engagement.

Syllabus sections 1, 2, 3, 4, 5.

LO1, LO2, LO3, LO4.

PQ Principles of Governance & Audit Paper Chs. 1, 4, 5, 6, 7.

(a) Factors to be considered prior to accepting an engagement:

    (i) Whether the audit firm, audit engagement partner and all members of the audit team are independent (as indicated above)

    (ii) Whether the audit firm/team is competent to conduct the audit. You want to ensure that the auditor has:

        a. adequate professional staff members to resource the audit (in numbers and level of seniority) so that it can be conducted to a high standard and in reasonable time

        b. knowledge of company's industry and business

        c. knowledge of applicable ISAs and how to apply them in the client's audit

        d. knowledge of laws and regulations that apply to the client's industry

    (iii) The integrity of the client (explain this point – what it means and why it is important)

    (iv) Any particular risk factors associated with the audit both business risk to the auditor and audit risk in itself.

(b) Report format should be adopted

Students should set out pros and cons of each option – for example:

Company X – possible problems from rapid growth (incentive to manipulate financial statements) and possible ineffective internal controls. But, the auditor has knowledge of the industry. Potential conflict of interest with the other client if it is a highly competitive industry.

Company Y – Little prior knowledge available from previous years' financial statements; potential problems from desire to go public (incentive to manipulate figures) and also from controlling shareholder. Opportunity to be the first auditor and to explain requirements of conducting an audit in accordance with ISAs. Additional costs associated with first year of audit.

Conclusion (will depend on students' reasoning for each company).

> **Additional areas where credit might be given, note this is not an exhaustive list:**
> - The suggested answers are not exhaustive. Credit can be given for other relevant points presented.

Question 2

Internal control. This short form question assesses the students' knowledge of the importance, components, and limitations of systems of internal control.

Syllabus sections 2, 3, 4, 5.

LO1, LO2, LO3.

PQ Principles of Governance & Audit Paper Chs. 4, 5, 6.

(a) A system of internal control consists of the following components:

   (i) The control environment – the environment created by the entity's directors and managers through their attitudes to, awareness of, and actions in respect of, the entity's internal controls and their importance to the entity.

   (ii) The entity's risk assessment process – the process adopted by the entity for identifying business risks relevant to financial reporting, deciding how to respond to these risks and the results of those responses.

   (iii) The information system relevant to financial reporting and related communication – the financial reporting system and its procedures for initiating, recording, processing and reporting entity transactions, events and conditions, and accounting for related assets, liabilities and equity; also the means by which the entity communicates financial roles and responsibilities and significant matters relating to financial reporting within the entity.

   (iv) Control activities – policies and procedures designed to ensure that responsibilities delegated by management are fulfilled and performed in the intended manner. It includes control activities that relate to information technology (IT) environments. These include general controls (such as restricting access to computers, programs, data and files to authorised personnel; and ensuring there are adequate backup facilities for both hardware and software; and ensuring all computer applications are fully documented and application controls (such as controls to ensure that (a) all transactions input to the system are properly authorised; (b) output is checked against input data and (c) transactions are properly, accurately and completely recorded and processed).

   (v) Monitoring of controls – a process designed to assess the effectiveness of internal control performance over time. It includes assessing the design and operation of the controls on the timely basis, taking corrective action when required and modifying the controls, as appropriate, for changed conditions.

(b) The importance of effective internal controls for (a) the company, and (b) the external audit:

   (i) For the company:

   Internal controls are important to ensure that all tasks delegated to company employees are performed as intended. Internal controls help to ensure that the company's objectives are met, the company complies with relevant laws and regulations and its financial and non-financial information (required for decision making) is reliable. Effective internal financial controls help to ensure that the company's external financial statements do not contain material misstatements and that fraud (and other irregularities) is prevented and detected.

   (ii) For the external auditor:

   The auditor undertakes a preliminary evaluation of the company's internal financial controls to identify internal control strengths (internal controls which appear to be operating effectively and on which the auditor may rely to reduce substantive testing) and weaknesses (internal controls that are required to prevent or detect material misstatements in the financial statements which are ineffective or absent). Before the auditor can rely on internal control strengths to reduce substantive testing, they must be tested (by compliance testing) to ensure they are working effectively and have been so working throughout the financial year. If the internal controls appear to be working effectively, the auditor will tend to rely more on compliance testing, will conduct more testing during the interim audit and will conduct less overall testing than if the internal controls do not appear to be operating effectively.

(c) Irrespective of how well designed a system of internal controls may be, and how effectively it operates, it will always possess inherent limitations. These include the following:

(i) Internal controls must be cost effective – beyond some point, the cost of instituting additional control activities will exceed the benefits to be gained from accurate financial data or increased safeguarding of assets.

(ii) Unusual transactions – internal financial controls are designed to prevent and detect errors in normal, frequently recurring transactions but errors are more likely to occur when recording and/or processing infrequent, unusual transactions.

(iii) Employees are human – the potential for error is always present because accounting personnel are human and therefore prone to making mistakes.

(iv) Errors in the design of a control activity - a person responsible for performing a particular control function (for example, reviewing exception reports) may not fully understand or appreciate the purpose of the function and fails to take appropriate action. Thus, iii and iv show that internal controls may not always operate as intended, and can have unintended effects.

(v) Management override – there is the possibility that management will override the controls, or two or more employees will collude to circumvent controls, or a computer operator may override or disable checks within a software program.

(vi) Controls outdated – internal controls may become inadequate or inappropriate as a result of changes in the entity's internal and/or external environment and, as a consequence, the effectiveness of (or employee's compliance with) the controls may deteriorate.

Additional areas where credit might be given, note this is not an exhaustive list:

- The suggested answers are not exhaustive. Credit can be given for other relevant points presented.

Question 3

Analytical Procedures. This short form question assesses the students' knowledge of meaning, use and importance of analytical procedures.

Syllabus sections 3, 4, 5, 6.

LO2, LO3, LO4.

PQ Principles of Governance & Audit Paper Chs. 7, 8, 12, 13, 14, 15, 16.

(a) Analytical procedures are the means by which meaningful relationships and trends in both financial and non-financial data may be analysed, actual data may be compared with budgeted or forecast data, and the data of an entity may be compared with that of similar entities and industry averages. By these means, any unusual or unexpected characteristics in the audit client's data may be identified and investigated.

(1 mark per relevant point, maximum 3 marks)

EXAM ANSWER BANK

(b) Stages in which analytical procedures are used (Candidates should capture key ideas shown in table below).

Stage in Audit	Objectives	Nature of Procedures Used
Risk identification and assessment	• To understand the client's business • To assess the likelihood of material misstatements in the financial statements • To identify high risk audit areas (i.e. significant risks) • To set materiality limits • To plan the nature, timing and extent of further audit procedures	• Trend analysis • Ratio analysis of entity data (e.g.: working capital ratio, debt to equity ratio – using figures from part-way through year) • Comparative analysis of entity data with previous years and that of other similar entities and industry averages • Relationship between financial and non-financial data (focus on the entity's overall financial position and performance
Substantive procedures	(a) To assess reasonableness of account balances (to determine nature and extent of further testing) (b) To obtain evidence to confirm (or refute) the truth and fairness of individual account balances (c) Substantive analytical procedures that can be performed on classes of transactions.	e.g.: Accounts receivable to sales, inventory to sales, rate of stock return e.g.: Interest paid, average debt held
Final Review	To confirm (or question) conclusions reached with respect to the truth and fairness of: • Profit and loss statement amounts • Statement of Financial Position amounts • Cash flow statement amounts • Financial statement note disclosures	• Trend and percentage analysis of individual accounts • Ratio analysis of financial statement data similar to initial stage but using finalised end of year figures (Focus is on the truth and fairness / fair presentation of the financial statements as a whole in portraying the entity's financial position, performance and cash flows

(c) Analytical procedures are efficient and effective audit procedures which assist the auditor in three different stages of the audit as indicated above. However, it must be remembered that their effectiveness is dependent on the quality of the underlying data.

The answers obtained from the analytical procedures need to be evaluated in the light of the auditor's expectations and other audit evidence obtained. Any unexpected answers or unusual explanations need to be thoroughly investigated.

> **Additional areas where credit might be given, note this is not an exhaustive list:**
> - The suggested answers are not exhaustive. Credit can be given for other relevant points presented.

Question 4

The Gym plc. This question is a case study (scenario based) and assesses the students' ability to analyse a number of issues during an audit and the impact the issues would have on the audit opinion.

Syllabus sections 4, 5, 6, 7.

L03, L04, L05.

PQ Principles of Governance & Audit Paper Chs. 8, 9, 10, 11, 12, 13, 14, 15, 15, 16, 18.

(a) (i) Absence of verification of the audited financial statements of the Philippine subsidiary.

The subsidiary contributed about 15% of The Gym's net profit and net assets. These amounts are material to, and have a pervasive effect on, The Gym's financial statements. Therefore, steps must be taken to ensure the amounts and disclosures in the subsidiary's financial statements are 'true and fair' and comply with International Financial Reporting Standards (note plc – IFRS apply).

Initially, you (as the engagement partner) should request the directors of The Gym to contact the directors of the subsidiary company to 'pressure' the local firm of auditors to provide you with the audit working papers and/or 'pressure' the local firm of auditors directly to provide the audit working papers.

If The Gym's directors are reluctant to take this action, or their efforts do not result in the provision of the audit working papers, advise The Gym's directors that International Standards on Auditing require you to obtain sufficient appropriate audit evidence to enable you to reach a conclusion about the truth and fairness of the subsidiary's financial statements and their compliance with IFRS. As a consequence, you will need to arrange for either some suitably experienced members of your audit team or a respected firm of local (Philippine) auditors to:

- visit the local audit firm to try to obtain the audit working papers;
- if the latter are obtained (through the directors' or your own actions – as above), evaluate the quality of the audit work (this may involve selectively re-auditing key financial statement amounts and disclosures);
- if the working papers cannot be obtained, have members of your audit team, or a local Thai firm you appoint, to selectively audit key financial statement amounts and disclosures in the subsidiary's financial statements to ascertain their 'truth and fairness' and compliance with IFRS.

The directors should be advised that any such action will almost certainly result in an increase in the audit fee and in the time taken to complete the audit. Note from the scenario that the company have requested a deadline of mid-July for the audit completion and it is now 30 May. They also need to be informed that, if you are unable to verify the amounts and disclosures shown in the subsidiary's financial statements and included in the consolidated financial statements, International Standards on Auditing prevent you from expressing an unmodified audit opinion in the auditor's report.

(ii) Potentially uncollectible account receivable.

The failure of Big Tech to pay outstanding invoices suggests that the amount is unlikely to be collected. You should review the correspondence file and minutes of directors' meetings for any evidence which suggests the amount of £1.2 million is in dispute or the IT company has signalled that it will not pay. Review business publications and media attention to ascertain if there is any press that would indicate Big Tech have going concern issues.

Assuming no such evidence is obtained, the Directors of The Gym should be advised that the Allowance for Bad Debts/Provision for Doubtful Debts should be increased by £1.2m. If this change is made, net profit and net assets would each decrease by £1.2 million.

(iii) Delayed occupancy of new spa and fitness centre.

As the new spa and fitness centre is yet to be completed, The Gym should not include the completed value of the facility on its balance sheet. From the information provided, it seems that the contract is only ¾ complete as it commenced in July 2020 and is due to complete at the end of June 2021.

You should ascertain the likelihood of the contract being completed by 30 June 2021 by enquiring of the Managing Director of the contracting company and reviewing Quantity Surveyor's reports and minutes of Board meetings. You should ensure the Managing Director's responses – especially any confirmation of the completion of the contract by 30 June 2021 – are confirmed by the Managing Director in writing.

Assuming such confirmation is obtained, the value of the contract (£88m) should be written down to its percentage of completion value (3/4 of £88m i.e. £66 m). You should ask the Finance Director to reduce the fixed asset by £22m and also reduce the corresponding liability by £22m. The directors should also be asked to include a note in the financial statements explaining the position – in particular, the commitment of £22m of funds for the remaining portion of the contract amount that will become payable upon completion of the project.

(b) (i) Impact on the audit opinion/report.

If The Gym' directors insist that no action be taken and the consolidated financial statements be published without further verification of the amounts and disclosures in the subsidiary's financial statements (and consolidated in the group financial statements), given the materiality and pervasiveness (about 15% of net profit and total assets) of the subsidiary's financial information, you will need to express a disclaimer of opinion. You have not been able to obtain and evaluate sufficient appropriate audit evidence on which to base an informed audit opinion. Students may suggest a qualified opinion rather than a disclaimer and, providing they have correctly argued their case for lack of pervasiveness, this should be accepted as correct.

(ii) Impact on the audit opinion/report.

If the Finance Director (supported by the other directors of The Gym) fails to make the requested adjustment, as the amount of £1.2 million is not material to either the net profit (1.2%) or the net assets (0.3%) as reported in the consolidated financial statements, you are unlikely to report your disagreement with the directors in respect of this matter.

Students may suggest a qualified opinion for disagreement – they should be given half marks.

(iii) Impact on audit opinion/report.

As both assets and liabilities are to be reduced by £22m the overall effect on net assets will be material (£22m is 5.8% of net assets). If the Finance Director refuses to make the adjustment and/or provide the information about the commitment in a note to the financial statements, the auditor may issue an unmodified opinion but is likely to refer to the matter in an emphasis of matter paragraph.

The impact on the audit report is uncertain and, as a result, students should be given credit for any correct reasoning.

> **Additional areas where credit might be given, note this is not an exhaustive list:**
>
> - The suggested answers are not exhaustive. Credit can be given for other relevant points presented.

Question 5

Dreamland Ltd. This question is a case study (scenario based) and assesses the students' ability to analyse a number of issues during an audit of current assets and identify/recommend actions re: identified matters, specifically re: *accounts receivable, inventory and cash*.

Syllabus sections 4, 5, 6, 7.

LO3, LO4, LO5.

PQ Principles of Governance & Audit Paper Chs. 8, 12, 13, 14, 15, 16.

(a) Actions re: identified matters.

    (i) Request the Finance Director to increase the provision for doubtful debts by £5.2 million – adjustable subsequent event (condition resulting in Hotels Galore's liquidation existed at year end). £5.2 million is just under 7% of accounts receivable balance and would increase the provision from £3m to £8.2m.

    (ii) Not a material misstatement but the error should be drawn to the attention of the Finance Director with the request that an adjusting entry be made.

    For both of the items above (i & ii), if the Finance Director decides not to adjust the account concerned, include the item concerned in the list of unadjusted errors to be reported in the communication to those charged with the company's governance.

    (iii) Recount a selection of stock counted by each employee to verify the accuracy of the count. If the count is found not to be accurate, request the company to conduct a further inventory count with the employees working in pairs. If taking inventory is considered impractical as it would now well be beyond year end, then it should definitely be an item in the letter of recommendation/ weaknesses and I would suggest increasing the risk assessment and performing more substantive testing of raw materials.

    (iv) Ensure that the sale has been recorded in the relevant accounts receivable and sales accounts and had also been excluded from the inventory account.

    (v) Ensure that the raw materials purchased for £865,000 have been included in both the inventory and trade payables accounts.

    (vi) Explain to the Managing Director that, in accordance with International Auditing Standards, auditors are required to be responsible for all aspects of external confirmation of receivables.

(b) (i) Accounts Receivable

        i. Prepare, or obtain a client prepared, an aged accounts receivable schedule as at 31 March 2021.

        ii. Randomly select a sample of receivables from accounts under 90 days old and below a certain amount (for example, £1,000,000). Send negative confirmation requests to all receivables in the sample selected. (These require the customer to reply only in the event that they disagree with the amount shown in the confirmation request).

iii. Send positive confirmation request to all customers whose accounts are more than 90 days old or whose accounts are greater than – say - £1m. (These require the customer to confirm whether or not they agree with the amount shown in the confirmation request).

iv. For all positive confirmation requests for which no answer is received, follow up with a second and, if necessary, third request.

v. For positive confirmation requests for which no response is received or for all confirmation request responses that indicate the information shown in Dreamland Ltd's records is incorrect – follow up to ascertain correct amount:

- inspect subsequent/ post year end cash receipts to see if payment relating to the item(s) constituting the receivable's balance has been received since 31 March 2021.

- inspect sales journal to see if subsequent sales have been made to this customer and to which any cash received might relate.

- inspect sales returns journal to see if goods sold and recorded as all or part of the receivable's balance have been returned.

- inspect correspondence files (disputed accounts file) to see if the customer has disputed the amount owed.

vi. For any confirmations returned to the audit firm marked 'not known at this address' investigate procedures for recording and updating customers' details (this may result in a re-assessment of relevant internal controls).

Also check for the ownership of accounts receivable by enquiring of the Finance Director and, if necessary, reviewing correspondence files and minutes of directors' meetings for any indication that the accounts receivable may be factored (owned by a finance house).

Check the collectability of accounts – especially those over 90 days old – by enquiring of Finance Director about efforts to obtain payment and reviewing disputed accounts and correspondence files for evidence which indicates the accounts will not be paid.

Review the client's calculation of the Provision for Doubtful Debts. Review the reasonableness of the assumptions made when selecting the percentage applied to the gross Accounts Receivable balance. Recalculate the Allowance for Bad Debts.

(ii) Inventory

i. If not present when the inventory count was conducted (which seems to be the case) discuss with the Finance Director how the inventory was counted and if this is acceptable, inspect the raw materials, work in progress and finished goods inventory to confirm existence and condition and conduct some test counts. If the stocktaking was not conducted satisfactorily, request that the stock be recounted. Students may argue that auditor inspection and test count and request for a recount will only work if there are continuous inventory records and an integrated system

ii. Review the inventory held by Dreamland Ltd for indications of diminution in the value of the stock held – whether due to damage or obsolescence. (If the value of any portion of the inventory is lower than its cost price, design a test for this to ensure that its net realisable value is used to value this inventory). Students may design/outline a test.

iii. Discuss with the Finance Director the accounting policy adopted for valuing inventory and confirm this complies with the financial reporting framework adopted by Dreamland Ltd. (Different portions of stock may be valued using different valuation methods).

iv. Confirm that the correct purchase prices have been applied to raw materials inventory on hand (unless its value is lower than cost).

v. Check that sales made in the few days before and after 31 March 2021 have been recorded in the correct accounting period.

vi. Check that raw materials (and any other 'bought in' inventory) purchased in the few days before and after 31 March 2021 is (a) owned by Dreamland and, if so (b) recorded in the correct accounting period. If ownership has not passed to Dreamland, ensure the relevant purchase is excluded from inventory.

vii. Enquire of the Finance Director and review correspondence files and minutes of directors' meetings for evidence of inventory being held on consignment etc. by a third party or being held by Dreamland on behalf of a third party.

viii. Recalculate the inventory figure.

(iii) Cash

i. Send a confirmation request to Dreamland's bank(s) to verify the amount of cash in Dreamland's bank accounts on 31 March 2021.

ii. Confirm the accuracy of Dreamland's records for cash held on the premises (petty cash). Count cash on premises and compare with company's records.

Additional areas where credit might be given, note this is not an exhaustive list:

- The suggested answers are not exhaustive. Credit can be given for other relevant points presented.

Question 6

Pre-engagement procedures and initial stages of an audit engagement (ISA 200, 210, 220 (Revised), 240, 250 (Revised), 260 (Revised), 320, 450). This question is a case scenario and assesses the students' knowledge of factors to be considered by the auditor prior to accepting an audit engagement.

Syllabus sections 1, 2, 3, 4, 5.

LO1, LO2, LO3, LO4.

PQ Principles of Governance & Audit Paper Chs. 1, 4, 5, 6, 7.

(a) (i & ii) Students need to explain the factors considered before acceptance (i) and their importance to the audit (ii):

- Does the firm have the required competence to perform the audit?

    Students need to explain what is meant by competence, mentioning characteristics such as:

    – Knowledge of the client's industry.
    – Knowledge of relevant accounting and auditing standards.
    – Adequate human resources in terms of number and experience of audit staff.
    – Adequate time to perform the audit.
    – Experts and the engagement quality reviewer available when needed.

Without competence the audit team might miss material misstatements and thus arrive at an inappropriate audit opinion.

- If the firm accepts the audit, will it result in a threat to the firm's or to any member of the team's ability to comply with the ethical principles of independence and objectivity, professional competence and due care, confidentiality, professional conduct (and behaviour), ability to consistently apply professional scepticism at an appropriate level?
  - If so, can appropriate safeguards be applied to reduce the threat to an acceptably low level?
  - If firms and audit teams do not comply with the ethical principles, there is a danger of the audit not being performed to the required standard (link to, for example, lack of independence and lack of due care), the breaching of the duty of confidentiality (link to disclosing confidential information to competitors of the potential client, etc.)?
- Does the client, its directors and/or senior managers lack integrity (Do we want the audit?). The firm can assess this by discussions with the previous auditor, speaking to independent but knowledgeable third parties, media search, etc.

  If the client lacks integrity:
  - There is a greater chance that the draft financial statements will contain material misstatements, and
  - There is a greater chance that the audit team will not be given full and accurate answers to their questions and/or otherwise not be able to gather sufficient and reliable audit evidence.

(b) Answers below are indicative of material the students could include in their answer.

(i) Gain a thorough understanding of the client.

- Understanding the client is very important because without the understanding:
  - Auditor does not have the context for evaluating the validity of evidence.
  - Client personnel are in a stronger position to deceive the auditor.
  - The value of accounts like inventory might be materially misstated without the auditor's knowledge.
  - The auditor is not in a position to assess the appropriateness of the design of certain internal controls (e.g. those of safeguarding assets).
  - The auditor may not be aware of legal, regulatory and reporting requirements to which the client may be subject.

How is this understanding acquired?

- Visiting the client, touring the premises, speaking with key personnel (e.g. managing, sales, production, HR etc. directors.)
- Reading trade magazines, newspapers, other media.
- Speaking with others in the industry.
- Reviewing the client's documents such as memorandum and articles of association, important contracts, accounting records, job descriptions and manuals, organisation chart.

- Reading the minutes of Directors' and Board committees' (especially audit committee) meetings.

(ii) Evaluate the risk of material misstatements in the company's financial statements:

- Assessing the risk of material misstatements is important as it determines the nature, timing, and extent of audit tests (the candidate should cross reference to earlier answer or provide an explanation of the three terms) for the audit as a whole and in each audit segment.
    - Assessing the risk also enables the auditor to identify areas of significant risk (areas of the audit that require special audit attention).
    - The level of risk will affect the number of hours required for the audit and the level (junior and senior) of staff required.
- The risk of material misstatement is determined by:
    - The performance of analytical procedures (this needs to be explained and examples of ratios performed provided).
    - Assessing inherent risk (explain the three components – management integrity, business risk and account risk and how each may be assessed).

Assessing internal control risk (how this is established through understanding and documenting each accounting sub-system and identifying and testing internal control strengths).

(iii) Determine materiality limits appropriate to an audit of the company's financial statements

- Setting materiality limits is important as the auditor is required to express an opinion in the audit report as to whether the financial statements are free from material misstatements.
    - Thus, the auditor needs to determine the size and nature of misstatements that are likely to affect the economic decisions or actions of users of the financial statements.
    - Determining the materiality limits for the financial statements as a whole and for each account balance and disclosure contained therein is important as it determines the **nature, timing and extent** of the audit tests to be performed (*each of these three characteristics needs to be explained*).
- Planning materiality is the maximum amount of error in the financial statements as a whole the auditor can accept while still concluding that the financial statements are true and fair. The concept of materiality is fundamental to the audit.

Three steps are involved in determining an appropriate level for planning materiality (each of which needs to be explained by the students).

- Selecting an appropriate benchmark, e.g. total sales, total assets, total equity, profit before tax).
- Identifying financial data to represent the benchmark (e.g. last year's figures, budgeted amount, extrapolate from year to date)
- Identifying an appropriate percentage (threshold) to apply to the benchmark (e.g. 1% of total income, 5% of profit before tax, but note that one size does not fit all, there are single rule methods and sliding scale or variable methods, blended methods, and formula-based methods)

- Auditors usually use a number of answers to arrive at a range of amounts to represent planning materiality
- Tolerable error is the maximum amount of error the auditor can accept in an account balance or financial statement disclosure while still concluding the item in question is fairly stated
- Starting point is planning materiality – typically start at between 50-75% of planning materiality and adjust for things like the nature of the account (the amount of estimation involved), its importance to users of financial statements, whether it is required by law.
- Some issues of materiality are not necessarily quantifiable, but are required by law (Qualitative materiality refers to the nature of a transaction or amount and includes many financial and non-financial items that, independent of the amount, may influence the decisions of a user of the financial statements), or by their nature could be misleading users even if below threshold, see ISA 450 for examples).

- Performance materiality – both planning materiality and tolerable error allow for detected but uncorrected misstatements and misstatements not detected because they fall outside the auditor's samples.
  - Before the audit commences, auditors are required to specify an amount for performance materiality – an amount of effort which, if detected, will signal to the auditor that there is a danger that planning materiality or tolerable error may well be exceeded (hence adjustment to further audit testing is needed!).
  - Typically set at about 10% of planning materiality or tolerable error, as applicable.

(Total 20 marks)

Additional areas where credit might be given, note this is not an exhaustive list:

- The suggested answers are not exhaustive. Credit can be given for other relevant points presented.

Question 7

Auditor's independence (ISA 200, 240, 320). This short form question assesses the students' knowledge of the importance, components, and limitations of and threats to auditor independence.

Syllabus sections 2, 3, 4, 5.

LO1, LO2, LO3, LO4, LO5

PQ Principles of Governance & Audit Paper Chs. 1, 3, 4, 5, 6, 7, 8, 9, 17, 18.

Students should:

- Define auditor independence mentioning both independence in mind (or fact) and independence in appearance.

- Explain that it is important because if auditors are not independent, they may well miss material misstatements they should detect (e.g. because of not being sufficiently sceptical) and thus arrive at an inappropriate audit opinion; if auditors are not perceived to be independent, users will not rely on the auditor's opinion – in either case, the audit will not fulfil its function and will have no value.

- Identify about five threats to auditors' independence and provide a specific example to illustrate each – self-interest threat, self-review threat, advocacy threat, intimidation threat, familiarity or trust threat. They may also mention management threat (APB Ethical standard 5 revised, FRC Ethical standard 2024, revised).

> **Additional areas where credit might be given, note this is not an exhaustive list:**
> - The suggested answers are not exhaustive. Credit can be given for other relevant points presented.

Question 8

Auditor's communication with shareholders (ISA 200, 210, 260 (Revised), 265, 300, 580, 700 (Revised), 720 (Revised))

Syllabus sections 2, 3, 4, 5.

LO1, LO2, LO5

PQ Principles of Governance & Audit Paper Chs. 2, 5, 7, 8, 9, 11, 17, 18.

Students should provide their own answers but will likely mention and explore some of the following points:

- The present report explains the responsibilities of the directors and the auditors for the financial statements, explain the level of assurance that should be derived from the auditor's opinion and outlines the audit process.

- However, the report is long and complex and the auditor's opinion is not always easily seen or understood

- The outline of the audit process may provide an incorrect impression of the complexity and extent of (auditor) judgement involved.

- The standard language used in the auditor's report is legalistic and contains technical terms that are not (fully or not at all) defined (hence is not easily understood)

- The content of all audit reports is virtually the same, and as a result, financial statement readers may not read them (carefully) but assume they already know what it says. They may, therefore, miss something of importance.

- Little if any company specific information is provided. Company specific information is provided by the auditors to the company's directors – why not also to shareholders, at least why not to a larger extent?

- Instead of including information in the audit report about the directors' responsibility for the financial statements (all listed companies are required to do so in the company's annual report), provide only a reference in the audit report to the information provided in the annual report.

- Instead of including information in the audit report about the auditor's responsibility and the audit process, provide this information on the audit firm's website or in an appendix to the audit report or in a note in the company's annual report and cross-reference this from the audit report.

- Include company specific information in the audit report (for e.g. in the 'Other matters' paragraph – this could include information about the auditor's assessment of the company's risk exposures, disagreement between company and the auditors, etc.

- Candidates may consider the use of free-form rather than standardised wording (should give pros and cons).

EXAM ANSWER BANK

> **Additional areas where credit might be given, note this is not an exhaustive list:**
> - The suggested answers are not exhaustive. Credit can be given for other relevant points presented.

Question 9

Cablecard. Auditor's responsibilities relating to fraud in an audit of financial statements (ISA 200, 230, 240, 250 (Revised), 260 (Revised), 300, 315 (Revised), 320, 330, 500, 505, 520, 530, 540 (Revised), 550, 560, 580, 600, 700 (Revised))

Syllabus sections 2, 3, 4, 5, 6, 7.

LO2, LO3, LO4, LO5.

PQ Principles of Governance & Audit Paper Chs. Introduction, 1 - 18.

(a) (i) Candidates should outline the key responsibilities as stated in ISA 240, touching on issues which include, inter alia, the following:

- The primary responsibility for the prevention and detection of fraud resting with both those charged with governance of the entity and management.
- Responsibilities of the auditor for obtaining reasonable assurance that the financial statements are free from material misstatement whether due to error or fraud.
- Planning and performing the audit to obtain reasonable assurance about whether the financial statements are free of material misstatement due to fraud.
- Auditor undertaking risk assessment procedures and design in a manner that is not biased towards obtaining evidence that is corroborative only or exclude evidence that is contradictory (re managerial assertions or auditor assumptions).
- For group audit, discussion among the group engagement team about the susceptibility of a significant component to material misstatement of the financial information of that component due to fraud.
- Evaluation of Fraud Risk Factors.
- Written representations from management and those charged with governance that they acknowledge their responsibilities for the design, implementation, and maintenance of internal controls to prevent and detect fraud.
- Does the auditor's report explain to what extent the audit was considered capable of detecting irregularities, including fraud?

(ii) Any five of the following objectives (some might be grouped by candidates, which may require some flexibility when marking) and any appropriate test(s) for each, additional suggestions to be considered:

- Are sales authorised
- Have they been recorded at their correct amount?
- Have they been recorded in the correct account (are they sales of long-term assets?)
- Have they been recorded in the correct financial reporting period?
- Are the sales transactions those of the entity (are they valid?)
- Are any sales transactions missing (are they incomplete)?

- Discussion amongst the engagement team regarding the susceptibility of the client to fraud.
- Consider the risk of fraud when documenting and testing internal controls;
- Asking management how they: assess the risk of fraud; and identify and respond to the risks of fraud.
- Asking management whether they have any knowledge of actual or suspected frauds.
- Enquiring of internal audit whether they have any knowledge of actual or suspected frauds.
- Enquiring of those charged with governance how they exercise oversight of management's process for identifying and responding to the risk of fraud.
- Enquiring of those charged with governance whether they have any knowledge of actual or suspected frauds.
- Do these overseas partners actually exist?
- Is there sufficient evidence of the validity of the transactions that are claimed to have taken place and the amount thereof, given their importance to the group's income?

(b) This is a wide ranging question which allows/requires critical reflection and where candidates may reflect on and explore a wide range of issues which span from their interpretation of the auditor's responsibilities re fraud in the audit of financial statements (possibly going beyond purely technical interpretations), expectations (some might formally explore or note the expectations gap), common law interpretations (e.g. limitations with regard to whom the auditor is liable to, liability to particular parties, issues of auditor negligence, duty of care, potential value of a Bannerman clause), ethical considerations, the social role of audit, reputational impact on the audit partner and the firm from getting it wrong, and potentially contrasting this against business priorities of completing the audit in time and on budget, keeping the client on good terms, and gaining future business. Candidates may reflect on recent accounting/governance/audit scandals, regulators' audit quality reviews which found many audits wanting, weigh the internal investigation which provided a clean bill of health against the need for a critical internal investigation, a potential onus on conservative interpretation and processional scepticism, an enhanced internal review of procedures and processes and the audit trail by the lead partner and/or the audit manager, and/or the internal reviewer. Potential impact of a review by the regulator which might deem the firm's processes wanting. It is not expected or likely that candidates will touch on all of these issues, and the level of engagement will differ, but some engagement with some of these issues is expected.

(c) That "auditors have no responsibilities for detecting fraud, as primary responsibility for detecting fraud lies with the Directors and management of the entity" is a contentious statement. Technically, this might be deemed incorrect as ISA 240 (inter alia) outlines auditors' responsibilities relating to fraud in an audit of financial statements with reasonable clarity. However, this and other relevant ISAs are subject to interpretation and nuance in application, and hostage to circumstances, and underlying motives. Noting that an auditor has 'no' responsibilities might be considered incorrect in a strict sense, but this has not stopped some commentators and firm representatives from effectively or verbatim claiming this, even at quite high formal level. The public frequently has a different opinion as to auditors' responsibilities re corporate fraud, as do many formal inquiries into corporate scandals, albeit after the fact. Some academics are adamant of a crucial role of audit in the detection of corporate fraud. Issues of materiality may come in as well. At the end of the day, it is the courts that might need to decide on whether or not an auditor has done their job as expected by standards and laws, weighing interpretation, expectations, standards, and evidence against each other. Candidates will likely reference ISA 240, in reflection of their answer under point 1., but will be expected to expand on this to bring in their own critical interpretation of this standard, and may also reflect on recent cases of governance/accounting/audit failures (established or alleged), may reflect on audit quality reviews, may reflect on recent fines extended to audit firms, may reflect on the audit reform debate. Candidates may reflect on standards in addition to ISA 240, such as ISA 315 (Revised) *Identifying and Assessing the Risks of Material Misstatement*, and a raft more which touch on responsibilities of audit to provide a true and fair opinion on client financial statements, reflecting on issues of materiality, communication with those charged with governance, the audit committee, and wider stakeholders. Candidates may extend their reflection on the development of standards on auditor's responsibilities re fraud (for example on the revised ISA 240 and what may have prompted these revisions; for very eager students, reflection on SAS 82 and SAS 99; or that SAS 99 not only requires auditors to be reasonably sure that financial statements are free of material misstatements, whether caused by error or fraud, but that this standard provides a focused and clarified guidance on meeting their responsibilities to uncover fraud; comparing the need to document meeting their requirements as per ISA 240. A more general criticism of some standards may be that many procedures are suggested rather than required, and that the devil in the interpretation as to whether a standard was met lies in the detail. Again, it is not expected or likely that candidates will touch on all of these issues, and the level of engagement will differ, but some engagement with some of these issues is expected.

> **Additional areas where credit might be given, note this is not an exhaustive list:**
>
> - The suggested answers are not exhaustive. Credit can be given for other relevant points presented.

Question 10

Internal control and going concern (ISA 240, 260 (Revised), 265, 315 (Revised), 320, 570 (Revised)). This case study/scenario-based questions assesses the students' knowledge of the importance, components, and limitations of systems of internal control, and also their understanding of the importance of the going concern concept.

Syllabus sections 2, 3, 4, 5.

LO1, LO2, LO3, LO5.

PQ Principles of Governance & Audit Paper Chs. 4, 5, 6, 18.

(a)(1) (i,ii) Deficiency – only a limited number of authorised personnel should have access. Store raw material in an area where they can be safeguarded – e.g. in a locked room or fenced and gated area with access only gained by pass or inputting correct code (or similar).

(2) (i,ii) Deficiency – While it is a strength to have sequentially numbered receiving reports but these need to be **matched** with the goods order forms, and related credit notes, etc., before the invoice is cleared for payment. Unless this is done, there is no guarantee that the goods ordered were actually received.

(3) (i,ii) Deficiency – high probability of cash being lost. All cash received should be banked daily.

(4) (i,ii) Deficiency – leaves open the possibility of theft of cash received.

(5) (i,ii) Deficiency – if person handling the cash also records it, it opens the door to the theft of cash and covering the traces. Incompatible duties (handling and recording of assets/transactions) should be segregated.

(6) (i,ii) Not a deficiency (explanation required of why not). Not material.

(7) (i,ii) Deficiency – leaves open the possibility of someone stealing the cheque books and writing cheques for personal gain. Should be kept in a secure location (safe or similar).

(8) (i,ii) Not a deficiency (explanation required of why not). No conflict of interest/not an incompatible function/sales staff expected to know prices.

(b) An entity is a going concern if it is able to continue in business for the next financial reporting period (although there is an increasing emphasis on longer viability). Candidates may expand, for example mentioning the ability to realise assets and discharge debts in the ordinary course of business.)

The auditor is required to assess the propriety of the directors adopting the going concern basis for preparing the company's financial statements, inter alia, at following stages:

(i) During the preliminary stage of the audit – establish whether there are events or conditions that might cast doubt on the ability of the entity to continue as a going concern and establish whether the directors have conducted a going concern assessment (candidates should give examples of events and conditions that might cast doubt on the ability of the entity to continue as a going concern).

(ii) *During the evidence gathering stage – the auditor needs to evaluate the directors' going concern assessment – establish and evaluate the reasonableness of assumptions underlying the assessment, establish whether they have given due consideration to events and conditions that might cast doubt on the ability of the entity to continue as a going concern; consider the period for which they have considered the future viability of the company.*

(iv) In the completion and review stage – re-assess the propriety of the client adopting the going concern assumption in the light of the audit evidence collected and the understanding of the client and its prospects obtained as the audit has proceeded. Also, in applicable cases, evaluate management's plans for overcoming any financial challenges it is facing – what are the plans? Are the underlying assumptions reasonable? Are the plans feasible and, if so, are they likely to be effective? Is management likely to implement them successfully?

(v) In the reporting stage – the auditor must consider if the directors have adequately disclosed any uncertainties that may cast doubt on the ability of the company to continue as a going concern. In the case of a listed company, the directors must report risks and uncertainties the company faces, together with assumptions or qualifications as necessary, in their directors' report. *Other companies only need to make disclosures when there is some doubt about their status as a going concern.*

If the auditor considers the adoption of the going concern basis for preparing the financial statements is appropriate and uncertainties relating to the company's ability to continue as a going concern are properly disclosed, s/he should express an unqualified opinion. Where there are uncertainties, these should be highlighted in an Emphasis of Matter paragraph which should include reference to the note in the financial statements where relevant details are provided.

If the auditor considers adoption is appropriate but there is inadequate disclosure of information relating to uncertainties – a qualified opinion should be expressed.

If the auditor considers that the company is not a going concern but has prepared its financial statements on this basis, an adverse opinion should be expressed.

Additional areas where credit might be given, note this is not an exhaustive list:

- The suggested answers are not exhaustive. Credit can be given for other relevant points presented.

Question 11

Audit of current assets. This question is a scenario based case study assessing students' ability to analyse matters arising during an audit of current assets. They are asked to recommend actions with regard to identified matters, particularly as they pertain to accounts receivable, inventory and cash.

Syllabus sections 4, 5, 6, 7.

LO3, LO4, LO5.

PQ Principles of Governance & Audit Paper Chs. 8, 12, 13, 14, 15, 16.

(a) Request that the Finance Director increases the provision for doubtful debts by £6.5million – this is an adjustable subsequent event (IAS 37 *Provisions, Contingent Liabilities and Contingent Assets* – condition resulting in BigHotel's liquidation existed at year end). £6.5m is just over 8% of Goodnight Ltd's accounts receivable balance and would increase the provision for doubtful debts from £4.1m to £10.6m.

(b) Verify that the sale has been recorded in the relevant accounts receivable and sales accounts and has also been excluded from the inventory balance at the year end.

(c) Recount a selection of inventory counted by each employee to verify the accuracy of the count. If the count is found not to be accurate, request the company to conduct a further inventory count with the employees working in pairs. If taking inventory is considered impractical (as it would now be well beyond year-end), then it should definitely be an item in the letter of recommendation/ weaknesses and it will increase the risk assessment requiring more substantive testing of raw materials.

(d) Explain to the Finance Director that, in accordance with International Auditing Standards (ISA 505 *External Confirmations*), it is the external auditors, not the company's management, who are responsible for all aspects of external confirmation of receivables.

(e) Verify that the raw materials purchased for £1 million have been included in both the inventory and trade payables accounts.

> **Additional areas where credit might be given, note this is not an exhaustive list:**
> - The suggested answers are not exhaustive. Credit can be given for other relevant points presented.

Question 12

Auditor's communication with users of financial statements. The external auditor's report is the final step in the audit process and typically the auditor's only communication with the company's shareholders and other external parties interested in the reporting entity (ISA 200, 210, 260 (Revised), 265, 300, 580, 700 (Revised), 720 (Revised))

Syllabus sections 2, 3, 4, 5.

LO1, LO2, LO5

PQ Principles of Governance & Audit Paper Chs. 2, 5, 7, 8, 9, 11, 17, 18.

(a) Unqualified and unmodified opinion, and note compliance with the applicable financial reporting framework and relevant legislation.

(b) Unqualified opinion but modified with an emphasis of matter paragraph drawing attention to the contingent liability and referring to the relevant note in the financial statements.

(c) Modified – qualified "except for" opinion as a result of disagreement which is material but not pervasive – include an explanation of the value of the inventory the auditor deems appropriate and disclosing the net profit and total assets that would be shown if this value of inventory had been included in the financial statements.

(d) Limitation in scope however as it is immaterial it would not require a modification in the financial statements. Therefore unmodified – destroyed records are immaterial – two months records is $1/15\text{th}$ (6.7%) of the inventory.

(e) Unqualified opinion but with a modified report to include an 'Other matters' paragraph drawing attention to the inconsistency.

> **Additional areas where credit might be given, note this is not an exhaustive list:**
> - The suggested answers are not exhaustive. Credit can be given for other relevant points presented.

Question 13

Audit evidence and sampling as an auditing technique (ISA 200, ISA 530). This question assesses students abilities to explain the meaning, importance, type and appropriate use of audit evidence and sampling in audit.

Syllabus sections 2, 3, 4, 5.

LO3, LO4, LO5

PQ Principles of Governance & Audit Paper Chs. 1, 2, 5, 7, 8, 9, 11, 17, 18.

(a) Audit evidence is all the facts, observations, information, impressions, insights, etc., the auditor gains throughout the audit (ISA 500 *Audit Evidence*).

Sufficiency refers to the quantity of evidence the auditor collects.

Appropriate refers to the quality i.e.: the reliability and relevance of the evidence.

Reliability refers to how reliable the evidence is. This may depend on the source – personal knowledge of auditor (e.g. reperformance of an activity) – very reliable; from an external source (e.g. confirmations) – reliable, from an inside source (e.g. client's accounting records or answer to enquiry) – least reliable. There is a hierarchy of reliability.

Relevance refers to how well the evidence gathered answers the question (audit objective) (e.g. observing the inventory provides evidence of the existence and condition of the inventory, but not its ownership).

The more appropriate the evidence, the less the auditor needs to collect in order to form an opinion about the truth and fairness of the financial statements and their compliance (or otherwise) with the applicable financial reporting framework and the Companies Act 2006.

(b) Sampling is the examination of only a selection of items (sampling units) drawn from a defined mass of data (population), with view to inferring characteristics about the mass of data as a whole. In the modern business environment, and in large, complex audits, it is not economic nor feasible to examine the details of every transaction and account balance. Testing a sample of transactions is faster and less costly than testing the whole population and enables the audit to be completed within a reasonable time. Furthermore, auditors are required to form an opinion about the truth and fairness of the financial statements, a task that can usually be accomplished by testing relevant and appropriate samples of evidence; there, typically, is no need to test the whole population.

(c) Judgemental sampling refers to the use of sampling techniques in circumstances where the auditor relies on his or her own judgement to decide:

- on the sample size
- which items from the population to select
- whether to accept or not accept the population as reliable based on the results obtained from the sample units examined.

Statistical sampling refers to the use of sampling techniques which rely on probability theory to help determine:

- the sample size
- whether to accept or not accept the population as reliable based on the results obtained from the sample units examined.

When statistical sampling is used, sample units *must* be selected at random.

The use of statistical sampling requires large homogenous populations (and meeting certain other assumptions re: the population distribution). In an ideal world, statistical sampling allows each sampling unit to stand an equal chance of selection. The sampling units could be physical items, such as sales invoices or monetary units. Judgemental sampling is useful when the auditor wishes to examine particular elements of an account (e.g. large and 'old' accounts receivable balances) or particular source documents, for example copies of sales invoices issued during the period when the credit manager was away. The approach has been used for many years and is understood and refined by experience. Because of the sixth sense of some auditors, they can bring their expertise and judgment into play. No special knowledge of statistics is required.

Audit sampling might not be appropriate, hence judgemental sampling may be more appropriate, or actually be required, in situations, where:

- the auditor is put upon inquiry.
- the internal control procedures are weak and 100% audit testing is feasible.
- the transactions under review are non-recurring in nature and material.
- the items are unusual or extraordinary.
- the items are specially required to be disclosed in the financial statements by law or other professional requirements.
- the items within the class of transactions, assets, liabilities and owner equity items are few and are individually material.

Additional areas where credit might be given, note this is not an exhaustive list:
- The suggested answers are not exhaustive. Credit can be given for other relevant points presented.

Question 14

Internal controls (ISA 265, ISA 315 (Revised)). This question is a case scenario and assesses the students' understanding of the importance, components, and limitations of systems of internal control, the identification of internal control deficiencies and potential remedies, and relevant communication to client (MOU).

Syllabus sections 2, 3, 4, 5.

LO2, LO3, LO4, LO5

PQ Principles of Governance & Audit Paper Chs. 2, 5, 6, 7, 8, 9, 11, 17, 18.

(a) Students should note that the auditor must exercise professional judgement in deciding if deficiencies in internal control are of sufficient importance to merit the attention of those charged with governance. See paragraph 6 (b) of ISA 265 *Communicating Deficiencies in Internal Control to Those Charged With Governance and Management*. Paragraphs A5 to A11 of this ISA are those that deal with significant deficiencies in internal control, and paragraph A6 gives examples of matters that the auditor may consider in determining whether a deficiency or combination of deficiencies in internal control constitutes a significant deficiency:

- The likelihood of the deficiencies leading to material misstatements in the financial statements in the future.
- The susceptibility to loss or fraud of the related asset or liability.
- The subjectivity and complexity of determining estimated amounts
- The financial statement amounts exposed to the deficiencies.
- The volume of activity that has occurred or could occur in the account balance or class of transactions exposed to the deficiency or deficiencies.
- The importance of the controls to the financial reporting process. (The standard gives examples of such controls, including general monitoring controls; such as oversight of management, controls over significant transactions outside the entity's normal course of business, and controls over the period end financial reporting process).
- The cause and frequency of the exceptions detected as a result of the deficiencies in the controls.
- The interaction of the deficiency with other deficiencies in internal control.

As a staff auditor you should seek advice from peer members of your audit team and your audit manager. You may also consider discussing the situation with other professional colleagues, but you should not break client confidentiality requirements. You could seek advice as to what extent the internal control weaknesses are material and also advice on your ideas for presenting solutions for improvement of internal controls to the client. You may also wish to discuss with your audit manager what the impact of these weaknesses could be on the overall control environment and the planned audit procedures. You can consult with the previous audit files / previous auditor to identify if similar weaknesses were identified in earlier years, as this will give you an indication of management's integrity and regard for internal controls.

(b) Memorandum with a covering note to the company's management

> To: The Directors and Chair of the Audit Committee of Fab Fashions Ltd.
> From:
> Date:
> Subject: Deficiencies in Internal controls
>
> As you are aware we have recently completed our interim examination of the books and records of your company for the year ended 30 September 2022. As part of our examination, we reviewed and tested the company's systems of accounting and internal control. We did this to the extent we considered necessary to evaluate the systems with the objective of establishing the nature and extent of our audit procedures necessary to express an opinion on the truth and fairness of the financial statements at 30 September 2022. During our review and testing of the aforementioned systems, certain deficiencies in internal controls came to light which we believe are significant enough to be brought to your attention. We believe that this will assist you in your duty of safeguarding the assets of the company and of maintaining reliable accounting records for the preparation of financial statements required by law to give a true and fair view. We have discussed the internal control matters contained in this memorandum with your chief accountant, and they are in agreement with our comments unless otherwise stated. We would mention that none of the comments made below should be taken as questioning the integrity of any member of the staff of your company. Should you require more information about the matters in this memorandum, please do not hesitate to contact us.
>
> Yours truly,
>
> Partner

General

We note that your internal audit department is currently being used in a very restricted fashion in that it is only conducting regular inventory counts at the company's stores. We believe that you should reconsider its role, as a properly constituted internal audit function can be an excellent support to management and those charged with governance. We believe too that the overall audit function (external and internal) would be much strengthened as a result. We suggest that we discuss this matter further with you at a suitable time. A number of our recommendations will require more investment in systems and the appointment of additional staff. However, we believe that our recommendations would result in considerable cost savings and increased income over time.

Area	(i) Deficiency (1 mark per relevant point, maximum 3 marks)	(ii) Implication (1 mark per relevant point, maximum 3 marks)	(iii) Recommendation (1 mark per relevant point, maximum 3 marks)
Nature of business	(a) The business is in the fashion industry and inventory write downs have become necessary when the company misses a fashion trend.	This clearly results in lower profits than should have been the case.	The company should appoint competent staff in each country to assess likely fashion trends – and to exchange ideas about promotions. Their work should be co-ordinated by the sales director.

Area	(i) Deficiency (1 mark per relevant point, maximum 3 marks)	(ii) Implication (1 mark per relevant point, maximum 3 marks)	(iii) Recommendation (1 mark per relevant point, maximum 3 marks)
Ordering	(b) The just in time system is currently not providing goods when the company needs them. For instance, it came to our attention that it can take 4 weeks for goods ordered to be delivered (see point (d) below).	This means either that inventory levels in each store are higher than should be the case, or that the company loses customers because they have to wait for goods to be supplied.	For a just in time system to work properly there should be good communication links to suppliers so that they are ready to dispatch goods when they are needed. Suppliers almost become part of your organisation.
	(c) The purchasing manager (PM) orders goods without reference to the store and sales managers. He will not be as well-informed as to needs of the stores as those on the ground.	Goods may be received in stores that are not needed and may become unsaleable without price reductions because they have been over-ordered or of the wrong quality. Alternatively, goods needed may not be ordered, resulting again in loss of custom.	Communication lines should be established prior to inventory ordering between the PM and the store and sales managers who know the demands of the market.
	(d) The purchasing director only receives information about total quantities for each region.	There is insufficient detail for the director to assess whether the ordering decisions are valid.	The order quantities for product lines should be analysed for each store and country. A responsible official should discuss the figures with local purchasing managers, before passing them to the purchasing director for their agreement.
	(e) The store managers are not always aware of the length of time it takes for goods re-ordered to arrive.	Loss of custom and therefore turnover.	Minimum inventory levels should be established until such time as the just in time system has been improved. Some minimum inventory levels for more popular items should continue to be maintained even then.
	(f) Stores out of particular products cannot currently order them from stores, which have them. When a customer orders such goods they are asked to contact that other store themselves.	It is unlikely that the customer will take that action. More likely is that the customer will go to a competitor, resulting in lost custom. It is also possible that the goods in the other store are surplus to requirements in that store and may become unsaleable.	There should be a system for transferring goods from one store to another. It is also desirable that a system for identifying slow-moving inventories in stores on a timely basis be introduced.

Area	(i) **Deficiency** (1 mark per relevant point, maximum 3 marks)	(ii) **Implication** (1 mark per relevant point, maximum 3 marks)	(iii) **Recommendation** (1 mark per relevant point, maximum 3 marks)
Receiving goods	(g) Goods received are only checked against the supplier delivery note – and for quantities only – not quality.	Goods may be received that are not in accordance with company orders, either as regards quantities and quality. Suppliers may be unwilling to take back goods delivered in error.	Stores should be given copies of orders (prenumbered) and stores should check goods received for quantity and quality received against the order.
	(h) GRNs are prepared by sales assistants at the stores when they have time by reference to the suppliers delivery notes (SDNs). As SDNs are not numbered on receipt, there is no certainty that GRNs are prepared in each case. GRNs do not appear to be numbered consecutively.	GRNs are the source document for checking purchase invoices from suppliers. Sales assistants are responsible for selling and may not be properly trained to recognise the importance of accurate recording of goods received. Invoices may be paid for goods not received or for wrong quantities and qualities	A responsible official should be appointed at each store to receive goods and should compare SDNs with the pre-numbered orders. They should prepare GRNs in duplicate, containing store reference number, date of receipt, quantity, quality and order number. GRNs should be numbered consecutively. One copy should be sent to head office for checking to the supplier's invoice, when received.
	(i) Stores do not currently know if goods have been ordered and cannot therefore chase them up.	Sales may be lost and customer may not return.	Copies of orders should be sent to stores so they can follow up missing deliveries.
Matching of purchase invoices	(j) There is likely to be a very high volume of purchase transactions and manual checking of GRNs to invoices received is very time consuming.	Pressure on staff is likely to mean an inefficient checking process, leading to potential overpaying of invoices.	This process should be computerised. If details of orders and GRNs were entered into a purchases system, they could be easily identified by reference to order number on the face of the invoice. Unmatched orders and GRNs could be chased up.

Area	(i) Deficiency (1 mark per relevant point, maximum 3 marks)	(ii) Implication (1 mark per relevant point, maximum 3 marks)	(iii) Recommendation (1 mark per relevant point, maximum 3 marks)
	(k) There are delays in recording of purchase invoices because of (j) above and they are not recorded until the time consuming matching process is completed.	Delays may mean that invoices can be easily mislaid. This combined with the fact that orders and GRNs do not appear to be numbered means that purchases and trade payables may be understated at any point in time. This may result in bad relations with suppliers and may make it more difficult to determine unrecorded liabilities at period ends.	Invoices should be logged onto the system as soon as possible in an unmatched invoices file. After matching and passed by the purchase director, they should be recorded in the purchases and trade payable files. At the year end, the unmatched invoices file would be the basis for journal entries to determine outstanding liabilities.

Additional areas where credit might be given, note this is not an exhaustive list:

- The suggested answers are not exhaustive. Credit can be given for other relevant points presented.

Question 15

Planning. Pre-engagement procedures and initial stages of an audit engagement (ISA 200, 210, 220 (Revised), 240, 250 (Revised), 260 (Revised), 320, 450). This question is a case scenario and assesses the students' knowledge of factors to be considered by the auditor prior to accepting an audit engagement.

Syllabus sections 1, 2, 3, 4, 5.

LO1, LO2, LO3, LO4.

PQ Principles of Governance & Audit Paper Chs. 1, 4, 5, 6, 7.

(a) Provide possible reasons for a client to change its external auditor.

> A change in external auditor occurs when an organisation's external auditor resigns or is dismissed. The facts or circumstances surrounding the change may not always be public knowledge. Below are several examples for changing external auditors:
>
> - Client-service provider relationship – the perceived lack of attention received from the professional service provider in the form of not meeting deadlines, insufficient communication, unreturned telephone calls or not communicating problems
> - Perceived lack of industry knowledge by the service team
> - Lack of involvement from senior executives from professional service provider with the business entity
> - Change as a result of a merger or acquisition to have a uniform professional service provider for a group of companies

- High fees, an unexpected increase in fees or an inability to afford the fees for professional services
- Concern surrounding audit quality – the removal of an auditor due to an actual or perceived decline in the quality of audit services
- Changes due to statutory requirements for firm or partner rotation or the decision of the audit committee to rotate audit firms to safeguard independence.

The professional service provider may opt to resign for the following reasons:

- Risk profile of the business entity is no longer acceptable in terms of its professional firms' risk management policies
- The professional service providers' ethical independence requirements cannot be maintained by the firm or network of firms
- The fees generated from providing services to the client are not sufficient to cover the audit firm's risk exposure and/or costs.
- Other valid points

(1 mark per relevant point, 11 marks available – max 5 marks)

(b) Analyse the factors which the RBA engagement partner should consider when evaluating whether or not to accept SC Plc as an audit client.

- Since this is a listed client, has a suitable engagement quality review partner been appointed?
- Has the engagement leader met with the client's audit committee to discuss any independence/quality management concerns? (Note: elaborations on corporate governance requirements can be awarded marks)
- Have terms of engagement been completed and signed by the parties?
- Will any non-audit services be rendered which are precluded by regulation (such as SOX or the FRC or the local regulator)?
- Have the implications of mandatory audit firm rotation been considered?
- Other valid points e.g. ability to pay audit fees etc.

(c) Using the information in Working Paper A-100, provide 4 examples of business risks.

SC Plc faces the following business risks:

- Due to the nature of the business (waste disposal) there is a risk of material environmental damage/contamination. This could have reputational consequences for the company and affect its ability to engage with customers/other stakeholders.
- Similarly, the company may be subject to adverse media attention or public scrutiny if its environmental policies and practices are weak. This could have adverse reputational consequences.
- The company will probably be subject to numerous environmental laws and standards which increases the risk of non-compliance. This can result in operational delays, additional financial costs and worsening relationships with key stakeholders.
- Operations in multiple jurisdictions can result in supply and other logistical challenges.

- The company will need to deal with employees and stakeholders with different cultures, values etc.
- Liquidity problems and leveraging point to operational challenges and financial concerns (including cash-flow problems)
- Changing auditors could have an adverse impact on management's standing with key stakeholders.
- Any other valid business risks

(d) Using the information provided in Working Paper A-100, analyse the risk of material misstatement at the overall/financial statement level for SC Plc.

#	Risk	Analysis
1	**SC Plc is a New client (Recently employed)**	The client knows that the auditor is new and this will allow them to engage in fraudulent financial reporting if they are inclined to.
		SC Plc may not have applied accounting policies consistently as the client is aware that the auditor is new.
		Material misstatements in opening balances may go undetected, especially if access to the predecessor auditor is restricted.
2	**Tight deadline on the audit**	The auditor may be under pressure to complete the work on time and may not take **events after reporting date** into consideration (IAS 10 *Events after the Reporting Period*) which could increase the risk that errors are made.
		There is an increase in the risk that errors are made by SC Plc. in the preparation of the financial statements due to the tight deadline to finalise the financial statements.
		The tight audit deadline gives management the opportunity for fraudulent financial reporting as they are aware that the auditors are under pressure to test transactions and balances.
3	**Listed on the FSE**	The Annual Financial Statements might be materially misstated as the company might not comply with the FSE Requirements resulting in the delisting of the company and affecting the company's ability to continue as a going concern.
		Management may manipulate financial statements to meet stakeholder expectations.
		There may be going concern issues due to non-compliance with the FSE listing requirements, poor stakeholder relationships and the allegations of fraud and corruption against the CFO.
4	**Directors are aggressive/ management lack integrity**	There is possible manipulation of financial statements (fraud) as management might want to manipulate the financial statements to ensure that more financing can be obtained from the banks to finance any further expansions of the group.
5	**Management style (autocratic)**	Management appears to have an autocratic management style, increasing the risk that the financial statements might be manipulated to meet expectations of the group as well as shareholders. This is evidenced by the fact that Tom Bull is running the company with an "iron fist", which increases the propensity to override controls (increases control risk).

		There is an increased risk that management might be bypassing controls which would give them an opportunity for fraudulent financial reporting. This is especially true if the CEO and the CFO (being husband and wife) collude.
6	Group structure (parent/ subsidiary relationship)	Intercompany balances may not be eliminated, or errors may occur in the consolidation process, which may result in non-compliance with IFRS.
		Risk of incorrect accounting treatment such as:
		IFRS 10 *Consolidated Financial Statements* requirements for determining control might be applied incorrectly due to the complex nature of the changes and board structures in the group.
		There is an increased risk that divisions might be accounted for as subsidiaries, or subsidiaries accounted for as divisions, which would lead to a misstatement at the overall group financial statement level.
		Incorrect accounting for or elimination of inter-group balances and transactions.
		There is a risk of fraudulent financial reporting because the complex group structure provides an opportunity for management to use intercompany transactions (or subsidiaries) to conceal fraud and to manipulate the results reported.
7	Fraud / Bribery	Financial statements might be misstated to hide fraud/bribes, given the various locations where operations are located.
		The risk that the opening balances are misstated is high due to the alleged fraud reported in the previous year. This is evidenced by the discussions held with the previous auditor.
8	Operations in regions or countries with strict regulations/ different regulations	The annual financial statements may be materially misstated as the entity might not comply with the relevant laws and regulations in Freedonia or other countries in which it operates (e.g. India). This could lead to unrecorded liabilities and fines.
9	Going concern	The company is struggling to pay debts and is struggling to obtain financing, increasing the risk that the going concern basis for accounting might be inappropriate.
		There is a possibility of the company not being a going concern, as bribes (an illegal act) have to be paid to obtain/maintain licenses in various jurisdictions.
10	Non-compliance with laws and regulations	There is a risk that the company is not complying with the relevant laws and regulations related to the waste disposal legislation that can affect the financial statements. For example, provision for environmental rehabilitation and legislative requirements with regards to the disclosure.
		There have been instances of non-compliance with the Companies Act (the long tenure of the auditor), indicating that the company has a weak control environment as it relates to laws and regulations (control risk).

11	Weak governance structure in the company	The CEO and the CFO are married, which can lead to governance compliance issues as there would not be appropriate oversight
		The company has had the same auditor for an extended period indicating the company is not complying with best governance practices.
		As explained above, management's autocratic style may result in an override of controls.
12	Rapid expansion	The company is currently expanding at an increased rate, increasing the risk that not all expansion costs are correctly treated and classified, which could affect multiple line items and disclosures in the company resulting in errors in the financial statements
13	Related parties	There may be various related party transactions that are taking place in the group and these transactions stand the risk of not being at arm's length or being disclosed per IAS 24 *Related Party Disclosures*, increasing the risk of material misstatements due to management having the opportunity to use these transactions to perpetrate fraud

(e) Determine (using appropriate examples) two fundamental principles of ethical behaviour.

Fundamental principle	Requirement	Example
Integrity	• A professional accountant should be straightforward and honest in all professional and business relationships. • The accountant must be truthful and not knowingly be associated with reports, returns, communications or other information which (1) contains false information; (2) contains statements or information provided recklessly or (3) omits or obscures required information where such omission or obscurity will be misleading.	• Any reasonable example
Objectivity	• A professional accountant should not allow bias, conflict of interest or the undue influence of others to compromise professional or business judgements.	• Any reasonable example
Professional competence and due care	• A professional accountant has a duty to maintain professional knowledge and skill at the level required to ensure that a client or employing organisation receives appropriate competent services based on current legislation, standards and legislation. • This will require the professional accountant to take reasonable steps to ensure that those working in a professional capacity under their authority have appropriate training and supervision. • A professional accountant is not permitted to continue with an engagement which they are not competent to perform unless advice and assistance are obtained to ensure that the applicable service is carried out satisfactorily.	• Any reasonable example

EXAM ANSWER BANK

Fundamental principle	Requirement	Example
Confidentiality	• A professional accountant should not disclose confidential information acquired as a result of his professional or business relationships unless there is a legal or professional right or duty to disclose such information. • Confidential information should not be used for the personal advantage of the professional or third parties. • The professional accountant will take steps to ensure that the confidentiality of the information is maintained.	• Any reasonable example
Professional behaviour	• In addition to complying with the relevant laws and regulations, a professional accountant should avoid any action which discredits the profession.	• Any reasonable example

Additional areas where credit might be given, note this is not an exhaustive list:

- The suggested answers are not exhaustive. Credit can be given for other relevant points presented.

Question 16

Case Study: Execution. This question is a scenario based case study assessing students' ability to analyse matters arising during an audit of current assets. They are asked to recommend actions with regard to identified matters.

Syllabus sections 3, 4, 5, 6, 7.

LO3, LO4, LO5.

PQ Principles of Governance & Audit Paper Chs. 8, 9, 12, 13, 14, 15, 16.

(a) Determine 5 possible controls which Pepper Ltd can implement to limit duplicate creditor balances.

To avoid duplicate creditor contracts from being recognised and loaded it is important that only reputable creditors are contracted with by Pepper. On applying for a contract, creditors, can be required to submit, for example:

- Draft financial statements/audited financial statements
- Proof of valid name changes to identify whether the creditor is already on the system
- Evidence of company registration (if no financials are available) to confirm registration numbers
- Company tax numbers to confirm the validity of tax claims as well as registration for sales tax purposes

To avoid duplicate creditor contracts the financial manager can perform month on month comparisons to identify potential duplicate creditors and requests these be removed from the approved supplier list.

Creditors can be sequentially numbered based on tax numbers to prevent duplicate numbers on the system.

Creditor invoices must be matched against purchase orders and goods/services received notes to prevent duplicate recognition of invoices.

The creditor reconciliations should be reviewed for duplicate invoices on statements to prevent recognition of duplicate amounts or unreconciled balances.

Purchase orders should be flagged as closed on the system once goods/services have been received to avoid duplicate orders.

(b) (i) Prepare a schedule of substantive procedures which can be performed on the completeness of trade creditors:

Obtain a schedule of the total trade creditors balance for the current period.
- Cast and cross-cast the schedule
- Agree the totals to the amount per the trial balance and Pepper's financial statements

Compare the current period's approved suppliers list to the prior period list to:
- Identify any missing creditors from the prior period
- Identify any creditors with a Nil balance in the current period and a balance in the prior period.

Enquire of management why there have been creditors removed in the current period to determine if there is a reason for any missing or nil balances and agree to the email communication requesting their removal.

Inspect a sample of creditor contracts for the signatures of the creditors, key terms and evidence of any amendments which would give rise to penalties or additional costs.

For a sample of purchases/expenses in the current period:
- agree the amount per the ledger to the amount per the invoice (accuracy; completeness).
- inspect the goods received note and agree it to the amount per the invoice (occurrence, accuracy, completeness).
- inspect the goods received note for the signature of the creditor.

For a sample of payments post year end trace the amount to the invoice to confirm the liability is recorded in the correct period.

Select a sample of expense invoices from 5 days before and after the end of the financial year:
- Inspect the purchase order to confirm it has been matched to the goods received/services rendered note and the associated liability recorded in the correct period.

Perform an analytical procedure on the balance per creditor and in total. For example:
- Total creditor days per creditor against credit terms per the contract agreement
- Compare current period balance per creditor with the prior period and month-on-month to identify unusual trends

Inspect media releases and minutes of meetings to identify any potential liabilities or contingencies which need to be recorded/disclosed in the financial statements

(ii) Prepare a schedule of substantive procedures which can be performed on the disclosure of trade creditors:

> Obtain the draft financial statements of Pepper and the accounting policy for trade creditors and
> - Compare to the prior period financials to identify any changes in disclosure
> - Agree the totals on the face of the statement of financial position to Pepper's trial balance
> - Agree the opening balance to the prior period financial statements
>
> Enquire with management whether there have been any changes in the accounting policies for accounts payable in the current period and if these have been disclosed in terms of IAS 8 *Accounting Policies, Changes in Accounting Estimates and Errors*.
>
> Inspect the disclosure checklist for any relevant changes in the accounting disclosure.
>
> Inspect the trade creditors for any debit balances and follow up with management on any material disclosure/amounts to be reclassified.

(c) Advise on the difference between a control deficiency and a misstatement.

> A control deficiency may increase the risk of the financial statements being materially misstated but is not the same as an identified misstatement.
>
> Per ISA 265 (para 7) *Communicating Deficiencies in Internal Control to Those Charged With Governance and Management*, a deficiency in internal control exists when:
> - Control is designed, implemented or operated in such a way that it is unable to prevent, or detect and correct, misstatements in the financial statements on a timely basis or
> - A control necessary to prevent, or detect and correct, misstatements in the financial statements on a timely basis is missing.
>
> In terms of ISA 450 *Evaluation of Misstatements Identified During the Audit*, a misstatement is a difference between the amount reported, classified, presented or disclosed per the financial statements and the applicable financial reporting framework (IFRS).
>
> As a result, misstatements have a direct and quantifiable effect on a client's financial statements while the implications of a control deficiency can be understood as being indirect.

> **Additional areas where credit might be given, note this is not an exhaustive list:**
> - The suggested answers are not exhaustive. Credit can be given for other relevant points presented.

Question 17

Case study: Audit evidence and ethics. This question is a scenario based case study assessing students' ability to analyse matters arising during an audit specifically re accounts receivable balances, repercussions from extended outstanding debts, and to identify ethical considerations arising from potential conflict of interest and familiarity. They are asked to recommend actions with regard to identified matters.

Syllabus sections 1, 2, 3, 4, 5.

LO1, LO3, LO4, LO5.

PQ Principles of Governance & Audit Paper Chs. 4, 8, 9, 12, 13, 14, 15, 16.

(a) The memo should be correctly formatted, addressed and dated with ownership and purpose stated. Contents could include:

(i) General audit work:

- Agree materiality for this area of work.
- Seek balance confirmations for all customers with >90 days debts.
- Find out why only the balance for Alsace is insured.
- Complete analytical review of overall accounts receivable balance and its ageing.
- Test ageing report with a sample of invoices.
- Check cash received post year end for all material >90 days balances.
- Calculate a provision for doubtful debts and check that any differences with the provision calculated by the client are not material if they raise an audit adjustment journal.
- Consider any suggestions to be made to the client to improve the controls in this area.

(ii) Specific work on individual balances, where material:

Evenbetter: Verify that cash was received as anticipated, verify that this cash relates to the >90 days receivable balance through a review of the remittance advice received with the payment.

Bale: Verify that the contra accounts payables balance exists and check that there are no terms of trade with would prohibit a contract (contact Bale, review terms of trade and contract).

Out: Check that the debt collection contract has been completed and check for onerous terms. Check that the debt has been collected and that a suitable provision for collection costs was established at year end. If the collection has not occurred, calculate an appropriate provision.

In: Review assurances received and come to an opinion on to what extent we can rely upon this.

Alsace: Review the relevant insurance agreement. Check that it is currently in operation and check that the terms allow for the recovery of this debt and that all relevant terms have been complied with by the company.

Other small balances: Review for material balances and determine if any should be written off and if so identify the relevant audit adjustment journal.

(b) Areas which should be considered in accordance with ethical standards, including various areas of potential threat to auditor independence:

- Interim credit controller appointment: Assess the level of involvement of audit firm staff, e.g. would the staff member be posting journals or assuming any management work – **self-review threat,** strictly separate roles from audit team.
- Ensure appropriate letters of engagement are in place and any staff providing accounting services are not involved in audit work due to potential **self-review threat.** Ensure that audit staff providing accounting services have not previously involved in audit work with this client.
- There is a possibility of **familiarity threat** from the staff member who recently left to take up a consulting position at Allgood. If the role is substantive it is not relevant that this position

is a consulting position rather than a permanent position. Ensure that audit staff on the engagement this year have not previously worked closely with this ex-employee.

- The unpaid audit fee could be perceived as a loan to the company and could threaten perceived independence. **Self-interest threat.** Ensure this is paid before audit work on the year end commences.

> **Additional areas where credit might be given, note this is not an exhaustive list:**
> - The suggested answers are not exhaustive. Credit can be given for other relevant points presented.

Question 18

Audit Risk. This question assesses students' ability to analyse issues related to materiality, setting appropriate materiality levels and to distinguish between components of audit risk directly controllable by the auditor vs those not directly controllable. They are asked to recommend actions with regard to identified matters and support their answers with explanations and elaboration, as appropriate.

Syllabus sections 2, 3, 4, 5, 6.

LO1, LO3, LO4, LO5.

PQ Principles of Governance & Audit Paper Chs. 1, 3, 4, 7, 8, 9, 17, 18.

(a) (i) An item is said to be **material** if its presence or absence, its accuracy or inaccuracy is likely to affect the decisions or actions of a reasonable user of the financial statements. The size or nature of an item can cause it to be material (some explanation of the latter point is needed – e.g. if the item is required to be disclosed by law, it must be disclosed irrespective of size; its absence will always be material).

(ii) **Planning materiality** – the maximum amount of error the auditor will accept in the financial statements as a whole while still concluding that they are true and fair (determination follows below).

Tolerable error – maximum amount of error auditor will accept in a class of transactions, account balance, or financial statement disclosure and still conclude it is not materially misstated.

(iii) **Setting planning (overall) materiality:**

(1) Selecting one or more appropriate benchmark(s) (e.g. profit before tax, total sales, total assets, total shareholder funds);

(2) Identifying appropriate financial data for the selected benchmark(s); problem is, setting materiality levels is done part way through the financial year, and therefore, end of year data are not available. Can use figures from prior year, or budgeted figures, or figures extrapolated from year to date, etc.;

(3) Determining a percentage to be applied to the selected benchmark(s). This is a matter of professional judgement, but will vary according to the benchmark selected (e.g. 1% of sales; 1.5% of total assets, 5% of shareholders' funds).

Setting tolerable error:

For each account, the starting point is ~50-75% of planning materiality. This will then be adjusted depending on the type of account and its likelihood of misstatement (candidates are expected to explain the factors which result in accounts like cash having a tolerable

error of 50% or less of planning materiality and provision for doubtful debts having a tolerable error closer to 75% or planning materiality). Some mention is needed of the impact of legally required disclosures, or items in which the financial statement users have a particular interest, which result in a very low tolerable error (zero in the case of legally required disclosure that may be absent).

(b) Candidates should convey the ideas outlined below, but some explanation and elaboration of the components shown below is required to obtain full marks.

(i) Controllable risk: Risk of failing to detect material misstatement (Sampling risk, Quality management risk)

(ii) Non-controllable risk: Risk of material misstatement occurring (Inherent risk [management integrity, account risk, business risk]); Internal control risk.

> **Additional areas where credit might be given, note this is not an exhaustive list:**
> - The suggested answers are not exhaustive. Credit can be given for other relevant points presented.

Question 19

Case study: BlockRon Ltd – Planning. This question is a scenario based case study assessing students' ability to analyse issues arising in the planning stage, specifically to identify issues which may indicate increased risk(s) of material misstatement after review of working papers, outline an appropriate audit approach, and analyse the nature, timing and extent of the audit procedures to be performed over revenue.

Syllabus sections 1, 2, 3, 4, 5.

L01, L02, L03.

PQ Principles of Governance & Audit Paper Chs. 1, 2, 3, 5, 6, 7, 8, 9, 17.

(a) With reference to working paper PLN-01, identify and analyse the risk of material misstatement at the overall/financial statement and assertion-level. Indicate clearly if each risk is at the overall/financial statement or assertion-level.

Issue	Overall (O) or assertion-level (A)	Explanation of risk
The company is listed on the FSE	O	This can increase the risk of non-compliance with regulatory requirements, listing provisions and applicable governance prescriptions. Management also has the incentive to overstate assets/incomes to meet earnings targets/outperform prior period results/achieve a higher share price.
There is a tight audit deadline	O	This increases the risk of material misstatement due to fraud as the management of BlockRon could use this as an opportunity to misstate financial results because they know AAA will not have time to test everything.

Issue	Overall (O) or assertion-level (A)	Explanation of risk
Mr Santoro and Mr Bong both hold significant equity interests in the company.	O	This can add to the incentive to misstate financial results to achieve targeted share prices for their benefit.
Lack of appropriate skills and experience on the Board of Directors	O	The CEO had a career in acting, the CIO is a part-time waitress and the FM has a PhD in palaeontology. The lack of financial expertise and business experience on the Board of Directors could lead to an increase in the risk of material misstatement due to error because the Board is incompetent.
All of the members on the Board of Directors are best friends, and two of the members are siblings	O	The friends spend a lot of time together outside of business hours. In addition, Monica Greenstein is the sister of Peter Greenstein, which means that she is not an independent director as it is stated. This could result in an increased risk of collusion, override of controls or weaknesses in the overall control environment.
BlockRon has experienced rapid growth	O	BlockRon is expanding rapidly which increases the risk of material misstatement that the controls are not adapting or expanding at the same rate as the company is growing resulting in material misstatements not being detected, prevented or corrected.
Accounting for intangible assets under IAS 28 *Investments in Associates and Joint Ventures* is complex	A	Complex accounting increases the risk of non-compliance with or misapplication of IFRS. The patents and copyrights might be amortized over the incorrect useful life/over an indefinite useful life incorrectly (valuation, accuracy). Research costs might incorrectly be capitalised to the carrying value of intangible assets (valuation, accuracy, classification) There is an increased risk of undetected fraud when transactions are unusual or complex
Management performance bonuses are based on the annual amount of joining fees earned, as well as the number of subscription renewals	A	Management has an incentive to overstate joining fee sales to earn performance bonuses (occurrence). This increases the risk of fraudulent reporting and override of controls.

Issue	Overall (O) or assertion-level (A)	Explanation of risk
Management integrity is questionable	O	Mr Santoro is closely involved in determining his remuneration. He could use this as an opportunity for personal gain.
		In addition, the Board is composed of majority non-executive directors (most of whom should be independent), nor is it composed of the appropriate mix of skill and diversity. This increases the risk of material misstatement due to fraud.

(b) Determine what is meant by an "audit approach" and explain the relationship that exists between the various components of an audit approach

The audit strategy and audit plan when combined, make up the audit approach.

The audit plan is more detailed than the overall audit strategy.

Audit strategy

The audit strategy deals with the nature, timing and extent of audit procedures at the overall financial statement level.

The auditor must establish an overall audit strategy that will set the scope, timing and direction of the audit and guide the development of the audit plan.

Audit plan

The audit strategy deals with the nature, timing and extent of audit procedures at the financial statement line item level.

The auditor's assessment of the identified risks at the assertion level provides a basis for considering the appropriate audit approach (combined audit approach or substantive audit approach) for designing and performing further audit procedures (ISA 330 *The Auditor's Responses to Assessed Risks*, par A4).

A combined approach entails a combination of tests of controls and substantive procedures.

A substantive approach entails both tests of detail and substantive analytical procedures.

The audit plan occurs once the risks of material misstatement at the overall and assertion level have been developed and the materiality is set.

It is the plan the auditor will follow to obtain sufficient and appropriate audit evidence.

The auditor needs to assess whether audit evidence should take the form of a test of controls and substantive tests or substantive tests only.

Alternative

Audit approach (AA) = audit strategy (AS) + audit plan (AP)
AS – Nature, timing and extent at the overall financial statement level
AP – Nature, timing and extent at the assertion level

(c) With reference to working paper REV-01, analyse the nature, timing and extent of the audit procedures to be performed over revenue. Your answer must NOT include any substantive procedures or tests of controls.

The accounting process is complicated because there are different streams of revenue (joining fee, annual fee and merchandise). The joining revenue is recognised at a point in time, whereas the annual fee is recognised over time. This increases the inherent risk of errors.

According to ISA 240 *The Auditor's Responsibilities Relating to Fraud in an Audit of Financial Statements*, there is a rebuttable presumption that revenue is susceptible to fraud. There is no evidence that this presumption can be rebutted for BlockRon, and so revenue has an increased inherent risk of fraud and is a significant risk.

Nature of testing

The necessity to rely on controls

The accounting system operates automatically on the e-Portal system. Revenue transactions are therefore highly automated, which increases the necessity to rely on application controls due to such automation.

There are more than 1 million subscribers to the BlockRon channel, and a large volume of merchandise sold. As such, there is a large volume of transactions that occur, increasing the necessity to rely on controls.

This is because high volumes of transactions cannot be tested substantively without causing a significant constraint on AAA's resources.

ATTS can be made use of to substantively test a greater sample of the population, however.

The need to rely on controls is based on the fact that performing substantive tests over the revenue transactions may not be sufficient and effective, as this would place strain on the resources AAA has available.

Due to a large number of transactions and the integrated online e-Portal system, there will be limited input documentation available to perform substantive tests over. This further increases the need to rely on controls.

Due to the above, it would be necessary to rely on the controls with regard to revenue.

Possibility to rely on controls

The e-Portal was created using a widely available online accounting package. This implies that AAA has the necessary IT Audit software, making it possible to test automated controls.

As the automated e-Portal system appears to have controls at regular intervals there is the possibility to rely on controls.

Desirability to rely on controls

To test controls would be cost-effective and beneficial as testing controls is generally quicker to perform, decreasing pressure on the AAA audit team.

Furthermore, through testing controls the audit team can make recommendations over BlockRon's revenue cycle based upon risks that might have been identified, increasing the value added by the audit service.

As there is a tight audit deadline, it would also be beneficial to perform tests of controls to reduce pressure on the AAA engagement team to adhere to the deadline, reducing detection risk.

Conclusion

Based on the above, AAA can follow a combined approach to gain sufficient and appropriate audit evidence over revenue.

Such an approach is a combination of tests of controls and substantive procedures.

There are no controls over cut-off, and as a result, the substantive-based approach should be used to test cut-off of BlockRon's revenue.

Timing of testing

The substantive tests related to cut-off will attract larger sample sizes because no controls can be relied upon.

In terms of timing of the audit procedures, cut-off can only be tested post-financial year-end, and no roll forward testing can be performed. Therefore this large sample size will have to be tested at the financial year-end.

As a result of the above, the implication is that the testing over the remaining assertions should be performed at an interim period and the revenue amount rolled forward to financial year-end due to the tight audit deadline.

This will ensure that sufficient time is provided to obtain sufficient and appropriate audit evidence, reducing the detection risk.

Extent of testing

As controls over completeness, occurrence, accuracy and classification can be relied upon; this reduces the substantive sample sizes for the tests of details with regard to these assertions.

> **Additional areas where credit might be given, note this is not an exhaustive list:**
> - The suggested answers are not exhaustive. Credit can be given for other relevant points presented.

Question 20

Case - BlockRon Ltd – Completion. This question is a scenario based case study assessing students' ability to identify audit opinions which an auditor can provide and the circumstances in which each would be appropriate (after review of relevant information), and to identify and name case specific issues which may necessitate modification during the completion phase.

Syllabus sections 2, 3, 4, 5, 6, 7.

LO3, LO4, LO5.

PQ Principles of Governance & Audit Paper Chs. 1, 2, 3, 5, 8, 9, 11, 17, 18.

(a) Explain the difference between a qualified audit opinion, a disclaimed audit opinion and an adverse audit opinion.

A qualified opinion is issued when the auditor has obtained sufficient appropriate audit evidence, concludes that misstatements, individually or in the aggregate, are material, but not pervasive, to the financial statements or the auditor is unable to obtain sufficient appropriate audit evidence on which to base the opinion, but the auditor concludes that the possible effects on the financial statements of undetected misstatements, if any, could be material but not pervasive.

A disclaimed audit opinion is issued when the auditor is unable to obtain sufficient appropriate audit evidence on which to base the opinion, and the auditor concludes that the possible effects on the financial statements of undetected misstatements, if any, could be both material and pervasive.

An adverse opinion is issued when the auditor, having obtained sufficient appropriate audit evidence, concludes that misstatements, individually or in the aggregate, are both material and pervasive to the financial statements.

Respond to the email sent by the Audit Manager using **WP – 027**. Your answer should include the following: A schedule of unadjusted differences which shows the proposed correcting entries and the effect on the audit client's assets, liabilities, equity and profit or loss

(b) (i) Schedule of unadjusted differences.

Issue No.	Type of Misstatement	Correcting journal entry	Assets	Liabilities	Equity	Profit/ loss
1	Factual	Dr. Intangible Asset (SOFP) FM120,000 Cr. Profit or Loss (P/L) FM120,000	+120,000			120,000
2	Judgmental	Dr. Provision for Bad Debts Expense (P/L) FM110,000 Cr. Provision for Bad Debts (SOFP) FM110,000	-110,000			-110,000
3	Factual but see next column	Immaterial				
4	Factual	Dr. Profit or Loss (P/L) FM300,000 Cr. Intangible Asset (SOFP) FM300,000	-300,000			-300,000
		Dr. Intangible Asset (SOFP) FM12,000 Cr. Profit or Loss (P/L) FM12,000	+12,000			+12,000
5	Factual	Dr. Prepaid Expense (SOFP) FM40,000 Cr. Profit or Loss (P/L) FM40,000	+40,000			+40,000
Total			-238,000			-238,000

(ii) Analyse the issues and conclude on the effect on the audit report

Issue 1:

This is a factual misstatement as the Intangible asset should be amortised over the correct useful life of 24 months and not 12 months as per IAS 38 *Intangible Assets*.

The difference due to error is FM120,000 which is above the materiality amount of FM100,000 and is therefore quantitatively material.

The error is not qualitatively material because it is not a result of fraud or gross misapplication of IFRS – it was a once-off error.

Issue 2:

This is a judgemental misstatement as there is a difference in the auditor's estimate of the provision for bad debts amount and management's estimate of the provision.

The value of the misstatement is FM110,000 and is quantitatively material as it is above the materiality level of FM100,000.

Justification for qualitatively material.

Issue 3:

This is a factual misstatement as the amount has been incorrectly recorded from the amount stipulated in the invoice.

The difference of FM72 is not quantitatively material as it does not exceed the materiality level of FM100,000. Does not/will not appear on the schedule of unadjusted misstatements as it is below the clearly trivial threshold of FM5,000.

The amount is not qualitatively material either as it is a transcribing error and is not as a result of fraudulent conduct.

Issue 4:

This is a factual misstatement as the research costs should have been expensed and not capitalised as an intangible asset as per IAS 38 *Intangible Assets*.

The amount is quantitatively material as the FM300,000 exceeds the materiality threshold of FM100,000.

Quantitatively material justified.

Issue 5:

This is a factual misstatement because only the portion of the insurance premium consumed in the current financial year should have been expensed as per the accrual basis of accounting in terms of the Conceptual Framework.

The difference of FM40,000 is not quantitatively material as is below the materiality level of FM100,000. The difference will not appear on the schedule

The amount is also not qualitatively material as it does not appear to be a result of fraudulent conduct.

Overall

If the errors are material, then the auditor will only be able to issue a clean audit report if the client adjusts the financial statements. If no adjustment is made, the auditor will need to modify the audit report.

In total, the errors are quantitatively material as the accumulated adjustment required is greater than the materiality level. Several of the errors are also individually material as explained above.

Corresponding adjustments may be required for current or deferred tax depending on the resulting tax implications.

The following matrix, reproduced from Büchling et al. (2019), indicates the type of opinions which an auditor can provide and the circumstances in which each would be appropriate.

Table 1: Modification to the audit opinion

Nature of matter giving rise to the modification	Auditor's judgement about the pervasiveness of the effects or possible effects on the financial statements	
	Material but not pervasive	**Material and pervasive**
Financial statements are materially misstated	Qualified	Adverse
Inability to obtain sufficient appropriate audit evidence	Qualified	Disclaimer

Reference: Büchling, M, Cerbone, D, Kok, M, Maroun, M, Marques, G, Segal, T (2019). ASSURANCE, RISK AND GOVERNANCE: AN INTERNATIONAL PERSPECTIVE. Juta & Company Ltd.

> **Additional areas where credit might be given, note this is not an exhaustive list:**
> - The suggested answers are not exhaustive. Credit can be given for other relevant points presented.

Question 21

Self-regulation. This question assesses the students' knowledge of the statutory and regulatory framework governing or regulating the audits of public companies' financial statements in the United Kingdom.

Syllabus sections 1, 2, 5, 6.

LO1, LO3, LO4.

PQ Principles of Governance & Audit Paper Chs. 1, 2, 3, 4.

(a) **The Companies Act 2006**

The Companies Act 2006 provides the administrative framework for company audits. It specifies:

- which companies must have an audit.
- who may be the auditor of a company (including the requirement to be a registered auditor).
- how auditors are appointed.
- how their fees are set.
- how they can resign or be replaced or removed.
- their statutory duties.
- their rights.
- the directors' responsibility to include in their directors' report a statement that they have each provided the auditor with all relevant information.

(b) **Common (or case) law**

Common law determines the required standard of auditors' performance.

- general standard set out in *Re Kingston Cotton Mill* case.
- what amounts to reasonable skill, care and caution varies as changes occur in the social, economic and technological environment.
- other cases have highlighted what is required when auditors perform various aspects of an audit (e.g. *Leeds Estate Building and Investment Co.* v *Shepherd*; *Re London and General Bank* case, *London Oil Storage* case, *Arthur E Green*, *McKesson Robbins*.... Citing one or two as illustrative examples).
- some cases bring together findings of previous cases and outline what is expected of auditors in the performance of their duties at that time – eg, *Pacific Acceptance* case (a couple of points made in the case may be used as examples).

(c) **Regulations and Standards – in particular, Auditing and Ethical Standards and the Corporate Governance Code (UK).**

Auditing Standards specify details of what is required of auditors during the acceptance, planning, performance and completion stages of an audit and when forming and expressing an opinion on the audited financial statements (citing examples of the Standards to illustrate the point).

Ethical Standards – the FRC's Ethical Standard for Auditors (*Revised Ethical Standard 2024*) provides details of what is required of auditors in respect of maintaining their objectivity and independence. International Ethical Standards (e.g. those of AIA, ACCA, AICPA-CIMA, FASB and IFAC's International Ethics Standards Board for Accountants 'INTERNATIONAL CODE OF ETHICS FOR PROFESSIONAL ACCOUNTANTS (Including International Independence Standards), 2023') and the profession's Code of Ethics provide details of what is required of auditors in respect of their independence, objectivity, professional competence and due care, confidentiality and professional conduct.

The Corporate Governance Code (UK) requires public companies to provide, in their annual reports, a statement of their compliance with the Code's provisions. Auditors are required to review their public company auditees' statement in so far as it relates to the Code's accountability and audit provisions. The auditors are required to report any instance where the company reports it has complied with one or more of these provisions and it has not done so or the reasons given for its non-compliance are not fully and properly disclosed.

> **Additional areas where credit might be given, note this is not an exhaustive list:**
> - The suggested answers are not exhaustive. Credit can be given for other relevant points presented.

Question 22

Overall objective of the independent auditor. This question assesses the students' knowledge of the overall objective of the independent auditor, with focus on evidence, compliance and substantive procedures, and understanding client, industry, business and operations.

Syllabus sections 1, 3, 4, 5.

LO1, LO2, LO3, LO4.

PQ Principles of Governance & Audit Paper Chs. 1, 4, 5, 6, 7, 8, 10, 11.

(a) **There is usually a great amount of evidence available to the auditor. Discuss the factors auditors should consider when deciding which evidence to gather.**

The auditor should consider the following five factors:

- **Relevance** – how well the evidence gathered answers the question (audit objective) addressed. (e.g. observing the inventory provides evidence of the existence and condition of the inventory but not its ownership)

- **Reliability** – how reliable the evidence is. Depends on its source – personal knowledge of auditor (e.g. reperformance of an activity) -very reliable; from external source (e.g. confirmations) – reliable, from inside source (e.g. client's accounting records or answer to enquiry) – least reliable.

- **Availability** – how readily available the evidence is: personal knowledge – readily available; outside source- less readily available, inside source – readily available

- **Timeliness** – whether information can be obtained in a timely manner (as for availability)

- **Cost of obtaining the evidence**: directly obtained by auditor – very costly; obtained from outside source – costly; obtained from inside source – least costly.

(b) **Relating to the above case scenario for examples for your answer, demonstrate the difference between compliance and substantive procedures (or tests) and explain the importance of each of these types of procedures in the audit process.**

Compliance procedures – testing to see if client personnel have complied with internal controls (e.g. if the mail is expected to contain customer remittances, observing to see if two people are present when the mail is opened; checking for the initials of the credit manager as evidence that credit sales have been authorised).

Substantive procedures – testing to see if the amounts and other disclosures in the financial statements are fairly stated (in accordance with the applicable financial reporting framework and are true and fair). (e.g. Analytical review for immaterial balances such as interest paid; checking the accuracy of extensions and footings on invoices, confirmation of bank and accounts receivable balances).

If the internal controls are found to be operating effectively and have been so operating throughout the financial year, the auditor will be able to (i) reduce the extent of audit testing, (ii) conduct more testing during the interim audit and (iii) place emphasis on the (less costly) compliance testing than substantive testing. But, because the auditor is required to express an opinion on the financial statements (not on the effectiveness of the internal controls, unless SOX applies) and as all systems of internal control have inherent weaknesses, auditors must always conduct some substantive testing.

(c) **Auditing Standards require auditors to gain a thorough understanding of their client's industry, business and operations. Explain:**

  (i) **the importance of this step in the audit process, and**
  (ii) **how auditors may perform it.**

  (i) The student needs to convey an understanding of the ideas conveyed below and appropriately reflect on the case scenario for examples (e.g. new company, new area of operation, recent listing, rapid growth, numerous acquisitions, limited prior experience of the auditor, potential cost and time pressures from company management):

  It is essential that the auditor has a sound understanding of the client and its environment. It is only with such an understanding that the auditor can:

  - understand the classes of transactions, account balances and disclosures expected to be present in the financial statements;
  - identify factors that may give rise to the risk of material misstatement in the financial statements (whether through fraud or error) and to assess the likelihood of such misstatement occurring;
  - plan the nature, timing and extent of further audit procedures.

  (ii) A thorough understanding of the client entity and its internal and external environment is thus necessary for planning the audit and exercising appropriate judgment throughout its progress. It is also essential so the auditor can understand 'how the client ticks' and to provide a background (or context) against which the credibility of evidence gathered during the audit, and responses given by the client's management and employees to the auditor's enquiries, can be evaluated (in the light of the auditor's knowledge of the business, its circumstances, and its internal and external environment, does the evidence gathered and responses given 'make sense' and 'ring true'?).

Gaining an understanding of the client may be obtained by:

- visiting the client and touring the premises;
- having discussions with key personnel inside and outside the entity;
- inspecting the client's documents and records;
- reviewing industry and business data and publications;
- reviewing previous years' audit working papers and, if relevant, drawing on previous experience with the client;
- discussion among engagement team members;
- performing analytical procedures (or analytical review).

Additional areas where credit might be given, note this is not an exhaustive list:

- The suggested answers are not exhaustive. Credit can be given for other relevant points presented.

Question 23

Case study: ABC (I). This question assesses students' knowledge of benefits of audit to a private company, key elements of assurance engagements, and the identification of material misstatements at assertion level.

Syllabus sections 1, 3, 4, 5, 6.

LO1, LO2, LO3, LO4, LO5.

PQ Principles of Governance & Audit Paper Chs. 1, 4, 5, 6, 7, 8, 10, 11.

Note. Q3 and Q4 share the share the same case information. This is only provided under Q3. Both questions include a note to the requirement to read the information under Q3.

(a) Determine the objective of an audit and the benefits of a private company like ABC having its financial statements voluntarily audited.

The objective of an audit is to express an opinion on whether or not a client's financial statements are materially misstated ('true and fair').

To achieve this objective, the auditor first needs to gain a sufficiently detailed understanding of the client, its environment and its internal controls to be able to assess the risk of material misstatement whether due to fraud in error, in order to gain sufficient and appropriate audit evidence to form an opinion.

In the context of an audit of financial statements, reasonable assurance is given and not an absolute level of assurance.

The auditor is required to apply an adequate level of professional scepticism and professional judgement during the course of the audit engagement.

All assurance engagements contain the following elements:

A three-party relationship: the practitioner (the auditor), a responsible party (the audit client) and intended users (shareholders and other stakeholders).

Appropriate subject matter: this is the financial statements or a portion thereof being audited.

Sufficient, appropriate evidence to support the conclusion (and managerial assertions): to provide their audit opinion, the auditor needs to obtain enough and high quality audit evidence to support the opinion.

A conclusion contained within a written report: this is the audit opinion given by the auditor to the audit company.

The benefits of a private company such as ABC being audited include:

Deficiencies can be identified by the external auditors, whilst gaining an understanding of the entity, its environment and controls and the auditors can make recommendations to improve the efficiency of the business.

An external audit opinion will give the entity (some) credibility on whether its financial statements are free from material misstatement, which could attract new investors and creditors, supports funding applications such as the additional bank financing ABC are hoping to secure, and reassures current shareholders and creditors.

(b) Identify and demonstrate the risks of material misstatement at the assertion level for ABC's new patent.

There is a risk that the patent for the taste tester has not yet been included as part of intangible assets as it was relatively recently registered which may affect the completeness of intangible assets.

A risk of material misstatement pertaining to the existence of the "taste tester" patent arises as there is an incentive by management to overstate its intangible assets.

There is a risk that research costs have been incorrectly classified as the intangible asset, instead of as an expense.

There is a risk of material misstatement that the valuation of the patent has been incorrectly calculated due to the complexity of the calculation and requirement of significant judgement which would affect the valuation of intangible assets. **(IAS 38 *Intangible Assets*)**.

Costs capitalised

There is a risk that research costs have been capitalised to the intangible asset, when the criteria for a development cost has not been met.

Amortization

There is a risk of material misstatement that the incorrect useful life has been applied to the intangible asset, resulting in an overestimation or underestimation of the accuracy of the amortization expense, which will impact the valuation of the intangible asset.

Impairment

There is a risk of material misstatement that the recoverable amount of the new patent at year end is lower than the carrying amount of the patent which would affect the accuracy, valuation and allocation of intangible assets.

There is a risk of material misstatement that the recoverable amount has been calculated incorrectly due to errors in judgements and complex calculations affecting the accuracy and valuation of intangible assets if impaired at year end.

Additional areas where credit might be given, note this is not an exhaustive list:

- The suggested answers are not exhaustive. Credit can be given for other relevant points presented.

Question 24

Case study: ABC (II). This question assesses students' knowledge of ethical concerns and consideration related to acceptance of client, and whether or not a client should be accepted.

Syllabus sections 1, 3, 4, 5, 6, 7.

LO1, LO2, LO3, LO4, LO5.

PQ Principles of Governance & Audit Paper Chs. 1, 4, 5, 6, 7, 8, 9, 10, 11, 13, 16, 17, 18.

Note. Q3 and Q4 share the share the same case information. This is only provided under Q3. Both questions include a note to the requirement to read the information under Q3.

(a) Prepare a short report which:

(1) Analyses any ethical concerns which Miss Cecile Speyer should have considered before accepting ABC as an audit client;

(2) Demonstrates other considerations which should have been factored into the client acceptance process; and

(3) Concludes on whether or not the audit should have been accepted.

(i) **Ethical Concerns**

The audit engagement was accepted at a fee lower than what was paid to the previous auditors. This could create a self-interest threat to professional competence and due care of the audit team as they may not have enough resources to perform the audit with the necessary level of competence and skill required.

The audit has a tight deadline despite Cecile only being assigned to the audit 2 months before year end. This could create a self-interest threat to professional competence and due care as it is doubtful that Cecile will be able to complete the audit with the necessary competence and diligence required.

A year's supply of jellybeans was accepted by the engagement partner as part of the agreement. This could create a self-interest threat/intimidation threat to objectivity as the acceptance of the gift creates a conflict of interest and could compromise Cecile's ability to remain objective when performing the audit.

The acceptance of the gifts may compromise Cecile's independence of mind and appearance, which is also reason not to accept the engagement, as it may reduce the professional scepticism applied during the audit.

The audit is significant to ACME, as it will be an important addition to diversify their range of clients. This creates a self-interest threat to objectivity/independence as Cecile is likely to oblige to ABC's requests in order to ensure that they remain a client.

Cecile accepted the offer of the new Every Flavour Jelly bean being named after Cecile as part of advertising the firm. This creates a self-interest/ advocacy threat to objectivity as Cecile and her staff are likely to allow this to impair their judgement.

This inducement cannot be seen to be an ancillary part of the professional service offered to ABC.

The gift of the year's supply of jellybeans and the advertising for ACME can both be seen as an incentive to persuade ACME to accept the audit. This creates a self-interest threat to professional behaviour as accepting a bribe would undoubtedly bring the profession into disrepute.

Miss Weasely prescribed the 'type' of testing to be performed. This creates a self-interest threat to objectivity and professional competence and due care breach of due care because Cecile's agreement to this may not allow her to perform the audit in accordance with ISAs and CPC.

Georgia specifically requested that the audit team do not contact the previous auditors. A self-interest threat to professional competence and due care is created because Cecile's agreement to this term has hindered her abilities to act in accordance with the ISAs and CPC.

There is also an intimidation threat around not contacting previous auditors and suggestions not to undertake substantive testing.

In addition, based on this request, ACME should have declined the engagement of ABC.

(ii) **Audit Acceptance Considerations**

It appears as though Cecile accepted the audit engagement without performing a formal client investigation.

Cecile did not consider the consequences and reasons for management specifically instructing them not to contact the previous auditor.

Cecile accepted the audit without investigating whether the reason the previous auditors resigned could affect ACME's decision on whether to accept the audit of ABC.

Cecile did not consider or gain an understanding of the entity, including the shareholders and whether any of them have negative publicity which could increase the risk of accepting the audit.

Cecile did not consider the ability of ABC to pay the audit fee in light of going concern issues and the fee being significantly less than it was previously.

Cecile may be a very competent auditor, but it appears as though she only has audit experience in the energy and renewables industry. As such, it may not be appropriate for her to be the assigned as the partner on the ABC audit as this may impact her ability to guide the audit team.

Cecile's lack of experience in the industry could result in risks of material misstatement, not being identified and responded to appropriately.

It is uncertain whether the audit team has the necessary competence and capabilities to undertake and perform the audit with proficiency.

There is a tight audit deadline which could impact the ability of the team to assign appropriate resources to engagements (including human resources, technological resources, and financial resources).

The fee accepted for the engagement is significantly low which could impair the amount of resources which can be allocated to the audit.

There is no formal written arrangement to perform the audit of ABC.

(iii) **Conclusion**

Based on the concerns raised above, the audit should not have been accepted.

(b) Determine and demonstrate the risks of material misstatement at the overall level for ABC Ltd (ABC)

There may be a risk of material misstatement (ROMM) due to error as controls implemented may not be keeping up with the rapid growth and expansion to ensure proper financial reporting.

There is a ROMM due to error as a result of incomplete financial statements, in relation to fees and penalties as a result of non-compliance with laws and regulations.

ABC is a new audit client, as such, there is a ROMM due to error as there may be errors in the opening balances since they were not given permission to contact the previous auditors.

There is a ROMM that financial statements are fraudulently altered as ABC knows that Cecile is a newly appointed auditor which provides an opportunity for fraud.

There is a ROMM due to fraud as management may not consistently apply accounting policies as they know that Cecile is newly appointed.

There is a ROMM due to error as management may be under pressure to meet audit deadlines and to focus entirely on compliance testing rather than substantive testing.

There is a ROMM due to fraud as management may utilise the opportunity of the tight audit deadline to conceal fraudulent activity as they are aware that the auditors cannot test all transactions.

There is a ROMM that assets and income are overstated, and liabilities and expenses are understated fraudulently in order to obtain the loan.

There is a ROMM due to fraud that management have manipulated the financial statements to cover up going concern issues.

There is a risk of material misstatement that the financial statements have been prepared on an incorrect basis (e.g. on the going concern basis).

There is an increased ROMM due to fraud as the CEO and CFO are related (twins) providing an opportunity to collude.

There is a ROMM due to fraud as management lacks integrity as can be seen by their willingness to incentivise the auditors with the Every Flavour Jellybeans.

There is a ROMM due to error as a result of the changes in accounting policy which may have occurred during the current year (see WP P102), and not taken into account.

Additional areas where credit might be given, note this is not an exhaustive list:

- The suggested answers are not exhaustive. Credit can be given for other relevant points presented.

Question 25

Lovely Toys Ltd. This question assesses students' knowledge of internal controls, specific control weaknesses related to the case, and mitigation recommendations.

Syllabus sections 1, 3, 4, 5, 6

LO2, LO3, LO4.

PQ Principles of Governance & Audit Paper Chs. 1, 4, 5, 6, 7, 8, 10, 11, 14.

(a) Analyse the controls which should be in place over the addition of suppliers to the Masterfile.

Note. You do not need to deal with automated controls over data input and passwords.

Suppliers should fill in and sign a sequentially numbered application form detailing relevant details such as name, address, company registration number, contact details, bank details and tax number.

The order clerks should complete a Masterfile Amendment Form (MAF) with the required information.

The MAFs should be signed by Doug Stevens as the purchasing manager, after agreeing the details of the amendment to the supporting documentation including the supplier application form.

Access to the Masterfile must require a username and password.

Write access to the supplier Masterfile is to be restricted to order clerks.

All Masterfile amendments should automatically be logged by the computer on sequenced logs and there should be no write access to the logs.

Doug Stevens, on a monthly basis, should review the log to ensure that the amendments were approved and sign the log as evidence of a review.

A log of Masterfile amendments completed but not approved should be maintained and followed up on by Doug.

Sequence checks must be performed on the MAFs entered into the Lampoon system to confirm that there are no incomplete or duplicate MAFs.

(b) Assume that the Lampoon system operates effectively. Prepare a table which:

(i) Determines control weaknesses in the inventory acquisition process including stock despatch to the stores.

(ii) Provides a recommendation for improvement for each weakness.

(i) Weakness	(ii) Recommendation
No review of the purchases orders is performed before the orders are sent through to the suppliers via Lampoon, and this may result in incorrect orders being processed (descriptions and quantity of toys) and purchases from suppliers that are not approved which may result in having excess stock or stock shortages or the clerks engaging in kickbacks.	Doug Stevens should review the orders before they are sent to the suppliers against the approved requisition and supplier list to ensure that the purchases orders are correct and an approved supplier is used.
The order clerks do not follow-up on long outstanding orders and this could result in delays of delivery of toys and shortages of stock at the stores which customers will not be happy about, hence may result in loss of customer goodwill.	The order clerks should follow-up on long outstanding orders with the supplier to ensure that the toys are delivered by the supplier to avoid stock shortages.
The receiving bay clerks accept the order without first agreeing the order to the relevant purchases order and the delivery note and this could result in accepting incorrect orders (description and quantity) or having to pay the supplier for toys not received as the invoice will be on the basis of the delivery note.	Upon the delivery of the orders, the receiving clerks should agree the quantity and description of the order to that on the relevant purchases order and delivery note to ensure correct orders are accepted.
No superficial check of the condition of the toys is performed before accepting the order, and this may result in accepting toys that are damaged.	Before accepting the orders, the receiving clerks should perform a superficial check of the condition of the toys to ensure that no damaged orders are accepted.

(i) Weakness	(ii) Recommendation
No check is made for potential differences between the goods received note and delivery note.	The receiving clerks should prepare the goods received note based on the actual toys accepted from the suppliers and any differences between the goods received note and the delivery note, should be clearly marked on the delivery note and signed to by both the receiving clerks and the delivery personnel of the supplier.
The receiving bay manager has decided, the purchases orders for which toys have been received should not be marked as such, and this may result in accepting duplicate orders from suppliers.	After accepting the order, the receiving clerks should clearly mark the corresponding purchases order(e.g. ticked as resolved in the file) to ensure no duplicate orders are accepted from suppliers.
The toys are sent to the warehouse without the accompanying goods transfer note, and this could result in theft or loss of the toys as they are being transferred which the warehouse manager will not be able to detect as there's no goods received note nor a goods transfer note accompanying the goods.	Toys transferred from the receiving bay to the warehouse should be accompanied by a copy of the corresponding goods received note and goods transfer note and both documents should be signed by the receiving clerks and the warehouse manager to acknowledge the transfer and receipt of the toys respectively.
The warehouse manager does not review the toys picked by the warehouse clerks before they are sent to the despatch area, and this could result in incorrect toys (description and quantity) being despatched to the stores which will result in delays when correcting the matter.	The warehouse manager should review the toys picked by the warehouse clerks before they are sent to the despatch area to confirm that the quantity and descriptions matches details on the orders sent by the store managers.
No picking slips are prepared and sent to the despatch area together with the toys, and this may result in some toys being lost or stolen as they are being transferred. The despatch area clerks do not sign any documentation to acknowledge the receipt of the toys, hence no one can be held responsible if the toys are stolen or lost (no Isolation of responsibilities).	The warehouse manager should review the toys picked by the warehouse clerks before they are sent to the despatch area to confirm that the quantity and descriptions matches details on the orders sent by the store managers.
No background checks are performed on the delivery personnel, this may result in dishonest people being hired to transfer the toys which could result in them stealing some of the toys.	The HR department of TOYS should perform background checks on the delivery personnel before being hired to ensure only trustworthy individuals are employed.
No picking slip/delivery note is given to the delivery personnel to sign and acknowledge the receipt of the toys and this could result in loss or theft of the toys on delivery to the stores for which the delivery personnel cannot be held responsible.	The delivery personnel should be given delivery note/picking slips which they should sign after agreeing the quantity and description of toys loaded in the truck to the details on the pickling slip to ensure that they acknowledge the receipt, completeness and accuracy of the toys.

(i) Weakness	(ii) Recommendation
No delivery note/picking slip is signed by the store manager to acknowledge the receipt of the toys and no subsequent review is performed on the delivery note by the warehouse manager. This could result in some of the toys not being transferred at all to the stores(due to loss or theft by the delivery personnel) without any detection.	The store manager should sign the delivery note after agreeing the toys delivered to details on the delivery note to ensure they acknowledge the receipt, completeness and accuracy of the delivery. The warehouse manager should review the signed delivery note for the signature of the store manager to confirm the receipt of the toys by the store manager and should follow up on any delivery notes not signed or marked for issues by the store manager.

Additional areas where credit might be given, note this is not an exhaustive list:

- The suggested answers are not exhaustive. Credit can be given for other relevant points presented.

Mock exam questions and answers

Question 1

You are an internal audit manager, working for SportRTW plc within the UK. SportRTW plc sell high end sports fashion, through a shop network which has outlets within all of the major UK cities (totalling 25 stores). The company's reputation has been built upon the fact that all the products are sourced and manufactured within the UK.

The audit plan for the next quarter includes a review of the Human Resources (HR) department. This department is principally located at the head office of the business, however, certain aspects of the function are devolved to local shop managers. The manufacturing facilities and distribution hub are also located at the head office location. All employees are invited to join the trade union.

The business profits have been negatively impacted by the government's requirements for a 'national minimum living wage' for all UK based employees. As a result of this, the HR department management group have been reviewing policies and procedures for recruitment, remuneration and retention of staff. In the meantime, a number of cost saving directives have been issued until these policies are reviewed and finalised including:

- All shop managers are to review payroll budgets and plan for a reduction in staff costs of 10%.
- All pay rises and bonus payments have been deferred for the foreseeable future. Current pay scales are below market rate.
- There will be no promotions given for the next 12 months.
- Staff training budgets are reduced in comparison to the prior year's budget.
- The payroll function is to be outsourced in order to benefit from cost efficiencies. This will be effective immediately.

As a separate part of the overall company cost control process, you have also been informed by the senior manager of the Internal Audit department, that the Board are also considering outsourcing of the Internal Audit function within the next three years.

Required

(a) One of your friends (who does not work in the accounting profession) has asked you to explain your role in the company. Differentiate how your role as an internal auditor contrasts with the role of working on external audits. **(5 marks)**

(b) Describe the risks that exist in SportRTW's HR function. Explain the tests of control that would be performed.

(9 marks)

(c) Discuss the advantages and disadvantages of outsourcing of the internal audit function to an external provider. **(6 marks)**

(Total 20 marks)

Question 2

Advocard is a small business which was started several years ago by two friends Jim and Aziz operating in partnership together. Over the years, the firm has grown and expanded its range of activities and customer base. It now consists of five partners and approximately 60 employees, operating from several locations throughout the country. To accommodate this growing business, the partnership is considering the purchase of a new building to be used as the Head Office. Jim is now reaching retirement age, and is thinking about leaving the partnership, and one of his business contacts has expressed an interest in joining.

Lauren, one of the more recent partners to join the firm, is keen that Advocard should appoint an independent auditor. The other partners are reluctant to incur unnecessary costs, and at a recent partnership meeting, Aziz pointed out that since the firm already employs a qualified accountant as a member of staff, there is no need to appoint an external auditor. He asked Lauren to prepare a memorandum for the next partners' meeting explaining why an audit would be useful.

Required

Draft the memorandum from Lauren to the partners, explaining:

(a) The difference between auditing and accountancy work. **(5 marks)**

(b) The advantages to Advocard of having an independent audit. **(10 marks)**

(Total 15 marks)

Question 3

You are the auditor of Digital Images Ltd, a small mail order photographic processing company. You are planning the company's audit for the current financial year.

Customers can order prints online or by post, and have them delivered directly to their home address. The company also sells a selection of personalised gifts including greeting cards, photo books, photo mugs and calendars. All sales must be paid for along with the order, so there are no trade receivables. Customers pay in a variety of ways, using credit cards, cheques or cash.

The company's Managing Director, Jackie Lee, runs the company along with her two full-time assistants, Sean and Eileen. Miss Lee has been running the business for many years, and is satisfied that it now operates smoothly and efficiently, and requires only minimal supervision from her. She has therefore reduced her working hours to one day a week, although she still makes sure that she authorises all the major transactions such as payment of wages and large orders.

Sean orders the chemicals, paper, and other photographic materials needed for processing the orders, and is also responsible for maintaining the payables ledger and paying suppliers. Eileen records all customer orders as they are received, and is responsible for dispatching prints and other gifts to the customers, and for maintaining the cashbook.

Required

ISA 500 *Audit Evidence* details several different procedures that can be used to gather audit evidence. These procedures include:

(i) Analytical Procedures
(ii) Inquiry
(iii) Inspection
(iv) Observation
(v) Re-calculation

For each of the above audit procedures:

(a) Provide an example of how the technique could be used to gather evidence during the audit of Digital Images Ltd, and **(5 marks)**

(b) Discuss the suitability of each procedure for Digital Images Ltd, explaining the limitations of each. **(10 marks)**

(Total 15 marks)

Question 4

SpecialCycle UK Ltd is a family owned business, and your audit firm has recently been appointed to perform the external audit of this company. SpecialCycle UK Ltd's core business is the selling of a range of specialist equipment to cycling enthusiasts. SpecialCycle UK Ltd sells to customers through their website, and distributes directly to customers. It has also recently begun to operate cycling courses for school children, a part of the business which is expanding.

Historically, the core business has only distributed to UK-based customers. However, in the past year the company has decided to expand the internet business to sell to European customers. In addition, a number of independent cycle shops have agreed to sell the SpecialCycle UK Ltd branded products on a consignment stock basis.

The majority of the inventory balance is stored at the UK distribution hub centre, which is owned and operated by SpecialCycle UK Ltd. Products are sourced from a number of suppliers (with the majority of manufacturers, being based in China). All products are quality checked on receipt from suppliers and then booked onto the computerised inventory system. There are two inventory counts performed each year. Approximately 10% of inventory is now held on a consignment basis at independent cycle shops.

Due to business expansion into Europe, there are plans to open a secondary distribution hub in the outskirts of Amsterdam. The board of directors has identified a suitable location and is in negotiation with the bank to secure a loan to purchase the site.

A summary of the company performance is provided below:

	Year ending September X7 $'000	Year ending September X6 $'000
Total Revenue	10,021	10,125
GP %	51.2%	51.5%
Profit after tax	450	540
Net assets	3,388	3,233

Shortly before the year end SpecialCycle UK Ltd received legal notification of a claim being made by one of their school customers, relating to a specific family. The family's son had attended a course run by SpecialCycle UK Ltd and had been involved in a collision with another participant, which resulted in mild concussion. The child's doctor recommended that the family postpone their half term holiday to the Caribbean, which had cost the family $7,500. The family were claiming for damages against SpecialCycle UK Ltd. Despite the family signing a disclaimer for injury prior to the son attending the course, SpecialCycle UK Ltd's legal representative considered that there is a possible obligation to meet this claim.

Required

(a) Define inherent risk, and discuss TWO inherent risks associated with this business, with respect to inventory. **(4 marks)**

(b) Explain which factors would be considered in relation to setting materiality and how this would be calculated for this client. **(10 marks)**

(c) Describe audit procedures that would be carried out in relation to inventory. **(5 marks)**

(d) Explain the issues that would be encountered during the audit of the legal claim, with reference to IAS 37 *Provisions, Contingent Liabilities and Contingent Assets*. Recommend the audit work which would be required to gather audit evidence for this issue. **(6 marks)**

(Total 25 marks)

Question 5

You are an audit partner in the firm DWW LLP. You qualified with the AIA a number of years ago.

Your firm has been approached by ElectroNE1 plc, with a view for the board to appoint your firm as external auditors. ElectroNE1 plc is traded on the London Stock Exchange and you personally own a number of shares in the company. The board have approached DWW LLP as a result of a personal recommendation; the nephew of the Chairman has recently joined DWW LLP as an audit trainee.

The board of ElectroNE1 plc have informed you that there have been a number of issues relating to staffing in the finance department, which has resulted in the Finance Director leaving the company. This means that there is no Finance Director in post at present, so ElectroNE1 plc have also asked if a member of your firm could be released to act as interim Finance Director over the year end period, to oversee the preparation of the year end accounts.

ElectroNE1 plc operate within the electricity supply market within the south of the UK. Your firm also provides audit services to one of ElectroNE1 plc competitors, so your firm has experience within the audit of this industry.

Required

(a) Advise why independence and objectivity are so important to the audit profession. **(5 marks)**

(b) Explain the threats to auditor objectivity and independence, when considering whether to accept this invitation for engagement with ElectroNE1 plc and suggest suitable responses to these threats.

(20 marks)

(Total 25 marks)

Question 1

(a) The internal audit function performs assurance and consulting activities designed to evaluate and improve the effectiveness of the entity's governance, risk management and internal control processes.

The following table summarises the roles and differences between internal and external audit.

Internal audit	External audit
• Internal audit is designed to add value and improve an organisation's operation	• External audit is an exercise to enable auditors to express an opinion on the financial statements
• Internal auditors report to the board of directors, or other people charged with governance, such as the audit committee	• The external auditors report to the shareholders, or members, on the truth and fairness of the accounts
• Internal audit work relates to the operations of the organisation	• External audit work relates solely to the financial statements
• Internal auditors are often employees of the organisation, although sometimes the internal audit function is outsourced	• External auditors are independent of the company and its management. They are appointed by the shareholders.

(b) Risks in HR function

The pay freeze and halt on promotions may lead to staff leaving the company/or raising issues through the trade union, if the HR do not communicate the plan effectively to employees.

The cost cutting exercise may also impact staff training. With a reduction in training budgets staff may feel undervalued, and under prepared to meet their role requirements, which increases internal control risk.

Some HR procedures are devolved to shop managers, which may lead to inconsistencies in application of policies and procedures.

The new employment laws also pose a risk – given the cost cutting which is underway this may lead to problems with recruiting staff and complying fully with the new employment laws – shop managers may try to circumvent legislation to maintain staff cost budgets.

The plan to outsource payroll also poses a risk due to loss of control over payroll processing – the contract with the payroll provider will have to adequately address risks to avoid issues of misstatement, and accuracy and timely payment to staff.

Tests of control:

- Obtain a copy of the long term HR plan and review in light of the risks identified.
- Obtain evidence of how HR are intending to monitor pay levels in the market, and their plans to communicate the pay restructuring with employees.
- Review succession planning in light of the promotion freeze.
- Review training procedures and policies in light of the freeze on employee costs.
- Review contracts and KPIs agreed with new payroll provider.
- Review risk assessment made by management of use of new payroll provider.

(c) Advantages of outsourcing internal audit include:

- Staff retention and recruitment risk is transferred to the outsourcing partner, who are contracted to provide resource;
- The service provider will have wider specialist skills within resources in their overall organisation, and thus can tailor the internal audit plan using their access to a broader range of skills;
- Associated staff costs are eliminated i.e. training/pension – this is one of the key advantages for SportRTW who are looking for cost savings;
- Secondment opportunities may be possible from the outsourcing provider when additional resource is required, adding flexibility.

Disadvantages may include:

- Often internal audit outsourcing is provided by external audit firms, and the company may wish to use the same firm, leading to complications for the external auditors in terms of independence.
- The cost of outsourcing internal audit may be more expensive than employing staff;
- Outsourced internal auditors may have sector specific knowledge but may lack understanding as to how processes and controls operate at SportRTW.

> **Additional areas where credit might be given, note this is not an exhaustive list:**
> - **There are a number of extra marks available under each section for expanded discussion of roles, risk and advantages/disadvantages, with marks capped as appropriate. The examiner will consider any appropriate points raised by students which address the question in each section.**

Question 2

MEMORANDUM

From: Lauren
To: Advocard partners

(a) **Difference Between Auditing and Accountancy Work**

Accountants are responsible for handling the day to day financial affairs of a business. An audit, by contrast, is typically an appraisal of those financial affairs which is carried out by an independent organisation. Some businesses do employ their own auditors to oversee their accountants, but many bring in auditors from third-party firms.

Accountancy work involves keeping proper accounting books from which a trial balance can be extracted, followed by the preparation of final accounts and this is not part of the audit work.

There are often two stages to an audit: an interim audit which focuses on the effectiveness of an entity's internal controls and a final audit which seeks to gather evidence to support the audit opinion. An auditor will often report any deficiencies they identify in an entity's internal control to those charged with governance.

An audit on the other hand involves the examination of the financial statements by a professionally qualified accountant in his or her capacity as an external auditor with a view to expressing an independent opinion on the truth and fairness of the financial statements.

Auditors analyse the records kept by a company's accountants for accuracy and fairness. They help companies to ensure that they are performing within applicable regulations. Auditors then provide suggestions based on their findings.

(b) **The advantages to Advocard of having an independent audit**

Carrying out an objective independent examination of Advocard's financial statements would increase the value and credibility of the financial statements produced by the partnership's accountants, and would therefore increase the partners' and other users' confidence in the financial statements.

The audit will provide assurance that accounting estimates made by management are reasonable, and information presented in the financial statements is relevant, reliable, comparable and understandable.

More specific advantages of having an external auditor for the partnership accounts include the following points:

Providing assurance that the partnership's financial statements are not affected by material fraud, error or other misstatements that should have been detected in the course of the audit. If the audit is well planned and conducted with reasonable skill and care, material errors and fraud should be discovered in the process of the audit work.

It will also help prevent any errors or frauds, through the deterrent effect of the audit. Advocard employees will be less tempted to act fraudulently or carelessly if they know that their work will be subjected to an audit.

Having an audit will facilitate the agreement of tax assessments with the tax authorities, who are more likely to accept as accurate figures presented to them when they have been subjected to an independent audit.

As the partnership is considering buying a new property, it will most likely need to raise finance. Having an audit will help with obtaining a loan or obtaining other forms of credit, since applications to banks and other lenders will be greatly enhanced if supported by audited accounts.

As part of the work, the auditor will carry out an objective review and evaluation of the effectiveness of Advocard's accounting and internal control system, and will report to the partners on how the system could be improved.

Any disputes between the partners and other business associates may be avoided, especially in relation to the partners' profit-sharing arrangements. In particular, it will ensure the soundness of the financial information used in calculating any capital repayment to Jim from the partnership when he retires, and provide reassurance to prospective new partners who are considering joining the firm.

Finally, an independent audit will enable the partnership to obtain up to date financial advice from a firm that will have access to expertise in various financial matters, such as current company law, taxation, and other legal and professional pronouncements.

Additional areas where credit might be given, note this is not an exhaustive list:

- **Additional marks will be awarded in part (a) for alternative approaches to the difference between accountancy and audit work. In part (b), and well-argued and sensible advantages for Advocard of having an independent audit will be given credit.**

Question 3

	(a) Example	(b) Suitability and limitations
Analytical Procedures	Review income from sales for the past several years to try to identify whether income has been understated, possibly by cash being taken prior to banking. There is no control over the opening of the post so cash could be withdrawn by Eileen, who also has control over the cash book.	This method of collecting evidence will be useful in the audit of Digital Images Ltd because it will help to identify unusual changes in income and expenditure. As Digital Images Ltd is a small company, monitoring gross profit will show relatively small changes in sales margin or purchasing costs. However, the technique may be limited in its application because it will not detect errors or omissions made consistently year on year. If Miss Lee or one (or both) of her assistants is regularly defrauding the business each year, then analytical procedures will not be able to detect this.
Inquiry	Obtain statements from suppliers to check for completeness of liabilities at the year end. As there are no controls over purchases, invoices could have been misplaced resulting in lower purchases and trade payables figures.	Inquiry evidence will be very useful in the audit of Digital Images Ltd, especially where this is derived from third parties. Third party evidence is generally more reliable than client originated evidence, as there is a decreased likelihood of bias. Suppliers can therefore be verified using supplier statement reconciliations. External inquiry evidence will be less useful in the audit of sales and receivables because goods are paid for prior to dispatch, and there are no receivables. Internal evidence will be available from Miss Lee and the assistant; however the lack of segregation of duties means that this will not be so reliable.
Inspection	Inspection of the company's stock of chemicals and other photographic materials held at the end of year to ensure that all inventory is recorded and are usable in their current condition.	Inspection of documents within Digital Images Ltd will be helpful, particularly regarding checking whether expenses are bona fide. All purchase invoices, for example, should be addressed to Digital Images Ltd and relate to purchases expected for the company, such as photographic materials. The fact that an invoice is addressed to the company does not confirm completeness of recording so inspection of the cash book for unusual payments verified by checking the purchase invoice will also be required. Inspection of documents is time consuming, but, given the poor system of internal control within Digital Images Ltd, the auditor may have no

	(a) Example	(b) Suitability and limitations
		choice but to use this method of gathering evidence. Note however that a specialist may be required to assist the auditor in their assessment of the condition of inventory.
Observation	Look at the process of opening of the post and recording of customer orders to ensure that Eileen is recording all orders as they are received, to ensure that none of them are being omitted.	Observation may be useful because it will show how the assistants check documents. However, no information is provided on any internal controls within Digital Images Ltd so simply viewing how documents are checked without any evidence of checking has limited benefit. Observation tests will be of limited usefulness because the assistants may act differently when an auditor is present. The same problem will apply to any observation checking carried out by Miss Lee.
Re-calculation	Check the additions in the cashbook to confirm that the total amount of cash recorded in the cashbook is accurate and can be included in the sales figure. Here cash receipts should be the same as sales as there are no trade receivables.	Re-calculation evidence is very useful for checking additions on invoices, balancing of control accounts etc. This means that the arithmetical accuracy of the books and records in Digital Images Ltd can be confirmed. The main weakness of re-calculation checking is that calculations can only be carried out on figures that have been recorded. If there are any omissions then checks cannot be carried out.

Question 4

(a) Inherent risk is the susceptibility of an assertion about a class of transactions, account balance or disclosure to a misstatement that could be material either individually or when aggregated with other misstatements, before consideration of any related internal controls.

Inherent risks related to inventory include:

- Majority of inventory held at one location – susceptibility to material misstatement due to loss/theft/inventory system issues at one distribution hub.

- Proposed expansion leads to new warehousing/distribution hub – increasing complexity of monitoring of inventory.

- Nature of consignment stocks – again recording of such items may lead to misstatement without relevant control framework/good relationship with suppliers.

- Nature of product – specialist, and may quickly go 'out of fashion', leading to valuation difficulties.

- Family owned business, is there a risk of family removing inventory for own use without disclosure (this appears to be a high margin/desirable inventory from summary financials).

(b) There are several factors that auditors consider when setting materiality benchmarks, including:

- Elements of the financial statements i.e. profits, assets, revenue. There appears to be a focus on inventory, and mortgaged non-current assets in this client given the limited information provided.

- Whether there are key elements in the financial statements for users e.g. profit.

- Ownership structure and finance. In this instance, this is a family owned business so related parties will most likely be involved. Thus materiality will need to be adapted for the nature and disclosure of such transactions.

- Relative volatility of the benchmark chosen, althoughthere does not seem to be particular volatility in these numbers.

A range of values for materiality may be calculated by considering the percentage of total balances reviewed. This may be applied based on the information available for this client including:

- Consideration of total revenue at ½ to 1% i.e. approximately $50,000 to $100,000.

- Consideration of total gross profit at ½ to 1% i.e. ($10,021,000×51.2%×½ to 1%) approximately $25,000 to $51,000.

- Consideration of profit after tax at 5% to 10% i.e. approximately $22,000 to $45,000.

- Consideration of net assets at 2% to 5% i.e. approximately $68,000 to $169,000.

(c) The following audit procedures relate to inventory:

- Attend the inventory count at the UK distribution hub centre to ensure that the inventory count is being conducted in accordance with inventory count instructions, perform test counts and observe the condition of inventory.

- Consider whether auditor attendance is required at the secondary distribution centre in Amsterdam or whether written confirmation of inventory from the centre manager is sufficient.

- Request direct written confirmation of quantities of consignment inventory balances held at year end by the owners of the independent cycle shops and request confirmation of any damaged or slow-moving parts.

- For a sample of inventory items, vouch the item's cost to supplier invoices and compare this to the cost included in the financial statements.

- For a sample of items, review the sales price charged post year end to sales invoices/price list to determine whether the item's net realisable value is above cost.

- Discuss any slow moving inventory items with management to identify items where the net realisable value may be less than cost. Recalculate any write down made in relation to these inventory items.

(d) IAS 37 states that:

- A provision is a liability of uncertain timing or amount

- A contingent liability is a possible obligation that arises from past events and whose existence will only be confirmed by the occurrence or non-occurrence of one or more uncertain future events not wholly within the control of the entity.

The event described in the scenario is 'possible' indicating a contingent liability, however, the auditors will need to confirm this with further audit evidence.

Relevant audit procedures would include:

- Determining whether the company had a present obligation through review of the initial disclaimer and the resulting legal correspondence.

- Determine whether it is probable that transfer of economic benefit will be required to settle the obligation by review:
  - Any payments to the family after the end of the reporting period.
  - Updated correspondence from legal team/sending a letter to the legal team.
- Recalculate the basis for the estimate of $7,500.
- In the event it is not possible to estimate amount/or determine likelihood, ensure appropriate contingent liability is disclosed in the accounts.

Question 5

(a) It is essential that the auditor is impartial and independent of management, so that they can give an objective view. The auditor not only must be ethical, but must be seen to be ethical. Independence and objectivity matter, because there is an expectation of those members of the company that are directly affected, that the auditors provide a level of objective assurance on the financial statements that the directors never could. In addition, it is important that the general public have confidence that the audit profession is independent and objective as auditors may sometimes need to disclose information which is in the public's interest.

(b) There are a number of threats to independence and objectivity in this case. These issues will require judgement by the audit firm on the risk, and then considering relevant safeguards to address the risk, prior to moving forward with engagement.

Threats and suitable responses include:

- Financial Interests – members of the audit firm have a financial interest in the client, in the form of share ownership. The following safeguards could be put in place: disposing of the shares, appointing another member of the audit partners to engage the firm, making the client's audit committee aware of the issue, or using an independent partner for review purposes.

- Family relationship – the auditors have been approached as a result of a family recommendation. However, this is a junior member of the team, and therefore this risk may be considered minimised as the likely responsibilities of the junior member of the team are unlikely to cause risks within the engagement. A safeguard would be to remove the junior member of the team from the engagement.

- Employment with the audit client – the client has requested a seconded employee, which compromises independence. This causes two issues as the seconded employee from the audit firm may wish to impress ElectroNE1 in an attempt to gain future employment, and also because the seconded employee will have too much knowledge about the audit firm's approach. The seconded employee may exert too much influence over the more junior members of the audit team, in his capacity as interim Finance Director at the client. A potential safeguard would be to decline the request for secondment and recommend another audit firm for the client to approach regarding secondment. Another safeguard would be to modify the audit plan i.e. unfamiliar to client and seconded employee, and to implement additional quality review within the engagement.

- Another area to consider is conflicts of interest with other audit clients of the audit firm. The case suggests that the audit firm is already engaged with firms in the same industry, therefore, an assessment will need to be made to ensure there are no conflicts of interest e.g. advocacy issues, and if so an alternative audit partner may need to be appointed.

- Furthermore, DWW LLP must ensure that confidentiality is maintained where they have clients which are competitors, safeguards should be put in place such as obtaining written consent from both parties giving DWW LLP permission to act, establishing information barriers, the use of separate teams and the signing of non-disclosure agreements.

MOCK EXAM ANSWERS

> **Additional areas where credit might be given, note this is not an exhaustive list:**
> - Any other suitable threats suggested by students will be considered for merit by examiners, subject to appropriate application to the case.

Bibliography

Bibliography

Companies Act 2006. [Online]. Available from: www.legislation.gov.uk/ [Accessed 31 October 2016]. http://www.nationalarchives.gov.uk/doc/open-government-licence/version/3/ Contains Parliamentary information licensed under the Open Parliament Licence v3.0.

IESBA. (2023) *Code of Ethics for Professional Accountants*. [Online]. Available from: https://ifacweb.blob.core.windows.net/publicfiles/2024-03/2023%20IESBA%20Handbook%20-%20Updated%203-26-24_0_0.pdf [Accessed 20 June 2024].

IFRS Foundation. (2019) *IFRS*. [Online]. Available at: http://eifrs.ifrs.org [Accessed 14 May 2020].

International Auditing and Assurance Standards Board. (2018) *2018 Handbook of International Quality Control, Auditing, Review, Other Assurance, and Related Services Pronouncements*. [Online]. Available from https://www.ifac.org/system/files/publications/files/IAASB-2018-HB-Vol-1.pdf [Accessed 14 May 2020].

Organisation for Economic C0-operation and Development. (2023) *Principles of Corporate Governance 2023*, OECD Publishing, Paris [Online]. Available from: https://doi.org/10.1787/ed750b30-en [Accessed 12 June 2024]

UK Corporate Governance Code 2024. [Online]. Available from: https://www.frc.org.uk/library/standards-codes-policy/corporate-governance/uk-corporate-governance-code/ [Accessed 12 June 2024]

UK Corporate Governance Code 2024 Key Changes [Online]. Available from: https://media.frc.org.uk/documents/UK_Corporate_Governance_Code_2024_Key_Changes.pdf [Accessed 12 June 2024]

Corporate Governance Code Guidance. [Online]. Available from: https://www.frc.org.uk/library/standards-codes-policy/corporate-governance/corporate-governance-code-guidance/ [Accessed 12 June 2024]

The Cadbury Code - The Financial Aspects of Corporate Governance. [Online]. Available from: https://media.frc.org.uk/documents/Cadbury_Code_-_The_Financial_Aspects_of_Corporate_Governance.pdf [Accessed 12 June 2024]

Financial Reporting Council. (2024) *Revised FRC Ethical Standard 2024*. [Online]. Available from: https://media.frc.org.uk/documents/Revised_Ethical_Standard_2024.pdf [Accessed 20 June 2024]

The Global Reporting Initiative, Resource Centre. [Online]. Available from: https://www.globalreporting.org/media/s4cp0oth/gri-gristandards-visuals-fig1_family-2021-print-v19-01.png [Accessed 18 June 2024]

Unilever GRI Content Index 2021. [Online]. Available from: https://www.unilever.com/files/df81b5e7-2913-4e89-90a9-18868f7355a3/unilever-gri-index-2021.pdf [Accessed 18 June]

Nestle Global Reporting Initiative and Sustainability Accounting Standards Board Indexes 2023. [Online]. Available from: https:/www.nestle.com/sites/default/files/2024-02/gri-sasb-index-2023.pdf [Accessed 18 June]

Siemens Sustainability report 2023. [Online]. Available from: https://assets.new.siemens.com/siemens/assets/api/uuid:00095b96-4712-4cd1-b045-19d5df704358/sustainability-report-fy2023.pdf [Accessed 18 June]

IBM Impact Report 2023. [Online]. Available from: https://www.ibm.com/impact [Accessed 18 June]

IBM GRI Content Index 2022. [Online]. Available from: https:/www.ibm.com/impact/pdf/2022_GRI_Index.pdf [Accessed 18 June 2024]

Integrated Reporting Framework. [Online]. Available from: https://www.ifrs.org/issued-standards/ir-framework/ [Accessed 19 June 2024]

BIBLIOGRAPHY

Deloitte UK Accounting Plus. [Online]. Available from: https://www.iasplus.com/en-gb/resources/sustainability-en-gb/iirc#:~:text=The%20Framework%20sets%20out,information%2C%20both%20financial%20and%20other. [Accessed 19 June 2024]

IFRS S1: *General Requirements for Disclosure of Sustainability-related Financial Information*. [Online]. Available from: https://www.ifrs.org/issued-standards/ifrs-sustainability-standards-navigator/ [Accessed 19 June 2024]

IFRS S2: *Climate-related Disclosures*. [Online]. Available from: https://www.ifrs.org/issued-standards/ifrs-sustainability-standards-navigator/ [Accessed 19 June 2024]

GRI publication: Double materiality. The guiding principle for sustainability reporting. Available from: https://www.globalreporting.org/media/rz1jf4bz/gri-double-materiality-final.pdf [Accessed 26 June 2024]

PwC article: 10 pitfalls companies should avoid when conducting a CSRD-aligned double materiality assessment. Available from: https://www.pwc.com/us/en/services/esg/library/csrd-double-materiality.html [Accessed 26 June 2024]

Index

> Note. **Key Terms** and their page references are given in **bold**.

Ability to perform the work, 112
Acceptance procedures, 109
Accepting appointment, 108
Accountability, 2, 3
Accounts receivable listing, 335
Accruals, 362, 364, 366
Adverse opinion, 419, 422
Advocacy, 79, 93
Advocacy threat, 79
Aged analysis, 335
Agents, 3
AIA's Code of Ethics, 78
American Institute of Certified Public Accountants, 24
An **Emphasis of matter, 427**
Analytical procedures, 150, 160, 183, 186
Analytical Procedures, 189
Annual general meeting (AGM), 43
Anomaly, 201
Information processing controls, 132, 133
Appointment ethics, 109
Appointment of auditors, 28
Appropriateness, 180
Association of Chartered Certified Accountants (ACCA), 22
Association of International Accountants (AIA), 22
Assurance, 2, 15
Assurance engagement, 4, 15
Audit, 2, 5, 58
Audit committee, 53
Audit documentation, 203
Audit engagement letters, 113
Audit evidence, 180
Audit files, 206
Audit plan, 146, **147**
Audit procedures, 182
Audit regulation, 22
Audit report, 427
Audit risk, 153
Audit risk model, 154
Audit sampling, 197, **198**
Audit software, 194
Audit strategy, 146
Auditor liability, 36
Auditor rights and duties, 31
Auditor's expert, 220
Auditor's report, 9, 408
Auditors' responsibilities, 56
Automated working papers, 207

Bank, 278
Bank confirmation, 278
Bank reconciliation, 280
Basic elements of the auditor's report, 411
Best estimate of other misstatements, 400
Business relationships, 82
Business risk, 60, 156

Cadbury Report, 42
Capital and revenue expenditure, 264
Capping liability, 37
Cash count, 284
Cash system, 256
Changes in nature of engagement, 115
Charities, 6
Checklists, 134
Client screening, 112
Close business relationships, 82
Close family, 96
Clubs, 6
Combined Code, 53
Compagnie Nationale des Commissaires aux Comptes, 24
Companies Act 2006, 31
Compensation and evaluation policies, 83
Completion checklists, 400, 401
Compliance with accounting regulations, 397
Automated tools and techniques (ATTs), 194, 195
Automated tools and techniques (ATTs), 186, 193
Conceptual framework, 79
Confidentiality, 79, 208
Confirmation, 183
Confirmation of receivables, 335
Confirmation of trade payables, 359
Conflict of interest, 98
Constructive obligation, 369
Consultation, 171
Contingent asset, 369
Contingent fees, 84
Contingent liability, 369
Contract, 342
Control activities, 126
Control environment, 124
Control risk, 154
Corporate finance, 90
Corporate governance, 4, **42**, 58
Corporate objectives, 58
Cost, 316, 317

INDEX

Creditors, 3
Current audit files, 206
Customer, 342

Deficiency in internal control, **269**
Design of the sample, 198
Detection risk, 154
Difference method, 201
Direct assistance, 216, 218
Direction, 170
Directors, 3
Directors' emoluments, 375
Directors' responsibilities, 55
Directors' service contracts, 376
Disclaimer of opinion, 419, 423
Dismissal of auditors, 29
Duty of care, 36, 37

Economy, 61, 62
Effectiveness, 61, 62
Efficiency, 61, 62
Eligibility/ineligibility, 27
Emphasis of matter, 419
Emphasis of matter paragraph, 409, 428
Emphasis of matter paragraphs, 427
Employees, 3
Employment with an audit client, 95
Engagement economics, 112
Engagement performance, 170
Entity's risk assessment process, 125
Ethics, 78
EU 8th Directive, 22
EU Audit Regulation, 101
Evaluating the effect of misstatements, 400
Exception, 338
Expectations gap, 14, 163
Exposure draft, 33
External audit, 8, 15, 58
External confirmations, 335

Factual misstatements, 398
Fair, 9, 13
Familiarity, 79, 93
Familiarity threat, 79
Fee negotiation, 108
Final audit, 161
Financial, 64
Financial Accounting Standards Board, 24
Financial audit, 64
Financial interest, 81
Financial Reporting Council, 23, 99
Financial statement assertions, 181, 187

Finished goods, 317
Flowcharts, 134
Framework for International Education Standards for Professional Accountants, 26
Fraud, 64, 131, **163**
Fraudulent financial reporting, 164
FRC ES Part 1 Integrity, objectivity and independence, 100
FRC ES Part 2 Financial, business, employment and personal relationships, 100
FRC ES Part 3 Long association with the audit engagement, 101
FRC ES Part 4 Fees, remuneration and evaluation policies, litigation, gifts and hospitality, 101
FRC ES Part 5 Non-audit services provided to audit clients, 102
Fundamental principles of professional ethics, 78

General IT controls, **132**
Gifts and hospitality, 83
Going concern, 384
    key audit matter (KAM), 418
Going concern basis of accounting, 384
Goods on sale or return, 345, 346
Governance, 270

Hampel Committee Report, 43
Haphazard selection, 198
Human resources, 66, 268

IAS 1 *Presentation of Financial Statements*, 384
IAS 2 *Inventories*, 261, 316
IAS 7 *Statement of cash flows*, 415
IAS 10 *Events After the Reporting Period*, 390
IAS 16 *Property, Plant and Equipment*, 296
IAS 37 *Provisions, Contingent Liabilities and Contingent Assets*, 369
IAS 38 *Intangible Assets*, 300
IESBA *Code*, 78, 169
IESBA *Code of ethics*, 78
IESBA *Code of Ethics*, 35, 78
IFRS 15 *Revenue from Contracts with Customers*, 342
Immediate family, 96
Income, 342
Independence, 80
Independence in appearance, 81
Independence of mind, 81
Ineligible for appointment, 27
Information system, 126

Information system relevant to financial reporting, **126**
Information technology, 63
Information technology audit, 63
Inherent risk, 154
Initial communication, 109
Inquiries, 150
Inquiry, 183
Inspection, 153, 183
Institut der Wirtschafstprüfer, 24
Institute of Internal Auditors, 69
Intangible asset, 300
Intangible non-current assets, 300
Integrity, 79, 80
Interim audit, 161
Internal audit, 108
Internal audit assignments, 61
Internal audit function, 8, 55, **58**, 60, 64
Internal audit reports, 68
Internal audit services, 89
Internal auditing, 8
Internal auditors, 54
Internal control, 55, **124**
Internal control effectiveness, 55
Internal Control Evaluation Questionnaires, 135
Internal review assignment, 68
International Accounting Education Standards Board, 26
International Audit and Assurance Standards Board (IAASB), 25, 33
International Education Standards, 26
International Federation of Accountants (IFAC), 25
International Standard on Quality Control 1 Quality Controls for Firms that Perform Audits and Reviews of Financial Statements, and Other Assurance and Related Services Engagements, 170
International Standards on Auditing, 24, 33
Intimidation, 79, 97
Intimidation threat, 79
Inventory, 308
Inventory system, 260
Inventory valuation, 317
ISA 200 *Overall Objectives of the Independent Auditor and the Conduct of an Audit in Accordance with International Standards on Auditing*, 153
ISA 210 *Agreeing the Terms of Audit Engagements*, 113
ISA 220 (Revised) *Quality Management for an Audit of Financial Statements*, 169, 221
ISA 230 *Audit Documentation*, 161, 203

ISA 240 (Revised) *The Auditor's Responsibilities Relating to Fraud in an Audit of Financial Statements*, 131, 165
ISA 250 *Consideration of Laws and Regulations in an Audit of Financial Statements*, 99, 166
ISA 260 (Revised) *Communication with Those Charged with Governance*, 270, 432
ISA 265 *Communicating Deficiencies in Internal Control to those Charged with Governance and Management*, 269
ISA 300 *Planning an Audit of Financial Statements*, 146
ISA 315 (Revised) *Identifying and Assessing the Risks of Material Misstatement*, 124, 148
ISA 320 *Materiality in Planning and Performing an Audit*, 162, 399
ISA 330 *The Auditor's Responses to Assessed Risks*, 159
ISA 450 *Evaluation of Misstatements Identified During the Audit*, 398
ISA 500 *Audit Evidence*, 180, 221
ISA 501 *Audit Evidence – Specific Considerations for Selected Items*, 308, 370
ISA 505 *External Confirmations*, 278, 335
ISA 520 *Analytical Procedures*, 190
ISA 530 *Audit Sampling*, 198
ISA 560 *Subsequent Events*, 391
ISA 570 (Revised) *Going Concern*, 384
ISA 580 *Written Representations*, 394
ISA 610 (Revised) *Using the Work of Internal Auditors*, 216
ISA 620 *Using the Work of an Auditor's Expert*, 221
ISA 700 (Revised) *Forming an Opinion and Reporting on Financial Statements*, 409
ISA 701 *Communicating Key Audit Matters in the Independent Auditor's Report*, 416
ISA 705 (Revised) *Modifications to the Opinion in the Independent Auditor's Report*, 419
ISA 706 (Revised) *Emphasis of Matter Paragraphs and Other Matter Paragraphs in the Independent Auditor's Report*, 427
ISA 805 (Revised) *Special Considerations – Audits of Single Financial Statements and Specific Elements, Accounts or Items of a Financial Statement*, 432

Judgemental misstatements, 398

Key audit matters, 387, **416**
Key audit matters (KAM), 416

INDEX

Law and regulations, 166
Leadership responsibilities, 169
Legal obligation, 369
Liability, 369
Liability limitation agreements, 37
Limitations of accounting and control systems, 131
Limitations of audit, 14
Limitations of controls system, 131
Litigation and claims, 370
Loans and guarantees, 82
Long association of senior personnel with audit clients, 93
Lowballing, 84, 108

Management integrity, 112
Management's expert, 220
Marketing, 65, 266
Material uncertainty, 387
Materiality, 12, 161
Minimum business controls, 245
Misappropriation of assets, 164
Misstatement, 398
Modified opinions, 11, 419
Modified reports, 427
Monetary Unit Sampling, 199
Monitoring, 171
Monitoring of controls, 129

Narrative notes, 134
Negative confirmation request, 336
Negligence, 36
Net realisable value, 316, 317
Non-Compliance with Laws and Regulations (NOCLAR), 99
Non-current asset register, 292
Non-current liabilities, 367
Non-executive directors, 49
Non-response, 338
Non-sampling risk, 155, **200**
Non-statutory audits, 6

Objectives of the auditor, 8
Objectivity, 79, 80
Obligating event, 369
Observation, 153, 183
OECD Principles of Corporate Governance, 43
Operational audits, 64
Operational work plans, 59
Opinion, 5, 8, 15
Ordre des Experts-Comptables, 24

Organisation for Economic Co-operation and Development (OECD), 43
Other matter paragraph, 427, **428**
Outsourcing, 70, 71
Overall responses, 159
Overall review of financial statements, 397
Overdue fees, 84
Overhead absorption, 318

Package programs, 194
Partnership, 6
Payables, 362
Performance materiality, 162
Performance obligation, 342
Periodic plan, 59
Permanent audit files, 206
Perpetual inventory, 309
Pervasiveness, 419
Physical inventory count, 309
Planning, 146
Population, 198
Positive confirmation request, 336
Preconditions for an audit, 113
Preparing accounting records and financial statements, 87
Prepayments, 346
Principles of the UK Corporate Governance Code, 45
Problems of accounting treatment, 398
Procedures after accepting nomination, 110
Procurement, 65, 265
Professional behaviour, 79
Professional competence and due care, 79
Professional indemnity insurance in place, 37
Professional scepticism, 12, **153**
Projected misstatements, 398
Projection of misstatements, 201
Proportionate liability, 37
Provision, 369
Provisions, 362
Public, 3
Purchases cut-off, 360
Purchases system, 234
Purpose-written programs, 194

Qualified opinion, 419, 420
Qualitative aspects of misstatements, 201
Quality control, 169
Quality control review, 171
Quality of evidence, 181
Questionnaires, 134

INDEX

Random selection, 198
Ratio analysis, 191
Ratio method, 201
Reasonable assurance, **12**
Reasonableness test, 191
Reassessing sampling risk, 201
Recalculation, 183
Recent service with an audit client, 94
Recognised Qualifying Bodies, 22
Recognised Supervisory Bodies, 22, 24, 30
Recognised Supervisory Bodies (RSBs), 22
Recording of accounting and control systems, 134
Recruitment services, 85
Recurring audits, 114
Relative size of fees, 83
Removal Of Auditors, 30
Remuneration of the auditors, 29
Reperformance, 183
Reporting internal control deficiencies, 269
Reservation of title, 362
Resignation of auditors, 29
Retention of working papers, 208
Revenue, **342**
Review, 170
Rights to information, 32
Risk management, 55
Risk-based approach, 153
Romalpa case, 362

Sales, 342
Sales cut-off, 345
Sales system, 228
Sampling risk, 155, **200**
Sampling units, **198**
Schedule of unadjusted errors, 399
Segregation of duties, 127, 129, 245
Self-interest, 79, 81
Self-interest threat, 79
Self-review, 79, 87
Self-review threat, 79
Sequence or block selection, 199
Serving as a director of officer of an audit client, 83
Share (equity) capital, reserves and distributions, 373
Share register, 373
Shareholders, 3
Significant deficiency in internal control, **269**
Significant risk, **158**, 161
Small companies, 129
Small company audit exemption, 20
Small entity, **20**

Sole traders, 6
Specific misstatements, 400
Stakeholders, 2
Standard costing, 317
Standardised and automated working papers, 207
Standards for the Professional Practice of Internal Auditing, 70
Statistical sampling, **198**
Statutory audits, 5
Statutory books, 374
Stewardship, 2, **3**
Strategic plan, **59**
Subsequent events, 390
Substantive procedures, 160, **183**, 186
Sufficiency, 180
Summarising misstatements, 398, 399
Supervision, 170
Supervisory and monitoring roles, 28
Suppliers' statements, 359
Systematic selection, 198

Tangible non-current assets, 292
Taxation authorities, 3
Taxation services, 89
Temporary personnel assignments, 90
Tendering and obtaining work, 108
Tests of controls, 160, **182**, **185**
Tests of detail, 160, 186
The public, 3
Those charged with Governance, **270**
Three Es, 62
Tolerable misstatement, 162, **200**
Tolerable rate of deviation, **200**
Trade accounts payable, 354
Transaction price, **342**
Treasury, 66, 267
Trend analysis, 191
True, **9**, 13
Truth and fairness, 8, 9, 11, 12
Truth and fairness, 8

UK Corporate Governance Code, 44, 45, 58
Uncorrected misstatement, **398**, 399, 400
Unmodified opinion, 9, **409**
Unqualified audit report, 418
Utility programs, 194

Valuation services, 88
Value for money, 61, 63, 64, 65

Wages and salaries, 364
Wages system, 240
Window dressing, 280
Work in progress, 317

Working papers, 203
Working procedures of the IAASB, 33
Written representations, 394, 398